Praise for *American Rifle*

Named One of the Best Books of 2008 by *The Economist*

"Like David McCullough in *The Great Bridge,* Rose has the rare ability to make technology come alive even for the non-technology-minded. He is not only a good historian but also a gifted storyteller, and I hope his book will make its way beyond the readership of *American Rifleman* and *Shotgun News* to everyone who wants to read about a singular and enduring artifact in American life and history."
—MICHAEL KORDA, *The Washington Post*

"One of the most interesting nonfiction books of the year . . . packed with fascinating anecdotes . . . and keen insights into the nexus of civilian politics, business, and the military."
—*National Review*

"It is not often that I am taken completely by surprise by a book, but that was the case with accomplished military historian Alexander Rose's *American Rifle*. . . . Simply brilliantly written."
—*American Rifleman*

"*American Rifle,* Alexander Rose's irresistible history [is] a biography of a revolutionary idea . . . ingeniously conceived, deftly written and thoroughly engrossing."
—*The Dallas Morning News*

"Regardless of your stance on firearms, it's true that the rifle holds an iconic place in the forming of our nation. This definitive treatise is full of lost historical fact and intriguing anecdotes."
—*The Sacramento Bee*

"This fascinating book shows how the history of the U.S. is mirrored in the history of one of its technological achievements, the rifle. . . . It is impossible not to get caught up in this rich, surprising, and engrossing story."
—*Booklist*

"Provides surprising insight into the country's history . . . ingenious and satisfying."
—*Kirkus Reviews* (starred review)

"In his entertaining history, Rose engagingly chronicles Americans' peculiar quest to build a more refined and effective firearm."

—*Publishers Weekly*

"An exhaustive history of the rifle's place in American culture . . . Once you start, *American Rifle* will have to be pried from your cold, dead hands before you put it down."

—Amazon "Best of the Month" Selection

"Historian Rose . . . is at his best with the Colonial, Revolutionary, and Civil wars, explaining in great but absorbing detail. . . . Well documented . . . Recommended for most libraries, this will find readers among historians, militarists, gun enthusiasts, and Americana buffs."

—*Library Journal*

"Thoughtful, illuminating exploration of the rifle's deep roots in our cultural history . . . good reading for those on either side of the gun-control debate." —*The Sunday Oregonian*

Also by Alexander Rose

Washington's Spies: The Story of America's First Spy Ring

Kings in the North: The House of Percy in British History

AMERICAN
RIFLE

A Biography

ALEXANDER ROSE

Delta Trade Paperbacks

2009 Delta Trade Paperback Edition

Copyright © 2008 by Rosewriter Inc.

Published in the United States by Delta,
an imprint of The Random House Publishing Group,
a division of Random House, Inc., New York.

DELTA is a registered trademark of Random House, Inc.,
and the colophon is a trademark of Random House, Inc.

Originally published in hardcover in the
United States by Delacorte Press, an imprint of
The Random House Publishing Group, a division
of Random House, Inc., in 2008.

Photo credits and permissions appear on pages 477 and 478.

Library of Congress Cataloging-in-Publication Data
Rose, Alexander.
American rifle: a biography / Alexander Rose.
p. cm.
Includes bibliographical references and index.
ISBN: 978-0-553-38438-3 (trade pbk.)
1. Winchester rifle. I. Title.
TS536.4.RR67 2008   2008023170
683.4'22—dc22

Printed in the United States of America

www.bantamdell.com

2 4 6 8 9 7 5 3 1
Text design by Virginia Norey

TO REBECCA

"I am my beloved's, and my
beloved is mine."

"Among all this people there were seven hundred chosen men lefthanded; every one could sling stones at an hair breadth, and not miss."
—Judges 20:16

* * *

"Without gunpowder there can be no freedom!"
—German-American proverb during the War of Independence

* * *

"Now then I'll dwell upon the GUN.
When first this weapon was invented
It had no lock; men were contented,
Or rather were oblig'd, 'tis said,
To use a lighted match instead.
At length, the very things they needed,
Hammer, and flint, and steel succeeded;
Then, probably, the shooter thought
His piece was to perfection brought;
But ev'ry age improv'd it still,
And so, perhaps, the future will."
—W. Watt, *Remarks on shooting*, 1835

* * *

"Each civilized nation is found to choose a rifle, and it is curious study to discover the reasons for the selection each of a different pattern."
—Chief of Ordnance Stephen Vincent Benét, 1879

* * *

"The old musket was the arm of the masses, and the rifle is that of the individual."
—J. Walter, *The Volunteer Force*, 1882

* * *

"You must not forget that the rifle is distinctly an American weapon. I want to see it employed."
—General John Pershing, 1917

* * *

"The weapon had to be adapted to the man; measured to fit his intelligence and his training. A rifle suited to the use of a Russian peasant soldier would not efficiently serve the American infantryman. A rifle designed for an expert marksman would not efficiently serve an army put into the field with but little training."
—S. Brown, *The Story of Ordnance in the World War*, 1920

☆ ☆ ☆

"Augsburg, Germany, May 1 (AP)—Pvt. Wyatt Virgil Earp, a direct descendant of the legendary sharpshooting Earp brothers, has qualified as an expert with the M14 rifle, a U.S. Army spokesman announced. Earp, 17, is serving as a tracked vehicle mechanic with the 24th infantry division. He is a grandson of Virgil Earp, who, with his brother, Wyatt, tamed Tombstone."
—*The Washington Post*, 1965

Contents

AMERICAN
RIFLE

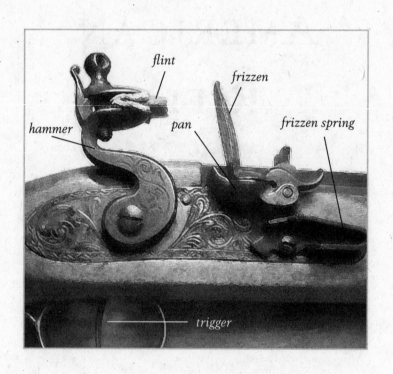

Chapter 1

THE MYSTERY OF
WASHINGTON'S RIFLE

George Washington, never exactly a cheerful or chipper soul, was today even more glum than usual.[1] It was May 21, 1772, and all day he had been posing for his portrait motionless, awkwardly dressed in an antique uniform originally tailored for a younger, slimmer man.[2] The painter—an up-and-coming artist by the name of Charles Willson Peale—was certainly taking his time about it.[3]

And then, at last, Washington was allowed to see the result. There he was, looking suspiciously more youthful (Peale knew how to flatter his subjects) than his forty years might suggest, but otherwise the likeness was most accurate. There he stood, Colonel George Washington of the defunct Virginia Regiment, officer, gentleman, loyal servant of His Majesty, and veteran of the French and Indian War.

Peale's portrait of Washington—the earliest authentic likeness of the man that is known to exist—is distinguished from hundreds of other pictures of eighteenth-century soldiers hanging in the world's museums in one remarkable respect. It's easy to overlook, but, subtly protruding from behind Washington's left shoulder, is the muzzle of an American rifle.[4]

This particular arm had probably been commissioned two years before, in early 1770. In March of that year Washington was staying with his friend Robert Alexander, and according to his diary, they often "went out a hunting" foxes; but he one day rode to "George Town" (then a small place eight miles upstream from Alexandria, Virginia) to pick up "my rifle" from the gunsmith John Jost (or Yost) for £6 and 10 shillings. (An exact conversion to today's dollars is extremely difficult to determine, but $1,400 is a very rough approximation.) Gratifyingly, the cost of the firearm was partly offset by Washington's winning of £1 and 5 shillings from his host at cards, while its fineness can be gauged by the fact that during the Revolution Jost would make rifles for American troops invoiced at £4 and 15 shillings each—and this *after* prices had already soared owing to inflation.[5] Washington may well have paid more than a 100 percent premium for the privilege of owning a custom-made Jost.

Few but Washington would have instructed their portraitists to add such a weapon. Rifles, at the time, were rarities among common soldiers and were carried by officers only in the field—the hunting field, that is, for the noble pursuit of shooting game, not the battlefield.[6] Among civilians, many Americans weren't even sure what exactly a rifle was. As late as June 1775 John Adams mentioned to Abigail that he had recently heard about this "peculiar kind of musket, called a rifle" which had "grooves within the barrel, and carries a ball with great exactness to great distances."[7]

All of which makes Washington's insistence on including one of these "peculiar" firearms in his portrait all the more mysterious. Indeed, a man who wished to use an object as an emblem of rank might have brandished it openly, but he didn't. The rifle is instead discreetly tucked away in the background, serving, it seems, as a reassuring symbol, for those in the know, that this individual, dressed in a uniform last donned two decades before, is *one of them.* So what was Washington telling his fellow Americans? The answer lies hidden somewhere amid the vast, remote American wilderness, an unconquered territory densely thicketed by forests, rumpled by towering mountain ranges, and watered by unbridgeable rivers. For newcomers to this land, it was a terrifying place such as had not existed in Europe since the dark and cold days of the Neanderthals. It was the frontier.

* * *

The great Spanish conquests did not hinge on firearms. Columbus brought with him just one for his infantry—a gun weighing about thirty pounds aptly named the "hand-cannon"—on his voyage to the New World in 1492. This type of weapon, which consisted of an inch-or-so-wide iron tube mounted on a broomstick-sized pole, could be lethal up to a few dozen yards, but its noise, smoke, and flash were undoubtedly its scariest qualities.[8] Thirty years later Hernán Cortés brought down King Montezuma and his mighty Aztec empire with 110 sailors and 508 soldiers, of whom only twelve carried guns.[9]

Owing to the unwieldiness of guns, as well as the impossibility of obtaining extra supplies for them, the conquistadors preferred to use simple, low-tech weaponry and sheer will to carry the day.[10] In 2004 in Peru archaeologists excavated the remains of a man thought to be the earliest known gunshot victim in the Americas. He was lying in a mass grave with five hundred–odd other victims—Inca Indians who had rebelled against the Spaniards in 1536—with a bullet wound to the head from a ball fired from a hundred feet away. Since then, several other skeletons have been found with similar injuries. However, the vast majority of those killed exhibit signs not of gunshot trauma but of wounds caused by violent crushing (by horses' hooves), impalement by pikes, or hacking, smashing, and tearing by other iron weapons.[11] The Amerindian empires were undone not by European technological superiority but by their own internal dissension, germs, their leaders' indecision, the Spaniards' employment of Indian allies disaffected from their overlords, and the foreigners' use of war dogs and horses to cow foes.[12]

Firearms genuinely came into their own only in the early seventeenth century: on July 30, 1609, to be exact, when Samuel de Champlain, the French explorer and fur trader, accompanied his sixty Montagnais and Huron allies on a raid near the Ticonderoga peninsula against their mutual enemies, the Mohawks.[13] Just two volleys from a couple of muskets put to flight a numerically superior force of two hundred. Admittedly, however, Champlain's shots had inflicted more damage to morale than to flesh and bone.

The Mohawks eventually recovered from their fear of the Europeans' thunder-making machines, but even then they and many other tribes were reluctant to dispense with their traditional weaponry. Being heavy, inaccurate, useless in the rain, instantly spottable at night, and based on iron and gunpowder (two elements requiring specialized production facilities), the early gun initially found few takers.

The increasing use of the serpentine, an idea borrowed from crossbows, began to change these attitudes. This was a freely pivoting, S-shaped metal arm attached to the breech—that part of the gun behind the barrel—that served simultaneously as a rudimentary trigger and as a clamp to hold the match, a lengthy wick that burned at an even rate. By suspending the match above the priming powder until the shooter pulled the trigger, the serpentine allowed the firer to hold the "matchlock" gun with both hands—unlike the old harquebus, which had to be steadied with one hand as the other manually applied the match to the powder. As a result, accuracy greatly improved, though the issue of long-glowing, slow-burning matches giving away one's position remained nettlesome.

With the arrival of the flintlock, which used flints to ignite sparks on demand, shooters could forever dispense with sputtering matches. While Europeans saw this new type of gun as merely a gentle evolutionary progression past the basic matchlock, Indians quickly realized that flintlocks comprised an entire replacement technology that rendered their bows and arrows obsolete. To them, the flintlock was a sudden, punctuated revolutionary leap forward.

At that point the Indian adoption of flintlock firearms became extraordinarily rapid.[14] As early as 1628, wrote William Bradford, an early governor of Plymouth Colony, the moment the Wampanoags "saw the execution that a piece [musket] would do, and the benefit that might come by the same, they became mad (as it were) after them and would not stick to give any price." They reckoned "their bows and arrows but baubles in comparison to them."[15] Exactly a century later the Indians used "nothing but firearms," remarked William Byrd, a Virginia lawyer who traveled the area widely. "Bows and arrows are grown into disuse, except only amongst their boys."[16]

Purchasing firearms was one thing: as with most forms of technology (such as cars and computers), *maintaining* them in decent condition over the long term added considerably to their cost in time, effort, and cash. Not only needing spare parts to remain in working order, guns also required a constant supply of powder and ammunition. Neither the parts, nor the powder, nor the bullets, let alone skilled gunsmiths, were easy to come by.

The Indians were quick to learn how to make rudimentary repairs and basic lead ammunition. For parts, they cannibalized unsalvageable weapons. According to Bradford, they soon owned "moulds to make shot of all sorts, as musket bullets, pistol bullets, swan and goose shot, and of smaller shots," then moved on to forging "screw-plates to make screw-pins themselves when they want them." Given that settlers generally took their firearms to smiths if they were broken, the Indians' ability to take care of the bare essentials meant that they were soon "better fitted and furnished than the English themselves."[17]

Still, performing a simple repair on a gun was a far cry from manufacturing one. Aware of the necessity of keeping certain forms of knowledge and technology out of Indian hands, in 1630 New England colonial governments forbade whites to teach any Indian how "to make or amend" firearms. A decade later gunsmiths were banned from repairing seriously damaged Indian-owned weapons; in reaction, Indians took up blacksmithing. In the 1650s, in a final effort at gun control, New Englanders outlawed the sale or distribution of key specialized parts, such as barrels and firelocks, that only experienced artisans could produce.[18]

Not surprisingly, the talents of competent gunsmiths became highly prized—so much so that their skills could save their lives if captured in hostile territory. During Lewis and Clark's expedition to the Pacific, Le Borgne, a one-eyed Indian chief, threatened to massacre the Corps of Discovery but said he would make an exception for "the worker of iron and the mender of guns."[19] During the Pontiac uprising of 1763, when Shawnee, Delaware, and Seneca warriors laid siege to Fort Pitt (now Pittsburgh), they demanded that English soldiers and settlers leave or be killed but that the gunsmiths must stay—and they promised them fair treatment.[20]

At least New Englanders did not have to worry about the Indians making their own gunpowder, which was the product of a multistep, highly specialized chemical and industrial process. Gamely, if unsuccessfully, they tried alternative means of acquiring the gray powder more desired than glimmering gold. In 1637 Pequots kidnapped two young English girls and asked them, according to Edward Winslow, the lordly Plymouth governor, "whether they could make gunpowder. Which when they understood they could not do, their prize seemed nothing so precious a pearl as before." (Dutch traders later freed them.)[21]

As early as 1639 Massachusetts attempted to establish its own powder mills, and three years later the colony's General Court ruled that every plantation and town must build its own saltpeter house. Gunpowder, said its elders, was "the instrumental means that all nations lay hold on for their preservation." Because natural deposits of saltpeter, the key ingredient of gunpowder (it provides the oxygen needed to burn the powder rapidly at high temperature), were unknown in New England, the colonists used a special shed to mix limestone, old mortar, and ashes with animal and vegetable refuse gathered from slaughterhouses and farms, which was then moistened with urine. That of a horse was most often used, but a heavy wine drinker's was much sought, for it was reputed to make the mightiest powder. After decomposing, the compound was leached with water and the crystallized saltpeter extracted. Note that this was a pretty rough-and-ready method for harvesting saltpeter (and would not have passed muster in the finer European armories), but it had to do.[22]

Despite Massachusetts's best efforts, all its powder mills failed either financially or productively. Not until 1675, about thirty-five years after the colony's initial attempt, did a mill at Milton, on the Neponset River, at last succeed in making sufficient quantities of powder to supply the provincial troops and militias. In October 1676 Edward Randolph reported back to London that "the powder is as good and strong as the best English powder."[23] Even so, until the Revolution gunpowder could be hard to come by in parts of America.

The great paradox of gunpowder was that although it was enormously difficult to make, it was also, owing to its lightness and its fluid shape, ridiculously simple to smuggle. A pound or two in a deerskin pouch was sufficient to make a long trip for an illegal transaction economically worthwhile. At the opposite end of the spectrum, musket balls were easy to make—all one needed was a flame, a cheap pair of tongs, and a spherical bullet mold—but the raw lead was so heavy that it was too burdensome to sell in bulk at a profit. The gunpowder shortage combined with ammunition self-rationing encouraged gun owners not to waste their shots. Aim carefully, fire once, was the rule. The habit died hard: in the future the thriftiness and marksmanship of American shooters would become renowned throughout Europe.

The government's efforts initially succeeded in reducing the number of new weapons and the amount of gunpowder available, but their effectiveness was slowly eroded by gunrunning during the Thirty Years' War (1618–48). North America became a proxy battlefield for the great powers of Europe. Native tribes who were allied to the English, or who were regarded as being useful irritants to the French, accordingly received shipments of guns, either as a reward for their loyalty or as a bribe to induce it. The English were by no means alone in this practice. At various times before the Revolution, they, the French, the Swedes, the Germans, and the Dutch denounced one another for trading in munitions while busily selling weapons to their own Indian allies.[24]

Europeans expertly manipulated the Indian hunger for guns for profit and control. By the 1720s Indian dependence on European firearms was well established. No one dissented when Long Warrior observed to his fellow Cherokees that the warriors today "have all their goods of the English arms to defend themselves [without which] they could not go to war and that they'll always be ruled by them." For some colonists, nevertheless, the gun trade was an altruistic one. The British often claimed that by arming the native Americans with modern weaponry, they were raising the savage to civility. To that end the South Carolina governor James Glen reminded an audience of young Cherokees what life was like before his kind arrived: "Instead of the admirable firearms that you are now plentifully supplied with, your best arms [were] bad bows and wretched arrows headed with bills of birds and bones of fishes or at best with sharp stones . . . Your knives were split canes and your hatchets were of stone, so that you spent more days in felling a tree than you now do minutes."[25]

Despite Glen's optimism, the trade was not always equally beneficial.

From the Indians, the British needed only skins and pelts; from the British, the Indians wanted—in addition to weapons, powder, and parts—ironware, clothes, shoes, utensils, bric-a-brac, food, medicine, and liquor. Owing to this imbalance, if a particular tribe was not being cooperative, the British could easily threaten to switch suppliers; that same tribe, however, would have a hard time weaning itself from British goods if relations worsened. For dedicated officials the gun trade was key to maintaining imperial order and realizing peaceful stability on the frontier. "Trade governs these people," observed Colonel Charlesworth Glover in the late 1720s as he counseled *against* sending troops to beat down the Creeks.[26] He was right. By the 1780s the Creeks were finished, undone by rampant consumerism and rum.[27]

The irony of the early firearms business was that even as the British succeeded in creating an ever-greater Indian dependency on them for guns, they became increasingly vulnerable to lethal Indian attacks using those very same weapons. The preservation of their own security, in short, was based on undermining it.

Indeed, despite their low rate of fire, guns escalated the level of violence ever higher from what was once a modest base. When Europeans first arrived, they were sometimes shocked, but more often amused, by how bloodless Indian warfare was. The early colonist Captain John Underhill, witnessing a clash between his Mohegan allies and the Pequots, jeered that "they might fight seven years and not kill seven men." He thought their fighting was "more for pastime than to conquer and subdue enemies."[28] Observed the eminent theologian Roger Williams, seldom were more than twenty combatants killed in any "battle."[29]

Few Europeans understood that in Indian culture death in battle was terrifying to contemplate: warriors who perished were consigned to wander eternally in the afterlife to seek vengeance on their killers. No Valhalla and no Heaven welcomed fallen heroes; they would know only bitter solitude and separation from friends and family. Thus it was that a war band, even when perched on the edge of victory, might retreat if it sustained a few casualties.[30]

Inter-Indian conflict rarely focused on the "serious" European objectives of territorial aggrandizement, religious supremacy, and economic gain. Instead, warriors were more concerned with settling feuds between kin, sorting out grievances, capturing prisoners to "adopt" into the tribe to replenish the population, defending personal honor, and on an individual level, improving one's chances of marrying a chief's daughter by displaying bravery on the warpath.[31] John Lawson, an experienced observer of the North Carolinian tribes, pithily stated that "the Indians ground their wars on enmity, not on interest."[32]

The spread of guns transformed Indian-on-Indian conflict into an economic struggle for survival. European-armed eastern Indians—who had shot unprecedented numbers of elk, deer, and bears in their own territories to pay for their weapons—were forced to surge westward, where those still using bows were inevitably at a disadvantage. As a result, several bands were simply exterminated. The Mohawks' original source of power, for instance, had been their connection to Dutch and English traders in Albany, in what is now upstate New York. Addicted to arms, the Mohawks relentlessly sought beaver pelts and had acquired three hundred muskets by the early 1640s. After quickly killing off their own beaver population, the Mohawks expanded into others' hunting grounds and used their guns to devastating effect against the French-backed Hurons. Over the decades they clashed with the nations of the St. Lawrence River region—the Erie, the Neutral, the Khionontateronon—and many other tribes to satisfy an insatiable hunger for supremacy. In 1661–62 alone the Mohawks and their allies in the Five Nations attacked the Abenaki of New England, the Algonquians of the subarctic, the Siouans in the Upper Mississippi, and other tribes in Virginia.[33] Their advantage began to erode in the 1660s, when they met the Susquehannock of southern New York and Pennsylvania, who were still more heavily armed.[34]

As the supply of ordnance increased, the butcher's bill toted up after each clash rose inexorably. Whereas Underhill had spoken of a few dead men here and there in the 1630s, the missionary Daniel Gookin reported in 1669 that when a force of Massachusetts warriors were ambushed by the Mohawks, "about fifty of their [the Massachusetts] chief men" were slain.[35] Within the decade the fearsome toll that the gun exacted on the Mohawk nation itself had become startlingly evident: in the 1640s they had been able to field between 700 and 800 warriors; by the late 1670s that number had been whittled down to 300.[36]

War between Indian and Indian was not the only sort of violence that the spread of guns magnified. Europeans and Indians increasingly found themselves *behaving* more violently toward each other.[37] Previously, hostile encounters had generally been limited skirmishes with a minimal level of casualties; but the "chivalric" traditions that had historically kept the practice of war within certain boundaries eroded. Colonists accused Indians of viciously torturing prisoners (in 1637 John Tilley was kidnapped and was kept alive, handless and footless, for three days) and of kidnapping women and children.[38] The Indians regarded these barbarous forms of behavior as either ritually blessed or militarily necessary. European-style "total" warfare, they said, was beyond the bounds of acceptability. Indians criticized the practices of razing crops, slaughtering livestock, and destroying property—regarded as perfectly aboveboard in Old World warfare—as condemning to lingering deaths warriors and noncombatants alike.

Only during the last quarter of the seventeenth century did the chivalric boundaries finally disappear. During the Pequot War the Indians had never thought to use fire to destroy Fort Saybrook and the other English settlements, but during that of King Philip, some four decades later, arson became a common Indian method of terrorizing the enemy.[39] As indeed it had long been among Europeans.

The rise of the gun also contributed to changing colonists' attitudes toward the Indians. Initially believing that the Indians were a lost tribe of Israel—in 1650 Thomas Thorowgood argued that Indians and Jews were mighty similar in their speech and customs—the Puritans had been intent on "civilizing" the savages by introducing them to the word of God, the wonder of Christ, and the works of John Calvin.[40] Indians, so the thinking went, would be assimilated into English mores, not only saving their souls but ending bloodshed. To this end, New Englanders strove hard to integrate Indian youths into churches, schools, and apprenticeships, and they invited their Christianized parents to move into "praying towns," where they were isolated from temptation (drink, gambling, and vices of all kinds). These towns, miniature simulacra of utopian life, were all overseen by the impartial workings of English common law. Residents were obliged to style their once-long hair in the English fashion, dress like Englishmen, adopt English names, maintain

English moral norms, and learn the English language. (An exception was made for Arabic numerals.)

By the turn of the eighteenth century, however, a harsher attitude toward the Indian was beginning to prevail. Europeans still widely saw them as God's errant children but as too different from His European offspring to be counted as kin. This unfortunate impression was not alleviated by the failure of the praying towns, which by 1764 had confirmed to Nathaniel Rogers, among many others, that "the [ferocious] manner of a native Indian can never be effaced . . . nor can the most finished politeness totally eradicate the wild lines of his education." By the time of the Revolution hardly anybody, outside the rarefied circles of well-meaning clergymen and liberal-minded reformers, believed that the Christianization of the Indian was a course worth pursuing.[41] If he could not be assimilated, some went so far as to speculate, it might be more merciful to exterminate his kind. From his pulpit in Boston in 1689 Cotton Mather exhorted his parishioners to "beat them small as the dust before the wind, and cast them out, as the dirt in the streets . . . those ravenous howling wolves."[42] (This likening of Indians to diabolically possessed wolves was common at the time, as were comparisons to such devilish beasts as serpents and dragons.)[43]

Perhaps paradoxically, the farther west one traveled from the cities, the less one heard such talk. On the frontier proximity fostered a more clear-eyed understanding of the Indian worldview. Usually quite pacific, the frontier could suddenly turn extremely violent, but these spasms of killing between Indians and frontiersmen were restricted to small groups or individuals and exhausted themselves once the score had been settled.

These isolated types of incidents nevertheless helped create the frontier's dreadful image as a hell deserted by Christ and his saints. For enlightened Europeans, taking a trip out there was like being hurled back to the Dark Ages; Connecticut Yankees might well have thought themselves in King Arthur's barbaric court. Bred on the Greek rationalist classics and bestirred by the great Roman republican orators, visitors were horrified to witness (or much more likely, to hear about at third hand) eye-for-an-eye blood feuds, ferocious plundering, and alien rituals set amid a pitiless moral universe reminiscent of *Beowulf* and the Gilgamesh epic.

That great chronicler of eighteenth-century American life, Hector St. John Crèvecoeur, was convinced that only extreme necessity, misfortune, congenital criminality, or unpayable debts would induce white men to enter "the great woods"—a place "beyond the reach of government." The frontier's inhabitants, he believed, "are often in a perfect state of war; that of man against man, sometimes decided by blows, sometimes by means of the law; that of man against every wild inhabitant of these venerable woods, of which they are come to dispossess them." In the backcountry "men appear to be no better than carnivorous animals of a superior rank, living on the flesh of wild animals when they can catch them, and when they are not able, they subsist on grain."[44] He believed that eating more vegetables cooled the passions.

Not quite as abhorrent to respectable opinion were the traders. These men, having spent a year or three living among Indians, enjoyed some experience of their culture. During their time away they became Indian in dress, language, protocol, and sexual mores.[45] For their part, a class of "trading girls" emerged to service the visitors. According to John Lawson of Carolina, those who made "money by their natural parts" soon affected a distinctive hairstyle to "prevent mistakes" by traders offering cash to respectable women "not of their profession."

Europeans criticized traders on various grounds, but not because they had become "savages." It was widely understood, rightly or wrongly, that traders' adoption of Indian customs was a temporary disguise and that underneath they remained white men. Most of them were runaway servants, former convicts, or rougher individuals making a buck well away from the watchful eyes of the law; their rowdiness and insolence were what most annoyed observers. James Adair, a trader himself but one blessed with a fine education, disliked the current crop because they taught Indians the most horrendous terms of "obscenity and blasphemy."[46]

Many residents of the frontier did not luxuriate in overly positive images of themselves. The Irish, who made up the majority of frontiersmen, "do not prosper so well; they love to drink and to quarrel; they are litigious, and soon take to the gun, which is the ruin of everything," according to Crèvecoeur (who confessed nonetheless that he always carried "my gun, for no man you know ought to enter the woods without one"). But one group stood out in contrast: German immigrants. Observers made exceptions for them, believing that they retained a strong sense of decency, community, and religion.[47] Unlike their Celtic cousins, in the eyes of Crèvecoeur and others, the Germans were just the kind of immigrants America needed more of. Perhaps so, for it would be they who introduced the rifle to this country and helped turn it into the national weapon.

The first recorded German immigrants arrived on October 6, 1683, when the *Concord* arrived in Philadelphia with thirteen Mennonite families aboard. Scraping their money together, they founded Germantown in a new colony euphoniously named Pennsylvania, which King Charles II had granted to William Penn two years before. For these seventeenth-century Israelites, Pennsylvania would become Jerusalem. There they could leave behind the dreadful bloodletting and persecutions of the Thirty Years' War and settle down in peace.

The Mennonites were soon followed by a variety of religious sects—Moravians, Schwenkfelders, Amish, Dunkards, Pietists, and others.[48] Owing to theological strictures, few of these arrivals brought or used guns of any kind (though Moravians and Schwenkfelders were permitted to bear arms in self-defense).[49]

This initial wave of emigration lasted until about the first decade of the eighteenth century. From then onward "religious" Germans were slowly outnumbered by their more secular Lutheran and Reformed compatriots, a good number of whom had performed military service in Europe. Less literate than their predecessors—Benjamin Franklin, annoyed that they were apparently ruining his Philadelphia, called them "Palatine boors" and opined that Germany's jails were being emptied to fill Penn's paradise—these immigrants were also less able to afford to buy farms, as the sects had done, and instead sold their skills as artisans.[50] Gunsmithing was a specialty for a significant number. Indeed, a favorite proverb came from the old country: *Ohne Schweffel und Salzpeter gibt's keine Freiheit!* (Without sulfur and saltpeter there can be no freedom!).[51]

Those accustomed to muskets found the typical German firearm an odd-looking piece. Significantly shorter and lighter than an English-made weapon, with a much narrower caliber and a finer set of rear and front sights than any musket, its most intriguing aspect was the grooves carved inside the barrel (which was smooth in other makes of gun). The weapon was commonly known as a "Jäger rifle."

The ancient Greeks had known that a well-fletched arrow flew truer, faster, and farther than one without vanes or feathers, but they had not understood precisely why. Likewise, in the late fifteenth century gunsmiths in the Alpine regions of southern Germany and northern Switzerland intuitively grasped the principle that a spinning projectile behaved differently from other types of bullets. The question was, how to rotate a bullet?

At the time some experimenters were carving several straight, parallel grooves inside a few musket barrels. They wanted to see whether they could reduce fouling, the sludgelike gunpowder residue blown down the barrel after a bullet was fired. Contemporary powder did not efficiently self-destruct, so whatever was left quickly built up and posed an explosive danger to the shooter if a stray spark ignited it. Frequent cleaning of the barrel, perhaps even every couple of shots, was required. The narrow grooves acted as canals, draining off residue from the bore's surface, which meant the cleaning had to be done less often. Then some bright (and as so often in the early history of firearms, anonymous) German gunsmith around 1450 wondered, why not cut spiraled grooves instead of straight ones? A helical pattern would not only present a greater surface area to trap residue, it might also impart spin to the ball so that it flew like an arrow.

Guns with these types of helical slots were soon dubbed *riffeln* (from the German verb for "to cut or groove") to distinguish them from ordinary smoothbores, whose bullet would erratically bounce and scrape along the inside of the barrel and assume whatever angle of flight its last contact with the muzzle imparted. The difference in bullets fired from the two was initially almost imperceptible, but velocity, weather conditions, and distance to the target amplified the smoothbore bullet's drift by as much as several feet. Still, long experimentation and competition among rival gunsmiths showed that a rifle bullet had to grip the inside of the barrel very tightly to pick up spin from the grooves. Whereas smoothbore shooters merely dropped a ball down the barrel, riflemen used bullets cast slightly larger than their weapon's bore and hammered them down the barrel as far as possible using a wooden mallet and a six-inch metal spike before shoving them into the chamber at the bottom with a strengthened ramrod. That took work—and precious time, though by 1600 they found that wrapping the bullet in a thin greased patch of leather eased entry.[52]

These changes improved weapons performance by a significant degree, but they remained hardly known outside their German homeland. Armies stuck with smoothbore arms for regular issue, partly because between 1470 and 1650 Europe experienced a dramatic rise in prices and the cost of living.[53] Rifle-boring was a skilled-labor–intensive, expensive process: carving the spiraled groove required a specialized machine. Ensuring that the barrel was absolutely straight needed a highly experienced craftsman who commanded among the highest wages then available. Because plain muskets could be produced without anywhere near as much care, they were simply much cheaper than rifles.

Hunters, however, found rifling a boon, for in the rugged and echoey Alps they could use rifles to stalk bears, stags, and chamois from as far as two hundred yards away—a range at which a musket was virtually ineffective. While amid the chasms and atop the peaks, swirling wind eddies wreaked havoc with a regular bullet's trajectory and velocity, with a rifle an experienced hunter could achieve a one-shot kill by compensating for the wind. As early as 1487 shooters were competing in target competitions.[54] By the 1580s the rifle was a relatively common sight in these circles, but it remained a niche product with a reputation as being for experts only. By 1650 its butt had been redesigned to fit sturdily against one's shoulder for greater stability, and it sported the most modern flintlock ignition system available.[55] This was the gun that the Germans took to America.[56]

These recently arrived gunsmiths soon found that, owing to the Quakers' pacifist dislike of their trade, they were unwelcome in Philadelphia, the city of brotherly love. So they departed to found communities in southeastern Pennsylvania, the most famous being Lancaster, established in 1718 about seventy miles west of the capital. Lancaster didn't have much to see—at first, it was just a trading post and several log cabins—but the surrounding area was blessed with seams of iron ore and tracts of maple and walnut trees, which the gunsmiths adopted as their favored materials for stocks. Moreover, the location was perfect: it was within reasonable traveling distance of Philadelphia, yet it also formed the gateway to the boundless wilderness beyond, ensuring a steady supply of rangers, trappers, explorers, and hunters needing well-crafted, reliable, accurate weapons.

Expansion was rapid as immigrants rushed to this new economic hot spot. In 1719 the Swiss-German Martin Meylan built a workshop to bore out gun barrels; two years later Peter Leman was making rifles at Leman Place, a village a few miles east of Lancaster. To serve gun buyers and the burgeoning population, taverns, stores, and inns sprang up along the winding trails linking the isolated settlements, as did posts providing frames for hunters to stretch and dry their deer, bear, wolf, and panther skins. By 1730 guns were the area's most lucrative business, and men with names like Roesser, Stenzel, Albrecht, and Folecht were making a good living manufacturing rifles. In 1815 no fewer than sixty gunsmiths, each with his own particular style and specialty, lived in Lancaster County alone.[57]

Between their arrival and the outbreak of the Revolution, these gunmakers created the very epitome of a firearm: the "Kentucky rifle." One theory surrounding the origin of its name is that in the early 1770s stories were circulating of Daniel Boone's distant explorations west of the Cumberland Mountains. At the time any territory there was generally referred to as "Kentucky" (today, the area making up the states of Kentucky and Tennessee), and because Boone carried a rifle made in Pennsylvania ("Pennsylvania rifle" never really caught on) out there, well, why not use "Kentucky rifle" to describe the typical firearm carried on the frontier? A second explanation traces the name to a song popularized after Andrew Jackson's victory over the British at New Orleans during the War of 1812. The lyrics to "The Hunters of Kentucky" contain the first use in print of the name "Kentucky rifle." It's equally possible, however, that the term was commonly used in speech for many decades prior to the battle but that no one thought to write it down.[58]

For several years after establishing themselves in Lancaster, gunsmiths restricted themselves to turning out run-of-the-mill Jäger rifles,

An early engraving of sixteenth-century German hunters in the wilderness. Immigrant gunsmiths from central Europe brought their specialist knowledge of rifle design to the New World.

the sort they had long been accustomed to making and their customers to buying. From about 1725, however, they gradually introduced a raft of changes that, taken together, spurred the relatively primitive Jäger to evolve into the distinct, if genetically similar, Kentucky.[59] The two most striking mutations were in length and caliber.

Whereas the average barrel length of a German rifle was between 30 and 36 inches, American ones grew to between 40 and 48 inches.[60] The extension allowed a more efficient combustion of the powder, thereby reducing fouling and maximizing the force propelling the ball from the muzzle. It also quieted the rifle's report and served to balance the weapon for improved handling. Aesthetically speaking, as the physical forces were more evenly distributed, gunsmiths could lighten the weight of the barrel so as to fashion a weapon more graceful and slender than the Jäger.

A key ancillary effect of the longer Kentucky barrel was the reduction of caliber. Jäger bores, and those of many smoothbore muskets, averaged .65 of an inch (and there were many monsters of .75 or even .80), while Pennsylvania makers slashed them to between .45 and .50. The smaller bullets made for major economies. Take a pound of lead. For a .75 rifle, one could mold from it 11 balls; for a .50, that figure more than tripled, to 36.[61] On a months- or even year-long expedition into the wilderness and with no way of purchasing more supplies, that difference could mean life or death.

Many Europeans believed that a large bullet was a more effective killer than a slighter one and refused on principle to "trade down" to a rifle. Intuitively, size would matter, but any projectile's lethality hinges on multiple factors, not least of which is the proportion of gunpowder a shooter uses relative to the size of the bullet. George Hanger, a British colonel regarded as one of the world's finest shots and who fought in America during the Revolution, observed that riflemen here "never put in more powder than is contained in a woman's thimble." Even so, owing to the bullet's smallness, "they will carry [i.e., load] more than *half the weight* of the ball in powder." By contrast, sportsmen in London used a quarter of their bullets' weight in powder. By this measure, an American ball weighing, say, 200 grains (a gram equals 15.43 grains) would be boosted by 100 grains of powder, and a British ball of 400, by an identical amount. Thus, a British shooter would load the same amount of powder as an American, but because the ball was much heavier, each grain would be forced to do more work. The projectile's velocity and kinetic energy consequently suffered. In Hanger's words, "what the smaller ball loses by its want of weight, is most astonishingly compensated for, by the triple velocity given to it, from the great increase of the powder."[62]

Hanger was convinced that the American method and style of shooting was distinct from anything found in Europe. He was right. Nowhere else was the cult of accuracy so rigorously worshiped as in colonial

America. Stretching the barrel, for instance, increased the distance between the rear and front sights, allowing the shooter to take a more precise bead on his target.[63] Some riflemen even purchased a long, narrow brass or iron tube about half an inch in diameter that could be screwed into the top of the barrel to function as a rudimentary "telescopic" sight. (The accessory lacked a magnifying glass but certainly aided concentration.)[64]

Only American riflemen refused to "guess" how much powder to use for their personalized weapon. When they purchased a new rifle, they would rest its muzzle on the snow or on a bleached cloth and fire it. If it spat out unburned residue, they gradually reduced the powder load until none stained the white background. Then they would fashion a powder flask or charger that would dispense exactly the right amount down the barrel.[65] For "tricky" shots, they would rely on long experience and a skilled eye to calculate whether to use extra or skim a little off. For longer ranges, where the ball would be buffeted by the wind and retarded by air resistance, they would add more powder for higher muzzle velocity and a flatter ballistic arc; to increase accuracy by reducing recoil at shorter distances, they would use less. In order to hit enemies laboring under the misapprehension that they were out of range, Davy Crockett occasionally inflated the muzzle velocity of a .40-caliber flintlock nicknamed "Old Betsey" (one of at least three rifles he owned) up to a remarkable 2,500 feet per second (normally, it was 1,600 fps) by loading it with six fingers of gunpowder. During hard times Crockett conserved his ammunition and powder by sawing bullets in two and halving his charge.[66]

In Europe hunting with guns was a pursuit reserved for the nobility, but in America, where gun ownership on the frontier was more common if not universal, even children were introduced to firearms from an early age. When a boy was twelve or thirteen years old, wrote Joseph Doddridge of the typical eighteenth-century Virginian and Pennsylvanian, he "was furnished with a small rifle and shot pouch. He then became a fort soldier, and had his port hole assigned him. Hunting squirrels, turkeys and raccoons soon made him expert in the use of his gun." He was taught never to shoot offhand—from a standing position, steadying the weapon against his shoulder—if he could help it. Rather, he was to use a rest—such as placing moss on a log or holding the rifle against the side of a tree—to aid steadiness.[67] Marksmanship was of paramount importance to the American frontiersman.

How accurate were Kentucky rifles? Compared to modern weapons, they were monstrously inaccurate, but *at the time* contemporaries regarded them as terrifyingly unerring instruments of death. A 1920s experiment pitted a grooved Kentucky rifle against a smoothbore musket by setting up man-sized targets at distances of 100, 200, and 300 yards. Each weapon was fired ten times at the three ranges. At 100 yards the rifle hit the target ten out of ten, as did the musket. At 200 the rifle retained its perfect score, but the musket plummeted to just four hits. At 300 the rifle hit five times, but the musket, a miserly once.[68]

The experimenters were expert shooters, firing a limited number of shots using modern gunpowder in ideal conditions. In reality, any number of factors could adversely affect accuracy, so firearms performance—even for rifles—was nowhere near as impressive in actual battle. The fault could lie with the gun itself: incorrect sight positioning, a barrel flaw, a faulty trigger pull, too wide a gap between bullet and bore, an overpowerful recoil, or barrel vibration. Or the gunpowder could be defective, owing to hurried measuring, mixed granulation, dampness, low quality, or indifferent ramming. The ammunition might also present a problem: weight and caliber deviation, rushed loading, or faulty casting, resulting in air pockets and spherical asymmetry. Finally, such external conditions as wind, temperature, air density, humidity, and sunlight all gently altered the flight of the bullet.

In battle soldiers would exhibit purely human defects, such as overloading their weapons multiple times, using old flints reluctant to spark, dropping the cartridges, experiencing burning smoke-blindness, becoming nauseous from the saltpeter in the gunpowder, bumping into the man reloading next to them, and even forgetting to withdraw the ramrod from the barrel so that it, along with the ball, was blown out of the muzzle. These errors could easily ruin even a shot fired at point-blank range. On dry days alone muskets misfired 15 percent of the time; on wet, one in four shots never left the barrel.[69]

With all these considerations taken into account, in the eighteenth century the British understandably insisted that shooters were exhibiting a "high degree of precision" when one of every five or six rounds they fired hit a three-foot-wide target at 100 yards. Even successful shots could be randomly dispersed, as demonstrated by a British test that fired ten rounds at a soldier-shaped target only 100 yards away. The result: six misses. Of the four successes, one thudded into the target's breast, another into its knee, another into its mouth, and the last, its ear. As painful, and perhaps as fatal, as these wounds might have been, there was no predictability as to where they would hit.[70]

Given its undoubtedly superior accuracy, the rifle did not long remain confined to Lancaster. Word of this intriguing hybrid spread to the west and south, as did a younger generation of gunsmiths who had learned the trade from their emigrant fathers. In 1784 Jacob Ferree moved to Allegheny County—twenty-four miles up the Monongahela from Pittsburgh—where he and his wife (a fine shot; she was his product-tester) opened a powder mill and a gunsmith shop popular with the hunting trade.[71] Other second- and third-generation sons like Henry Albright and Peter Resor joined him.[72]

As the frontier expanded, gunsmiths followed, making the identification of rifles with the American backcountry ever more inextricable. The Carolinas, the Ohio River country, Maryland, Kentucky, and Tennessee all witnessed an influx of German-trained smiths. Virginia west of the tidewater area, in particular, was a hotbed of rifle ownership from the early 1750s onward.[73]

Even as gunsmiths diffused outward from Lancaster, they jealously guarded their arcane knowledge of rifle-making. Until automation emerged in the first third of the nineteenth century, each and every piece of a rifle was manufactured in a gunsmith's own minifactory—which made between fifteen and thirty guns each year—thereby excluding outsiders from the process and preventing nonapproved competitors from setting up shop. To further protect the secrets of the craft, the gunsmiths' apprenticeship structure was by far the most onerous of any trade: teenagers served their masters for no fewer than eight years to imbibe the mysteries of engraving metal, casting brass, assembling complex firelocks, carving wood, forging metal parts, and rifling barrels.[74]

Over the course of the century, nevertheless, rifle-making progressively became less "German" and more "American" as gunsmiths married out of their traditional ethnic backgrounds or Anglicized their names.[75] Henry Albright's original name, for instance, had been Albrecht, and when Mr. and Mrs. Ferree's descendants fanned out to Kentucky, Virginia, Maryland, Massachusetts, and New Hampshire, they married spouses with names like Steele, Griffith, Critchfield, Marlott, Powel, and Gardner.[76] The distinctly non-German-sounding David and William Geddy advertised that they rifled gun barrels as early as August 8, 1751, in the *Virginia Gazette*.[77]

Apprenticeships too, once restricted to German youths, were eventually opened to Anglo-Americans—not always successfully. The drudgery of maintaining the forge fire, pumping the bellows, and polishing gun parts could grind anyone down. It evidently did one John McCan, a runaway apprentice whose master Christian Klein offered an eight-dollar reward in the September 16, 1795, issue of the *Lancaster Journal*. McCan, aged nineteen and five feet six inches tall, spoke "both English and German, but English best." As late as 1795, remarkably, apprentices were expected to learn German for shopwork.[78]

An exception to the diffusion of rifle knowledge and ownership was the East Coast. At the outbreak of the Revolution there were rifle shops in Baltimore, Alexandria, Cumberland, Charlotte, and Augusta—but not a single one east of the Hudson River.[79] If one earnestly desired a rifle, one could find one, but only by diligently scouring a newspaper's classified pages for a rare announcement that a couple were in stock. This ad, from the *New York Journal and General Advertiser* of March 16, 1775, no doubt caused some palpitations among the city's rifle cognoscenti: "Gilbert Forbes, Gun Maker. At the sign of the Sportsman in the Broad Way, opposite Hull's Tavern in New York. Makes and sells all sorts of guns, in the neatest and best manner; on the lowest terms; has for sale, silver and brass mounted pistols; *rifle barrel guns*, double swivel and double-roller gun locks; 50 ready made new bayonet guns, on all one size and pattern" (emphasis added).[80] Indeed, the few rifle fans (perhaps they had spent some time on the frontier) in New York and Connecticut were widely regarded as rather eccentric marksmanship fanatics.

If rifles weren't popular among easterners, they found eager customers among the Indians. Those who believed Indians were too ignorant to appreciate the distinction between Kentucky rifles and cheap muskets were refuted by the Shawnees' own vocabulary: muskets were called *teaquah*, but rifles were *pemqua teaquah*.[81] There was clearly something special about the firearms, which is why the Moravian missionary David Zeisberger noticed that the Delawares "use no other than rifle barrelled guns, having satisfied themselves that these are best at long range."[82]

Remarkably, the first mention of Indians possessing rifles had been in 1736—relatively soon after Lancaster began booming—when Colonel Auguste Chouteau noted in his journal that the anti-French Chickasaws of northern Mississippi were armed with them—and were counted as fearsomely good shots, so much so that even the Iroquois were wary of them.[83] Nine years later a Delaware sachem named Mussemeelin was captured and found to be carrying a rifle. Eleven years after that, James Smith, a prisoner in Ohio, recorded that his adopted brother Tontieaugo was a "first rate hunter [who used] a rifle gun and every day killed deer, raccoons and bear." King Hagler, sachem of the Catawbas, was buried in 1763 with his prized "silver mounted rifle and a fine powder flask."[84] By that time possession of a rifle had become much more common, and the Pennsylvanian gunsmiths who had moved westward were selling rifles in large quantities to the fur-dependent Delawares, Shawnees, and Mingos.[85]

The catalyst for this expansion and extension of the Indian rifle market had been the British triumph over their French, Spanish, and Dutch rivals in the race to arm the Indians. Their winning strategy in the 1750s had been to provide high-quality merchandise at lower prices than their competitors, adding, as a bonus, inexpensive and sometimes even free repairs.[86]

Over the previous decades one of the British purveyors' most successful products had been the "trade fusil," an affordable, utilitarian musket imported under contract with the Hudson's Bay Company.[87] These smoothbores had significantly longer barrels than the German Jäger rifles then being made by the Pennsylvanians.[88] Perhaps they were inspired by suggestions from their Indian customers; or perhaps they noticed that weapons with extended barrels outperformed their Jäger equivalents, but the Pennsylvania gunsmiths began lengthening their rifle barrels—making them up to forty-eight inches long, the same as a standard trade fusil. The contemporaneous shift toward smaller bores may also have been partly prompted by the trade fusils' example. The original Jäger rifle's caliber averaged, as we have seen, about .65, while from 1730 onward the fusil's was about .56 or .58.[89] From about that time the Kentucky's bore fell to between .45 and .50. This melding of German engineering with English style had created a specifically American rifle.

Indians admired the rifles as ideal hunting weapons and objects of status, but they also quickly recognized that rifles represented their best shot at freedom. In his report of 1764 discussing British Indian policy, Colonel John Bradstreet astutely divined the native Americans' desire for rifles: "All the Shawanese and Delawar Indians are furnished with rifled barrel guns, of an excellent kind, and that the upper Nations are getting into them fast, by which, *they will be less dependent upon us, on account of the great saving of powder, this gun taking much less, and the shot much more certain, than any other gun, and in their way of carrying on war, by far more prejudicial to us, than any other sort*" (emphasis added). He urgently recommended that the government "stop the making and vending of any more of them in the Colonies, nor suffer any to be imported," if it wanted to save its hide.[90]

The most alarming aspect of the Indian preoccupation with rifles was that the attributes of this particular type of firearm admirably fitted their traditional way of warfare—threatening to make it deadlier and more effective than ever before. When they had first experienced the Indian style of fighting, English settlers (especially those with a soldiering background) were amazed by how different it was from their own. In European warfare of the time troops formed into long, thin lines spread across a chosen field of battle and efficiently marshaled by their officers. They would fire a volley or two from their muskets, then attempt to advance toward the enemy army as quickly as possible to use bayonets against them. Essentially, then, late-seventeenth- and eighteenth-century warfare was based on three factors: volume of fire, officer-imposed discipline, and shock combat at close quarters. By contrast, the Indians relied on individual accuracy, initiative, and surprise.

Firepower was the realm of the musket, a weapon useless for fine marksmanship on an individual level but fearsome when numbers of them were massed together and fired simultaneously. European commanders had long recognized that a single man firing one shot with a musket at a small target 100 or 150 yards away was powerless since, owing to random dispersion and all the external variables involved, he would need extraordinary luck to hit exactly what he was aiming at. But if a commander packed together enough men along a sufficiently wide front, what the soldiers lacked in accuracy would be more than made up for in the sheer volume of lead unleashed.

The downside of this tactic was that much ammunition was wasted— a source of great worry in an era when every pound of lead and ounce of gunpowder had to be transported by horse and wagon at no little expense and danger. Analyzing data from several recent wars, the French found that just one out of every ten thousand cartridges supplied to the army would subsequently hit an enemy. A Prussian military writer claimed that a soldier using a musket required his own weight in lead to put a single man out of action. A widely accepted rule of thumb, however, held that it actually took seven times that. Sir Richard Henegan, who witnessed the fighting in the Peninsular War against Napoleon, calculated that an infantryman needed to fire 459 shots in order to hit an enemy.[91] Using Henegan's figure, a skilled musketman who fired five shots a minute, and who often had just five minutes of firing time before a charge, could participate in up to nineteen battles before he actually killed a man using his firearm.

That sobering fact mattered little to commanders of the time. Battles were mostly won not with muskets—firepower served as a kind of appetizer for the main course—but by soldiers' obedience to orders. Ferocious discipline was key to ensuring simultaneous fire along the line, to preparing to receive a volley, and to mounting an assault. Since the complex maneuvers and clockwork tactics of contemporary warfare hinged on large numbers of men unquestioningly adhering to their officers' commands, soldiers, from the minute they enlisted, were subjected to tedious drills and exercises designed to extinguish individual thought and initiative. Men who used their own minds were menaces to morale and the mass.

A core assumption among commanders was that men were little more than tamed beasts: they could be trained to perform tricks and whipped into fearful subservience, but in battle they must ultimately be unchained to indulge their bloodlust by ravaging the enemy. That was what bayonets were for. During a battle, once the initial rounds had been loosed, infantry would advance with bayonets fixed and seek to break the enemy. The true test of an army was not how well it fired its weapons at a distance but how lustily it fought hand-to-hand.

The Indian way of warfare was wholly removed from these European tactics. Where the Europeans insisted on decisive clashes of arms in the open field, Indians preferred guerrilla attacks in the woods.

The practice of invisibly lurking with an intent to kill an unsuspecting enemy was integral to Indian fighting. Native American warfare avoided pitched battles in favor of low-level insurgencies that inflicted relatively few casualties but dragged on for years, tiring out nervous settlers, wearying militiamen with constant call-outs, and exhausting government treasuries unable to afford the cost of maintaining a permanent professional force for protection. Europeans naturally became frustrated by the Indians' refusal to stand and fight.[92] Cotton Mather quoted Julius Caesar (representing the forces of civilization, if not of Christianity) on the nomadic Scythians, whom he likened to the maddening Indians: *"Difficulius Invenire quam Interficere"* (It is harder to find them than to foil them).[93]

Frontiersmen popularized the term "skulking" to describe the Indian reliance on (in the worried words of William Hubbard) "ambushments, sudden surprises, or overmatching some of our small companies with greater numbers, having had many times six or seven to one."[94] Worse, European troops were used to fighting during good weather and in daylight—that was the only way a general could possibly direct the thousands of regimented men under his command—but the Indians subjected them to nighttime and dawn raids, as well as surprise attacks during thunderstorms and fog.[95]

The American terrain was particularly murderous. The forests that had once covered much of western Europe had long been cleared, but over here the whole country, as one general informed Prime Minister William Pitt, was "an immense uninhabited wilderness overgrown everywhere with trees and underbrush, so that nowhere can anyone see twenty yards."[96]

Wilderness fighting favored fleety, camouflaged, loosely organized bands of men traveling light and adeptly using trees, ravines, and rocks to pick their targets and snipe at the enemy before scuttling to another hiding place. The Indians' favored strategy was to dispatch scouts to detect approaching enemies, then ambush them in a vulnerable position, such as alongside a river or along a path passing through a ravine.[97] Upon deducing the enemy's weaknesses, Indian bands executed a complicated series of tactical maneuvers to deploy into a "half-moon" formation that would flank the unfortunates and pick them off.[98]

Such attacks nearly always occurred from a distance, using rifles or bows, for it was a rash chief who engaged trained soldiers in hand-to-hand fighting.[99] The tomahawk and club, accompanied by a war whoop, could be terrifying for raw militia and settlers, but disciplined redcoats accustomed to stopping cavalry charges in their tracks with "cold steel bayonets" proved tougher to break. General Jeffery Amherst was so confident in his soldiers' steadfastness that he often cut the time-honored number of ranks from three to two (the famous "thin red line" formation later seen at Waterloo and Balaclava) because "no yelling of Indians . . . can possibly withstand two ranks, if the men are silent, attentive, and obedient to their officers."[100] From even such an early date, facility with a bayonet-tipped musket was associated with mass discipline and hard fighting, the rifle with individual skill and enterprise.[101]

Eventually, Americans adapted to wilderness fighting (and frontier living) by adopting Indian tactics and tricks. So it was that while schoolboys in New York toiled over their Latin declensions, youths out west learned how to "imitat[e] the noise of every bird and beast in the woods," as Joseph Doddridge wrote of western Pennsylvanians after the French and Indian War. "The imitations of the gobbling and other sounds of wild turkeys often brought those keen eyed and ever watchful tenants of the forest within the reach of the rifle."[102]

Woodland skills once used for peaceful purposes could easily be turned to warlike ends—by both sides. That proficiency in turkey calls during the day, and of wolves or owls at night, also allowed Indian warriors and European rangers alike to locate each other in the deep woods without alerting their human quarry.[103] Likewise, camouflaging oneself to hunt beasts was a skill needed to hunt people. Accordingly, the Indians "apparel[ed] themselves from the waist upwards with green boughs, that our Englishmen could not readily discern them, or distinguish them from the natural bushes."[104] Whites soon abjured their bright-colored clothes for scruffy browns and greens.[105] Veterans of frontier fighting even began campaigning in the months of October and November, when expeditions into the forest were less risky because, as one soldier put it, "of the trees losing their leaves, by which one can see a little through the woods, and prevent the enemy's surprises."[106]

The Indians also kept "a deep silence in their marches and motions"— unlike newly arrived whites, who, complaining loudly about their rations and making lewd remarks, were blissfully unaware that their approach could be heard by awaiting attackers. Not only did the Indians keep their mouths shut, they traveled noiselessly thanks to their deerskin moccasins, while the interlopers heedlessly clumped around. One friendly Indian scout guiding an inexperienced British unit through the woods became incensed by a soldier's "new pair of shoes that made a creaking noise as they travelled." He refused to continue until the fellow borrowed his moccasins. Another time the same guide ordered a man wearing leather breeches that were making "a rustling noise" to soak them in the river to quiet them.[107] Any frontiersman worth his salt quickly threw out his boots and wore moccasins each and every day.

Men unaccustomed to frontier fighting found swamps and forests to be the most dangerous and terrifying places on earth. With their "arms pinioned with the thick boughs of trees" and "feet shackled with the roots spreading every way in those boggy woods," local militiamen likened the experience to "fighting with a wild beast in his own den."[108] Perceptive commanders soon ended the typical European practice of marching in a body through the woods.[109] They instead advanced with at least several yards separating each man and were directed to scatter and take cover if attacked.[110] No longer, either, would they attack in line but would creep silently forward on their bellies once a scout detected the enemy. Most important, to avoid ambushes the best officers and frontiersmen never left a swamp or forest by the same path they entered.[111]

Still, sometimes officers had to be sufficiently flexible to rely on the old, imported methods of mass, volume, concentration, and discipline. Consequently, between King Philip's War and the French and Indian War, an authentic *American* way of warfare evolved on the frontier. It was a doctrine based on an admixture of European and Indian practices. It relied much more heavily on individual enterprise (symbolized by the rifle and accuracy) than was acceptable in Europe, yet it was more disciplined (symbolized by the mass-firing musket and bayonetry) than anything previously seen in America. Americans on the defensive might still use the tried and true European tactic of forming the infantry into lines, but they were lines that took advantage, Indian style, of any available cover. Likewise, they learned that when taking the offensive, they needed to combine firepower with loose, fluid movements rather than remaining in a static line and moving directly forward.

In the hands of the most masterful commanders, the fusion of New and Old World ways could be devastating against both stiff European formations and mobile Indian ambushes alike. The young George Washington would perfectly embody the meaning and methods of this American way of warfare.

★ ★ ★

Notwithstanding the blazing temperature, just after midday on July 9, 1755, General Edward Braddock and his aides (including a very young Washington) were justly confident: their objective, the French Fort Duquesne (now subsumed within Pittsburgh) was but a few days' march away, and resistance so far had been light. Braddock's 1,469 men comprised two British regiments, three companies of Virginia provincial troops (two of rangers and one of "carpenters"—axmen and bridge-builders—all experienced at frontier fighting), and three "independent" companies from New York and South Carolina. They exultantly marched in an extended column along a narrow path through the woods.[112]

As Colonel Thomas Gage's vanguard of grenadiers reached the top of a hill, it marched headlong into a French and Indian ambush. Under heavy fire, the grenadiers retreated while the nine-hundred-strong enemy splayed out into a half-moon shape, surrounding the British on three sides. In the confusion of the grenadiers' withdrawal, panic spread among Braddock's officers and men. Within minutes the soldiers were completely entangled, and no man could find his lieutenant or sergeant. It was impossible to organize an efficient defense against the Indian marksmen briskly picking them off from the hill, a ravine to one side, or the thick trees to the other.[113] One veteran remembered that he never saw more than "five or six" of the enemy at a time, and even then they were "either on their bellies or behind trees or running from one tree to another."[114] Another spoke of incoming fire "like popping shots, with little explosion, only a kind of whizzing noise; (which is a proof the enemy's arms were rifle barrels)."[115] It would be hours before the pummeled, bloody remnants of Braddock's force managed to retreat to safety.[116]

Braddock himself was just one of the astounding 997 casualties: since 60 of the 86 officers present were killed or wounded early in the battle, the Indians had clearly been targeting epaulettes. Washington himself had helped the mortally stricken general onto a cart. A little later, worried that those back home presumed him dead, Washington assured a kinsman that "I now exist and appear in the land of the living by the miraculous care of Providence, that protected me beyond all human expectation." He had escaped unscathed from the slaughter, though "I had four bullets through my coat, and two horses shot under me."[117]

Raised since birth to worship the professionalism and bravery of the British Army, Washington was disheartened by what he witnessed that terrible day. The redcoats had "behaved with more cowardice than it is possible to conceive," and their "dastardly" reluctance to stand and fight had condemned the Virginians, who had been "inclined to do their duty, to almost certain death."[118] These provincial troops, in the words of Captain Robert Cholmley's servant, had kept their heads and, in true frontier style, "fought behind trees and I believe they did the most execution of any."[119] But it was all for naught: while "the Virginian companies," reported Washington, "behaved like men, and died like soldiers . . . I believe out of the 3 companies that were there that day, scarce 30 [men] were left alive." The British panic made it inevitable that the Virginians would eventually "br[eak] and run as sheep before the hounds."[120] Even so, Washington's uncle Joseph Ball assured him that back at home "every body commends the courage of the Virginians" and blamed Braddock's "rash conduct" for the fiasco.[121]

Even if Virginians had only praise for Washington's actions, the aftershocks of Braddock's defeat put paid to his efforts (which had included lessons in the social sport of fencing) to acquire a much-desired commission in the royal army. Though he was not condemned publicly for the catastrophe, Washington, like the other aides associated too closely with Braddock, was held to be guilty of helping to lose an army. No evidence was ever produced, and no accusations were published, but in London and Boston army commanders began saying his name with a silent question mark after it. The young man's hitherto meteoric career turned earthward, and he was obliged to console himself with a distinctly provincial appointment as "Colonel of the Virginia Regiment & Commander in Chief of all Forces now raised & to be raised for the Defence of this His Majesty's Colony."[122] It was a sweet-sounding title, but it was no colonelcy in a smart British regiment of the line. Still, his loss would be America's gain, for that battle affirmed two of the most important lessons that Washington ever gleaned from his bloody experience on the frontier.

He witnessed at first hand the necessity of discipline and efficient officering to any army. The Virginian companies were brave, but bravery alone did not win victories. And to be perfectly honest, Virginians, like other American militia and provincial troops, could be a slovenly, ill-behaved lot. "If left to themselves," drolly observed the British general Jeffery Amherst in 1759, the provincials "would eat fried pork and lay in their tents all day."[123]

Washington's first priority was to whip his regiment into shape. For this task, his lack of a king's commission turned out to be fortunate. Not beholden to the fanatically enforced regulations laid down by the army, and liberated from the brown-nosing and glad-handing that young officers hopeful of preferment had to perform, Washington was able to train his Virginians as he thought fit.

Turning his attention first to the officers, Washington insisted that in the Virginia Regiment a meritocratic (if not democratic) ethos would be the rule. Men, he believed, will follow only leaders they respect. In this sense, the Indian practice of electing their commanders was the example Washington intended to follow (within limits). "Remember," he told his subordinates on January 8, 1756, "that it is the actions, and not the commission, that make the officer and that there is more to be expected from him than the title." (Washington meant what he said: he exiled an ensign from the regiment that day for dishonoring himself by cheating at cards.)[124] Officers would gain respect through the display of personal competence and fairness to all ranks: henceforth enlisted soldiers would be paid, fed, and equipped on time and according to what they were promised at their recruitment. Skimming the men's pay for personal gain, showing favoritism, and lying about the men's conditions of service—time-honored practices in European armies—would no longer be tolerated.

Virginia volunteers had duties as well as rights. In return for decent treatment, command by sound officers, and fair justice, they would submit to drill and ceremonial regulations conceived by Washington "even in the most minute punctilios."[125] The deal included also accepting his exertion of discipline. When he discovered that his men had been deserting, Washington tempestuously ordered a "gallows near forty foot high erected" and sentenced fourteen deserters to death, five more to fifteen hundred lashes, and two others to a thousand. (Governor Robert Dinwiddie, a longtime ally, helpfully provided sixteen blank death warrants.) As time went on, however, Washington's ardor for capital punishment dissipated, and he ended up pardoning all but two—one an incorrigible deserter and the other "one of the greatest villains upon the continent." His mercifulness did not extend to the guilty's method of execution: once benoosed on the gallows, they were to be raised slowly so as to be strangled, rather than dropped so that their necks broke instantly. Dinwiddie would, Washington hoped, excuse him the decision, for the method "conveyed much more terror to others; and it was for example sake we did it."[126]

The colonel's efforts paid off when two of his companies were sent to South Carolina in 1757. Though Washington stayed at home, one of his most promising captains and a fellow veteran of Braddock's lost army, George Mercer, proudly boasted to his chief that "we have been told here by the [British] officers that nothing ever gave them such surprise as our appearance." They had been "expecting to see a parcel of . . . disorderly fellows headed by officers of their own stamp (like the rest of the Provincials they had seen)." But "behold they saw men properly disposed who made a good and soldierlike appearance and performed in every particular as well as could be expected from any troops."[127]

There remained, nonetheless, distinct differences between the Virginia Regiment and the British infantry, not least of which was Washington's emphasis on marksmanship. In selecting soldiers for his elite Virginians, Washington insisted that "great care should be observed in choosing active marksmen; the manifest inferiority of inactive persons, unused to arms, in this kind of service to lively persons who have practised hunting, is inconceivable. The chance against them is more than two to one."[128] To get the best shots, he beat up for many more recruits than he needed and put them through their paces at the target range to find the naturals and the exceptionals.[129] The men were to be trained to hit targets on the bull's-eye at a variety of distances because Washington had imbibed the lesson that the Indian way of warfare, developed and honed over innumerable generations, paid lavish dividends.[130]

He was certainly keen to put principle into practice. The *New-York Mercury* reported in the spring of 1756 that French-backed Indians "have drove in all the inhabitants on the frontiers for 50 miles" and that the Indian bands "very dextrously avoid large parties, while they make a prey of the smaller ones, so great is their cunning in warlike matters." But one "Col. Washington . . . intends to scour the woods, and find them out, if possible. If he does, I hope it will deter them from coming again soon, as we shall have several good woodsmen with us, who are so dextrous with their rifles, that they generally make sure of their mark."[131] (The anonymous officer upon whom the story relied was possibly Washington himself, who was rarely averse at this time to self-advertisement.)

Washington, almost uniquely among officers of his upscale social background, had been a rifle aficionado from at least the moment he re-turned from his initial baptism in frontier warfare, which actually oc-curred a year before the slaughter at Monongahela. In July 1754, during a fruitless expedition to oust the French from the forks of the Ohio, the twenty-two-year-old commander was humiliatingly forced to surrender at Fort Necessity (at Great Meadows, Pennsylvania) but was allowed to return to Williamsburg with his four-hundred-man force (including about one hundred South Carolina regulars under Captain James Mackay). Among the weapons confiscated by the French were "7 rifled guns" valued at £6 each and belonging to John Frazier, the expedition's armorer.[132]

None of these weapons belonged to Washington, but he had lost his own anyway. Nearly two months after the surrender, following up on an inquiry from his comrade-in-arms, Mackay informed Washington that "I shall take care that you shall have your rifle."[133] It seems another man had it and hoped that Washington would exchange another rifle for it. How this fellow came by it remains a mystery, but because Mackay noted that Washington himself had ordered that every soldier should carry his own weapon, the letter suggests that the man had been present at Fort Necessity. It's likely that during the desperate defense of the fort, Washington had lent his rifle to a soldier whose own weapon had mis-fired and had asked Mackay to get it back.[134]

Washington was virtually alone in the officer corps in carrying a per-sonal rifle in the hinterland, and this particular weapon was special to him. It is a pity, then, that he doesn't seem to have reacquired it, for we find him three years later purchasing another rifle, this time from Aaron Ashbrook, for £4 and 15 shillings on February 22. Perhaps it was a sec-ondhand one, for later that year he brought it in for repair to Joshua Baker, an upmarket gun-maker in Frederick County, Virginia, who spe-cialized in the rifle business and often worked as armorer for the Virginia Regiment.[135]

In 1758 Washington's efforts with his Virginians at last paid off. That year the British, now under General John Forbes, set out to avenge Braddock's defeat by conquering Fort Duquesne—Braddock's original objective. Forbes, now in his late forties, had won his spurs fighting guerrillas during the War of the Austrian Succession (1742–48) before becoming adjutant general to John Campbell, Earl of Loudoun in Nova Scotia in 1757. Loudoun himself had been blooded in counterinsurgency fighting during the Jacobite uprising in the Scottish Highlands a few years previously. The earl was among the few senior officers in North America who understood the need for light troops, or regular troops who were more agile, and less encumbered with accoutrements, than the typical soldier, so that they could scramble up ridges and skirmish with enemy scouts in the woods.[136]

Forbes was less enamored of imported light troops, and, believing that he could benefit from the presence of both bayonets *and* rifles, he preferred to rely on regulars backed up by frontiersmen and native American allies. Adamant that "we must comply and learn the art of war, from enemy Indians or anything else who have seen the country and war carried on in it," in the woods Forbes employed frontiersmen to screen his regulars and Indians to scout ahead of the army; in battle the redcoats would fix bayonets and bring the enemy down at close quarters.[137]

For the Forbes expedition, the general chose two subordinates, both experts in frontier fighting: Colonels George Washington (of the Virginia Regiment) and Henry Bouquet (of the Royal American Regiment of Foot). Bouquet (1719–65) was a Swiss working in the British service whom Washington regarded as the leading wilderness soldier on the continent. Believing frontiersmen to be superior to redcoats at trekking over mountainous terrain, snowshoeing, swimming, working individually and yet rallying when needed, finding cover, deploying camouflage, and leaping over wide ditches and fallen trees, he enlisted them as auxiliaries to his regular troops.

Before the expedition left, Washington and Bouquet were regularly exchanging ideas. Washington told Bouquet that his men had few regimental uniforms, but "far from regretting" this fact, he confessed that "were I left to pursue my own inclinations I would not only order the men to adopt the Indian dress, but cause the officers to do it also, and be the first to set the example myself [in order to proceed] as light as any Indian in the woods." "Indian dress"—by which he meant the frontiersman's version, consisting of hunting shirts, moccasins, and leggings—"is an unbecoming dress, I confess, for an officer; but convenience rather than show" should be the watchword in the backcountry. "Soldiers in that trim," he argued, "are better able to carry their provisions; are fitted for the active service we must engage in; [and are] less liable to sink under the fatigues of a march." Bouquet readily agreed that "their dress should be our pattern in this expedition."[138] Privately, Washington was thrilled that the more experienced warhorse had accepted *his* recommendations, and he boasted to his friends about it.[139]

Likewise, Washington followed Bouquet's counsel in how to get his men up to speed on wilderness fighting. One effective method, he was told, was to send out "scalping parties" to "harass the enemy (by keeping them under continual alarms)." These units comprised an officer, about a score of Cherokees, and a small detachment of his frontiersmen. These patrols allowed the men to practice operating as an Indian-style squad while honing their survival, marksmanship, and combat skills.[140]

Forbes eagerly sought Bouquet's and Washington's advice on the best way to advance through the woods. Washington insisted that Forbes's regulars must not repeat Braddock's mistake of marching in a single column; instead they must be divided into three small divisions flexible enough to form "instantly" into an "order of battle in the woods" if attacked. Each division must be further subdivided into three separate sections—each "to be in readiness *always* to oppose the enemy," he specified—working strictly along a chain of command to avoid the confusion that had beset Braddock.

If the vanguard division was attacked, Washington stipulated that its members were not to form up in a line or retreat to the main body but instead were to file smoothly off to the right and left "and take to trees, gaining the enemy's flanks, and surrounding them." Simultaneously, most of the second division was to split off to the right and join their comrades in the flanking parties, while the third, the rear guard, would do the same, but leftward. Their Indian allies should in the meantime "get round, unperceived, and fall upon the enemy's rear." His plan, Washington promised, would be "different from any thing they have ever yet experienced from us."

Forbes adopted this farsighted scheme and handed Washington command of the right division, composed of his Virginia Regiment veterans plus several provincial companies of North Carolinians, Marylanders, and Pennsylvanians (mostly armed with rifles), as well as two units of rifle-equipped backwoodsmen. The force was almost sundered by colonial and royal rivalries, was hampered by a lack of both transport and funds, and was deserted by its Indian allies; nonetheless Forbes brought it through the Pennsylvania fastness safely thanks to his deputies' counsel. On November 25 the Anglo-American army marched into Fort Duquesne. Abandoned by the alarmed French, the stronghold was renamed Fort Pitt and the frontier inexorably moved westward. The popular Forbes, nevertheless, was so weakened by the campaign that he died, emaciated and deathly pale, in Philadelphia less than three months later. Notwithstanding the loss of Forbes, the conquest of Fort Duquesne was the crowning moment, thus far, of Washington's military career.[141]

The Forbes expedition, ironically, also marked the end of that career—for the next twenty-odd years. That fall, with a marriage in the works, Washington was elected to the Virginia House of Burgesses as the representative of Frederick County and resigned his command of the Virginia Regiment. Which brings us back to the mystery and history of Washington's rifle.

In the 1770s, for those staid Virginian planters sitting in the clubby House and reluctantly steeling themselves for the final showdown with London that would erupt at Lexington and Concord, that rifle in the Peale portrait symbolized something meaningful. Washington's rifle was carefully calculated to prompt a certain reaction. It was a deliberate effort to capture the image of the frontiersman, then as now a halcyon icon of very American—or in the political context of the 1770s, anti-British—traits: doughty individualism, rugged self-reliance, and an independent spirit determined to defend hearth and home against the predations of outsiders.

The uniform of the Virginia Regiment that Washington wore could only cement this impression. Here the burgesses had before them a master of war, the only American who had turned a ragtag provincial outfit of "broken innkeepers, horse jockeys, and . . . traders" into the equal of the finest fighting soldiers on earth—the British infantryman and the

Indian warrior.[142] By identifying himself simultaneously with the American frontiersman and with the professional soldier, Washington succeeded in squaring an obstinately round circle. One day, and that day was fast approaching, this feat would lead to his unanimously approved elevation to commander in chief of the American forces for a war of independence.

The Kentucky Rifle

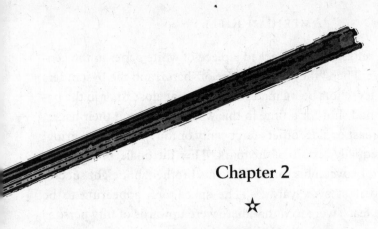

Chapter 2

☆

THE RIFLE AND
THE REVOLUTION

The riflemen were coming! That August of 1775, among the dispirited American troops besieging the British in Boston, exciting rumors spread of the imminent arrival of these mythical creatures from the backwoods and the frontier. Few, if any, of the New Englanders had ever before glimpsed one, but their fighting powers were considered to exceed those of any mortal, at least according to the newspapers and popular gossip.

A correspondent for the *Pennsylvania Packet* wrote that in Lancaster he had seen a force of frontiersmen "bear[ing] in their bodies visible marks of their prowess, and show[ing] scars and wounds, which would do honor to Homer's *Iliad*." One in particular "show[ed] the cicatrices of four bullet holes through his body"—a fact that would have impressed the young, unblooded volunteers camping in Massachusetts. "With their rifles in their hands they assume a kind of omnipotence over their enemies," he added.[1]

Indeed, the frontiersmen well knew the image they projected. Their appearance alone inspired fear and wonder in their foes: one witness noticed them passing by "painted like Indians, armed with tomahawks and rifles, dressed in hunting-shirts and moccasins."[2] During their march they invited locals to come watch them in action. They propped up a board five by seven inches and tacked a piece of white paper in the center as a bull's-eye. Then "they began to fire off-hand, and the bystanders were surprised, few shots being made that were not close to or in the paper. When they had shot for a time in this way, some lay on their backs, some on their breast or side, others ran twenty or thirty steps, and firing, appeared to be equally certain of the mark."[3] For the finale, one of them placed the board between his thighs while his brother shot eight successive bullets into it at sixty yards.[4] "The spectators, appearing to be amazed at these feats, were told that there were upwards of fifty persons in the company who could do the same thing; that there was not one who could not plug 19 bullets out of 20 (as they termed it) within an inch of the head of a ten-penny nail."[5]

Later that night, the frontiersmen kindled a bonfire in the courthouse square, around which the company, "all naked to the waist and painted like savages (except the captain, who was in an Indian shirt)," awed onlookers with an "exhibition of a war dance, and all the manoeuvres of Indians holding council, going to war, circumventing their enemies, by defiles, ambuscades, attacking, scalping, etc."[6]

This particular company of 130-odd riflemen and their Indian-shirted captain consisted of Michael Cresap's Marylanders, Pennsylvanians, and others from places yet unsettled. The son of an English immigrant who became a prominent Appalachian, militia officer, and Indian trader, Cresap was a twenty-three-year-old Marylander with long experience fighting Indians in the Virginia militia, as well as an unenviable, if perhaps not entirely warranted, reputation for massacring the families of his native American foes.[7]

When Cresap's company arrived in Boston, they shocked the New Englanders with their insouciance. The frontiersmen were certainly not what the Bostonians had been expecting after Congress—still a little unsure as to what a rifle was—voted on June 14 to augment the New England militias by raising "six companies of expert riflemen . . . in Pennsylvania, two in Maryland, and two in Virginia; that each company consist of a captain, three lieutenants, four sergeants, four corporals, a drummer or trumpeter, and sixty-eight privates." These units were ordered to "march and join the army near Boston, to be there employed as light infantry." (Historically speaking, they were the first troops recruited for the nascent Continental Army.)[8]

Among Cresap's men, there didn't seem to be any kind of hierarchy, let alone the traditional captain-lieutenant-sergeant-corporal-private structure envisaged by Congress. The Marylander was merely an Indian-style chief for whom they consented to work, yet the frontiersmen willingly did as they were told.[9]

Another rifle company under Daniel Morgan was run on almost identical lines. A frontiersman through and through, but one not born and bred, Morgan was probably conceived in 1735, in New Jersey, the son of Welsh immigrant farm-laborers. He first traveled to western Pennsylvania, Maryland, and Virginia in the early 1750s, where he became acquainted with Kentucky rifles. An itinerant worker who enjoyed a good bar brawl, the six-foot Morgan eventually became a wagoner and transported goods into the hinterland to sell to settlers. When General Braddock set off on his fateful march to Fort Duquesne, Morgan accompanied the army as a teamster. Fortunately for Morgan, in order to travel faster, Braddock left his wagons behind, and so the Welshman missed the slaughter at the Monongahela.

After the Braddock debacle, Morgan joined a band of Virginia rangers, fought Indians while imbibing their "skulking" skills, and hunted in his spare time before returning to the wagoning business and buying farmland. With the outbreak of the Revolution and Congress's call for riflemen, he held (just as Washington had done with his Virginia Regiment and other rifle commanders were doing) shooting trials to determine the best shots for his company. His men must have been singularly excellent because he actually took on ninety-six privates (rather than Congress's stipulated sixty-eight). All were armed with rifles—Morgan even bought a brand-new one for the occasion—and they carried the usual terrifying complement of tomahawks and scalping knives.[10]

The alacrity with which backswoodsmen leaped to join the service surprised almost everyone and shooting competitions caught on everywhere. John Harrower, a Scottish merchant who had been ruined by the financial panic of 1772 and indentured as a schoolmaster on Colonel William Daingerfield's Virginia plantation, wrote that the local commander held one because "those that insisted on going far exceeded the number wanted" and he wanted to "avoid giving offence" to those not selected. Such competitions were often close-run things. For the one witnessed by Harrower, the target was set 150 yards away, and each man was given one chance to place his single shot closest the mark. So adept were the Virginians, however, that by the time the fiftieth man took aim, nothing remained of the bull's-eye.[11]

On a broader level, while Congress had authorized ten companies, fully twelve were raised—eight from rifle-mad Pennsylvania alone, a couple of them composed of German speakers (the rest being Scots-Irish).[12] The celerity of their arrival in Massachusetts was in itself extraordinary, especially considering the glacierlike slowness of eighteenth-century logistics. The first company appeared on July 25 (just five weeks after Congress's order), and eight others arrived by August 14. All had undertaken journeys of between 400 and 700 miles by foot.[13]

Symbolized by the shooting competitions, a major distinction between riflemen and musketmen was already emerging: entry into the army was virtually guaranteed for any comer, especially since Washington was crying out for soldiers, but joining a rifle company depended strictly on one's proficiency with a weapon. The job, of course, came with perks.

One was that Washington relieved them of the fatigue duties imposed on regular Continental soldiers. Another was that riflemen were *expected* to "skulk" in the Indian manner as part of their responsibilities; yet Washington ordered that if any other kind of soldier "shall attempt to skulk, hide himself or retreat from the enemy without orders of his commanding officer, he will instantly be shot down as an example of cowardice."[14] Skulking clearly had two meanings, depending upon what kind of gun you were carrying. Such mollycoddling of riflemen would soon begin to rankle regular troops and their officers.

Officers, in particular, were alarmed that the riflemen's absence of hierarchy and the complete lack of concern for precedence might have adverse effects on their own units. Morgan once saw soldiers struggling to move a large rock blocking a road. An ensign was nearby, looking on haughtily. "Why don't you lay hold and help these men?" asked Morgan, only to be told, "Sir, I am an officer!" "I beg your pardon," Morgan replied sarcastically, "I did not think of that!" before lending a hand himself.[15] The ensign's reply may have offended any rifleman's latitudinarian social views, but he was only following a tradition upheld by Alexander the Great, Julius Caesar, and Frederick the Great.

Frontiersmen were less concerned than regulars with bureaucratic nitpicking, discipline, and precedence. In the army, much valuable time and effort (to their minds) were wasted debating precisely the difference between a lieutenant colonel and lieutenant colonel commandant.[16] Manuals were devoted to teaching minute details of drill, the proper ways to polish buttons and place epaulettes, and the intricacies of saluting superiors; there was a fascination, too, with how hair was to be worn—"plaited and powdered or tied"—and how many times a week men were to shave (thrice).[17] Punishment was harsh. For small infractions, the men were subjected to "the wooden horse," "the Whirligig," "the picket," "the ganteloupe," whippings with the switch or cat-o'-nine tails, hanging, shootings by firing squad, or being drummed from camp.[18]

Among the riflemen, corporal punishment was administered but occasionally and often never. Morgan banned flogging on the grounds that it was degrading.[19] Nor did the riflemen have an official uniform—another source of resentment (and admiration, as well, at their exotic look) among the regulars, who were forced into rough woolen coats and blister-popping shoes. Instead, the riflemen dressed as they did at home: like Indians, with a few concessions to European sensibilities. Moccasins, leggins, furred or buckskin caps with tassels, breechclouts, and—of great symbolic importance—dead-leaf–colored hunting shirts were the most striking aspects of their outfits. Often the only difference between what captains and their men wore was a crimson sash, donned when in camp but left behind on missions—a custom left over from the days when Indians targeted officers.[20]

By the end of August, some fourteen hundred frontiersmen, described as "remarkably stout and hardy men; many of them exceeding six feet in height," had congregated outside Boston.[21] They were soon busy showing off to their gawping comrades, and morale within the American camp, hitherto sagging, soared. "They are the most accurate marksmen in the world," boasted John Adams to his wife, Abigail, while Dr. Thacher opined that "their shot have frequently proved fatal to

British officers and soldiers, who expose themselves to view, even at more than double the distance of common musket shot."[22] The Bradford brothers of Philadelphia, publishers both, went so far as to tell the *London Chronicle* that "this province has raised 1,000 riflemen, the worst of whom will put a ball into a man's head at a distance of 150 or 200 yards, therefore advise your officers who shall hereafter come out to America, to settle their affairs in England before their departure."[23] A particularly patriotic Church of England minister played his part in the Revolution by writing directly to the Earl of Dartmouth (then the colonial secretary) about the breed of men whom British troops were going to face.

Rifles . . . are daily made in many places in Pennsylvania, and all the gun-smiths everywhere constantly employed. In this country, my lord, the boys, as soon as they can discharge a gun, frequently exercise themselves therewith, some a fowling and others a hunting. The great quantities of game, the many kinds and the great privileges of killing, making the Americans the best marksmen in the world, and thousands support their families principally by the same, particularly riflemen on the frontiers, whose objects are deer and turkeys. In marching through woods, one thousand of these riflemen would cut to pieces ten thousand of your best troops.

This same minister bragged that the American fortifications at Roxbury and Cambridge were "17 feet in thickness," that their forts were "bomb proof," and that of "provisions and money there are very plenty, and the soldiers faithfully paid." Indeed, "if your lordship knew but one half what I know of America, your lordship would not persist, but be instantly for peace, or resign."[24] The clergyman's efforts were commendable, but his claims were either patently exaggerated or blatantly false. Not for the last time would the exploits and talents of American riflemen be employed as a morale-booster.

Following the minister's lead, the papers were soon printing stories of feats, most embellished, some impossible. On August 5 the *Pennsylvania Gazette* reported that "a party of these men at a late review on a quick advance, placed their balls in poles of 7 inches diameter, fixed for that purpose, at the distance of 250 yards." The feat was difficult but not beyond the realm of possibility.[25] Eleven days later, on August 16, the same paper commented that "we are also told that the riflemen had in one day killed ten of a reconnoitering party; and it is added likewise, that they have killed three field officers. A sentry was killed at 250 yards distance."[26] Again, such a performance was possible, though a rival newspaper upped the ante by claiming that the unfortunate sentry had been assassinated "when only half his head was seen"—at 250 yards.[27] Within a week the exaggerations had spun out of control. The normally sober *Pennsylvania Gazette* of August 21 reported that "a gentleman from the American camp says—Last Wednesday, some riflemen, on Charlestown side, shot an officer of note in the ministerial service, supposed to be Major Small, or Bruce, and killed three men on board a ship at Charlestown ferry, at the distance of full half a mile." Half a mile is 880 yards, a miracle if ever there was one.[28]

The riflemen were only too happy to play along, even after the regulars lost their initial amazement at their sharpshooting and morale became as sodden as before. Admiration had given way to revulsion and envy: not only was the riflemen's camp kept a hundred yards apart from everyone else's, but they were paid more than ordinary soldiers, were excused from "all working parties, camp guards, and camp duty," and "were under no restraint from the commands of their officers, but went when and where they pleased, without being subject to be stopped or examined by any one."[29]

Heedless of their comrades' chagrin, by the end of the summer of 1775 the riflemen's reputation had been bloated by so much hyperbole that between their own egos and the impersonal force of hubris, they were heading for a major fall. Even Washington acidly commented that "there is no restraining men's tongues, or pens, when charged with a little vanity, as in the accounts given of, or rather by, the riflemen."[30]

Telling tall stories had been a soldier's pastime since time immemorial, so Washington was reluctant to chastise the riflemen, at least until their antics became too flagrant to ignore. At first he privately reminded their captains to control the men: this was not the frontier, after all, but a respectable war. When he ordered one rifle unit to Cape Ann to "do [their] utmost to distress and annoy any detachment from the ministerial Army that may be sent from Boston, to plunder, or destroy that settlement," he made sure to tell its chief that "upon your march, and during your residence at Cape Ann, as well as upon your march back to camp, you will observe strict discipline and on no account suffer any under your command to pillage or maraud."[31] Clearly there had already been some problems with looting.

By mid-September some of the riflemen had sunk to acting like children, or worse, if their whims weren't satisfied. Disliking camp regulations and tempted by the rich bounty that the British were offering for turncoats who brought "their rifled barrelled guns," quite a few deserted to the enemy. Scarcely a night passed, said one soldier, without at least one sneaking past the American sentries—no difficulty for those accustomed to Indian warfare—and demanding to be taken in by their red-coated opposites in Boston and Charlestown.[32]

Those malcontents who stayed were often little better. Sergeant James Finley of Captain Thomas Price's Maryland company was found guilty by a court-martial of "expressing himself disrespectfully of the Continental Association, and drinking Genl Gage's health." (Gage was the soon-to-be-replaced commander in chief of British forces in North America.) For once, and much to the satisfaction of the regulars, a spoiled rifleman discovered the meaning of army discipline: Finley was "put in a horse cart, with a rope around his neck, and drum'd out of the Army and rendered for-ever incapable of serving in the Continental army."[33]

Worse was the mutinying. Jesse Lukens, a rifleman, conceded that indulging his comrades had "rendered the men rather insolent for good soldiers." Not once but *twice* had Virginia riflemen broken into the guardhouse where their friends were being held on minor charges and released them. The colonel, William Thompson, had done nothing to punish the miscreants; indeed, he went so far as to pardon one serious offender who had been sentenced to a flogging. Then, one Sunday in early September, the company adjutant ("a man of spirit") actually dared confine a popular sergeant for "neglect of duty." When the men began "murmuring" and threatening to again storm the guardhouse, the adjutant forthrightly clapped irons on the chief mutineer and sent him to join his friend in jail. When the adjutant reported the matter to the colonel after dinner, they heard a "huzzaing" outside and found that the riflemen had sprung the mutineer. Now forced to act, the colonel and several of his officers seized the rebel again and conveyed him to the Main Guard at Cambridge under escort. They managed this without any violent opposition, but about twenty minutes later thirty-three men "of Capt. Ross's company with their loaded rifles swore by God they would go to the Main Guard and release the man or lose their lives, and set off as hard as they could run."

When Washington was informed of the matter, he "reinforced the guard to 500 men with fixed bayonets and loaded pieces." For all he knew, the rebellion might spread throughout the rifle companies and even infect the army if it were not put down with overwhelming force. The mutineers, in the meantime, had become frightened at what they had started and hid in the woods. Washington ordered them to down their weapons, and all immediately did so.

"You cannot conceive what disgrace we are all in," confided an embarrassed Lukens. Even so, the punishments handed down were (considering that the penalty for mutiny was death) absurdly benign. The ringleader John Seamon cooled his heels in prison for six days, but the men were each fined just 20 shillings, an amercement, thought Lukens, mitigated "on account of their having come so far to serve the cause and its being the first crime." The money didn't matter so much anyway, for the men "seem exceedingly sorry for their misbehavior and promise amendment." They were made still sorrier when they discovered that Washington had revoked their comfortable exemptions from fatigue, guard, and camp duties and had ordered the separated riflemen's camps to be integrated with those of the regulars.[34]

Most important, Washington had learned that riflemen were almost uncontrollable when left to their own devices. The catalog of minor infractions, the spate of spiteful desertions, and the breathtaking arrogance of the mutineers persuaded him that rifle units had to be leashed to regular army formations, so as to benefit indirectly from their good officering and steady discipline. Moreover, keeping the riflemen cooped up around Boston was dissipating their powers of mobility, stealth, and

A late eighteenth-century print, German in origin, illustrating the differences between an American rifleman (left) and his musket-armed equivalent in the regular infantry. Even at this early date, riflemen were distinguished from the army's disciplined ranks by their idiosyncratic dress and manners—to the annoyance of many generals.

marksmanship. To be sure, the riflemen had proved their utility on several occasions: in one covert operation they had crawled forward on their bellies, Indian style, toward the enemy's positions at Charlestown and captured two prisoners for interrogation. But their special skills were not being fully exploited.[35]

A jaunt up north was just the thing. That September Washington dispatched three rifle companies under Morgan to aid Colonel Benedict Arnold on his expedition to Canada, the plan being to harry the British deep behind their front lines. Ultimately the campaign failed, despite Arnold's best efforts. Morgan himself ended up a prisoner. But his riflemen (and one woman, Mrs. Warner, who, when her husband fell ill, borrowed his rifle and came along in his place) acquitted themselves honorably in the territory's wet, then snowy, but endlessly forested expanses. Washington, pleased with their improvement, told Congress on April 22, 1776, that this "valuable and brave body of men" now formed "a very useful Corps."[36]

Quite so. In Quebec the riflemen's prowess had astonished the Old English as much as it had the New Englanders. One time a squad of redcoats managed to kidnap George Merchant, one of Morgan's boys. He was taken to London as a kind of traveling exhibition of The American Frontiersman. A British newspaper of the time gasped that he "is a Virginian, above six feet high, stout and well-proportioned . . . He can strike a mark with the greatest certainty, at two hundred yards distance. He has a heavy provincial pronunciation, but otherwise speaks good English."[37]

Having been exchanged by the British, Captain Daniel Morgan was released from prison and returned home in January 1777. He was soon promoted to colonel and given command of a new regiment, the Eleventh Virginia. He spent the next few months staffing it with trusted friends as officers and found the best shooters in western Virginia by setting up a target depicting a British officer's head (some said it was of King George III) at one hundred yards and requiring his recruits to hit it on their first shot. In June 1777 Washington strengthened the regiment by attaching five hundred light infantrymen to it. Designated a "distinct" (independent) unit, they, according to the Marquis de Lafayette, were chosen "from parts of the country on the frontier of the savage tribes, and from amongst men whose mode of life, and skill in firing their long carbines, rendered them peculiarly useful in that service."[38]

To this end Morgan stipulated that all members of the regiment be issued rifles. This request was almost as easily done as said. There were actually *too many* rifles available and not enough muskets. After Lexington and Concord state committees of safety had purchased as many firearms as they could for the influx of excited volunteers, without stopping to coordinate with one another or waiting to see what the army most required. Thus Virginia's committee, befitting its frontier heritage, bought 3,325 muskets and 2,098 rifles between September 18, 1775, and July 5, 1776.[39] The abnormally high proportion of rifles to muskets—two for every three—was vastly more than could be issued to competent marksmen, especially since most of the riflemen brought their own pieces anyway.

By October 1776 the secretary of the Board of War went so far as to tell the Maryland Council of Safety that "there is a superabundance of riflemen in the army." "Were it in the power of the Congress to supply muskets," he continued, "they would speedily reduce the number of rifles, and replace them with the former."[40]

Unfortunately, Congress was hardly likely to acquire that power, at least in the immediate future, since there were no large-scale production facilities, no centralized arms industry, and no major gunpowder refineries in the colonies. Indeed, the few small gunpowder mills that existed—mostly in Connecticut, Pennsylvania, New Jersey, and Massachusetts—were producing only "miserable trash" (in the words of one government inspector).[41]

The gun situation was not much better. Every weapon had to be made in a one- or two-man gunsmith's shop whose average output was twenty per month. There were just twelve such smiths in Maryland. At that rate Washington would need until the turn of the century to outfit his army with uniform muskets. Even that goal was bound to be frustrated, for each one's barrel length, caliber, and quality varied from state to state, county to county, and even town to town or smith to smith, depending on the maker's whims, experience, and talents.[42]

To make up for the musket shortfall, Congress relied on clandestine arms shipments from abroad. In January 1776 two enterprising French merchants, Messrs. Pliarne and Penet, approached Congress's Secret Committee and divulged that the French royal armories might be persuaded to sell some surplus stocks on the quiet. Armed with a congressional contract, Pliarne and Penet sailed home and sent ten thousand model 1763 "Charleville" muskets.[43]

Domestic gunpowder production was still lagging. In 1777 the French again came through. King Louis XVI created a dummy corporation theatrically named Roderique Hortalez and Company that was run by Pierre-Augustin Caron de Beaumarchais—author of *The Barber of Seville* and a prodigiously talented gunrunner. Hortalez & Co. arranged to smuggle another 30,000 Charlevilles and 300,000 pounds of prime-grade gunpowder to America in the spring of 1777. Some of these shipments were intercepted, but no fewer than 21,000 muskets and 100,000 pounds of gunpowder were issued to American troops.[44] The imbalance between the numbers of rifles and muskets was well on its way to being righted.

Hence, Colonel Daniel Morgan was able to outfit his regiment as he wished—and with Washington's blessing. For his part, Washington had come a long way from his Virginia Regiment days.

His key insight was that the ultimate success of each style of warfare—traditional European in-line formation and dependency on fire volume, and the Indian reliance on guerrilla fighting—partly hinged on its geographical context. In the eastern states set-piece battles of army versus army would necessarily be the rule owing to the preponderance of open fields, cities, sufficient supplies, adequate communications, and good roads. In these surroundings small, dispersed parties of riflemen would be easy pickings for the columns of bayonet-armed soldiers and cavalry units sweeping the terrain. Musket fire would have to be fought with musket fire.

In the forested West and North, however, regular armies would be as vulnerable as Braddock's had been back in the French and Indian War. In those verdant landscapes, however, homegrown riflemen would be in their element. And in the swampy South, though it would become horrifically apparent only after 1780, unbridled guerrilla warfare would find its zenith.

Soldiers from the East cried out for muskets; irregulars and troops drawn from frontier provinces wanted to stick with their rifles.[45] Accordingly, at the beginning of the war, when the army was preponderantly populated with New Englanders, Washington was besieged with requests from senior officers to replace their new recruits' rifles with muskets.[46] Thanks to the newly arrived Charlevilles, the solution in 1777 was a straightforward exchange.

First, Washington assured those officers who had begged him to convert their regiments from rifles to muskets that he had "determined to have as few [of the former] used as possible. He will put muskets into the hands of all those battalions that are not very well acquainted with rifles."[47] True to his word, Washington then ordered that "such rifles as belong to the States, in the different brigades, [are] to be immediately exchanged with Col. Morgan for muskets."[48]

With Morgan's weapons problem solved, in mid-June Washington commanded the colonel's riflemen to "gall" General William Howe's troops "as much as possible" by worrying at their flanks and rear as they traveled through New Jersey on their way to draw out Washington to open battle in Pennsylvania. Knowing that many of Howe's soldiers were new to America and green to boot, Washington advised Morgan—in inimitable frontier fashion—to "dress a company or two of true woodsmen in the right Indian style and let them make the attack accompanied with screaming and yelling as the Indians do," because "it would have very good consequences."[49] It did. Morgan's riflemen, in combination with General Anthony Wayne's brigade, attacked the British rear guard and drove it across the river to seek cover.

Not long afterward Washington transferred the regiment to the north—the perfect hunting ground for Morgan's riflemen—this time to blunt General John Burgoyne's thrust southward from Canada through the woods in the (forlorn) hope that Howe's forces in New York would advance north. Once they met halfway, they would amputate the upstart New England states from the rest of the country and cause the rebellion to collapse.

On August 16 Washington instructed Morgan to proceed with all haste to Peekskill and thence to Albany, as "the approach of the enemy, in that quarter, has made a further reinforcement necessary, and I know of no Corps so likely to check their progress in proportion to their number, as the one you command." By now, as is evident from his warm words and his happily confessed "great dependence on you, your officers and men," Washington regarded Morgan's riflemen as his joy and pride.[50] To him, they were the Virginia Regiment resurrected.

In the runup to the Saratoga campaign, Morgan rapidly aligned himself with an old Monongahela comrade, General Horatio Gates, who had commanded an independent company under Braddock (and had been severely wounded in the fighting).[51] In order to protect Morgan's vulnerable riflemen from a redcoat assault, Gates took the precaution of assigning an additional three hundred musketmen under Major Henry Dearborn to them—an early instance of combined operations.[52]

The country was absolutely perfect for frontier fighting: forest-shaded creeks wended through it, the lush undergrowth disguised movement, there were deep ravines, and the hills provided excellent cover for skilled marksmen. At the battle of Freeman's Farm Morgan's riflemen hid in the bushes and climbed trees in order to target Burgoyne's infantry officers as well as known Tories (there were about 150 of them), a practice that, as a British sergeant drily noted, "accelerated their estrangement from our cause and army."[53]

At the end of that bloody day, September 19, Burgoyne had lost 600 men, compared to Gates's 320. Of the American dead, just *four* were riflemen (another eight were wounded, and three were missing), even though Morgan's force had been involved in the very thickest of the battle. Morgan's unit had disproportionately killed officers, and by pinning down the enemy while the infantry attacked, it had been responsible for reducing the once-proud 62nd Regiment, the rock holding the British center, down to a mere sixty men, and had killed or wounded every officer but one of the 53rd Regiment.[54] It was an incredible performance by any standard, demonstrating the devastating effect of the rifle when properly protected by regular infantry. When Washington asked Gates to send Morgan's riflemen south to aid him, the general demurred by stating that "Your Excellency would not wish me to part with the Corps the army of General Burgoyne are most afraid of."[55] On that note a Hessian officer serving with Burgoyne wrote that "in the open field the rebels do not count for much, but in the woods they are formidable. Thus far, however, we still live, walk, dwell, and march in the woods. There they lie like bacon hunters behind the trees and slip from one tree to the other."[56]

The same lesson was applied on October 7, when the two armies again clashed. "Order on Morgan to begin the game," Gates directed his aide.[57] Morgan this time led his riflemen to the left and inflicted casualties, while Dearborn's troops rushed past them and drove Lord Balcarres's infantry back at the points of their bayonets. "Morgan, you have done wonders," exclaimed Gates.[58] During this battle rifleman Tim Murphy famously shot General Simon Fraser of the 24th Regiment. Many years later Morgan described what happened in his own rough-hewn way. He boasted that his riflemen had "whopped" Burgoyne's redcoats "tarnation well" back in September, then recalled that "me and my boys" were getting whopped themselves on October 7 until "I saw that they were led by an officer on a grey horse—a devilish, brave fellow." So "says I to one of my best shots [Murphy], says I, you get up into that there tree, and single out him on the . . . horse. Dang it, 'twas no sooner said than done. On came the British again, with the grey horseman leading; but his career was short enough this time, I jist [*sic*] tuck my eyes off him for a moment, and when I turned them to the place where he had been—pooh, he was gone!"[59]

Murphy, an experienced Indian fighter with twenty unfortunates' scalps to his name, seems to have owned a rare piece indeed: a double-barreled, probably double-triggered rifle, the kind of advanced sniping weapon that only a frontiersman would have commissioned.[60] And proving that a rifleman's aim was superb but not unerring, it took him three shots to wound Fraser fatally: the first hit the back of his saddle, the second blazed through the horse's mane (a little behind the ears), and the third struck Fraser in the breast.[61] Even so, it was a magnificent kill, considering that all three bullets landed within a yard of each other at no little range and that Fraser's horse was moving at some speed.

One British soldier who surrendered to Gates alongside his chief, General Burgoyne, on October 17 was the eccentric Major George Hanger—a creature of such odd habits that he could not find a female willing to put up with them and he would die unmarried in 1824.[62] Hanger, the son of a baron, was the best marksman in the British Army: to an insolent questioner of his abilities, he replied, "Sir, I do not know whether I am a gentleman, but I do know I am a *dead shot.*" He actually preferred to serve in a Jäger regiment, all the better to practice using his rifle.[63] During his captivity Hanger incessantly quizzed Morgan's riflemen about their weapons and techniques.[64] "I never in my life saw better rifles (or men who shot better) than those made in America," he was forced to conclude.[65]

⋆ ⋆ ⋆

Despite the triumph over Burgoyne, military opinion by no means universally condoned Morgan's tactic of targeted assassinations, just as it harshly condemned the Americans whose fine shooting had killed so many at the Battle of Bunker Hill in what was, as one Briton enviously had to admit, an impressive display of martial vigor.[66] Even on the

American side, the so-called "Indian" habit of taking shots at officers to sow confusion in the ranks was thought to degrade the Continental Army, which some commanders wanted to act in a more "European" manner.

General Anthony Wayne epitomized these apprehensions and strove hard to prove that the American army was worthy of the name. In Wayne's eyes, the frontiersmen's uncivilized practice of shooting generals out of their saddles did not improve the army's respectability; moreover, it handed ammunition to the Tory newspapers that identified the Continentals as drunken, irreligious brutes who did not abide by the accepted laws of war. Indeed, of all the weapons employed by either side during the Revolution, just one—notwithstanding its effectiveness— was "singled out as intrinsically inhumane" by participants like Wayne: the rifle.[67]

Many officers, British and American, regarded the practice of taking aim and deliberately shooting an officer or even a sentry, as opposed to firing randomly into an undifferentiated mass, as tantamount to murder. This view stemmed from an aristocratic suspicion of projectile weapons that dated back to at least the time of the ancient Greeks and Romans: their nobles killed man to man, with swords and thrusting spears, while the poor and the barbaric murdered from afar with their cowardly bows and slings.[68] By the Middle Ages and Renaissance, the snobbery was directed more toward bullet-launching firearms than toward longbows, which had by then won so many battles for the English that they were exalted as a national symbol. Shakespeare nicely captured the prevailing ethos in Henry IV, Part 1, when "a certain lord, neat and trimly dressed" who has hitherto avoided having to fight claims that "but for those vile guns, he would himself have been a soldier."

Barons and gentlemanly knights particularly disliked guns, mostly because commoners proved themselves dab hands at piercing their extremely expensive armor with bullets, necessitating ever thicker steel and thereby limiting their usefulness on the battlefield. These lumbering metal behemoths eventually became so cumbersome that while they could suffer no wounds, they could not inflict them either.

As muskets became more common (so to speak) and remained instruments designed for indiscriminate use against faceless masses one hundred or more yards distant, the commanders' mental link between unsoldierly conduct and the use of firearms was transferred to the rifle exclusively. Indeed, quite a few commanders were adamant that their men, even those armed with muskets, *should not aim at all* for fear of appearing unsporting. For decades training handbooks insisted that soldiers should merely "level" their muskets and "pull the trigger briskly" or "jerk the trigger smartly"—a habit that would cause many a bullet to overshoot the heads of the enemy. They even admonished the British soldier to *close his eyes* as he fired. Instead of teaching men how to hit the target, they made them memorize the precise chronology of the movements for loading and ramming a bullet into the chamber. One English manual printed detailed instructions for the twenty-nine steps this action required but left number thirty simply as "Give fire" before explaining at great length the subsequent fourteen steps needed to prepare the next round.[69] Understandably, the devastating losses suffered by the British at the Battle of Bunker Hill would be sniffily attributed to the unfortunate American habit of "taking sight" and pulling the trigger slowly to reduce movement.[70]

The image of the rifle as the chosen weapon of low-born cheats prompted all sorts of atrocity stories about the craven practices of their owners. The *London Chronicle* shocked its readers by alleging that Americans used "rifles peculiarly adapted to take off the officers of a whole line as it marches to an attack," pointing out that "this is the real cause of so many of our brave officers falling, they being singled out by these murderers, as they must appear to be in the eyes of every thinking man."[71] Hearing that the Americans were planning to post sharpshooters to target officers in Boston, an enraged British lieutenant sputtered, "What a set of villains must they be to think of such a thing!" It only went to show that there was nothing "these people will stick at to gain their ends."[72]

This distaste for the rifleman's trade meant that after they surrendered, a higher proportion of them than regular soldiers were executed.[73] The same principle had once applied to Indian raiders who sniped at their targets: for this reason in 1759 Colonel Thomas Gage informed Major James Clephane, commanding Fort Stanwix, that "I look upon these partys as so many assassins, not soldiers, therefore they have no quarter."[74]

During the Battle of Long Island in the summer of 1776, the Hessian Colonel von Heeringen witnessed the corpses of riflemen "pierced to the trees with bayonets" and left there as a warning.[75] On the last day of 1776 the *Middlesex Journal* quoted a British officer as saying that those carrying Kentuckys often "find themselves run through the body by the push of a bayonet, as a rifleman is not entitled to any quarter."[76] Eleven months later some of these contemptible Americans still had not learned their lesson. Near Philadelphia in mid-November 1777 Lord Cornwallis and the 33rd Regiment were advancing through the town of Darby when his trusted sergeant-major suddenly collapsed. One of a team of presumably Pennsylvanian snipers had shot him from their hiding place in a nearby house. "The troops entered it and bayoneted the whole," noted Captain John Montrésor of the Engineers.[77]

Morgan, blooded on the frontier, cared nothing for European niceties. To him, killing officers was like killing Indian troublemakers: it shortened a conflict's duration and so saved thousands of men's lives. Many other American officers, however, were not so immune to the temptation to make themselves "respectable" in the eyes of their enemy.

The issue of weaponry even had implications for the kind of society that Americans wanted to build after the war. Those officers—usually social and political conservatives—who were keen to keep the fighting strictly between armies along European lines tended to plump for muskets-and-bayonets and backed the creation of a British- or Prussian-style professional force equipped with those arms.[78] They saw rifles as relics of an embarrassing frontier past, to be discarded as America joined the civilized present.

To that end, General Anthony Wayne insisted that he had "an insuperable bias in favour of an elegant uniform and a soldierly appearance," so much so that he would prefer to lead troops armed "merely with bayonets and a single charge of ammunition" than to command unkempt backwoodsmen with sixty rounds apiece.[79] Bayonets in particular were believed to be conducive to fine soldiering: in the Paoli Massacre of September 20, 1777, British infantry had surprised an

American force (commanded, embarrassingly, by Wayne) who were sleeping by their fires and bayoneted 150 of them without a shot being fired. Notwithstanding its moral questionability, the massacre was a testament to brilliant discipline, untold hours of training, and firm officering.[80] In 1781 Wayne—by now garlanded with the nickname "Mad Anthony"—repaid the insult by launching a bayonet attack with his 800 Pennsylvanian Irishmen against Lord Cornwallis's entire army of 6,000. Rebuffed by fierce musketry, the Americans stood their ground (fighting off two first-class British regiments) and would have kept on doing so had not Lafayette ignored Wayne's objections and ordered a retreat. For Wayne, the eternal principle of war was simplicity itself: Man was supervised by a "sanguine God [who] is rather thirsty for human gore."[81]

This potent combination of cold steel, hot blood, and total control proved irresistible to many American observers, who felt that soldiers shouldn't think for themselves. European societies commonly regarded regular infantrymen as the least productive and most degraded members of society. In Paris signs hung outside cafés reading "No dogs, lackeys, prostitutes or soldiers." Believed to lack any sort of moral quality—courage, loyalty, self-reliance, sacrifice—soldiers were, at best, animals who, with stern mastership and up to two years' training, could be taught to attack.[82]

Over here, Alexander Hamilton, then a captain, voiced suspiciously similar sentiments. He wanted to "let officers be men of sense and sentiment, and the nearer the soldiers approach to machines perhaps the better." This was because under "sensible officers soldiers can hardly be too stupid."[83] The upshot was that frontiersmen were too independent-minded to be useful.

The upper-class General Philip Schuyler certainly believed that they were more trouble than they were worth, remarking that "gentlemen in command find it very disagreeable to coax, to wheedle, and even to lie" to frontiersmen to get them to do what they were told. They should just snap to it and follow orders unhesitatingly, like his servants. Wayne dismissed riflemen out of hand with the comment that "to say anything severe to them has just as much effect as if you were to cut up a butcher's chopping block with a razor." The only way a commander had any chance of controlling them was to inflict "downright blows which, with the dread of being whipped through the small guts keeps them in some awe."[84]

Wayne's outlook had been formed by his favorite reading, Marshal Maurice de Saxe's *My Reveries Upon the Art of War,* first published in 1757 after the brilliant commander of the French armies during the War of the Austrian Succession had retired with an extraordinary record of victories under his belt. From the *Reveries* Wayne learned that "it has always been noted that it is with those armies in which the severest discipline is enforced that the greatest deeds are performed." Wayne took the advice to heart and immediately sentenced to death soldiers who rebelled against their leaders ("a soldier who lifts his arm against an officer ought not to be permitted to live").[85] Under Wayne and his ilk, the Continental Army would fight for democracy, but it would not be one.

The assumption that fighting men were no better than beasts of burden drove Thomas Jefferson to apoplexy. He charged that their "native courage and . . . animation in the cause" was their greatest asset, not a liability. After all, at Bunker Hill the enemy had obtained its objective "by superiority of numbers, but their loss was five times greater than ours."[86] Following Jefferson, red-hot radicals like Generals Charles Lee and Horatio Gates (who penned a couplet condemning moderation and compromise: "The middle way, the best, we sometimes call, / But 'tis in politics no way at all") felt that fighting for independence along genteel European principles would result, even if successful, only in the preservation of the "royalist" social hierarchy.[87]

The Revolution, they believed, was a *people's* war of national liberation. Sustained by the power of patriotism, Americans could dispense with what Charles Lee disparagingly called the hidebound "Hyde Park" tactics and "puerile reviews" of the British Army and instead allow the "active vigorous yeomanry, fired with noble ardour . . . all armed, all expert in the use of arms," to shoot their own firearms.[88]

That weapon was, more often than not, the rifle and the two factions split bitterly over its role in the war. Jefferson was convinced that American success could be ascribed to "our superiority in taking aim when we fire; every soldier in our army having been intimate with his gun from his infancy."[89] Likewise, Charles Lee avidly favored rifles and was a stout proponent of riflemen adopting unconventional guerrilla tactics. Naturally, he also loathed Alexander Hamilton, whom he called a "son of a bitch," and Anthony Wayne, whom he regarded as a reactionary crypto-monarchist.[90]

As blunt as Lee was sharp, Wayne replied, "I don't like rifles—I would almost as soon face an enemy with a good musket and bayonet without ammunition."[91] The general, during his extraordinary 1779 storming of Stony Point, proved as good as his word when he had his men advance with bayonets fixed and muskets *unloaded*. Observed General Nathanael Greene, Wayne's method was "the perfection of discipline."[92]

Quite aside from its utility as an assassination device, what offended Wayne and his allies was not the existence of the rifle per se but how it was used: to be a successful rifleman, one needed coolness under fire, calm nerves, independence of mind, a personal desire to improve oneself through intense individual training, and a honed ability to evaluate external factors objectively (i.e., weather, distance, ballistics) in order to judge their potential effect on the shot. The rifleman had no practical need for an officer to tell him what to do. All these features were precisely the opposite of the martial values and practices espoused by traditionalists like Wayne.

At heart, the rifle-versus-musket controversy was a conflict between the heralds of *self*-discipline and the advocates of *imposed* discipline, a debate representative of the greater one raging between the apostles of individual liberty and the pharisees upholding traditional government authority. The seismic political, economic, and social reverberations of this very eighteenth-century divide are with us still. At the time, however, the antirifle military traditionalists would gain the upper hand once the initial fervor of 1776 wore off.

Their success was owed partly to accident. Wayne's and Hamilton's Europhile views eventually dominated the officer corps not because of their inherent value but because of their antagonists' failures and weakness. Wayne too was immensely aided by the good fortune of having on hand Baron von Steuben, the German officer who, during the dismal winter at Valley Forge, forged Washington's battered, miserable collection of barkeeps, schoolmasters, farmers, and fishermen into the Continental Army. Steuben had been a captain in the Prussian army during the Seven Years War before serving on the general staff of

Frederick the Great. Departing the Prussian court under a cloud—a bout of unsavory conduct was to blame—he was hired by Benjamin Franklin and Silas Deane (both agents of the U.S. government in France) and arrived in America in December 1777. Though in reality he was just a disgraced captain in desperate financial straits armed only with a dodgy pedigree, Steuben quickly went to work by incessantly drilling and disciplining the buff-and-blues. He was particularly disgusted to discover that their bayonets had turned rusty with lack of use. So successful was he that during the three most dire months of deprivation, just once (when two brigades refused to march against the enemy unless sufficient supplies were secured) did the soldiers turn insubordinate.[93]

Steuben's reforms were indispensable to American victory. His star spectacularly rose with the incompetent failure of Charles Lee at the Battle of Monmouth and the fall of Horatio Gates at the Battle of Camden—which proved to military observers that the revolutionary radicals were responsible for a lengthening series of defeats.[94] Despite his long-standing affection for his riflemen, Washington in particular was persuaded that over-reliance on them and on militia, no matter how fiery their patriotic devotion, risked harming military effectiveness. By trying to save the Revolution, they might well doom it. The radicals continued to praise the "great achievements" of the Romans and Greeks to justify their patriotic calls to service, but by April 1778 Washington had firmly decided that those who believe that "a few examples from ancient story" are "sufficient basis for conducting a long and [bloody] war, will find themselves deceived in the end." Without the creation of a functioning, effective army, eventually all that would be left would be a shriveled band of brothers "without discipline, without energy, [and] incapable of acting with vigor."[95]

During the September 1781 prelude to the Battle of Yorktown, the army's increasing reliance on shock attack and volume of fire became so total that Washington specifically ordered that "the troops [are] to place their principal reliance on the bayonet, that they may prove the vanity of the boast which the British make of their particular prowess in deciding battles with that weapon."[96] The Continental Army had come a long way from that summer of 1775 outside Boston, but it's interesting to speculate whether the rifle would have been integrated earlier and more completely into America's armed forces if Lee and Gates had been more effective generals—or Wayne less of one.

✫ ✫ ✫

It was October 7, 1780, an overcast day with an occasional light, misty rain falling. Major Patrick Ferguson, an ambitious British officer, was spoiling for a fight. That day he got one: at King's Mountain rifle-armed (many made by Deckhard, a well-known German smith in Lancaster) frontiersmen and mountain men from Pennsylvania, North Carolina, Virginia, and Tennessee would besiege his force of 1,125 Tory loyalists and British regulars.[97]

Unlike Yorktown and Saratoga, King's Mountain is today, alas, not numbered among the great or famous battles of the Revolution. But it was remarkable in one particular respect: it was the single significant clash in which rifles alone were pitted directly against musket-and-bayonet.[98]

The "mountain" was actually a narrow, stony ridge, 500 yards long and between 70 and 120 wide, and raised 100 feet higher than the land surrounding it. Its sides, however, were rugged and steep. Ferguson, knowing that at least five units of Americans were closing in, declared himself king of King's Mountain and "defied God Almighty and all the rebels out of Hell to overcome him" atop his densely forested fastness.[99]

So they did. Ferguson had miscalculated, possibly because his attention had wandered after a night gallivanting with two amours (a talented buxom redhead named Virginia and her pleasing friend, also named Virginia).[100] The frontiersmen and mountaineers fanned out, shouted Indian war whoops and climbed the hill, took cover behind the trees and boulders, and loosed rounds into Ferguson's closely packed platoons. (The redheaded Virginia was shot and killed at this point.) Whenever a body of Americans hove into sight, the British charged time and time again with fixed bayonets, but the riflemen simply retreated, firing all the time, and melted away into the landscape.

The enemy's return musket-fire proved impotent. Trained to fire over flatland at greater distances, the British tended to raise their muskets slightly to compensate for gravity pulling the ball downward and for their lack of adjustable sights. A soldier fighting on flat terrain, advised a manual of 1800, should "strike a man in the center of his body, up to 100 meters aim at his chest, 100–140, at the height of his shoulders; 140–180, at the height of his head; 180–200, at the top of his head-dress; over 200, aim over the head-dress."[101] Hence, owing to the mountain's steep slope, "they overshot us altogether, scarce touching a man, except those on horseback," said one American participant.[102]

Surrounded, hemmed in, and losing men one by one from the "constant and well-directed" rifle shots that emerged from the forest, the hapless Ferguson retreated to one end of the ridge, but it was all for naught.[103] As the Americans tightened the noose, James Collins, a seventeen-year-old American new to fighting who had briefly considered deserting before the battle ("my feelings were not the most pleasant . . . but I could not well swallow the appellation of coward"), was thrown into the battle's epicenter and saw a mounted Ferguson encouraging his men to stand fast. Ferguson soon fell and disappeared from view.[104] With some four hundred of their comrades already dead and wounded, the British and Tories, seeing their chief downed, threw down their arms and called for quarter. Of that there was little. As they pleaded down on their knees, scores were shot, and nine more—who were found to be the most egregious war criminals—were hanged after a court-martial. (One of them was a captain who had recently knocked on the door of a local Whig and shot the man's young son in the head with a pistol when he said his father wasn't home.) American losses amounted to 30 dead and about 50 wounded.[105] The rifle's devastating accuracy had just been demonstrated in the most violent way possible.

Shortly after the British surrender, Collins—who had fired his rifle six times, though he saw others do so nine or ten times—stumbled over the slaughtered to see the "dead body of their great chief." "It appeared," he remembered, "that almost fifty rifles must have been leveled at him, at the same time; seven rifle balls had passed through his body, both of his arms were broken; and his hat and clothing were literally shot to pieces."[106] Others found the bodies of at least twenty Tories, each with a rifle bullet hole in his forehead—they had been shot as they poked their heads above the rocks shielding them.[107]

King's Mountain aside, the rifle played a marginal *military* role during the War of Independence. But the reverberations of its cameo appearances could still be felt generations later. The legend of the American Rifleman, the bitter divide between officers enamored of disciplined musketry and those of independent riflemanship, the cult of accuracy versus faith in firepower: these legacies would be repeatedly resurrected down the ages.

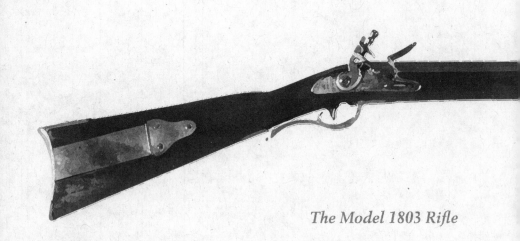

The Model 1803 Rifle

Chapter 3

THE RISE OF THE
MACHINES

Amillion square feet of floor space. Thirteen thousand exhibits. A unique building 1,850 feet long and 450 feet wide constructed entirely of glass and iron, with a central, barrel-vaulted transept and a mammoth nave lined with chapel bays along its sides. A cathedral dedicated not to an ethereal God but to the thrusting new religion of commerce. *This* was the Crystal Palace in London, site of the 1851 "Great Exhibition of the Works of Industry of All Nations," a world's fair demonstrating the majesty of empire and the contribution of free trade to the emancipation of all mankind.

More than six million people visited, all curious to see the wondrous things that twenty-eight countries had dispatched, almost as tribute, to London, the Victorian era's Rome. Americans, recognizing a commercial opportunity when they saw one, devoted a herculean effort to creating their country's pavilion.

Proclaimed the *New York Herald,* "We are as yet unknown in the market of Europe as the producers of raw material. Now we can show them that we not only produce cotton, iron, coal, copper and gold in greater abundances than any other nation, but that we can work them up into manufactures often equally, sometimes surpassing the oldest nations in a perfection and with a facility unknown to them."[1]

The call was answered. Of the many thousands of proposals that deluged the government, 599 were chosen for inclusion in the American pavilion, a two-story affair lorded over by a gigantic golden eagle and a mighty organ that put to shame anything even Bach, the instrument's maestro, could ever have conceived. Most of the exhibits were either agricultural or industrial in nature—a result of the tug-of-war between rural southern interests and northern manufacturers. Innovative plows, scythes, and reapers were popular attractions, as were "unpickable" locks, "meat biscuits," rubber lifeboats, and sewing machines. Two exhibits in particular, however, were of immense interest to the representatives of Her Majesty's Government who toured the American section: Samuel Colt's revolvers (which, in an early example of an "interactive" display, visitors were encouraged to pick up and shoot) and a set of six military-grade rifles made by a new Vermont firm, Robbins & Lawrence.

Their like had never before been seen. As astounded visitors goggled, Colt's salesmen informed them that these pistols had been *made by machines,* while the Robbins & Lawrence people disassembled the six rifles, mixed up the pieces, and put them back together again.[2] Their various metal parts were perfectly interchangeable; one rifle was exactly the same as another. Cynics, who knew such a thing was impossible, suspected that a trick was being played upon them.

Unlike today, interchangeability and machine production were not synonymous. An advanced machine of the time could make *uniform* parts, but because they did not mesh perfectly, a trained artisan had to fine-tune them, finish them, and fit them together. Parts that appeared to be similar would be loose or grind together, or they might be slightly misshapen and mismatched. *Interchangeable* parts, however, were identical and could be slotted together by a semiskilled worker following a set procedure. Machine-produced uniformity was in itself a tall order, but true interchangeability was regarded as the Holy Grail of industrialism by some (and as a fool's errand by most others).

Robbins & Lawrence, and for that matter Colt, had not invented machine production; nor had they conceived the principle of interchangeability. Despite Colt's boasts, the pieces of his weapons were not truly interchangeable, and armorers were still required to fit them together, filing and bending them when necessary.[3] But Colt, and many others,

A lethal symbol of the "American System of Manufactures": An inter-changeable Robbins & Lawrence percussion rifle, the same model that amazed spectators at the 1851 Crystal Palace exhibition in London.

had benefited from several decades of firearms development funded by the American government—most particularly in the field of advanced rifle design—which had diffused technology to, and seeded know-how among, to a wide array of private companies. By such means manufacture of the rifle kick-started American industrialism, shaped the rise of modern capitalism, changed society (for better or worse), and propelled the United States to world economic mastery.[4]

In that single Robbins & Lawrence demonstration at the Crystal Palace, the world in which a single craftsman painstakingly created one product at a time vanished. "The old universe was thrown into the ash-heap," Henry Adams once curmudgeonly commented, and in its place would rise the tyranny of time-punching, the machine epoch, and later the era of mass production, when millions of identical rifles (and cars, and appliances, and plastic products) would be churned out by sleepless robots and tired workers.[5]

This wrenching economic change occurred neither painlessly nor overnight, and its success depended heavily on locality. In the industrialized North many former artisans adapted relatively quickly to wage-labor work. Factory production surged, though income declined, as did working conditions, which led to often bitter class conflicts. In the rural South the natural rhythm of the weather and the unhurried ease of life bestowed by slavery (on prosperous whites) continued to dominate the pace of production. Partly because they could always look down on blacks as being more subordinate and miserable than they, small yeoman farmers did not suffer from the same travails afflicting northern industrial workers. This absence of rancor had the benefit of defusing social agitation, but at the price of remaining defiantly, and nostalgically, antimodern.[6]

The new federal armories at Springfield (Massachusetts) and Harpers Ferry (Virginia) provide a most striking example of the differences between North and South at the time. Both had been established in the 1790s to ease the weapons-supply issues that had dogged the American forces during the Revolution, but from the beginning Harpers Ferry had been a major headache. Whereas Springfield benefited from its New England geography and a pool of business and artisan talent, Harpers Ferry began as a pork-barrel project, advised against by surveyors but pushed by George Washington, to aid local commercial development. Being closer to the new federal capital, the armory was subject to intense political pressure from whichever administration happened to be in power. It was distant from established roads, lacked natural resources, and every summer was stricken by devastating diseases that sent the armorers (many lured away from the gunsmithing workshops of Pennsylvania) to their sickbeds.[7]

A harbinger of the chaos to come was the Model 1803, the first official production rifle to emerge from Harpers Ferry and the first official U.S. military rifle. Before the Model 1803, the armory had made a small quantity of the experimental Model 1800, which was originally envisaged as a high-performance heir to the Kentucky rifle but actually seemed to have been designed by committee—and not a very competent one either. The weapon certainly looked a bit like the graceful Kentuckys of ages past, but it had clearly inherited the stout, heavy genes of its German Jäger ancestors. This unfortunate familial trait was mostly the result of the War Department's insistence on a larger caliber and a much shorter barrel than the Kentucky, so that the weapon would be easier to clean and load. To compensate for its "sawn-off," big-caliber specifications, shooters had to use very fine powder to burn off the charge. The price was that the gun kicked with a colossal recoil.[8]

The Model 1803 rectified some, but by no means all, of the 1800's deficiencies and it remained an inaccurate weapon, at least compared to a customized Kentucky. As a by-product of its large caliber, it did enjoy significant knockdown power, while its short barrel made it easy to carry slung across one's back through tangled forests. For these reasons Captains Meriwether Lewis and William Clark settled upon an advanced prototype of the Harpers Ferry Model 1803, fifteen of them to be exact, to equip their Corps of Discovery on its mission to extend the American frontier to the Pacific. Lewis and Clark also ordered basic Model 1795 smoothbore muskets for the army volunteers attached to the corps, as well as tomahawks and knives. The nine frontiersmen who accompanied the team refused, however, the Harpers Ferry rifles and instead carried their own Kentuckys as well as a host of Indian weapons. Clark himself had a personal weapon of which he was most fond: a specially made Kentucky "small rifle" with a tiny caliber of .33.

If it had been detailed to make limited batches of custom rifles, the Harpers Ferry armory would always have done a fine job, but it wasn't: its task was to produce many thousands of them, and in that respect it was a failure. This was primarily owing to the way it was run. In Massachusetts the superintendent was the no-nonsense Roswell Lee, who was intent on making the Springfield Armory the most efficient, progressive, and economical arms manufacturer in the region; but for two decades from 1807 onward, Harpers Ferry was controlled by James Stubblefield, a man in whom patronage and paternalism were inextricably entwined.

In conjunction with the local gentry, which controlled the schools and stores, Stubblefield ran the armory as a personal fiefdom. He rarely bothered to keep accounts, he installed his relatives and cronies at every level of power, he contracted out work to whichever firms his friends owned, and any employee who dared rock the boat was shoved overboard. The oligarchical web of personal fealties and kinship at the armory became familiarly known as the "Junto." Still, the armorers at Harpers Ferry were fond of their feudal master: unlike the hyperefficient Roswell Lee, Stubblefield was happy to allow them to work when they wished, to drink and carouse on the job, and to take days or weeks off as the mood struck them—all while he protected their artisanal privileges and paid them lavishly.

Stubblefield did not invent this system; he inherited it. As early as 1806, even before he appeared on the scene, making 4,000 muskets at Harpers Ferry required more than 140 men, while half that force at Springfield sufficed to produce the same number.[9]

While working conditions were certainly more pleasant at Harpers Ferry than at Springfield, the dark side of the merry old ways was everywhere evident. Corruption, back-scratching, and bullying were endemic, and the armorers fiercely resisted any kind of innovation or reforms. One went so far as to shoot a manager who hoped to introduce more regular hours.[10]

★ ★ ★

The old guard at Harpers Ferry would soon meet its match in a Yankee from Maine: John H. Hall.

Son of a Harvard divinity graduate, Hall was born in 1781 and in 1803 joined, as many young American males did, a militia company, where he developed a lifelong interest in firearms. Seven years later his mother (the father having predeceased her) died, leaving him a comfortable, if not lavish, inheritance that he invested in his own small carpentry firm making barrels, cabinets, and boats. In his spare time Hall tinkered with rifles, always mindful of what he had witnessed during his time in the militia. "Among those things which appeared to me of the greatest importance and particularly attracted my attention," he later wrote, "was that of improvement in firearms regarding their accuracy and dispatch." No mere technician he, Hall ambitiously dreamed of "render[ing] the issue of battle less dependent upon that perfect discipline, subordination, and unison, in which regulars may always excel a militia composed of all the citizens."[11]

Whereas the Revolution had ended with the domination of European-influenced views on discipline and musketry favored by Alexander Hamilton, Anthony Wayne, and Baron von Steuben, Hall wanted more heed paid to the country's militia traditions—even as he acknowledged that battles would henceforth be fought mostly between professional soldiers. His gun, Hall believed, would permit regulars to fight like militia.

Standing up for the militia was unpopular. For years the Federalists had attacked the very idea of civilian defense. In today's more complex society, they emphasized, the division of labor into specialized tasks was critical: universal militia duty took men away from their occupations, detracting from their ability to produce goods and condemning America to the poorhouse.[12]

They thought it more sensible to make military service a paid, voluntary job. Warfare, no longer the province of amateurs, now required expertise in strategic theory and the scientific disciplines, an understanding of the logistics of supply, distribution, and stockpiling, and a mastery of intricate battlefield tactics. Part-time colonels and weekend sergeants were no longer up to the job of running a modern army.

The force of this argument was not lost even upon Thomas Jefferson, the high priest of republicanism, the militiaman, and the frontiersman. The United States, he knew, still faced French incursions in the Floridas and Louisiana, British adventurism in Canada, and Spanish machinations in the West. During his administrations (1801–1809), while still paying lip service to the ideal of a citizen army, he recruited no fewer than ten thousand men into a professional one and established the U.S. Military Academy at West Point to train the army's nascent officer corps.[13]

Jefferson had concluded that the nation's fundamental republican ethos now required for its protection an antirepublican institution. In this respect, his and John Hall's views were identical. For Hall, arming America's soldiers with an American rifle so that they could beat Europeans became a lifelong obsession.

Improving its "accuracy and dispatch" were his two immediate concerns. Enhancing the accuracy of a weapon already famed for that attribute was too tall an order, however, so Hall initially focused on accelerating the speed of reloading. His *Eureka!* moment happened sometime in the winter of 1811. The main factor retarding the number of shots per minute that a rifleman could fire, he had noticed, was the necessity of ramrodding ball and powder down a lengthy barrel. Hall adapted a pistol design and then integrated it into the rifle's firing mechanism. Pistols also required muzzle-loading, but because their barrels were so short, charging them was a relatively rapid and easy job; some barrels could even be unscrewed and the bullet and powder placed directly in the chamber. Unscrewing a rifle barrel would have been as time-consuming as loading from the muzzle, but Hall did insert a solid metal block—a "receiver"—containing the flintlock fire-mechanism and hollowed-out chamber into the breech. The block was hinged and was kept in place with a spring-catch that the shooter released to raise it. All the rifleman had to do then was pour in powder, drop a bullet on top, snap the receiver back into place, prime the pan, and fire. With this one shortcut, Hall had circumvented the entire centuries-old, laborious process of muzzle-loading.[14] He was not the first to ever think of loading a gun at the breech, but he pioneered a safe, effective, and reliable method of doing it.

Excited about his invention, Hall sought to patent it, but in so doing he learned that the apparently ever-upward line of technological progress is often frustrated by the crooked timber of humanity. In his case, the crook was Dr. William Thornton, a pious Quaker whose religious principles may well have included pacifism but not, apparently, honesty. Thornton, a well-connected Jefferson toady, ran the Patent Office, and soon after Hall filed his application, he sent him a letter regretting that a patent on such a mechanism had already been taken out. By one Dr. William Thornton, as it happened, back in 1792. Still, Thornton proposed that he was "desirous of sharing the invention with me and hoped that there would be room enough for both of us."

Hall, intrigued and perhaps a tad suspicious of this remarkable coincidence, traveled to Washington to see Thornton's prototype. With a flourish, Thornton produced, of all things, a Revolutionary-era British rifle that bore no resemblance whatsoever to Hall's version. The two guns were so dissimilar that Hall told Thornton that "we might each have obtained patents for our respective developments without any risk of ever interfering with each other." Thornton refused to budge, so Hall approached Secretary of State James Monroe. In the secretary's office, Hall remembered, "I was advised that it would be more to my interest to be connected with Doct. Thornton even at the expense of half my right than have it wholly to myself." If he played by the unwritten rules, Monroe said, Thornton's influence "would be exerted in my favor but otherwise would be exerted against me." If the latter, Hall could expect no assistance "in case of any attempts by others to interfere with my rights by attempting the obtainment of patents for the same invention connected with alterations, an event frequently occurring with patents likely to prove important."[15]

The fix was in. If Hall dared contest the decision, he would find himself tied up in legal knots for years to come and never see a penny from his invention; however, for just a modest one-off concession, paths would be cleared, red tape cut through, and obstacles miraculously hurdled. For his payoff, Thornton declared himself content to receive half the proceeds arising from the sale of the patent rights to private manufacturers, but he generously would allow Hall to keep the profits from any rifles made in his own factories. As would so many others, Thornton underestimated Hall's stubbornness and determination to have his own way. Hall, having no choice, agreed to the terms but immediately frustrated his tormentor by refusing to sell the patent rights to anyone and then established his own business to escape Thornton's extortionate "tax."

The bold scheme was doomed to fail. Employing between six and eight men, Hall concentrated on manufacturing his patent rifle, as well as a series of pistols and smoothbore muskets based on his hinged-receiver concept, but he never managed to produce more than fifty weapons a year. His primary market was restricted to Maine, and he did a brisk business there during the War of 1812, when locals were threatened with British invasion. The *Eastern Angus* of September 8, 1814, commented—Hall was one of the paper's major advertisers—that "at the present time of danger and alarm, when all are anxiously seeking means of defense of their families and firesides, we would recommend to our fellow citizens as the most effective defensive weapon for light troops in use, the improved fire arms made by MR. JOHN H. HALL."[16] At this time Hall married Statira Preble, a "tall, elegant woman" whose even temperament counterbalanced her husband's "mad genius" character, and she proved a rock in the troublesome decades to come. No firmer advocate of Mr. Hall's breech-loader could be found than Mrs. Hall, and a good thing too, for between 1811 and 1817, Hall had blown through his mother's inheritance and was $6,000 in debt to Statira's family.[17]

As bankruptcy threatened, Hall was sustained by a glimmer of interest from the War Department. Hall tried to obtain a government arms contract, despite Thornton's poisonous whisperings in Washington to scotch it. Thornton, already frustrated once by Hall's shenanigans, was determined not to lose out twice. He knew, as did Hall, that if the government stepped in to purchase his breech-loaders, the patent rights could never be sold off privately and he would wave goodbye to any windfall. This was because in an era of scarce capital and few banks, the government's ability to provide funds to subsidize the cost of labor, raw materials, shop construction, and tools made it indispensable as a source of financial security, but its largesse came at the cost of permanently taking the vendor off the market. Gaining access to the charmed circle of sumptuous government contracts was exhilarating for anyone, but the price exacted was never-ending subservience to the vagaries of Washington politics and War Department infighting.

Hall, however, was caught desperately between Thornton and imminent financial meltdown. He wrote to Secretary of War William Eustis in 1811, but because the department had recently contracted for 85,200 conventional muskets, Eustis passed on funding Hall's rifle. Two years later Hall tried again, this time with Eustis's successor, John Armstrong. Armstrong passed his letter on to Colonel George Bomford, an uppercrust, West Point–trained engineer who was friendly with Andrew Jackson and serving as Colonel Decius Wadsworth's deputy at a new agency, the Ordnance Department. Bomford was intrigued by Hall's invention and asked him to send eight sample breech-loaders for trials.

Between December 1813 and November 1814 Bomford experimented with the guns and submitted a favorable report recommending their adoption into the service. He ordered two hundred rifles just before Christmas 1814. There was one problem: Bomford wanted the firearms delivered by April 1, 1815—an impossibility given Hall's limited production runs and the need to handcraft each one. Disappointed, Hall was obliged to turn down the request, though he did spend the subsequent year refining his rifle design. Two key innovations that he introduced were adding an attachment for a bayonet and moving the priming pan from the traditional right-hand side to the top of the receiver so that, as he explained, "the powder in the pan is not blown violently against the left cheeks of all the right hand men [in an infantry line], and does not induce that injurious habit of *starting* [flinching] so injurious to marksmanship."

Hall was intent on turning his experimental rifle into a viable replacement for the entire army's muskets. Said Hall, men armed with his rifles would outshoot those carrying muskets because "they can load and fire with certain aim more than twice as fast as musketry can load their pieces with their cartridges."[18] If adopted, the Hall rifle would turn the American army into the most lethal force in the world, in terms not only of volume of fire but of accuracy as well.

Bomford, to Hall's mind, was not thinking ambitiously enough. He had ordered only two hundred rifles, evidently intending that they should merely form the nucleus of a specialized rifle unit, like those of the Revolution. If Hall were to persuade the brass to replace the army's muskets, he would have to find some way of churning out more of his own rifles, faster. To that end, just as he had dreamed up a simple method to shorten loading time, Hall also thought long and hard about how to improve the speed of production.

The greatest time-waster, Hall noticed when watching his employees, was the handcrafting of each individual piece of a gun to mesh snugly with its neighbors. While every hammer or trigger looked basically the same, on closer inspection they weren't. That was because a workman generally constructed a weapon from scratch: carving and polishing the wooden stock, boring and rifling the barrel, fitting the sights and fire-lock, and fashioning each piece according to his own dictates and judgment. Taking the Harpers Ferry Model 1803 rifles as an example, between 1804 and 1807 the armory made about four thousand of them, but barrel lengths could be an inch shorter or longer than regulations stipulated depending on the maker's whim, and the style of rifling carved on the inside of the barrel also varied widely, leading to enhanced or diminished performance.[19] Though all the Model 1803 rifles were superficially similar, in other words, each weapon was individualized and its finished quality hinged on the skills and experience of the armorer. Some rifles might fire beautifully, while others tended to hang fire, and still more fell apart because the armorer had been in a hurry to go home and hadn't bothered to securely fit together its parts.

The solution, Hall deduced, lay in removing the randomness introduced by individualization and in perfecting the manufacture of each rifle's components. Since the human factor was causing the errors and slowing down production, the most obvious fix was to replace people with machines that would produce identical parts. Even so, several major problems remained. These extraordinary machines had to be designed and built; skilled armorers would still be required to assemble the pieces; the machine-built parts might not fit together as intimately as those made by hand; and lastly, taking into account the cost of developing these machines plus labor expenses, would it even be financially worthwhile? For the five sample rifles, Bomford had offered to pay $40 each—about $500 in today's dollars—a price that Hall reckoned would cover the production costs, but that was for a tiny order. If Hall was serious about gaining a government contract for a significant number of rifles, Washington would not likely be willing to pay such a high figure.

Hall, for the moment, pushed these concerns aside. His immediate aim was to get Bomford's signature on the dotted line before he went bust. To that end, and having successfully introduced his bayonet and priming-pan refinements, he approached the Ordnance Department in June 1816—and wrote what should be counted as among the most important letters in American history:

> Only one point now remains to bring the rifles to the utmost perfection, which I shall accept if the Government contracts with me for the guns to any considerable amount, viz: to make every similar part of every gun so much alike that it will suit every gun, e.g. so that every bayonet will suit every barrel, so that every barrel will suit every stock, every stock or receiver will suit every barrel, and so that if a thousand were taken apart and the limbs thrown promiscuously together in one heap, they may be taken promiscuously from the heap, and will all come right—This important point I conceive practicable, and although in the first instance it will probably prove expensive, yet ultimately it will prove most economical and be attended with great advantages. [20]

Here, for the first time, Hall was confidently proposing the mass·production of a good on the principle of pure interchangeability. In this respect he had gone further than anyone before him.

* * *

Hall was about to get his big break thanks to an astoundingly fortunate constellation of factors. The first was a defiantly igneous rock lurking in the sedimentary pile of the War Department by the name of Major Louis de Tousard.

After narrowly avoiding losing his head to the guillotine during the French Revolution, Tousard settled down on a hundred-acre farm near Wilmington, Delaware, where he served as a conduit of French military theory for America's postwar army. At the time American officers looked to the British for military-*tactical* advice; but for military-*technical* advice, France remained their beacon. In his widely read *American Artillerist's Companion,* an 1809 study commissioned by the late President Washington, Tousard neatly outlined the virtues of a weapons "system of uniformity and regularity" based on scientific observations and mechanical experimentation.[21]

Tousard had not invented the concept of "uniformity and regularity," though another Frenchman had: General Jean-Baptiste de Gribeauval, a mentor of Tousard's who in 1765 applied Enlightenment precepts to the art of war. If one man was born equal in reason to every other man, and if each soldier, thanks to strict discipline, was replaceable in the line with his comrades, then why, asked Gribeauval, should not his weapons also be identical? Uniform men with uniform firearms would surely produce a uniform army of mechanical precision. The idea appealed to his superiors, and Gribeauval was eventually permitted to rationalize the national armories with the aid of Honoré Blanc, a firearms designer. The rise of Napoleon—who prized personal loyalty and nationalist zeal over harmony of mechanical parts—put paid to these remarkably prescient efforts.[22]

But meanwhile Thomas Jefferson, the American minister in France, had noticed the commotion going on at the French armories. His interest in the project was unsurprising, for Jefferson himself was mad on guns—pistols mainly, particularly ones he commissioned with twenty-inch barrels for fine shooting—it being his considered opinion that ten-year-old boys should be handed a firearm and urged to go hunting in the forest because it "gives moderate exercise to the body . . . and independence to the mind."[23]

Given the depth of Jefferson's knowledge of firearms, when he informed John Jay of his findings after visiting Blanc, he was certainly listened to. The French advance in standardized production, he concluded, "may have influence in the plan for furnishing our magazines with this arm."[24] Unfortunately, Blanc turned down Jefferson's invitation to emigrate to America and put his talents at the disposal of the government. Hoping instead that an American could divine the secrets of standardization, Jefferson sent six of Blanc's improved muskets to Philadelphia in 1789 for examination.

Following the XYZ Affair—a financial scandal that almost led to war with France—the need for a reliable domestic manufacturing base became ever more urgent. Finally in 1798 Eli Whitney, a well-connected machinist, unlucky businessman, and future inventor of the famous cotton gin, won the first government contract for army muskets: ten thousand, standardized, with delivery two years later. Given the state of technology, this goal was forbiddingly implausible to begin with, but Whitney talked such a good game that he was advanced $5,000—the first of several huge payments based on his assurances that he was close to emulating Blanc's success. In the end Whitney didn't deliver a single musket until the summer of 1801, and he completed the order only in 1809, eight years after the guns' scheduled delivery date. And even then, they were seriously flawed. Nevertheless, there were so few gunmakers in the United States capable of producing the number of weapons needed that Whitney was able to sign another contract three years later, this time with Secretary of War John Armstrong for fifteen thousand Model 1812 muskets. Between Tousard's call for basic uniformity and Whitney's failure to achieve it, Hall's proposal to forge fully interchangeable firearms could be assured of at least a friendly hearing.

The second factor in Hall's success came in the form of Callender Irvine, the new commissary general of purchases for the army, who had begun casting a beady eye Whitney's way. In June 1813 Irvine, a man who hated waste and extravagance, began targeting greedy arms manufacturers who "did not expect in the beginning to be able to comply with their [contractual] engagement nor do they now intend it."[25] Four months later the first warning shot from Irvine blazed across Whitney's bow when he rejected as worthless a batch of his Model 1812s. "These defects must be remedied," he warned, "or the muskets will not be received or paid for by me."[26] When Whitney complained, Irvine airily replied that "your opinions and criticisms on the exceptions taken to your musket have little weight in my mind." Either supply the muskets in perfect condition immediately, he concluded, or "refund, promptly, the money with interest, which has been advanced to you by the United States."[27] Irvin wanted to terminate the contract because "no good arms can be expected from him," but Whitney was saved by the War of 1812, when the American government was crying out for guns, any guns, even Whitney's guns.[28]

Despite (or because of) Whitney's lucky escape, reform was in the air. Colonel Decius Wadsworth, a colleague of Tousard's and Irvine's, was appointed head of the newly founded Ordnance Department, an agency carved out of the War Department whose specific task it was to improve efficiency in arms procurement and manufacture.[29] His motto? "Uniformity, Simplicity and Solidarity."[30] It would soon become his fiefdom's mantra.

Wadsworth was a man whose clockwork mind functioned along precisely dotted and plotted lines, much as did his "uniformity system." In 1815, with his deputy George Bomford's assistance, he undertook a major reorganization of the American military-industrial complex. Henceforth, he directed, the two national armories at Harpers Ferry and Springfield would pursue uniformity in all things, from using precision gauges and standardized accounting to constructing "model" or "pattern" weapons (i.e., perfect specimens issued to private makers that they would copy to the millimeter) before production began.[31] Thanks to Hall, Ordnance would soon be able to put principle into practice.

The third factor militating in Hall's favor was Andrew Jackson's surprise victory at the Battle of New Orleans in January 1815, which

produced a flurry of interest in rifles.[32] Jackson's triumph over the
British general Thomas Pakenham's veteran troops was an extraordinary event in American history. Just five months before, the White
House and Capitol had been burned by the enemy, and public opinion
had turned despondent, but news of New Orleans, recalled one contemporary, "came upon the country like a clap of thunder in the clear azure
vault of the firmament, and travelled with electromagnetic velocity,
throughout the confines of the land." The battle, boasted the papers,
amply demonstrated the "rising glory of the American Republic" and
placed "America on the very pinnacle of fame."[33]

The Battle of New Orleans was the culmination of two weeks' bitter
fighting around the city. On January 8, on the plains of Chalmette,
Jackson and Pakenham had faced each other for the final trick. The
Americans were entrenched behind a long wall of sugar casks and barrels, mortared together with mud. They were protected by a ten-foot-
wide ditch, with a cypress swamp on Jackson's left and a river levee
to his right. In short order Jackson's outnumbered forces—consisting
of between 3,500 and 4,500 assorted U.S. Marines, navy sailors,
Baratarian pirates, freed black soldiers, Choctaw warriors, and large
complements of Tennessee, Kentucky, Mississippi, and Louisiana militiamen—had inflicted an extraordinarily one-sided defeat on the enemy.
American losses were 13 killed, plus 58 wounded and 30 captured,
compared to the astounding figure of 385 redcoats dead, 1,186
wounded, and 484 taken prisoner or missing.

Given Jackson's favorable defensive deployment, Pakenham had been
forced to mount a frontal assault (with a small flank attack) using his
troops in compact formations, bayonets at the ready to storm the wall.
The task of his subordinate commanding the van, Colonel Thomas
Mullins, had been to ensure that ladders were available in the ditch so
the regulars could climb the sides; Mullins, however, failed miserably
(for which he was ignominiously cashiered after the war), leaving the
redcoats and the doomed Pakenham stranded helplessly at the mercy of
the American artillery, musket fire, and rifle shots.

The most deaths, as well as the most hideous wounds and gaping
maws, were caused by the cannons firing grapeshot into the dense,
writhing ranks. After the battle, however, observers noticed that many of

BATTLE OF NEW ORLEANS
AND DEATH OF MAJOR GENERAL PAKENHAM
On the 8th of January 1815.

A contemporary engraving of Andrew Jackson's victory at the Battle of New Orleans.

the fatalities had been shot precisely in the forehead and that scores more had been shot at least twice in the head.[34]

These were the unmistakable calling cards of Jackson's rifle-armed, camouflaged militiamen, the same ones who in the weeks previous had made a specialty out of shooting British sentries. One of them, from Tennessee it is said, had crept through the long tall grass and underneath bushes to a place where he succeeded in shooting a guard, then his replacement, and then the replacement's replacement. After that the outpost was abandoned.[35] Reflecting contemporary opinion of down-and-dirty sharpshooting, George Gleig, a British observer, contrasted the American behavior with European manners. Whereas European armies, when they weren't shooting at each other, kept a civil truce—he himself had seen French and British soldiers standing guard just twenty yards away from each other—"the Americans entertained no such chivalric notions. An enemy was to them an enemy, whether alone or in the midst of five thousand companions."[36]

Before the battle, it was reported, a British officer out reconnoitering the American line had been hailed by a Tennesseean and directed to surrender. Rapidly weighing his options—a running retreat was still possible—the officer raised his hands. When asked why, he said that ultimately "I had no alternative; for I have been told these damned Yankee riflemen can pick a squirrel's eye out as far as they can see it."[37]

Immediately after the battle Jackson's riflemen were lauded as heroes across the land, and their peculiar weapon suddenly (if temporarily) became the darling of Washington. So when John H. Hall wrote to the Ordnance Department in June 1816 proposing to build a factory on the interchangeability principle that would produce rapid-loading rifles en masse, his timing was impeccable. The Ordnance Department quickly seized the opportunity to investigate this promising arms-maker and his intriguing invention.

In January 1817 Wadsworth informed Hall that he should send one hundred rifles and bayonets (quoted at $25 each) by year's end—an order Hall fulfilled, much to Wadsworth's surprise, by October. The weapons were quickly issued to a rifle unit based in Missouri for testing under actual field conditions. Wadsworth was also pleased to hear from one of his deputies, Captain George Talcott, who had initially been skeptical of the breech-loading mechanism but was converted to its advocacy after a careful examination.[38] In April 1818, while the rifles were still being tested, Wadsworth raised the cheering possibility that Hall might transfer his operations to Harpers Ferry and run an autonomous factory under government aegis. The offer was most tempting, for under the wing of the Ordnance Department, Hall would be forever protected from the predations of Dr. Thornton.

Two issues, though, were beginning to gnaw at Wadsworth. First was the rifles' expense: each specimen had actually cost $200 to make. To be fair, Hall had warned that until he had his system properly set up, prices would remain high. Then again, whereas Hall had contracted for rifles at $25 each, the current cost of a regular Harpers Ferry musket was $14.73—quite a price difference.[39]

The other worry was largely philosophical, but it would continue to bedevil rapid-firing weapons for many decades to come. And that, in Wadsworth's words, was "whether the facility of [rapid] firing will not occasion an extravagant use and waste of ammunition and whether the means of transporting all the ammunition which will be required can be obtained in actual service—These are consequences to be taken into view before we can safely decide upon such an important alteration in our military system." As it was, just test-firing the four Halls at the armory according to regulations would require no fewer than 25,000 rounds—"a piece of extravagance," opined the thrifty Wadsworth.[40]

Hall's very success in finally overcoming the rifle's traditional inferiority in rate of fire might actually, in other words, turn out to be a fatal liability. As Wadsworth said, soldiers armed with rapid-firing rifles would be tempted to replace their weapon's parsimonious single-shot accuracy with musket-style wastage, leading to a potential shortage of ammunition, which was by no means cheap or particularly easy to come by in the required quantities. If use of the rifles was restricted to specialized units of sharpshooters, ammunition costs could be regulated, but issuing such an advanced weapon to small numbers of troops made little sense while regular infantry was forced to make do with muskets.

From the army's point of view, such a result would be unacceptable. While muskets were prodigious consumers of lead and powder, officers strictly controlled the precise rate of fire along their section of line and tamped down on excessive use. If, say, the usual rate of musket-fire was three shots a minute, and the addition of a Hall mechanism raised that figure to six, how long would the men's fire-discipline hold? And how great would be the concordant diminution of respect for their commanding officer, now reduced to an impotent figurehead? Would the regular army turn into nothing but an undisciplined rabble of militia, as Anthony Wayne and others had feared?

On a broader level, one had to query whether switching the army over from flintlock muzzle-loaders to Hall-enabled breech-loaders was worth it in the foreseeable future. Undoubtedly, nightmarish logistical, financial, and organizational problems loomed in Wadsworth's imagination. As always with a radically new technology, decision-makers are confronted with a set of unpleasant trade-offs that often result in sticking with the old system simply because it is easier that way.

Hall, in this respect, was fortunate in having a staunch defender in George Bomford, who was certain to inherit the chieftainship of Ordnance once Wadsworth retired (as he would in 1821); what was more, every test the government armorers threw at the breech-loader confirmed its superiority over its competitors. In November 1818 a preliminary trial comparing a Hall rifle to a Model 1817 army rifle found that no difference in accuracy was discernable (as was only to be expected) but that when it came to celerity in loading, the difference was startling: the Hall rifle was twice as rapid. Durability-wise, it had been assumed that the breech receiver would not withstand severe punishment, but the armorers simulated "a fatigue at least equal to what those pieces would be exposed to in 14 or 15 campaigns, and probably more than they would ever be required to undergo" by firing the Hall thousands of times without incident. It had also been widely predicted that troops would find the Halls confusing and difficult to load, but that expectation was quickly dashed by the testers, who reported the opposite. The testers' "only objection to these [Hall] arms proceeds from the expense of their fabrication," leading them to conclude that the time was not yet right to introduce them "*generally* into the service." Before "so great a change in the armament of the troops be made," they required "the most unequivocal proof" of the Hall's superiority, so for the moment, they recommended that Hall rifles be given to rifle units to conduct further trials.[41] To which Hall, always brusque, rhetorically asked whether it would be "improper to reject a species of firearms which will do twice as much execution as common ones merely because they cost more?"[42] He knew he was right.

Impressed by his own armorers' enthusiasm, a few months later Wadsworth offered Hall a contract to build one thousand rifles at Harpers Ferry in his own self-run Rifle Works. In making the offer to set up shop at faraway Harpers Ferry rather than at Springfield—a more natural home for Hall—Wadsworth and Bomford's strategy was to use him as a Trojan horse to subvert Superintendent Stubblefield's fortress from within. As a private contractor answerable to the Ordnance Department, Hall would not be subject to Stubblefield's writ and would provide a useful counterweight to his reign. Upon hearing the news, Stubblefield correctly suspected an intrigue but could do nothing but make his hatred of the interloper apparent from the moment he showed up. The feeling was mutual. Hall, outspoken and stubborn, and Stubblefield, jealous and threatened, fought over absolutely everything, from the allocation of raw materials to the choice of postmaster for the town.[43]

Stubblefield liked to blame the armory's chronic deficit on having to subsidize the Rifle Works, but Hall himself cost the government very little (while snitching to Washington that Stubblefield's unwillingness to allow competitive bidding raised the cost of materials by up to 20 percent). His pay, after all, was just $60 (about $920 in today's dollars) a month, but to supplement this modest wage, Hall arranged to receive a royalty of $1 (i.e., $15) for each rifle manufactured.[44] This was nowhere near enough to retire on, but Hall had high hopes of eventually obtaining contracts for tens of thousands of rifles, which would set him up very nicely, especially if he could bring the price of each gun down.

It was Hall's responsibility to build the machines that would enable this scale of economy and identicalness of form, but even he, in his jubilation, underestimated just how arduous this task would be. Interchangeability on paper sounded easier than it actually was. Take such a simple object as a screw. To manufacture it in quantity requires a thorough understanding of such technical matters as its pitch diameter, thread angle, crest, root, pitch, and flank. Traditionally, each craftsman had made his own screws; only in the 1770s had Jesse Ramsden conceived a lathe that cut a fine pitch—crucial for making the kind of precision screw necessary for the construction of steam engines and machine tools. Gunsmiths, however, still relied on their own preferences and made small batches when necessary, none of which were perfectly identical to those preceding or succeeding. The variety of available screws rendered Hall's efforts to make them interchangeable using a specialized screw-lathe a thankless task, particularly after Bomford, in an expensive attempt at thriftiness, ordered that the available stocks of screws be used up before making new ones.[45]

Though Hall's mechanics could use one another's screws (by hammering them in, if necessary, when the boss wasn't watching), employing a screw that was not precisely machined for its hole or nut resulted in metal fatigue, considerable loss of holding force, and uncertain strength. For everyday uses it still might suffice, but in a gun, subjected to immense physical forces and burning-hot temperatures, such convenient workarounds could lead to a short life span—for both weapon and shooter.

In early 1823, confronted by this and other daunting obstacles, Hall came close to resigning his position, citing his maudlin reflections "upon the excessive and unavoidable slowness of our progress in the construction of the tools and . . . viewing my time passing away by years in their completion."[46] His old patron, Bomford, calmed Hall down and urged him to press on, though later Hall's supreme confidence in his talents again wavered, and he confessed that "had I been aware, in the first instance, of the intense application, excessive mental exertion, and great length of time necessary" to build his factory, "I should not, perhaps, have ventured upon it."[47] Originally, "from an unswerving reliance on my own abilities I [had] expected to accomplish [designing and building the machines] in a *short* period," but through a dogged perseverance and his own stout bloody-mindedness to see the job done, Hall did succeed in setting up several of his contraptions by Christmas 1824.[48]

What he had not succeeded in doing was producing actual rifles. By 1824, when he was supposed to have finished making the thousand stipulated in the contract, Hall had manufactured the grand total of twenty. Bomford, now head of Ordnance, was a patient master, and having received Hall's assurances that he had surmounted the most troublesome mechanical obstacles, he not only allowed him as much time as he needed but sweetened the pot by adding another thousand rifles to the order. This was a remarkably brave show of support, particularly considering the judgment of a visiting government inspector that "Mr. Hall . . . is too fond of projects, too much of an innovator ever to have been entrusted with public means to complete machinery of his own invention."[49]

Bomford's confidence was not misplaced, and just two months into 1825 Hall had churned out the first thousand of his rifles. Best of all, the gunmaker observed jauntily, he had brought "every thing relating to my arms to its utmost point of perfection." It was a technical triumph; for the first time, anywhere, Hall had achieved interchangeability. Now that each piece of his rifles would "suit all their corresponding parts in all of the arms," he predicted that from now on costs per firearm would begin to fall.[50] The average cost of each of the first batch of rifles was, Hall calculated, $20.59—significantly below the $25 Wadsworth had originally budgeted for—and he was confident he could reduce that figure to $14.71 for the next thousand.[51]

Bomford was most relieved to hear it: over seven years Hall had burned through $57,022—about $1.12 million—of taxpayers' money (at a time when the country's tax revenue was a minuscule fraction of today's) on fewer than a dozen wood and iron machines. Stubblefield's allies in Congress were beginning to ask probing questions about the Harpers Ferry accounts.[52] Once Bomford's vainglorious expenditure on the rifles came to light, they believed, Hall's project would be shut down.

Their hopes were to be dashed. Prompted by the Stubblefield faction, three inspectors sent along in December 1826 to watch the Halls in action reported to the government that the experiments at Harpers Ferry were certainly not a waste of public monies; quite the opposite, in fact. They were bowled over.[53] They had never before seen arms "made so exactly similar to each other," and they fell over themselves recommending that Hall receive "that patronage from the government his talents, science, and mechanical ingenuity deserve."[54] A tactic that had been intended to highlight Hall's weaknesses had actually backfired on Stubblefield by calling attention to his own lackadaisical management and accounting practices.

That month as well the Artillery School at Fortress Monroe, Virginia, reported on the results of its exhaustive five-month-long trials of the Hall, of a regular Harpers Ferry rifle, and of brand-new Springfield-made muskets. For Bomford and Hall, everything hinged on this test, but even they might have been surprised by the artillerists' conclusions. The school's testing staff "expresses its perfect conviction of the superiority of this [Hall's] arm over every other kind of small arm now in use; and this opinion has been formed after having seen two companies armed with them for five months, performing all the duties to which troops are liable in garrison." Further, the rifles' interchangeability of parts "is peculiar to this arm, and it is considered a great improvement."

Nobody had ever witnessed this kind of performance from a prototype weapon, the testers excitedly proclaimed. Its celerity of fire was incredible. Five Halls had discharged 77 times in 4.5 minutes, compared to 54 in the same time from the muskets and 37 from the regular rifles. Whereas ten men loaded and fired their Halls ten times each in an average of 3.75 minutes, the musket took 6.5 minutes, and the regular rifles, 16.75 minutes.

In terms of accuracy, the Hall won hands down against the musket. Thirty-eight men fired at a target 100 yards away for ten minutes at their own speed. The testers found that the Harpers Ferry rifles had discharged 494 times (with 164 rounds, or 33 percent, hitting the target) and the muskets 845 (with just 208, or 25 percent, in the target), but the Halls toted up the extraordinary figure of 1,198 shots, of which 430, or 36 percent, were in the target. All the examiners could gasp was that a Hall-armed unit would achieve a *guaranteed* victory "over an adversary of equal numerical force, armed with the common muskets."

They had just one or two minor criticisms. The most important was that concerning "the mass of filth" that accumulated in the chamber and barrel after rapid firing. They recommended that Hall supply a "small cylindrical wire brush" with each gun and make cleaning the breech part of every rifleman's drill. Aside from that, they had little to add.[55]

The report had exceeded even Hall's and Bomford's most optimistic expectations. A modern-day test has confirmed the Artillery School's plaudits for Hall's brilliant achievement of near-perfect interchangeability. In the late 1980s Robert Gordon, a professor of applied mechanics at Yale University, took precise measurements of the eleven critical dimensions of two early machine-made Hall rifles. Perhaps the most crucial measurement, that of the "head space" between the breech block and the barrel, averaged 0.003 inches on a brand-new arm, while the average deviation of the other ten dimensions was 0.0027 inches. For comparison's sake, the average deviation on Springfield firearms, then the most precisely hand-tuned weapons in the country, with their every piece individually crafted, was a relatively massive 0.0042 inches. By any standard, even those of today, Hall's success was impressive.[56]

Hall, however, was uncomfortably aware that he was hampered by a lack of space. He had too little room for all the machines he needed to build. Making a rifle required stock-carvers, drop hammers, forges, a complex pulley system, drilling implements, and machines able to straight-cut, curve-cut, and lever-cut, plus sufficient men to operate the apparatus, examine their output, and store the guns. One recurrent worry was finding enough water power to animate the machinery. Hall was obliged to use one machine to perform several tasks, rather than having several machines each performing one task, a deficiency that hampered efficient production as a single operator had to constantly readjust and remeasure the jigs and settings.

Also weighing on his mind was money. By this time his original patent on the firing mechanism had expired—a gratifying event, in that the malevolent Thornton would never see a penny from his scam. Hall's solution was to take out a patent on the *machinery* he had developed over the years while negotiating a $1,500 salary and retaining the one-dollar royalty.[57] Almost immediately Hall at last began to garner the rewards due him. The battery of Artillery School tests and inspectors' visits had convinced the government that the Hall was viable, even if it remained reluctant to replace the entire army's muskets, and Hall received a contract for no fewer than six thousand rifles over two years in April 1828.

Thanks to the favorable publicity inadvertently produced by Stubblefield's clumsy inquiry, no fewer than ninety-six congressmen asked for samples, as did the Marine Corps and even the governments of France and Prussia.[58] In December of that year, in response to requests from state militias, Hall and Bomford signed a contract with the gunsmith-industrialist Simeon North that allowed him to make another five thousand rifles for them, with the royalties paid to Hall. There was but one nonnegotiable condition: North's products had to be perfectly interchangeable with Hall's military-grade Harpers Ferry rifles.[59]

On that date Hall reached the meridian of his career, and despite the imminent departure of the loathed Stubblefield (Andrew Jackson's election ensured that he and his Junto would be cast out, like biblical unfortunates, into the wilderness), henceforth his victories would be tempered by failures and beset by aggravations. The most pressing problem confronting him was time. In the beginning his rifle had been the most advanced firearm in the world, but here it was, seventeen long, hard years after he had first approached the War Department, and the rest of the world was inexorably catching up. Though Hall's receiver retained its formidable technological lead, knowledge of the principle of interchangeability had filtered out to the wider business world. Johann Nikolaus von Dreyse in Prussia was quietly working on the still more futuristic "needle-gun" (which would become the first breech-loading rifle with a bolt-action mechanism), and a Scot, the Reverend John Forsyth, had invented the precursor of the percussion cap, the mechanism that would break that centuries-long supremacy of the flintlock.

Forsyth was a peculiar mixture of Enlightenment scientist and conservative divine who ministered to his human flocks on Sundays and devoted Mondays to Saturdays to shooting the feathered kind. In 1805 he had been struck by a genuinely inspired revelation. He noticed, while out hunting, that the sparks (actually, minute pieces of red-hot metal) lit by the flint's scraping and the puff of smoke emanating from his priming pan alerted his sitting prey to imminent danger. The birds got a moment's head start before the gunpowder ignited and the ball reached them. Hoping to reduce the delay, Forsyth began investigating the alchemical wonders of fulminates.

Fulminates (aptly derived from the Latin word for "lightning") were the eighteenth century's miracle chemical. A new class of compounds, they were exceedingly explosive, to such an extent that a few dozen grains were sufficient to demolish a lab. One version was so sensitive that a falling drop of water could detonate it; it could even blow up under the shifting weight of its own crystals. After several, almost lethal, attempts to develop fulminates for military use, scientists decided to stick with regular gunpowder.[60]

Forsyth's great insight was to realize that if one used fulminate as *priming* powder, not as a replacement for the gunpowder itself, an explosion could be controlled. When concussed by a metal object, a fulminate would detonate so rapidly that a bird would have no time to react, and when used in really tiny quantities, it presented little danger to the shooter.

It took him two years of hard work and lonely experimentation, but in April 1807 Forsyth patented a workable formula, in addition to a perfume-bottle–shaped dispenser that deposited the requisite amount in the pan, to which he attached a tube leading into the chamber. When the hammer hit the minute dot of "super-primer," ignition was instantaneous, and the flame descended the tube to burn the powder and propel the bullet.

It was a brilliant innovation, and like Hall, Forsyth soon found himself embroiled in patent problems. In Forsyth's case several other inventors came forward and claimed the concept for themselves. In 1819 the matter finally reached the courts, where Lord Abbott ruled in Forsyth's favor on the grounds that when other parties claim the right of simultaneous discovery, the first to patent it should legally be recognized as the inventor. Despite his victory Forsyth had grown weary of the years of incessant legal challenges to his idea. He quit his patent and retired to his little church in Belhelvie to harangue his congregants for the next two decades about the Eighth Commandment.[61]

Forsyth's withdrawal left a vacuum that others were all too willing to fill, and his rivals focused on making priming more convenient. At least four inventors—Joseph Manton, John Day, and Joseph Egg, all of England, as well as a recent English immigrant to Philadelphia, Joshua Shaw—laid claim to the idea of filling with fulminate a small copper "nipple" that would be detonated by a hammer striking it. Hence "percussion caps," their rather less powerful descendant being the caps used in children's toy guns. Perhaps Shaw should properly be called the percussion cap's father: he originally applied for the patent in 1814, but it was rejected on the grounds that he had lived in the United States for not long enough to qualify for patent protection. In 1815 he began using pewter caps before switching to copper ones a year later. His story had a happy(ish) ending, something of a rarity in the history of gun development. In 1846, following a lengthy investigation, the American government awarded him $25,000 (about $635,000) for what it called "one of the most ingenious, and one of the most useful inventions in modern terms." (It was so ingenious and useful that Washington later reduced its prize to $18,000.)[62]

Forty years later Shaw's caps were still being used, though Edward Maynard, a Washington, D.C., dentist and former gun designer, eased the process by developing the "Maynard tape primer" in 1845. Shaw's caps each had to be inserted individually, whereas Maynard's adaptation consisted of a roll of fifty caps encased between two strips of varnished paper. (Again, toy guns operate on the same principle.) Maynard soon sold the rights to the U.S. government, and from the 1840s onward the army's muskets and rifles were percussion-based.[63]

Early caps tended to be unstable because the copper sheathing was too thin or too cheap to contain the blast, and miniature shrapnel flew outward. But within a few years that problem had been surmounted, and designers turned their attentions to exploiting the new technology.[64] As the quality of fulminates improved, caps needed less to fill them, and in 1831 the British Board of Ordnance found to its delight that not only had the traditional wastage of expensive priming-powder ended (the wind blew a lot of it away, and men poured more than was needed into the pan to ensure that it lit) but also that the mammoth annual bill for gunpowder could be slashed by a fifth. This was because the fulminate allowed a more efficient detonation of the powder, and so less of it was required to produce the same projectile force.[65] Because of the reduction in the amount of unburned residue inside the chamber and barrel, infantrymen were not obliged to swab their guns as often, and the weapons benefited from not being subjected to as much wear and tear.

Armies also found that their supply headaches were eased somewhat by the caps. Historically, cumbersome wagon trains had prudently moved at a slow pace to prevent friction from causing accidental powder explosions, but caps were safe to transport and were more compact than barrels of priming-powder. Mr. Lovell of the Royal Arms Factory in England once conclusively demonstrated their safety by the simple expedient of thrusting a red-hot hammer into a tin box of five hundred caps. The only ones that exploded were those directly touched by the tool. His colleagues fired rounds into other boxes, with the same effect. The only way to blow up the entire box was to pour in gunpowder and ignite it.[66]

The cap led not to a revolution but to a reformation of military thinking. Since caps were waterproof, armies now had the option of campaigning in the winter and fall (even if gunpowder remained vulnerable to dampness), whereas the summer had been the age-old season for fighting. In order to man their armies for the longer duration, generals recruited more troops and generally incurred higher casualties, owing to the simple fact that a greater number of soldiers were being shot at for more extended periods of time.

The percussion cap arrived just as Hall was perfecting his rifle. Nevertheless the order came down from on high at the War Department that he was to redesign the gun using a percussion mechanism. The change did not require a thorough overhaul of the weapon, but Hall knew it meant inventing yet another machine and certainly a whole new round of tests. Not for *years* would his gun again reach the production stage.

By 1830, however, Hall had lost his youthful energy, and he was growing ever more irascible, carbuncled, and stubborn with age. He truckled to the War Department's commands but was reluctant to introduce the new technology. Continually beset by money problems, Hall convinced himself—with some justice—that enemies lurked everywhere, and he turned increasingly operatic, secretive, and controlling.

The rest of the decade tried Hall's soul, and he received no relief from the War Department, where the new guard began urging him to retire gracefully, to allow younger managers into his fiefdom of the Rifle Works, so that it could move with the times. Truth be told, Hall's unwillingness to keep up with the pace of technological development was delaying production of the breech-loading percussion carbines that the army wanted for the cavalry, and by now he was refusing to make even important revisions to his rifle.[67] To give him a gentle nudge, which the prickly Hall interpreted as a violent shove, in 1834 the department demoted him to the rank of master armorer, cutting his pay to a risible $600 a year. Bomford reassured his old friend that, no, it wasn't a *real* demotion, but Hall knew different and ascribed the move to his unseen foes in Washington. Though Bomford managed to get him a temporary raise to $2,646, Hall was confronted by a highly visible enemy in 1837, in the form of Edward Lucas.

As the new superintendent of Harpers Ferry and a Jacksonian appointee, Lucas was levelheaded but ruthless at playing politics at the armory, a habit that further contributed to Harpers Ferry's decline relative to Springfield. Between 1837 and 1840 Lucas fired thirty-four highly skilled employees (of whom twenty-eight were enemy Whigs) and replaced them with less-talented men more to his liking, who just happened to be Democrats.[68] He was most displeased by what he incorrectly thought were the continuing problems with interchangeability, a prejudice no doubt exacerbated by Hall's refusal to toe the party line. Convinced that "arms cannot be made, that will interchange, and at the same time closely and accurately, at a reasonable price, and without sacrificing other and greater advantages" (such as mass production), Lucas thought that "the sooner the attempt to accomplish it be dispensed with, the better."[69] Support for the Rifle Works was hence slowly, but inexorably, withdrawn, but the interchangeable genie was already out of the bottle.

Models of rifles and muskets from the early 1840s onwards would be fully interchangeable. Nevertheless, they would be muzzle-loaders—despite Hall's heroic efforts to supersede them.

Hall would never see the death of his breech-loader. His health had greatly deteriorated, and in 1840 he went on leave of absence.[70] Few, apart from Bomford (who was weakening himself), were keen to see him return. In the succeeding winter Hall's symptoms worsened, and he died on February 26, 1841. He chose to be buried in Darksville, Missouri, as did his wife, Statira, and as late as the 1970s their tombstones were visible, enclosed by a rusting iron fence. Bomford, now left isolated at the Ordnance Department, resigned in 1842 and followed his friend to the grave six years later.

It was John Hall, nevertheless, who had the last, if posthumous, laugh over his rivals. Since the days when he had struggled to persuade official Washington and the army that rifles were a feasible alternative to muskets, the world had changed.

No longer were riflemen regarded as ornery, uncouth backwoods folk; they instead occupied a plinth in the pantheon of American heroes. A major agent for this image turnaround was show business. In 1822, seven years after Jackson's victory over the British, Noel Ludlow, a theatrical impresario, was performing at a New Orleans playhouse and decided to keep the locals entertained with a rousing song. Recently his brother had sent him a copy of "The Hunters of Kentucky," a patriotic broadside written by Samuel Woodworth (now better known for his pretty poem "The Old Oaken Bucket"). Ludlow thought it perfect for his audience and set it to the music of "Miss Baily," a catchy tune from a comic opera, *Love Laughs at Locksmiths*.[71] As Ludlow remembered:

> *I dressed myself in a buckskin hunting-shirt and leggins . . . and with moccasins on my feet, and an old slouched hat on my head, and a rifle on my shoulder, I presented myself before the audience. I was saluted with loud applause of hands and feet, and a prolonged whoop, or howl, such as Indians give when they are especially pleased. I sang the first verse, and these extraordinary manifestations of delight were louder and longer than before; but when I came to the following lines:*

> > *"But Jackson he was wide awake, and*
> > *wasn't scared with trifles,*
> > *For well he knew what aim we take*
> > *with our Kentucky rifles;*
> > *So he marched us down to Cypress Swamp;*
> > *The ground was low and mucky;*
> > *There stood John Bull, in martial pomp,*
> > *But here was old Kentucky."*

> *As I delivered the last five words, I took my old hat off my head, threw it upon the ground, and brought my rifle to the position of taking aim. At that instant came a shout and an Indian yell from the inmates of the pit, and a tremendous applause from other portions of the house, the whole lasting for nearly a minute . . . I had to sing the song three times that night before they would let me off.[72]*

Quite a show-stopper, made all the more remarkable by what appears to be the first use in print of the term "Kentucky rifle." (In 1828 the song was such a national hit that it was adopted as Andrew Jackson's presidential-election anthem, sometimes amended to "The Voters of Kentucky.")

James Fenimore Cooper, the best-selling novelist, also played a major role in fixing the rifle in the American mind in the 1820s. Between 1823 and 1827 three volumes—*The Pioneers, The Last of the Mohicans,* and *The*

Prairie—appeared, recording the exploits of hardy frontiersman Natty Bumppo.

In *The Last of the Mohicans* Bumppo is forced to abandon not only the women accompanying him but also Killdeer (his treasured rifle) to capture by the Indians. "He gave Cora an affectionate shake of the hand," Cooper wrote, "lifted his rifle, and after regarding it a moment with melancholy solitude, laid it carefully aside." Natty is, evidently, a great deal more concerned about Killdeer than Cora falling into the enemy's hands. The Indians, led by the deceitful Magua, also seem more interested in the rifle than in the woman: "'La Longue Carabine! La Longue Carabine!' passed from mouth to mouth, until the whole band appeared to be collected around a trophy, which would seem to announce the death of its formidable owner."

Killdeer itself "was a little longer [in the barrel] than usual, and had evidently been turned out from the workshops of some manufacturer of a superior order. It had a few silver ornaments, though, on the whole, it would have been deemed a plain piece by most frontier men, its great merit consisting in the accuracy of its bore, the perfection of the details, and the excellence of the metal." Indeed, when Bumppo first sees Killdeer he exclaims, "This is a lordly piece, and would make a steady hand and quick eye the King of the Woods!" And so it eventually does.[73]

Cock-a-hoop about the impending death of Bumppo, the Indians (rather unrealistically, but Cooper needed a plot point) leave the vaunted firearm unguarded, which allows Natty to recapture it. Such was Killdeer's value to him that, before he rescues the girl, Bumppo spends precious minutes "examining into the state of his rifle with a species of parental assiduity."[74]

But a catchy variety-hall ditty and a few thrillers did not a legendary weapon make. Timing had much to do with Americans' newfound love for the rifle. The fiftieth anniversary of 1776 fell in 1826, and Americans were celebrating a half-century of independence. A fast-diminishing number of the Revolution's band of brothers were still alive—James Monroe, the country's fifth president between 1817 and 1825, was the last incumbent to have been an adult at the time of the Declaration of Independence—and it was only natural for the next generation of Americans to look back and wonder what had gone right, and what wrong, and compare their achievements to those ideals envisaged by the Founding Fathers.[75] Would they have been disappointed in their children? Proud, or merely bemused? The heroism of Jackson's boys in carrying out yet another whupping of the British suggested that George Washington himself would have been proud of his republic's citizens.

Politics, too, intruded. Anti-Jacksonian Whigs—heirs to the Hamiltonian Federalists and the National Republicans—caviled at Jackson's appropriation of the famous song's lyrics to serve his own ends, but they appreciated the Kentucky riflemen's self-reliance and ethical uprightness. While Jacksonians tended to assign responsibility for poverty and inequality to socioeconomic factors beyond the individual's ken, Whigs were adamant that personal flaws—laziness, priapism, godlessness— were the real cause. No such failings were evident among the riflemen, they argued.

In order to demonstrate their loyalties to the Common Man and to outflank Jackson, the Whigs coopted their own superstar rifleman and congressman: Davy Crockett, described by one contemporary reviewer of his memoirs as a "product of forests, freedom, universal suffrage, and bear-hunts."[76] Outsiders found his celebrity status inexplicable: Tocqueville, author of the classic *Democracy in America,* wonderingly recorded that Tennessee voters had rejected a candidate "of wealth and talent" in favor of a man who "has had no education, can read with difficulty, has no property, no fixed residence, but passes his life hunting . . . and dwelling continuously in the woods." But Crockett—bluff and plain spoken, possessed of a mother wit, perseverance, and courage—ran against Jackson, and the country took him readily to heart.[77] When he traveled to Philadelphia for a tour of the East during his last congressional term in 1834, it was only natural that the city's Whigs presented him with Pennsylvania's finest product: a Kentucky rifle that he quickly dubbed "Pretty Betsey" to distinguish it from her predecessor, "Old Betsey," given to him by his constituents back in 1822. Describing it as "just about as beautiful a piece as ever came out of Philadelphia," Crockett told the adoring crowd that "I love a good gun, for it makes a man feel independent, and prepared either for war or peace." It was exactly what they wanted to hear.[78]

Jackson's Democrats were uncomfortably aware of the corruption and favoritism endemic in American politics, just as they were disturbed by the rise of gauche stockjobbers, rich slaveowners, and merchant princes. It was understandable that they, like the Whigs, exalted the manly, selfless, simple patriotism of grizzled frontiersmen volunteering for duty armed only with their trusty Kentuckys. The British troops vanquished at New Orleans could even be conveniently reimagined as proxies for bankers' capitalism and royal despotism.

Once looked down upon by civilized easterners as a brute, the rifleman had transformed into an American, and his firearm, a symbol of independence and tradition, not of backwoods wildness. The irony was that the nineteenth century was a time of tumult and displacement, of the rise of machines and centralized management. That brave new world beckoned enticingly (or beguilingly), and John Hall's children—the modern-minded mechanics and managers of the Rifle Works, and those manufacturers and officials who learned the secrets of interchangeability—were going forth into the world, multiplying, and prospering. In their vast diaspora they applied the teachings of their high priest to every sector of American business enterprise. To them, the rifle—once lovingly handcrafted in small workshops by skillful artisans—happily signified the shock of a new industrial age.

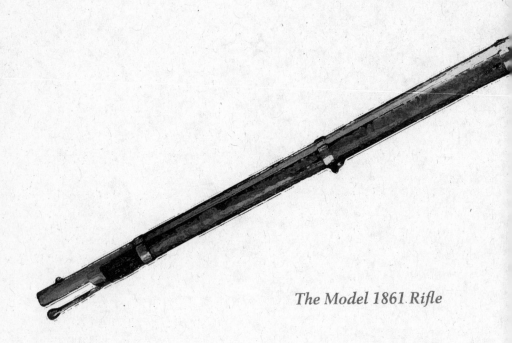

The Model 1861 Rifle

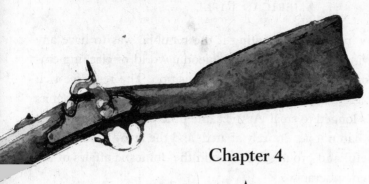

Chapter 4

☆

THE BIG BANG

By the time John Hall died, the U.S. Army was beginning to resemble a business corporation, while U.S. companies were assuming the characteristics of an army. In the mid-nineteenth century this extraordinary melding of organizations and outlooks, dedicated, respectively, to making money and making war, combined to produce a "big bang" in weapons development that ultimately raised the rifle to supremacy over all other infantry firearms. Truly, proclaimed an excited magazine in 1858, "in no branch of scientific industry have there been greater strides in improvements" than in that of "weapons of destruction." What had been scarcely heard of five years before, it continued, "already we have grown to consider . . . obsolete."[1] By the end of the Civil War, the debate was no longer between the rifle and the musket, or the breech-loader and the muzzle-loader. The breech-loading rifle had no peer, no rival. Put into hard numbers, between 1811 and 1860, inventors patented 135 breech-loading longarms, but between 1860 and 1878 alone, that figure ballooned to no fewer than 624.[2]

☆ ☆ ☆

By the second decade of the nineteenth century, American soldiers and government officials realized that the army desperately needed to be

placed on a new, professional footing if the republic was to have any
chance of surviving the tough post–Napoleonic world of clashing empires, gunboat diplomacy, and ruthless acquisition. The resource-rich
United States might be an infant, but it was heir to a vast fortune that its
European uncles longed to steal. At the same time popular suspicion of
standing armies had not yet entirely abated, and the army tried hard to
prove itself a useful and progressive force in the domestic affairs of the
great Jacksonian democracy.

To this end, the secretary of war's annual report of 1828 took pains to
explain that soldiers should not be seen "in the light in which standing
armies in time of peace have usually been regarded, as drones who are
consuming the labor of others." The army was instead "a body of military and civil engineers, artificers, and laborers, who probably con-
tribute more than any other equal number of citizens not only to the
security of the country but to the advancement of its useful arts."[3]
Henceforth the army was to be not only the sword and shield of the republic but its pruning hook and plowshare as well.

The armed forces provided private manufacturers with the venture
capital, infrastructure, freely distributed government patents, tax exemptions, and talented brains that they needed to set up shop and
compete with foreign firms. In order to oversee its burgeoning responsibilities to soldiers, the army also established distinct pay, quartermaster,
judge advocate general, and medical bureaus, as well as specialized departments dedicated to Indian affairs, veterans' pensions, and land surveying. In this respect the army provided the organizational blueprint
for the corporations that were then gestating. The latter would acquire a
phalanx of legal, pension, planning, pay, human resource, overseas, financial, medical, operations, marketing, inventory, strategy, and advertising departments run by a legion of vice presidents answerable to a
board and chief executive. Their bureaucratic resemblance to a military's chain of command, with ultimate authority residing in its senior
general and his staff, was not coincidental.

War was business, and business, war.[4] Indeed, the very first popular
"business best seller" was a guide to efficient factory management written by the army captain in charge of Frankford Arsenal.[5] Accordingly, the
ways of the army and its subsidiaries—in particular, the Ordnance

Department, the national armories, and the Corps of Engineers—were diffused and cross-pollinated throughout the rest of American industry by their former employees. When they left government service at, say, John Hall's Rifle Works, these men collectively carried in their heads decades of experience with advanced manufacturing processes that they donated to their new civilian employers. Hall himself was most annoyed, for instance, by the loss of five highly skilled workmen—fully a third of his workforce—over the spring of 1827 to private firms in New England. Within a decade many more had left for higher-paid jobs and promotions at factories as far afield as Pittsburgh, St. Louis, Augusta, and Cincinnati. The last, thanks to an influx of expert armory machinists, eventually emerged as a leader in the burgeoning machine tool industry.[6]

Others, who joined as apprentices at Harpers Ferry and Springfield, learned their trades, rose rapidly up the ranks, and then departed to found their own businesses around the country. From there they interacted with other companies and thereby introduced the new technology and their specialist knowledge to a rapidly enlarging circle of firms. By the 1840s and 1850s America was home to an entire generation of talented, armory-nurtured mechanics, engineers, artificers, and inventors familiar with modern production processes and determined to make them personally profitable.[7]

Most of the firms set up by former arms makers—men accustomed to twisting, planing, cutting, turning, shaping, polishing, drilling, welding, and boring metal parts—were in the machine tool industry. Only by learning on the job had they imbibed the esoteric knowledge of how machines made machines. Not simply a matter of pushing a button or manipulating a lathe, it required an understanding of such technical issues as friction reduction, power transmission (gearing, shafting, belting), control devices, feed mechanisms, heat resistance, and the stress tolerances of metal.[8]

These individuals' well-paid, much-coveted expertise provided a boost for the nascent mass-production industries of manufacturing shoes, watches, clocks, bicycles, typewriters, ready-to-wear clothing, elastic and rubber goods, and later, cars.[9] The most famous of these former arms-makers-turned-industrialists was Henry Leland. Upon leaving Springfield Armory, he went to the Brown & Sharpe Manufacturing

Company, which made machine tools and sewing machines for Wilcox & Gibbs, and he would go on to found the Lincoln and Cadillac car companies.[10]

As production techniques mutated away from their armory-bred genetic inheritance, manufacturers began experimenting with materials unused by the arsenals, such as glass, silk, rubber, and sheet metal, to forge new consumer durables that were eagerly purchased by the growing middle class.[11] Shopping at the mammoth new "department stores"—such as Macy's, founded in 1858—American consumers loved their products' affordability and uniformity.[12]

While armory-trained mechanics could always find a supervisory job on the shop floor, the managerial expertise of army officers, especially engineers, was highly prized by private companies, particularly by the railroads.[13] Between 1827 and the 1850s the railroads recruited significant numbers of them to run their operations, reform their administrative procedures, and improve efficiency across the board.[14] It was a natural match; who better than an army man knew how to transport matériel over vast distances, delegate responsibility to subordinates located in far-flung places, and coordinate supplies and financing with a large number of contractors? With some reason, then, for ninety-six years of its first hundred, the Pennsylvania Railroad would be presided over by former military engineers.[15]

Ex-officers, often irked by the snail's pace of promotions and mediocre pay in the army, flooded the nation's other great businesses. Of the 1,058 graduates of West Point between 1802 and 1866, no fewer than 35 became corporate presidents, 48 chief engineers, 41 superintendents and senior managers, and eight corporate treasurers.[16] Fully one in eight West Pointers, therefore, left military service for senior positions in private ventures. If one includes the number of graduates who became middle-ranking civil engineers, electrical engineers, attorneys, banking executives, and so forth, that figure balloons to a third or more.

These men had learned their good habits from General Winfield Scott's four-hundred-page *General Regulations for the Army* of 1821, once called "the first comprehensive management manual published in the United States," whose chapters exhaustively covered every facet of army life and procedure. As Congress sometimes still suspected the army of being an imposition on civil society, the *Regulations* focused on instilling financial accuracy, personal accountability, and individual probity, and thus it laid down exact methods of compiling monthly, quarterly, and yearly reports on performance targets and cost-effectiveness, as well as budgetary breakdowns, supply bottlenecks, personnel assessments, and inventory figures. These were pored over in Washington, and inefficient or lazy officers were weeded out, and instances of corruption severely punished.[17]

Such diffusions of technological and managerial knowhow had profound implications for the development of the rifle. Between the 1790s and the 1840s the general emphasis in weapons development had been not on making firearms more lethal but on making factories more efficient at producing them. From the mid-nineteenth century, however, innovators applied an array of new techniques and technologies to firearms development. Moreover, the American market and the managerial revolution offered the enticing possibility of profits and fame to talented men who had previously been confined to working in government armories for government wages. No longer beholden to the superintendent, the clock, the War Department's edict, or the master armorer's whim, they could work alone or with their business partners to find ways of breaking the technological stranglehold held by ball-and-powder ammunition and muzzle-loading firearms. In so doing, they transformed the rifle into the American weapon par excellence.

During this period of fierce ferment government arsenals and private weapons manufacturers took diverging paths. For a mixture of economic, political, and logistical reasons, the arsenals insisted on manufacturing muzzle-loaders, whereas their private competitors mostly saw a future for breech-loaders. By 1860 there were twenty-four major gunmaking businesses; just six of them made traditional muzzle-loaders, but of the eighteen others (including Colt, Remington, and Smith & Wesson), no fewer than fifteen concentrated on making advanced breech-loading guns, including revolvers and repeating rifles that relied on a magazine to feed newly invented metallic cartridges into the chamber.[18]

How and why had this happened? The Ordnance Department, which had once been in the forefront of nurturing *homegrown* technological innovation, had begun looking to Europe for inspiration. This transatlantic shift is a significant reason why, after John Hall's death, further official interest in breech-loading declined in favor of a new French idea called a "rifle-musket" that used an innovative type of projectile: the conoidal minié bullet. In short, the competition between muzzle-loaders and breech-loaders pitted two *advanced* technologies against each other, not, as one might intuitively think, "backwards" or outdated muzzle-loading technology holding out against the futuristic, and allegedly superior, breech-loading system. The choice was never as simple as that.

The rifle-musket's origins lay in the absence of a French John Hall. Abroad, breech-loaders had retained their traditional reputation as gas-leaking, underpowered, easily fouled contraptions. The whole idea of opening the breech to permit faster loading was regarded as an evolutionary dead end in firearms development. The most promising way forward, the French thought, was to retain the muzzle-loading method but enhance performance by concentrating on the *bullet*. If their attempts panned out, they would end up with a hybrid that combined the power and speed of a musket with the accuracy of a rifle: a rifle-musket.

Captain Henri-Gustave Delvigne of the French royal guard grasped that reducing windage—the gap between the sides of the barrel and the ball—was key to raising the musket's accuracy. The problem here was that muskets loaded faster than rifles because their bullets slid easily down their smooth, wide barrels. Reducing the windage would make loading only more difficult, thereby lowering the musket's rate of fire to that of the rifle.

Delvigne's novel solution was conceptually similar to a ship-in-a-bottle, in which the folded, flattened vessel is slipped through the narrow neck and unfurled inside. He placed a "rebated," or slightly smaller, chamber at the bottom of a broad but rifled barrel. The soldier poured the powder down so that it settled into this cramped space and, after rolling down a spherical ball, used a heavy ramrod to stamp on the soft lead bullet so that it flattened and expanded its diameter. Upon firing, the bloated ball gripped the grooves, spun, and turned the musket into a rifle.

After its 1834 trials, Delvigne's gun was sufficiently impressive to persuade the army to issue it to the reinforcements being sent to North

Africa, where the French were confronted by Kabyles adept at seeking cover in the rocky desert sands, taking shots with their old, Kentucky-style long-barreled rifles, and vanishing. The troops already there had discovered that their smoothbore muskets lacked sufficient range and accuracy to cope with the "skulking" tactics of these marauders.

Despite its effective range of four hundred yards (roughly double that of their most modern muskets), troops soon found that under tropical conditions the Delvigne performed poorly. The barrel had to be kept well lubricated, but the sun's heat melted the grease, and it dripped into the chamber, wetting the powder. Consequently, a portion of the charge didn't burn, not only making the gun prone to fouling but reducing the ball's velocity. More damningly still, in any kind of weather the act of bashing the ball deformed it and therefore made its course erratic, which led to inaccuracy. The Delvigne died a sudden death soon afterward.[19]

Around this time several British and French inventors, working independently, had grasped that since it was the human act of flattening the ball that made it irregularly shaped, what if the projectile *self*-expanded to fit the rifling? That is, the shooter would harness the physical and thermodynamic forces unleashed by the exploding powder to transform the bullet into a predictable shape, thereby eliminating the element of randomness. But what kind of bullet?

Relying on recent scientific investigations into the nature of projectile flight, gunsmiths, sporting shooters, and ballisticians were beginning to understand that an *elongated* bullet was subjected to weaker air resistance than a spherical one.[20] The former retained a greater proportion of its muzzle velocity, or the speed at which the projectile leaves the gun, for longer. It would also fly straighter—thereby improving accuracy—but only so long as the rifling in the barrel imparted a far higher rate of rotation than was customary with the older rifles. From the mid-1830s onward, as a result, arms-makers tightened the rifling's "twist" to intensify the new type of bullet's spin before it left the muzzle. The advent of these more modern-looking, if stubby, projectiles meant the end of the spherical ball was nigh—though soldiers, tipping their hats to the past, continue to fire "rounds" today.

The first popular "cylindro-conoidal" bullets had a broadly pointed nose that rather resembled a Romanesque arch atop a short, almost hollow cylinder. Fighting off the competition, it was Captain Claude-Étienne Minié of the French Army whose design became the standard.[21] According to one historian, so remarkable was this cartridge that the entire history of infantry tactics can be divided into two eras: before Minié and after Minié.[22]

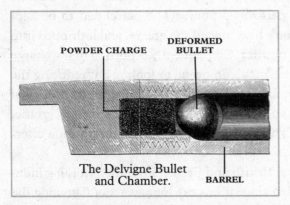

The origins of the modern bullet. Captain Delvigne's design improved accuracy but was ultimately superseded by that of his French compatriot, Captain Minié.

Minié placed an iron plug at the hollowed bottom of the cylindrical bullet so that the combusting powder's gas forcefully thrust it forward. As the plug expanded, the bullet's sides were pushed outward; it gripped the rifling and began spinning. The beauty of Minié's design was its ease of loading: a bullet went in one size and emerged miraculously larger.

The minié was by no means perfect. It tended to foul the guns, and if it was poorly manufactured, the thin iron plugs were liable to over-expand and shatter the bullet in the barrel. Still, in the late 1840s the minié was an instant success, and no wonder, given its unbelievable accuracy rates. In a competition between minié rifles and smoothbore muskets, twenty men fired ten shots with each weapon, or 200 rounds per gun, at a target six feet high and twenty feet across. The results were striking. At 100 yards, three-quarters of musket shots hit compared to 95 percent of minié shots, though that was only to be expected given the musket's traditional scatter-shotting. But at 400 yards, just nine (or 4.5

percent) of the musket shots found their mark, while more than half of the minié's did.[23]

Ordnance experts around the world delighted in the minié's technical aspects. The French armories, as well as their Russian, Austrian, Saxon, Belgian, Portuguese, and British counterparts, were besotted with the new technology. The British finally got around to thinking about a replacement for the venerable, if unvenerated, Brown Bess musket and began making the .577-caliber, minié-enabled Enfield rifle-musket in the mid-1850s.[24]

In the United States, the Ordnance Department was at first cautious about the rifle-musket hybrid and instead focused on integrating the percussion mechanism into its next-generation, interchangeable Model 1841 *rifle* and Model 1842 *musket*. Here, then, the two types of weapons continued to be regarded as distinct. Over the course of the decade Ordnance sat on the sidelines, watched European developments, and slowly modernized its stockpiles of old flintlock muskets by converting them to percussion. It was a simple if time-consuming task: in 1850, 56,134 flintlocks were converted, followed by 30,431 more (of Model 1822s) in 1851, and another 26,841 Model 1840s a year later. By the mid-1850s, after the experimental minié bullet had proven itself, many of these percussioned muskets were subsequently rifled and given long-range sights.[25] These firearms worked satisfactorily, but by that time the United States had clearly fallen behind Europe.

Consequently Secretary of War Jefferson Davis authorized the Ordnance Department to design a weapon from scratch that properly exploited the minié's advantages. The Model 1855 was the result.[26]

Its caliber was .58—a huge decrease from the .69 of the previous generation of muskets and slightly more than the rifle's typical .54. The Model 1855 was also designed to take advantage of America's productive prowess. Soldiers were finding that the minié's ease of loading enabled them to fire more often, with a consequent rise in ammunition expenditure (in terms of cost as well as of frequency). At Pennsylvania's Frankford Arsenal, in an ominous hint of the coming era of mass firepower, a single workman could oversee two machines churning out one hundred percussion caps a minute. During a regular day some 60,000 by his hand alone would roll off the line, with a labor cost of just $1.20. In two years Frankford made 16,842,250 caps, with officials predicting that annual output would more than double when additional machines were installed.[27] Clearly the good old days of soldiers using fewer than a score of bullets during an entire campaign were gone forever.

The Model 1855's appearance also marked two major milestones: henceforth the U.S. government produced no more smoothbores, and after nearly 150 years the accurate rifle and the fast-loading musket finally converged into the hybrid then known as the rifle-musket and eventually—for convenience's sake—just "rifle."[28]

The decision to proceed with the muzzle-loading Model 1855 rifle-musket was a momentous one. But by following the path beaten by Europe's armories, Ordnance ignored the trail blazed by America's private gun-makers.

★ ★ ★

The most influential of these privately made arms in the pre–Civil War years was the Sharps, named after Christian Sharps, born in 1811 in New Jersey. A mechanic and machinist formerly employed at Hall's Rifle Works, Sharps improved on his boss's breech-loader by adding, among other things, a percussion-cap dispenser (for fast loading) and a platinum ring to reduce gas leakage at the breech.[29] He also developed a cartridge containing powder and ball made out of linen, a definite advance over the easily damageable paper cartridges that troops had long used. These linen cartridges were self-consuming in that (unlike their paper predecessors, which were torn open and emptied down the muzzle) they were loaded in one piece at the opened breech and had their rears sheared off by closing the breechblock, thereby exposing the propellant and bullet to the flames unleashed by the hammer hitting the percussion cap. The linen would quickly burn—especially if it was soaked in nitrates—and little residue would be left in the chamber to foul the piece. It was completely different, conceptually, from the minié bullet.

During the early and mid-1850s the Sharps was enormously popular, but only among civilians, owing to the military's fascination with muzzle-loading European rifle-muskets. A March 1850 article in *Scientific*

American had captured many people's attention. According to the writer, the Sharps was so simply constructed and so easy to use that a man with no previous weapons experience could fire it up to *nine times* a minute and place every bullet within a six-inch circle forty yards away.[30] Practice made only more perfect: Sharps himself, it was said, could fire his invention eighteen times a minute.[31] Even a total neophyte, however, could pick up a Sharps and stand a pretty good chance of hitting a malevolently inclined individual at least twice before he got too close for comfort.

Understandably, the Sharps became the weapon of choice for inexperienced settlers, jumpy officials, and nervous prospectors headed out to the faraway West. Helpfully, the coach lines used to give travelers coming from the East a lengthy itemized list of useful things to bring: occupying first place was "one Sharp's [*sic*] rifle and a hundred cartridges." ("Three or four towels" was figured the least important.)[32]

Professionals also relied on them. The half-dozen grizzled guards for the U.S. Mail coaches bumping over the hazardous trail between Santa Fe, El Paso, and San Antonio all carried Sharps rifles. They agreed with their boss, Henry Skillman, who had been a "frontier man for fourteen years," that there "was no arm that in all its attributes begins to compare with the Sharps' arm."[33]

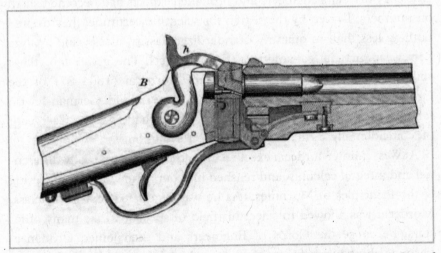

The Sharps mechanism made the gun so easy to use, anyone could fire it and stand a fairly good chance of hitting something—or someone. It became the preferred rifle of those heading, nervously, out West.

The Sharps received its biggest boost from the "Bleeding Kansas" clashes following the passage of the Kansas-Nebraska Act of 1854, when Senator Stephen Douglas declared that the inhabitants of the new territories ought to be allowed to determine for themselves whether to permit slavery. Soon afterward abolitionist (Free-Stater) and pro-slavery (Border Ruffian) guerrillas arrived to try to swing the vote either way.

The abolitionists were armed by the Emigrant Aid Society, and up to twelve hundred Sharps rifles were illicitly sent to Kansas. They were popularly known as "Beecher's Bibles," since the preacher Henry Ward Beecher (brother of Harriet Beecher Stowe, author of *Uncle Tom's Cabin*) had reportedly told his congregants that while it was as pointless to read the Bible to slavers as it was to buffalo, the former nonetheless had "a supreme respect for the logic that is embodied in Sharps rifles."[34] Taking their cue from Beecher, the junior class at Yale presented a local infantry captain with a Sharps that was inscribed *Ultima Ratio Liberarum*—"the final argument of liberty."[35] Indeed, the abolitionist John Brown, a veteran of the Kansas wars, liked his Sharps so much that he outfitted his raiding party with them for his famous attack on the Harpers Ferry Armory in 1859.[36]

The army, for its part, was not impressed in the slightest. As part of its efficiency drive, its engineers and ordnance experts had become fixated on numbers. Driven by the search for scientific certitude, they desired nothing less than to quantify, standardize, classify, assess, and analyze new weaponry, its capabilities, and its effects. The greatest of these soldier-technologists was Major Alfred Mordecai (1804–87) of the Ordnance Department. The Mordecais were an old German-Jewish family long settled in America; his father, Jacob, had served as a sergeant of, coincidentally, a rifle unit during the Revolution.[37]

At West Point, Mordecai excelled in mathematics, especially differential and integral calculus, and relished his courses in "Civil Engineering & the Principles of Machines." As he was graduated first in his class, Mordecai was allowed to select his field of specialty. Like many other stars, he chose the Corps of Engineers and then joined Ordnance. Distinguishing himself from the outset, Mordecai was given command of the Washington arsenal in 1833, then Frankford in 1836, then

Washington again, and finally Watervliet (New York) in 1857. In 1854 he was made major.

Mordecai's prewar career was devoted to the principles of interchangeability, standardization, testing, and production, as well as to refining the army's appreciation of military science. He did his most memorable work at the behest of Secretary of War Jefferson Davis, who sent him and two colleagues (Major Richard Delafield and Captain George McClellan, future commander of the Union Army) abroad to observe the Crimean War and to survey the state of European armaments and military organization.

Mordecai's subsequent report, *Military Commission to Europe in 1855 and 1856,* is a landmark in military literature. Even at the time, it was considered so important that it was published by order of Congress.[38] Its most striking aspect is Mordecai's fascination with the minute variations between the types of weapons issued by each nation to its soldiers, and their almost infinite complexity and splendor. To him, the differences—imperceptible to the uninitiated—between, say, the Hanoverian seven-grooved rifle-musket, the Hanoverian eight-grooved rifle, and the English two-grooved rifle, or the precise degree of deviation between shots fired by Swedish and Norwegian breech-loaders—were endless forms most beautiful and most wonderful.

His report is a masterpiece of unbiased scholarship, carefully weighing the pros and cons of each system, compiling intricate tables to demonstrate contrasts and similarities, tracing every historical variation in bullet design back to its original source, and motivated above all by the belief that if a given variation proved unsuitable to its surroundings, it would eventually disappear and be replaced incrementally by ones more adaptable.

Mordecai's grand vision of the origins, efflorescence, and evolution of the rifle and its projectiles was the martial equivalent of Charles Darwin's theory of natural selection; not coincidentally *On the Origin of Species* was published in 1859 to worldwide acclaim and *Military Commission to Europe* less than a year later. By linking the evolution of weaponry to Darwinism, Mordecai helped inspire a tradition of interpreting rifle development as a line of progression moving endlessly upward. Thus the matchlock naturally gave way to the wheel lock, which was superseded by the flintlock, inevitably rendered obsolete by the superior percussion lock.[39]

In truth, science and technology rarely march so neatly forward. The number of false starts, strange flukes, and odd decisions that afflicted arms-makers over the centuries would reduce any strict evolutionist to tears. Indeed, the existence of a viable rival technology—represented by the Sharps rifle, among others—should have demonstrated to a man of Mordecai's intelligence that the evolutionary tree sprouted many branches, not just the one supported by the Ordnance Department.

Mordecai was nevertheless too mesmerized by the fruits of his own research to realize this significant reality. To him, breech-loaders were patently useless. Referring to the breech-loading rifle newly issued to the French Cent Gardes, who served in the emperor's palace, he said that their weapon might work tolerably well "under cover of a roof; but it would not seem to be adapted to use in the ordinary vicissitudes of military service."[40] Bafflingly, despite all his decades in the Ordnance Department, where he was undoubtedly familiar with the Rifle Works, the name of John Hall makes no appearance in this massive report; and neither does the Sharps. It was as if they, and their magnificent guns, had never existed.

Mordecai's essential complaint about breech-loaders was that they fired rapidly. Rapidity resulted in waste and inaccuracy, which upset Mordecai's painstaking compilations of barrel lengths, angles of elevation, and precise ranges. The ballistician in him objected to messiness and disorder—the unwavering indicators of mass firepower, terror, and the spattered guts of the battlefield that would characterize the awful war between the states that was soon to come.[41]

Mordecai, like other scientifically minded Ordnance men, was hypnotized by the prospect of achieving perfect accuracy. To them, *that* quest was the be-all and end-all of rifle development, and other considerations—such as hitting power and celerity of fire—were distinctly secondary. By the outbreak of the Civil War the department was wholly concerned with neatly placing bullets inside a given area at long distance. Whether those bullets were capable of killing a human target at four hundred or more yards was disparaged as an irrelevant question.

Rather than encouraging technology to develop in diverging directions just to see where they led, the Ordnance Department's policy from the 1840s onward amounted to pursuing a single-track strategy. Owing to their myopia, Mordecai and virtually the entire staff of the Ordnance establishment missed the most radical innovation of all: the all-in-one metallic cartridge and the consequent and lethal rise of the repeating rifle.

How could this development have escaped the brightest lights in the military firmament? It was the spirit of the age that ultimately told against them. Jacksonian America was a nation engulfed in violent, and often contradictory, tumult. At once "the people" were democratically exalted as the highest moral, intellectual, and political authority, while the individual "self-made man" (a term invented at the time) improved himself by sheer will, brilliance, and discipline. For such superachievers, tenacity, individualism, enterprise, and the arrogant defiance of conventional belief were the determinants of success. A self-made man got ahead by relying on his eye for seizable opportunities, his calloused hands, and his nose for profit.[42] Business entrepreneurs and armorers who started their working lives as apprentices were practical fellows. Not for them the rigors of logical induction, syllogism, and mathematical analysis. Convinced that a refined intellect was inferior to the raw power of emotions, the narcotic delights of the senses, and good old common sense, they read men, not books.

The Ordnance Department, unfortunately, was completely out of step with the social and political hurricane represented by Jackson and his allies. Bewitched by European design and innovation and obsessed with which weapons the European governments were using to arm their troops, they wanted to introduce them to America. The department, too, was crammed with the cleverest book-learners, the elite of West Point's elite, and the country's most proficient masters of obscure scientific and technological detail. Ordnance even made a point of advertising its exclusivity and necromantic character. According to George Bomford, the department's work "is of a character so peculiar to itself, that a separate . . . provision for it is believed to be indispensible." The only people suitable for Ordnance work, it seems, were cherry-picked West Pointers.[43] He meant it: between 1832 and 1903, of the 166 officers commissioned in the department, fully 155 of them were West Pointers.[44]

By 1830, accordingly, West Point was being subjected to numerous offensives by Jacksonians. "There is not on the whole globe an establishment more monarchial, corrupt, and corrupting" than the academy, exclaimed one. (Jackson's opponents shot back that, yes, in fact there was: Jackson's White House.) Of particular irritation—even to Jackson's enemies, like Davy Crockett, who sided with him on this matter—was West Point's creation of a European-style "military aristocracy"; but no less annoying was the habit of these elite graduates, educated at public expense, to leave the army after a couple of years for more lucrative occupations in private business.[45]

No breed of men more aptly represented the spirit of Jacksonianism than America's gun-makers. Unlike the Ordnance and Engineers' finest, the greatest among them—Winchester, Colt, Spencer, Hall—lacked formal higher education, and most had barely attended a school. The sum total of Christopher Spencer's time, for instance, in any educational establishment consisted of twelve weeks at an academy for apprentices. Yet these men were collectively responsible for creating a true revolution in weaponry by perfecting the metallic, all-in-one cartridge and the repeater rifle.

Cartridges and repeaters, *as concepts,* were not new. In the early 1600s the warlike prince King Gustavus Adolphus of Sweden directed his troops to carry preprepared cartridges made of a cylinder of paper ("cartridge" stems from the Latin *charta,* "paper") containing powder and ball and twisted closed at both ends. In America and in Europe, some regulars adopted the practice and stored their cartridges in a pouch on their hip; it was thought to hasten loading and to avoid wasting precious gunpowder. For the next two centuries, while muzzle-loading smoothbores reigned, cartridge development remained static.

That began to change around the first decade or so of the nineteenth century with the advent of the metal-canning industry. In 1795 the Revolutionary French government offered a 12,000-franc prize for a successful method of preserving food for long periods. Nicolas Appert, a pickler, spent fifteen years trying to solve the problem. In 1810 he presented the emperor Napoleon with a solution to the problem of keeping his soldiers and sailors healthy over the months they would be away on service. After partially cooking the food, Appert sealed it in glass bottles with airtight corks, as one did with wine, and then immersed them in boiling water to kill the bacteria. In that same year King George III of England granted Peter Durand a patent for a similar idea to preserve food in "vessels of glass, pottery, tin, or other metals or fit materials." Durand's key improvement over Appert's method was to use sealed, airtight metal cylinders instead of breakable glass and undependable corks. By 1814 even Napoleon, then cooling his heels on the isle of Elba and plotting his return to the helm of France, was eating tinned British food—a punishment nearly as dreadful as exile.

Meanwhile another Englishman, Thomas Kennett, had set up shop on the New York waterfront to can hermetically sealed fruits, vegetables, oysters, and meat. In 1825 President James Monroe granted him a patent to use "vessels of tin." Over the next twenty years the American canning industry exploded as the hordes of prospectors and settlers heading out west brought tinned food (corn, tomatoes, peas, and fish mostly) along with them.[46]

It was a simple conceptual jump from using a metal container to hold food to using a smaller one to hold gunpowder. Sealed airtight with the bullet, a metallic cartridge preserved powder and primer for years on end while protecting its precious contents from rain, snow, and most important, fire. From the point of view of America's private arms-makers, an all-in-one cartridge released them from the age-old dilemma of how to seal a breech against spewing gas after the powder ignited. A cartridge contained the explosion within its strong walls and efficiently directed the pressure toward the front to blast the bullet up the barrel.

The French, as in so many other matters military and technological, had initially been at the forefront of development but dropped sharply behind as time went on. In 1812 Samuel Pauly (who was actually Swiss but lived in Paris) was awarded a patent for an innovative breech-loader that relied for ignition not on an external flintlock but on a hammer that cocked a firing pin or internal striker. The weapon itself went nowhere, but the little descendants of the special ammunition that Pauly designed for it were destined for greater things.

He had added a metal base packed with fulminating primer to a conventional paper cartridge containing powder and ball. When the shooter cocked the hammer and pulled the trigger, the striker hit the base's rim with such force that the fulminate exploded and sent the bullet on its way.[47] Essentially Pauly was using a regular percussion cap, but instead of loading it separately and letting the hammer hit it directly, he had integrated it into the cartridge. It was the first example of that type of cartridge soon known as a "rimfire."

The next, crucial stages occurred in America, where for the first time the twin concepts of the metallic cartridge and rapid fire were linked. The original genius who made this connection was Walter Hunt (1795–1859), one of those mechanically minded polymathic types so common in the nineteenth century. Hunt is best known today as being the inventor of the safety pin (conceived while fiddling with a piece of wire as he worried over how to repay a small debt) and builder of America's first sewing machine, though he also came up with a fountain pen, a streetcar bell, a heating stove, a knife sharpener, a road sweeper, and most intriguingly, what he called his "Antipodean Apparatus"—a pair of shoes that allowed a person to walk "upon a polished ceiling with HEAD DOWN-WARD."[48]

In 1848 (a year before his safety pin triumph) Hunt birthed a new and improved type of cartridge, which he vividly dubbed the "Rocket Ball," noting in his patent application that it was "well adapted to firearms made to be charged at the breech."[49] The Rocket Ball was actually a hollowed-out conical bullet containing powder whose open rear end was stopped up by a cork wad with a small hole in the center. When the cartridge was chambered, a separate primer cap was also automatically loaded, the hole in the cork serving to admit the fulminate's flame.

A year later Hunt returned to the Patent Office with plans for a rifle named the "Volition Repeater," designed for use with his Rocket Ball. Hunt's gun was a remarkable weapon, one that eclipsed every other design on the market. The Volition Repeater had a movable trigger that did double duty as a "lever" to feed cartridges contained in a long tube underneath the barrel repeatedly into the chamber. Its main problems were that it was too complicated a mechanism for popular use (the shooter also had to operate a second lever to make it work) and that the tube chambering proved unreliable. The concept, though, was brilliant.[50] For the first time, a shooter could carry a supply of ammunition in the gun itself rather than insert rounds individually by hand. Loading and firing was thus a mechanical process, not a physical one.

Despite his sparkling inventiveness, Hunt was a poor businessman: he sold the rights to the safety pin for $400 and never bothered to patent the lock-stitch needle that was crucial to a sewing machine's operation. Lacking the funds to market the Rocket Ball and Volition Repeater—only one of the guns was ever made—Hunt assigned the rights to a well-off New York machinist named George Arrowsmith. He set one of his employees, Lewis Jennings, on to the problem of simplifying the firearm. By the end of 1849 Jennings emerged with a prototype (called the "Jennings rifle") that improved upon the Volition (he integrated the two levers into one, among other things), but while the ammunition-chambering process was much smoother, now the separate primer-loading mechanism was buggy.

Nevertheless Arrowsmith sold the Jennings patent for the huge sum of $100,000 (about $2.5 million in today's dollars) to Cortlandt Palmer, a wealthy former president of the Stonington & Providence Railroad who enjoyed a spot of speculative financing. Palmer contracted with Robbins & Lawrence, the Vermont arms firm that was then preparing the six interchangeable firearms for the Crystal Palace Exhibition, to make five thousand .54-caliber Jenningses.[51]

Ultimately Palmer was the one left holding the (very expensive) bag. Despite Jennings's improvements, the gun still could not be made to work reliably, and Palmer was forced to market it not as an epoch-shaking "mechanical" repeater but as a run-of-the-mill single-shot "physical" rifle. It did not sell. Determined to give his investment one last try, Palmer asked Horace Smith, who was supervising production of the Jennings at Robbins & Lawrence, to look into refining both the Rocket Ball and the lever operation; shortly afterward Smith asked a friend of his, Daniel Wesson, to fiddle with the gun's firing mechanism and see if it was worth salvaging.

Smith was another archetypal gunsmith of the time. Born in 1808, the son of a carpenter, at sixteen he was apprenticed to the Springfield

Armory, where he specialized in gun-making machinery. After eighteen years there he left the Armory for the private sector and worked at a variety of plants, including a tool factory, Allen, Brown & Luther. It was while employed there that Smith had first met Wesson. The two kept in touch and became still closer friends after Smith joined Robbins & Lawrence up in Vermont sometime in 1849.[52]

As for Wesson, he was seventeen years younger than Smith, and their age difference was reflected in their career paths, a consequence of the rapidly changing times. Whereas Smith had come up the traditional way through the government arsenals, Wesson from the get-go was strictly a private businessman. Though their father was a farmer, Wesson's older brother Edwin had established a rifle-making workshop in Massachusetts to which young Daniel was apprenticed at seventeen. Early on the teenager had been fascinated, not with guns, but with the mechanics of guns. In 1842 Edwin had told their father that "Daniel likes to hunt, but he had rather be at work in the shop on gunlocks, springs or something of that kind." Unfortunately, just after Daniel completed his apprenticeship, Edwin died, leaving behind unsurmountable debts. The promising little business was wound up, leaving Daniel not just with debts but with nothing, not even a set of tools. He took a superintendent's job with the Leonard Pistol Works, whose guns were made under contract at Robbins & Lawrence. As such, Wesson oversaw operations and ensured quality control up in Vermont. Hence his working alongside Smith.[53]

At this early date it was Smith, not Wesson, who did most of the work for Palmer, and a modified Smith-Jennings rifle was patented in August 1851.[54] The priming mechanism worked better, but the Rocket Ball was less a majestic *Saturn V* than an underpowered piece of lead. Most important, Smith used the now-ring-shaped trigger as both the firing trigger and as a lever that, when pulled downward and forward, shoved a cartridge into the chamber from the underbarrel tube. When pushed back into position, the gun was ready to fire. Just over a thousand of the Smith-Jenningses were made.

While worldly success still eluded the increasingly frustrated Palmer, Smith and Wesson were forming a close bond, a union of like minds and equal talents. One of their early meetings was particularly momentous: together they decided that a repeating rifle with a magazine (the underbarrel tube, in this case) was simply not practicable with the Rocket Ball. Hunt's design was inherently flawed. Instead of relying on a ball-and-powder cartridge ignited by a separate primer, they now believed that ball, powder, and primer must instead be seamlessly one.

By good fortune, Smith and Wesson had both become interested in a French gun that was used for short-range indoor-target shooting: more specifically, various dandies prepared for duels by aiming it at targets shaped like themselves. Sold in 1849 by the Parisian Louis-Nicolas Flobert, the pistol itself was little more than a .22-caliber toy, but what had attracted Smith and Wesson's attention was the ammunition Flobert had engineered for it. He used a metallic cartridge containing fulminate at the bottom and a bullet at the top. Just a few grains of powder were present, for the cartridge was too delicate to withstand the shock of a full gunpowder charge—and in any case, salon shooters would find the experience too alarming.

Target-range owners were also accommodated. In order to prevent fouling of the barrel, the constant cleaning of which would annoy them, Flobert had thoughtfully left a large amount of empty space inside the cartridge so as to "confine the burning inside."[55] Little did Flobert know (and he certainly wouldn't profit from it), but his fops' ammunition would form the foundation of the American gun industry in the second half of the nineteenth century.

Smith and Wesson continued working with the long-suffering Palmer, who fronted them additional funds to finish and patent a prototype of a Flobert-based salon pistol—but one integrating a simple lever-action firing mechanism.[56] No one paid it any attention, which was all very well for Smith and Wesson (and Palmer), since at the same time they were secretly refining a new, somewhat more powerful type of all-in-one cartridge based on Flobert's basic design. Four months after patenting the pistol in February 1854, Smith, Wesson, and Palmer formed a limited partnership company, and two months after that Smith & Wesson patented their upgraded metallic cartridge, the forerunner of those used today.[57]

Even Palmer, by this time, was running short of cash, and the new partnership was reorganized as the Volcanic Repeating Arms Company with the financial backing of a consortium of New Haven and New York investors. Most of the twenty-nine new shareholders were local Connecticut businessmen or respectable white-collar employees—six clockmakers, a railroad conductor, a shipping merchant, a shoe seller, and a grocer, for instance—but there was one among them who would achieve lasting fame: Oliver Winchester, of 57 Court Street, New Haven, who described himself as a "shirt manufacturer."[58]

At this point the original partners transferred the patents on their various firearms and cartridges and went their separate ways. Palmer, having received $65,000 in cash and 2,800 shares of stock in the new Volcanic company, retired from the arms-making business and nursed his huge losses back in New York. Smith and Wesson meanwhile took their profits and established their own pistol-making company, which still exists.[59] In league with Rollin White, another inventor, they soon produced a six-shot revolver firing a modified Flobert cartridge.[60]

Winchester, in his midforties and well-to-do thanks to his shirt selling, was among the first of a new breed of Yankee businessmen.[61] They were more marketers than makers, more moneymen than mechanics. Unlike Smith, Wesson, and Hall, Winchester himself had no gun experience but entered the trade because he saw a profit in it.

Another member of this club was Samuel Colt, who emerged from a very American tradition of fast-talking, hard-sell showmanship. After all, anyone who could immortalize a .45 revolver as the "Peacemaker" was not just an advertising natural but a gunsmithing superstar.[62] This same man gave a shooting display at his own brother's trial for murder (with an ax) just to prove the revolver's effortless superiority over any kind of bladed weapon. It didn't help the sibling, but Colt might well have sold a few guns to the jury afterward.[63]

From his youth Colt, the son of a cloth merchant, adored guns, and by seven he had illicitly acquired a pistol; at twelve he was making his own bombs and detonated one spectacularly in the middle of a local pond. At school in 1830 his education was cut very short owing to another unfortunate pyrotechnics display, and his father sent him to sea. Aboard the *Corlo*, whiling away the time on a voyage to Calcutta, Colt whittled a wooden pepperbox pistol, a clumsy type of handgun with revolving barrels. Quite brilliantly, he realized that a more effective design would have a single barrel that was serviced by a revolving cylinder containing multiple loads. Returning home, Colt presented a wooden specimen to a local gunsmith, who made a cheap, and evidently shoddy, metal version—which blew up on the first shot.[64]

Undaunted but penniless, Colt decided he needed to make some cash before setting up a business. First he grew a beard so as to look older than his eighteen years and grandiosely styled himself "Dr. Coult of New York, London, and Calcutta." Then he manufactured a supply of laughing gas and gave streetcorner demonstrations around the country. Having sold enough of the stuff to various practical jokers to keep himself afloat, Colt obtained a rather vague patent on his revolving-cylinder idea on February 25, 1836.[65] He then set sail for London and Paris to apply for patent protection abroad (Samuel always thought ahead—and big), and on his return he established the Patent Arms Manufacturing Company in Paterson, New Jersey, with the help of several friendly investors. The firm went bust pretty soon afterward but not before producing fifty Colt revolving rifles based on his cylinder idea. Hoping to interest the military—"government patronage . . . is an advertisement, if nothing else," Colt once said—he sold them for $125 each to Colonel William Harney, who was down in Florida fighting the Seminole War.[66]

The hapless Seminoles saved Colt because soon afterward, with the princely sum of $6,250 in his pocket, his vessel was shipwrecked and he lost everything. Helped by Colt's nonstop marketing drives, however, word had spread of these strange repeating rifles among the soldiers, and they happily provided Colt with sufficient testimonials ("I honestly believe that but for these arms, the Indians would now be luxuriating in the everglades of Florida," wrote Harney) to prompt the Ordnance Department into taking a look at them.[67] The department dismissed them as too complicated and unreliable for military use, but Colt realized that while soldiers might be armed with army-issue rifle-muskets, he could sell them pistols as personal sidearms.[68] So he began making handguns *and* rifles.

Already legends, the Texas Rangers became keen customers, as did John Frémont and Kit Carson during their surveys of the West.[69] Flightly riders for the Pony Express bought Colt revolvers for their protection while each of the eight men guarding the dangerous mail-stage run between Independence, Missouri, and Santa Fe carried a Colt revolving rifle, a massive .44-caliber, six-shot "Dragoon" Colt revolver weighing nearly five pounds that pretty much stopped anything in its tracks, and a smaller "back-up" .36-caliber version. When the public expressed skepticism that their letters would get through Indian and bandit-infested territory, the Missouri government declared that "these eight men are ready in case of attack to discharge 136 shots without having to reload. We have no fears for the safety of the mail." It went through, safely.[70]

The gun's widespread use during the Mexican War finally persuaded Ordnance to adopt the revolver for service use, though it must be said that the department had been quite right in expressing doubts about the Colts' reliability in the field. In 1848 Captain John Williamson informed Colonel George Talcott of Ordnance that of 280 revolvers issued to five companies of Texas Rangers eight months before, only 191 were handed back after the men had been discharged. Apart from a few lost to the enemy, the remainder had "bursted in their hands." And of those 191 left, just 82 he judged serviceable: the rest were damaged by firing, or their barrels and cylinders were irreparable, or their muzzles had been torn asunder by the blast.[71] Nevertheless, Colt was well on his way to making a fortune, and his display at the 1851 Crystal Palace Exhibition turned his new company into an armaments superpower. Colt died of inflammatory rheumatism in 1862, aged just forty-eight.

Regarding Oliver Winchester, he too suffered the usual trials afflicting private arms-makers at the time. Like Colt's Patent Arms Manufacturing Company, his undercapitalized Smith and Wesson–less Volcanic Company lurched into insolvency, but when its president died, Winchester bought out most of the shareholders and assumed almost complete control. Renaming it the New Haven Arms Company in 1857, Winchester set out not only to cultivate a network of retailers and suppliers but to hire skilled staff. Always a keen talent spotter, Winchester knew exactly who he wanted to head the factory: Benjamin Tyler Henry, a former Springfield Armory engineer who had gone to work for Robbins & Lawrence in 1842. There (the arms world being a small one) he had become friendly with Wesson and helped him out with the Jennings firelock;

then when Palmer went into business with Wesson and Smith, Henry had gone with them. Taking a shine to the thirty-something, Winchester hired him as master mechanic at his shirt company before promoting him to the superintendency of the new arms company. His primary responsibility was making Winchester's newly purchased gun patents work.[72]

Key among them was the metallic cartridge. Henry began experimenting with the cartridges during the fall of 1858, and by the end of the year he had designed a .44-caliber rimfire bearing a conical bullet. The choice of caliber is interesting. Smith & Wesson's Flobert-based .22-caliber was nice and light, but it lacked stopping power and was therefore unsuitable for military use; then again, .44 was still much smaller than the usual army rifle caliber of .58 and above. Henry, however, had a practical reason for deciding to shift toward a smaller caliber: with the company's sales still anemic, and now that the rifle's firing and chambering actions were working smoothly, neither he nor Winchester wanted to delay production by having to readapt the breech to accommodate the lengthier, wider .58s.

Once he was finished with the ammunition, Henry began making improvements to the Volcanic Company's version of the Smith-Jennings rifle. Most of his work was devoted to adapting the breech and lever mechanism so that it could load, fire, and then *eject* the spent all-in-one rimfire cartridge while pushing a fresh round into the chamber. By October 1860 he'd done it, and what's more—thanks to keeping the caliber size down—he had managed to squeeze no fewer than fifteen cartridges into the underbarrel tube. When added to the live round in the chamber ready to fire, these made the "Henry," as Winchester had generously christened the newly patented weapon, the world's first dependable "16-shooter."[73] His sales agents boldly claimed to potential customers that "a resolute man, armed with one of these rifles, particularly if on horseback, CANNOT BE CAPTURED."[74]

The Henry did have competition, strong competition, from a rival arm, the Spencer repeater. Christopher Spencer was a perhaps unique combination of Yankee businessman and skilled gunsmith, thereby blending the best attributes of Colt and Winchester. Born into a Connecticut farmer's family in 1833, which made him about twenty years younger than Winchester and Colt and a fortunate heir to the can-do spirit of Jacksonian America, Spencer was taught the fundamentals of gunsmithing by his ninety-year-old grandfather, a veteran of the Revolutionary War. In 1847 the wispy boy with piercing eyes was apprenticed as a machinist at the Cheney brothers' silk mill, soon becoming an accomplished workman in his own right by designing new machines for his employers. The Cheneys and Spencer rattled along very well, and the brothers encouraged the youth to branch out by working at the New York Central Railroad locomotive repair shop. During a subsequent secondment to the Ames Manufacturing Company in Massachusetts, he shifted his attention to firearms and temporarily transferred to Colt's factory in Hartford in the early 1850s. Again returning to the Cheneys, Spencer began patenting labeling and thread-spooling machines, but in his off time he engineered guns.

Taking his cue from Smith & Wesson and Winchester, Spencer was intrigued by the new rimfire-cartridge technology and conceived a repeater of his own—but with a twist. Instead of storing the ammunition in a tube under the barrel, he kept it in a tube contained in the wooden butt *behind* the breech. Pulling a lever under the breech drew a spring-loaded bullet from the stock and pushed it into the chamber. After cocking the hammer and firing, the shooter pulled the lever down again to eject the spent cartridge and load a fresh round. In the winter of 1859, he patented a .36-caliber prototype and devoted himself afterward to enlarging the bore to .44 in order to compete with the Henry's heavier ordnance, though at the cost of fitting fewer cartridges into the magazine.

At .44, let alone .36, the new repeaters were distinctly underpowered, at least according to the Ordnance Department's stricture that ammunition should conform to the standard rifle-musket's caliber of .58. Spencer nevertheless felt his weapon would pass muster, if only given the chance. Lacking Winchester's and Colt's money, and finding it impossible to establish a connection with Ordnance, at the outbreak of the Civil War Spencer turned to his old patrons, the Cheneys, and assigned them the rights to the rifle in exchange for a royalty of one dollar per gun made.

Charles Cheney happened to be a neighbor of Navy Secretary Gideon Welles, who asked the commandant of the Washington Navy Yard, John

Dahlgren, an experienced firearms designer himself, to test the weapon. The hope was that the navy would be more open to new ideas than the army, and that Welles could press Spencer's case with President Lincoln.

Dahlgren was mightily impressed with the rifle, having fired its entire seven-round magazine in ten seconds and additionally shot it 91 times in 29 minutes. Over the course of two days five hundred rounds were fired with but one failure (caused by a faulty cartridge). In his report Dahlgren supported adopting the piece for naval use, and the *navy's* Ordnance Bureau ordered seven hundred Spencers at $43 each plus 70,000 rounds. By this time, the army's Ordnance Department could not afford to look as if it were dragging its feet, and Captain Alexander Dyer carried out a few preliminary tests. He too reported favorably, but nothing happened. Silence.

Wondering what was going on, in October 1861 the Cheneys retained R. S. Denny, a Washington lobbyist, to prod the Ordnance Department into action. Despite several letters, there was no follow-through from the department. It was almost as if Ordnance had decided that Spencer didn't exist.[75]

He wasn't the only one having problems. Oliver Winchester was suffering the same befuddling experience. No one could understand why. After all, for arms-makers those times were indeed auspicious. Lincoln had been elected president of the United States, and after Fort Sumter in April 1861 he had called for 75,000 volunteers, all of whom, Winchester and Spencer had shrewdly predicted, were in desperate need of weaponry. But strangely, when Winchester wrote to the new chief of ordnance, Brigadier General James Ripley, about the Henry rifle, his inquiry also went ignored.

Ripley represented all that was best about the Ordnance Department and all that was worst. Dignified and regal with his swept-back hair, impressively aquiline nose, and towering forehead, Ripley was notorious for his starchy bearing, absolute incorruptibility, and unyielding adherence to The Regulations. With Ripley, no corner could be cut, no rule bent, no blind eye turned. His stiff-neckedness permitted him a resolute independence—even at the risk of infuriating his superiors—but also rendered him impervious to change, even when change was patently necessary.

The sixty-six-year-old Ripley was born in Connecticut in 1794, entered West Point in 1813, was commissioned a second lieutenant of artillery after graduating a mediocre twelfth in a class of thirty, and was promoted to first lieutenant in 1818. That is the sum total of our knowledge of Ripley's first twenty-four years of life; he steadfastly refused ever to provide editors of encyclopedias or biographers with any other details. Ripley felt that such matters were irrelevant and wished to be judged solely by his military accomplishments.

In 1818 we gain our first glimpse of Ripley's mettle. During the Seminole War the lieutenant received an urgent requisition order from a high-ranking officer, which Ripley, as he proudly declared, "refused to comply with, on the ground that it had not reached him through the channel pointed out by the regulations." General Andrew Jackson (for it was he who had made the requisition) was livid at this insolence. A message was sent. If Lieutenant Ripley did not instantly fulfill the order, Jackson "would send a guard to arrest and bring him into camp, and there hang him on the first tree." Ripley blinked and "promptly complied." Only on a few other occasions would he back down, at least without fighting a ferocious rearguard action.

Ripley's saving grace was his efficiency and dogged adherence to duty. General Winfield Scott, later commander of the Union forces, thought Ripley had "no superior in the middle ranks of the Army, either in general intelligence, zeal or good conduct." In 1832, as a reward for his sterling work, Ripley was allowed to transfer to the Ordnance Department. In 1841 he was granted the plum post of superintendent of Springfield Armory and immediately began refashioning it after his own image. Ignoring a slew of lawsuits and the effigies of him burnt atop the armory's flagpole, Ripley converted workers to his own upright creed of Episcopalianism and fired those who subscribed to subversive newspapers. The armory's grounds, which had become overgrown, were laid out symmetrically according to the best military principles, a verdant simulacrum of Ripley's neat and tidy mind. That mind even reduced the average cost of producing a rifle from $17.50 to $8.75.

Soon after the guns fired at Fort Sumter, Ripley arrived in Washington and was elevated to the chieftaincy of Ordnance.[76] On April 24, 1861, he entered for the first time the dingy, cramped Winder

Building on 17th Street, the wartime headquarters of the Ordnance Department (or Ordnance Bureau, as it was often called). The clerks shuffled to attention as he shimmered by. Papers were piled up higgledy-piggledy on the dark heavy desks, and wooden models of various guns were scattered around. The disorganization offended Ripley's sensibilities, and he quickly instituted a complex set of procedures to impose order.

Order, but not necessarily efficiency. Under Ripley, papers were no longer piled but were neatly stacked, and the model guns were placed tidily on a special desk; but he preferred to generate red tape rather than cut it.[77] His unfortunate staff found themselves engulfed by interdepartmental memoranda, dictated missives, forms to be filled out in duplicate and triplicate, signatures and countersignatures. Ripley, who was becoming an avid Washington turf warrior, was apparently less concerned with increasing the number of Ordnance officers to conduct experiments, run the arsenals, and arrange contracts than with enlarging his staff of filing clerks. Between 1860 and 1863 the number of officers rose from 41 to 45, but that of clerks from 8 to 36, and even then Ripley complained there were too few to handle all the paperwork.[78] At one point he became obsessed with the lovely, neat "hand" of one Private William O'Brien, then serving in the western theater, and wrote to his captain, then to his general, then to the secretary of war, then to all three simultaneously in an effort to have him assigned to his office.[79] (He did get him, so it wasn't a complete waste of time.)

Ripley drew Samson-like strength from his Ordnance background. Like Mordecai, he accepted as divine revelation the modern methods of interchangeability. Also like Mordecai, he believed unshakably in the efficacy and superiority of the muzzle-loading rifle-musket.

Ripley believed his task was simple. The Union needed to arm at least tens, probably hundreds, of thousands of volunteers and conscripts with a satisfactory firearm, and that firearm must be the rifle-musket—tried, true, and tested. Nothing else mattered, certainly not the imprecations of Winchester, Spencer, and the hordes of other non-Ordnance-approved amateurs all claiming to have invented war-winning, revolutionary weapons, and especially not these newfangled repeating breech-loaders with their metallic cartridges. When he eventually did get around to replying to Winchester and Spencer, Ripley was unmovable. He told Winchester that his Henry repeater was useless for war, despite its "singular beauty and ingenious design." As for Spencer, his wasn't the kind of weapon "which I would be willing to adopt for the military service."[80]

Before condemning Ripley too harshly for his inflexibility, bear in mind his predicament. Swarms of inventors showed up at his office, all claiming to have conceived a miracle weapon. Some were well-meaning patriots, others hoped to make a quick profit, but a significant minority were simply cranks. A few of these souls were genuinely unhinged, such as Edward Tippett, a machinist who snowed the White House with rambling letters quoting the Book of Joshua and fantasizing about a gravity machine; one time President Lincoln, tired of him, scribbled on one such letter, "Tippett. Crazy-man." Others were respectable businessmen or lawyers, outwardly well grounded and blessed with wonderful families, who had got hold of one Big Idea somewhere along the line and turned it into a mind-warping, monomaniacal obsession. And still others were merely dreamers, such as the man who proposed outfitting the army with "water walkers" (small watertight canoes that fit on a man's feet), the investors who wanted soldiers to be encased in heavy metal body armor (perhaps not such a bad idea, and one given serious consideration until it was realized that unarmored troops thought wearers cowards), and the advocates of steam-powered "centrifugal guns," a weapon that could fire four hundred bullets simultaneously, "enemy-slaughtering, far-shooting, spider-wheel-mounted, two-ounce-ball rifles," and double-barreled cannons that fired two balls connected by a chain to scythe through the rebel ranks.[81]

Whereas Lincoln tended to treat inventors with good-natured forbearance, Ripley was obnoxious to any who dared show up on his doorstep. Horror stories about Ripley's behavior became common knowledge. *Scientific American* magazine blasted Ripley for his "rudeness and circumlocution of the rankest kind" and asserted that because of him "inventors are shy of presenting plans that have to be experimented upon by Government before acceptance, and the consequence is that the country suffers."[82]

Within a few months of Ripley's arrival at the Winder Building, governors and generals too were complaining about the haughtiness of Ordnance and about Ripley's impertinent habit of ignoring their letters demanding guns.[83] (His nickname became "Ripley Van Winkle.")[84] The editor of the Washington-based *National Republican,* whose inept brother Ripley had turned down for a patronage position in the department, roared about his "disdainful refusal to examine and adopt the improvements in arms and matériel by which the superior civilization of the free States could have put down this semi-barbaric rebellion."[85] Ripley ignored him too.

In response, Ripley had one of his deputies, Captain Kingsbury, write an amusingly ironic letter to his military critics observing that "the Ordnance Department has been compelled to supply both armies," since the struggling Army of the Potomac had managed to lose 53 cannons and 25,000 firearms to the enemy during its brief and embarrassing course of operations.[86]

In June 1861 Ripley launched another offensive by circulating a memorandum on the subject of small-arms contracting. He complained of "the vast variety of new inventions, each having, of course, its advocates, insisting upon the superiority of his favorite arm over all others and urging its adoption by the Government." Reportedly soldiers were already carrying some of these weapons, a situation that Ripley declared was "very injurious to the efficiency of troops." The only way to stop this "evil" was by "adhering to the rule of uniformity of arms for all troops." At bottom, felt Ripley, the Union forces simply had no need to waste time with these "untried" weapons because "the U.S. [rifle-]muskets as now made have no superior arms in the world." In any case, he was convinced that many of the claims made by private makers were just hooey: "I know of none, and I do not believe there are any, who have the requisite machinery, tools, and fixtures for making such arms, and but few who can prepare them in less than one year's time."[87]

Ripley's snottiness notwithstanding, he was right about many things. He correctly highlighted the perils of outfitting troops with a myriad of weapons, some good, many bad. At the beginning of the war the Union Army recognized as "official" ordnance no fewer than 79 models of rifles, muskets, and rifle-muskets, 23 models of carbines and musketoons, and 19 models of pistols.[88] Ripley additionally had to consider the vast amount of ammunition the new Union Army would require for battle operations. By issuing a single, affordable model of rifle-musket, he could ensure sufficient ammunition by making just one type of standard bullet.[89] The alternative was a logistical nightmare: at the Second Battle of Bull Run an officer horrified Ripley by demanding no fewer than eleven different calibers (ranging from .52 to .71).[90]

He was also correct to be skeptical about the optimistic claims made by inventors that they would hit their production deadlines. Even Colt's factory, which was probably the most efficient in the United States, could not hope to be ready and tooled up for mass production in less than six months.[91] As for Winchester and the rest, they were accustomed to handling outputs of a couple of hundred rifles a month, not the several thousand the army would require.[92]

In any case, Ripley was already confronted by major delivery failures on the part of officially approved factories making standard models. Typically, one contractor, John Rice of Philadelphia, had promised to supply 36,000 regulation rifle-muskets in November 1861 but could not deliver a single one. And another eight businesses, which together contracted for a total of 351,000 rifle-muskets, produced precisely zero.[93] Scores of similar cases beset the ordnance chief.[94]

Despite these letdowns, Ripley performed sterling service in rapidly outfitting Union troops with the weapons they needed to fight. Six months or so before the war's outbreak, federal stocks of shoulder arms totaled the seemingly impressive figure of 610,598. But just 28,207 of them were first-class modern arms (.58-caliber rifles and rifle-muskets), while some 503,664 were twenty-year-old smoothbore .69-caliber muskets that had been converted into percussion firearms.[95] They would do in a pinch, but the soldiers must also have more up-to-date weaponry.

Between April 1861 and November 1862, by way of contrast, Ripley's arsenals made or acquired 263,182,600 small-arms rounds, 422,198,600 percussion caps, and 867,303 guns for the infantry (plus another 393,294 for the cavalry). Initially, most of these firearms—rifles and rifle-muskets particularly—were purchased abroad, but whereas in 1860 Harpers Ferry and Springfield had together been able to produce 22,000 weapons annually, Ripley forecast that by January 1863 Springfield alone would be making 24,000 *per month*. Harpers Ferry was destroyed at the beginning of the war, so Ripley built replacements at Rock Island and Governor's Island, and by standardizing the output of private manufacturers—thereby preventing them from squandering their efforts on innovative guns—he believed that by mid-1863 the Union would be churning out upward of 700,000 small arms annually.[96]

He underestimated. Before the Civil War arms manufacturers had still been imbibing the Ordnance Department's lessons about interchangeability while exploring the new cartridge/repeater technology and raising financing. Their production runs and factories remained quite small, at least compared to the output of the national armories. During the Civil War the task of arranging funds at least became relatively easier thanks to the government's largesse when awarding contracts. Private firms also found that if they took a step back from Ordnance's emphasis on seamless interchangeability, their cost per unit fell while output rose. So while they relied on machines as much as possible, in the very final stage they still used specialized labor to "fit" the parts exactly. The process lacked the precise perfection demanded by John Hall and his successors, but that was offset by the advantages of building faster and shipping weapons on schedule.[97] As a result, while the total output of the entire American private sector in 1860 had been just 50,000 shoulder arms and pistols, by the end of the war it had produced between 2.5 and 3 million, a number exponentially beyond anything the Europeans or British could even imagine.[98]

Abroad the rifle remained the property of professional soldiers and well-off hunters: the British regarded their gunsmith as they did their tailor, as the chap who made firearms on a bespoke, personally customized basis. But in the newly united States after 1865 the rifle became the common man's gun, mainly because there were so many floating around and so many ex-soldiers who knew how to use them.[99] In less than a century, the American rifle had transformed from being the specialized firearm of frontiersmen to the tool of Everyman.

During the war, too, the differences between Northern and Southern business styles—that division between the Springfield way and the old Harpers Ferry way—helped break Dixie's back. While both sides struggled to harness managerial expertise to the industrial, technological, and logistical demands of the war, Lincoln emerged as more competent than Jefferson Davis at exploiting the talent at his disposal, despite the South's many able engineers and organizers.[100]

Ripley's Confederate counterpart as chief of ordnance, for instance, was Josiah Gorgas, but he forever lacked the mammoth resources enjoyed by his opposite. Cantankerous and impatient, the Pennsylvania-born Gorgas had married an Alabama lass and fondly dreamed of buying a plantation staffed by a retinue of slaves. As the war came closer, Gorgas's sympathies turned strongly secessionist as northern abolitionists threatened his retirement plan. The ideology of states' rights attracted him, and aware that his impertinence toward his superiors at the Ordnance Department had doomed him to a captain's rank for the rest of his career, Gorgas made noises about joining the fledgling Confederate Army.[101]

Jefferson Davis, however, was keener to acquire Major Mordecai and made him an offer on March 4, 1861. Mordecai refused. Davis then turned to Gorgas, who accepted the post of chief of Ordnance, an offer that came attached with a promotion to a majority and the prospect of eventual elevation to the rank of general.[102] On March 21 Gorgas resigned his commission with the Union Army and headed south.[103]

Until the last his faith in inevitable victory remained unswerving, though it did waver once or twice (after Gettysburg he wondered whether "we [can] believe in the justice of Providence, or must we conclude that we are after all wrong?").[104] The peace at Appomattox devastated him, and Gorgas transformed into an unpleasant racist bestirred by visions of a resurrected Confederacy. Suffering a stroke in 1878, the same year he assumed the presidency of the University of Alabama, he died half a decade later.

Upon first arriving in Richmond, Gorgas found just 159,010 weapons in the Southern arsenals, and about 3.2 million cartridges, plus sufficient gunpowder to make an additional 1.5 million bullets. There were also 2 million percussion caps (and nine musicians' swords).[105] The capture of Harpers Ferry by Confederate troops in April 1861 netted about 4,200 minié rifle-muskets and sufficient parts to finish up to 10,000 more. Most important, at least in the long term, were the armory's 300 machines and crates of specialist tools that fell into their hands. Two weeks later John Hall's old Rifle Works was stripped bare of its own equipment (most designed and built by the great man himself) and sent to Richmond.[106]

The haul was a good one, but nowhere near enough to supply the new army, especially over several campaigns. The Harpers Ferry machinery formed the foundation of wartime production, but to raise output Gorgas needed the South's foundries to make still more, a task rendered impossible by the shortage of iron.

Gorgas also strove to improve distribution but was continually frustrated by the South's decrepit railroads and transport networks, and his centralization of production at the Richmond Armory owed more to necessity than to choice. It, and a smaller plant at Fayetteville, North Carolina, were the only two armories in the entire South. Together they could manufacture 1,500 firearms per month, hardly anything considering that the Confederacy lost 70,000 weapons at Vicksburg and Gettysburg alone.[107] By 1862 the Confederacy's resources were so stretched that the desperate chief planned to issue medieval-style pikes to the infantry.[108]

Unable to improve domestic production, Gorgas zealously sought alternative sources of weaponry. He purchased substantial numbers of foreign-made firearms (such as British Enfields) at exorbitant cost with cotton, even as he contended with Union agents sent abroad with orders to buy up any guns for sale, no matter the expense. His Ordnance Bureau also bought four vessels to smuggle weapons from Nassau and Bermuda; but while gunrunning from the Caribbean or from Mexico through Texas along the "Cotton Road" helped relieve the chronic arms crunches, the 182,000 pieces that the Ordnance blockade runners sneaked past Union patrols between September 1862 and December 1864 could not hope to compete against the North's home advantage.[109]

What Gorgas lacked in resources, he made up for in ingenuity. The bureau relied on work-arounds, makeshifts, and expediencies to a remarkable degree. When the importation route was closed after the Confederacy lost the Mississippi River, the bureau replaced mercury, a key ingredient of percussion caps that was available in quantity only in Mexico, with a compound of chlorate of potash, sulphuret of antimony, and nitric acid. Gum arabic, used in Enfield cartridges, was ingeniously replaced by flour paste. Gorgas even told his officers to cut down on their correspondence to save paper that could be used as cartridges.[110]

Given the difficult circumstances, Gorgas performed miracles, and it was testament to his unflagging perseverance that after General Lee abandoned Richmond in April 1865 and retreated to Amelia Court House, where he expected to find crates filled with rations for his hungry men, he found no food but instead a train packed with homemade ammunition.[111]

As northern production gained momentum, Ripley suffered from quite a different, indeed enviable, problem: too many guns. His primary concern now was the potential wastage of his precious, hard-won stockpiles. Repeaters, he was convinced, were the greatest threat in this regard. It was a standard Ordnance complaint that men blew through ammunition with repeaters, thereby causing supply headaches.

Theoretically the supply problem was a worrying factor. By 1865 soldiers armed with repeaters had to carry an average of one hundred rounds compared to the usual forty or so issued to rifle-musketed troops. As a practical matter, however, evidence gained from actual field experience was proving that soldiers soon learned to husband their ammunition: at Gettysburg, over the course of three days' hard fighting with a 20 percent casualty rate, one veteran unit with repeaters shot on average only thirty-two rounds per man.[112] The morale of troops armed with repeaters also tended to be higher and more resilient than those without. A perceptive Lieutenant Green of the U.S. Marines had reported on this unexpected phenomenon in February 1860 following his testing of a Sharps rifle. His report concluded that "the soldier in battle, possessed of a gun that can be instantly loaded, keeping his eye on the foe, confident of his power and strength (that he always is ready), naturally is inspired with courage and self-possession." Conversely, for the soldier carrying a muzzle-loading rifle-musket, his "severest trial occurs after he has discharged his piece, and during the interval of reloading." At that point panic sets in. "Hence it is, after an engagement, so many arms are found disabled by the insertion of the ball below the powder, or double or treble loading."[113]

In a controversial letter to *Scientific American,* Oliver Winchester opportunistically highlighted another advantage of repeaters over rifle-muskets and other single-shot weapons. Owing to their rapid rate of fire, a unit armed with a sixteen-shot "magazine gun like the Henry rifle" could "produce a sheet of fire and lead which no troops could stand to receive the last shot."[114] Then he damned Ripley by name for opposing the introduction of repeaters, cruelly remarking that the "saving of life does not appear an element worthy of [his] consideration." And then, resurrecting the florid Jacksonian distrust of the highfalutin, European-minded Ordnance boffins, Winchester sarcastically added that "this is West Point opinion—the deductions of West Point science!"[115]

"West Point science" or not, some of Ripley's worries, especially at the war's outset, were justified, but he was hopelessly wrong not only in his fanatical determination to stop *any* kind of trials with the new weaponry but also in his reluctance to approve the meanest issuing of breech-loading repeaters to specialist troops, even when ordered by the president himself.

Ripley had no time for "amateurs" like Lincoln. When the president sent a letter to the department directing Ordnance to conduct experiments with a new type of firearm, *Scientific American* reported that "some functionary" sneered, "What does Lincoln know about a gun?"[116] Readers were left in little doubt who the Ordnance "functionary" was.

Certain American presidents had been intensely interested in firearms: George Washington and Thomas Jefferson, of course, and Andrew Jackson. Lincoln, much to Ripley's unpleasant surprise, was another.

Lincoln may have lacked hard combat experience, but he certainly knew his way around a rifle. How could he not, given that his father was a Kentucky frontiersman who moved to Indiana when Abraham was eight. Then it was still a "wild region," in the president's words, "with many bears and other wild animals still in the woods."

When he was a boy, the Lincolns owned an "old smoothbore" and two "riffle" guns left behind by the late grandfather. Abraham himself sometimes went hunting with them and on one occasion shot a wild turkey.[117] Never a keen hunter, however, Lincoln did not set his sights on larger, more dangerous beasts. In 1832, as a young captain during the Black Hawk War, he drilled with muskets, and during the Civil War when Seth Kinsman, a well-known California hunter, brought his old Kentucky to the White House, Lincoln happily held it and marveled at its beauty.[118]

Lincoln was by no means an expert on ordnance, nor was he a first-class shot, but he was nevertheless able to grasp the essentials—and much more. As early as 1855 he was keeping abreast of ballistic developments. He knew, from his treasured copy of that year's *Annual of Scientific Discovery*, of the debate between advocates of the new breech-loaders and those of the minié-balled muzzle-loading rifle-muskets.[119] Indeed, when Lincoln discovered that his business acquaintance, George McClellan, then the chief engineer and vice president of the Illinois Railroad, had been a member of Major Mordecai's influential military commission to Europe a few years before, he quizzed him mercilessly about armaments.[120] Widely read newspapers and periodicals of the time also carried summaries of arms trials: in the summer of 1858 *The New York Times* and *Scientific American* printed detailed reports of an Ordnance competition to determine the best method of converting muzzle-loading firearms into breech-loaders.[121]

What specialist knowledge Lincoln lacked, he more than made up for in sheer curiosity about all things mechanical and scientific. One of his colleagues, Henry Clay Whitney, well recalled his friend's insatiable inquisitiveness. While on the road and traveling together, when they stopped at a local farmhouse for dinner, Lincoln would obtain

> some farming implement, machine or tool, and he would carefully examine it all over, first generally and then critically; he would "sight" it to determine if it was straight or warped: if he could make a practical test of it, he would do that; he would turn it over or around and stoop down, or lie down, if necessary, to look under it; he would examine it closely, then stand off and examine it at a little distance; he would shake it, lift it, roll it about, up-end it, overset it, and thus ascertain every quality and utility which inhered in it, so far as acute and patient investigation could do it.[122]

Given Lincoln's fascination with firearms technology, small wonder that he took a fatherly interest in the arming of his troops. Time and time again he would conduct his own experiments with a new weapon and report the results to an irritated Ripley—sometimes accompanied by an order to purchase several thousand of them, which irritated him still more. Thus, in the summer of 1861 Lincoln and his private secretary, William Stoddard, tramped across the White House south lawn for some shooting practice. Lincoln carried, most probably, one of Winchester's very early repeating Henrys, and Stoddard a Springfield rifle-musket specially modified into a breech-loader.[123] Lincoln himself at this point took only an "especial interest" in repeaters, having had little experience with them (the gun he carried that day was a prototype, not a finished model), and he was convinced the "single-shooting breech-loader" was "the army rifle of the future." Even on that point, Stoddard remarked, "the Bureau [i.e., Ordnance] officials" were "against him."[124]

At the bottom of the lawn there was a patch of ground picturesquely called Treasury Park (about where the Washington Monument is), though it was less a verdant park than weedy, gravelly turf enclosed by a shoulder-high wooden fence and containing a large pile of lumber that Lincoln used as a buffer for bullets gone astray. (Sometimes they went *too* far astray. In November 1862 one such ball crashed through Mrs. Grady's nearby window, flew through her parlor, and lodged itself in the opposite wall.)

Having set up a target against the woodpile, Lincoln and Stoddard took their positions one hundred yards away. Lincoln fired, missed. Stoddard fired, hit. "I declare, you are beating me," said Lincoln. "I'll take a good sight this time." Hearing shots in the middle of Washington, where discharging firearms was banned, a passing sergeant and his men appeared, shouting, "Stop that firing! Stop that firing!" Seeing the president, the sergeant stopped short, did a comical double-take, and rapidly withdrew. "Well," remarked Lincoln, "they might have stayed to see the shooting."[125]

Shortly afterward, impressed by the modified rifle-musket's performance, Lincoln asked Ripley to look into placing an order for these rifles, the brainchild of one Samuel Wilmer Marsh. Expecting the president soon to forget about it, Ripley ignored him and went so far as to tell Marsh bluntly that "we do not want such arms as you offer." Hearing of this insolence, Lincoln instructed Ripley to purchase 25,000 of them

President Lincoln, like Washington and Jefferson, took a keen interest in firearms development. Here he tests a rifle on his firing range on the White House lawn, only to be challenged by a passing patrol alarmed at hearing gunshots in the capital.

immediately or perhaps consider looking for another job. Even then Ripley cunningly placed a clause in the contract that a late delivery at any point would nullify the contract. Again, the president overruled him.[126]

Ripley had come close to crossing the line, but at this moment, with the Union on the ropes and Lincoln facing mounting criticism for his conduct of the war, the chief of ordnance was unfirable. He remained the only man in Washington who was capable of producing the titanic numbers of weapons that the government needed. Besides which, there was no one of sufficient seniority or experience available to replace him. Lincoln bided his time, possibly comforting himself with the illusion that Ripley's insubordination had resulted from a miscommunication.

Over the following two years it would become evident that there had been no such thing. Ripley's intransigence on the subject of breechloaders and repeaters grew steadily more obnoxious. When Lincoln requested Sharps rifles for Colonel Hiram Berdan's famous Sharpshooters outfit, Ripley did not order them and instead issued them Springfield rifles. In the spring of 1862, after much backstairs maneuvering to circumvent Ripley, Berdan eventually acquired Colt revolving rifles that he was able to exchange for the much-desired Sharps. In November 1861, when General McClellan—who, despite his other faults, was keenly interested in repeaters—directed Ripley to provide one thousand Colt revolving rifles for one unit, the latter never deigned to exert himself.[127]

A look at the hard figures of what Ordnance bought for the army between April 12, 1861, and December 31 of that year demonstrates the success of Ripley's adamant refusal to introduce any kind of breechloader into the service. The bureau purchased 236,157 rifles and riflemuskets in that time, of which just 2,676 were breech-loaders—a shade over one percent.[128]

Eventually Lincoln tired of Ripley's machinations and obstreperousness, authorizing Edwin Stanton, his new secretary of war in 1862, to make "some changes" at Ordnance for "the success of military operations and the safety of the country."[129] Ripley's successor, secretly selected by Lincoln and Stanton, was to be Major Alexander Dyer of the Springfield Armory, but he declined the promotion, claiming that his work at Springfield was too crucial for the war effort for him to leave now.[130] At a loss as to what to do next, Lincoln and Stanton approached General Ethan Allen Hitchcock, a good old loyalist, to advise them.

Hitchcock, to their surprise, thought it unadvisable to remove Ripley, at least not yet. Like it or not, within Ordnance circles Ripley, despite his short-temperedness, was regarded as the Boss, a deadly Washington player who protected the department from outside interference and got things done. "If this belief be shaken" by his dismissal, said Hitchcock, "the operation of the whole system is endangered," and thus the Union war effort might well falter. Stanton was a little skeptical about this assertion, but nevertheless he "concluded not to make any change just at that time and not until I had become further acquainted with the business of the office."[131]

That didn't stop him from putting Ripley back in his place. Stanton first cut off most direct communication with him by appointing Peter Watson as assistant secretary of war. Henceforth Ripley would be answerable to Watson (an unofficial demotion, as Ripley well knew) while still subject to Stanton's whims. The secretary took to occasionally, and with sadistic high-handedness, summoning him to his office. One time in March 1862, when Ripley was ordered to come over, he found Stanton in the midst of dealing with a crowd of supplicant contractors and public visitors. The secretary of war was standing by the window holding a weapon, apparently fitted with a new type of firelock. After Ripley negotiated his way past the onlookers, Stanton asked him how many of the firelocks he had ordered. Ripley answered, citing the number. Thereupon Stanton harshly replied, "If you dare to adopt another musket of this kind, I'll dismiss you from the service." Ripley goggled at him for a second but managed a civil, if wavering, "But, Mr. Secretary . . ." "Not another word," Stanton loudly retorted, dismissing him with his hand, "you can return to your Bureau." For the first time Ripley had been torn off a strip in public, and the arms contractors and inventors present instantly knew that the once-feared chief of ordnance was wounded mortally.[132]

But not yet dead, since the calamitous decline of federal arms stockpiles after the battles of Shiloh and Second Bull Run and the bloodbath at Antietam necessitated keeping him on, simply because he was the only one capable of replenishing them.

Ripley might still have held gamely on and hoped for a change of personnel at the War Department to relieve him of the odious Stanton and Watson, but time was against him. The thing that really finished off the formidable chief was the one factor he could not control, despite his best efforts: for more than a year, in order to circumvent Ripley, individual commanders in the field had been securing their own repeaters and single-shot breech-loaders directly from the manufacturers, from friends in the War Department, or from navy stocks. Sometimes soldiers even used their own wages to pay for them in installments. General William Rosecrans, in charge of the Army of the Cumberland, a West Pointer who'd joined the Engineer Corps and was something of an inventor himself (kerosene lanterns and soap-making machines mostly), was a particularly keen customer, acquiring thousands of Colt revolving rifles for his cavalry and infantry. His subordinate, Colonel John Thomas Wilder, was still more enthusiastic: he once wrote directly to Oliver Winchester asking, "At what price will you furnish me *nine hun-*

*An early seventeenth-century matchlock in action. The sputtering "match,"
which ignited the gunpowder, gave away one's position at night and was
useless in the wet. The arrival of the flintlock spurred demand for firearms
among both colonists and colonized.*

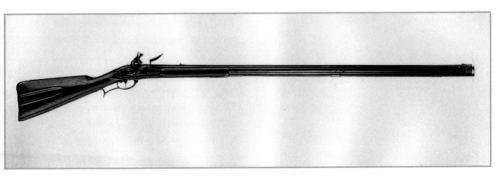

*A fine example of German worksmanship adapted for the American wilderness: A "Kentucky-
Pennsylvania" rifle of the eighteenth century.*

The magnificent weapon to which John Hall devoted his life: a breech-loader built on interchangeable principles, a machine made by machines. Hall helped lay the foundations of American economic supremacy.

A passion for precision was the key to successful arms production on a mass scale. To ensure perfection, workmen at the Springfield and Harpers Ferry national armories were issued with toolboxes containing dozens of gauges and other measurement tools. This one was used to inspect Model 1841s.

Major Alfred Mordecai—among the greatest of America's ordnance experts—during his 1850s tour of Europe that examined, quantified, and classified the small-arms arsenals of the Great Powers. His subsequent report, its outlook and conclusions inspired by Darwin's The Origin of Species, *was regarded as so important that Congress ordered it be made publicly available.*

What industrialization wrought (I): gunmaking machinery at Springfield Armory.

What industrialization wrought (II): stockpiling rifles at Springfield Armory. The sight of thousands of them inspired the visiting poet Longfellow to write, in a mixture of awe and horror: "From floor to ceiling,/Like a huge organ, rise the burnished arms."

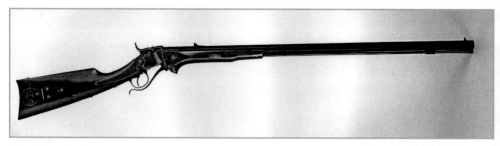

The Sharps rifle owned by John Brown. These rifles were popular among antebellum abolitionists, especially during the Bleeding Kansas clashes with proslavery guerrillas. The junior class at Yale presented a local infantry captain with one enscribed Ultima Ratio Liberarum—*"the final argument of liberty."*

This customized Henry repeater, the forerunner of the famous Winchester, was presented to Lincoln during the Civil War.

Sharpshooting riflemen were long regarded with distaste by regular soldiers. The regulars particularly disliked sharpshooters' insolence, their independence, and their habit of targeting officers. This picture of California Joe, a well-known marksman of the Civil War, captures the rifleman's prevailing image.

The talented General James Ripley, the Union's ordnance chief in the early stages of the Civil War. Imperious, all-knowing, patronizing, he was widely loathed—and yet brilliantly efficient at producing unparalleled numbers of firearms.

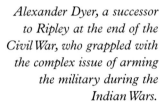

Alexander Dyer, a successor to Ripley at the end of the Civil War, who grappled with the complex issue of arming the military during the Indian Wars.

A contemporary engraving depicting breech-loader trials in 1867. The question by that time was not whether they would supersede muzzle-loaders, but if the future lay with accurate single-shot rifles or rapid-fire repeaters.

The great Spencer repeater, a favorite among Union soldiers and the bane of Confederate ones, but a weapon eventually overtaken by the Winchester.

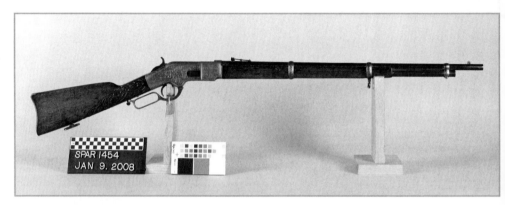

The Winchester Model 1866, the greatly improved successor to the Henry. Its popularity out West propelled its maker to the front rank of America's gun companies.

Repeaters were also popular among less upstanding citizens. This Winchester belonged to the outlaw Jesse James.

REPEATING RIFLES.

SAVAGE UTE:—"We want *no improvements* but this!"

By the 1870s, Indians were among the repeater's most zealous fans, and were widely (but falsely) believed to be better armed than the soldiers sent to fight them. This cartoon insinuates that Native Americans were keener on fighting than farming.

Since the Colonial era, Indians had decorated their rifles using a variety of brass tacks, leather, and silver inlays. This Winchester was once, evidently, a prized possession.

The thrill of "buff-running," or buffalo hunting on the Plains. Repeaters could be used only at close range, but professional hunters (like the young Wyatt Earp) kept their distance and insisted on employing only single-shot rifles.

The terrible aftermath of the buff-running craze.

dred of your 'Henry's Rifles,' . . . Two of my regiments, now mounted, have signified their willingness to purchase these arms, *at their own expense.*" Unfortunately Winchester didn't have enough available, but Christopher Spencer was on a marketing tour of Tennessee at the time (March 1863) to drum up interest in his repeater, and he was only too glad to arrange a shipment to Wilder.[133]

On May 15, 1863, the first Spencers arrived at Wilder's camp. The men were so excited by their amazing guns, they scarpered into the woods to try them out on any squirrels, rabbits, and turkeys unlucky enough to be in the vicinity. Three weeks later, on June 4, Wilder's brigade engaged a small detachment of the First Kentucky Confederate Cavalry outside Liberty, Tennessee. The firefight was short but ended with twenty cavalrymen taken captive. It was the first time a Spencer had been used in battle.[134]

The second happened the following day. Wilder's mounted infantry skirmished with a significant force of Confederate foot and horse and put them rapidly to flight. One southern lieutenant, a prisoner, couldn't believe what he'd seen. He had to ask one of Wilder's officers, "What kind of *Hell-fired* guns have your men got?" Near the end of June, after the Spencers again rattled a Confederate unit, one of the fleeing cavalrymen warned an advancing soldier, "Those Yankees have got rifles that won't quit shootin' and we can't load fast enough to keep up."[135]

By mid-August of that year Lincoln had heard enough of these colorful stories (and had read, as well, the laudatory press accounts of the Spencer's performance at Gettysburg a month earlier) to prick his interest, and he summoned Spencer to the White House for a demonstration.[136] Spencer arrived with one of his repeaters and handed it to the president. Betraying his curiosity in all things mechanical, Lincoln asked to be shown "the inwardness of the thing," so Spencer took the piece apart and screwed it back together, to the president's boyish delight.

At two P.M. the following day (August 18), Spencer accompanied the president, Lincoln's son Robert, and his private secretary John Hay out for a demonstration on the shooting range at Treasury Park. A wooden plank three feet long and six inches wide to use as a target was set up for them. Lincoln took the first shot, from 40 yards away. It hit five inches below, and somewhat to the left, of the bull's-eye. His next hit the spot, and by furiously working the lever, he rapidly placed five more in the neighborhood. "Now," he said, "we will see the inventor try it." Spencer, "a quiet little Yankee" (in the words of Hay), then performed "some splendid shooting" and beat the president's score. Lincoln, amused, defended his inferiority by remarking that Spencer was younger than he was. Then Hay had a try, but his efforts were "lamentably bad." (Being younger than either, he blamed his poor eyesight.) A naval aide brought the board with them back to the president's office. Bidding farewell to Spencer, Lincoln gave him the target, saying that "it might be a gratifying souvenir." In his diary Hay echoed his boss's thoughts on the Spencer: "a wonderful gun, loading with absolutely contemptible simplicity and ease with seven balls and firing the whole readily and deliberately in less than half a minute." The president liked it so much he went out the next evening and fired off many more rounds.[137]

Lincoln could not help wondering why Ripley had been so adamantly opposed to this "wonderful gun" and why he was continuing to drag his feet issuing it to the troops. A month after the shooting exhibition, the inevitable decision was made.[138] Ripley had to go. This time Lincoln was helped by a recent Act of Congress declaring the president's power to retire officers of more than forty-five years' service. With forty-five already on the clock, Ripley knew his day was done, and on September 14 he resigned his commission.[139] (Two years later he was breveted a major general for his long and faithful service. Until 1869 the crusty old soldier worked as an inspector of the coastal New England forts, a position that kept him out of Washington politicking. In March of the following year he died at his home in Hartford, Connecticut.)[140]

Now that Ripley was at long last out of the picture, there remained the problem of a successor. Lincoln wanted Colonel George Ramsay, the wholly uninteresting, dutiful superintendent of the Washington Arsenal who was guaranteed not to cause as much turmoil as Ripley had. Unfortunately Stanton loathed Ramsay, but he also understood that his own ambitious favorite, Captain George Balch, was outranked. Giving in, Stanton accepted Ramsay but stipulated that Balch be made his deputy.

It took six months for Ramsay to realize that Balch had been sending out imperious demands to one and all using his signature. Following a full and frank exchange of views, Balch tendered his resignation, only to be "persuaded" to return to his post. Round one to Balch. Following yet another unpleasant altercation in the summer of 1864, Balch again resigned. Round two to Ramsay. But Stanton refused to accept it. Round three to Balch. Then Stanton fired Ramsay on September 12 and exiled him, à la Ripley, to the inspection of coastal fortresses. Round four and knockout to Balch.

Lincoln had now noticed the distinctly strange goings-on at Ordnance and insisted on Major Alexander Dyer, who was still at the Springfield Armory after previously turning down the post. With Dyer, even Stanton could find little to complain about. Aware of the lion's den he was entering, Dyer's first act was to banish Balch to "special duty" at West Point.

Dyer remained as chief of ordnance until 1874, dying in harness. Three years before his appointment he had actually been the first ordnance officer to test the Spencer, which he regarded as the finest breech-loading arm he had ever seen. In October 1864 Dyer even approved releasing Ramsay's final report, which noted that the army was intending to adopt the breech-loading rifle as the infantry and cavalry's standard arm following "full and thorough tests and trials."

Ramsay had been far-seeing enough to grasp the importance of repeaters and metallic cartridges, as well as breech-loaders. It was he who recommended gradually shifting production away from linen and paper cartridges and investing more resources in metallic technology. "The repeating arms," he noticed, "are the greatest favorite with the army . . . the demand for them is constant and for large quantities. It seems as if no soldier who has seen them used could be satisfied with any other." Of these repeaters, Ramsay believed the Spencer to be the "cheapest, most durable, and most efficient." In August 1864, just before he was sacked, Ramsay announced that he had ordered 78,000 repeaters and 89,950 single-shot breech-loaders.[141]

The "details for effecting these measures," Dyer pledged in turn, "will receive the early attention of this Bureau."[142] He was as good as his word. The January 2, 1865, issue of *Scientific American* cheered, "BREECH-LOADERS TO BE ADOPTED—The Government has appointed a commission of seven military officers, to meet at Springfield Armory on the 4th of January, for the purpose of testing breech-loading carbines and muskets, in order to select the best for army use."[143] It marked the end of the muzzle-loader and the final victory of the breech-loading rifle.

Not so readily apparent was whether *single-shot* or *repeating* breech-loaders were the coming thing. Deciding the issue boiled down to weighing the pros and cons of mass firepower versus one-shot marksmanship in the modern age. There was no clear-cut answer to the dilemma, which was fraught with complications and contradictions.

Ripley had been castigated as simply an out-of-touch reactionary, but by insisting on retaining single-shot muzzle-loaders, he had in fact struggled to reconcile the most advanced European and Ordnance thinking on scientific ballistics with the superior proficiency of American riflemen to hit their targets. Likewise his foes, such as Oliver Winchester, who boasted of their weapons' technologically advanced ability to unleash dozens of bullets, were unwittingly rehearsing the antique, eighteenth-century justifications for rapid-fire, unaimed musketry.

Both sides' advocates were further frustrated by the Civil War's ambiguous lessons. Ripley's partisans pointed to the impressive hit rates—as measured by the number of bullets expended for every casualty inflicted—racked up by combatants compared to their extravagantly wasteful overseas equivalents. Union and Confederate troops did not need repeaters precisely because they made their shots count.*

---

*The eighteenth-century French tactician Guibert had calculated that of 1 million shots fired, just 2,000 struck home (a 0.2 percent hit rate), and the Duke of Wellington's redcoats at the Battle of Vittoria in 1813 had achieved a 0.125 percent rate (or one out of every 800 rounds). Those figures were in keeping with enemy soldiers' performance during the Mexican-American War of the late 1840s and that of the Austrians at the 1859 Battle of Solferino, where they loosed 8.4 million rounds in exchange for 2,000 deaths and 10,000 wounded on the Franco-Piedmontese side, or one casualty for every 700 shots (0.14 percent).

By way of comparison, in Mexico American troops had inflicted a hit every 125 rounds (0.8 percent), and Civil War numbers bore out the same story. During the Battle of Murfreesboro, one Confederate was killed or wounded for every 145 small-arms rounds, for a 0.69 percent hit rate. At Gaines' Mill the figure was about 1 percent. The rate at Chickamauga (September 1863) ranged between 0.6 percent and 0.8 percent, while during the Battle of the Wilderness it fell between 0.99 percent and 1.5 percent. In short, an American infantryman of the time was *five times* as effective at hitting his foe than his Mexican, British, and European counterparts.

This remarkable disparity was produced by several factors, not least of which was Americans' greater familiarity with firearms before they ever donned a uniform. Confederates, drawn more from rural areas, enjoyed an advantage in this respect over urban Northerners. Then again, Union men were generally armed with more modern, more accurate weapons than their Southern foes, who often carried ancient pieces into action. The Confederate advantage in experience could be canceled out by Northern manufacturing prowess.

Not every American was a fine shot. Still, they did not all have to be for their armies to rack up impressive scores. Careful observers perceived that overall unit lethality hinged on the performance of a few key individuals. Take a hundred-man company whose hit rate is a mediocre 0.5 percent, and replace just ten of the laggards with the same number of new sharpshooting recruits who achieve a 10 percent rate. The unit's subsequent hit rate will be a spectacularly deadly 1.45 percent.

Such skilled killers were spoken of with no little reverence. Lieutenant Josiah Favill, commanding a detachment of civilian volunteers at First Bull Run, recalled that among them was a "tall, elderly gentleman, wearing plain clothes and a tall silk hat, in the front rank, who loaded and fired away in the most deliberate manner, apparently wholly indifferent to danger; he must have done a great deal of execution, as the excitement did not seem to affect him in the least." The mysterious sniper was "a noted abolitionist, and desired to do his share in the field."[144]

Firepower advocates dismissed the presence of talented individuals in the line as merely fortuitous. Perhaps at the long ranges (four hundred yards and above) that Ordnance claimed were the average battlefield distance between opposing sides, sharpshooters could work wonders picking off glinty-epauletted officers, but hard fighting was close fighting.

During Civil War firefights—including battles, skirmishes, and low-level actions—the average distance between Confederate and Unionist was a mere *127 yards*.[145] Yardage varied widely, with the prime killing ground being between 80 and 120 yards. There were even firefights at the terrifying distance of 10 or 20 yards. These nightmares nearly always happened either in darkness, or when one side coolly held its fire until the last moment, or when combatants came to grips in the woods. During the latter instances the Confederates, harking back to colonial days, would shout Indian cries, and at times the brush was so impenetrable that soldiers were blasting each other at fifteen paces.

Those favoring repeaters highlighted the danger of relying on careful marksmanship in the fluid circumstances of the modern battleground: a small error in precisely judging range and wind resulted in a miss. That was why one Confederate infantryman at Drewey's Bluff, Virginia, in May 1864 noticed a tall pine behind him riddled with bullets from top to bottom; cones and needles from its loftiest branches kept falling onto his breastworks.[146] Far better, it was argued, to close the distance as quickly as possible and devastate the enemy with hailstorms of lead.

The experience of war had wrought a radical shift in attitude. Only two years before its outbreak Lieutenant Cadmus Wilcox had published an encyclopedic volume entitled *Rifles and Rifle Practice* that could be regarded as the bible of the accuracy school. Hundreds of its pages were devoted to the scientific minutiae of various ballistical measurements and statistical comparisons and their impact on marksmanship. The army even purchased one thousand copies for general edification. But it soon fell into obscurity, victim to the slaughterhouses of Maryland, Virginia, and Pennsylvania.[147]

More in keeping with real-world conditions was Major G. L. Willard's exhaustive *Comparative Value of Rifled and Smooth-Bored Guns,* which in 1863 went so far as to call for the return of *smoothbore* muskets. On the grounds that rifles equipped with precise, elevating sights (which Wilcox had counted as one of the finest devices ever conceived by the wit of man) were too slow for use in battle, wise commanders, Willard advised, should tell their men to bash off their fiddly elevating sights and simply "wait until the enemy are within point blank range, where the old arms [begin] to act with real effect."[148]

Willard was killed during just such a charge at Gettysburg—though a fragmented artillery shell ripping off most of his head was the cause, not a musket ball. Given the Civil War's hundreds of thousands of other dead and maimed men, it was understandable if Ripley's promotion of individual talent in the field of battle seemed a quaint throwback to the days of yore. Now the apostles of firepower, not the evangelists of accuracy, were the industrial age made flesh.

The Henry Rifle

Chapter 5

THE "GREWSOME GRAVEYARD"

No sooner had that national convulsion, the Civil War, passed than the country began dismantling its colossal martial apparatus and attempted a return to normalcy. Fleeing the blasted South and the over-crowded North, hundreds of thousands of emigrants set their sights westward—to the alluring Plains, to the Rockies, to the Southwest, even to fabled California. They traveled by horse, wagon, foot, and stage-coach along the Oregon-California Trail, the Santa Fe Trail, and the Smoky Hill Trail, or they bought berths aboard the trains skimming over the Union Pacific's skeletal iron fingers that stretched, at the beginning of 1866, already as far as the Missouri. By the end of that year they were approaching the Nebraska-Wyoming border. Thrusting eastward from Sacramento, California, the coolies of the Central Pacific line were bor-ing, digging, and blasting their way through the Sierra Nevadas. In May 1869 the two railroads rendezvoused seventy miles northwest of Salt Lake, and within the week trains were running daily from coast to coast. By 1880 the European population of the West had swollen by three and a half million, nearly quintupling the number of its prewar inhabitants.

To make room for the new arrivals, the West's *other* prewar inhabi-tants—some 270,000 Indians, divided into about 125 tribal groups—would have to make way. The official policy was to chivvy them onto reservations, establish a Bureau of Indian Affairs to oversee matters, teach them how to cultivate their land, Christianize them, and gradually wean them off the traditional ways so that ultimately their grandchildren could leave the reservation and join civilization. Another school, more romantically minded, felt that the Indians were the last remaining free spirits, poignant and potent reminders of what life was like before the onslaught of the modern industrialized age, that era of hourly constraints, starched collars, and weekly pay packets.

Even at the height of the Indian wars, fewer than 100,000 native Americans were counted as active hostiles, and they were, in any case, greatly outnumbered by European settlers.[1] The tribes basked in widely varying reputations among the soldiery. Some bands of the Plains Sioux were regarded as treacherous, barbaric, and vicious (though the Yankton and Santee bands were very friendly), while the Utes of the Rocky Mountains were seasoned warriors who unfortunately practiced the most terrible mutilations of corpses. The Cheyennes, thought George Custer, were "the Dog Soldiers, the most mischievous, bloodthirsty, and barbarous band of Indians that infest the Plains." The Crows were widely believed to be amicable but "arrant thieves" and "beggars." Pawnees were the "most reliable friends of the whites." The Nez Percés, who did not scalp their enemies, were seen as the most honorable of Indian foes, while the Apaches of the Southwest, ferocious as they were ("tigers of the human race" was what General George Crook called them, not a little admiringly), were easy enough to get along with so long as they were "treated right," in the words of Sergeant George Neihaus. Corporal Emil Bode thought the Comanches were overrated, for they "generally frightened a timid person half to death with their yells" but nevertheless lacked the martial swagger of the Apaches.[2]

Many of the Indian tribes historically detested one another, but the European settlers needed to keep them divided, for the 100,000 hostiles greatly outnumbered the U.S. Army, which averaged about 25,000 soldiers. Worse, during the Civil War soldiers had been able to count on decisively engaging the enemy en masse on the field of battle, but in the postwar West (as the pre–Revolution British had discovered to their cost and as Americans were painfully relearning) Indians adhered to their age-old guerrilla tactics of swooping ambushes, sneak flank attacks, and lightning raids on the enemy's vulnerable points. "Their tactics are such as to render the old system [of army-versus-army battles] almost wholly impotent," noted the experienced western hand Captain Randolph Marcy.[3]

Whites were again confronted by a "skulking" enemy who was far more adept than they at exploiting the natural environment.[4]

Whereas eighteenth-century fighting had been confined to the dense, forested tracts of New England and the Appalachians, the Indian wars of the latter part of the nineteenth occurred in a far more diverse set of terrains. In the dark, entangled woods where the likes of Washington and Morgan learned their trade, single, accurate rifle shots had counted for more than a volley of musket rounds: a combatant might catch sight of an opponent only briefly before he disappeared into the undergrowth or behind a tree, and if waiting to spring an ambush, one would want to preselect a target.

In the West soldiers rarely fought in such cramped environments. Instead they found themselves on the ceaseless plains confronting horse-borne Sioux who swept across the flats like fleets atop the ocean before vanishing. In the words of Colonel Philippe Régis de Trobriand, "The movement of Indian horsemen is lighter, swifter, and longer range than that of our cavalry, which means they always get away from us." Only in the winter, when the Indians' grass-fed ponies proved less hardy than the troopers' grain-fed mounts, was it possible to keep pace.[5]

In the Southwest the sedentary desert-dwellers were less mobile but knew how to survive for months beyond the reach of soldiers who were rendered helpless by soaring temperatures and parched throats. In the mountains, natural fortresses all, tribesmen outraced their slower hunters through the contorted passes, across the roaring rivers, and between the ravines.

The army was pitted against an enemy, observed Captain Marcy,

who is here to-day and there to-morrow; . . . who is everywhere without being anywhere; who assembles at the moment of combat, and vanishes whenever fortune turns against him, who leaves his women and children far distant from the theatre of hostilities, and has neither towns or magazines to defend, nor lines of retreat to cover; who derives his commissariat from the country he operates in, and is not encumbered with baggage-wagons or pack-trains; who comes into action only when it suits his purposes; and never without the advantage of numbers or position.[6]

Owing to the more open, fluid geography of the West, pinpoint accuracy was now of far less importance than raw, sudden violence employed against army units or lumbering wagon convoys. Once masters of marksmanship, Indians suffered from a newfound reputation for being poor shots.[7] The change had been forced upon them, not least by their lack of modern accurate firearms, and in their preference for swooping fast and close on horses they adapted their buffalo-hunting technique of riding among a stampeding, jostling herd and picking off beasts willynilly with bow and arrow. The confusion and swirling action that ensued resembled nothing less than combat at close quarters.

Unable to detect and destroy the enemy forces, the army focused on depriving the Indians of their means of sustenance. General William Sherman, whose march to the sea during the Civil War had taught him the importance of making "old and young, rich and poor, feel the hard hand of war," ordered his men to slaughter the teeming buffalo herds roaming the Plains.[8] The campaign's strategic goal was to remove Indians in the central plains territory between the Platte and Arkansas rivers who were obstinately standing astride the routes used by settlers traveling westward. By liquidating the buffalo from the contested area while leaving the northern and southern herds unharmed, Indians would be compelled to seek refuge on reservations north of Nebraska and south of Kansas.[9] With the center cleared, there would be nothing left to fight over. With a single stroke, then, both the Indians' casus belli would vanish and the Union Pacific could build its railroad unhindered by raids.

It would not work out that way, of course: poachers hunted the northern and southern herds, riling tribes whose peace treaties had promised them exclusive rights to hunt.[10] Settlers too—including those who had never hunted a buffalo in their lives—suffered from roving assaults on their lives and property. Even when they strictly adhered to the terms of the latest treaty, said one Indian superintendent named Murphy, local whites had been murdered, raped, and attacked by Cheyennes and

Arapahoes. Originally sympathetic to the Indians' plight, he now judged that the custom of giving presents and signing treaties had allowed Indian chiefs to conclude that the government was weak and vacillating. Murphy recommended that they "be left to the tender mercies of our army."[11] Despite its best efforts to disengage from the Indian and settler "problem," the army found itself being drawn in only deeper. Small wonder that General Crook, probably the most masterful of frontier commanders, laid down at the end of his career that "Indian warfare is, of all warfare, the most dangerous, the most trying, and the most thankless."[12]

In December 1866 the army experienced the blunt, horrific force of a new-style Indian strike. The Civil War veteran Captain William Fetterman, 49 soldiers (armed with muzzle-loading Springfields), and 27 cavalrymen (with Spencers) left Fort Phil Kearny, an outpost at the foot of the Bighorn Mountains, to chase a band of Lakota Sioux, Northern Arapaho, and Northern Cheyenne that had been harassing wood-gathering parties from the fort, whose presence they naturally resented on their domain. Before the captain left, James Bridger—the fort's chief scout—said ominously, "Your men who fought down South, are crazy! They don't know anything about fighting Indians."[13] He was laughed at. Setting off along the Bozeman Trail, Fetterman soon disappeared from sight of the fort as he ascended into the hills.

The band sought by Fetterman was actually just a decoy to lead him to a narrow ridge, where between 1,500 and 2,000 warriors had hidden themselves in the snow-covered ravines alongside it. The army column was quickly sliced into three groups that were too isolated to lend fire support to one another.

When the troops of the relief force arrived an hour or so later, they found only corpses, or rather parts of corpses, in this "grewsome graveyard."[14] Every man but one in Fetterman's command had been stripped naked and mutilated—a ritualistic act of revenge that must have taken longer than the actual fighting. (The "lucky" exception was Adolph Metzger, the bugler. He had desperately killed several Indians by battering their heads with his instrument; as a mark of respect, a buffalo robe was laid over his undefiled corpse.)[15] Fetterman had been killed by American Horse, an Oglala warrior who clubbed the captain to his knees and slashed his throat with a knife.[16]

The local commander, Colonel Henry B. Carrington, summarized the grisly scene for his superiors in Washington:

Eyes torn out and laid on the rocks; noses cut off; ears cut off; chins hewn off; teeth chopped out; joints of fingers; brains taken out and placed on rocks with other members of the body; entrails taken out and exposed; hands cut off; feet cut off; arms taken out of sockets; private parts severed and indecently placed on the persons; eyes, ears, mouth, and arms pene-trated with spearheads, sticks, and arrows; ribs slashed to separation with knives; skulls severed in every form, from chin to crown; muscles of calves, thighs, stomach, breast, back, arms, and cheek taken out. [17]

What is striking about the colonel's description is its focus on the damage wrought by spearheads, sticks, arrows, and knives. Skulls were severed, not exploded by metal projectiles; ribs were slashed, not broken by the force of a bullet's impact; hands and feet were cut off, not holed by lead. Though some of the wealthier or more accomplished warriors were armed with both bladed and ballistic weapons, very few of the Indians at the Fetterman fight bore firearms, and the vast majority of those who did carried old muzzle-loaders. The fort's assistant surgeon, who examined the corpses, believed just six men had died exclusively of bullet wounds. [18]

It was a common misapprehension on the frontier that Indians were not only firearmed but were *better* armed than the whites. Fetterman's infantry may have carried Civil War–era .58 Springfield muzzle-loaders, but his cavalry had good Spencers. Two ill-starred civilians who went along on the jaunt had brought Henry repeaters. It was the overwhelm-ing waves of braves that did for Fetterman, not his being outgunned. Even when Indians did own guns, they tended to be old. When Lieutenant George Belden later visited the Fetterman site, the rocks were still stained with blood and covered in hair where the Indians had bashed out the soldiers' brains; there he found a flintlock musket, an Indian heirloom, engraved "London, 1777." [19]

The great Wagon Box Fight—eight months after the Fetterman Massacre, and again involving the beleaguered occupants of Fort Phil Kearny—further demonstrated that at this early stage in the Indian wars

Red Cloud's Sioux were not only poorly armed but were unfamiliar with modern weaponry. On August 2, 1867, Captain James Powell and a detachment of twenty-six infantrymen escorting four woodcutters—the size of the bodyguard was testament to the prevailing sense of danger—were assailed by a force of anywhere between one and two thousand Indians. As the men sought shelter within an oval-shaped ring of wheelless wagons, the outlook did look grim.

Since Fetterman's death, "thanks to God and Lieutenant-General Sherman" (in the words of Private Samuel Gibson), the men at Fort Phil Kearny had received brand-new Springfield breech-loaders. Even so Gibson, fearfully sitting alongside Sergeant McQuiery and Private John Grady in a wooden wagon box, watched them take their shoes off and pull out the laces. He wondered why. Each man in the detachment, they explained, was making a loop to fit over his right foot and would tie the other end to his Springfield's trigger "to kill themselves when all hope was lost." His companions told Gibson that when the Indians overwhelmed them, "every man would stand erect, place the muzzle of his loaded rifle under his chin and take his own life, rather than be captured and made to endure the inevitable torture." A splendid idea, thought Gibson, who "had just taken off my own shoes and made loops in the strings when the firing began."

Once Gibson and his colleagues had fired their first shot, a group of Indians charged within 150 yards of them and halted. Gibson realized that "they were sitting on their ponies wait[ing] for us to draw ramrods for reloading, as they supposed we were yet using the old muzzleloaders." Their flipping open the breechblocks to reload "puzzled the Indians, and they were soon glad to withdraw to a safe distance."[20]

Sergeant Max Littman remembered that some three hundred Indians advanced on his side of the corral on foot, very slowly, and after a volley they began running forward. Following a second volley, they "still came on with wild cries and shrill war whoops, thinking, no doubt, that once our guns were empty they could break over the corral and score an easy victory." But after a third volley at two hundred feet, the mystified attackers "broke and fled for the hills."

The new Springfields had performed wonders, but still Littman admitted that if the enemy had "advanced steadily with their entire force,"

the fight would have lasted but five minutes, as "it would have been simply impossible on our part to have loaded and fired rapidly enough to
have prevented" them from overrunning the wagons.[21] Numbers still
counted, and though breech-loading, single-shot Springfields were
powerful, they were nowhere near as fast as a Spencer repeater. Other
soldiers and settlers would soon take this lesson to heart.

Nevertheless, when Custer's Seventh Cavalry—again armed with
standard Springfields, and again engulfed by an ocean of numbers—was
slaughtered to a man at the Little Bighorn, the conspiratorial idea that
Indians were armed with the most modern weaponry gained traction.
The government was blamed, mostly. Captain Charles King, a well-
known commentator, blamed the "silk-hatted functionaries" from
Washington whose "cheap oratory . . . about the Great Father and
guileless red men" prompted them to invite chiefs into the White House,
whence they returned to their reservations "laden down with new and
improved rifles and ammunition." In the meantime King and his men
were left to bury their dead.[22]

Notwithstanding King's accusations that advanced weaponry had
changed hands, the most common firearm among the minority of
Indians who actually owned one was, until the mid-1870s, an old
muzzle-loading, smoothbore musket. Though they lacked the finish and
precision of arsenal-made guns or the wares sold by upmarket gunsmiths, all these weapons were perfectly serviceable, and their plainness
was regarded by the Indians as a virtue. Just as eighteenth-century
Indians had decorated their firearms, so their descendants studded the
stocks with brass tacks and affixed eagle feathers to the wooden forearm.

Government efforts largely succeeded in staving off the threat that
caches of surplus Civil War weapons would reach the Indians. But still a
steady, if leisurely, stream of firearms flowed westward. Not all of them
were illegal; some were in fact sold to Indians by government-licensed
traders operating through the Interior Department's civilian Indian
Bureau. That policy was dictated by the bureau's effort to reward com-
pliance: tribes that promised to use firearms solely for hunting would be
allotted more, if not better, guns, than those that didn't. For this reason
Agent Edward Wyncoop in Kansas provided the Arapahoes with eighty
muzzle-loading rifles while the less accommodating Apaches received

just twenty.[23] The army, echoing Charles King's suspicions about Washington's collusion with insurgents, was less enamored of such artfulness and demanded the cessation of all arms transfers whatsoever.

Eventually the two institutions reached a tenuous accommodation that would prevent the distribution of newer and more powerful weapons yet allow limited numbers of older ones to be used for legitimate purposes. Reflecting the new arrangement, Agent A. J. Simmons of the Milk River Agency in Montana Territory informed traders in his jurisdiction that they were no longer "permitted to dispose of . . . any breechloading fire arms, cartridges, or fixed ammunition . . . to any Sioux Indians." Only muzzle-loaders "in quantities sufficient for hunting purposes"— twenty-four maximum at a time—plus sufficient gunpowder (25 pounds per month) and lead for ammunition (75 pounds)—were allowed.[24]

The agreement proved unworkable. There were plenty of traders, licensed or not, willing to work off the books for favored clients. Joseph Taylor knew that "the great Durfee & Peck trading company" did an excellent trade selling illegal arms and munitions to the Sioux.[25] Because the new restrictions raised the black market price of firearms, profits were easy—and tempting. At Fort Phil Kearny, of all places, the Sioux pestered soldiers to sell them powder and ammunition: at one point they were offering $4 (about $61 in current dollars) for a single charge, or $40 for four ounces of powder.[26] Andrew Garcia, a dubious if entertainingly self-aware operator—he swore he had only ever one friend, "a man I was low-down enough to stab in the back"—reminisced about the time when the Blackfeet gave him thirty-six buffalo robes (worth $360 back east) in return for just four old muzzle-loading rifles and a dozen boxes of cartridges.[27]

In the Southwest, buffalo robes were rarely used as currency. Instead, Mexican black marketeers and American merchants used rifles and pistols to pay Kiowas and Comanches for horses stolen in Texas. According to John Cremony, a former U.S. boundary commissioner, "not a few [of these weapons had been] sold by immigrants to obtain food and other supplies while crossing the continent."[28] Up north Louis Boucher, a French Canadian married to the daughter of Chief Spotted Tail, ran guns hidden under sacks of flour for his father-in-law—all unwittingly courtesy of the Union Pacific Railroad.[29]

Just as the New England and Appalachian tribes had particularly esteemed rifles over muskets as being better suited to their style of fighting and the terrain, especially prized among later Indians were Colt revolvers and repeater rifles. One major stationed at Fort Dodge loudly complained that for a Colt, Indians were offering "ten, even twenty times its value, in horses and furs."[30] Plenty Coups, chief of the Crows, said that after he saw his first breech-loader, "I did not rest until I owned one, giving 10 finely dressed robes for it . . . I laid away my bow forever." That gun was two-thirds more expensive than a muzzle-loader, but that mattered not to Plenty Coups when it "could be loaded on a running horse."[31]

During the 1870s, efforts to staunch the flow of modern guns were clearly failing. As early as 1873 Custer noticed during his expeditions along the Yellowstone River that he was up against Indians armed with "the latest improved patterns of breech-loading repeating rifles, and their supply of metallic rifle-cartridges seemed unlimited . . . Neither bows nor arrows were employed against us."[32]

That was something of an exaggeration, but Custer's observation was nevertheless a telling one. At the Little Bighorn in 1876, remembered Medal of Honor recipient Sergeant Charles Windolph of Captain Frederick Benteen's Troop H, at least half the braves brought bows, arrows, and lances (as well as clubs, axes, and knives), and about a quarter used "odds and ends of old muzzle-loaders and single-shot rifles of various vintages." Thus "not more than 25 or 30 per cent of the warriors carried modern repeating rifles."[33] Assuming fifteen hundred Indian warriors fought, then there were between 375 and 495 repeating rifles at the battle, the lower number being the more probable (according to statistical projections based on artifacts found at the battlefield).[34] Whatever the exact number, Custer's 220 men, armed with their single-shot Springfields, were hugely outmatched by just the repeater-armed Indians, let alone those carrying traditional weapons and old muskets.

In the early 1880s, having quit trying to reduce the supply of weapons—General Crook admitted in 1883 that "the Indians are now no longer our inferiors in equipment"—the government instead concentrated on controlling that of *ammunition*.[35] The thinking was that since the newer types of cartridges could be manufactured only in specialist workshops and armories, eventually the Indians would be left with empty repeaters and forced to parley. Accordingly President Grant banned the sale of such ammunition in "country occupied by Indians, or subject to their visits, lying within the Territories of Montana, Dakota, and Wyoming and the states of Nebraska and Colorado."[36]

Initially the prohibition seemed to work. On his first brush with renegade Indians, Private James Gillett of the Texas Rangers was confronted by one armed with a repeater but lacking any cartridges. Nevertheless Colonel Dodge soon noticed that the shortage had stimulated the "ordinarily uninventive brain[s]" of the Indians, and they had begun jerry-rigging their own ammunition. After buying from a trader "a box of the smallest percussion caps," they forced one into the base of a spent casing until it was flush, then poured in some easily available powder before inserting a lead bullet produced by means of a conventional mold. Voilà, a homemade cartridge. The "Indians say," reported Dodge, "that the shells thus reloaded are nearly as good as the original cartridge, and that the shells are frequently reloaded forty or fifty times."[37]

By 1886, said Captain John Bourke, who attended a meeting between General Crook and his old foe Geronimo, any hope of controlling either firearms or ammunition had disappeared: "Twenty-four warriors listened to the conference or loitered within earshot; they were loaded down with metallic ammunition; some of it reloading and some not. Every man and boy in the band wore two cartridge belts."[38] Nevertheless Dodge's claim that their recycled shells were "nearly as good" as virgin ones is unlikely, especially after the first ten or twenty times, when their rims would have been battered out of shape.

The ballistical quality of recycled cartridges was, at bottom, tangential, since the new Indian way of warfare was based not on accuracy but on mass firepower. With reused cartridges, homemade bullets, and crushed percussion caps, no man could hope to hit a barn door at two hundred yards. So long as the cartridges worked at close range, that was what counted.

The degree to which Indians had cast off their famed shooting ability is revealed by an 1879 Ordnance report listing 284 shoulder arms that had recently been turned in by captured Sioux and Cheyennes. Many of them were classified as unserviceable, at least by arsenal standards. A large number suffered from cracked stocks and faulty lock mechanisms, but most revealingly, a majority had broken, loose, or missing *sights*. Those remaining had been hacked down, the jagged ruins suitable only for short-range use. Captain O. E. Michaelis of the Ordnance Department commented that the modern Indian warrior "steals upon his quarry and fires *at* it." By shooting at point-blank range, they overcame "the difficulty attending fine sighting and the accurate estimate of distances."[39]

Knowing the Indian disinclination to take sight, experienced riflemen grew cocky. During the retreat from the Little Bighorn, Captain Winfield Edgerly noticed one Private Saunders with "a broad grin on his face, altho' he was sitting in a perfect shower of bullets." When the fighting was over, Edgerly asked Saunders what he found so funny at the time: "I was laughing to see what poor shots those Indians were; they were shooting too low and their bullets were spattering dust like drops of rain."[40]

To compensate for their lack of long-distance accuracy, Indians would first collect in great numbers, then close rapidly with the enemy and destroy him with intense free fire before he could take cover. Alternatively, they would strike in small numbers out of nowhere very fast, as happened to Custer's unit during a foray along the Yellowstone River when six mounted Sioux dashed boldly into their midst and attempted to stampede their horses.

And sometimes both methods would be used in tandem. After driving off the six horsemen into the woods, Custer's "suspicions were excited by the[ir] confident bearing," and he ordered a cautious advance toward the "heavy growth of timber which stood along the river bank above us." His caution was warranted. Suddenly, "with their characteristic howls and yells over three hundred well-mounted warriors dashed in perfect line from the edge of the timber and charged." The Indians outnumbered Custer's force by five to one, but his men held them off with furious hails of fire.[41]

In this instance Custer's deploying his troops into defensive positions saved the day, but in general soldiers were finding their single-shot Springfields outmatched by Indian swarming tactics. Designed to hit individuals at a distance, the Springfields simply could not fire quickly enough to keep up. The soldiers demanded to fight rapid fire with rapid fire.

The stream of complaints flummoxed the Ordnance Department, which had spent decades perfecting the long-range, single-shot, pinpoint-accurate rifle and had striven ceaselessly to place one in every soldier's hand. Between 1865 and 1876 the department had finally succeeded in doing so—just in time for its coming eclipse.

Single-shots would nevertheless long enjoy a fan base. Like many other dated technologies, they would continue to find favor for decades to come.[42] Certainly an element of snobbery was involved. Among expert hunters, professional lawmen, and the hardier sort of frontiersman, single-shots were prized items, one reason being that carrying one marked you as a killing gent, as opposed to the amateurs and tenderfoots showing off their brand-new repeaters bought at some fancy emporium back east.

Buffalo Bill Cody called his modified Springfield Model 1866 breech-loader "Lucretia Borgia" and used it to slaughter herds of buffalo for admiring spectators. The Ballard belonging to hunter Theo Davis "never failed me . . . More than one antelope has been brought down at three hundred yards. During our Indian fights it was the treasure of our party."[43] Lieutenant George Baylor of the Texas Rangers tried one of the new repeaters but got rid of it "after the first Indian fight." He needed an arm that would ghost on the first shot, and so began using a Springfield.[44]

Another attraction of the single-shot rifle was the splendid array of ammunitions available, enabling shooters to fine-tune their requirements as the situation demanded. For smaller prey like wolves (or men), the shooter could buy, say, the .40-100-190—the first number denotes the caliber, the second, the powder grains in the charge, and the third, the weight of the bullet expressed in grains; this one was a small cartridge whose light bullet and large charge allowed a very high and accurate velocity at the expense of penetrating power. By way of comparison, the Sharps company's monstrous "Big Fifty," which first appeared in 1872, bore a bullet weighing between 335 and 550 grains powered by 90 grains of powder. Over time American ammunition manufacturers would introduce such cartridges as the .50-70, .45-550, .44-60, .44-90, .45-100,

.40-50, and a dozen others, for as many market niches and specialized tasks as they could conceive.

The most famous cartridge of all would be the .45-70-405, selected by the government in 1873 as its standard-issue army ammunition for the Springfield. The .45-70—fondly known as the "ounce of lead"—was widely copied by civilian manufacturers (Winchester, Sharps, Remington, Marlin, and Hotchkiss, among others), and part of its universal appeal was that with its customary 405-grain bullet, it was effective against Indians at long range—at 700 yards, the .45-70 drilled 7.3 inches deep into white pine boards—but when customized with a 500-grainer, it killed the horses they rode on, or a buffalo.[45] It was by no means a coincidence that the "furor of slaughter" (in Colonel Dodge's words) of the buffalo reached its zenith in 1873, the exact moment when lethally accurate single-shot breech-loaders were achieving theirs.[46]

The most perfect single-shot breech-loader of all was undoubtedly the Remington rolling-block rifle. The Remington company had been founded in Ilion Gulph, New York, in 1816 by the rake-thin, stiff-collared Eliphalet Remington II, a man who even his enthusiastic biographer concedes had "no trace whatever of humor."[47] For fun, he repeatedly read Milton's *Paradise Lost*.

In the 1840s, taking a leaf from John Hall's Rifle Works at Harpers Ferry, the company began experimenting with the use of machine tools to increase production. Then on a business trip in 1845 Eliphalet met William Jenks, inventor of a breech-loading weapon lately sold to the navy. Remington liked him so much, he bought the company. Two years later the improved Remington-Jenks rifle was in the hands of the Marines who immortally stormed the "Halls of Montezuma" at the Battle of Chapultepec during the Mexican War. Jenks himself died soon afterward by falling off the top of a hay wagon as it entered a barn whose door was somewhat lower than he expected.[48]

From midway through the Civil War, Remington rifles (and pistols) found a customer in the U.S. government, which had been impressed by the sturdy single-shot weapons and negotiated contracts with Eliphalet's three sons—Philo (the mechanic), Samuel (the salesman), and Eliphalet III (the manager)—who had inherited the growing company upon their father's death from overwork in August 1861. Two years later one of

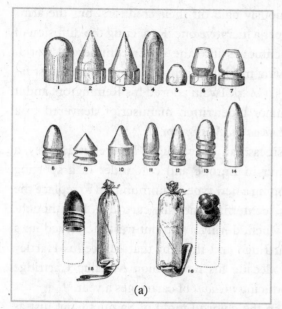

(b)

(a)

a) The range, evolution, and multiple forms of bullet technology in the nineteenth century. This is merely a small selection. Numbers 1 to 3 are traditional minié balls; Number 4 is a hexagonal bullet; Numbers 5, 6, and 7 are French bullets used in the Crimean War; Numbers 8 and 9 are German bullets; Number 10 is a Sardinian bullet; Numbers 11 and 12 are Swiss ones; Number 13, the bullet of an American .45-70; Number 14, a new type developed specifically for long-range sharpshooting (note aerodynamic shape); Numbers 15 and 16 are old-style paper cartridges, the first being a minié and the second "buck-and-ball" (used for point-blank assaults). b) The immortal .45-70-405 cartridge of 1873. This contemporary illustration patriotically contrasts smooth, machined American-made ammunition with its English counterpart.

their employees, Leonard Geiger, developed a curious "split-breech" rifle in which the hammer blocked an opening at the back of the breech. Intrigued, the post–Ripley Ordnance Department ordered twenty thousand of them at $24 each. As a present to the troops, every fifth Geiger version of the Remington was equipped with a miniature coffee-grinder embedded in the wooden stock, but more important, it formed the basis for the rolling-block breech mechanism to come.[49]

The end of the war witnessed the mass cancellation of Remington orders; like the Spencer company, having invested tens of thousands of dollars in new machinery and plant, the firm found itself deeply in debt. The

Remington brothers assiduously paid off their creditors, but the arms business was clearly no longer a lucrative one. Reflecting the diffusion of firearms-manufacturing techniques into the wider commercial world, they branched out into sewing machine, farm implement, and most famously, typewriter ventures. (Mark Twain adored his Remington, and it is thought that the first major typewritten manuscript delivered to a grateful publisher was his *Life on the Mississippi*.)

At the time another businessman, New Yorker Marcellus Hartley, a former Union arms-procurer in Europe and cofounder of a sporting goods company, was developing a new type of ammunition to replace the rimfire—what was called a "centerfire" metallic cartridge. It is thought he entered the arms trade when, during a trip out west, he picked up a shoddily made metallic cartridge and thought that Marcellus Hartley could do better. Within a decade his new Union Metallic Cartridge Company (UMC) was producing *millions* of cartridges a year.[50]

Hartley was a gun man in the colorful mold of Samuel Colt, just as the Remingtons were cut from the same sober cloth as Oliver Winchester. He owned two houses, the first at fashionable 232 Madison Avenue in Manhattan, and the other, a gigantic turreted Gothic mansion near Orange Mountain, New Jersey, where his friend Mr. Wu also lived. Wu had arrived in America as the personal agent of the Dowager Empress of China—she needed some weapons to put down a couple of unpleasant peasant revolts—and Hartley had invited him to spend the weekend in New Jersey. That had been ten years before. Now comfortably at home, he wore blue, rose, and gold brocaded robes with a peacock feather in his cap and would mysteriously shimmer into the room whenever Hartley had dinner guests, much to their surprise. Mr. Wu's own servant was named "John Chinaman," who opened the door to visitors and shouted up the stairs, "Hey, Hartley, man come see you!"[51]

Hartley, who was married, confined the fun and games to his free time; when it came to business, he, like Colt, was as straitlaced as any Remington and as merciless toward competitors as Winchester.[52] His mechanical whiz for the centerfire project was Alfred Hobbs, a man who once had won a $1,000 bounty offered by the British government to anyone who could unpick a massive new lock guarding the vault of the Bank of England. It took Hobbs fifty-one hours of continuous concentration, but he did it—and was decorated by the king into the bargain. Together with Colonel Hiram Berdan, the Civil War sharpshooter, he created the centerfire, though there is some evidence that Berdan, who was not unfamiliar with "borrowing" ideas without crediting their conceiver, had first seen an experimental version during a visit to the Frankford Arsenal, traditionally a leader in ammunition technology.

Centerfires outwardly resembled the older rimfires, but instead of packing the fulminate around the cartridge base's circumference, Berdan and Hobbs thickened the brass rim and inserted what was essentially a small percussion cap in the center. When struck by the hammer, the cap exploded, setting the powder afire. By means of this refinement the centerfire suddenly allowed metallic cartridges to increase vastly in power. The problem with rimfires was that their hollow rims and necessarily thin walls had rarely been strong enough to withstand the pressure blast of loads greater than about 50 grains; the centerfire suffered no such weakness. From 1867 onward rifles were capable of firing bullets farther and faster than ever was possible before.[53]

The Remingtons, meanwhile, had been encouraged to reenter the firearms trade by the expansion of the West and by settlers' demands for weapons. Stumped for ideas, they directed their plant supervisor, Joseph Rider, to have another look at the Geiger rifle. In the winter of 1865–66 Rider showed the brothers the rolling-block rifle. Instead of Geiger's split-breech, a pioneering concept but in practice one inherently weak and too mechanically complex for sustained use, Rider used a solid block of metal to house the firing mechanism. The shooter simultaneously cocked the hammer and "rolled" back the breechblock with his thumb. A cartridge was inserted into the open chamber, and the breechblock flipped forward to shut it. Once the trigger was pulled, the hammer slammed into the breechblock, creating a perfect seal against gas leakage. Recocking the hammer ejected the spent casing. It was a magnificently simple system using few moving parts and can justly claim to be the finest single-shot firelock ever produced. With some experience, a shooter could fire up to seventeen shots per minute, slower than a repeater admittedly but spectacular for a "single-shot" weapon. Better still, the breech was virtually unbreakable. In one test Alphonse Polain crammed a .50-caliber Remington with forty small balls and 750—750—grains of powder (the usual charge was 70 grains) and fired it. "Nothing extraordinary occurred," he reported of the bomb that had just detonated.[54]

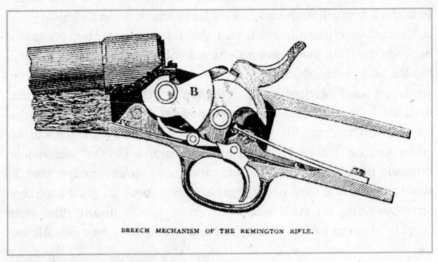

BREECH MECHANISM OF THE REMINGTON RIFLE.

The famed Remington rolling-block rifle.

Though understandably impressed by the Remington, the army was loath to order large numbers, not at a time when secondhand, wartime Springfields were hoarded in the arsenals. Remington, however, was happy to sell to foreign governments. Samuel Remington, the salesman son, was made president and dispatched abroad to glad-hand potentates, despots, emperors, voluptuaries, and even a few mere kings. He was a fine choice: unlike his abstemious brothers, Samuel was not averse to the aristocratic style of life, and he quickly settled in to his new corporate quarters in Paris. Although the American was a businessman, Napoleon III welcomed Remington to the Tuileries, while the spendthrift (he was rumored to be "indifferent" to interest rates) Ismail Pasha, Khedive of Egypt, consulted him personally about outfitting his army with Remingtons. "A sword and a strong arm are no longer sufficient for victory," the khedive proclaimed. "Only the most modern rifles will do." Oddly, the Mahdi of Sudan informed his followers after defeating the

Remington-armed Egyptians in 1881 that "the Prophet has repeatedly informed us that our victory is through the spear and the sword, and that we have no need for the rifle." That unfortunate occurrence lay in the future, but in the meantime so pleased was the khedive with his "most modern" Remingtons that he donated a prime parcel of land in central Cairo to Remington—upon which the American built a compact, but exquisitely formed, marble palace to use as the firm's regional sales office.[55]

The one dark spot amid all this celebration was Remington's reception in Prussia. Initially the heroically whiskered Wilhelm I was enthusiastic ("My friend, Remington, the gun man!"), but that rapidly subsided when he fired a faulty cartridge and heard nothing but a click. Throwing the accursed weapon to the ground, the king galloped off with his retinue of silver-helmeted staff officers. Disappointed but undaunted, Remington was overjoyed to hear soon afterward that at the 1867 Imperial Exposition in Paris, a commission of ordnance authorities from France, Britain, Austria, Russia, Spain, Italy, Sweden, Holland, Belgium, and yes, Prussia (which must have required some explaining when the official reported to Wilhelm) voted the Remington the best rifle in the world.[56]

High praise indeed, but still, selling batches of 10,000 to Spain, 60,000 to Egypt, or 30,000 to Sweden was not sufficient to keep the concern a going one, even if Remington's ally Napoleon III came through with an order for 150,000.[57] The embarrassing failure of a single cartridge in front of the King of Prussia had lost the firm a potential order for 200,000 Remingtons worth several million dollars; worse, a deal for 400,000 rifles arranged with the Sultan of Turkey had been about to close when an Ottoman vizier demanded a bribe so exorbitant that even the urbane Samuel Remington gasped—and refused to pay.[58] That was the end of that. Even Remington's old friend, Khedive Ismail, perhaps unsurprisingly, defaulted on his $1 million bill. Frustrated and facing bankruptcy, an agitated Remington went so far as to draw a sword in the office of yet another senior official who was shaking him down for a sweetener. He was told to leave Egypt immediately, "or there might be serious results."[59]

American hunters came to the Remington company's rescue, especially the "buff runners," the professional buffalo killers who then occupied the same place in the romantic imagination that World War I fighter aces, Mercury "Right Stuff" astronauts, and Special Forces commandos later would.[60]

Buffalo hunting served several purposes, aside from the visceral and the political. Buffalo meat supplied workers who were building the railroads and settlers founding towns in the new territories; their hides were used for myriad applications, including winter boots and overcoats for soldiers; and their tongues were considered a delicacy on the East Coast. Indians were angered at the liquidation of their ancient source of food and shelter, and their search for happier hunting grounds often led to clashes with either neighboring tribes, soldiers, or settlers. The arrival of hordes of rich amateurs and "sporting" incompetents merely left thousands of tongueless, meaty carcasses littering the plains. During an Arkansas trip in 1873, where the year before there had been "myriads of buffalo," observed Colonel Dodge, now "the air was foul with sickening stench, and the vast plain . . . was a dead, solitary, putrid desert. . . . The loin, the ribs, the hump, all the best and most savoury parts of the animal, are left to rot, or are eaten by wolves."[61] By the late 1880s, some think, where once up to 30 million bison had roamed, fewer than a thousand were left. Not all of these animals died by human hand: so cold was it in 1841 that the Wyoming prairie was left thickly covered in ice and millions of bison starved to death.[62] Still, Mother Nature had nothing on the Brotherhood of the Rifle.

A professional hunter could clear $10,000 a year (about $183,000 in today's dollars) once he had paid off his considerable setup and recurring costs, running at least $1,400. He needed a cook and skinners, plus a covered wagon drawn by mules or horses for hauling his treasure to the trading post, a good pony of his own costing between $250 and $500, a couple of hundred pounds of lead, thousands of primers, and hundreds of shells (if he preferred to load his own ammunition) or thousands of cartridges (if he didn't).[63] The young Wyatt Earp went into buffalo running in the early 1870s, though he was honest enough to admit that "no buffalo hunter of my acquaintance—myself, least of all—

planned his work as a crusade for civilization [against the Indians]. . . . I went into the business to make money while enjoying life that appealed to me."[64]

A hunter's most critical tool was his weapon. Anyone worth his salt used a single-shot rifle, for repeaters were still, as Smith and Wesson had found when developing their first metallic cartridges, obliged to use smaller-caliber ammunition and much less powder than single-shots in order to avoid fragmenting the bullet in the barrel owing to the enormous stresses and heat generated by rapid firing.

Repeaters lacked range, velocity, and killing ability. Thus, a Remington bullet would whiz past a cruising repeater round and travel about double its distance. For a brute as formidable as a buffalo, only a single-shot would suffice. "With the Henrys and Spencers" at any range beyond point-blank, rued Andrew Garcia the unscrupulous trader, "half of the time the buffalo did not know that you hit them."[65]

Hardened hunters regarded the traditional Indian method of riding among stampeding buffalo and killing at close range as crude, haphazard, and worse, unprofitable. To them, the whole point was to kill individually and with pinpoint accuracy while not startling a grazing herd. They devoted days to stalking the creatures and spent hours selecting a camouflaged position and patiently watching the quarry from a distance too far away for a gun's report to be heard. Then, after affixing a newfangled telescopic sight to their weapon, one shot, one kill, always to the neck or heart.[66] A single laggardly buffalo would fall unnoticed by the rest, and so mercilessly on and on until none were left. By such means the legendary buff runner Bob McRae, carrying a Remington .44-90-400 mounted with a Malcolm telescopic sight, once demolished a fifty-four-buffalo herd—in fifty-four shots.[67] Another frontiersman, shooting with regular sights, used a .45 Sharps to kill 121 buffalo in a little over three hundred shots.[68] And the aptly named Buffalo Bill, probably using his favorite Springfield, single-handedly bagged forty-eight in half an hour in a competition against a team of Pawnee scouts (who scored twenty-three).[69]

Makers of single-shot rifles adored the publicity such exploits garnered, but from a commercial standpoint, the professional market was insignificant compared to the wider, growing civilian demand for re-peaters. The leading single-shot companies consequently fell into seri-ous financial distress. The hallowed Sharps firm ended production sometime in 1881 or 1882 and disappeared.[70] By the time of Samuel's death in 1882 Remington was again deeply submerged in debt and went into receivership, whence it was bought out by Marcellus Hartley's UMC in 1888 for the knockdown price of $200,000.[71]

The general shift toward repeaters had multiple causes. Many users discovered that single-shots were too powerful and weighty for their needs and plumped instead for a nice light repeater at the local store; these switchers were often settlers or fortune-hunters, and over time they numbered in the scores of thousands. It also helped that used repeaters were cheap (the government auctioned off its surplus Henrys and Spencers for around $12 and $6 respectively, or about 20 percent of their cost price), while a customized, specialized single-shot cost significantly more.[72] Frank Collinson, a naïve seventeen-year-old Yorkshireman trav-eling out west for the first time, purchased a "ten-pound, forty-caliber, muzzle-loading rifle" from a wily outfitter but quickly discovered it was "too long and too heavy for a saddle gun." So when he reached Arkansas, he sold it to a wagon-maker and bought a repeater.[73]

Annie Oakley, who owned hundreds of shotguns, rifles, and pistols and could justly claim to be the finest exhibition shooter in the world, proved to all that switching to a repeater did not automatically mark one as an amateur. She began her career in the early 1870s using Stevens .22-caliber single-shot sporting rifles, but by the 1890s even she had converted to a .32-caliber Winchester Model 1895 lever-action and a Marlin .22 repeater.[74]

Much to honest Annie's disappointment, outlaws too were quick to adopt the repeater for professional business reasons. The troublemaking cowboys who would meet the Earps and Doc Holliday for that fatal gun-fight at the O.K. Corral were all known to be armed with products of the Winchester company.[75] James Hobbs, a notorious scalp-hunter in Arizona and Nevada, never failed to carry two Henrys for his bloody oc-cupation. In 1868, when he and his men chased one hundred Paiutes into Owens Lake (Nevada), his Henrys' combined thirty-two-shot reserve proved useful. More than half the Indians were killed thrashing in the water.[76]

Inevitably, in order to keep pace, Texas Rangers and other lawmen also started using repeaters.[77] In May 1866 Steve Venard, Nevada City's former town marshal, tracked down three outlaws who had robbed a Wells Fargo stagecoach to a steep canyon crowned by a waterfall. Clambering to the top, Venard was greeted by a Colt .44 revolver wielded by Jack Williams. Venard's trusty Henry leaped to his shoulder and drilled Williams through the heart. Nearby, Venard could see the fiend's villainous accomplice, Finn, struggling with his piece, and according to Neill Wilson's vivid *Treasure Express: Epic Days of the Wells Fargo,* he worked the trigger guard "and another half-ounce cone of lead was in firing position." This second shot was "despatched before echo of the first had caromed off the cliffs, sped upward and spattered on the canyon wall, having entered Finn's skull below the right eye and toured his skull en route." Prying the Wells Fargo bag from the late Finn's cold, dead hand, Venard sought the third man: "The next shot out of the pursuing Henry explored his heart, sent his spirit winging and his person crashing downhill into the canyon." For his heroics, the governor of California made Venard a lieutenant colonel of militia and Wells Fargo awarded him $3,000.[78]

There was something comforting about having a repeater close to hand when a man was in a tight spot. Finn Burnett, who was present at the great Hayfield Fight of 1867, witnessed the civilian D. A. Colvin in action there and believed there wasn't "another man living, or that ever lived, who has killed as many Indians in a day." The unruffled Colvin, using a Henry, "fired about 300 shots" at ranges of between 20 and 75 yards.[79]

On the narrow trail near O'Fallon's Bluffs on the South Platte River on June 12, 1867, eight herders armed with Spencers and tending 340 mules held off 125 mounted Indians "yelling and shouting like fiends" by throwing "themselves down on the ground, and commenc[ing] firing." By the time the rest of the wagon train arrived, the herders had killed at least nine of them.[80] Hearing inspiring stories like that, was there ever a tenderfoot or greenhorn who wouldn't rush to the nearest outfitter and

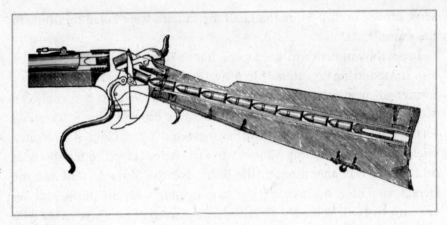

The Spencer action

plunk down his money to buy the firearm that might very well save his life?

The second factor working in the repeater's favor was Oliver Winchester, the former Connecticut shirt-maker who was now ruthlessly intent on ruling the range (and prairie). He was aided immeasurably by the travails suffered by his great rival, Christopher Spencer, in the years following the Civil War. Despite General Ripley's best efforts, by its end the federal government had bought 12,471 Spencers (plus another 94,196 carbines) while Winchester had sold just 1,731 Henrys.[81] But after 1865 Spencer's very success turned against him. With former soldiers opting to stick with their wartime Spencers—no less a personage than General Grant said they were "the best breech-loading arms" available—he found few buyers for his newer products. In 1868, Spencer already having left the company, the firm, flailing in debt, was wound up. The remaining assets—machinery, finished weapons, and patents— were bought by Winchester for $200,000. The machinery and inventory were flogged at auction for $138,000, thereby enabling Winchester to retain the rights to Spencer's inventions for the knockdown price of $62,000.[82] By such means, between 1869 and 1899, Winchester's once tiny company's share of the *total* American firearms and ammunition industry rose from 8 percent to 29 percent.[83]

As early as mid-1865, however, Winchester had begun thinking about phasing out the Henry. The treachery of its disaffected creator, Benjamin

Henry, sealed Winchester's decision to forge ahead with an updated replacement.

In the spring of 1865, while Winchester was on a sales trip to Europe, Henry, working in league with the company's secretary Charles Nott, had mounted a shareholder coup and tried to rename the firm the Henry Repeating Rifle Company. Winchester desperately fought back but could not prevent the name change. Instead he financially crippled Henry's firm by establishing his own, the Winchester Repeating Arms Company, took all the assets with him, and left Henry and Nott with all the debts. (Henry later became an independent gunsmith and died in obscurity in 1898.)[84]

For understandable reasons, Winchester wished to erase the memory of his nettlesome former mechanic's name and asked his loyal superintendent Nelson King to make improvements to the product. First to go was the Henry's somewhat annoying design that required the shooter to load cartridges into the underbarrel magazine from the muzzle end; King kept the magazine where it was but made an opening in its rear so that the operator simply pushed cartridges in and they were driven forward. Winchester claimed that his weapon, dubbed the Model 1866, could fire thirty rounds a minute.

The newly renamed "Winchester" Model 1866 went into production in August. Initially its standard round was a .40-28-200—far too light for the big-gamers—but King managed to cram in seventeen of them, as opposed to the Henry's sixteen. By the spring of 1867 the first Winchesters were being seen in the West, though they seem to have been limited-edition trial specimens. After Winchester authorized a full-scale advertising campaign in the newspapers out there, demand began to take off, then rocketed.[85] Indeed, most of the Indian warriors who used repeaters at the Little Bighorn used Winchesters—ironic testament to their popularity.[86]

The Model 1866 and its successor, the legendary Model 1873 (or "Winchester '73," Billy the Kid's weapon of choice), was popular with settlers and travelers—the company sold 100,000 of the Model 1866 alone. But it did not make inroads into the professional or military market, mostly owing to its reputation for being underpowered. Comparisons between a Winchester and a Springfield Model 1873 showed that at one hundred yards, the Springfield drilled its bullet ten inches into a block of white pine, double that of the Winchester.[87]

Hence, according to P. C. Bicknell, who accompanied a team of buffalo hunters in 1876, "the Winchester is the laughing stock among these men—they would not take one as a gift if they had to use it."[88] As late as the end of the 1880s, according to Dr. William Allen, one grizzled frontiersman named Hiram Steward "looked at my Winchester with contempt, calling it an old popgun." And with that he "slid down from his jackass, pulled his old Sharps from the sling and inserted a .44-75."[89]

Yet Steward, by that time, was in the minority, a tetchy holdout clinging to the old ways. During the mid-1870s some experienced warhorses and hunters had come around to recognizing the virtues of repeaters. In 1874 the Indiana-born and Civil War–blooded Lew Wallace (six years later he would write *Ben-Hur: A Tale of the Christ*) was already using a Winchester for up-close buffalo hunting in northern Mexico: "The time came to use my Winchester. I selected the place to shoot at—just below the shoulder . . . Goodness!"[90] Ten years later, writing in *Harper's* magazine, the accomplished huntsman G. O. Shields described his pursuit of antelopes in Montana and proudly said the once-unsayable: that he used a repeater, a Winchester.[91]

A catalyst for the hunters' change of heart had been the increasing availability of centerfire ammunition, which helped repeaters erode the single-shot's superiority in terms of power. Moreover, as the buffalo vanished from the Plains, need diminished for the single-shot's Big Fifty and its like, since the prey that remained lacked their toughness, size, and vitality. Downing medium game like elk, deer, and antelope simply did not require the heavy loads once thought necessary.

However, the military market remained stoutly impenetrable to Winchester's salesmen. Had the Indian wars—which were characterized by police actions and small-scale skirmishing, ideal conditions for repeater fire—not already begun to wind down, Winchester and his ilk might have enjoyed more success, but already officers were looking ahead to the army-on-army battles that they believed would typify the defense of American interests against European imperialism. Would short-range repeaters really prove superior to well-aimed single-shot rifles in the maelstrom of war? They suspected not.

For this reason the ambiguous lessons raised by an obscure battle fought between Russians and Turks in 1877 at Plevna, a town in northern Bulgaria, exerted a powerful grip on America's brightest military minds, popular commentators on army affairs, and the highest reaches of command alike.

Galvanized by pan-Slavic feeling, refreshed by the recent abolition of serfdom, angered by Turkish atrocities, and roused by centuries of war between Christianity and Islam in the Balkans, Tsar Alexander II declared war on Turkey on April 24, 1877. Some fifteen thousand Turks under Field Marshal Osman Pasha readied to meet them at Plevna.

Though no Americans were involved in the hostilities, and no American interests were endangered, Plevna would be the first time that American weapons would be put on vivid display before the world. Indeed, Hartley's UMC factory at Bridgeport had actually supplied both sides with ammunition because Russians and Turks alike had long known that a war was in the offing and had seen to securing the millions of cartridges that they expected to use. Hartley had helpfully separated two workshops, one devoted to Russian cartridges, and the other to Turkish, each overseen by its empire's official representatives—who, when they met in the corridor, treated each other with a distinctly formal coldness.[92]

Oliver Winchester, having also seen war in Turkey's future, dealt only with the Ottomans: he had opened contacts with Constantinople as early as 1870. Following a gift of sixteen specially made Winchesters—including a gold-plated one and five silver-plated—to the Supreme Council of War, the company received an order for 50,000 Model 1866s from the Turkish government. Thirty-nine thousand were sent, and of them between 8,000 and 12,000 would be present at Plevna, where they would play a key role in the fighting.

Winchester was also responsible for brokering the sale of Peabody-Martini rifles to the Turkish government. These firearms had an interesting backstory. In 1862 Mr. Henry Peabody of Boston had brought an elegant, slimline rifle to the (in)attention of General Ripley at Ordnance. Rebuffed, he sold the patent to the Providence Tool Company of Rhode Island.[93] At the very end of the Civil War, the authorities toyed with the idea of adopting the Peabody as the standard infantry arm but decided instead to keep the Springfield.[94] The Providence Tool Company, still hoping to make a profit, offered its weapon for sale abroad and enjoyed modest success among the lesser powers, such as Switzerland, which purchased fifteen thousand of them.[95]

In the late 1860s Friedrich von Martini, a Swiss, used one of those fifteen thousand as the basis for his own version incorporating the firing action into the breechblock, patented it under his own name, and licensed it to the British. In turn, the British had one of their own technicians, Alexander Henry (no direct relation to Winchester's benighted Benjamin Henry), make further adaptations to ensure its suitability for army use. That gun, the .45 Martini-Henry, would be the official weapon of the British Empire for some three decades. It would find immortality at the defense of Rorke's Drift against the Zulus, an event majestically depicted in the Michael Caine film *Zulu*. In *another* Caine (and Sean Connery) movie, *The Man Who Would Be King*, the British troops carry Martini-Henrys. And Rudyard Kipling's poem "Fuzzy-Wuzzy," which celebrates the doomed, heroic Sudanese warriors who broke a British square at the battle of Abu Klea, concedes that while "our orders was to break you, an' of course we went an' did," we had "Martinis, an' it wasn't 'ardly fair."

Henry Peabody was unamused to hear about Herr Martini's appropriation of his design and sued the British government for compensation. He lost, the government position being that his issue was rightly with Martini, not with London. Here Oliver Winchester's patriotic (and commercial) instincts flared up. Using his contacts in Constantinople, he arranged on behalf of the Providence Tool Company a stupendous order for 600,000 Peabodys, though even he could not avoid paying a royalty of two shillings per gun to Martini, much to the original inventor's annoyance. The Turkish version was thus unavoidably dubbed the Peabody-Martini, in itself an irritant to Alexander Henry, who then sued the Providence Tool Company, which pointedly ignored his suit. By the time of the Russo-Turkish war, about 442,240 of the Peabody-Martinis had been shipped to Turkey. (Owing to a later financial crisis, the Turks reneged on payment for the rest of the 600,000, and the Providence Tool Company lurched into bankruptcy in 1885.)[96]

Winchester, as usual, did very well for himself out of these arms deals.

Not only was a lavish commission undoubtedly involved for arranging the Peabody contract, but in the early 1870s his ammunition division had been embroiled in an expensive patent-infringement battle with its main competitor, Hartley's UMC. Planning to give Hartley one in the eye, the Winchester company acted as a covert cutout for the British government (which was unofficially backing the Turks against the Russians) and supplied 280 million empty but primed rimfire cartridges to the Sublime Porte between 1874 and 1877. However, Winchester and Hartley each soon realized that if their rivalry turned so bitter that third-party competitors saw an opening and entered the fray, they would both lose, so the two firms soon came to terms on their patent problems. For all concerned, the sensible thing to do was to cooperate and ensure that the UMC-backed centerfire—which Winchester first integrated into the Model '73—became the standard form of ammunition here and abroad.[97]

While Winchester and UMC were making peace, the Turks bravely awaited the Russian onslaught. In the trenches outside Plevna, Osman Pasha had placed thin lines of skirmishers as a decoy to lure the enemy closer. When 7,500 Russian infantry advanced on July 18, they quickly put the Turks to flight. Assuming the town was lightly defended, they pushed forward into Plevna. All was quiet. But behind each door and on each roof and below each window lurked a Turk armed with a Winchester. The Russians, armed with dated but serviceable single-shot rifles, plodded forward. At Osman Pasha's signal, every man broke cover and poured in round after round at point-blank range. The two Russian commanders were among the first to fall. Within twenty minutes, in a horrific scene reminiscent of Braddock's defeat and of Custer's last stand, no fewer than 74 Russian officers and 2,771 of their men were slaughtered in the crowded alleys. Turkish losses were twelve killed, 30 wounded.

Stunned by the defeat, Grand Duke Nicholas, supreme commander of the Russian forces, ordered his generals to attack or die. When they explained that the Turks, having received reinforcements, now outnumbered them 50,000 to 26,000, Nicholas dismissed their fears. On July 30 the Russians were again ready to force the issue with a hopeless plan to attack from the north and east simultaneously. Quite how the two distant wings were expected to communicate and coordinate with each other was never discussed. Meanwhile Osman Pasha had distributed his men in three staggered lines on the reverse slopes of hills and ridges overlooking open plains. Carefully dug in, they would have ample opportunity to fire at the enemy as he crossed the country toward them.

In the north, the extreme left of the Russian advance, General Mikhail Skobelev's Cossacks reached within six hundred yards of the Turkish positions but came under withering long-range rifle fire and withdrew. On the inside left Prince Schachowskoi's lancers and infantry managed to occupy the lightly held village of Radisovo. The emboldened prince decided to press on and lined up his two brigades to assault the Turkish lines. To the Russians' surprise, men began dropping at about 2,500 yards' range, with Peabody-Martini rifle bullets embedded in their torsos. Since no shoulder arm could achieve that range, the Turks had evidently elevated their rifles midway between zenith and horizon to achieve maximum trajectory. When the enemy advanced, the Turks lowered their rifles' angle as their officers accurately estimated and called out the diminishing range. At 2,000 yards, the casualty rates started rising fast, and at 600 the once-orderly Russian line was looking distinctly ragged. At that point they were easy targets for men equipped with movable sights.

Beside each Turk lay a Winchester, fully loaded, with five hundred spare rounds within reach. At 200 yards the Turkish officers commanded their men to lay aside their single-shots and use the repeaters. The Russians came on, bayonets fixed. With the Winchesters squirting bullets, the Russians were suffering enormous losses, yet goaded by their officers, they kept advancing. At 50 yards the Turks fell back to the second line of entrenchments and continued firing. Now the Russian push was stalling, as had the attack from the east. General Baron Nikolai Krudener, in charge of the reserves, threw the Serpoukhof Regiment into the center to restore his side's flagging spirits. They got no closer than 100 yards. By seven that evening, harassed by Turkish sharpshooters, Prince Schachowskoi's forces were in full retreat, and every one of his bodyguards lay dead on the field. The prince dispatched a rider to Skobelev with the panicked message "Extricate yourself as best you can. My companies (originally 200 strong) are coming back 5 and 10 men strong!" Later that evening the Russian wounded were killed by the Turks: Turks did not take prisoners.

The official Russian report on the day's fighting declared that "Turkish rifle fire was infernal on the flanks and center and seemed to increase greatly as our men neared the trenches." Tsarist losses this time dwarfed even those of July 18: 169 officers and 7,136 enlisted, fully 30 percent of all the troops committed to action.

On September 7 the Russians again gamely attacked. Now they were determined to crack this small but exceedingly troublesome nut at Plevna. Joined by Romanian units, the Russians now numbered 80,000, divided into two divisions, each of 40,000. Digging in to the north, south, and east, their artillery bombarded the Turkish positions for four days nonstop but killed few of the enemy. The Turks were entrenched in zigzag trenches fifteen inches wide; nothing but a direct hit could hurt them. The battle's third phase was virtually a repeat of the second: long-range fire followed by close action with Winchesters—only this time losses increased to 300 officers and 12,500 men, with another 56 Romanian officers and 2,500 men added to the butcher's bill. The sole bright spot was Skobelev's storming of two Turkish redoubts in the south, but he was soon forced to relinquish them, losing 8,000 men—half his force—in the process.

Russian doggedness, understandably, was faltering, but the Romanians had not yet had the stuffing knocked out of them. It took more than a month, but their sappers eventually succeeded in burrowing under one of the largest Turkish redoubts. The Turks, unfortunately, were well aware of this and waited until the Romanians expectantly approached their position before opening up with their Winchesters. In the subsequent twenty-minute fight some 400,000 bullets were launched at the Romanians, who retreated with the loss of 1,000 men. This .25 percent hit rate was not impressive by traditional American military standards, but by now the Turkish high command was so impressed by these magical, murderous Winchesters that they ordered 140,000 more from the maker.

The latest bloodbath was quite enough for the Russians and Romanians. They mounted no more assaults. Instead, they besieged Plevna and waited for tens of thousands of reinforcements to arrive. When they did, their combined army had swollen to 150,000; this against the 40,000 defenders of the town. By December, Osman Pasha knew he must abandon his positions. On his way out he surprised the Russians with a beautifully planned frontal assault, but the attack nevertheless failed and the marshal was captured. He was visited by Grand Duke Nicholas, who was curious to meet this extraordinary commander. "I congratulate you on your defense of Plevna. It is one of the most splendid exploits in history," he proclaimed before returning his foe's surrendered sword.[98]

Plevna and 30,000 Russian casualties demonstrated the superiority of American armaments to an astonished world. Before the Civil War the great majority of American weapons shipped abroad had been Colt revolvers, but the carnage inflicted by the Winchester repeaters, Peabody-Martini single-shots, and UMC/Winchester cartridges (in addition to the hard-earned American reputation for delivering high-quality merchandise on time and on budget) helped boost foreign demand to unprecedented levels. Between 1867 and 1880 U.S. companies sold close to $100 million worth of weaponry and ammunition to eager foreign customers, close to $2 billion at today's prices.[99] The positive effect on the balance of trade of this influx of money and credit helped lay the foundations of American economic power over the coming century.

It could not have come at a better time for Winchester. Between 1868 and 1872 domestic sales had been buoyant, but in 1873 a national depression lasting until about 1879 was hurting manufacturers in every industry. To stimulate demand at home, Winchester had been forced to slash prices: the cost of a Winchester '73 nearly halved from $50 in 1874 to $28 six years later, and for the Model 1876 Winchester the company was never able to charge more than $32.[100] The foreign deals certainly helped Winchester, and other gun-makers, reduce their surpluses and stabilize prices while simultaneously serving as portable advertisements for U.S. manufacturing prowess.[101] Three years after the battle Winchester died a happy man.

Military observers drew conflicting lessons from the Plevna fight. Advocates of the repeater pointed to the Winchesters' lethality at close range while conceding that success was contingent on having hundreds of millions of cartridges available to feed their greedy maws. Alternatively, one could highlight the accuracy of the single-shots' long-range fire, an advantage that broke the enemy's spirit and disrupted his assaults before they came anywhere near bayonet range. The Winchesters, according to this interpretation, merely mopped up *already demoralized* troops. In many respects, this debate echoed the older one between supporters of rapid-firing muskets sweeping the enemy's ranks at one hundred yards or so, and those who preferred to rely on riflemen's ability to hit their targets dead-on many hundreds of yards away.

The pity of it all was that there seemed to be no right answer, no obviously correct lesson to learn. Or perhaps there was: combine the virtues of accuracy and firepower in a single infantry weapon rather than emphasizing one *or* the other. Easier said than done, as the United States Army was finding out.

The Springfield
Model 1873

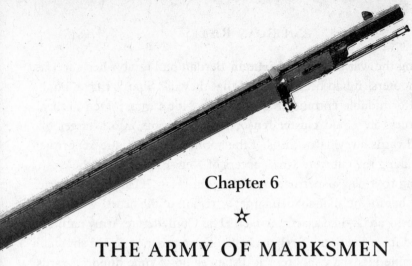

Chapter 6

⋆

THE ARMY OF MARKSMEN
AND THE SOLDIER'S FAITH

Officially, at the close of the Civil War and for decades afterward, the U.S. Army was committed to the single-shot rifle. Though many officers in the field profoundly disagreed with the policy and purchased their own repeaters, it remained a fact nonetheless that every single infantry recruit was issued with a standard Springfield rifle. The Ordnance Department said they must be, and the Ordnance Department made the rules. The department's creed was based on one unshakable conviction: that the American soldier was the finest marksman on earth. He did not require a repeater because he hit what he aimed at—with a single, lethal shot.

If anyone disagreed, the department would recite the figures favorably comparing American hit rates with European and British ones. As the experience of the Civil War testified, however, these figures were severely flawed. True, generally speaking and averaged out, American soldiers really were superior to their overseas equivalents, but the quality of their marksmanship was by no means universal. Some units were uniformly excellent; some poorly performing outfits could have their hit rates goosed by the arrival of a few talented killers; and still others were unbelievably incompetent. The latter were more common than many realized.

During the war the Union's Hiram Berdan had established the U.S. Sharpshooters (it had been intended that they use Sharps rifles), but he had set formidable entrance requirements. Not a man joined his regiment unless he could cluster ten consecutive shots into a target two hundred yards away. Two-thirds of the applicants failed; the majority of those making the cut were "the hunters of New-England and the West," according to a newspaperman attending the trials. That same reporter noticed that the human-shaped target's "region of the heart" was particularly perforated—like a sieve, in fact.[1] The Confederate Army naturally benefited from the South's relatively greater number of skilled shooters, and it trained its sharpshooters at distances up to nine hundred yards. Accurate records were kept for each man's performance, and those congenitally unable to improve their scores were sent back to their regular units.[2] But outside the specialized units, the experience of Captain George W. Wingate was more usual: he discovered that most of his New York company couldn't hit a barrel lid at one hundred yards and so was forced to use an imported British manual on riflemanship to teach them the rudiments of shooting.

Escaping Ordnance's notice was the fact that their fine theories had long ceased to bear much resemblance to the reality of military training and campaigning. Line officers (those commanding troops that were engaged in fighting or other operations on the frontier or in the field) ignored, by and large, the dictates and regulations issued by Ordnance staff officers. The farther a commander was from Washington, the less likely he was to pay any attention to his colleagues in the capital.

Even before the war officers overseeing the western territories had given marksmanship training short shrift. Regarded as a quaint affectation of the East Coast staff elite, "target practice" before the mid-1850s had often consisted of a soldier whose watch was over firing a round at a crude bull's-eye painted on a guardhouse. (And even that was only because live weapons had to be deactivated after guard duty—by laboriously using a screwlike instrument to "pull" the ball out—so that soldiers saved time by pulling the trigger instead.) Wrote a private in the Second Dragoons, so few officers believed the men required any more practice with their weapons that, in his five months of wearing "Uncle

Sam's livery," he had been taken out for proper target shooting just twice.[3]

In 1854 officers were ordered to train their men with the new rifle-muskets being issued, but they were given no means of standardizing results. Many simply invented their own standards, which happened, for instance, at the forts along the Rio Grande, where a target eight feet tall and eighteen inches wide—presumably representing a gangly beanpole of an Indian—was used and any hits were reported to Washington as "bull's-eyes." Even then two-thirds of the rounds fired at one hundred yards missed. A few companies actually used blanks. Similarly, the colonel in charge of Fort Laramie on the northern Plains reported that about half his troops might one day "become expert enough to shoot at a crowd," while the rest could be counted as just moderate shots.[4]

Three years later a captain in the Tenth Infantry with sound connections to the Ordnance Department, Henry Heth, was given the task of producing a uniform manual of small-arms instruction. It was unoriginal stuff but was still greatly needed, considering that in 1855 an inspection of 325 recruits' rifles at Santa Fe revealed that 140 of them had been loaded with the ball first and powder second.[5]

Heth copied a French textbook that was intended for teaching recruits wholly unfamiliar with firearms, ballistics, or the basic principles of shooting. First it explained to the soldier how to assemble and disassemble his weapon, giving the names of its parts, illustrated what a cartridge was, and so forth. Then it described how to point a rifle at a simple target across the room. There followed instructions on maintaining the proper firing stance and on how to squeeze a trigger without throwing off one's aim. The next stage took place outdoors: an officer placed a man at various distances and asked the recruits to gauge how far away he was, the aim being to teach them to judge range using relative size as a yardstick. Only when they had passed the test would recruits be allowed to fire their rifles using live ammunition at six-foot-high, twenty-two-inch-wide targets set at distances from one hundred to four hundred yards.

Heth's manual was certainly a leap forward, but the outbreak of war put paid to its widespread adoption (and it didn't help that Heth joined the Confederacy). During that conflict a new soldier's first shot often coincided with his first battle, and in any case, the fierce frontal attacks popular among generals ensured that the cultivation of marksmanship was given little emphasis.[6]

By the war's end and well into the 1870s, many line officers were even less convinced of marksmanship's merits, believing that the focus on single-shot accuracy was undermining their men's fighting efficiency by restricting their ability to rapid-fire. During a firefight, stipulated General John Gibbon of the Seventh Infantry, anything "beyond one hundred or one hundred and fifty yards . . . is pretty much a matter of chance."[7] In the heat of battle his men were naturally more interested in firing off as many rounds as they could, usually at close range, than in scoring hits at one thousand yards.

Gibbon's words were borne out on June 17, 1876, when General George Crook's two thousand foot and horse clashed with the Sioux and Cheyenne at the Rosebud River. In the vicious melee that followed his forces hardly had a chance to take a bead on the enemy. The mounted Indians swept in close and very fast; Captain Anson Mills wrote that they "overwhelmed them, charging bodily and rapidly through the soldiers, knocking them from their horses with lances and knives, dismounting and killing them, cutting the arms of several off at the elbows in the midst of the fight and carrying them away."[8] Amid the stormy sea of men and neighing beasts, the soldiers had to fire as fast as they humanly could. Sergeant Louis Zinger of Company C, Third Cavalry, recalled that at the beginning of the fight each soldier carried 150 rounds; by its end, they were down to five rounds apiece.[9] Company C's fifty-eight men alone had fired something like 8,400 shots in fewer than six hours, while in total Crook's force blew through about 25,000 rounds. For this remarkable expenditure of lead and powder, just thirteen Indians lay dead on the field (though Crazy Horse later pegged casualties at 36 killed and 63 wounded).[10]

In that kind of desperate environment, Ordnance's precious hit-rate statistics were worthless; what counted was raw firepower—which inevitably meant shockingly low scores. Eight days after the Rosebud clash, at the Battle of the Little Bighorn, the doomed troopers of Custer's Seventh expended 38,030 rounds (plus about 2,954 pistol rounds) to kill roughly sixty Indians and wound a hundred more.[11] These figures equate to a minuscule 0.16 kill-rate (excluding the wounded and pistol shots).

Postwar marksmanship training was, if possible, even more lax than it had been in the 1850s. First, owing to budgetary constraints, the army decided to restrict each soldier to ten rounds per month for practice and left it to individual commanders to decide whether to bother training their men.[12] Many did not—with predictable results. At the Battle of Slim Buttes, for instance, a colonel remarked of his own skirmishers that "they couldn't hit a flock of barns . . . much less an Indian skipping about like a flea."[13] "Compared with the white hunter of the plains, the Indian is a wretched shot. He is about equal to the United States soldier, being deficient for the same reason—lack of practice," remarked Gibbon sardonically.[14] Into this breach stepped William Church, the editor of the *Army and Navy Journal.*

In 1870, alarmed by the army's insouciance, Church launched a campaign in his journal (which he would edit until 1917) to expose what he believed was the shameful decline in American shooting prowess. He took particular delight in publishing not only embarrassingly critical analyses of units' performances on the range but letters from officers whistleblowing about their men's terrible aim. Bolstered by the reaction he had inspired, Church asked a friend, George Wingate—the very same man who had discovered that his company couldn't hit a barrel lid during the war—to publish a series of six articles on rifle practice and target shooting to enlighten his military readers. Those issues quickly sold out. Wingate, a thirty-year-old New York lawyer, then published them as a book, *Manual for Target Practice,* which went through at least seven editions and caused a surge of interest in marksmanship.[15]

From the beginning, concerned that Americans' enthusiasm for all things martial had dimmed after four blood-drenched years of warfare and 620,000 fatalities, Church and Wingate sought to create a forward-thinking, positive ethos around the figure of the American sharpshooter. Unlike the ill-trained cannon fodder of the Union and Confederate armies, the sharpshooter would bypass the sordid, squalid battlefield and fight his battles cleanly and humanely, with a single shot to the head at eight hundred yards. If Americans adopted marksmanship as their creed, the duration and intensity of future conflicts would be greatly reduced, leaving no more thousands of veterans without jaws, eyes, legs, or arms. The cult of accuracy that Church and Wingate nurtured was a *progressive* one—not in political, but in military terms—somewhat analogous to today's theories about technological superiority erasing the need for traditional means of fighting.

The duo drew inspiration from the Germans, who had themselves recently fought several wars of unification and had won them speedily and bloodlessly (at least compared to the Civil War). Impressed by their prowess, and hoping that some of the magic might rub off, the army even began specifically looking for German recruits. An officer in the Fourth Cavalry, while believing the Irish to be "more intelligent and resourceful as a rule," thought that "if a German was fit to be a noncommissioned officer he usually made a good one—he was feared by the men, did not curry favor, but was rigid in carrying out orders."[16] Similarly, in 1872 the army started to copy Prussian style for its dress uniforms, and it outfitted the cavalry and artillery with German spiked helmets—better known as *Pickelhauben*—sporting a metal eagle and a horsehair plume (yellow for cavalry, red for artillery).[17]

In Church and Wingate's opinion, the Germans had clean hands, virtuous minds, and pure hearts; one could easily extol the similarities between Prussianism and Puritanism. The two countries' standards of morality and work habits were alike, both were predominantly Protestant, and they shared a federal political system. (True, the Germans were ruled by an emperor, but according to George Bancroft, the American "envoy extraordinary and minister plenipotentiary" to Berlin between 1867 and 1874, he observed republican niceties.) Among intellectuals such German philosophers as Hegel and Marx were coming into vogue, and perhaps most important the "Iron Chancellor" and architect of German unification, Otto von Bismarck, had been sufficiently foresighted during the Civil War to have backed the Union.[18]

Napoleon III of France, conversely, had played his cards disastrously. Instinctively siding with the more "aristocratic" South, the emperor had further inflamed tensions with the Lincoln administration by toppling the U.S.-backed president Benito Juárez and placing Archduke Maximilian of Habsburg on the Mexican throne. Napoleon's adventurism was soon rewarded with Maximilian's execution, all of which left a sour taste in many American officers' mouths. General Sherman, tired of hearing that the postwar U.S. Army should adopt, as in days gone by, French doctrine and standards, remarked that "our people are not French but American and our army should be organized and maintained upon a model of our own, and not copied after that of the French, who differ from us so essentially."[19]

Napoleon III's humiliating defeat in 1870 at the hands of Bismarck's Prussians was greeted joyously, or perhaps with a scintilla of schadenfreude, throughout the United States.[20] "Anything that knocks the nonsense out of Johnny Crapaud will be a blessing to the world," as James Russell Lowell had commented to Charles Eliot Norton just before the war.[21] The French, already suffering from a reputation for dandyism—many Americans were adamantly convinced that French officers wore saucy makeup—suffered still more when measured against their warlike neighbors to the east.[22] At about this time the seemingly ineradicable "feminine" stereotype of France—fashion-obsessed, pretentious, elegant, brittle, frivolous—yet again bloomed.[23] Indeed, compared to *Colt* or *Winchester*, even the name of their army rifle sounded a bit girly: *chassepot.*

Given the Germanophilia of the era, it was hardly surprising that William Church looked to the *Schützenbünde*—social and fraternal clubs for avid shooters—to save the American tradition of fine shooting. These organizations were made up of German-Americans or recent immigrants who had brought their country's hunting traditions along with them; in this sense they were descendants of the eighteenth-century emigrants to Pennsylvania who had created the Jäger-Kentucky rifle tradition in the first place.[24] The *Schützenbünde* held dinners, fairs with merry-go-rounds and singers, and popular shooting competitions. Members gloried in medals and secret handshakes, and sundry Rhine maidens bestowed kisses and garlands on those anointed *König* (king) of the competitions. The largest *Schützenbünde* were especially prominent in the cities of the East Coast and in those with significant Germanic populations (Chicago, Milwaukee, and Cincinnati, for instance). New York mayor John Hoffman was proud to declare that the upright behavior of *Schützenbünde* members proved that "love of the rifle is not incompatible with respect for the law."

Encouraged by the success of the *Manual for Target Practice* and inspired by the Schützenbünde, Church and Wingate conceived a bold plan to introduce marksmanship to the general public. They approached New York National Guard officers to help them set up an organization they called the National Rifle Association, which they founded on November 21, 1871.[25]

The NRA and the nascent National Guard were bound to share close genetic connections. Not only would Wingate become president of the National Guard Association (established in 1879), but originally both began as fraternal organizations; their officers were mostly upper-middle-class gentlemen in the industrial cities of the North; and their membership quickly spread across the country, altering their character and composition. Perhaps most important, their cardinal principles were virtually identical. Both believed "in rifle practice [to promote] manliness, healthfulness, self-reliance, coolness, nerve and skill."[26]

With Church as vice president and Wingate as secretary (and Civil War general Ambrose Burnside, the inventor of a rifle himself, briefly installed as president), the association was granted $25,000 by the state legislature to purchase a rifle range. The NRA agreed to raise an additional $5,000, and the cities of Brooklyn and New York chipped in $5,000 each.[27]

Colonel Henry Shaw, charged with finding a suitable piece of land for the new rifle range, bought a plot owned by the Central and North Side Railroad of Long Island for $26,250. Originally the site of a farm run by the Creed family, its seventy-acre flat expanse of brambles and grass resembled an English moor, thought Shaw, who christened it Creedmoor. Its 1,200-yard length could easily accommodate a pavilion and a spectacular thousand-yard range. On June 21, 1873, Wingate fired a few rifle shots at an iron target, officially opening the range. What was intended to be the high temple of target shooting was at first used almost exclusively by New York Guardsmen. Within the month, however, NRA shooters held their first Creedmoor match, the winner—shooting at five hundred yards—being John Bodine of Highland, New York.[28]

Meanwhile in Britain, where target shooting as a sport was longer established, an Irish team jubilantly beat the English and Scottish squads. The Irish victory counted as a major upset, for the English were traditionally regarded (at least by themselves) as the best shots in the world. Having achieved the highest score ever seen at Wimbledon, the Irish then vanquished Canada and Australia and were considered unbeatable. Their muzzle-loaders—you could always tell the old-school shooters by their antiquarian preferences—had been specially made for them by John Rigby, the finest gunsmith in Dublin (and also a member of the team) and were equipped with exquisitely sensitive Vernier elevation sights and wind-gauge scales.

Looking for fresh laurels but unaware that the NRA existed, the Irish captain, Major Arthur Leech (or Leach), issued a plucky challenge to the "Riflemen of America" in the pages of the *New York Herald* on November 22, 1873: one six-man team (plus a nonshooting captain) versus another, using only domestically made rifles, at ranges of 800, 900, and 1,000 yards. Despite its inexperience, the NRA's sixty-two-member Amateur Rifle Club could not refuse the good-hearted provocation and canvassed widely for the best riflemen to come to Creedmoor and give the cocky Irish a lesson in how to shoot.

The slack response sorely disappointed the NRA. Most of the newspapers in the West had carried its advertisements, but hardly a doughty frontiersman replied. Given the distance they were expected to travel at their own expense for a mere competition, this may not have been so surprising; but the appearance of the Winchester Models 1866 and 1873 also meant that the repeater was gaining adherents and that fewer men did know how to shoot.

Over subsequent heats the thirty men who volunteered were winnowed down to seven. Wingate served as captain; the others were Colonel Bodine (who had won the 1873 competition), General Dakin, Lieutenant Fulton, Colonel Gildersleeve, Mr. L. Hepburn, and Mr. Yale. (These ranks were mostly honorific, dating from the Civil War and Guard duty.)[29] The question arose, which rifles to use? American gunmakers came through for their boys: Remington and Sharps, desperate to claw ground back from Winchester, turned out special customized breech-loaders, both firing .44-550-90 loads. The Amateurs split equally in their choice of rifle: Bodine, Fulton, and Hepburn selected Remingtons, while Yale, Gildersleeve, and Dakin picked the Sharps. The sights were of excellent quality. The front sight was minutely adjustable for wind, and the rear included precision-adjustment scales. Part of the assembly was adapted for optimum sighting in different weather conditions.[30]

By this time, to Church and Wingate's delight, the upcoming match was unexpectedly attracting national interest. In so many ways it made for prime entertainment. The Americans were certainly the underdogs, so their even accepting the Irish challenge had a charming element of "supremest American cheek," as *Forest and Stream* magazine put it.

Unfortunately, what the NRA had originally thought would be a fine opportunity to demonstrate the progressive benefits of marksmanship was interpreted rather differently by the media. Many newspapers pitched the story as a tale of gruff, grizzled Americans up against effete foreigners. The editorialists at Chicago's *Inter-Ocean* enthused that while the Irish "have been practicing under scientific teachers, and popping away at a bull's-eye in a carefully constructed gallery, our boys have been shooting buffaloes upon the plains or taking a wild turkey on the wing." (This wasn't exactly true, considering the absence of actual frontiersmen on the team.) The match at Creedmoor would "be a contest between trained efficiency and native skill, between the dainty hand of the city and the rough grasp of the woodsman." (Again, that was not exactly true, given that a large number of NRA members were New Yorkers.)

Accordingly, the press made much of the "aristocratic" Irish versus the self-made American businessmen. In fact, the Irish team wasn't a particularly noble one, consisting as it did of three merchants, two gunmakers, and a jeweler alongside just two country gents. But an unfortunate photograph of them spoke a great deal more than a thousand words: looking for all the world as if they'd just taken a break from administering their sprawling estates, the Irish were lounging around in tailored shooting jackets nursing hugely expensive, custom-made rifles. They presented a jarring contrast to the Americans, who were outfitted in identical suits and appeared suitably serious. Among the Americans, the papers loved to point out, only Dakin did not work for a living, and that was solely because he had retired. The gunsmith Hepburn was promoted as a humble mechanic who had made good through his own efforts and talents, whereas his unfortunate Irish opposite, Rigby, was cast as a haughty plutocrat who owned a large gun company.

Even so, the tensions of the past could not wholly be erased. In the press, westerners carped at the ascendancy of easterners on the team; eastern newspapers chortled that the New York boys excelled at the "intellectual" sport of riflery while westerners dumbly plinked at tin cans and massacred Indians; and southerners, infuriated by Reconstruction and ignoring a plea from the NRA to come to New York "to revive the feelings of fraternity between North and South," simply refused to attend.

Intrigued by the sensational reports of a world-shaking showdown, more than five thousand people traveled to Creedmoor on September 26 to cheer their heroes. The rules were straightforward: The sharpshooters were allowed no practice or sighting shots, and no artificial rests. Each rifleman was to fire fifteen shots at three-foot-square bull's-eyes set at 800, 900, and 1,000 yards; the bull's-eye was in the middle of a "center" (six-foot-square) section, which in turn was surrounded by an "outer" area extending three feet on either side. In total, the target measured six feet high by twelve feet across. Shooters would earn two points for every shot in the "outer" area, three in the "center," and four for the bull's-eye. Thus, the highest possible score for a set of fifteen shots would be 60 points, and a team's perfect score would be 360.

After the first eight-hundred-yard round, the Americans were in the lead, 326 to 317, but the bookies following the telegraphic results around the world weren't surprised, since they had been heavily favored at the shortest range. During the second round, however, the Irish pulled off a 312-to-310 win. The third and last round proved the hairiest. Milner, for Ireland, made a rare and terrible mistake when he scored a bull's-eye—on the wrong target. Zero points. But thereafter the Irish scored almost perfect bull's-eyes, compensating for Milner's error. Then only the American, "Old Reliable" Bodine, was left to shoot. The bookies' nails must have been bitten to the quick, because after fourteen excellent shots, the score was Ireland 931, America 930. Everything—the whole match, and a colossal number of wagers—hinged on Bodine's very last shot.

And that was when he, parched on this hot and humid summer's day, asked for a sip of ginger beer.[31] A teammate passed him an unopened, and inadvertently shaken, bottle. When Bodine pried off the cap, the glass exploded, sending shards of glass into his hand. Gore flowed from the shredded veins, staining his starched white cuffs. How could he now hope to save American honor?

In one of those immortal sporting moments, as delicate ladies swooned and hearty men gasped, Bodine unflappably withdrew a large handkerchief from his pocket and wrapped it tightly around his injured hand. Taking his usual shooting position—he favored lying prone—he stared down the Remington's long barrel through his pale-blue shooting spectacles, keenly aware of the breeze and the deceptive shadows cast by the clouds. Then, holding his breath, he slowly pulled the trigger. *Crack.* For four seconds the bullet traveled the thousand yards. Then a whiff of white smoke puffed from the target. "He's on!" roared the crowd when they saw the bull's-eye. The Americans had won by three points.[32]

The Irish graciously admitted defeat, and the Americans were cheered as conquering heroes. Target shooting instantly became the most popular sport in the country and was practiced with consummately "scientific" skill and seriousness (exactly the qualities for which the Irish had been lambasted). Within a month of the match there were no fewer than four rifle clubs in Chicago alone; within a year dozens more sprang up as far afield as Florida and California. There was even one in Peru, established by American expatriates. The New York Rifle Club was by far the most opulent. Equipped with a parlor, a piano, "soft yielding carpet, heavy window curtains, elaborate chandelier, bronzes, and works of art," the club was intended solely for the wealthy—the same people who had, just a short time previously, regarded rifle users as incorrigible philistines living in backwoods shacks. At Harvard, Yale, Columbia, and the other great universities, students founded rifle clubs, though they were allowed to fire only short-range, low-power bullets. The restrictions didn't blunt their keenness, and by 1888 some fifty schools and colleges were receiving government-supplied ammunition and teaching marks-manship—considered to be the character-building touchstone of cool nerves, grace under pressure, and steely discipline.

Preachers, pleased that abstinence from alcohol and tobacco im-

The "cult of accuracy" and riflemanship became a national phe-
nomenon after the Civil War. Between 1870 and 1885, when the
craze reached its height, popular songs were whistled, strummed,
hummed, and danced to across the country. Dating from 1880,
this example—which requires five rifle shots to ring out, like the
booming cannons in Tchaikovsky's 1812 Overture—*commem-*
orates the victorious Americans, but there were also, among
many others, "The Gallant Rifles Parade" (a jaunty quickstep),
"Maguire's Rifle Corps," the "International Rifle-Match" (a
waltz sportingly dedicated to the English team), the "National
Rifle Quickstep," the "American Rifle Team March," and, of
course, the "American Rifle Team Polka."

proved target scores, lauded shooting's practitioners in their Sunday sermons, and matches were held in church basements around the country.
Forest and Stream commented that "it has become quite the fashion for

ladies to practice rifle shooting." Soon all-women clubs were flourishing in half a dozen cities. Female participation in the manly pursuit—which required the same type of masculine, practical clothes that the bicycling craze would subsequently popularize—might have even encouraged the nascent suffragette movement. Unlike bicycling, though, shooting, according to the *Chicago Field,* allowed women to defend themselves and their families against criminals and as such was a worthy endeavor in its own right.[33]

Church and Wingate had scored a spectacular triumph by making the cult of accuracy an essential creed of Americanism.[34] At last the army began to pay attention. Before Creedmoor, Wingate—mindful of the military's sharply reduced budgets—had advocated using cheaper, reduced-charge cartridges for practice and had nevertheless failed to interest the Department of War; but two years later the department agreed to double the number of training rounds per month to twenty. That figure was still nowhere near enough to turn men into marksmen, but it did allow commanders to hoard their monthly allotment and use them all at once if they wished. Some fortunate soldiers were thus enabled to fire their annual allocation of 240 rounds over the course of an intense day or two.[35] It was a small change but one, at least, in the right direction.

The percolating influence of the military reformer General Emory Upton elevated marksmanship to the pinnacle of army concerns. Originally of a New York farming family, Upton had fought a brilliant war. An extreme rarity in that he served in all three branches of the army (artillery, cavalry, and infantry), he achieved notable success in each. After the war he returned to West Point to teach cadets. There he produced *A New System of Infantry Tactics, Double and Single Rank* (1867), a brilliant manual that paid little heed to the traditional French influences but instead described a system of tactics that exploited the new breech-loading rifles' power in a specifically American environment. He urged the end of heavy, clumsy line formations advancing across open ground to engage the enemy with the bayonet, and promoted in their place a squad-based "skirmish" formation consisting of light teams that could march, deploy, wheel, and shoot in teams of four. A sergeant or corporal would be in charge of several squads separated from one another, and the "line" that advanced toward the enemy would be a ragged, staggered one that would minimize casualties from artillery and defensive fire.

On the strength of his book, Upton, still only in his midthirties, was sent abroad in 1875 for an official tour of the world's armies. His instructions from the army were to "examine and report upon [their] organization, tactics, discipline, and . . . manoeuvres." His eighteen-month trip produced 1878's *The Armies of Asia and Europe,* a work heavily influenced by his favorable impressions of the German Army.

Upton's recommendations amounted to radical army reform. To replace the lumbering conscript armies of the Civil War, he advocated the creation of a relatively small but highly professional and expertly officered regular force during peacetime, supported by large "National Volunteer" units. In wartime, using the army as a core, the National Volunteers could be grafted onto the armed forces, thereby vastly and rapidly multiplying the country's military strength. In peacetime a regular company, for instance, would comprise three officers and fifty-four men, but a declaration of war, thanks to the influx of National Volunteers, would expand its strength to five officers and 242 men. Using Upton's figures, the peacetime army's twenty-five regiments would balloon from 12,500 to 100,075 trained effectives in very short order. Any enemy, expecting to find weak forces confronting them, would be unpleasantly surprised by the American ability to field a first-class army within weeks.

For Upton, the country's ability to manufacture an effective fighting service hinged on meritocracy and hard training. No officer in the National Volunteers would owe his place to political connections; he would instead prove himself in a special examination or attend courses in military science, and he would demonstrate his competence during field training exercises. The same applied to regular officers: if inept, they would be removed; if doddering, retired; if overpromoted, relegated.[36]

A key aspect of Uptonian doctrine was marksmanship. Constant practice would create a nation of lethal riflemen ready and able to spring into action against a foe. Upton's focus on squads deployed in skirmish formation dovetailed nicely with the need for good shooting. From a command perspective, because the men would be more spread out, an officer could not retain strict European-style control over everyone in his unit. "In this all important matter of firing," grumbled Lieutenant P. D. Lochridge, "a captain used to be able to control his company. Now, a corporal may ruin it."[37] Each man had to be sufficiently proficient with a rifle to look after himself and his squadmates. On the tactical side of things, Upton emphasized the importance of standardized target practice out to as much as eight hundred yards.[38]

Upton had some powerful allies, not least Church (at the *Army and Navy Journal*) and William Sherman (the former commander of military operations in the West and currently in charge of waging the Indian wars). The trio were keenly interested in raising the standard of military education and in improving the standing of the postwar army, but Sherman expressed particular interest in developing new ways of combating Indian successes against the frontier regulars.

In this respect Upton's preparedness scheme proved politically useful. Sherman might be able to squeeze extra dollars for the army and the "National Volunteers" out of a penny-pinching Congress that was relieved that the country's defense needs could apparently be fulfilled on the cheap. Meanwhile, the patent inability of American soldiers to hit anything with their Springfields was becoming, thanks to the target-shooting fad and Church's cascade of editorials, hugely embarrassing. The Legend of the American Rifleman remained potent, and considering that the army was avidly recruiting German and Irish immigrants, as well as liberated blacks, into the ranks, perhaps teaching them how to shoot accurately—and thereby "Americanizing" them—might not be such a bad thing?

To this end, Sherman ordered a wholesale revamping of the army's regulations on marksmanship. Colonel Theodore Laidley, who had been an Ordnance officer since the 1840s, was given the task of replacing Henry Heth's antebellum system of training. In 1879 his *Course of Instruction in Rifle-Firing* appeared, and following a short, nasty, but rather entertaining legal spat launched by George Wingate of the NRA, the Department of War gave it its imprimatur. Wingate accused Laidley of plagiarizing his own *Manual for Target Practice,* which the latter disputed by alleging that Wingate's *Manual* bore a suspicious resemblance to his own official work, the *Ordnance Manual* of 1861. The case never came to court, and Laidley in the end salved Wingate's amour propre by making it more apparent that his basic principles "followed" those laid down by the NRA at Creedmoor.[39]

Laidley ruled that each garrison should appoint an "instructor of musketry" (strange how the old terminology lived on) to ensure standard training for enlisted men, and he insisted that officers, hitherto absolved from shooting practice, must also take lessons. Soldiers, following Upton's emphasis on small squads, would train in teams of six; each man would fire in turn rather than simultaneously, as had formerly been the case, so that his mistakes could be corrected.[40]

Marking the end of strictly regimented eighteenth-century line volleys governed by officers, this innovative reform heralded the rise of individual or squad-level initiative on the battlefield, a method of fighting particularly apposite to the frontier and other guerrilla-type environments. Thus, instead of being drilled solely in the regulation pose of standing upright—a relic of the Musket Age and the Napoleonic Wars—men would be taught to fire while kneeling, prone, and lying on their backs with their Springfields' muzzles resting on their thighs (a position known as the Texas Grip). These positions had all been developed by American riflemen before and during the Revolution, not only to take advantage of any available cover but to ensure a better, surer shot.

Laidley additionally increased the variety of ranges. Instead of restricting target practice to the usual 100 or 200 yards, he laid down new regulations that the men must be competent at up to 600 and sometimes up to 1,200. Further, in order to ensure that none became too accustomed to a certain range (a technique called "known distance firing"), Laidley told instructors to surprise their pupils with random distances, to test them at no more than two ranges per session, and to allow each man no more than fifteen rounds to achieve his task.[41] You have "an army of marksmen," the chief of Ordnance exultantly informed the secretary of war once the reforms were in place, "and this gratifying result is due largely to Laidley's *Rifle Firing*."[42]

The army also introduced a practice known as "skirmish firing," in an attempt to simulate the combat experience. The traditional battered iron plates hanging forlornly on the range and the lead-bespattered bull's-eyes painted onto walls were exchanged (in the words of Mr. Powhatan Clarke in *Harper's Weekly*) for "ingenious targets of the revolving and disappearing type" that were often placed at random distances, at varying heights, in unexpected places, and partially hidden by brush or rocks.[43]

The need for such "realistic" practice was vividly borne out by one innovative officer at Fort Mackinac. He decided to test his men's combat efficiency by having a kneeling silhouette pulled back and forth laterally across the range. Out of 120 shots fired at 185 yards, just 23 hit. A little later, at Fort Niagara, a similar test held at 175 yards resulted in 15 hits out of 170 rounds. Two hunters were then asked to undergo the same test. Each fired 20 rounds; the first man hit the moving silhouette 18 times, the second, 10. The test demonstrated that practice with rifles could not fully replace actual experience with them.[44]

For honing similar skills, the army encouraged its soldiers to go hunting whenever they had a free moment.[45] Following guard duty, any trooper was granted "permission to take his horse and rifle and go where ever his fancy may lead him," reported *Turf, Field and Farm* magazine. "The majority provide themselves with a liberal stock of ammunition and seek for sport in the chase." Hunting had the happy dual benefit of allowing soldiers to practice shooting at moving targets at varying ranges, and at the same time encouraged thriftiness. One fall, F Troop of the Sixth Cavalry helpfully saved the army "$300 on bacon alone."[46]

To inspire competition among units, Sherman and Laidley instituted shooting matches (the prizes were gold medals and handmade Springfields) and then sent teams up against the NRA's crack shots at Creedmoor. Initially, they went home with their tails between their legs, but by the early 1880s the military's overall marksmanship was rapidly improving.

Accuracy had become the army's watchword. John Gibbon, the officer who had once averred that for a soldier to hit anything "beyond one hundred or one hundred and fifty yards . . . is pretty much a matter of chance," became something of an authoritarian on the issue: in 1883 he ordered his company commanders to hold target sessions six days a week beginning at seven a.m., and no man, unless he was sick, was to be

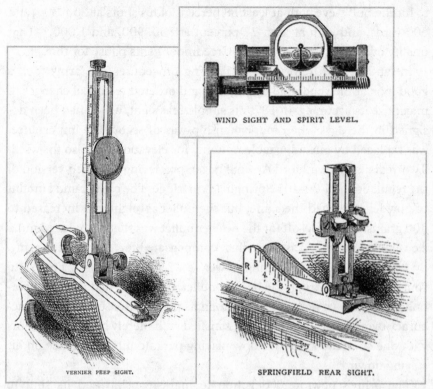

WIND SIGHT AND SPIRIT LEVEL.

VERNIER PEEP SIGHT.

SPRINGFIELD REAR SIGHT.

An array of military and civilian sights from the heyday of marksmanship. The precision demanded of these once-primitive devices is remarkable.

excused. Army-wide, a complex system of scoring was developed to keep track of each unit's progress. Men were divided into "marksmen," and then into first-class, second-class, and third-class "shooters," whose scores were weighted differently. In 1883, by using Laidley's new methods and computing his soldiers' ability according to the scoring matrix, Major General John Pope of the Department of Missouri proudly reported that his command had 883 marksmen: three years previously, there were just two.

The system's success resulted in so many marksmen that the army had to invent a new, elite category of "sharpshooter." (In 1909 a *super*-elite category of "expert" would come into being, members receiving a monthly five-dollar bonus.) To achieve that rank and gain the Sharpshooter's Cross—based on the German Iron Cross and worn at the neck (the Marksman's Pin was attached to the breast)—a soldier had to hit the bull's-eye with at least 88 percent of his shots at 200, 300, and 600 yards, and with at least 77 percent at 800, 900, and 1,000.[47] That quality of shooting gave even the Creedmoor gents pause for thought.

In tandem with reforming its training procedures, the army took a good look at the venerable Springfield and ordered technical changes to maximize its accuracy. In 1879 its simple rear sight, which had been designed in the days when marksmanship was of secondary importance, was replaced by one adjustable not only for elevation but also for wind. Two years later Frankford Arsenal began producing a refined version of the regulation .45-70-405 Springfield cartridge. The caliber and amount of powder remained the same, but the bullet's weight was increased to 500 grains. The trade-off for the heavier bullet was slightly reduced muzzle velocity, but that was more than compensated for, thought the army, by its greatly improved hitting power (a 22 percent boost). Thanks to some ballistic tinkering, the heavier bullet, moreover, had less of a parabolic trajectory (it flew straighter) than its predecessor, enhancing its accuracy over longer distances. Not satisfied with merely hitting the enemy with one shot, the army was now placing paramount importance on his staying down.[48]

The army's newfound devotion to marksmanship and its shift to Uptonian doctrine was not without its critics. (So fierce were their attacks on Upton and his thinking that they may well have contributed to his suicide on March 15, 1881.)[49] Congress and leading businessmen were in the forefront of the assault upon Upton. Having learned his trade during the Civil War and learning from the Europeans, he had originally designed his expansible force for fighting army-on-army battles. It was a flaw that his civilian critics were quick to exploit. If the army were intended for major strategic operations against a Great Power rival, they asked, then where were all those enemies?

None were on the horizon, so what was the point of his mooted army of up to 150,000 men? Congress instead cut back the defense budget. (Ordnance alone had its funds slashed from $31 million in 1865 to $700,000 a year later.) In 1866 it had limited the size of the army to 54,000 men, and three years later it further reduced the number of infantry regiments from 45 to 25, instantly slashing the number of troops to 37,313. In 1870 it abolished the ranks of general and lieutenant general and instituted a further decline to 30,000 effectives. In 1874, about the time Upton began promoting his ideas, a proviso stated that the government was to maintain no more than 25,000 troops. In less than a decade Washington had more than halved the size of the U.S. Army.[50] The policy had bipartisan support: northern Republicans abolished regiments that were no longer needed for policing duty during Reconstruction; southern Democrats vengefully targeted regiments that had policed them during Reconstruction.

Businessmen, for their part, found the very concept of a huge army alarming. For them, and for settlers intending to go west, the army's job was to provide domestic security by acting as a national police force to catch outlaws, keep the flags flying atop the forts, and put down the occasional bit of Indian troublemaking. In the absence of a genuine threat from abroad, the temper of the times clamored for "business pacifism."[51] The Civil War had drained the blood and treasure of the nation, and Lincoln's assassination seemed to signal the end of an era of barbaric ferocity. When George Wingate of the NRA pleaded with New York governor Alonzo Cornell to restore the organization's state funding, Cornell had high-handedly replied that "there would never be any war in my time or in the time of my children," and that all the army needed to do was "to march a little through the streets" during parades. Rifle training, the governor added, was a foolish waste of time.[52] Cornell was by no means alone in holding optimistic views of the peaceful utopia to come in the twentieth century. In 1886 an Iowa congressman asked, "What is the necessity of having any fighting men now?" to which his colleague Representative Foney of Alabama countered, " 'In time of peace prepare for war': that is the only reason I know." The classical allusion garnered Foney only mocking laughter.[53]

Unsurprisingly, within the army morale plummeted. Officers stationed on the frontier found themselves condemned back east as exterminationist Indian-killers. ("I only know the names of three savages upon the plains," announced the former abolitionist Wendell Phillips in 1870: "Colonel Baker, General Custer, and at the head of all, General Sheridan.")[54] Adding to their troubles, junior officers found that their path to promotion was blocked by Civil War relics who were simply counting the days until their retirement; some of these officers stayed

put until the turn of the century. In 1877 a newly minted second lieutenant would have to wait between thirty-three and thirty-seven years to
attain a colonelcy. Most made it nowhere near that high up the ranks:
John Summerhayes of the Eighth Infantry languished as a lieutenant for
twenty-two years before he was finally promoted to captain, and another
long-serving officer retired, still a captain, at sixty-four.[55]

In the ranks below them the situation was still worse. Men who enlisted were commonly regarded, in the words of the *New York Sun,* as
"bummers, loafers, and foreign paupers." In fact, of the 7,734 enlistees
in 1882, about a third described themselves as laborers, and nearly ten
percent as farmers. The remainder tended to be bakers, blacksmiths,
teamsters, and clerks, and most were in their midtwenties.

There were also quite a few exceptions, such as the Harvard man
serving in C Troop of the Eighth Cavalry, the exiled Russian aristocrat
doing a fine job as a sergeant of the First Cavalry, and the former divinity student who as a well-read private in the Third Cavalry subscribed
to the *New York Times,* the *New York Herald,* the *Kansas City Times,* the
St. Louis Globe-Gazette, the *Police Gazette,* and the *New York Clipper.*[56]
Indeed, among the hundred men in his company, said a trumpeter of
the Seventh Cavalry in 1877, there was a printer, a telegraph operator, a
doctor, two lawyers, three professors of languages, a harness maker, and
three schoolteachers.[57]

In short, thought Corporal Emil Bode (whose drill sergeant was
Jewish and who himself was acquainted with Lieutenant Henry Flipper,
the first black graduate of the United States Military Academy), the
army really was made up of all sorts. "We found men of intellect and
stupidity, sons of congressmen and sons of farmers, rich and poor, men
who are willing to work and can not find it in civil life, men who are
looking for work and hope that they never may find any: gamblers,
thieves, cutthroats, drunkards"—and that was just among the officers,
Bode laughed. As for the recruits, "Oh what a variety of humanity, from
a very intelligent society man, to Darwin's missing link [from] some
backwoods" to "a real Yankee" who had "read too many dime novels,
poor boy, and wanted to go west to kill Injuns, and wished he'd never
left home."[58]

Given the appalling conditions, the frequency of bullying, the prevalence of homesickness, and the risks soldiers ran for only a few dollars a day, disheartened officers found it almost impossible to keep their companies' numbers up. Desertion was rife. Of the 255,712 men recruited between 1867 and 1891, fully 88,475—a third—went AWOL, many absconding with their rifles and equipment, to sell to whoever offered a price, be he brigand or Indian. In some units turnover was so high that one officer remembered drilling with a company consisting of four men.[59]

Sometimes, lured by offers of amnesty or because they had nowhere else to go, deserters came back to the army and took their chances with a new alias. Captain King recalled hearing a working-class New Yorker, sounding for all the world like he'd stepped out of a moonlight-and-magnolia southern romance novel, announce that he was "Jackson Bewregard," while a hulking Scotsman with an incomprehensible accent claimed he was christened "Jooles Vern." Playing along, the recruitment adjutant exclaimed, " 'No. 173—Jules Verne.' Ha! Yes. The party that wrote *Around the World in Eighty Days*. Have we any more of these eminent Frenchmen, sergeant?"[60]

With army morale alternating between low and very low, heavy drinking was the force's bane. When the idealistic young West Pointer George Duncan arrived at his first posting at Fort Wingate, New Mexico, in 1886, he found every man, from the commanding officer down to the freshest private, dead drunk after a five-day binge.[61] Booze-fueled brawling was common, and many a soldier could recall rotgut-maddened enlisted men pummeling (and sometimes murdering) their corporals, sergeants, and even lieutenants. During the 1880s fully one out of every twenty-five enlisted men was hospitalized for alcoholism—and this at a time when only the most serious cases were classed as such.[62]

Partly caused by the tedium of garrison life, alcohol and drug abuse pervaded the officer corps as a whole. Colonel Ranald Mackenzie of the Fourth Cavalry ended up, in the words of Corporal Emil Bode, "in Washington, D.C., in an asylum, crazed from drink." His colleague, Lieutenant Colonel John Davidson of the Tenth Cavalry, became an opium and morphine addict.[63]

More alarmingly, a significant number of junior and middle-ranking officers, no longer satisfied with the bottle, relieved their boredom and frustration by intoxicating themselves on battle—or rather, the thought of it. By the 1880s, the backlash to the backlash *against* war had well and truly set in, for at that time the first of a slew of hugely popular battle reminiscences appeared. Carlton McCarthy, a former Confederate, published *Detailed Minutiae of a Soldier's Life* in 1882, celebrating his "joy at the prospect" of fighting the Yankee enemy. General Ulysses Grant's mammoth autobiography appeared in 1885–86, at the same time as the *Century* magazine began publishing its realistic series "The Battles and Leaders of the Civil War," the editor of which claimed he was "telling it like it was." By such means the gory episodes in any soldier's life, the ones most often suppressed by veterans, slowly transformed into romantic imaginings by their younger successors.

The Union veteran Colonel B. F. Scribner, in his *How Soldiers Were Made,* full-throatedly sang war's praises when he claimed that "there is nothing that produces upon a man so profound an impression as a great battle; nothing which so stirs and tests the soul within him; which so expands and strains the functions of sensation and so awakens all the possibilities of nature! There is nothing which so lifts him out of himself; so exalts him to the regions of heroism and self-sacrifice; nothing which so surcharges him and permeates his receptive faculties, and so employs all the powers of his mind and body as a great battle!"[64] In similar vein the jurist and wounded Civil War veteran Oliver Wendell Holmes, Jr., declared in a speech called "The Soldier's Faith" that those who "shared the incommunicable experience of war" have felt, and still feel, "the passion of life to its top." While others may have asked what war was good for, Holmes was adamant that it was good for many things.[65]

Postwar officers of like mind—called "diehards," to distinguish them from military progressives like William Church and other accuracy advocates—believed that easterners had abandoned them, and they exhibited an unexpected empathy with and respect for their Indian protagonists. (This sentiment was not confined to officers. When Buffalo Bill Cody exhibited in New England the splendid war bonnet, shield, and weapons of his slain opponent, the heroic young chieftain Yellow Hair, the local press and clergy—much to his disgust—forced him to withdraw "the blood-stained trophies of his murderous and cowardly deeds." Bill had experienced no problem whatsoever in the West. Even the Indians there thought the exhibition was a signal mark of respect, with one warrior commemorating another's deeds.)[66]

Diehards not only expressed sympathy for the Indians' plight but romanticized their willingness to war to the death.[67] General Charles King lost himself in reverie for the "grand revel in blood, scalps, and trophies" that characterized western fighting, a zone where "the love of rapine and warfare is the ruling passion."[68] To men like him, war was glorious, and the bloodier the better. ("When at war, it was kill them all," fondly recalled George Whittaker of the Sixth Cavalry.)[69] Like medieval barons, with armor clanking and banners unfurled, such soldiers preferred a heroic, honorable death on the field fighting their martial equals to a tedious, comfortable life of peace. Peace, to them, was the prerogative only of "civilization," the oft-praised virtue of those denuded fools who refused to acknowledge that man is wolf to man. Killing was the natural order of things. As General George Schofield, in charge of the Department of the Missouri, put it, "Civilized man never feels so happy as when he throws off a large part of his civilization and reverts to the life of a semi-savage."[70]

Progressive officers were shocked at the romantic bloodthirstiness inherent in the diehard view of the world. They believed in the redeeming benefits of Science and were convinced that Indians would shuck off their savage habits if given the chance at respectability. The burden of the white man, they claimed, was to extend a helping hand to those still mired in ignorance. Like all other societies, Indian societies must (and this was a very nineteenth-century conception) pass "through the stages of the hunter, the herdsman, [and] the agriculturalist" to reach the exalted realms of "commerce, mechanics and the higher arts," wrote General Nelson A. Miles, a leading progressive (though stoutly conservative politically).[71]

Hoping to show recalcitrant Indians the way ahead, Miles argued that access to "modern appliances" would persuade them to accommodate themselves to the inevitable. After Custer's death at the Little Bighorn he had divided some Sioux veterans of the battle into two groups, separated them, and allowed them to talk to each other on the telephone. "They recognized the voices of their friends so clearly . . . it was surprising to see the effect upon these aborigines, stalwart, bold, hard-nerved men as they were who scorned to show the least emotion." Holding "the little telephone instruments," their hands shook visibly, their bodies trembled with emotion, and great drops of perspiration rolled down their bronzed faces," he reported. Awestruck by the power of Alexander Graham Bell's magical invention, they said they would war no more and turned instead to Christ.[72]

Diehards dismissed their progressive counterparts as wide-eyed appeasers who shuddered at the horrid necessity of whites fighting the untamable Indian on his own terms. For the diehards, allowing a Plains-bred Sioux to chat on the phone for a minute or two would never suffice to erase thousands of years of breeding for war; hostiles respected only troopers who were equally adept at jerking open their entrails with a serrated bayonet. They were wild people accustomed to the open prairies and would never settle down to a life of happy respectability. After all, in 1876, when the government built ten grand houses at Fort Sill for those chiefs who had stayed peaceful, the Indians proudly showed them off to their comrades but continued to camp and sleep outside. Their dogs lived in them instead.[73]

On the issue of marksmanship, the differences between diehards and progressives were perhaps nowhere more blatant. Always preferring the civilized way, progressives preferred the distant clean shot to the up-close dirty kill. Naturally they found common ground with the gentlemanly eastern shooting establishment, whose abstract Creedmoor rules were the deliberate antithesis of brutal frontier warfare. For that reason, in his analysis of the lessons of the Battle of Plevna between the Russians and Turks, William Church of the *Army and Navy Journal* completely omitted any mention of the Winchester repeaters' devastating close-range fire. Instead, he concentrated exclusively on the Turks' "firing at distances ordinarily regarded as not to be compassed by anything except the fancy shooting of rifle ranges or the tentative practices of sharp-shooters."[74]

Battles could be won, Church argued, antiseptically. In the future, any man could be a "sharp-shooter" and stand well back from the dangerous front line. For the first time in history, war could be *safe*. Marksmanship was thus identified with rationalist, modern, enlightened aims. To be a good target-shooter, progressives claimed, a soldier must be deliberate and logical; he must be able to function on his own and not rely on the orders of his superiors; he must not follow the dull herd's instinct but work together with his teammates; he must be fully aware of the scientific calculations involved in gauging wind speed, adjusting for elevation, and determining range. He must, in short, be a modern can-do man capable of independent thought and not beholden to military tradition. Whereas in times of yore, mused Colonel Henry Closson, the military was expected "to teach one man how to handle many" as part of its top-down emphasis on the chain of command, these days its task was "to teach every man to handle himself."[75] The army was to be of one.

The modern fighting soldier, progressives thought, should resemble his self-sustaining Colonial and Revolutionary forebear, the American frontier rifleman who felled his foes with a single shot. "In an Indian fight," opined one, "the best marksman is the strongest man. Victory is not for the man of muscle, but the result of the quick eye and cool nerve of the fine shot."[76] One exponent went so far as to assert that "rapid firing is in itself evil."[77] They now called his form of prowess the "new courage" to distinguish it from the inferior, dated martial virtues—men's instinctive emotions, brute force, and valorous ferocity tightly harnessed by officers and unleashed at the enemy—revered by the diehards.

This debate between progressives and diehards over shooting theory had profound public reverberations. At a time when the harsh ethos (and lavish rewards) of industrialized capitalism was reflected in the garish, cruel glow of the Gilded Age, Americans were beginning to wonder if all was right with their Great Republic. Walt Whitman perfectly enunciated those fears when, after seeing three men "of respectable personal presence . . . plodding along, their eyes cast down, spying for scraps, rags, bones," he worried that "our republican experiment, notwithstanding all its surface-successes, is at heart an unhealthy failure."[78]

That hardy national sense of "all pulling together" in the common cause was dissipating, Americans could not help feeling, and was being replaced by atomization, overconsumption, and greed during the boom times, and by poverty, torpor, and violence during the busts. The American "character" was disappearing before their very eyes, a victim of mass immigration, uncertainty, and financial panics.

Perhaps, to reinvigorate the republic, applying the ideals and values of the military to the wider society might pay dividends. William Church certainly believed so. Inspired by the first army-navy football game of December 1, 1890—in which the midshipmen's quarterback called out his plays in nautical language ("clear deck for action") and his opposite used army expressions ("right front into double line")—he and other progressives encouraged college students to take up football chiefly "for its influence in developing the qualities especially required in an officer of the army or navy—qualities which it is at the same time well for every young man to cultivate." Progressive officers felt that football was war; one alleged that the game required the same "tactical and strategical combinations for the accomplishment of the desired end."[79]

From the diehard point of view, football had rules, just as the firing range at Creedmoor had rules, but the same could not be said for the scalp-littered battlefields of Dakota where, if any football was going to be played, it would be more like *The Longest Yard* than *Knute Rockne, All American.* Yet they too believed in the virtues of the game, if only because they found its violence and roughhousing a salutary method of unleashing the innate "savage" in men. Battering the defense into submission or sacking the quarterback was more their style.

But as Shakespeare warned, if one let slip the dogs of war, havoc would unfold. War dogs, even as they sank their fangs into the enemy, had to be kept on a tight leash—or they might very well turn and attack their owners. For this reason General George "Blood and Guts" Patton, future exemplifier of all things diehard, once asked, "Where would an undisciplined football team get?" Nowhere, of course, because, like hounds, "all human beings have an innate resistance to obedience," and it is only the smack of firm "discipline [that]removes this resistance and, by constant repetition, makes obedience habitual and subconscious."[80]

Diehards, like such Revolutionary forebears as Alexander Hamilton and Anthony Wayne, were concerned solely with ensuring that men did as they were told by their superiors—a subject of particularly wider import at this later time, when violent industrial unrest, sabotage of railroad property, and angry strikes were becoming increasingly common.[81] Diehard officers were particularly exercised by the prospect that individual soldiers would *choose* when to advance (or worse, retreat). To them, the so-called new courage was merely old-fashioned cowardice dolled up as virtue. A favorite progressive statistic was that in the Civil War sharpshooting skirmishers had a hit-and-kill rate double that of the infantry regimented into lines for volley firing; diehards retorted that those very same sharpshooters often retreated after suffering a mere two percent loss, while disciplined infantry did not break until sustaining *at least* a 40 percent casualty rate.[82]

Then diehards drew attention to the prima-donna reputation of the progressives' favorite marksmen. Back in the war, critics remembered, sharpshooter units on both sides had been less than ideal. Union ones had, outrageously, been permitted to carry their own choice of rifles and, in homage to their hunting ancestry, had worn green uniforms when they complained about regulation blue ones. Even then, carped an officer who had reviewed them in December 1861, they were "perfect slouches and slovens in appearance [of whom] hardly any two are uniformed alike."[83] As for the Confederate battalions, despite their skills they had been bywords for delinquency and orneriness.

To that end, one Lieutenant Frost argued, the recent rage for target shooting was unconducive to maintaining tight discipline: "In the race for a record, men known to be good shots have been coddled and petted until there was no living with them." More shockingly still, "men of this class have even set up their will against that of the officer, and too often, it has been overlooked."[84]

Intending to break the progressive stranglehold on marksmanship training, diehards counterattacked. Reliance on wind gauges and advanced, elevating sights was ruining the art of soldiering, said Captain James Chester—a man so Old School, he was the school they knocked down to build the Old School—and he proposed to replace them with a simple spirit level. His ally Captain Frank Ely even developed a mechanism that prevented a platoon's lined-up rifles from being raised (or fired) past the angle set by their officer.[85]

In Germany a new technique of fire control, called "field fire," had swept the army, and it quickly gained a following among American diehards.[86] According to this method, officers estimated the range to the enemy, and their men followed the command to fire, thereby removing individual riflemanship from the equation and restoring the traditional top-down hierarchy. If the officer made a correct estimate, the enemy received a mighty broadside; if he didn't, everyone missed and their shots sailed high or low; the key thing was to keep order and strict fire discipline. Essentially, Chester, Ely, and their German equivalents wanted to ensure that weapons were pointed straight forward and leveled; they wanted to force soldiers to get so close to the enemy that marksmanship didn't matter. That was the *old* courage, and it still worked.

The progressive-diehard antagonism was reflected in the decades-long clash over the army's rifle. The .45-70 single-shot Springfield that, after much effort and expense, had been converted after the Civil War from a muzzle-loader into a breech-loader, was a fine weapon and a popular one as well. In 1870, following a two-year field trial in which the Remington rolling-block rifle was pitted against the Springfield, company commanders reported by a ratio of eight to one that they preferred the latter—despite an earlier Ordnance board recommendation that the Remington be adopted as the universal service arm.[87]

During this time repeaters were not even being considered. In the lead-up to the 1870 trial, forty-one rifle models had been submitted by inventors and various companies, but among them was just one repeater (a Spencer). Winchester, knowing the army's views, did not bother to even enter the heats. The Americans were not alone in their conviction that repeaters were unsuitable for military use: the War Office in London had held a similar competition in 1866, and not one of the 112 entrants had been a repeater.[88]

For progressives, repeaters had two insurmountable drawbacks. The first was their sorcerous power to hypnotize enlisted men into forgetting to aim. The second concerned storing their cartridges in a tube running under the barrel. As cartridges were fired, the ejection of their spent casings slightly shifted the weapon's center of gravity. Unless the shooter readjusted his aim each time he pulled the trigger, the muzzle would elevate and send bullets high. The built-in flaw made it impossible to achieve consistently pinpoint shooting.

Diehards, on the other hand, were more open to bringing more repeaters in the fighting services owing to their belief that ammunition magazines (either in a tube running beneath the barrel or hidden inside the butt stock) were a useful addendum to a bayonet. A soldier, before an assault, prepared a bayonet (by fixing it to the muzzle) and used it at close quarters to inspire both fear in the enemy and fortitude in his own men; so too the magazine in a repeater was preloaded and held in reserve. Initially the troops would fire at the command of their officer, but as the fighting grew more heated and the two opposing forces came closer, soldiers would unleash the fifteen or so bullets in their magazine in short order. The enemy, brutally assaulted at close range, would falter, fall back, or just fall, while one's own men would fight harder, knowing they would never be left exposed while fumbling for a cartridge to load. If surrounded, they could even blast their way out, just as the bayonet, too, was sometimes used as a weapon of last resort.[89]

Nevertheless, at least during the 1870s, even the diehards weren't confident that repeaters were up to military-grade performance requirements, and in any case the technology of that decade heavily favored the progressive case. The science of metallurgy was rapidly advancing, and after 1873 newly decarbonized Bessemer steel was adopted for rifle barrels. It permitted the use of larger powder charges and reduced imperfections within the barrel.[90] Those attributes, in turn, aided long-range accuracy, much to the delight of progressives and Creedmoor shooters, but they did little to address the repeater's inability to handle large loads. What was now a doddle for a Remington to shoot was, owing to its delicate firing, lever, and extractor mechanisms, well-nigh impossible for a Winchester.

Ordnance's decision in 1873 to use the centerfire .45-70-405 cartridge as its standard infantry caliber was another body blow for the diehards. The "forty-five seventy" was way out of the Winchester's league; the Winchester's more usual ammunition was the pint-sized .44-28-200 or .44-40-200 rimfires, capable of only short ranges. Put more vividly, the .45-70 was almost 2.75 inches long, about double the length of the .44-40. The company nevertheless produced a special model repeater for the sole purpose of impressing Ordnance, but even then the largest cartridge it could handle was a .44-70-caliber topped by a 360-grain bullet. Firing it so stressed the Winchester during tests that it left a twelve-inch split along the stock.[91] It was close, but not close enough, though objective observers predicted that one day Winchester might manage it. (The paradox, unnoticed at the time, was that caliber sizes were slowly shrinking, thereby putting Winchester ahead of the curve, not behind it.)

Anticipating that day, diehards managed to insert a clause into Ordnance's 1873 conclusions judging that the "adoption of magazine-guns for the military service, by all nations, is only a question of time." When a repeater was considered "as effective" as the Springfield and possessed "a safe and easily manipulated magazine," it added, "every consideration of public policy will require its adoption."[92] The clause contained a sufficient number of get-out phrases, loopholes, tall orders, and ifs-and-buts to lull the board's progressives into believing that nothing would ever come of it.[93]

Their certitude was shaken the following year when the longtime chief of ordnance, Alexander Dyer, died. Replacing him was his forty-seven-year-old assistant, Brigadier General Stephen Vincent Benét, who would serve until 1891. If there ever was a stereotypical Ordnance officer out of central casting, it was Benét. Born in Florida and something of a prodigy, Benét had read Blackstone's legal *Commentaries* by the time he was thirteen and had attended the University of Georgia before heading to West Point. In 1849 he graduated third in his class and, like many Academy stars, was ushered straight into the Ordnance Department. Reflecting the department's antebellum Francophilia, Benét translated Jomini's *Political and Military History of the Campaign of Waterloo* from the French and was posted to the Watervliet and Frankford Arsenals. In his spare time he composed poetry, prefiguring the literary talents of two of his grandsons, who would both be awarded Pulitzer prizes. (The first, in 1929, would go to his namesake Stephen, for *John Brown's Body,* an epic poem; the other, in 1942, to William, for *The Dust Which Is God,* an autobiographical "novel in verse.")

Benét's Civil War was not a glittering one: he never commanded troops in the field (automatically a source of suspicion among line officers) and spent much of the conflict at West Point as a captain teaching geography, history, ethics, and gunnery to cadets. Following a stint as commandant of Frankford, he was lucky to be bumped down only to major in the postwar downsizing.[94]

Benét trod a moderate path between the progressive and diehard cliques. As Dyer's man, his reputation and career were invested in the

Springfield single-shots, but he was also aware that repeaters were the coming thing. His personal preference, he said, would be to commission "a gun that will carry a few rounds in the magazine for a reserve supply, but will be ordinarily used as a single[-shot] breech-loader."[95] Notice (because the Winchester people certainly did) Benét's assertion that any repeater would be restricted to carrying "a few rounds" as a reserve, essentially for close-range work. With that hint Benét was alerting the Winchester company that the standard Winchester, with its tubular cartridge capacity in the midteens, was never going to be accepted. Whereas the company had traditionally tried to cram as many cartridges as possible into their weapons, now the arms-maker was expected to reduce the number to fit army requirements.

To junk existing models and start over with a new design would have been too painful and would have hurt civilian sales, so Winchester reverted to form and simply sought out and bought out a competitor. Company agents sallied into the field to track down a firm making a suitable weapon. At the Philadelphia Centennial Exposition in 1876, Winchester men were scouring the firearms displays when they discovered a prototype that they thought would perfectly fit the bill: a *five*-shot rifle whose magazine was located in the butt stock (as in a Spencer).[96]

This piece had been invented by an expatriate Connecticut machinist in his midforties named Benjamin Hotchkiss, once a formidable name in Civil War artillery-shell design but currently finding Europe more to his taste. In America metallic cartridges were old hat, but after the war Hotchkiss discovered that the French were still using paper cartridges, and he quickly sold their army on the idea of switching to metal ones. Flush with lavish government contracts, Hotchkiss applied himself to designing a magazine rifle, the one subsequently exhibited in Philadelphia, that employed a bolt-action system: the firing mechanism was contained inside a metal tube that, when pulled back by means of a knob set to the side, opened the chamber for loading and then sealed it by pushing or rotating the knob back into position. The beauty of the Hotchkiss's bolt action was that it lent itself either to single-shot loading *or* to magazine firing, *and* it was comfortably at home firing the army's high-power ammunition. Perfect, thought the Winchester people, who purchased the rights to manufacture the weapon on February 14, 1877.[97]

Why the hurry? Custer's shattering annihilation at the Little Bighorn fifty days after the Centennial Exhibition had led to calls to reopen the question of issuing Springfield single-shots to the troops. During the furious fighting of the last stand, it was reported, the Springfields' breeches had badly fouled and become jammed by empty casings. The only way of extracting them had been to insert a hunting knife and force them out. Indian prisoners testified that they had seen Custer's doomed soldiers desperately trying to clear their Springfields, and military investigators recorded broken knife blades scattered around the battlefield.[98]

Custer's defeat was partly attributable, some contemporary observers darkly hinted, to an inherent flaw in the Springfield's design. Not so, Ordnance experts countered, blaming poor maintenance and dirty cartridges for the jamming. The gun itself, they stoutly declared, was not to blame.[99] In truth, neither side was completely right. Later ballistic and archaeological research has found that five percent of Custer's Springfields suffered from extraction failure. It was a high rate—more than double that recorded during experimental trials (held under ideal conditions)—but faulty loading on the part of terrified, panicked soldiers doubtlessly contributed to the failures.[100]

The accusations might have been ignored, but 1876 was a particularly bitter election year, and Democrats keen to attack Ulysses Grant's Republican administration made the Little Bighorn a rallying point. Custer's defeat allowed them to hit Grant hard, repeatedly. Democratic newspapers led the charge from several different directions. The *New York Herald* linked the administration's ever-widening corruption scandals to the president's peace policy: Custer's death symbolized the incompetence of Grant's Indian Bureau, it thundered, "which feeds, clothes and takes care of their noncombatant force while the men are killing our troops." The president was "what killed Custer," its editorialists concluded. Anti-Reconstructionist papers below the old Mason-Dixon Line, such as the *Mobile Register* and the *New Orleans Picayune*, used the slaughter to tell Grant to end U.S. troops' "political services at the South and send them where the honor of the flag . . . may be redeemed. The five massacred companies of Custer attest the inhumanity and imbecility of the republican administration."[101]

The Republicans lost the election, and as a result, the outcry over the "needless" sacrifice of the Seventh Cavalry prompted Congress to approve the modest sum of $20,000 to let Benét evaluate (not select) a potential magazine arm for the service. From the get-go, the experimental Hotchkiss was rumored to be the one. If all went well, thanks to Winchester's opportunistic purchase of the rights, he would have a lock on the market. The reports streaming in from the Russo-Turkish campaign at Plevna in the second half of 1877, during which Winchester's Winchesters had cut themselves quite a dash, only added to the growing feeling that maybe, just maybe, the repeater's day had come.

In April 1878 a new Ordnance board met at Springfield. Twenty-seven firearms, all chambered for the regulation .45-70, were submitted by various inventors and firms. Winchester, determined to win an army contract, submitted no fewer than four versions of its new Hotchkiss. Just seven rifles survived the rigors of the initial heat, and in the end the Hotchkiss was judged the most "suitable for the military service." It looked as if Winchester's gamble had paid off, in spades. If Washington gave its approval, overseas orders would inevitably flood the company coffers—indeed, the celestial Chinese Empire alone ordered 100,000 Hotchkisses that year just to be first in line.[102]

Benét immediately directed that a small number of Hotchkisses (1,015) be issued to soldiers in the Dakota Territory and the Texas frontier for field trials. Unfortunately, however, Winchester had rushed through production, and mechanical defects were all too common. The company replaced nearly half the original batch with improved versions, but officers remained ambivalent about the Hotchkiss. For every soldier who praised it, another preferred the Springfield, with opinion often dividing along diehard-progressive lines. Bluntly reported one progressive officer, "I am . . . not in favor of a magazine gun for general armament." Another, of diehardist persuasion, thought that his "men have more confidence in it then they have in the Springfield."

Fatally, no one, even among diehards, could work up much enthusiasm for the Hotchkiss: one colonel (a persistent advocate of repeaters) went so far as to confess that even he was "not especially wedded to the Hotchkiss." In 1880 about half of all company commanders said they wanted to stick with the Springfield and returned their Hotchkisses.[103] Benét remarked that the Hotchkiss, once considered so promising, "is an improvement on the present Springfield arm only in its ability to empty its magazine of cartridges in one-half the time that the same number could be fired by the latter."[104]

Oliver Winchester did not live to see the formation of another board in July 1881, this time to trial a new batch of magazine rifles, including ones from a fresh competitor, the Lee Arms Company (run by James Paris Lee), as well as a Colt-sponsored Chaffee-Reece. (Winchester, now the long shot, submitted new, improved versions of its lackluster Hotchkiss.)

Lee, a Scot, was born in August 1831, the son of a watchmaker. The family had emigrated to Canada when he was an infant, and Lee started work in his father's jeweler's shop when he was seven. Fascinated by the complex mechanics of watches, and boyishly intrigued by firearms, Lee opened his own workshop and store in 1850, worked on his beloved rifles in his spare time, and married one Caroline Chrysler, of the family that would found the car company. In 1862, now based in Wisconsin and a naturalized American citizen, he patented his first weapon, a single-shot rifle with a then-innovative breech-loading mechanism. Not until April 18, 1865—nine days after General Robert E. Lee surrendered his army to Grant—did Ordnance get back to him; Dyer, the chief, ordered a thousand of his rifles for trials. Unfortunately, the instructions weren't quite clear, and Lee submitted his batch in the wrong caliber. The department, understandably, refused to accept them, and Lee sued the government for $14,350 in costs. He won, but not without making himself unwelcome at Ordnance for some time to come.[105]

In 1874 he tried again with an updated design but was brazenly rebuffed: "The Department does not intend, at the present, to consider the subject of breech-loading guns, with a view to their introduction to the service." That was completely untrue, of course. Ordnance was at that very moment considering the subject very carefully. It was just that Ordnance refused to consider the subject of *Lee's* breech-loading gun.[106]

By the end of the decade Lee had found, or purchased, enough friends in Congress to ensure a proper trial, whatever Ordnance's feelings on the matter, for any rifle he submitted in the future.[107] Lee didn't waste the opportunity. For the 1881 round of trials he submitted a radical design for a magazine rifle. (The basic version would go on to enjoy a long life—some sixty-plus years—in the British Army, and its genes are present in even today's small arms.) Whereas the Colt-backed Chaffee-Reece and the Winchester-owned Hotchkiss were *tubular*-magazine rifles, the Lee was the first to use a five-shot *detachable* magazine in which the ammunition was contained in a narrow, vertical metal "box" inserted beneath the breech. As the shooter pulled back the bolt, the empty casing was ejected, while as the bolt was pushed forward, a Z-shaped spring at the bottom of the magazine pushed a new round upward into the chamber. The bolt action automatically cocked the rifle, so all the soldier had to do was pull the trigger.[108] When the magazine was empty, the shooter would merely detach it and quickly replace it with a full one, so that, in Lee's words, "the rapid firing can be continued with great rapidity." Though its reserve held only a third of the ammunition of a standard Winchester, the Lee compensated by being far faster to load: other repeaters had to be manually reloaded by pushing cartridges individually into their magazines—which took no little time—but a Lee magazine came preloaded. It was ready to go in seconds and the gun could be used either as a single-loader or as a repeater.[109]

The board was dazzled by the Lee's action but also a little worried that it was *too* drastic a change. Having only recently come around to the idea of testing repeaters at all, the army was wary of adopting a futuristic novelty like a detachable magazine. The Chaffee-Reece and Hotchkiss, despite their other problems, were at least based on widely tested mechanisms. In September 1882 the board passed the buck upstairs to General Sherman, who felt the Lee was the best and appropriated $50,000 to manufacture a batch of three thousand for field testing. But Benét, not yet content to let Lee have his victory over Ordnance, insisted that all three rifles be put out for trials. With any luck, the Lee would falter under real-world conditions.

In the end, 750 each of the Hotchkiss and Lee, and 200 of the Chaffee-Reeces, were ordered made. Lee by this time had contracted the rights to his rifle to Winchester's archrival Remington, and the two companies furiously competed to gain the military's favorable attention. While Winchester offered its batch at $15 apiece, with delivery in seven months, Remington bid $16 but promised its Lees within three months.

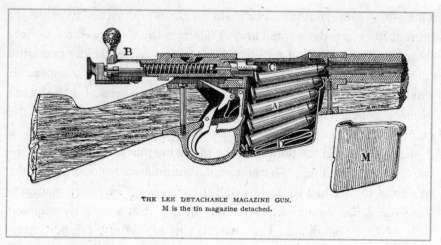

THE LEE DETACHABLE MAGAZINE GUN.
M is the tin magazine detached.

The Lee design (with detachable magazine).

Chaffee-Reece badly stumbled when Colt optimistically quoted a price of $150 each—in a leisurely eight months.

Despite their sunny promises, Remington-Lee, Winchester-Hotchkiss, and even Colt-Chaffee-Reece all ran late on their deliveries. It wasn't until the early fall of 1884, or nearly two years behind schedule, that all the firearms were received and sent out to company commanders around the country. In the summer of 1885 the results of the field trials dribbled in. Reports on the Lee were favorable, though opinion as usual divided on the entire issue of distributing magazine arms at all. Most of the complaints about the Lee centered on the soldiers' dropping the rifle's empty magazines on the ground—they were quite expensive. More positively, much to his surprise, a captain of the progressive school found that eight of the ten sharpshooters in his command preferred the Lees to their Springfields.

Benét had asked each of the 149 company commanders testing the weapons to express a definite preference for just one of the experimental arms, then to compare that favorite against the Springfield. Unfortunately, some performed one task but not the other, some neither. It didn't help that some units received all three rifles, and others just one or two.

Of the ones who did complete the requirements, 55 voted for the Lee over the other repeaters, giving it a wide margin over the Hotchkiss (26) and the Chaffee-Reece (14). In the end no one preferred the Chaffee-

Reece over the Springfield as a single-shot weapon; just one did for the Hotchkiss; and an unimpressive five for the Lee. Asked which weapon they considered the best for general use, ten plumped for the Lee, three for the Chaffee-Reece, and four for the Hotchkiss, but forty-six felt the Springfield was the best in all respects. Faced with such a wall of opposition, Benét concluded that "I am satisfied that [none] of the magazine guns should be adopted and substituted for the Springfield rifle as the arm for the service."[110] The Springfield would stay.

While the Lee certainly had its problems, it was still in the experimental stages. Given proper encouragement, its defects would have been remedied in time, and the U.S. Army might have enjoyed the distinction of possessing the world's first magazine service rifle once the Springfield, a first-class arm but one showing its age, was gradually phased out. With five-odd years to go until retirement, and with forty years of sterling service behind him, Benét had taken the easier route. Not for him the rigors of introducing a brand-new weapon into the service with all the attendant army infighting and Washington intriguing. He left that to someone else.

Benét's decision to kill the Lee led to stultification within the Ordnance Department for close to a decade and eroded traditional American superiority in the rifle business. In the meantime the European powers had not stood still. On this side of the Atlantic the Indian wars were subsiding, but on the other the ravenous hunger for new territorial acquisitions resulted in intense competition to have the best rifle first—or risk losing the struggle for mastery.

In Germany, Peter Paul Mauser and Ferdinand von Mannlicher were competing for supremacy. Mauser, born in 1838, the thirteenth of thirteen children, was the son of a gunsmith and the brother of four more. In the early 1880s, he had successfully converted his bolt-action *Infanterie-Gewehr* (Infantry Rifle) Model 71 into a magazine weapon for the army. Strikingly, while the American government was requiring firms to standardize their calibers to .45, Mauser insisted on reducing them, first to 11mm (.433) and then, he predicted, to 9mm (.354). Mannlicher produced a bolt-action repeater in 1885, using metal clips to feed its maw that automatically dropped out when empty. The time-saving idea would be integrated into German arms and used until the Second World War.

In Britain, by 1886 the Small Arms Committee was taking a serious look at Lee's improved magazine rifle. (Lee, miffed, had given up on ever finding success in the United States while Benét reigned.) The following year the committee chose the Lee as the army's replacement for the Martini-Henry, though its adoption was delayed owing to concern that the Lee's ammunition might be distinctly cumbersome: the German and the Swiss (who had introduced a .295 for their service rifle) had recently moved toward reduced calibers. So the momentous decision was made to adopt what would become one of the most famous rounds of all time, the .303.[111]

The French, as always, plowed their own quirky furrow. In 1886–87, the Lebel appeared, named after the colonel who developed its ammunition. It was, again in traditional French fashion, designed by military committee rather than conceived by individual inventors. (The German individualist tendency was replicated in American workshops.) Remarkably, the Lebel also integrated German and American styles: boasting a Winchester tubular magazine under the barrel, the rifle fired its loads using a Mauser bolt action.

The Lebel left the German, British, and American high commands gasping with astonishment. It was not the rifle itself that shocked them (though the *New York Times* did dub it "the most vicious small arm in existence") but the gunpowder that fired it.[112] It was the first weapon in the world to use "smokeless powder." Black powder, that mixture of saltpeter, sulfur, and charcoal, had served for half a millennium as the charge for every pistol and rifle in existence. It had just been rendered instantly obsolete.

The Krag-Jørgensen Rifle

Chapter 7

THE SMOKELESS REVOLUTION

Smokeless powder was discovered, quite by accident, in the impeccable, bourgeois kitchen of Frau Schönbein in 1845. One day when she was away, her husband, Christian Friedrich (1799–1868), a Swiss-German professor of chemistry at the University of Basel, was toying with a vial of nitric acid—in violation of Frau Schönbein's express orders not to play with such stuff in the house—and spilled it over the table. Worried about his formidable wife's reaction, he quickly mopped up the mess with one of her cotton aprons and tucked it away near the stove to dry. Frau Schönbein, he thought, would be none the wiser. Then the apron blew up.[1]

A year later, presumably after Frau Schönbein's fury had been assuaged, the professor addressed a meeting of Basel's august Society of Scientific Research on the subject of his work treating cotton with nitric and sulfuric acids. The professor was closed-lipped about his exact process—he had a mind to patent his combustible invention—but there was no doubting that "nitrocellulose" (soon dubbed guncotton) was an intriguing idea.

Journalists present at the talk dispatched their stories home, and overnight Herr Professor Schönbein became famous. *Scientific American* commented in November 1846 on "a curious discovery in Europe, by which cotton was so prepared as to explode with all the force or effects of gunpowder." The journal professed itself "suspicious of the genuineness of the report," but even after discounting for gossip, "we are left to conclude that *cotton* (like saltpeter) *will explode*." The magazine humorously warned that henceforth "young ladies who travel by railroad will have more than ordinary occasion to 'beware of sparks.' " More seriously, *Scientific American* published a rudimentary guide to the process, which it claimed consisted of "simply dipping common cotton in nitric acid, and immediately washing it in water and drying."[2] There was a little more to it than that, as several subscribers soon discovered.

One eager amateur explained that he had loaded his old .75 musket with twelve grains of guncotton, less than a quarter of his usual gunpowder charge, and rammed a ball down on top. "On discharging the rifle, about five inches of the breech end of the barrel together with the lock, were completely blown to pieces. One piece weighing eight ounces was carried through the roof of the building."[3] And Mr. J. H. Pennington, "who has been trying to fly for two or three years," told the editors that he was going to turn himself into a human rocket by strapping on a few pounds of homemade guncotton.[4] His fate remains unknown.

Schönbein was even invited to Osborne House in London to demonstrate guncotton's properties to Prince Albert, Queen Victoria's consort. First, of course, they needed a guinea pig. The prince selected a colonel of the Household Regiment, who recoiled from the idea. Albert, always interested in scientific endeavor, then himself volunteered. The professor placed a small amount in his hand, and "off went the cotton, without smoke, stain or burning of the skin." Then the colonel consented, but the sample was not as high quality, and "it gave him such a singeing that he leapt up with a cry of pain. A hearty laugh was all the commiseration he received."[5]

Cruel laughs aside, every army in the world was clamoring to try out this miraculous substance, which looked like cotton wool. Major Alfred Mordecai, the leading American ordnance specialist, soon managed to acquire a sample. He too "used to burn little bits of it in the palms" of his children for entertainment, but his tests revealed that "gun-cotton seems to produce in the musket an effect equal to about twice its weight of good rifle-powder."[6] After firing 60 grains of guncotton (the equivalent of 120 grains of regular gunpowder), Mordecai found hardly any visible residue in the barrel—though it did leave behind water and nitrous acid, which could corrode the metal if not cleaned properly—and even after eight shots, "there was scarcely any perceptible heat."[7]

In short, guncotton fired clean and cold. Its "smokeless" explosion produced only gas, while that of black gunpowder comprised 31 percent gas, the rest being carbon dust and acid. (To get some idea of how quickly residue could accumulate, consider that every time a 110-ton artillery cannon was fired, 528 pounds of waste was expelled. Most of it was blown into the surrounding air, but significant amounts remained inside the barrel.) Another experiment showed that after firing 75 rounds with small amounts of guncotton, a rifle's barrel temperature rose from 94 degrees to 128, but after just 45 rounds using regular powder, it heated up to 144 degrees.[8]

The implications of guncotton for the conduct of warfare and for rifle design were startling. Needing only half the amount of powder as before, soldiers could not only carry more cartridges but would not tax the army's limited transportation capabilities. The commanders' oft-expressed fear that their men would run out of ammunition if permitted to fire freely would no longer cause nightmares. And since guncotton was cheap to produce compared with prime-grade gunpowder, military accountants would also sleep better. Better news was still to come. In Britain a wad of guncotton was experimentally submerged in water for sixty hours, extracted, and dried out; it was then found "to possess all its original inflammability and strength."[9] The stuff was basically impervious to water, and if kept moist it could be safely transported with virtually no risk of a stray spark setting it off.[10]

For the generals, a waterproof propellant meant an end to the tyranny of the weather. For the first time since firearms had replaced bladed metal weapons during the Renaissance, armies could *fight in the rain,* or at least in damp conditions, thus extending each campaigning season from the traditional summer into the fall and spring.

Once the initial celebrations subsided, however, ordnance experts and military writers began to notice guncotton's drawbacks. Experiments were showing that in fact guncotton was not, in Mordecai's words, "well adapted to use in firearms."[11] The problem lay mostly in its enormous explosive force: no shoulder arm in existence could handle more than a dozen successive loads without bursting. Guncotton may have burned at a much lower temperature than gunpowder, Ordnance discovered, but it burned far *faster*. As a result, immense pressure accumulated within the firearm before the projectile exited the muzzle, rupturing the breech and barrel and shearing off the rifle grooving. Until the rate of combustion could be controlled, Ordnance recommended postponing its adoption by the military.

Other voices, too, were urging caution. The longer campaigns permitted by smokeless powder might have the adverse effect of greatly increasing the cost of war, since extended periods in the field required larger armies and therefore higher expenses for pay, supply, and maintenance of weapons—and all that was before factoring in rising casualty lists and pension registers. To a budget-minded military complex, such concerns were painfully relevant.

Tactically speaking, guncotton's smokelessness meant that a man could loose a shot and then, no longer blinded by the traditional fog of the battlefield, immediately fire again. For progressives, the advent of smokeless powder "set a premium upon marksmanship" because soldiers "will have no excuse for wild firing at clouds of smoke" and "each shot will be directed at the men of the enemy."[12] Then again, smokelessness also meant that the enemy marksmen would be more likely to hit one's own troops. In the future, for precisely that reason, armies that were once garishly and gorgeously uniformed (so that friendly soldiers could see each other in the smokestorms darkening the battlefield) began outfitting their troops in muted colors to camouflage them.[13] By the turn of the century the once-red coated British Army, for instance, was kitted in khaki.[14] From 1902 the U.S. Army relegated its Revolutionary War–era dark blue to formal use only and switched to khaki in the summer and olive drab in the winter for its service uniforms.

Less tangibly, the advent of smokeless powder also changed the experience of combat. Throughout history men in battle had been fearful of *what they could see*, usually the enemy directly ahead of them; that localized, immediate fear had disappeared as soon as the foe did. But now that the enemy could fade into the landscape, soldiers grew alarmed at *what they could not see*; death might strike suddenly at any time, from anywhere, and emanate from the long-range rifle of an invisible, lurking assailant. Terror was about to become universal and opaque.

The most practical argument to be made against guncotton, however, was that it was too dangerous to manufacture. During the initial wave of excitement various countries had built factories to produce the substance in large quantities. But careless preparation, unfamiliarity with the process, and other factors resulted in a series of horrific explosions. In July 1847 Hall & Sons of Faversham, in Britain, blew up with the loss of twenty-one lives. In July 1848 sixteen hundred kilograms of guncotton exploded at a factory at Bouchet, France, killing a large number of civilians and employees. Major industrial accidents occurred in Prussia and Russia as well. By 1850 guncotton production had been almost wholly outlawed throughout Europe. In the United States such disasters had not occurred, mostly because manufacturers had been awaiting Ordnance approval before investing in large factories. They had a lucky escape.[15]

Chemists, however, continued to discuss the substance's properties in the new scholarly journals, so specialized that not even *Scientific American* carried summaries of their findings. Scientists were fascinated by guncotton, for unlike gunpowder, which explodes owing to the physical proximity of its ingredients, guncotton's constituent molecules were bound organically to one another.

The one place where practical research on guncotton for military purposes continued to be quietly carried on was Austria. In the late 1850s and early 1860s Baron von Lenk, an intimate of the Habsburg emperor, maintained a small, secret project to investigate the use of guncotton as a bursting charge in howitzer shells. Lenk's experiments were only partially successful, but he did achieve the purification of guncotton's ingredients so as to better stabilize the substance and regulate the rate of combustion. Based on his research, the baron went so far as to speculate that if sufficient acid were removed during processing, guncotton could possibly be used in small-arms production.[16]

Although the United States lacked the requisite manufacturing facilities, it had maintained a highly covert interest in guncotton ever since publicly disclaiming it as a small-arms propellant. During the Civil War both North and South made some limited forays into guncotton production, only to be frustrated by the Union's lack of cotton and the Confederacy's lack of acid. In 1863, probably using Lenk's office as an unofficial channel, Lincoln's consul in Vienna, Theodore Canisius, obtained a small number of experimental guncotton cartridges and shipped them to the Ordnance Department. Colonel Theodore Laidley reported favorably on them but cautioned that they were too few for the department to carry out exhaustive research. A secret telegram was then dispatched to Canisius, directing him to obtain as many cartridges as he could. The consul, pulling every string in Vienna and then some, succeeded in acquiring a batch of one thousand and smuggled them home in the diplomatic bags. Though this number was nowhere near sufficient to render an accurate judgment, and even considering that the army's Springfields could not handle the Austrian cartridges, Laidley believed that Washington should in any case purchase the rights to Lenk's purification process. And that was the last anyone heard of guncotton officially until 1879, the year when the Ordnance Department first mentioned the subject again in its reports.[17]

The department remained firmly convinced that guncotton was too unstable for everyday service use. In any case, neither the advocates of military repeaters nor the backers of the Springfield were keen on the introduction of a new powder: Winchesters, Hotchkisses, and the like had a hard enough time handling a service load, let alone one of guncotton, while the Springfield, according to its most ardent exponents, was near to reaching its apex of perfection. A switch to guncotton would require a wholesale revamping of the weapon. Returning the new Springfield, perhaps not to square one but certainly to square two or three, would require years of testing and render obsolete all the results so painstakingly gathered from various experiments and trials over the decades.

By the mid-1880s rumors circulated within Ordnance circles that the French had made a top-secret breakthrough. Whereas British, German, and American chemists had discussed each other's academic papers, the French had remained mysteriously aloof ever since the discovery of guncotton. Then, from nowhere seemingly, they announced the appearance of the Lebel rifle, powered by a propellant named Poudre B. It was the invention of a young military chemist, Paul Vieille, who blended guncotton with ether and alcohol to produce a gelatinized mass that could be thinly rolled, cut, and dried for easy cartridge loading. Poudre B thus successfully retarded and stabilized guncotton's furious burn rate.[18] Moreover by keeping the bullet inside the barrel for longer, so as to better exploit the burgeoning pressure behind it, the new propellant permitted the projectile to achieve amazing speeds. Consequently, just 43.25 grains of Poudre B produced an incredible velocity of 2,020 feet per second for a bullet weighing 232 grains. The Springfield .45-70-405's velocity, by way of comparison, was roughly 1,350 feet per second. "These are about the best results ever given with a small arm," judged a studiedly phlegmatic *Scientific American.*[19]

The magazine's calmness notwithstanding, Vieille's taming of guncotton understandably sparked a frantic powder race among the Great Powers. Poudre B was a single-base powder—it used only one explosive as the active ingredient—as opposed to the still more powerful double-base powders soon conceived by the Swede Alfred Nobel in 1888 and Hiram Maxim a year later.[20]

In the United States, Ordnance looked distinctly inept and behind the times. Its pooh-poohing of guncotton's possibilities as a small-arms propellant—now proved wholly erroneous—had lost it pride of place in the global constellation of first-rate arms and munitions manufacturers. Mesmerized by its internal debates over repeaters versus single-shot weapons, over Indian fighting versus European warfare, and over firepower versus marksmanship, the country's military had collectively missed the greatest ammunition development since the beginning of the metallic-cartridge era.

In 1889 the chief of Ordnance was forced to confess grimly that every attempt his department had made to reproduce smokeless powder had failed. As the new double-base smokeless powders, being highly classified, were impossible to purchase on the open market in Europe, it was alarming that "all effort, official and otherwise, to date, to obtain a smokeless powder has been abortive." Even American military attachés to the chancelleries and palaces of Europe, whose job it was to procure secret intelligence, could do no better than file sparse reports gleaned from sources of dubious accuracy.

Given these failures, Benét felt it was imperative that the United States develop its own powder and produce it. To this end, the Ordnance chief decided to make his memorandum on smokeless powder public in the hopes of stimulating some American company or entrepreneur to concoct a suitable substitute. *Scientific American* readers were additionally tipped off by his hint-hint comments that since "no American has yet submitted for trial a smokeless powder," evidently "American powder makers and chemists have not yet awakened to the lucrative opportunity presented them."[21]

Never before had a senior Ordnance officer been forced to admit openly that private industry could compete with—nay, might even exceed—the best that Springfield had to offer. Benét's confession was a humiliating one and surely hastened his retirement in 1891. Ordnance, after all, had long had a mutual "like-dislike" relationship—"love-hate" is too strong a term—with private business. Ever since the department had fostered the interchangeability revolution and sent its employees out into the world to found their own firms, Ordnance staff had, as federal officials, believed themselves effortlessly superior to those who lacked their scholarly, social, and military credentials.

Businessmen irritated by Ordnance's smugness, on the other hand, pointed out that all those lucrative foreign arms contracts streaming in were not for Springfields and armory-produced ammunition but for Remingtons, Winchesters, and the little products of the Union Metallic Cartridge company. For them, Benét's comeuppance was the delicious climax to a long-running fight between private firms and the government.

From the 1870s onward major and minor gun-makers alike, to take on the Ordnance monolith, had formed themselves into the Association of Manufacturers of Arms, Ammunition and Equipment. To its members' collective mind, only the association's intense lobbying efforts had obliged Ordnance to allow Winchesters, Remingtons, Lees, Hotchkisses, and so forth into its weapons trials to compete against the department's precious Springfield. The president of the Whitney Arms Company, Eli Whitney, Jr.—the son of the Whitney who invented the cotton gin— acted as the association's spokesman and went so far as to say in 1878 that had the government taken the "millions of dollars that have been spent upon the National Armories" and diverted it to the private sector, then the United States would today be "the best armed country in the world." The entire armory system should be shuttered, he argued, and its budget parceled out among association members.

The association's criticism of Ordnance for favoring its own weapon could be justified, but its proposal to terminate all government arms production and research in order to scoop up its appropriations was too patently self-interested for most congressmen to stomach. The whole affair appeared to be an effort by manufacturers to shore up their own failing businesses at the expense of the government. (Confirming these suspicions, Whitney's company would be liquidated in 1888, the same year in which Remington was divided up between Marcellus Hartley's United Metallic Company and Winchester.) It was no great surprise, then, that the association's campaign in the late 1870s to privatize the arms business was quashed.[22]

Times had changed by 1890. Thanks to the smokeless-powder debacle, to Lee's immensely profitable defection to the British with his rejected, superb rifle, and to continuing French and German weapons advances, Ordnance could no longer lord it over private makers and was compelled to plea humbly for its profit-making rivals to help save American face.

The arms-maker Maxim and the black-powder producer Du Pont, as well as the Belgian Wetteren company, were among the first to present their wares to Ordnance. None were wholly satisfactory: Maxim's could be loaded into the cartridge only one grain at a time, Wetterin's smelled disconcertingly of pineapple when fired, and Du Pont's was difficult to load because it was cut into rectangles. These defects could soon be rectified, but more seriously, none of the competitors had succeeded in making a powder as powerful as that used by the French. On average, their powders propelled a bullet at 1,700 feet per second, faster than regular black powder could, but the army had stipulated at least 2,000.[23]

Ordnance, however, was not entirely down for the count. In 1892 the department successfully lobbied for funds to establish a chemical laboratory at Frankford Arsenal, the government's traditional center of ammunition manufacturing. By the end of 1893 what might be called the cooperative competition between Ordnance and private enterprise had allowed the United States to catch up to its European rivals, and the larger firms were even forging ahead with improved forms of powder. Even so, the actual output of powder lagged behind ideal requirements. In 1895 Frankford struggled to produce three million smokeless cartridges, barely sufficient for the army's everyday needs for a year, and Ordnance warned that if war broke out in the near future, an adequate supply might not "be relied upon from American manufacturers." Recalling the hard-won lessons of the Revolution and the War of 1812, when soldiers suffered from ammunition and powder shortages, Ordnance tried hard to ensure that production was divided up among several firms—itself quite an accomplishment, considering that six years previously, there had been none at all—each prepared to expand capacity to a limited degree upon the declaration of hostilities. A year after the department announced the shortage of smokeless cartridges, the staff could congratulate themselves on a job well done: there was now sufficient powder for all the army's service rifles and even enough to replace black powder for target practice and ceremonial shooting using blanks.[24]

The most immediate effect of the smokeless revolution was felt on bullet design. The deleterious impact of air resistance on a bullet's flight path and range heavily depends on its velocity; the projectile's size and shape also play a role. A bullet propelled by guncotton is so much faster than one propelled by regular powder that greater air resistance threatened to offset any gains in accuracy caused by the flatter trajectories of the speeding projectiles. In order to lower air resistance, ballisticians began reducing caliber and lengthening and narrowing ammunition to create a more aerodynamic bullet. A consequence of this change was that the spiral grooves inside a rifle's barrel had to be "twisted" more tightly than ever before, to impart increased spin, so that these light, elongated projectiles did not tumble end over end in midflight as air resistance pushed against them.

A by-product of the tighter twists was that normal bullets—from time immemorial fashioned from soft, malleable lead—were being torqued literally to pieces as they hurtled up the barrel. To prevent the immense centrifugal forces from ripping the bullets apart, arms-makers began jacketing them in either copper or cupro-nickel.[25]

The infuriating problem, then, was that these small-caliber bullets—even with their jacketing—could not match the killing ability of the good old one-shot, one-kill .45-70. The solution was inescapable: guns would have to fire more bullets, more quickly, to compensate for the loss in hitting power. No matter what advocates of the Springfield might say, the day was coming when the exclusively single-shot military rifle must pass into history.

The *New York Times* summarized the problem: "As a serviceable weapon there is, perhaps, none better than the Springfield," but compared to the products issuing from European arms-makers, it was distressingly antiquated. The average caliber of the British, Austrian, German, Belgian, Swiss, Portuguese, French, and Danish service rifles had fallen to .31 (roughly two-thirds of the Springfield's weighty .45), while their average muzzle velocity was 2,008 feet per second (about a third more than the Springfield's 1,300).[26]

Ordnance had, in fact, been looking into the issue of smaller-caliber rifles for some time. In 1887 Benét had concluded that because there was "a movement in that direction in military circles both here and abroad," a reduced caliber for the next generation of small arms was a certainty. A .30 was even mooted—quite a comedown from the mighty .45. The choice of caliber was arbitrary: Springfield's commanding officer told the chief of Ordnance that .30 (rather than .29 or .31) had been selected "not from any special principle involved," but because it was easier for tool-makers to work with "even" numbers.[27] On such small accidents are the tidal waves of history based. The Ordnance Department accordingly developed blueprints for a suitably shaped and charged cartridge, but it could do nothing tangible—either in ammunition manufacture or in rifle procurement—until sufficient supplies of smokeless powder had been obtained.

Brigadier General Daniel Flagler, a New York–born Ordnance lieutenant during the Civil War and superintendent of three arsenals (Rock Island, Frankford, and Watertown), replaced the aged Benét in early 1891. His job, as he saw it, was twofold. First, he needed an American-made powder; and second, he needed an American-made rifle to fire it. The 1890s were perhaps the high point of nationalist fervor, and while he could simply have bought Mausers and Mannlichers from the Germans, the very idea of outsourcing U.S. military requirements to foreigners was abhorrent. "It is hoped," wrote Flagler, "that this country can produce a better arm, and until it can, or certainly until it has been demonstrated that it can not, it would be wise to defer a change from the excellent single-loader now in service to a magazine system."[28] To those who complained that Ordnance was desperately grasping on to an outmoded weapon (the *New York Times* accused him of dithering), Flagler retorted that an infantryman using one of these apparently obsolete Springfield single-shots could fire up to twenty rounds per minute "with the accuracy generally needed in action."[29]

His opponents immediately attacked by highlighting the disingenuousness of that reply. What did "accuracy generally needed" mean? At what range? How likely was it that a soldier could load, aim, and fire a bullet every three seconds in battle for a sustained period? To them, soldiers obviously needed a modern rifle with a magazine designed so that they could choose to fire singly or quickly, depending on range and conditions. Moreover such a rifle would finally allow diehards and progressives to reach compromise after so many decades of infighting. If progressives accepted the diehard emphasis on rapid, intense firing at close quarters, and if diehards accepted that marksmen could be used to harry the enemy at long distance with accurate fire, then surely peace between the warring camps was nigh.

The *principle* of a magazine being mutually agreed upon, the last point of contention, then, would be the *type* of magazine. Diehards tended to favor a Mannlicher-style clip that would slot into place and be instantly ready to unleash hell. More progressive soldiers were keener on a Winchester-style magazine that needed to be loaded one cartridge at a time, both as homage to the single-shot rifleman's traditional skills and also to remind troops not to waste their ammunition like the musketmen of yore and the repeater-armed civilians of then.

To make the final decision, Flagler set July 1, 1892, as the deadline for the submission of rifles for a new board to test. Fifty-three arms were sent to Ordnance; all but one or two were bolt-action pieces, and most were magazines (some in the forestock, some in the buttstock, some rotary, some box). Thirty-seven were quickly rejected as poor to useless. Then, surprisingly, the British-made Lee, the vaunted Mauser, and then a highly experimental .30 single-shot Springfield flopped out. Neither the Lee nor the Mauser company was quite out of the running, since they both had other models entered, but still their missteps were embarrassing. As for the Springfield, it had been patched up many times in its twenty-six years of faithful service, but this was once too often. Even Flagler had to admit that the United States was "suffering in a military reputation" from its reliance on the single-shot Springfield.[30]

The next round saw further culling, and by the third heat there were just seven left, including a Mannlicher, a Mauser, a Lee, and a Krag-Jørgensen—a Norwegian rifle developed by Captain Ole Krag, superintendent of the Königsberg arsenal, and Erik Jørgensen, its civilian master armorer. It was quickly emerging as the surprise star of the competition.[31] "Greatly to the surprise of the average American inventor of the small-arm mechanism," commented the *New York Times,* "the board of army experts [has] decided upon adopting a weapon of foreign design rather than a child of their own creation."[32] First place was awarded to this obscure, foreign-made rifle. Lieutenant Colonel Hall of the Sixth Infantry, the president of the board, praised it as a "suitable and satisfactory arm to be adopted for the United States military service."[33]

Crucially, though it had a magazine, the Krag had a mechanical cut-off so that it could be loaded and fired as a single-shot arm, thereby appeasing the most vocal of the army's marksmen, though some feared that its bullet's small caliber (.30), modest charge (40 grains), and light weight (220 grains, jacketed in cupro-nickel) would not kill when it connected—even if smokelessly traveling at 2,000 feet per second.

The diehards' temper was, however, assuaged by the Krag's jam-proof, rapid-action firing and by its sights, which even one of its greatest fans described as "an abomination" and "truly primitive—music to their ears, for it meant that long-distance accuracy was out of the question." On the Continent armies used sights that were not adjustable for windage, barely for elevation, and not at all for barrel twist. Instead, they were designed to fire at a set range of standard distances in increments of one hundred yards—which made it easier for officers to retain control over their men's shooting. These attributes made them distinctly inferior to the Springfields' exacting "Buffington sights," which had been developed with Creedmoor-style shooting in mind. Though marksmen could customize their Krags with infinitely better sights, they would be issued as they were to regular troops.[34]

American makers complained about the choice of the Krag and begged to be given another chance. Domestic and political pressure from Congress induced the board to agree to retest some fourteen arms, only to (again) reject them all in May 1893.[35] One month later, on June 1, the Springfield .45-70 single-shot rifle ceased production, and remaining stocks were passed on to the various state National Guards.

Yet a lingering desire for an American-made arm remained, and Flagler privately assured domestic manufacturers that the Norwegian interloper would be sent back to the Nordic wastes once Americans developed a suitable replacement.[36] Until that happy day, Ordnance bought the patent rights (a royalty of one dollar per gun) from its inventors to manufacture the weapon entirely in the United States (so that at least it didn't seem as foreign). After a lengthy process of converting its arsenals over to the new machinery, the United States succeeded in outfitting the entire army (of 28,000-odd soldiers) with the new service arm within a year.[37]

Being handed a Krag and then firing it for the first time must have been a jarring experience for the regular American soldier accustomed to his trusty Springfield .45-70. Where was the belching smoke, the bruising recoil? What were these pipsqueak cartridges? Why had the reassuring roar of his Springfield been replaced by a distinct "crack" from this rifle? The Krag was the first service weapon to use smokeless powder, and many had never heard of the stuff. Their bafflement might have deepened when they aimed their Krags at, say, a tree trunk or a thick wooden board. A Springfield, using the usual .45 round propelled by a charge of 70 grains of black powder, could push a bullet 3.3 inches deep into oak, or 5.3 inches when the projectile was protected by a cupro-nickel jacket. In both instances, the bullet left a thick gash in its wake and was badly deformed by its rough passage. A .30 Krag round, powered by 37 grains of smokeless powder and similarly jacketed, managed the astounding feat of penetrating 24.2 inches into oak. And at its terminus the bullet was barely damaged. Those witnessing such a performance could justly speculate that this bullet would not only disable an enemy soldier but might very well pass through two or three soft-bellied men standing too close together.[38]

The outbreak of war with Spain in 1898 caught the army off guard and critically undersupplied. Nevertheless, Americans were chipper since, for the first time since the War of 1812, they had a real European army to fight—even if it belonged to a Great Power that was long over its powerful greatness. (Spain did manage to field a force of 150,000, however, six times larger than the U.S. Army.) At the time Ordnance had stockpiled some 50,000 Krags (in addition to those already issued), but by August of that year the armed forces had swollen to 275,000 men, overwhelmingly National Guardsmen who had volunteered for overseas service.[39]

All could be given Springfields from the vast reserve, but they were equipped to fire only traditional black-powder rounds. When it came to smokeless cartridges, Ordnance had 4.5 million on hand, which amounted to just 60 rounds per Krag, hardly enough for even a single engagement considering that the rifle could fire around 50 shots in three minutes. Even Ordnance officials estimated that each man should carry 175 rounds as standard, and that 300 rounds at a minimum were needed for a battle.[40]

The shortage had been caused partly by the financial panic of 1893 and the resulting depression, which prevented private manufacturers from fulfilling their contracts, as well as by delays in selecting the optimum smokeless mixture. Ordnance eventually managed to extricate itself temporarily from the bottleneck by reserving Krags for the regulars and Springfields for the Volunteers, apart from those serving with the Rough Riders. Colonel Leonard Wood, commanding the Riders, had realized (according to Theodore Roosevelt) "the inestimable advantage of smokeless powder," and by agitating for Krags, he managed to get them for his men. Even so, because the Krags were issued so shortly before sailing, the Riders had to drill without cartridges.[41]

Arms-makers were told to urgently devote more resources to turning out smokeless .45 rounds so that at least the Springfield-armed Volunteers would have modern ammunition. Consequently, the earlier a

Volunteer departed for the front, the less likely he was to be carrying smokeless rounds. Thus when the first complements of Volunteers arrived in Cuba, they were greeted by Spanish troops whose first-rate modern Mausers shot into the billowing, sulfurous clouds of smoke coming from the Americans, at once obscuring the latter's line of sight and revealing their position. If the Spanish took cover, it was difficult for the Americans to return fire, and the Volunteers took heavy losses. By July, when the fighting had moved to Santiago, Springfield-armed troops had been transferred away from the front line and combat was left mostly to soldiers with Krags and smokeless rounds.

This experience showed that while the progressive emphasis on marksmanship and self-initiative still had its adherents, and while diehards remained convinced that officer-led discipline created efficient soldiers, small wars in the real world confounded (and confirmed) the assertions of both. Thus General Shafter of the Fifth Army Corps proudly claimed that 80 percent of his men "wore on their breasts the marksman's badge" and that in two hours' fighting they had fired fewer than ten rounds apiece—presumably to great effect.[42] Several officers also testified that their riflemen had displayed a heroic willingness to rely on their own enterprise and a can-do spirit instead of dully waiting for orders. Private William Beatty—an "experienced hunter and good shot," according to his regimental chief—of the First Colorado decided to sally out alone from his outpost to take care of a Spaniard who had been plaguing the regiment all day. After stripping off his uniform and negotiating a ditch, Beatty shot him at 150 yards.[43] While William Church and his fellow progressives had predicted an end to martial barbarism thanks to the marksman's unerring aim, it was discovered that sharpshooting did not necessarily make for gentlemanliness; if anything, it could extend the killing to targets previously held sacrosanct. Richard Harding Davis, the war correspondent, reported that enemy snipers "spared neither the wounded nor the Red Cross, they killed the surgeons and the stewards carrying the litters."[44]

On the other side of the fence, Leonard Wood was pleased that his Rough Riders, adhering to the finest diehard traditions, maintained strict discipline and obediently waited for their officers' commands before firing—the racket of hundreds of magazines simultaneously being opened, loaded, and shut must have been quite a sound; but once the shooting started, it unexpectedly became impossible to maintain any sort of control.[45] The smarty-pants commentators back home, noted Davis, had "foretold that the cowboys would shoot as they chose and . . . would act independently of their officers." But "as it turned out, the cowboys were the very men who waited most patiently for the officers to give the word of command." All the same, he added, once that word was given, the fighting turned "breathless and fierce, like a . . . street-fight."[46]

The fetish for disciplined fire was hard to maintain once commanders began realizing that aggressive attacking *combined* with massive fire-power worked wonders against even entrenched infantry.[47] "By sweeping the ground that we were advancing over with a storm of bullets," wrote Brigadier General Frederick Funston, "we could so demoralize the enemy that his fire would be badly directed."[48] Dug-in defenders subjected to such a fusillade refused to stand up and fire back, testament to the long-held diehard conviction that repeaters and magazine-fed rifles, not marksmanship and mastery of the single-shot Springfield, were key to emerging triumphant from any modern battle.

Crouching and crawling at San Juan Hill, and harassed by the spat and whine of Mauser bullets, some seven thousand American troops unleashed upon the tiny outpost at its brow one of the greatest concentrations of rifle fire hitherto ever delivered. So intense was the American fire that their Krags' metal parts became burningly hot as the men pulled the trigger and bolt without rest up to 150 times in rapid succession. The soldiers took to pouring the precious contents of water bottles over their rifles to cool them down.

The vast majority of the tens of thousands of bullets hit nothing but wall, air, or dirt; but even so, after Roosevelt's triumphant charge up San Juan Hill, it was noticed that every Spanish casualty in the trenches had been shot several times in the face or had "little holes in their heads from which their brains were oozing" (Roosevelt's words). Any Spaniard unwise enough to poke his head above the parapet for a look-see had run smack into a fusillade of fire. They weren't killed by American sharpshooters. Quite the opposite, in fact. Roosevelt later said his orderly "had stopped to shoot, and two Spaniards fell as he emptied his magazine.

These were the only Spaniards I actually saw fall to aimed shots by any of my men, with the exception of two guerrillas in trees." The latter might have been downed by someone like Lieutenant Charles Muir of the Second Infantry, who was officially recorded as being "of the class of distinguished sharpshooters" and, in classic progressive style, a "man who mixes brains with gun powder." He shot two Spaniards, both at an impressive eleven hundred yards.[49]

Aside from its heroic splendors, San Juan taught American troops distinctly unmythical lessons about the realities of modern combat. With respect to Lieutenant Muir's sharpshooting talents, the two unlucky Spaniards would almost certainly have survived being hit. Roosevelt's men had quickly discovered that it was difficult to wound the enemy grievously, let alone kill him, using their new Krag ammunition.

The old .45 rifles, conversely, used by guerrillas and the Spanish irregulars had inflicted terrible wounds. ("There was one thing to be said for those old Springfields," reflected General Funston, "and that was that if a bullet from one of them hit a man he never mistook it for a mosquito bite.") But as Roosevelt noticed, "the Mauser bullets themselves made a small clean hole, with the result that the wound healed in a most astonishing manner." Much of the time "the wounds from the minute steel-coated bullet, with its very high velocity, were certainly nothing like as serious as those made by the old large-caliber, low-power rifle. If a man was shot through the heart, spine, or brain he was, of course, killed instantly; but very few of the wounded died—even under the appalling conditions which prevailed." One of his Rough Riders, for instance, was shot no fewer than seven times over the course of half an hour, but only when he was at last hit in the neck and losing blood quickly did he consent to leave the battlefield.[50] Captain Munson, one of the surgeons at the field hospital, confirmed that "wounds by the Mauser bullet were apparently either immediately fatal on the field or trivial in their subsequent course." Exit wounds were "scarcely larger than [those] of entrance," and the jacketed bullets "did not make the ghastly wounds that were expected."[51] Unfortunately, the Mausers' lack of killing power inspired an element of hubris among some Americans. "There is no Spanish bullet made that can kill me," boasted Captain

O'Neill of the Rough Riders a few heroic seconds before realizing that, yes, in fact, there was.[52]

Hard figures confirmed the anecdotal evidence of reduced morbidity and mortality from Mauser bullets. During the war U.S. troops incurred 1,320 cases of gunshot wounds in combat; of them, more than nine in ten were caused by rifle bullets—a figure tracking with the Civil War's average of 90.1 percent. Slightly more than a quarter of these battle wounds were in the upper extremities, and a third were in the lower ones; owing to the likelihood of rapid blood loss if the major femoral and popliteal arteries were holed, death from being hit in the legs was commoner than if shot in the arms (2.6 percent to 1.1 percent). Even so, that percentage was not high, and had been hugely reduced from the Civil War figures of 13.8 percent and 6.5 percent respectively. Compared against the wounds men suffered in the Civil War, the Spanish-American casualties showed impressive improvements in survivability when they were shot in the rectum, genitals, bladder, prostate, and back (excluding spine): 1.9 percent, down from 11.7 percent. Abdominal injuries still remained by far the most lethal ones, accounting for about half of all deaths by gunshot, but in the Civil War 89.5 percent had proved fatal. Usually these remarkable improvements are attributed to prompt and antiseptic first aid, the increasing popularity of "surgical conservatism" (leaving wounds to heal rather than amputating at the first opportunity), and the advent of X-rays. These factors, of course, made a great difference in *after*-battle care. But in fact the diminished lethality of small-caliber Krag and Mauser rounds relative to the Civil War's heavy .45s, .577s, and .58s was primarily responsible for the decline in mortality during combat.[53]

Roosevelt may have been astonished that the much-feared Mauser's high-velocity bullet inflicted so little damage, but he was by no means the only one. Until then virtually every ordnance expert, casual shooter, gunsmith, and soldier in the world had assumed that the faster a bullet traveled, and the greater its mass, the more shocking would be its impact as it thudded into the victim, pierced his skin, ripped his innards, and emerged on the other side. Thus caliber (which primarily determined projectile mass) and velocity were key to inflicting the kinds of gruesome wounds likeliest to result in the death of a bullet's recipient. Centuries of

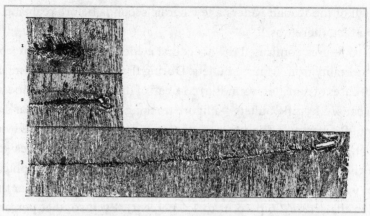

Number 1 is the traditional lead .45 powered by 69 grains of black powder (penetrating just 3.3 inches into oak); Number 2 is the same but the lead has been jacketed by German silver (penetrating 5.3 inches); Number 3 is a new, jacketed .30 propelled by 37 grains of Wetteren smokeless powder (penetrating 24.2 inches into oak). Such performance amazed ordnance specialists, but they overlooked a major factor: Notice that the .45 in both cases is badly deformed, while the .30 has retained its shape. Though possessing significantly slower velocity, the .45s would inflict much greater trauma in tissue; the .30s would often simply perforate the skin and drill sleekly through muscle and organs before exiting cleanly.

ammunition development and rifle technology had been based on precisely this principle, thereby partly explaining why armies had been obsessed with increasing muzzle velocity and sticking fast to large calibers for so long.

What Roosevelt (and everybody else) had misunderstood was that caliber and velocity were certainly factors critical to a bullet's behavior *before* impact, but once metal hit skin, the projectile's shape, construction, and eventual destination heavily influenced the extent of actual damage. Though the metal-jacketed Krag (or Mauser) slugs penetrated deeply into tissue, owing to their hardened sheathing the bullets did not fragment or deform within the victim—unlike the old lead ones that on impact transformed into a mushroom shape or shattered apart against bone. Hence Colonel Senn, the Americans' chief operating surgeon, was surprised to find relatively few Mauser bullets lodged in the body. It seems they were passing straight through the victim in one piece.[54]

Whether a soldier survived hinged on what the bullet hit as it toured his body. The primary purpose of a projectile is to disrupt tissue: when a bullet enters a human, it crushes the tissue directly in front as it drills forward. The channel created by its passage is termed the permanent cavity. In addition, it pushes or "stretches" the meaty tissue, as well as the bloody juice surrounding the channel, centrifugally, rather as a stone hitting water sends ripples outward, thereby creating a temporary cavity, which is many times larger than the permanent cavity. After expanding to a certain volume, these temporary cavities collapse behind the bullet. Thus the victim might very well have a small entrance wound, or even a small exit one, but experience an explosion inside his body. Gore splashes out at the points of entrance and exit, because the temporary cavity has torn muscle and connective tissue, ruptured small blood vessels, ballooned the larger ones, and compressed nerves. However, if a bullet fragments inside, its minute shards shoot radially outward like secondary missiles, each of them creating a new, smaller permanent cavity and minor temporary ones. As the shards are irregularly shaped and turn randomly on their axes, the extent and jaggedness of the permanent cavities they leave in their wake can vary widely. Thomas Longmore, a British war surgeon who was among the first to describe permanent- and temporary-cavity effects in the 1870s, wrote that there was generally "a huge hollow . . . formed inside the limb which, when it is fully laid open and the effused blood sponged away, offers to view a large mass of lacerated muscle intimately mixed with sharp-pointed and jagged-edge splinters of bone."

The body's ability to repair these cavities depends on the elasticity of the organs or tissue affected. Muscles, bowel walls, lungs, and skin are relatively "stretchy," and recovery from damage by Krag/Mauser rounds there was often a matter of time and decent care. Assuming their wounds did not become infected or they did not collapse from blood loss, soldiers suffering such wounds would often be nursed back to health. While during the Civil War 62 percent of perforating chest wounds caused by fragmenting minié balls were fatal, a few years after the Spanish-American War the American military attaché in Manchuria recalled seeing enemy soldiers walking eighteen miles to the rear after being shot in the lungs with Krag rounds. On the other hand, the liver is a brittle organ, and a hit there was a death sentence.[55]

Owing to the apparently reduced lethality of warfare, some well-meaning commentators even cheered that "the reduced cartridge accomplishes its object in a more humane manner [than the .45], in that it disables the soldier equally well for the time being without shattering in an unnecessary and brutal manner the bone which it may happen to strike." Indeed, "nothing is gained by excessive maiming."[56]

The troops disagreed, and American soldiers fighting in the Philippines (1899–1902) after San Juan Hill illicitly made their own dum-dum bullets out of their army-issue Krag rounds.[57] Dum-dums, invented in 1895 and named after a British military outpost near Calcutta in India, were bullets mutilated by grinding off the metal-jacketed tip and notching a cross into the lead with a knife so they would burst, mushroom, or expand upon impact (especially at close range), thereby helping overcome the Krag's small-caliber "humane" factor. As part of the general shift toward humanizing war, the International Peace Conference at The Hague in 1899 outlawed the "use of bullets which expand or flatten easily in the human body," but the mass industrialization of slaughter that erupted in 1914 made a mockery of such pretensions.

*The Springfield Model
1903 Rifle*

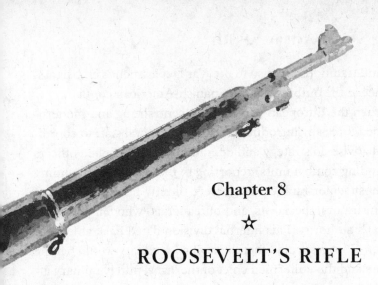

Chapter 8

☆

ROOSEVELT'S RIFLE

The final decade of the nineteenth century was among its most tumultuous. Beset by mass immigration, buffeted by violent strikes, amazed by the coming of the electrical age, cramped together by the new urbanization, subjected to new financial and social stresses by the incorporation of America and its transformation from a producer society into a consumer one, jingoed up by international naval geopolitics and the lingering desires of Manifest Destiny, stimulated by a weird interest in Social Darwinism, and rendered unemployed by a terrible depression between 1893 and 1896: people were alarmed and confused by all these developments and feared the future. By the late 1890s there was national support—perhaps not truly bipartisan, but certainly approaching it—for moderately progressive political, economic, and social reform to ready America for the excitement, or horror, of the coming century.

A key strut underpinning any reformer's platform was the urgent need to modernize the country's cobwebbed institutions, many of which either hadn't changed since about the time of the War of 1812 or had been contemptibly rotted from within by incompetence and self-dealing. In Washington the most patently obvious candidate for an astringent burst of spring cleaning was the army, owing not only to its creakingly archaic organization and traditions but also to the War Department's embarrassing performance at the outbreak of the Spanish-American conflict.

At a time when the European powers were centralizing and modernizing their armed forces by introducing a unified general staff to coordinate, plan, and advise on strategy and operations, American line officers (those commanding combat units) reporting to the army's commanding general (the most senior rank existing) were bitterly feuding with staff officers (administrators, specialists, and bureaucrats) who fell under the secretary of war's authority. This internal division dated back at least to the 1830s, when Congress ruled that the civilian secretary would handle all fiscal matters and the uniformed chief of the army, purely military affairs. With one man holding the purse strings and another grasping for them, the system was proving unworkable.

Presidents were all too aware of the system's built-in conflicts, but they did little to crack skulls. A strong president often preferred to keep his minions squabbling to prevent them from forming potentially rebellious alliances; a weak one tended to fall under the sway of the more powerful of two warring barons. A militarily experienced president naturally sided with his commanding general; an inexperienced one, with his chosen secretary of war. Worse, because they served for indefinite terms, commanding generals became accustomed to regarding themselves as virtually independent deities, not even subject to the commander in chief, the president. After all, presidents came and went every four or eight years, but commanding generals could stay in harness for *decades*. As for secretaries of war, the minuteness of the armed forces made the War Department something of a dead-end job. Incumbents had little incentive to do anything but keep the clock ticking until the next administration came along.

Lower down in the system, line officers hated reporting to staffers back in comfortable Washington, whom they imagined were rather more concerned with fighting turf wars than real ones. Instead of building a war machine, they complained, the red-tape brigade was turning the army into a paper mill. Line officers argued that the plethora of semiautonomous, closed-shop bureaus (like Ordnance) and technical departments was unwieldly, inefficient, and expensive. Bureau chiefs, fiercely protective of their rights and freedoms, retorted that they ran specialist outfits that were dependent on expertise and that no ordinary infantry captain could be expected to just "fill in" when it came to building bridges, designing advanced artillery, or practicing medicine.[1]

In the summer of 1898 the line-officer faction seemed to have pulled ahead when General Nelson A. Miles (anointed commanding general in 1895) began fancying a White House run to replace Republican president William McKinley in the 1900 election.

Miles was the very model of the traditional major general, and he knew it. His golden epaulettes glittering, his breast jangling with medals, his legs encased in the most polished of leather boots, Miles was a military hero who adored the peacockery of Victorian-style uniforms. He was now a far cry from his obscure beginnings as a clerk in a Boston crockery store with a basic grammar school education; through sheer application and unrelenting will, he had gained his lieutenancy without either a West Point or Ivy League pedigree.[2]

Miles, despite his accomplishments, was perpetually disappointed that his heroism had never translated into public acclamation. So desperately did he want to be popular that he launched a quixotic quest to weaken McKinley by embroiling McKinley's ally, Secretary of War Russell Alger, in a scandal over military food supplies. The general publicly claimed that the War Department had sickened the troops by feeding them contaminated beef in Cuba. In so doing, Miles not only forced McKinley to oust the colorless Alger but strengthened his own position as commanding general against the War Department staffers.[3]

Miles's luck, however, was running out. A board of inquiry investigated his accusations of beef profiteering and departmental ineptitude and found insufficient grounds for them. Public opinion, which had recently lauded him as a valiant whistleblower, rapidly soured on the aging warhorse. Miles's ambitions were finally quashed when Republicans, casting about for a suitable military hero to buttress McKinley for his 1899–1900 presidential campaign, chose as his vice-presidential nominee not the tainted Miles but the sainted Theodore Roosevelt, victor of San Juan Hill. Just as unfortunately, Alger's replacement at the War Department in August 1899 was Elihu Root, a far more dangerous and cunning adversary than his hapless predecessor.

Born in 1845, Root, the son of a professor of mathematics, attended law school at New York University and made a name for himself defending Tammany Hall capo William "Boss" Tweed during his criminal trial for corruption. After serving as U.S. attorney for the Southern District of New York, he chaired the Republican County Committee during Roosevelt's 1886 run for mayor of New York City. Roosevelt's bid failed, but Root again proved his indispensability and his fidelity two years later when he suppressed some pernickety questions about whether Roosevelt, in an effort to "minimize" his taxes, had fulfilled the state's residency requirements during his governorship campaign.[4]

As he was a lawyer with no military experience, Root's appointment as secretary of war came as a surprise to most everyone, not least himself. But McKinley felt that the very absence of a soldierly background was an asset, for it meant, ostensibly at least, that Root had no dog in the unending feud between the line and staff army factions. He was touted to suspicious staffers and line officers as merely an ombudsman, not as an advocate. "I took the United States for my client," he reassured them as he acceded to Alger's vacated chair.[5]

Perceptive observers of the Washington *mischianza* understood that the Roosevelt-Root team would inevitably drive through major reforms—either by sheer force of character (in Roosevelt's case) or by craftily indirect means (in Root's).

Roosevelt had already earned his stripes during his Police Commission days, shaking up sleepy, broken departments. His first victim had been New York Police Department chief Thomas Byrnes, whom he forced to resign on corruption charges; his second was the brutal inspector "Clubber" Williams. (His suspiciously large retirement fund, Clubber claimed, stemmed from land speculation in Japan and had nothing whatsoever to do with shaking down Lower East Side shopkeepers.) Roosevelt soon proved himself no easy roll by closing all the saloons on Sunday—as the law stipulated—and going out on the rounds late at night to catch patrolmen dozing on the job.[6]

Detail-obsessed and exacting, with a rather strange hairstyle that resembled shortened bangs and with a voice that was always soft and hoarse, Root was a perfect complement to Roosevelt's booming personality, and the two men rattled along for decades with barely a cross word. When such an incident did occur, it was hardly serious. One time they were in the dining car aboard a train returning from an inspection of West Point and fell into an argument over a particular aspect of army reform. Exasperated and irritated by Root's wiliness, Roosevelt exclaimed, "Oh, go to the devil, Root!" To which the secretary raised his champagne glass and urbanely replied, "I come, sir, I come."[7]

While Roosevelt, the politician, investigated police corruption, chased robber barons, advocated promotion strictly by merit, conserved forests, and broke up price-gouging monopolies, Root, as a great corporate lawyer, immersed himself in the most fashionable business movement of the time: "scientific management," often better known as Taylorism.

Progressively minded people (such as Louis Brandeis, the future Supreme Court justice, and Ida Tarbell, the "muckraking" journalist) saw scientific management as a hypermodern method of *liberating* workers. Scientific management, it was claimed, would eliminate unnecessary motions during production, reward conscientious employees properly with incentive pay, promote meritocracy, eradicate favoritism, remove sources of friction between management and workers, and improve all-round efficiency and productivity. Later observers would complain that scientific management reduced men to "mere mechanical instruments" (as the novelist D. H. Lawrence put it in *Women in Love*), but the world's first management consultant, Frederick Taylor (1856–1915), countered that he was offering workmen the freedom to exercise their natural abilities with steady employment at regular wages and standardized hours, using the finest machines and tools money could buy.[8]

Root wanted to bring Taylor's business methods to the business of army reform. "It does seem a pity," he argued, "that the Government of the United States should be the only great industrial establishment that cannot profit by the lessons which the world of industry and of commerce has learned to such good effect."[9]

Once esconced at the War Department, and puffing on one of his countless daily cigars, Root rapidly whipped his staff into shape along "scientific" principles. No more would they arrive at 10:30; the workday would start at 8:30 precisely. No more would they take leisurely lunches at the Metropolitan Club; coffee and sandwiches would be sent in. No more would they read newspapers all afternoon in comfy chairs; memoranda, directives, and reports would be dealt with the moment they arrived.[10]

In his own time Root soaked up the military classics so diligently that within months he could out-quote and out-analyze any West Pointer on tactics and strategy. Working late into the night, he pored over the organizational charts of the French, British, and German armies. He was particularly impressed by the work of a British military writer, Spenser Wilkinson, whose *The Brain of the Army* examined the workings of the German general staff. Root was also impressed by a long out-of-print edition of Emory Upton's *The Armies of Europe and Asia*, and discovering from reading Peter Michie's 1885 biography that Upton had written a text, now lost, on what to do with the U.S. Army, he obtained from the D. Appleton & Company publishing house the musty manuscript of Upton's unfinished masterpiece, *The Military Policy of the United States*. Root ordered it published and made it required reading among officers.[11]

Within six months of taking office, Root's first annual report (taking its cue from the French system) recommended that line officers be rotated to staff positions for three-year tours. The nucleus of the German concept of a general staff can be found in his proposal to establish a War College to allow young officers to undertake professional study. Presumably they would then join the staff, though for the moment Root steered clear of openly advocating such a scheme, owing to its explosive implications.[12]

Roosevelt, among others, cheered Root's report ("It does look as if at last light was breaking for the Army now that you have charge of it," he wrote), and it found some adherents among the younger men and up-and-comers.[13] But the report alarmed staffers and line officers alike. By introducing the principle of rotation, it threatened to break up the cozy arrangement by which staffers held their positions permanently; and by hinting at the creation of a general staff, Root was signaling that the era of the autonomous commanding general was passing, to be replaced by a chief of staff reporting to the secretary of war.

After the deranged anarchist Leon Czolgosz assassinated McKinley in September 1901, Roosevelt became president, and Root's position was strengthened. Roosevelt went on record to announce that there must be not only a general staff but "freer flow and closer touch between the line and the staff." In February 1902, consequently, Root submitted a bill calling for the army's two heads to be united.

Correctly anticipating trouble from Miles (who claimed that he had always gotten by without a staff but that now he would have to "get around a dozen or more majors" to execute the smallest decision), Root took care to offer the proud old man a choice of exits: either the general staff would be born immediately *after* he stepped down (Miles's mandatory retirement date was scheduled as August 8, 1903, when he would be sixty-four), or he could become the first chief of staff on the understanding that he would soon step aside. Roosevelt was rather less appeasement-minded than Root on the matter. He felt Miles was so selfishly ambitious that he "ought to be employed only when we are certain that his own interests and the interests of the country" coincided.[14] But Root persuaded the president to let Miles resign rather than spark a riot by sacking him.

Some fire still burned in Miles's aged belly. In front of the Senate Committee on Military Affairs, which was heavily packed with the general's comrades from the Civil War, Miles declared, in a flash of rhetorical brilliance, that the general staff concept was "more adapted to the monarchies of the old world" than to the republic of the new. He would never, he grandly announced in the best tradition of the martyr, truckle to the new un-American "despotism" of 1600 Pennsylvania Avenue.

At a stroke, Miles had reversed the perception of the Root reforms from being laudably progressive to being sinister harbingers of Euroautocracy. The *Washington Post* accordingly headlined a report from Berlin "Roosevelt His Own Warlord" and devastatingly quoted German officers as saying that the president "means to be head of the American Army de facto just as the Kaiser is his own minister of war." Root's reform bill suddenly stalled.[15]

Roosevelt, livid at Miles's draping of himself in the Stars and Stripes, now wanted him out by the end of 1902. The president's loathing for Miles never fell into remission, but Root, as usual, was more discreet and arranged for the retired commanding general John Schofield to tell a Senate committee that he backed the secretary of war and felt that his old office should be abolished. This country, Schofield added, should have "what other nations of the earth have, a chief of staff." Reassured by crusty old Schofield's appearance, many other senior officers soon outed themselves as Root backers. Miles, meanwhile, bloated by certainty that he had crippled Root, had embarked on a worldwide tour. It was a disastrous decision: during his absence, Root and Roosevelt lobbied congressmen hard, and on February 14, 1903, the bill was signed into law. A day later General Miles stepped ashore, now a powerless, forlorn figure.[16] He could only count the months until mandatory retirement.

When Miles departed on August 8, Roosevelt didn't bother sending the customary message of thanks, and Root failed to attend his leaving ceremony. Indeed, Roosevelt supplemented his formal announcement of Miles's departure with the cutting *envoi:* "Lieutenant-General Miles will now proceed to his home. The travel enjoined is necessary for the public service."[17]

Root's grand reforms signaled that the Miles-dominated era of the Indian-fighting Old Army was over. The new U.S. Army was to be a gleaming model of modernity, a bureaucratically designed example of scientific management and progressive ideals in action.

The deep and startling changes between 1898 and 1903, a half-decade that straddled the old iron-and-wood nineteenth century and the steel-and-glass twentieth, bore a lasting impact on the design and production of the army's weapons. For his new army Roosevelt wanted a new arm, a rifle that would properly represent all that the reforms stood for. In order to satisfy every army faction amid the uproar caused by Root's rout of Miles, he intended to strike the perfect balance between diehardism and progressivism while at the same time exemplifying the highest standards of scientific management. That new weapon would be the Springfield Model 1903—Roosevelt's Rifle.

★ ★ ★

The Krag symbolized the ancien régime and the Old Army. It was the legacy of Daniel Flagler, the chief of ordnance who had died in office in April 1899, and now that he had gone, it was time to clean house. Flagler's replacement had been Adelbert Buffington, the former superintendent of Springfield and the very last of the old-style Ordnance chiefs. (He even had an old-style name to go with his position.) The sole reason he got the job was that he was second in seniority behind the late Flagler, and everyone knew he was just a stopgap candidate ticking off the calendar until his retirement.

Buffington was scheduled to step down in November 1901. After him, in accordance with the Root reforms, there would be no more chiefs dying in harness at advanced ages after forty years' slow ascent up the promotional hierarchy; henceforth, there would be four-year renewable terms, a flow of new blood and fresh ideas as officers were rotated back and forth between line and staff, and selection for the top positions would be on merit.

Buffington's departure left the door open for Roosevelt and Root to select a successor who would be their trusty tool for implementing the reforms. They already had a particular man in mind. Roosevelt had talent-spotted him as early as October 1899, when Root received a note hand-delivered by Captain William Crozier. A Kansan and son of a U.S. senator, Crozier had gone up to West Point and joined an artillery regiment on the frontier in the late 1870s, then joined the Ordnance Department in 1881. Exacting and precise, he was a master of technical matters, as he showed by codesigning an advanced gun carriage for coastal artillery in the early 1890s.

As a delegate to the International Peace Conference at The Hague, Crozier had proved especially skilled at deflecting clever attempts to make the United States disarm. Upon his return in mid-1899 he approached Roosevelt and volunteered to help him implement any reforms deemed necessary within Ordnance. In order to introduce this ambitious young officer to Root, Roosevelt had given him a letter in which he asked the secretary of war to take its bearer under his wing.[18]

In the run-up to Buffington's expected departure in November 1901, the jockeying began for his replacement as chief of Ordnance. Acquiring it for Crozier—who was still merely a captain—would take some doing. That was because "all the mutton heads in the army," as Roosevelt commented to another military friend, Leonard Wood, "naturally object to anything resembling promotion by merit."[19]

The opposition's first assault against Crozier's candidacy was sounded in late September. At the War Department, reported the *Times,* officers had "been looking over the law" regarding promotions and had discovered that Crozier was "ineligible" to be made Ordnance chief since the rules stipulated that "the person selected shall not be below a Lieutenant Colonel in rank."[20]

These unnamed officers seemed to have no inkling that they were dealing with a formidable secretary of war: an admiring corporate client had once said that while he "had many lawyers who have told me what I cannot do; Mr. Root is the only lawyer who tells me how to do what I want to do."[21] Less than a fortnight after the officers' complaints, Root addressed them by promoting Crozier to . . . brigadier general—despite, or perhaps because of, the fact that twenty-nine officers had stood ahead of him in seniority at the department. The move, remarked the *Times* (clearly briefed by Root or an aide), "will mark another step . . . toward the vitalizing of the important army bureaus by placing young men at the head."[22]

The newly minted General Crozier was declared chief of Ordnance on November 22, 1901.[23] Officers who had previously been senior to Crozier but were now junior backed him, a sign that former enemies were coming to terms with the Root reforms.[24] On June 20, 1902, the Senate confirmed him 44 to 12, and on November 18, 1905, it reconfirmed him as chief for another four-year term.[25] By that time Crozier was unremovable—ironically, a system developed to replace ossified officers, who believed their tenured positions flowed from divine right, with innovative "young men" resulted in a young man who would stay in power at the president's pleasure until *July 1918.*

When he was first appointed, Crozier felt bound to justify Roosevelt and Root's confidence. Replacing the Krag—which had been in service for less than a decade—was his number-one priority. Crozier's need to prove, not only to his political masters but to the military men over whom he had leapfrogged to the top, that he was up to the task of overseeing the Ordnance Department was just one.

Another was that making a fresh start with a fresh rifle would demonstrate to all that it was no longer business as usual at Ordnance, which private arms-makers were still attacking as a closed shop that assigned lucrative government contracts to favored suppliers. A key plank in

Roosevelt's political platform was to eradicate the good-old-boy "interests" and self-dealing endemic to the Gilded Age and replace them with honest, transparent government. Cleaning out Ordnance's Augean stable would make an excellent start. Crozier, for his part, set an early example for his colleagues by announcing that, while in office, he would no longer accept royalties deriving from any of his inventions.[26]

Another factor against the Krag was that although it had performed adequately during the Spanish war, the Mausers used by the enemy enjoyed more of a positive "buzz" among soldiers and the public alike. The simplest solution would have been to purchase Mausers directly from their maker or, alternatively, acquire the rights to manufacture them in this country. But Roosevelt's patriotic senses rebelled at the thought that scientifically managed America couldn't produce its own homegrown guns.

Mausers, moreover, were German, and Roosevelt had personally grown wary of the German predilection for race-based nationalism. In the dangerous new world of the twentieth century, he wished to avoid creating a dangerous dependence on Berlin's continuing amity—particularly when the erratic Kaiser Wilhelm II was at the helm. To Henry Cabot

The lordly William Crozier.

Lodge, Roosevelt confided in March 1901 that "some friends of mine" who had attended German war games the year before "were greatly impressed with the evident intention of the German military classes to take a fall out of us when the opportunity offers." Not right now, but "in a few years they will be in a position to take some step in the West Indies or South America which will make us either put up or shut up on the Monroe Doctrine." To that end the German high command was counting on "our inability to assemble an army of thirty thousand men which would be in any way a match for a German army of the same size." In classic style, Roosevelt concluded that he wished "to see us act upon the old frontier principles 'Don't bluster, don't flourish your revolver and never draw unless you intend to shoot.' "[27] He and Root were forging ahead with strengthening the army, but still he needed a "revolver" made in America that could be drawn if the Kaiser's insolence became intolerable.

The Krag, of course, *was* made in America, but it was of foreign design and remained something of an underpowered weapon. Upgrading it would prove difficult. The tempo of technological change had accelerated, and the Krag was already showing its age. Though it was originally constructed to fire smokeless cartridges, its internal design struggled to keep pace with the newer, and more powerful, versions of gunpowder developed since. Its bolt had just one locking lug to secure it against the rearward blast of the exploding powder, and while that was adequate for the Krag's 2,000-foot-per-second velocity, Mausers were now firing at 2,300 fps. To match that, Springfield would have to make the Krag's chamber capable of withstanding 40,000 pounds per square inch of pressure.[28] At the moment the Krag could handle 30,000 psi. Attaining that extra 300 fps would therefore require an increase of a third in the Krag chamber's ability to withstand pressure—plus the problematic addition of a second lug to prevent chamber explosions. Even ignoring the pressure issue, adding the lug alone would demand a major overhaul of the firing mechanism; it would also involve a headache-inducing recall of all Krags currently in service.

In the late winter of 1899 Ordnance chief Buffington had tried to refashion the Krag in order to save it. In mid-August 1900 Springfield's experimental department succeeded in making a newly double-lugged Krag-derivative that could chamber the Mauser bullet *and* fire it at

2,300 feet per second, only to be told by a new Rifle Board that it must also be able to load, as the Mauser could, a preloaded clip.[29]

Springfield's technicians went back to work and eventually succeeded in turning this Krag derivative into a "a clip loading magazine gun . . . which enables the firer to use it as a single loader, with the contents of the magazine in reserve." The odd hybrid "embodies features of both the Mauser and the United States magazine rifle [the Krag]," noted an internal Ordnance report.[30]

Crozier's ascent to the chieftaincy assured the experimental weapon's redesignation as the .30-caliber, bolt-action Springfield Model 1901. When the Rifle Board examined the transitional M1901, its criteria gave some indication of the predominant attitude. Its primary concern was ensuring that the new Springfield combined "rapidity with accuracy"— a sea change from the nineteenth-century preoccupation with focusing on either one or the other. Having learned from the Indian-fighting experience, the board set up a man-sized target at the abnormally short distance of one hundred *feet*. Testers fired twenty shots using the five-round magazines; then twenty finger-loaded singly with an empty magazine; then twenty again singly but with the magazine cut-off engaged (a cut-off, a simple device beloved by progressive officers, consisted of a thin metal sheet hinged so as to swing horizontally over the top of the mag, thereby forcing men to rely on the clip only as an emergency reserve); and finally another twenty that were single-loaded for the first fifteen and fed from the magazine for the final five. Afterward there was a special test for accuracy with ten shots at five hundred yards.[31]

The rifle went back to the shop for additional work, then emerged as the prototype Model 1902. In early 1903 the Rifle Board reconvened to decide whether it was fit to replace the Krag and decided that it was. An experienced hunter himself, the president was a little concerned that the board had concentrated too intently on firepower at the expense of accuracy. Even if three of its four shooting tests had involved single-loading, they had been conducted at the distinctly diehard range of thirty-odd yards, and the board's trial of just ten shots at five hundred yards seemed a distinct afterthought.

As Creedmoor was receding into dim memory and as the experience of recent combat itself had amply demonstrated, the pendulum had swung against the school of marksmanship. The elderly George Wingate of the National Rifle Association went so far as to declare that "now rifle shooting is virtually an unknown art." As always, Wingate identified accuracy with American-ness, adding, "In the early years our ancestors won their liberties by their skill as marksmen, but now, with the cessation of those fighting days, little attention is given to the necessity of rifle practice."[32]

Aware of the progressives' complaints, Roosevelt proposed some trials of the rifle "at some place like that in Utah where several companies of men can be employed at firing [the weapon] at long ranges."[33] The board obliged and reported that at 1,500 yards the prototype Springfield penetrated pine boards 50 percent deeper than the Krag, while its accuracy at 500 yards was 14 percent better, and at 1,000, 4.6 percent. The board unanimously concluded that the "general design and ballistic qualities of this rifle are markedly superior to the present service arm."[34]

Crozier's new-look Ordnance Department celebrated June 20, 1903, as marking its liberation from the bonds of the past. That was the day the prototype M1902, having passed all its tests, was christened the "U.S. Magazine Rifle, Model of 1903, Caliber of .30" (better known as the Springfield Model 1903) and was authorized for manufacture.[35] Soon afterward, on January 31, 1904, an overworked, exhausted Elihu Root, his laborious task of army reorganization finally finished, and having shepherded the weaponly representative of his reforms into production, resigned as the secretary of war and was replaced by William Howard Taft.

Once the new gauges, machines, dies, tools, and fixtures for the Model 1903 had been installed, the Springfield Armory, it was thought, would start making 225 per eight-hour day; Rock Island Armory would build another 125. But progress was so rapid that within a month Springfield was producing 400 per day. A year and a half later the national armories had 74,000 Springfields in stock. Some delays ensued thereafter as, in response to continuing progressive alarm that riflery was dying out, existing Springfields were outfitted with upgraded front and rear sights.[36]

The greatest change was to come on October 15, 1906, when the new .30-06 cartridge was adopted. (The "06" designated the year, in order to distinguish the ammunition from the original .30s.)[37] This cartridge, explained Crozier to quizzical reporters, was markedly superior to its predecessor. It was tipped with what was known as a Spitzer bullet, a sharp-pointed projectile, as opposed to the old .30's rounded nose. German-designed, it was also significantly lighter—150 grains versus 220—and was powered by a modestly increased powder charge.

It was, Crozier boasted, an astoundingly aerodynamic bullet that was capable of flying greater distances, experienced reduced vulnerability to air resistance and wind drift, had less recoil kick, and enjoyed a flatter trajectory than a traditional .30. As Crozier pointed out, the .30-06 was "effective" against infantry at 600 yards, had a muzzle velocity of 2,700 feet per second (compared to the Mauser's 2,300), and at 500 yards would penetrate pine to a depth of 32 inches, as against 26 inches for the previous bullet.[38] With the .30-06, enthused *Harper's Weekly,* "trees will be of little protection to soldiers, for at close range the bullet would not only pass through the trunk of the tree, but through a couple of men hiding behind it."[39] If true, that would have been quite a bullet.

The downside of the .30-06 was that, for it to be usable in the rifles, the armories' workmen had to make exceedingly minor but time-consuming and unutterably tedious alterations to every single one of the roughly 100,000 Springfields then in stock. The new bullet's neck, for instance, was just 0.1 inch shorter than the regular .30, and thus for various reasons, the barrel of each and every rifle had to be shortened from 24.206 inches to 24.006 inches. As a result, the rear sights on all existing Springfields had to be removed and reattached painstakingly in a slightly different place. Small wonder that the arsenals fell way, way behind in production until the second half of 1907. By April 10, 1908, however, 160,000 of the updated Springfields were stockpiled, and by 1914 some 606,924 had been manufactured.[40]

So by 1903 Roosevelt's hope had been fulfilled: Crozier had made an American Mauser. Roosevelt got what he wished for, but in the end he got a great deal less than he desired, because the Springfield superrifle was in fact less all-American than mostly Mauser.

The trouble began in the spring of 1904, when government patent attorneys working for the Ordnance Department noticed that the Springfield's clips bore an uncanny resemblance to those used in the

Mauser. Hoping to prevent a public spat, Crozier immediately sent a letter to Waffenfabrik Mauser in Germany admitting that "an examination would seem to indicate that some of the features of the cartridge clip recently adopted for the United States Army . . . may be covered" by U.S. patents taken out by Mauser. Crozier was referring to patents registered as far back as 1889, when Paul Mauser had logged a "cartridge-package"—his clumsy name for a clip—that allowed the soldier to "increase the rapidity with which the arm may be fired . . . and to inspire [him] with confidence in his weapon by providing means whereby a magazine fire-arm may always be easily kept in readiness for rapid firing."[41] Three years later Mauser made some improvements and repatented it, doing it again in 1895.[42] There was thus no lack of a paper trail to follow, but Crozier hoped he could make the problem disappear if he made a preemptive offer. It was he, then, who requested Mauser— and not the other way around—to send a lawyer to determine "what, if any, of its features are covered by your patents and if so, to arrive at an agreement as to the royalties which should be paid therefore."[43]

Two months later Mauser attorney Arthur Frazier had a meeting with a distinctly edgy Crozier. Though Frazier knew there was a potential issue about the clips, one that could quite easily be made to go away with a large check, he couldn't understand why Crozier was so nervous. More mysteriously still, Crozier proposed sending him not only one of the clips to examine but an entire Springfield M1903 rifle as well.

Six weeks after that meeting, Frazier called Crozier to arrange another. On June 16 he told Crozier that the Mauser engineers had determined that the clip violated two of the company's patents; Mauser, however, would be more than pleased to settle this unpleasant business with a royalty of one dollar per thousand clips made. But there was one more thing: there were five patent infringements on the rifle as well, as Crozier had already gloomily surmised. Another dollar-per-rifle royalty was demanded. Before he left, Frazier added that his client was also convinced that U.S.-made Krags violated Mauser patents as well, but that the company was willing to overlook them if the Ordnance Department cooperated in the matter of the Springfields. In a sense, this last announcement must have come as a relief to Crozier, for now he could not be blamed for the fiasco: his expired predecessor Flagler had approved the Krag, and the now-retired Buffington greenlighted the early Springfield prototype. Crozier was just the poor innocent forced to clean up other people's messes—or at least that would be his excuse, if it came down to an investigation.

Still, better to have no investigation at all, which made it all the more necessary to pay off Waffenfabrik Mauser before the press heard about the scandal. Following secret negotiations between Crozier and Frazier, in early 1905 the United States and Mauser agreed on the terms of settlement. On April 5 the Treasury approved royalty payments of 75 cents per rifle plus 50 cents per thousand clips, up to a ceiling of $200,000. Seven months later, on November 6, Mauser's accountants were pleased to receive the first (for $11,367.53) in a four-year-long series of checks adding up to the $200,000 maximum.[44] Relieved that Crozier's sterling efforts had averted an embarrassing spectacle—the last thing Roosevelt needed, after apparently sweeping the army clean of deadwood and ridding it of the old practices, was the revelation that absolutely nothing had changed at Ordnance—the president appointed him to his second term as chief just thirteen days after the initial Mauser payout.

Believing that the whole unpleasant affair with the Germans had been safely buried, Crozier made an energetic start on the new .30-06 bullet, introduced on October 15, 1906. Early the following year he received an ominous visit from a very polite but insistent representative of Deutsche Waffen und Munitionsfabriken (DWM), maker of the Spitzer bullets for the Mauser rifle. The .30-06, he said, was a near-copy of DWM's "projectile for hand-firearms," which had been submitted to the Patent Office on February 20, 1905—about the same time, suspiciously, that Crozier had been finalizing the financial details of the settlement with Mauser—and approved on January 22, 1907.[45]

Yet another "complication" was looming very darkly. And this time the alleged infringement had happened entirely on Crozier's watch. The good news was that DWM had a far weaker case than Mauser's—it was difficult to demonstrate that the shape and dimensions of such a common item as a bullet were unique—and Crozier's patent attorneys advised him to fight the case. Crozier, again fearful that the newspapers would find out about this change (even if it was trumped up by an opportunistic DWM), decided to fend off the accusers by stalling. He appointed his deputy, Lieutenant Colonel John Thompson (inventor-to-be of the famous tommy gun), to take care of the negotiations in the hope that they would go on for years.

In the meantime Crozier was presented with a headache that, this time at least, was wholly American in origin. In fact, it might even have been partly to blame for his German-inspired mishaps. The prolonged campaign to modernize the army that had culminated in the Root reforms had inadvertently left Crozier with an inexperienced, understaffed department. Before Root and Roosevelt had pressured line officers to go on temporary secondments to the staff bureaus in Washington, Ordnance had enjoyed the pick of the litter for its new recruits. It tended to choose second lieutenants in the Artillery who, because the lowest rank at Ordnance was first lieutenant, automatically received a promotion just for joining. As a result, Ordnance's gentlemanly hours and relatively rapid promotional structure (especially when compared with that of the line) entailed no shortage of highly qualified applicants. *After* the reforms, however, line officers detailed to Ordnance received no automatic promotion for their voluntary secondments away from their units, and unless they were temperamentally inclined to the scientific, experimental nature of Ordnance work and were willing to study hard for the entrance examinations, they saw it as little better than enforced drudgery. Between 1901 and 1906 Crozier unexpectedly found himself trying to find often nonexistent applicants for Ordnance posts. For those five years Ordnance always had far fewer officers working there than prescribed by the new regulations. Even as late as 1913 the department's middle-management ranks were shorthanded.[46] The effect of this shortage was that corners were cut and fail-safes broken in order to keep pace with army requirements. Hence the continued, careless overlooking of such fundamentals as possible patent infringements.

A second incidental effect concerned the arsenals. Because Crozier was desperate to reduce his officers' workloads, he sought more efficient means of production and tougher managerial control. In a tradition stretching back to James Stubblefield's lax tenure at Harpers Ferry, arsenal employees had long enjoyed certain perks with their jobs, not least of which were eight-hour days (compared to the nine or ten common in private business), 28.5 paid days off annually, congenial working conditions, a seeming inability to get fired, and government-guaranteed wages. Owing to their extremely low rates of employee turnover and the relatively small salaries of the senior management, the arsenals were able to produce armaments at about the same price as their commercial competitors—but only when their production runs were long (as with 100,000 standardized rifles) rather than short (as with a half-dozen artillery gun carriages each with 4,500 separate parts). But their productivity rates were unspectacular by any standard, primarily because as life was so comfortable, there was no imperative to ruin it by working harder.

The mooted introduction of the Taylorite system threatened this agreeable status quo. But there was no question, to Crozier's mind, that scientific management worked wonders. After bringing in Frederick Taylor to analyze their operations, both the Bethlehem Steel Company and the Midvale Steel Company had realized significant gains in savings and productivity. The price of one of their gun carriages, for example, was quoted as $51,062.15—including a profitable markup—while the same equipment was sold by Watertown Arsenal to the government for $56,987.18. Crozier, continually besieged by his competitors' allies in Congress asking penetrating questions about Ordnance's mismanagement and cost overruns (or worse, about major royalty payouts to German companies, if they'd heard about it), thought it vital to cut costs and raise efficiency, even if that meant upsetting the settled way of doing things. What the unions would say, however, was quite another matter.

When Crozier first contacted Taylor in late 1906, he was particularly worried about the last point, but the management expert dismissed his concerns. There was no "occasion to bother much about what the American Federation of Labor wrote concerning our system."[47] Alas, Taylor was overly cavalier. His system had not yet been introduced into a workplace that had a strong union presence or where skilled craftsmen's associations could call on the support of sympathetic congressmen. Moreover, downing tools at, say, Bethlehem Steel, could be classed as a private management-worker issue, but a labor stoppage at the government arsenals might be defined as a matter of national security, thereby giving even the *threat* of a strike rather greater leverage than Taylor apprehended.

Crozier selected Watertown Arsenal, eight miles west of Boston, as the first place to receive the Taylor treatment. Detailed preparatory studies of the arsenal's workshops, machinery, accounting practices, and manufacturing processes, as well as the finalizing of the executive staff, began in April 1909, and the preliminary installation of the complicated new system was finished just two months later. By December 1910 the first phase (including inventory control, refurbishment of the tools and machinery, and construction of the central planning room) had been completed, but no time studies had been performed; nor had the employees heard about the revised, and bizarrely complex, premium-pay structure to stimulate productivity.[48]

The time studies started in June 1911, and initially all seemed well. The only machinist who complained about having one of Taylor's nerdish experts standing next to him and clicking his stopwatch was a famously ornery, elderly employee. But by mid-July trouble had emerged from the foundry, where the molders began objecting to any imposition of Taylorite control. The justice of their case was somewhat weakened by the foundry's reputation as a sinkhole of negligible productivity and towering costs, and their complaints went ignored. Taylor's inspectors reported that certain molders, despite the obvious benefits of the incentive-payment program, were actually reducing their output and taking *more* time to do their tasks. The workers retorted that the inspectors may have known a lot about keeping score with a stopwatch but they knew nothing about molding; each movement that an inspector noted down as superfluous, the molders demonstrated was not.

On the evening of August 10 the molders congregated after hours to compose a petition to Lieutenant Colonel Wheeler, commandant of Watertown, noting that the time study was "humiliating to us, who have always tried to give to the Government the best that was in us." Taylorism, they said, was "un-American in principle," and they were reaching "the limit of our endurance."

The petition was submitted early the next day. Management, which called it an "ultimatum," refused to budge, and by midmorning the molders were on strike. Later that afternoon the International Molders' Union and Boston Local No. 106 sent letters to every Massachusetts senator and representative requesting their support for a "fair deal" from Ordnance. Crozier rather quickly promised to investigate the molders' complaints, and on August 18, exactly a week after downing tools, the men were back at work.

On the face of it, the seven-day Watertown strike was not world-shakingly important, but it was in fact the first shot in the revolt to come against Taylorism in the workplace. The American Federation of Labor, contra Taylor's offhanded dismissal of any such possibility, took up the case, and its influential leader, Samuel Gompers, began agitating against this form of control, which he said would turn men into machines while reducing their wages. The International Association of Machinists joined him, threatening national strikes by its members if Taylorism continued to be introduced into American factories.[49]

Initially, organized labor could boast of making some telling hits on Crozier. Public opinion was naturally sympathetic to desperate tales of skilled artisans being underpaid and subjected to humiliating supervision with stopwatches, and later that summer the House Committee on the Taylor and Other Systems of Management held hearings into the matter. Reading its report in March 1912, Crozier was disappointed to find that the congressmen had reached no conclusion, and three years later the Senate prohibited Taylorism, in its most objectionable forms at least, in government work.[50]

The Senate ruling was but the latest in a series of setbacks for Crozier. In the summer of 1914 his deputy Thompson had finally run out the clock regarding Ordnance's alleged infringement of Deutsche Waffen und Munitionsfabriken's Spitzer bullet patents. DWM had made repeated offers to Thompson asking him to settle quickly, and each time they had been rebuffed (as per Crozier's directions). On July 18, 1914, less than a month before the outbreak of the cataclysmic Great War, in which millions of men would be killed by pointed bullets, DWM finally lost its patience and sued the government in the U.S. Court of Claims for royalties on 250 million Spitzers totaling $250,000. Ten days later, when Austria-Hungary declared war on Serbia, the suit was deferred.[51]

Crozier's position was saved by the sinking of the *Lusitania* in 1915 and the U.S. declaration of war on Germany in April 1917. Upon entry to the war, under authority of the Trading with the Enemy Act, the government created the Office of Alien Property Custodian to oversee the seizure of enemy-owned or enemy-controlled assets. To Crozier's immense relief, the DWM patent was ruled to be U.S. property, and the attorney general dismissed the company's suit out of hand. As if by a miracle, the second of Crozier's German problems had disappeared without the public finding out about it.

Crozier's streak of good luck was boosted by Taylorism's comeback. The unions' overly narrow focus on such ephemera as time studies and premium-pay schemes had resulted in poorly defined legislation. Thus the government had actually prohibited only isolated, practical aspects of Taylorism, not the philosophy or principles animating it.

Crozier and other senior managers discovered that so long as men with stopwatches weren't standing guard over their workers and incentive pay was abolished, there was nothing illegal about analyzing, reforming, and improving manufacturing processes, let alone performing time studies' more advanced successor, motion studies. Moreover, as Congress had barred only government-paid inspectors from performing time studies, Crozier could integrate data amassed by private industry for similar tasks into his own conclusions. He wasted no time. By the time the United States dispatched doughboys to the Western Front in late 1917, Watertown, as well as the other Ordnance installations at Springfield, Frankford, Watervliet, and Rock Island, had been almost totally Taylorized in all but name.

American entry into the war resulted in an exponential expansion of Ordnance, as its arms-procurement budget broke the $5 billion barrier. To give some idea of the scale of the expansion, consider that before the American declaration of war, some 97 officers worked for the Department; by the Armistice in November 1918—about a year and a half later—there were 5,800 (plus 79,720 civilian clerks). Again, before 1917 there were six government arsenals and two private plants making heavy armaments; by winter of the following year 5,000 factories were producing arms directly for Ordnance.[52]

Intending to keep pace with the thousands of contracts flooding in, and desperate to hire people who could coordinate the manufacturing process, Crozier Taylorized the staff of the department itself by bringing in newly uniformed members of the Taylor Society (the organization of managers and executives formerly known as Society for the Promotion of the Science of Management). By the beginning of 1918 fully a third of the society's membership worked for Crozier.[53]

Taylorism, combined with national industrialization and the mobilization for total war, produced a miraculous ability to raise output far above anything ever before imagined. Upon the outbreak of the war in Europe in 1914, the British contracted with American private companies (Winchester and Remington, primarily) to make their excellent Enfield .303 Model 1914 rifles. To fulfill their contracts, the gun-makers built three large plants and installed $15 million worth of machinery. All of this took time, and progress was relatively slow. By 1917 British factories themselves had tooled up for the switchover to Enfields, and the government scaled down its contracts, thereby leaving Remington and Winchester with excess capacity. When the United States entered the war in April of that year, there were roughly 600,000 Springfields in stock, an admirable total but insufficient to supply the million-man army that Congress thought would be the minimum required to fight. Ordnance then asked the Remington and Winchester factories to produce Enfields rechambered to the American .30-caliber on the Taylorite system. It was a capital plan and explained why a stunning 2,202,429 Model 1917 Enfields would be churned out in roughly eighteen months from just three factories.[54]

* * *

Migraine-inducing it might have been, but Roosevelt adored the Springfield Model 1903. So pleased was he with it that on November 17, 1903, just five months after the new service rifle was authorized for manufacture, he asked Crozier to obtain him one, stamped with the special serial number 6000 and suitably "sporterized." Being the commander in chief of the armed forces, the president thought it only right that he should use the army rifle as his chosen hunting weapon. Roosevelt went on to use it for a dozen years on three continents, bagging some three hundred head of all kinds, including lion, hyena, rhinoceros (square-mouthed and hook-nosed), giraffe, zebra, gazelle, warthog, hippopotamus, monkey, jaguar, giant anteater, ostrich, cougar, black bear, crocodile, and python.[55]

Considering his love for the Springfield 1903 and all its works, it was a good thing that Roosevelt, who died in January 1919, did not live to see the embarrassing finale to the ongoing legal battles over its "American-ness." As for Crozier, he yet again succeeded in not being left holding the bag, for he retired in the same month as Roosevelt's death. (His own would come in November 1942.) He thereby escaped censure for the fallout from a reinvigorated lawsuit launched by DWM in 1920. Having given up on obtaining a favorable patent-infringement judgment, DWM's lawyers focused on whether the alien property custodian's seizure of the patent had been lawful. Impressed by DWM's argument that its bullet patent was protected by previous treaty, a tribunal ruled the U.S. government in violation and awarded DWM damages of $300,000. Washington immediately appealed the decision, and the case lurched on interminably, like that of *Jarndyce v. Jarndyce* in Charles Dickens's *Bleak House* ("This scarecrow of a suit has, in course of time, become so complicated that no man alive knows what it means"), for another seven and a half years, until it was finally settled on the last day of 1928, a generation after its beginning. The judgment stood. With interest added on to the original $300,000, the United States owed $412,520.55.[56]

The M1 Garand

Chapter 9

THE PATHS NOT TAKEN

Though experts counted it as a modern weapon, the Springfield Model 1903, as a bolt-action magazine rifle with a five-round clip, was threatened with obsolescence from the moment it first appeared. Each time a cartridge was fired, the soldier would turn up the weapon's bolt and pull it back to open the breech and eject the spent casing; then he would shove it forward to insert a fresh cartridge from the magazine (or finger-load one by hand); and finally he would turn it down to lock the breech closed. Considerable muscular effort was required for this process if one wanted to fire rapidly, and a soldier had no evident way to accelerate his movements beyond a certain physical point. But if the process could be *mechanized* then, theoretically at least, a far greater rate of fire was possible.

To this end, a year before the Springfield was officially authorized for manufacture, chief of Ordnance William Crozier was musing on the possibility of "causing the musket itself to effect its own reloading upon discharge."[1] In the future, he thought, rifles based on just such a "semi-automatic principle" would recycle the energy released by firing a bullet by mechanically ejecting the spent casing and loading a new cartridge. The very act of pulling the trigger would allow the rifleman to pull it again.

Crozier neither expected, nor desired, anything ever to come of the self-loading idea, for two good reasons. In his carefully chosen words, "both *tactical* and *mechanical* questions are involved in the consideration of the possible desirability of the substitution of a semiautomatic musket for the hand-operated magazine rifle" (emphasis added).[2]

By "mechanical," the general was referring to the fact that the quest to make the semiautomatic principle a reality looked hopeless. Private firms were trying hard but had so far enjoyed little success. As early as June 1902 John Browning, one of the country's finest designers, patented a recoil mechanism that would form the basis of the Remington Model 8 Autoloader of 1906, while Winchester competed with a .22-caliber semiautomatic rifle and the Self-Loading Rifle Model 1905. The Standard Arms Company of Wilmington, Delaware, joined the fray in 1909 with its own model, which came in .25, .30, and .35 calibers.

But the Standard weapon jammed so often that the company eventually ceased operations; the Winchesters were clumsy and unbalanced owing to their heavy mechanism; and the Remingtons found few ringing endorsements. They "worked well," but that was all.[3] What all three had in common was their underpoweredness, the age-old criticism of repeaters now resurrected for their automated successors.

Just as Winchester's repeaters in the 1870s and onward had been forced to compete against the army's regulation cartridge, so too were the Springfield Model 1903's self-loading rivals. The .30-06 round was among the country's most formidable loads, but none of its competitors could sustainably handle such a high-power round; the heat buildup alone tended to make casing extraction buggy after just a few shots, and their wooden stocks were often found charred following a rapid-fire burst of a hundred rounds. In a manner reminiscent of the travails experienced by early breech-loader designs, the new semiautomatics were troubled by gas leakage owing to their moving breeches. Inventors tried several ways of solving this problem—including the development of straight-blowback, retarded-blowback, short-recoil, long-recoil, gas-operated, muzzle-cap, and primer-operated mechanisms—but all were forced to conclude that, at least for the foreseeable future, the semiautomatic was destined to use low- or medium-powered bullets.[4] The Springfield was safe, at least for the moment.

Crozier had also cited potential "tactical" issues raised by semiautomatics. By this he meant the inevitable resumption of infighting, recently quieted by the arrival of the Model 1903, between the army's progressive and diehard factions.

The advent of semiautomatics would immensely aid the diehard school in that their very raison d'être was to encourage the profligate use of ammunition at relatively close ranges. At the moment the only thing mitigating that temptation was the Springfield's miserly five-round clip; a semiautomatic, however, would burn through a magazine of that size in seconds, necessitating ever-larger clips and hastening the decline of marksmanship.

Contributing to progressive alarm over the "semiautomatic principle" was the terrible realization that much of the army had already fallen, or was poised to fall, under diehard control. In 1907 General Arthur MacArthur established the School of Musketry, where the principal focus was on the rapid-firing machine gun, and in 1909 new regulations directed that the diehards' Germanic favorite, field fire, would appear on the curriculum. In the latter year Captain Henry Eames's official instruction manual, *The Rifle at War*, stressed the centrality of officer-supervised field fire and rapid fire to modern warfare.[5] Attacks would henceforth be decided, he said, "by a psychically stunning rapid fire," in which the vast majority of shots missed but that "utterly paralyze[d] the fighting will" of the enemy.[6] Convinced, the army's house organ, *Infantry Journal,* converted almost entirely to diehard ideology, and virtually every issue of the pre-1914 period carried an article lauding the benefits of field and rapid fire.[7]

Not all was doom and gloom, however, for the progressive side. Even if they were sidelined within the military, politically speaking they were in fine fettle. Their civilian spokesmen, the National Rifle Association, was at the top of its form, following more than a decade of torpor and sagging popularity. In 1890 it had even suffered the ultimate indignity of having Creedmoor taken from its ownership and deeded to the state of New York.[8] In about 1900 the NRA slipped out of dormancy, repaired its chaotic finances and organization, and prepared to go forth into the new century.

Its first order of business was to combat the insidious Eames argument in favor of rapid and field fire. Whereas the captain had assumed that "a great volume of misses" (argued Lieutenant Colonel Smith Brookhart, captain of the Iowa National Guard rifle team and future president of the NRA) was part of any psychically stunning assault, in fact it only *emboldened* the enemy by letting him think he was pitted against green recruits.[9]

If anything, the diehard reliance on massive, clumsy assaults resembled nothing less than the outdated, bloody, officer-dominated tactics of old. Marksmanship, progressives had always proudly argued, was the modern, forward, even futuristic way, the thinking man's method of humanely winning wars. They could even point out that the first bullet fired from an aircraft emanated from a Springfield. On August 20, 1910, less than seven years after the Wright Brothers had achieved sustained flight and just two after the army had tested its first military aircraft, pilot Glenn Curtiss took a twenty-seven-year-old lieutenant named Jacob Fickel up in his biplane above Sheepshead Bay racetrack on Long Island, New York.

As Fickel clung with one hand to a wing strut for life and the other to his rifle, Curtiss ascended to three hundred feet and circled around a large target that had been set up in the middle of the racetrack. Four times Fickel steadied himself and fired the Springfield, hitting the bull's-eye twice and wowing spectators with his riflemanship.[10] Reporters began predicting that air fleets would one day transport legions of Springfield-armed skytroopers to the battlefront and evacuate them safely, their missions accomplished with barely a casualty. Given a chance, the progressive dream of clean, antiseptic wars would soon be a reality.

The NRA's desire to quash Eames and his cohorts was motivated not by self-interest but by its conviction that the diehard importation of authoritarian German concepts in the guise of firearms training undermined patriotically American virtues of liberty and self-improvement. Hence for decades afterward editorial after editorial, article after article, in the association's stable of magazines would hammer home the lesson that "today's tactics make the infantryman, more than at any time since the French and Indian Wars, an individualist . . . He must believe in himself, and to believe in himself he must believe in his rifle! He must know that he can deliver deadly individual fire! . . . This kind of individual marksmanship has its roots deeply bedded in the target ranges of America."[11]

President Theodore Roosevelt, always concerned with the question of what made an American an American, agreed with the NRA. In his 1906 State of the Union speech he went out of his way to praise the importance of American sharpshooting. To him, a soldier's "efficiency on the line of battle is almost directly proportionate to excellence in marksmanship."

When America entered the First World War in 1917, the NRA and its progressive friends could count on the support of the heaviest hitter of them all: General John Pershing, a ferociously competitive marksman (he placed second in the all-army championships) and son-in-law to a future NRA president (U.S. senator Francis Warren, who had won the Congressional Medal of Honor during the Civil War). Immediately before the main American forces arrived in Europe, Pershing had traveled to France to observe French and British maneuvers and to arrange for the training of his troops. Pershing informed Secretary of War Newton Baker that he wanted to "inculcate a strong, offensive, fighting spirit among our forces," but he was disappointed in the Allies' reliance on diehard tactics to carry out assaults.

The French and British, Pershing observed, "had all but given up the use of the rifle." Instead, blunt instruments like "machine guns, grenades, Stokes mortars, and one-pounders had become the main reliance of the average Allied soldier. These were all valuable weapons for specific purposes but they could not replace the combination of an efficient soldier and his rifle." Pershing added that he had heard "numerous instances . . . of men chasing an individual enemy throwing grenades at him instead of using the rifle."[12]

The general believed that British and French commanders had deluded themselves that "developments since 1914 had changed the principles of warfare." Fighting, his allies told him, had now become a static affair dependent on slow, grinding attrition to weaken the enemy. Pershing respectfully disagreed. "It was my opinion that the victory could not be won by the costly process of attrition, but it must be won by driving the enemy out into the open and engaging him in a war of movement." Alarmed that American troops were to be placed under

Franco-British command and taught the same pessimistic precepts, Pershing insisted on a separate American sector and control over his own armies on the Western Front.[13]

To further mark his turf and allow the unblooded Americans flooding into France to prove their spunk, Pershing fastened on to the legendary American proficiency with the rifle as a propaganda device. "You must not forget that the rifle is distinctively an American weapon," he stipulated. "I want to see it employed."[14] Grasping the emotional power of marksmanship, Pershing called upon the NRA version of history, the one genetically grafted onto elements stretching back to Colonial days, Jackson's victory at New Orleans, and the triumph at Creedmoor—all events where the rifle had liberated Americans from their self-created inferiority complex toward Europeans. Now rifle-bearing, crack-shooting Americans were to liberate stout Britain, cocky France, and plucky little Belgium from the jackboot of the Kaiser, leader of a nation of field firers.

Pershing quickly reinstated marksmanship as the most important part of the GI's education. While the men had many demands on their all-too-brief training time, nothing, he ordered, should "be allowed to interfere with rifle practice."[15] To further burnish the reputation of the American rifleman among friends and foes alike, a confidential pamphlet, *Training for Rifle Fire in Trench Warfare*, was circulated among officers at the Army War College; the manual proposed creating an elite "sniping" unit within each battalion that would consist of one noncommissioned officer and twenty-four privates. Those wanting to qualify for the unit would have to pass a still more onerous set of tests than those required for regular marksman status. Being "brave, yet cautious; cool, observant, patient, resourceful, and prompt," snipers would adhere to the traditional ideal of a sharpshooter and possess a "correct knowledge" of the influence that "a cold piece, a hot piece; clouds, heat, moisture, wind; a worn rifle; fouling; recent cleaning and oiling" would have on their shooting. Expertise in estimating range was absolutely required.[16]

American shooting superiority was often used as a rhetorical point to needle the Hun. Because the Germans had not participated in the great Creedmoor-style shooting competitions, *Scientific American*'s Edward

Crossman wrote, their infantry "turned out to shoot about as poorly as the infantry of most other nations not of Anglo-Saxon breed." Indeed, the Germans had deliberately designed their rifles' rear sights "so no man could do fine shooting, or stand a show in a long range rifle match, even if the desire . . . should enter his breast." The Teutonic rifle, devoid of "wind-gauges and devices for making fine changes in elevation," Crossman claimed, could at best place a bullet within six feet at one thousand yards, and even their finest shooters were "still pathetically insufficient in making what we consider first-class shots."[17]

So ingrained became these convictions that whereas the British and the French felt that the only way to overcome the Germans' tough machine-gun entrenchments was to flatten them with heavy artillery bombardments, progressives believed that a sharpshooter was more than a match for any machine-gunner. Spew hundreds of bullets wildly as he might, the man behind the machine gun was still prey to a single, precisely aimed shot.[18]

Chief among this class of supersnipers was Alvin York (1887–1964) of Pall Mall, located in remote Fentress County in Tennessee's Cumberland Mountains, the man destined to become the most famous American soldier of the Great War. Descended from, in his own words, "sharpshooters and pioneers and Old Testament folk," York was the son of a poor farmer who depended on hunting for meat. Because a flubbed shot by the boy meant no food on the table, his father "threatened to muss me up right smart if I failed to bring a squirrel down with the first shot or hit a turkey in the body instead of taking its head off."

Shooting the heads off turkeys was a long-established pastime in Fentress County. Regularly a turkey would be tethered behind a log so that only its bobbing head was exposed. Each contestant would take a shot until someone hit it. The winner wound up with the bird. York excelled at the sport but found himself drifting into mammoth moonshine-drinking binges, brawling, and gambling. By the time he was twenty-seven, however, "I knowd deep down in my heart that it was'nt [sic] worthwhile," and in December 1914 he began attending the Church of Christ in Christian Union, a fundamentalist sect that had split from the Methodists in the aftermath of the Civil War and discouraged any kind of political engagement.

Rigorously following his pastor's teachings, York paid no heed to the politics of wartime. (He was not alone in this respect: reflecting its readers' tastes the weekly *Fentress County Gazette* ran brief paragraphs on the European conflict while devoting multiple pages to livestock prices.) In any case, he had marriage on his mind (to Gracie Williams), Sunday school to teach, and sermons to give. Yet while he may not have been interested in the government, the government was interested in him and sent York a draft notice in June 1917.

Its arrival left York's mind writhing with indecision. "I loved and trusted old Uncle Sam and I have always believed he did the right thing. But I was worried clean through. I did'nt [*sic*] want to go and kill. I believed in my bible. And hit distinctly said 'THOU SHALT NOT KILL.' And yet Uncle Sam wanted me. And he said he wanted me most awfull bad. And I jest didn't known what to do. I worried and worried. I couldn't think of anything else."

York claimed conscientious objector status ("Don't Want to Fight," he scrawled on the form) and filed no fewer than four appeals. All were rejected, and Private York showed up for service at Camp Gordon, Georgia, and was assigned to Company G, 328th Infantry, 82nd Division. He soon made "good friends" with his Model 1917 Enfield, declaring it just as accurate as his old Tennessee muzzle-loader, at least to a hundred yards.

He proved it on October 8, 1918, when, during an American raid into the German lines, York's Enfield shot at least a score of Germans in the head, with nary a miss. In a replay of those Tennessee turkey matches, every time an enemy head appeared, York fired. After a time the German officer in charge, Lieutenant Vollmer, stood up and cried, "English?" "No, not English," York replied. "What?" persisted the German. "American," answered York. Whereupon a stunned Vollmer said, "Good Lord," and offered to surrender his unit.

York, promoted to sergeant, received the Medal of Honor for his feat (and was cited for killing 25 Germans, putting 35 machine guns out of action, and capturing no fewer than 132 prisoners while armed only with an Enfield rifle and a spare pistol). So remarkable was his heroism that even tiny Montenegro in the Balkans awarded him a medal. What was never mentioned was what York did the next day: he returned to the battlefield, knelt down, and prayed to the Lord to save the souls of those men he had killed. Over the decades that followed, whenever he was asked why he did it, York modestly refrained from saying anything more than, "Blessed is the peacemaker."[19]

York's miracle emblazoned the image of the clean-limbed, clean-living soldier in the American mind. While in France, he never smoked a cigarette, downed a shot, visited a brothel, or got into a fight. He never swore, not once, apparently.[20] He was exalted in the popular press and in biographies as embodying the spirit of the American Rifleman, that Jacksonian creature of rural virtue, plain speaking, patriotic devotion, time-honored skills, Christian values, and simple decency.[21] Even his lethal proficiency with the decidedly low-tech rifle stood out in stark relief to the impersonal mechanization of slaughter, the unstoppable grinding up of flesh and bone in the muddy gears of war.[22] He was one man with one rifle whose simple bravery had vanquished dragons.[23]

Newspapermen and propagandists portrayed York as an everyday man and reduced him to a "Mountain Man" stereotype, but he was by no means an ordinary person, and neither was his heroism anything but highly individualistic. Far from being a run-of-the-mill American Rifleman, York was in fact a freak, a statistical outlier, a unique fingerprint among U.S. servicemen. Once York had satisfied himself that America's duty was to punish Germany for her transgressions, the energy and devotion he had once applied first to boozing and carousing and then to his religious beliefs were diverted into a single-minded, unswerving willingness to kill without pause and without fear. Though he was kindhearted and charitable in peacetime, York's character under fire knew nothing of temperance but was quick to anger and quicker to avenge. The fanatical, fearless combination of faith and violence lurking deep in York allowed him to switch off the usual human emotions when punishing unbelievers.

Idealistic progressives at home invested far too much in York's example. General Pershing, however, schooled harshly on the Western Front, had learned otherwise and began calling for more training in "rapid fire" as the war continued. Though he still wished to distinguish his doughboys from their Allied comrades, Pershing was also becoming aware that relying exclusively on the accuracy of the rifle would be suicidal. The

French and British (and Germans, for that matter) had, after all, three years' worth of grim experience in trench fighting and knew what it meant to launch an infantry assault across no-man's-land and through bales of barbed wire against embedded machine guns. While Crossman over at *Scientific American* gloated that German recruits were never tested at ranges greater than 435 yards whereas American marksman could hit a dime at a thousand, Pershing soon realized the plain truth that little fighting, let alone sharpshooting, occurred at such extreme ranges. Artillery (the German 77mm shell burst into 500 lethal splinters) or machine guns (the .303 Vickers spat out 250 rounds per minute) were used for killing, not rifles.

Americans, in other words, were *over*skilled at long-distance shooting. True, they had a wonderful reputation for hitting their marks; a German report on the Marines noted the "high percentage of Marksmen, Sharpshooters, and Expert Riflemen" among them.[24] But the vast majority of hits took place at short range, often randomly during an attack or a skirmish, and weren't owed to a beautifully centered single shot.

Even when fine shooting was involved (as in the case of York), it usually occurred at typical Indian-fighting distances—not, as progressives at home imagined, at up to a thousand yards. Indeed, much of the fine shooting even *at home* was done at relatively close ranges, thus rendering parts of the American Rifleman image somewhat mythical. Back in Tennessee, when the locals had been competing against each other, they shot at targets at 40 yards "ef ye shot from a chunk" (a chunk being a rest, like the fork of a tree limb), but when shooting offhand (that is, standing and not using a rest) the ranges were set at roughly 27 yards.[25] (An honorable exception was Davy Crockett, who averred that when he shot offhand, his preferred range was 40 yards, at which distance he could hit a quarter-dollar.)[26] York himself, honest to a fault, told General Omar Bradley during the Second World War that "most of his effective shooting [during World War I] had been done at very short range—twenty-five to fifty yards."[27] On the day that York earned his Medal of Honor, the German positions had been 40 yards from his own.[28]

The all-too-real, wholly un-Creedmoorlike typical experience of

U.S. soldiers was well described by William Francis of the Fifth U.S. Marines. During an assault at Château-Thierry in June 1918:

> *After we made it to the top of the hill the Germans opened up with their machine-guns, hand and rifle grenades and trench mortars. Just then we all seemed to go crazy for we gave a yell like a bunch of wild Indians and started down the hill running and cursing in the face of the machine gun fire. Men were falling on every side, but we kept going, yelling and firing as we went. How any of us got through the murderous machine gun fire the Germans were putting up I will never be able to figure out . . . On this little hill were at least eight hundred dead men and several hundred wounded.* [emphasis added][29]

Pershing, once he realized that his desired "war of movement" could not happen until the Germans had first been bled white, played down his sunny attitude toward marksmanship and began calling for faster-firing, shorter-range weapons to help break the impasse—which is exactly what his French and British peers had been doing.[30] He was too American, however, to leave marksmanship entirely behind, and stood by his conviction that the "infantryman with his rifle" remained the fundamental military unit; all the other forms—aircraft, artillery, tanks—merely "supported" him.[31]

Accordingly, Pershing's general orders of April 9, 1918, laid down the new "middle way" of warfare, really a combination of good shooting and ferocious cold-steel diehardism. "The rifle and the bayonet are the principal weapons of the infantry soldier. He will be trained to a high degree of skill as a marksman both on the target range and in field firing. An aggressive spirit must be developed until the soldier feels himself, as a bayonet fighter, invincible in battle."[32] Pershing was searching for men who could shoot farther than any European soldier while outfighting him at close range.

Quite apart from the unlikelihood of doughboys crouching behind parapets within shouting distance of enemy trenches, jumping up and taking the time to target a helmeted German head while risking their own, Pershing had another reason to favor "skirmish firing." He had been presented with the "Pedersen device," one of the most secret inventions of the war.

It began in the late summer of 1917 when Mr. John D. Pedersen, a respected, independent designer of sporting rifles and shotguns based in Jackson, Wyoming, but born in Denmark, walked into Ordnance chief Crozier's office and offered him the chance to see something genuinely amazing. Soon afterward, intrigued, Crozier joined him on the Congress Heights Rifle Range outside Washington.

Producing a Springfield, Pedersen squeezed off a few shots in the regular manner, and then (in the words of Major Hatcher, an ordnance expert) "suddenly jerked the bolt out of the rifle" and quickly replaced it with a "mysterious looking" mechanism. As the observers exchanged wondering glances, "he snapped into place a long black magazine containing 40 small pistol size cartridges." The next thing they knew "Mr. Pedersen was pulling the trigger of the rifle time after time as fast as he could work his finger and each time he pulled the trigger the rifle fired a shot, threw out the empty cartridge and reloaded itself." Once he'd emptied the forty-round magazine, Pedersen broke it off, attached another, and continued his murderous firing. "It looked as though he had converted the Springfield rifle," recalled an astounded Hatcher, "into a one-man machine gun."

Confronted with this extraordinary demonstration, the Ordnance Department clamored to have a closer look at the strange semiautomatic device. Each cartridge, they found, was of the same caliber as the Springfield's standard ammunition but one-fifth the size. Whereas the .30-06 was a 150-grainer boosted by 45 grains of powder, the 80-grain Pedersen bullets were powered by a mere 3.5 grains of powder. These attributes translated into a highly diminished muzzle velocity—down to 1,300 feet per second from the .30-06's 2,700—and a muzzle energy one-tenth that of the Springfield.

For the Western Front, nevertheless, the Pedersen device was thought ideal. Soldiers facing an enemy onslaught could fire their modified Springfields, "and the entire zone in front of the trenches would be covered with such a whirlwind of fire that no attack could survive." If the troops were to attack the enemy, the Pedersen's tiny charge produced no noticeable recoil and "it could be fired from the hip while marching or running" across no-man's-land. Of course, under these circumstances fire would be all over the place, but each man would be producing a storm of bullets so dense that no German would dare to expose himself by returning fire. Moreover, for everyday use, because the device was so effortless to install and remove, a soldier had a choice between using his weapon's standard firing bolt to shoot his high-power Springfield ammunition and switching over to his low-power Pedersen's. Owing to the latter's compactness, Ordnance felt that every soldier should carry an additional ten magazines, each of forty cartridges, in addition to the hundred-odd .30-06s he was already forced to lug around. In that instance, the day of the five-round magazine would soon be over.

Following Pedersen's initial demonstration, Captain J. C. Beatty of Ordnance was sworn to secrecy and sailed to France with the device safely packed away. His orders were to explain its semiautomic mechanism to Pershing himself and give another demonstration to a board of senior officers. He did so on December 9, 1917. Just two days later, the board decided to order 100,000 Pedersen devices. If they worked out, they would eventually be issued to every American soldier. The board stipulated that the device was to be kept as secret as possible and distributed only after 50,000 of them had arrived so that a massive surprise assault could be launched. The term "Pedersen device," however, was sufficiently enigmatic to intrigue the overly curious, which is why it was soon colorlessly renamed the "Automatic Pistol, Caliber 30, Model 1918."

On January 23 Pedersen's employer, Remington-UMC, was informed that it would be the chief maker and was authorized to purchase the necessary machinery. By the end of March 1918 production began. Given the mammoth scale of the fighting on the Western Front and the coalescing Allied plan to smash Germany in a gigantic battle of annihilation in the spring of 1919, the order was upped to 633,450 "pistols," nearly 10 million magazines, and 800 million cartridges.

Then, just as preparations were well in hand with 65,000 devices in stock, the Germans signed the Armistice on November 11, 1918. There would be no Plan 1919, no half-million Pedersen-toting GIs simultaneously going over the top carrying four hundred rounds of ammunition in what would have been one hell of a surprise for the *boches*.

It was all over, and the first thing stopped was any more production of the devices, magazines, and cartridges. Nevertheless, the device was still classed as top secret, and on June 23, 1919, Ordnance directed Remington-UMC to transfer exclusive ownership and rights to the U.S. government so that the army could decide whether it wanted to declassify the invention and issue it universally to the 130,000 troops left after 128,436 officers had been demobilized and 2,608,218 enlisted men sent home.

Beginning that fall and extending into the following year, three new tests were conducted by boards of combat officers specially convened to make recommendations about the weapons needed in future. The Pedersen device did not make the cut. American soldiers, the boards said, were already overly burdened with equipment, and requiring them to carry an additional 12.125 pounds of Pedersen-related hardware was intolerable. They also cited as a liability the Pedersen bullet's comparative silence compared with regular Springfield or Enfield rounds. Because the latter flew faster than sound, they made a "sharp, menacing noise" as they passed an enemy soldier. Pedersen bullets, conversely, did not create an air wave, leading many officers to believe that they would not instill fear in the enemy. Lastly, the Pedersen bullet's underpoweredness was cited as an issue. Despite its inventor's last-ditch attempts to boost its performance by increasing the charge to 4.7 grains of powder and stretching the casing's length from .78 inches to .93 inches, the bullets would kill only if the target was closer than 350 yards—and even at that extreme range, one would have to strike a vulnerable organ, multiple times probably, to be lethal. Unfortunately, owing to the heat buildup caused by the rapid-firing, Pedersen simply could not enlarge his cartridges any more, and the boards' reports collectively rang the device's death knell.[33]

Taken together, all these criticisms added up to a single conclusion: the war experience had forged a common progressive and diehard desire to possess a light, full-powered, rapid-fire, semiautomatic rifle combining the best attributes of the standard Springfield and its Pedersen-enabled variant.[34] Importantly, it was no longer assumed that riflemen should hand-load their weapons with single cartridges by default while keeping clips in reserve. To appease the army's marksmen, however,

Ordnance emphasized that the accuracy of any future arm must be "comparable with that of the present service rifle" and have a wind-adjustable rear sight graduated out to one thousand yards.[35]

In 1921 the department began testing several experimental semiautomatic rifles that it hoped might serve as the Springfield's replacement, including one conceived by the aptly named Søren Hansen Bang of Denmark, another by General T. E. Liu of China, a recoil-operated version submitted by a Swiss named Rychiger, and a French gas-operated one named the St. Etienne. (Perhaps inspired by President Woodrow Wilson's campaign for a League of Nations, Ordnance had become rather more internationalist since the days of Crozier, recently retired, and the "American" Mauser.) None of them quite fit the bill.[36]

Pedersen then returned to the fray with a brilliant idea: instead of making the cartridges bigger, why not make both gun and ammunition *smaller*? Aside from tradition—the fondness for the good old .30—there was no overriding reason, as far as he could see, not to reduce yet again the caliber size. To do that one would need an entirely new semiautomatic weapon. By designing a new rifle and cartridge *together*, Pedersen could short-circuit the ponderous Ordnance procurement system that insisted on building weapons around an existing cartridge, a process that invariably resulted in unending compromises and adjustments.

After many furious sessions with his slide rule and ballistic charts, Pedersen emerged with a novel concept for a .276-caliber, 125-grain bullet that was half an inch shorter than the service standard (2.84 inches to 3.34 inches) and powered by 32 grains of fine-grained Du Pont No. 25—or 64 percent as much needed for the .30-06. Ideal for semiautomatic use, it produced just 60 percent as much heat as the .30-06, halved its recoil, and weighed 20 percent less. As an added bonus, a half-inch reduction in cartridge size enabled the designer to shorten the magazine and bolt by the same amount, plus the receiver behind the bolt, thereby shrinking the entire firing mechanism by no less than an inch. That cut, in turn, shaved half a pound of metal from the total weight of the rifle.

At the beginning of 1924, Ordnance, having been impressed by Pedersen's blueprints for the new cartridge, provided him with a large office in the New Experimental Department Building at Springfield and a salary of $10,000, along with a royalty of a dollar per rifle if it was adopted. Remembered one of his friends, Pedersen, not one of nature's gregarious souls, discouraged visitors, to protect not only his privacy but also his possible patent.[37] He had already been frustrated once—by the Armistice's kiboshing of his Device—and he had no intention of missing out again on a fortune.

Over the course of the year Pedersen made rapid progress with his envisaged semiautomatic rifle, which he intended to use in tandem with the new .276.[38] Gunsmithing seems to attract obsessive technical perfectionists like John Hall, the first of the species. John Pedersen was of like temperament. Ensconced in his new office, Pedersen followed in Hall's footsteps exactly, designing every single tool, jig, fixture, and gauge by himself and forgoing the scores of production specialists and engineers usually required to test successive prototypes, adjusting them minutely as problems and weaknesses were identified. Pedersen was fanatically intent on getting his rifle right the first time.

Eccentric as he was, Pedersen's reputation was second to none. Major Hatcher, the former works manager of Springfield before moving on to take over small-arms ammunition manufacturing at Frankford in 1923, once complimented John Browning on his mastery of gunmaking, only to be told that he regarded Pedersen as the greatest living arms designer. But, protested Hatcher, *you* are still alive. Ah yes, replied Browning (who was never overly modest about his talents), but I am an old man with his best work behind him while Pedersen is still young and yet has accomplished so much.[39] High praise, indeed.

Finally, in late 1925, the experimental Pedersen .276 was ready. Weighing eight pounds and two ounces and equipped with a ten-round clip, it was, said Hatcher, "a very finished-looking article, with all features such as the sights . . . worked out to the last detail, and in a form which fitted military requirements better than they ever had before been suited." With this gun "there was no cut-and-try," and it "worked well and looked good."[40]

On May 10, 1926, preliminary testing started and opinions were almost universally favorable, so much so that both the infantry and cavalry were keen to begin distributing samples to troops for field trials.[41] Pedersen may well have been disappointed by the slow death of his device, but his rifle at least looked a sure thing. Then John C. Garand came along.

Born the son of a farmer in the Quebec village of St. Rémi, just outside Montreal, on January 1, 1883, Garand moved to Denisonville, Connecticut (and afterward Jewett City) when he was eleven. With just four years' education under his belt—he was following the lead set by America's greatest gunsmiths—Garand quit school at twelve and, like Christopher Spencer, became a floor sweeper and bobbin boy at a textile mill. Also like Spencer and the other greats of American gunsmithing (as opposed to gun-selling), Garand was almost wholly uninterested in any intellectual pursuit beyond the practical arts: he never subscribed to any other journals but *Engineering, The American Machinist, Machinery Magazine, Metal Progress,* and those of similar bent.

By the time he was fourteen he had patented a new type of screw and by eighteen had worked his way up to the rank of machinist. Between 1908 and 1914 he worked for Brown & Sharpe as a tool- and gauge-maker, then moved to Providence, Rhode Island, as foreman and machine designer of the Federal Screw Corporation.

Modest, bespectacled, unassuming, permanently befuddled, and never quite losing his Quebecois accent (a fact he discovered only in 1940, when a friend played back a recording of his voice), Garand possessed an improbable competitive streak. In Providence he became a keen motorcyclist and, deciding that current machines were too slow, designed his own engine for racing. (In 1912 he won 19 of 21 starts.) He used to challenge auto racers to duels and regularly accelerated past 85 miles per hour.

Shortly after the outbreak of war, he again moved, this time to New York to work at a small micrometer firm and, motorcycle racetracks being in short supply in Manhattan, spent his weekends relaxing at a shooting gallery in Coney Island. (A place on Times Square, impressed by his aim, offered him free shooting in exchange for wowing the tourists who gathered around to watch.)

In 1916 Garand read of the army's search for a machine gun and applied himself to the task of designing one. What he came up with relied on an overly complex mechanism—but it worked. An impressed officer at the National Bureau of Standards gave him a position as "master gauge and gun experimenter" in Washington, starting August 18, 1918, to perform further work on the gun, but the Armistice halted any future progress. Even without the cessation of hostilities, the novel, expensive machine gun would probably not have made it to production stage, but Garand's thorough knowledge of advanced mechanical principles persuaded the Ordnance Department to bring him into the fold at a salary of $3,500 a year. After qualifying for civil service, Garand joined the semiautomatic rifle design unit at Springfield Armory on November 4, 1919, and became an American citizen the following year.[42]

He was blissfully happy at Springfield. During the winters Garand practiced ice-skating incessantly. Finding the ice at outdoor rinks insufficiently smooth for his fancy moves, he partitioned off a twelve-foot-square room in his (rented) house, opened the windows and chimney to create a draft, and flooded the floor with a hundred gallons of water. *Voilà*, lovely skating all winter, every winter—until his marriage in 1930 to Nellie Shepard, a salesgirl at a local department store, who promptly put an end to the bachelor's high jinks. She introduced him to the rather less blood-pulsing delights of gardening and bridge.[43]

Garand tried to develop a semiautomatic based on the same primer-operated principle (i.e., the firing pin performed double duty as cartridge-igniter and breech-operator) as his machine gun. In 1920 and 1921 he produced two models; both were respectfully, if not enthusiastically, received.[44] In 1922, after Garand simplified the mechanism, Ordnance asked him to make twenty-four specimens for field trials. It took the gun-maker four years—an indication that the mechanism was still too complex for easy production—to prepare all the samples, and it was only in June 1926 that all of them were issued to infantry and cavalry testers.[45]

Internal reports revealed that the "Garand" (as it was now called around the department) was noted for its smooth operation and could easily rapid-fire one hundred of the army's standard .30-06 rounds.[46] A *Washington Post* story on an early private demonstration of the Garand even speculated that it would "replace the Springfield" in coming years.[47] If he hadn't known it before, Pedersen was now certain he had a major rival in this Garand fellow.

For the moment, at least, he still held the upper hand, thanks to a wholly unexpected finding in the summer of 1928. The army, confronted by Pedersen's insistence that the .276 was the equal, if not the better, of the .30 in causing incapacitation (either by death or wound trauma), commanded three Medical Corps officers and an Ordnance representative to run tests on eighteen unfortunate swine selected for a grisly experiment.

Using .30-06, .276, and small .256 rounds (used in some European armies), the testers discovered, much to everyone's surprise, that at short range (defined as 300 yards) the .256 "gave by far the most severe wounds in all parts of the animal." It was the .276 that "must be considered as occupying second place" in causing trauma, with the .30-06 trailing behind. At 600 yards, however, the performance gaps narrowed significantly, and all the bullets inflicted almost equal amounts of wounding. In brief, at ranges of 300 to 400 yards, any bullet could be considered an excellent killer, though the smaller calibers tended to leave gorier wounds.[48] For Pedersen, the "Pig Board" results justified his caliber reduction and made the Garand's retention of the .30-06 look like overkill.

Cheering as the results may have been (except for the pigs), Pedersen was now confronted with a different kind of challenge, one related to his ammunition. The army had announced in 1925 that it would be replacing the storied .30-06 with another version of the .30 round called the M1 when the two billion .30-06s it had stockpiled were depleted. Under peacetime conditions that was expected to happen sometime between 1934 and 1936, but the Pig Board experiments threw the fate of the .30 into doubt.[49]

Garand, who had been lagging behind Pedersen in the popularity stakes, now made a radical decision to junk his primer-operated prototype, the one he had been working on for nigh on a decade. A solitary overachiever—how else to explain the strictly private ice rink, the single-minded motorcycle racing?—he would start all over again, this time designing his weapon to accommodate the M1 *and* the .30-06, thereby nailing his colors to the .30 forever and challenging the army to decide between himself and Pedersen, champion of the .276.

Garand's decision to throw away his primer mechanism was not strictly voluntary but was instead forced upon him by the fact that the

M1 ammunition would work poorly in his existing model. This was because the 150-grain .30-06 was packed with a type of smokeless powder known as Pyro D.G., a quick-burning propellant. As soon as the powder was ignited, the pressure inside the chamber rose to a peak and dissipated rapidly as the bullet zoomed down the barrel. The propellant inside the 172-grain M1, however, was of a more modern type called IMR (Improved Military Rifle) that was a progressive burner; that is, it burned slowly at first and gradually built up pressure as the bullet raced toward the muzzle, thereby avoiding the peak-and-valley profile of the Pyro D.G. The Garand's primer-actuated mechanism relied on an initial burst of energy to work, and so IMR left his semiautomatic system gasping for power.

After careful thought Garand settled on making a gas-operated rifle. This type of semiautomatic system used a tube connected to the muzzle to harness the high-pressure gas created by the explosion and recycle it backward to operate the firing mechanism.[50]

But was he too late? On September 21, 1928, impressed by the Pig Board results, the recently convened Army, Navy, and Marine Corps Semiautomatic Rifle Board stunned everyone by approving the adoption of the .276 "as the standard caliber for the semiautomatic shoulder rifle to replace the present shoulder rifle caliber .30."[51] Five months later Ordnance canceled all future development on the Garand gas-operated .30.[52] Fortunately, by that time Garand had a good handle on the workings of the new system and was able, thanks to copious amounts of burned midnight oil, to churn out a .276 version with a ten-round clip.

Suddenly the Pedersen—whose benighted inventor had been convinced he was a shoo-in *this* time—was again confronted by the infernal Garand. At this point Pedersen made a fatal error. Over in Britain, Vickers, the huge armaments concern, had been keeping abreast of the army trials and was convinced that Washington was poised to choose the Pedersen as the national rifle. Expecting that when it happened there would be a rush of foreign orders, Vickers wanted to be the firm ready to fulfill them. Knowing that Pedersen, unlike Garand, held the patent rights to his arm, the company invited him to oversee the retooling of its factories in preparation for that happy event. Accordingly, in 1930—at the exact moment when he should have been working flat out to beat Garand—Pedersen sailed across the Atlantic and stayed there, out of sight and out of mind, until the summer of 1931.[53]

During Pedersen's absence his rifle went head-to-head against the Garand .276. An infantry board's firing test in the early spring of 1931 found that the Garand was superior in rate of fire, in hits per minute, and in hits per pound of ammunition. It also gathered praises for its simplicity of operation and construction (just sixty parts now, compared to the Pedersen's ninety-nine). "A man who has never seen the rifle can be taught its stripping and assembling within a few minutes," said the impressed testers. "The Garand is the best semiautomatic rifle" presently available, they concluded.[54]

The most comprehensive test, the one intended to settle once and for all the question of what the next service rifle would be, convened on October 9, 1931. Before this combined-service board lay three weapons: the Pedersen .276, the Garand .276, and a Garand .30—"an almost exact duplicate" of its smaller-caliber twin, but one that developed a cracked bolt and had to be sent back to Springfield for refitting.

The board's summary proved devastating for the Pedersen's chances. Whereas the Garand .276 was "simple and easy to manufacture" the Pedersen "would be more difficult to produce interchangeably" owing to its relatively complicated mechanism. Revealingly, any defects of the Garand were classed as trivial "basic disadvantages" (i.e., "length of operating rod due to taking gas at muzzle"), while those of the Pedersen were defined as flaws "inherent in the mechanism and which do not appear easy to correct." It was curtains for the Pedersen. On December 9, 1931, the board recommended the Garand .276 as the United States' new service rifle.[55]

Three months later, just as plans to adopt the Garand .276 were speedily progressing, Ordnance received a letter from the adjutant general, John Shuman, writing on behalf of the chief of staff, General Douglas MacArthur. Its message, recalled one of the experts, "created a sensation among those who had been connected with the rifle development." Everyone involved with the various boards "seemed more or less stunned."[56]

Directly quoting the chief of staff, the letter stated that he did not consider the commitment to the .276 "wise or desirable," as it would "introduce an element of chaos, confusion, and uncertainty" into war preparations. Granted, said MacArthur, the board had made its choice based on the "technical perfection of the smaller caliber," but it had not paid enough attention "to the other important features involved." He felt that the development of a working .30 Garand semiautomatic had been overhastily curtailed, and he ordered the board to drop the .276 version immediately. The Garand .30's mechanical defects were to be fixed promptly and eighty models made for testing. "Even if a caliber .30 semiautomatic cannot be developed to the point of perfection desired by the Ordnance Department, it still probably would be advantageous to introduce such a type with its imperfections."[57]

This decision, which went against precedent by overruling the technical judgment of the Ordnance specialists, was based on extreme political and economic grounds. At the time MacArthur, aged fifty and the most decorated American soldier of the Great War, had been chief of staff for about a year and a quarter. In November 1930, when President Herbert Hoover appointed him, the nation had been on the verge of a calamitous economic slump, and it had fallen to MacArthur to defend the army as best he could from the inevitable budget cuts. Hoover was intent on balancing the books and wanted to pay for job-creating public works by taking money that had been appropriated for the armed forces. As the Commerce Department's index of employment in manufacturing industries plummeted from 100.6 in January 1930 to a catastrophic 61.9 in July 1932, Hoover cut army salaries by 10 percent (President Roosevelt would slash them by another 15 percent in April 1933), thereby lowering a private's monthly pay almost to the poverty line.

The only good news for MacArthur was that, despite the rotten pay, the army was having no problem filling its ranks, as recently unemployed men rallied to the flag for the free food and accommodation, and it was able even to *raise* its entry qualifications. Not that there were many slots available: by the spring of 1933, its 60,000 combat troops made the U.S. Army just three times the size of the New York Police Department.[58] The police were probably better armed, too, since MacArthur's men were still armed with World War I mortars and protected by obsolete, battered French artillery pieces. The total number of tanks made after 1918 in

U.S. service was an unspectacular twelve, and congressmen had begun joking (half-seriously) that they wanted to cut the army's toilet paper budget.[59]

At no other time in its history was the U.S. Army less able to fight than during this period. In 1936 the general staff concluded that should war break out, it would be able to feed, clothe, transport, shelter, and issue rifles to 110,000 soldiers within thirty days of initial mobilization. That sounds impressive until one learns what the general staff could *not* supply: "airplanes, tanks, combat cars, scout cars, antiaircraft guns, searchlights, antiaircraft fire control equipment, .50 caliber machine guns, [and] ponton equipment."[60]

For the Ordnance Department, the cutbacks were especially dire. Between 1910 and the outbreak of the First World War, the department's budget as a percentage of total War Department appropriations had hovered at about 8 percent. Between 1920 and 1935 it plummeted to an average of 3.37 percent. Not until 1938, when the Munich Agreement and Hitler's *Anschluss* with Austria signaled to perceptive observers that war was increasingly likely, would the Ordnance budget rise above 6 percent (then would quadruple to 24.27 percent in 1939).[61]

The late 1920s and early 1930s coincided, too, with the zenith of pacifist sentiment in the United States and Europe. In 1928 the international Kellogg-Briand Pact had optimistically "abolished" war between states; its signing had unloosed a torrent of antiwar works (Siegfried Sassoon's *Memoirs of a Fox-Hunting Man,* Robert Graves's *Goodbye to All That,* John Dos Passos's *U.S.A.,* Erich Maria Remarque's *All Quiet on the Western Front*). Despite their contrived plots and anorexically thin characterization, a slew of rather less well-written novels luridly highlighting the hideousness of future war became best sellers. So many of them focused on the horrors of chemical warfare unleashed by airplanes against an unsuspecting civilian population, or on the perils of Science Gone Mad, that they formed a distinct genre, known as the "Gas Bomb Novel."[62] In Britain alone, between 1930 and 1939, some seventy-five were published. Neil Bell's *The Gas War of 1940* predicted the deaths of 1.5 billion people in the next war ("a youngster had the face wiped off him down to the skull, nothing left in front but his teeth. And he was alive and screaming for several minutes") and sold 100,000 copies in hardback; in George Godwin's *Empty Victory* a nervous French air force preventively bombs Britain with "arsenic gas" and kills 950,000 Londoners in a single hour.[63]

Partly inspired by these widespread fears of the war to come, the World Disarmament Conference opened in Geneva in February 1932. Attended by 2,500 delegates and 4,500 journalists from sixty-four countries, the conference was an extraordinary affair whose vaulting ambition—the outlawing of "offensive" weapons (tanks, submarines, and military aircraft in particular), the reduction of armies to almost ceremonial status, the "internationalization" of civil aircraft, and even, in one of its sillier moments, a ban on the production of "warlike toys"— proved its undoing.[64] Hitler's withdrawal from the conference in 1933 ensured its descent into irrelevance and extinction.[65]

Thus, at the exact moment when he forcefully decided to keep the .30 as standard, MacArthur was contending not only with the greatest economic downturn that Americans had ever experienced but also with a powerful wave of public opinion hostile toward the idea of having an army at all, and the opening of an international conference intended to make that wish a reality.

Understandably, then, MacArthur had to make cuts wherever possible, and anyone could see that approving a "militaristic" service rifle with a new caliber when at least a billion perfectly good .30 bullets were piled up at the arsenals might not provide a good "optic" for the national media. So desperate was MacArthur to save money that one of the reasons his letter to the Rifle Board insisted that it make test models of the .30 Garand *immediately* was that, for the fiscal years 1932 and 1933, Ordnance had only the minuscule sum of $170,000 available for the production of prototype semiautomatics and of sufficient ammunition for testing. On June 30, 1932, a portion of the funds ($100,000) was due to expire if unused.[66] Approving at least eighty experimental rifles could save most of that money, even if part of the rest had to be "returned" to Congress to show that MacArthur was serious about budget cutting.

As MacArthur well knew, New Dealers and most Democrats in general detested him for his role in putting down marchers in Washington and for his denunciations of pacifism. (The mammoth floor-to-ceiling mirror that he installed in his War Department office, before which he admired his bemedaled self while striking Napoleonic poses and smoking Lucky Strikes, might have raised a few eyebrows as well.)[67] In early 1933 the accession of a new president, Franklin Delano Roosevelt, was an opportunity to make things right, or at least righter than they were following MacArthur's earlier outburst to him. During a full and frank exchange of views about cutting the army budget, MacArthur later recalled, "I said something to the general effect that when we lost the next war, and an American boy, lying in the mud with an enemy bayonet through his belly and an enemy foot on his dying throat, spat out his last curse, I wanted the name not to be MacArthur but Roosevelt."[68] This had not gone down so well.

Nonetheless MacArthur soon found a way to the president's heart. Roosevelt wanted, as part of the first stage of the New Deal, to create a Civilian Conservation Corps that would put 275,000 youthful enrollees to work in useful endeavors. MacArthur knew that only the army could possibly organize a scheme as quickly as Roosevelt was envisaging. Much to the president's delight, the general offered to set up training centers for the volunteers, run them with military precision, assign fully a third of his officers to overseeing the corps, and dispatch the participants off to their designated camps across the country. By being so cooperative, MacArthur saved his job, and despite much criticism from the press about this American Caesar "militarizing" the nation's youth, Roosevelt appointed him for a second term as chief.[69]

In 1934–35, as the First New Deal and its initial raft of legislation and government regulation (the Tennessee Valley Authority, the Securities and Exchange Act, the National Recovery Administration) wound down, Roosevelt and his advisers intended to stimulate the lackluster economy by encouraging consumption and demand-side growth. This proto-Keynesian fiscal policy, which came to be known as the Second New Deal, included such vast relief programs as the Works Progress Administration of 1935 (which employed roughly a third of the country's jobless), the Emergency Relief Appropriation (which distributed $5 billion to the needy), the Social Security Act, the National Labor Relations Act, and the Rural Electrification Act.

MacArthur, a Hoover Republican, was alarmed at the scale of

Roosevelt's social and economic interventionism, but he realized also that one had to adapt or die. Alternatively put, the army would stand a better chance of surviving if it evolved to suit Rooseveltism. To this end, the general smartly linked rifle development and procurement to New Deal virtues. Given the scale of modern industry and the need to put money in the pockets of the workers to spend on products, he said in effect, outfitting the army with a new rifle would be a massive undertaking that would employ many thousands of highly skilled mechanics and beneficially exercise a multiplier effect throughout the economy.

Hence the accelerated speed at which work on the Garand progressed. MacArthur wasn't concerned with the details; he needed only to satisfy Roosevelt that the army would do its part to help the country regain its footing. Thus on August 3, 1933, even before the eighty models were ready on Ordnance's rushed schedule, their experimental designation, T1E2, was changed to the more official, more positive "U.S. Semiautomatic Rifle, Caliber .30, M1."

With eighteen machinists detailed to help him, Garand completed the eighty as soon as May 1934. Marksmen, veterans, and recruits alike tested the weapons under the hardest possible conditions short of actual war. In October 1935, just as MacArthur stepped down as chief of staff to become the senior military adviser to the Philippine government, the trials were completed, and both infantry and cavalry unanimously approved adoption of MacArthur's rifle. On January 9, 1936, the "Garand M1" became the standard service arm of the American army.[70] For the first time in living memory, the United States was actually ahead of its traditional competitors in rifle development: Britain, France, and Germany all went to war in 1939 with the same rifles they had used in 1914.

The Garand couldn't have happened along at a better time. By 1936 the gathering storm in Europe was turning nasty, the Spanish Civil War had begun, the Disarmament Conference had finally dissolved after accomplishing nothing, Japan was becoming overtly aggressive in the Pacific, and Hitler's Germany had revealed the existence of a secret air force and announced that it was expanding the Wehrmacht to thirty-six divisions. Though Western governments continued to talk the language of peace, they were quietly beginning to rearm: across the Atlantic,

Neville Chamberlain was lobbying his Cabinet colleagues to construct a massive bomber deterrent, while Roosevelt belatedly approved enlarging the army from 118,750 to 165,000 troops.

Within two years the M1 rifle project, begun as part of an economic stimulus program, dovetailed into the campaign to strengthen national security by rearming America's antiquated army. On January 28, 1938, Roosevelt told Congress that "our national defense is inadequate for purposes of national security and requires increase."[71] Exactly one week (February 4) after that declaration, following the example of the earlier Roosevelt, the president wrote a letter to be read out at the NRA's annual banquet:

You are doing what I believe to be a meritorious work, contributing your efforts to carrying on the successful promotion, among citizens of this Nation, of rifle marksmanship—an accomplishment in which our forefathers so effectively excelled . . . Both national and international rifle competitions, which you encourage, have served to inject the idea of sports into rifle shooting . . . while encouraging a free spirit of rivalry [and which] also makes an essential contribution to the national defense.

Whereas in 1932, as the waves of pacifist sentiment rolled in, Roosevelt had felt that controlling handgun ownership in general would "tend to decrease crimes of violence in our State," by 1938 he believed that the NRA formed an existing corps of marksmen who could be used to train the new citizen armies that he was convinced would be needed. Over the course of the coming war, in fact, NRA instructors would train more than 1.75 million American soldiers.[72]

Setting up the manufacturing facilities and producing sufficient quantities of the M1 rifle were necessarily lengthy processes, even for as simple an arm as the Garand, which had been designed for easy mass production. One of the Pedersen's drawbacks had been its inventor's propensity to conceive, customize, and hand-engineer each and every piece, along with its associated machinery and tools. Garand, conversely, was more concerned with stripping each piece down to its very essence; he preferred to sketch out his concepts on rough blueprints and rely, if possible, on already available machinery.

b) A drill press installed in 1861 and still in use in 1935.

a) A rifling shop at Springfield.

Even so, making interchangeable rifles—as old John Hall had discovered a century before—was a colossal undertaking. Exacerbating the problem was the fact that except for two small programs to make machine guns and pistols during the war, the armories had not retooled since about 1900, when Springfield had set up shop for the Model 1903. Even then some buildings and machinery there antedated the Civil War. Staff and workmen were not only relatively few but tended to be soon headed into retirement, thereby leaving a potential vacuum of experience and talent behind.

All kudos to the Ordnance men, then, who pulled shift after shift to get production up and running in record time. The first step was the preparation of detailed production drawings for every part of the rifle and painstakingly ensuring that their tolerances (that is, the possible variations in a characteristic such as hardness, density, or weight) stayed well within fixed maximums so that each piece would fit together absolutely perfectly. If something went even slightly awry in the smallest minutiae of these blueprints, then interchangeability—the touchstone of the Ordnance Department for a hundred years—would be rendered impossible from the get-go.

Once the drawings were completed, the second step consisted of planning how each part was to be made in a sequence of operations. Every stage, from a piece's rough hewing to its exacting final state, was traced on a "route sheet" that also listed the manner of every operation, the type of machine that would perform it, and the gauges that would be needed to ensure the piece's standard dimensions.

With much of the paperwork done, the armory set about ordering the required amounts of material, a process that could take several months owing to the need for competitive bidding with outside contractors and possible delays resulting therefrom. Meanwhile, the planning division's production control section ensured that when the shops dealing with the smaller components received the material, they would have an efficient system of production ready so they could coordinate with the assembly room, which was where the major parts would be assembled.

As raw materials began to arrive, practical plans were drawn up to lay out exactly how each piece would be manufactured. During this stage the machines that would help make other machines were designed, adapted, or purchased and laid out on the factory floor according to the principles of scientific management. To make an M1 some two thousand separate operations were required, and nearly all of them called for a jig or a fixture to hold it still, a tool for the cutting, and several gauges to measure the finished article in all its dimensions. Thus multiple copies of, and spares for roughly six thousand pricey, precise accessories were required before manufacturing the M1 could even begin. Ammunition production was simpler but only relative to rifle manufacturing. Making a single cartridge took fully 111 operations from raw material to finished product: 64 mechanical operations, 19 washing operations, 16 drying operations, five pickling operations, and seven annealing operations (a process that softened the metal made hard and brittle by the mechanical procedures).

Now, some of these accessories were already available in the Springfield storerooms, owing to work on previous makes of rifles, and they could be quickly modified to fit the new model. But the great majority weren't, and because every single one had to be designed and made, an outside contractor for the armory estimated that twenty thousand hours of engineering study would be needed even to *plan* making these accessories, and two hundred thousand more to actually produce them. Moreover, over the past thirty years new machining methods, such as internal and surface broaching, and coining in cold dies instead of hot forging, had been developed, demanding additional research and investment in brand-new equipment. In turn, armory representatives had to canvass the market, advertise the open contracts, negotiate discounts with manufacturers, have the funds approved, and then wait for delivery and hope the manufacturer didn't screw up the order.[73] Ultimately, Springfield purchased nearly one thousand different machines at an average cost of $20,000 each, in addition to the jigs and fixtures.[74] Gunmaking is, it seems, more complex and wondrous a matter than most people assume.

Bearing all these considerations in mind, the speed with which the armory set up the M1 production line was remarkable, truly testament to the long shadows cast by John Hall over the American economic system. In September 1937—just eighteen months after the rifle had been authorized for use in January 1936—the first interchangeable Garands began rolling off the line at the rate of ten per day. Efficient mass-production methods rely on growing economies of scale, increasing automation, and steadily improving worker skill, so this figure gradually rose to twenty per day on March 1, 1938; to eighty per day on July 1, 1939; to one hundred per day on September 1, 1939 (the date Germany invaded Poland); to two hundred per day on January 22, 1940; to four hundred by July; to six hundred the following January; and to one thousand by June 1941 (when the United States was still at peace). By September 1943 production was averaging *four thousand* per day. By VJ-Day in the summer of 1945, Springfield and its associated arms-makers (such as Winchester, Remington, and Savage) had churned out 4,028,395 Garands.[75] To put those extraordinary numbers more graphically, whereas before the war it had taken four minutes and eight operations to make one particular small part for the Garand's rear sight, by the late spring of 1941 a single machine tool specially designed for the task cranked out six every twenty-seven seconds.[76]

Initially, the Garand M1 received a rough reception from civilian experts who were suspicious of rifles that appeared to soft-pedal the skill of marksmanship. Owing to the War Department's overly protective, or self-defensive, attitude toward its latest acquisition, the NRA was convinced that it was covering up something dubious about the Garand. In the late 1930s sample rifles were made deliberately difficult to get ahold of, and there was a persistent rumor—an accurate one—that early M1s suffered from a loose gas-cylinder assembly that rattled the front sight and threw off the shooter's aim.[77]

Admittedly, the government was concerned with secrecy at the time, but keeping the NRA—whose members were hardly likely to be enemy saboteurs—in the dark was neurotic. As a result, when the minor gas-cylinder problem was fixed, no one informed the NRA, let alone, bewilderingly, Major General Milton A. Reckord, member of the National Board for the Promotion of Rifle Practice, chief of the Maryland National Guard, and an extremely active executive vice president of the NRA. Owing solely to the army information blackout, Reckord continued to labor under the misapprehension that American soldiers were being issued a shoddy, unmarksmanlike arm—and he wasn't reluctant to call his friends in the press and on Capitol Hill to tell them about it.

In the winter of 1940 the storm broke. On February 22 Walter McCallum published the first part of a three-article series in Washington's *Evening Star* questioning the Garand's abilities and quoting Reckford extensively.[78] The outcry was such that the following month the House Military Appropriations Subcommittee convened to examine the evidence. In response to the charge that in 1939 the army had "discovered a defect so serious that a new barrel had to be designed," the Ordnance chief, Major General Charles Wesson (described in the papers as "cagey" but "capable"), said that the Garand was "the best semi-automatic rifle ever considered by the Army." A barrel defect there had been; serious it wasn't. Even so, Reckord testified to the subcommittee that "the War Department has made a very grave mistake," and he was backed up by Representative D. Lane Powers of New Jersey, who said that "we do not want to appropriate for . . . additional rifles if what we hear and what we read and what we are told by some well-informed people is true."

In May Reckord revealed what was up his sleeve in *The American Rifleman,* the NRA's house publication. Mr. F. C. Ness, an expert shot and frequent contributor to the magazine, had, through charm or guile or both, been able to borrow one of the jealously guarded Garands for three days and had fired off 692 rounds (not a large number, in test terms).[79]

Infuriatingly for Ordnance, and embarrassingly for the army, Ness concluded by rating "the Johnson" as better than the Garand. The Johnson—the creation of a tall young Bostonian and former Marine, Captain Melvin Maynard Johnson, Jr.—was the rifle of choice for discerning NRA members: they had been kept abreast of its evolution by *The American Rifleman,* which had run at least four articles on the subject.[80]

Johnson, born into an affluent family in 1909, was, like so many of America's firearms inventors, from an early age quite fascinated with these masterpieces of the mechanical sciences. A member of the Harvard class of 1931 (the same year he was commissioned in the Marine Corps Reserve), he was graduated from its law school in 1934. Though he practiced his trade until 1939, his childhood interest never died, and the Corps sent him to Quantico to attend its weapons schools. While serving as its observer at Springfield, he gained firsthand experience with the Pedersen and Garand rifles. In his off time, he tinkered with guns and founded Johnson Automatics, Inc.[81]

In 1935–36 he conceived a recoil-operated semiautomatic rifle based on a Mauser 98 action. The army tested it a few times, with fine results, in June and October 1938. Johnson had expressly designed his weapon for Creedmoor-style marksmanship and perfect handling: it would not even accommodate a standard bayonet for hand-to-hand combat and was handcrafted in every particular. Befitting its bespoke qualities, the Johnson consisted of 140 parts (compared to the M1's then-71).[82] As the Johnson was wholly unsuited to modern warfare, on February 23, 1940, Ordnance officially refused to consider it for adoption.

The NRA's reaction was not a favorable one (its April *American*

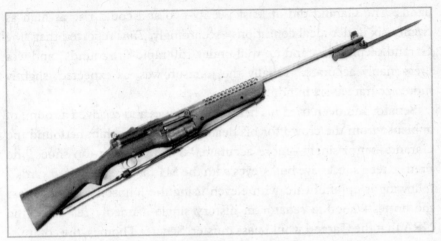

The contender: Melvin Johnson's semiautomatic .30 rifle.

Rifleman editorial was titled "The Courage to Be Frank"), reinforcing its position with Ness's critical review of the Garand in the subsequent issue. The army, which had hitherto been quite blasé about the matter (after all, Ordnance rejected dozens of prototypes each year; Johnson's was no different), was forced to take action before, in the words of an annoyed Ordnance officer, the army was forced to fight a war "not with the gun the soldiers wanted, but rather with the ones that someone had persuaded the public that the Army ought to have."[83]

To stifle the controversy, Ordnance believed that the Johnson had to be seen to fail. A competition was quickly arranged between the Garand and the Johnson for May 9, 1940, at Fort Belvoir, Virginia. Members of the press, army representatives, House politicians from both sides of the aisle, and the Military Subcommittee of the Senate Appropriations Committee attended, including its powerful chairman, Senator Elmer Thomas, and the man who would be the star of the day, sixty-one-year-old Senator Ernest Lundeen, a former captain in the army reserve.

The first set of targets was placed at six hundred yards, and in the first heat the Johnson narrowly outshot the Garand in accuracy 404 to 393; but in the second it faded as the Garand took 405 points to its 348. In the rapid-fire round there was no competition, for despite its semiautomatic action, the Johnson was hardly faster than the manual Springfield Model 1903 and could fire just fifteen shots per minute in experienced hands. The Garand did at least twenty-two and could rise as high as twenty-six under ideal conditions. Accordingly, *Time* reported that "the Garand seemed to stand up well under 150 rapid-fire rounds" and was "reasonably accurate." Finally the Johnson was, as expected, slightly more accurate at six hundred yards.

Senator Lundeen tried his hand at both rifles and received a round of applause from the crowd for his dead-eye marksmanship; he found the Garand—surprisingly—more accurate. "Sedate in high-top shoes," he fired sixteen successive bull's-eyes with the M1 (at three hundred yards), following it up afterward with eleven using the Johnson. With this feat the hottest-shooting senator in history single-handedly reassured the NRA that the Garand would pass muster. Senator Thomas, the committee chairman, put paid to Captain Johnson's hopes in his remarks to the press: "They are both mighty fine guns, and there is no particular difference. If the Garand is as good as the other, and we have the machinery already set up to produce it, I see no reason to go into production on a second good gun."[84] Chastened for the moment, the NRA grumbled a little that "the demonstration . . . proved absolutely nothing," but it ceased coverage of the Johnson.[85] Even before America entered the Second World War, the organization had shed its former skepticism and was numbered among the Garand's most vocal supporters.[86]

With the Johnson now a no-go for the regular army, just one holdout against the Garand remained: the U.S. Marine Corps, which insisted on keeping its Springfields. The Marines were adamant that the factor distinguishing them from the post-1914 army was their magnificent marksmanship training, and they felt that the Garand detracted from their skills.

To decide the matter once and for all, the Marines organized their own weapons competition in November 1940. The Garand—the Establishment weapon, the one backed by Ordnance, the general staff, the Washington political class, and the army—would be run directly against the Springfield, the Old School rifleman's rifle, in the most tightly administered and stringently measured test of all.

The Marines were most interested in, first, accuracy, and second, ruggedness and dependability in battle conditions. Though there was a war conveniently going on, America had not yet entered it, and so the

Marines were obliged to hold the trials at their base in San Diego using forty enlisted men, all marksmen. Beginning on November 18, the guns were tested to their limits in no fewer than thirty-seven shooting and abuse tests (timed shots, various ranges up to a thousand yards, firing under adverse conditions, differently sized targets, firing under fair-to-ideal conditions, prone shots, standing shots, and sitting-from-standing shots, among others).

In terms of accuracy, it turned out, the Garand was (in the words of the testing board) "comparable to the M1903" and far outclassed the Springfield in the number of shots per minute it fired. When it came to ruggedness, however, the Springfield triumphed: it survived a fourteen-hour-long test in which, to simulate a long march through rainstorms, the rifles were subjected to freshwater sprinklers for two hours off and on (the Garand suffered a 20 percent malfunction rate); it survived submersion in a mud bath (the M1 failed to work); and most impressively, it survived a test assuming that Marines (as these soldiers of the sea do) "have landed through heavy surf sufficient to break completely over men and equipment, and immediately engage in combat on a sandy beach." Repeatedly sprayed with salt water and dragged through sand, the Springfields could be operated with difficulty, while the Garands could not be fired.

Against Ordnance's expectations, the new rifle had not vanquished the old. The Marine Corps board concluded that while the Garand was an excellent semiautomatic, it was, at the end of the day, a semiautomatic. The forty-year-old Springfield remained the gold standard for tough dependability. Even so, soldiers using it were noticeably fatigued, thereby exacerbating the Model 1903's relative slowness of fire relative to that of the Garand, a firearm that could keep up a colossal volume of fire for sustained periods of time because the gun was doing the work. As always, the question came down to whether you wanted to kill the enemy with one shot or many. The Springfield remained "the darling of those who believe with Colonel William Prescott of Bunker Hill ('Don't fire until you see the whites of their eyes') in deliberate, sharpshooting marksmanship," summarized *Time*. "The Garand is three to three-and-a-half times faster, [and] is therefore the logical choice of those who put high fire power above all else."[87]

In actuality the Garand performed far *better* in the field than might have been expected from its test results. In late February 1942 General MacArthur told the press that during the fighting on the Bataan Peninsula the Garand developed no mechanical defects and did not jam up with dust and dirt, adding that in some cases it had been used almost constantly for up to a week without cleaning or lubrication.[88] Referring to the 1944 Normandy landings, Brigadier General Sidney Hinds would later point out that "most men who stopped, or were stopped, on the beach, probably became casualties themselves before the Garand was stopped by sand."[89]

Though in 1941 the Marines had finally signed on to issuing the Garand (mostly owing to the need to standardize weapons across services), owing to holdouts M1s remained relatively few in the Corps— despite a gracious article in the *Marine Corps Gazette* by the bested Melvin Johnson praising the Garand's rapid-fire ability and accuracy.[90] Sometime in early 1942 Brigadier General William Rupertus, commanding general of the Marine Corps base at San Diego, had a talk with his public relations officer, Captain Robert White. Rupertus was worried that the new men streaming into the Corps after Pearl Harbor did not understand "that the only weapon which stands between them and Death is the rifle." With the outbreak of war, the Corps had expanded from 18,000 to 25,000, and in order to train them all, the recruit syllabus was halved to just four weeks. Rifle qualification rates accordingly plummeted, as did training standards. The syllabus was soon returned to its previous status, but Rupertus insisted that recruits must have it hammered into them that "their rifle is their life . . . it must become a creed with them." The general scribbled down some lines on a "random scrap of paper" and handed it to White the next day. White typed it out, added a line or two here and there, and suggested a few word changes. The result, called "My Rifle" (sometimes known as the "Rifleman's Creed"), was first published in the San Diego *Marine Corps Chevron* on March 14, 1942:

1. This is my rifle. There are many like it, but this one is mine.
2. My rifle is my best friend. It is my life. I must master it as I must master my life.

3. My rifle, without me, is useless. Without my rifle, I am useless. I must fire my rifle true. I must shoot straighter than my enemy who is trying to kill me. I must shoot him before he shoots me. I will . . .

4. My rifle and myself know that what counts in this war is not the rounds we fire, the noise of our burst, nor the smoke we make. We know that it is the hits that count. We will hit . . .

5. My rifle is human, even as I, because it is my life. Thus, I will learn it as a brother. I will learn its weaknesses, its strengths, its parts, its accessories, its sights and its barrel. I will ever guard it against the ravages of weather and damage as I will ever guard my legs, my arms, my eyes and my heart against damage. I will keep my rifle clean and ready. We will become part of each other. We will . . .

6. Before God, I swear this creed. My rifle and myself are the defenders of my country. We are the masters of our enemy. We are the saviors of my life.

7. So be it, until victory is America's and there is no enemy, but peace!![91]

Still taught to recruits, the Creed has seeped into popular culture partly by dint of the films *Full Metal Jacket* and *Jarhead,* in which actors recite shortened versions of it. By identifying a man's rifle as "human," his constant companion, his own brother—indeed, his very savior—Rupertus's words struck a deep bass chord within the American soul with its mystical, collective memory of The Rifleman and his historical contribution to Liberty. On a less abstract note, the Creed's appearance coincides with the not overly popular decision by the Corps to adopt the Garand over the hallowed Springfield. Rupertus, who must have been present at the San Diego competition, thought it crucial to convince Marines new and old that the Garand was the official rifle of the Corps, and that even if they believed it inferior to the Springfield, the good Marine must become at one with his rifle—no matter what it was.

Rupertus's public relations exercise on behalf of the Garand did not, however, fully pay off until the Battle of Guadalcanal (August 7, 1942–February 7, 1943). There *Springfield*-armed Marines stormed ashore and entered the steaming rain forest—a place where thousand-yard headshots were in short supply and where overwhelming firepower quickly brought to bear was of prime concern. Lieutenant Colonel John George, who fought in the battle, recalled that the Marines "soon realized" they had made a mistake in sticking with the Springfield when the army units that followed them carried Garands.

> From almost the first minutes of the combat on Guadalcanal the Marines began wishing for a basic semiautomatic rifle. By the time we landed we had to keep ours tied down with wire. Leathernecks were appropriating all they could lay their hands on by "moonlight acquisition." In daylight, they would come over to our areas to barter souvenirs with the freshly landed doughboy units; any crooked supply sergeant who had an extra M1 rifle could get all the loot he wanted.
>
> When the Marines began to get a few Garands up to the front, the demand proportionately increased. They quickly learned that the M1 did not jam any more often than the Springfield, and that it was equally easy to maintain. The disassembly system, especially, made the M1 much easier to clean and oil.
>
> Yes, the Marines were justified in their yen for the Garand. Once in combat, no one could see the logic in remaining in the same armament class with the Japs. Most of the officers who had been appalled at the Garand's lack of target accuracy were quick to give it due credit in combat.
>
> The behavior of one Marine corporal seemed to epitomize this attitude. It was during the organization of a joint Marine-Infantry patrol, shortly after we had landed. I saw this Marine, a member of the 2nd Marine Raider Battalion, place and keep himself squarely behind one of the Army sergeants in the advance platoon. When the march was well under way, the sergeant inquired as to why the leatherneck kept treading on his heels.
>
> The answer came quickly: "You'll probably get yours on the first burst, Mac. Before you hit the ground, I'll throw this damn Springfield away and grab your rifle!"[92]

Key to the Garand's success among the Marines (and army soldiers) was its eight-round capacity, a 60 percent increase over that of the Springfield. His men "gained a certain assurance and confidence," recalled Colonel Whaling, a veteran of several Pacific campaigns, from being able to outfire the enemy.[93]

Marine Corps fears that the Garand was unacceptably inaccurate compared to the Springfield turned out to be unfounded. Marksmen, in fact, were well served by the Garand. One remembered that at Guadalcanal "Jap swimming holes and river crossings were ideal spots to watch, from any point not over 600 to 700 yards away." Happily, "the Japs could not believe that a kill at 700 yards was anything but accidental, so that the spot could profitably be watched three or more times a week."[94] Japanese troops, observed Colonel George, who enjoyed an immense amount of personal experience in the matter, were not trained in marksmanship to anything like the level in the U.S. Army and shot out only to four hundred yards ("Japs are poor belly shooters"), though they did (quite sensibly, he thought) compensate by using improvised rests as often as possible.[95]

Employed in combination with traditional American marksmanship, the Garand was a particularly lethal weapon that could be used in situations ranging from the toughest, bloodiest assault to pinpoint sharpshooting. It was the perfect everyday weapon of Everyman, and it seemed to possess an incredible ability to transform ordinary men into extraordinary soldiers. On January 26, 1945, in the final accounting, General George S. Patton would provide the ne plus ultra of celebrity endorsements: "In my opinion, the M1 Rifle is the greatest battle implement ever devised."[96] Garand himself, rather more modestly, averred that "she is a pretty good gun, I think."[97]

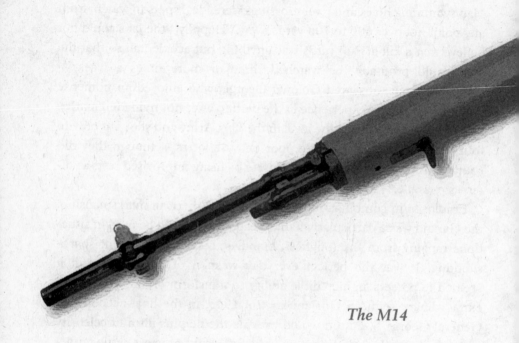

The M14

Chapter 10

★

THE GREAT
BLUNDERBUSS BUNGLE

Following Nazi Germany's surrender in the spring of 1945 Europe was a wasteland, a madhouse, a morgue. Aside from the tens of millions dead, 60 million people belonging to fifty-five different ethnic groups had been either uprooted or turned into refugees; coal production was less than half its prewar level; and a quarter of Europe's farmland lay fallow. Entire cities had been firebombed, and whole communities annihilated. Almost every country, from Albania to Norway, had been invaded and occupied, some twice. Their harbors were jammed with sunken vessels, their bridges sundered, their roads cratered.

Europe was no longer "Europe." It had been divided between the United States and Stalin's Soviet Union and was counted as either ours or theirs. Europeans swore to heal forever the bitter divisions that had caused the war—France and Germany alone had fought each other three times in less than a century. Never again must that happen, they resolved, especially in a nuclear age, when the consequences of a fourth war would be devastating.

The seeds of European union, of what Churchill called in 1946 "a kind of United States of Europe," were sown in the immediate postwar years. In 1949 the Council of Europe came into being, followed a year later by the European Convention for the Protection of Human Rights, and then came the pooling of coal and steel production, the European Economic Community, and the European Atomic Energy Community.

All these efforts to bind together former adversaries were taken with Washington's blessing and encouragement. As guarantor of European peace, the United States' interest lay in unifying the Western nations to blunt Communist expansion. To that end, it created the Marshall Plan in June 1947. The concept was simple: send sufficient supplies and donate enough money to allow Europe to recover and stand on her own two feet. Greece at the time was suffering a Communist insurgency, and the Soviets were pressuring Turkey to allow them free passage through the Dardanelles; if Europe remained bankrupt and stricken, the likelihood of Red gains, be they electoral, military, or terroristic, increased. On July 12 the representatives of sixteen European nations convened to accept the Americans' generosity. Amounting to five percent of the U.S. national income, some $13.5 billion in grants and credits, plus another $500 million in private gifts, flowed across the Atlantic from 1948 onward. The Marshall Plan was such a success that by 1951 European industrial production was 43 percent higher than it had been before the war. The recipients of the largesse mostly abjured the extremes of free-market capitalism and state-controlled Communism in favor of a regulated form of economic "planning" in which private enterprise coexisted with public welfarism. As the European economies stabilized, popular support for aggressively radical leftist and rightist parties subsided, and Continental voters turned instead to the consensus-seeking, moderate politics exemplified by Christian Democrat (for the conservatively inclined) and Social Democrat (for the liberally inclined) parties.

Just as trans-European politics and economics centered on the common middle, so too did the shibboleth of "commonality" affect the military. The term referred to the international standardization of armaments, so that a Soviet thrust into West Germany could be parried without having to worry about whether one country's weaponry would be compatible with the others'.

On April 4, 1949, when twelve countries (eventually joined by Greece, Turkey, West Germany, and Spain) signed the collective defense agreement known as the North Atlantic Treaty, arms standardization was high on the agenda. Owing to wartime commitments, geography, imperial obligations, and long-standing historical tradition, cooperation was particularly close between the English-speaking, or Anglospheric, signatories: the United States, Canada, and Britain. In the early summer of 1951, as a prelude to their wider adoption by the other NATO allies, the trio agreed to standardize some four hundred army items, including the new American light Walker Bulldog tank, various types of howitzers, fuels, electric system voltages, and lubricants.[1]

One issue remained particularly thorny: the lack of a common rifle caliber, and a common rifle to fire it. The Americans had assumed that the British and Canadians would choose the good old .30-caliber; they assumed wrong. While the Canadians tried to stay neutral, the British were determined to reduce the caliber to .280 and expected their American allies to do likewise. If Washington refused, London was willing to adopt its own rifle and caliber, thereby throwing into doubt the solidity of NATO solidarity. This spat over the longest fifth of an inch in history would almost tear apart the nascent Atlantic alliance and would ultimately lead to the M14 fiasco—the great blunderbuss bungle.

The trouble began in May 1944, when Springfield began investigating whether the semiautomatic M1 could be converted into a fully automatic weapon. With a semiautomatic the shooter must pull the trigger each time he fires; but an automatic weapon continues to fire so long as his finger is depressing the trigger. For automatics to work with any success, their magazines must be larger than the Garand's relatively miserly eight-shot one. Designers accordingly began drawing up plans for twenty- and even thirty-round clips—and immediately ran into the usual problem afflicting rapid-firing arms: they require lighter, smaller bullets because the heat buildup with full-power cartridges becomes intolerable, and because the repeated recoil and "bucking" of the gun makes a nonsense of accuracy. One solution to the heat issue was to add thickened wooden handguards to the weapon, a fix that would helpfully add several more pounds to the rifle's weight (in addition to the heavier clips). A heftier rifle dampened recoil and the rifle's tendency to jump upward and rightward as the spent casings were spat out. Unfortunately, even the Garand, which had not been counted as a particularly feathery rifle back in 1936, was already proving too much of a hump during tough campaigns, soldiers were complaining. Carrying an automatic version, with all the surplus ammunition that that entailed, would make an uncomfortable situation worse.

The army accordingly began asking Ordnance to see if it could do anything to lighten the soldier's load—to below nine pounds—while retaining the weapon's powerful hitting power with the .30, even when firing on automatic. Most important, Springfield's practical-minded production engineers (always on shaky terms with the armory's theoretical researchers) insisted that at least 85 percent of any new weapon must be able to be made using existing M1 tooling.[2]

Given these demands, there was no possibility of reducing the Garand's weight significantly. In the lead-up to the Normandy landings and a possible invasion of Japan, the Pentagon wanted to add all sorts of extras (bipod, flash hider, larger mags, telescopic sight, muzzle brake, and a grenade-launcher) so that the improved M1 could function as a one-stop shop for all its armaments needs. If all went well, the new, improved M1 could replace the Browning Automatic Rifle (powerful but not easily luggable at twenty pounds), the short-barreled carbines favored by paratroopers (light but underpowered), *and* the Thompson submachine gun (great volume of fire but very short-range, firing bullets as wildly as a Chicago gangster). In a perfect world, the new rifle would be as light as a carbine, as rapid-firing as a tommy gun, and as knockdown dangerous as the Browning. Ordnance, unfortunately, lived in an imperfect one.

John Garand, undaunted nonetheless, plowed ahead in his usual methodical way and produced a prototype in October 1944 dubbed the T20. Despite his best efforts, the weapon could not be all things to all men. For one thing, a rifle is an agglomeration of trade-offs. You could keep the .30 for the purpose of long-range hitting power, but you had hardly a chance of being able to use those cartridges *en masse* for short-range work (at 50 to 75 yards, the ideal range for urban warfare and jungle fighting); one reason was that at such close distances the .30 would wastefully "overkill," especially if fired automatically. Equally, as Garand found, if you fired .30s automatically at a rate of four to six hundred rounds per minute, only a Goliath could control the weapon as it spewed bullets every which way. You could add a reworked gas cylinder to better harness the energy, but then you would have to lose the bayonet.

Between October 1944 and the spring of 1945, Garand obsessively beavered away on the successor to his own M1. When he finally emerged from his cavernous workshop, he bore a miracle gun, made all the more so by its hasty genesis. Fitted with all its accoutrements, it weighed more than thirteen pounds, but stripped down to its absolute basics, it was just a few ounces heavier than a standard M1. It could be produced on existing tooling, and it had an innovative muzzle brake attached to reduce the fearsome recoil of its impressive, if theoretical, seven-hundred-rounds-per-minute capability. In August 1945, just before two atomic bombs forcibly induced Japan to surrender, 100,000 of them were ordered.[3]

In that halcyon period following VJ-Day, the last thing the world needed, now that it was finally at peace and had not yet been sundered into its Western and Eastern halves, was a new Garand of any kind. Just as Pedersen had had the bad luck to invent his device in the waning days of the First World War, so now did his former rival experience the pain of having his creation canceled—after only a hundred T20s had been made. Indeed, in a replay of the years immediately following the 1918 Armistice, Ordnance was among the first departments to have its budget slashed. By the fall of 1945 the number of employees in Springfield's manufacturing department had fallen from 3,100 to 900, with more cuts threatened.[4]

One of the lucky survivors was Colonel René Studler, chief of the Small Arms Development Branch. After graduating from Ohio State University and marrying Mildred, his college sweetheart, Studler had joined the army in 1917 as an enlisted man, and after six months he was commissioned a second lieutenant in the new aviation section of the Signal Corps. There he became a pilot, one of the few in this newest of military arms, and after five years he transferred to Ordnance. As one of its young stars, he was sent to MIT, where in 1923 he obtained a degree in mechanical engineering. He later helped supervise the Pig Board trials that compared the effect of various calibers on helpless swine. In the early 1930s, as one of the few Ordnance men who was conversant in several languages, he was dispatched to Europe in a kind of Major Alfred Mordecai role, his instructions being to file technical reports on the state of Europe's armaments. An assiduous, wiry fellow blessed with a snappy mustache and sufficient independent wealth to not have to worry about whether the bean counters would pay his travel expenses, Studler astounded his superiors by dutifully submitting no fewer than three hundred reports between July 1934 and February 1939. Owing to their tediousness, few, if any, of them were actually read, but on his return Studler (like Mordecai) could justly be regarded as knowing more about infantry small arms than any other American.[5]

Socially ambitious (he was a keen equestrian and tennis player) and described as being "impatient with delays and irritated by incompetence," Studler hoped to cap his career as a general and chief of Ordnance.[6] He therefore desperately craved a small-arms success. He had originally placed his hopes in the Garand T20, but talk of a new common NATO rifle revived his spirits. If the North Atlantic Treaty signatories adopted an American-made weapon, Studler would instantly outshine his predecessors: the Ordnance Department would be purveyor of fine arms not only to the U.S. armed forces but to those of a baker's dozen other nations. As armorer to the Free World, he might well end his professional life as a grand panjandrum at NATO headquarters.

Studler had two secret weapons. The first was a cartridge codenamed the T65, and the second was a man birth-named Earle Harvey. Regarding the former, the Western Cartridge division of Olin Industries had lately perfected a type of "ball" propellant powder that possessed several advantages over the standard smokeless, nitrocellulose powders: it could be manufactured in a fraction of the time; its burn rate was steadier, thereby producing stable velocities; and it was more powerful, grain for grain, so that a soldier could use less but get more bang. What the ball powder made possible, in sum, was a full-power .30 round whose *casing* was shorter than before—by five-eighths of an inch, to be precise—while its bullet retained its previous weight and velocity. Just as important, a shorter cartridge entailed a shorter breech mechanism that used less metal, and that in turn meant a lighter rifle.[7]

To accessorize the T65, Studler set in motion a new rifle project, trusting to Earle Harvey to see it through. The T25, as the Harvey rifle was called during its experimental stages, would be expressly designed to take advantage of the new, shorter cartridges that would, thought Studler, serve NATO as standard.

Harvey was in his late thirties, the Connecticut-born son of a lawyer's caretaker. Itching for the unindentured life, his father had purchased an eighty-two-acre farm a few miles south of Woodstock when Harvey was fourteen. Young Earle spent his youth learning about firearms from his father and grandfather, and he practiced his aim by shooting squirrels and grouse. Finishing high school in 1928, he attended the University of Connecticut, where for two years he studied engineering but found it too taxing. He then transferred to Brown University to study English. Graduating in 1933, he pursued graduate work at Yale before belatedly realizing that during the Depression English majors were hardly at the top of any employer's most-wanted list. In 1937, rather reluctantly, he returned to engineering but decided to specialize in his first love, firearms. Throughout his student years he had continued to hunt, and in the fall of 1934, while tootling down the street in New Haven, he had a vision of a new locking mechanism for a self-loading rifle. He mentioned it to Howard Newton, a partner in a local sporting goods firm, who advised him to go see Edwin Pugsley, an old Yalie and MIT man who currently headed research at Winchester. Pugsley advised the young man to draw diagrams of the mechanism and bring them in. Harvey purchased some brown wrapping paper from the Whitney Avenue Pharmacy on the way home and began sketching. Within a few hours he'd finished. Back at Winchester, Pugsley examined them for about ten minutes with Frank Burton, one of his arms designers. The mechanism had promise, they concluded, but probably would not work. Even so, Harvey was clearly talented, and Pugsley offered him work at the firm. The job was a low-paying, low-status one, and Harvey still dreamed of becoming an English professor, but after eighteen fruitless months of unemployment, he belatedly agreed to take the position. By then, however, there was no work at Winchester, and Pugsley tipped him off that there were better opportunities at Remington, which had recently been bought by the Du Pont Company and was rapidly expanding.

The 1930s were a dire time for dear old Winchester, as Pugsley was well aware. After the Great War its management had disastrously decided to expand its core business into cutlery, radiator tubes, lawn mowers, washing machines, electric irons, padlocks, flashlights, roller skates, and dry-cell batteries. Despite the company's optimistic advertising slogan ("As Good As the Gun"), few of these products had gained traction with the public, and the arrival of the Depression sent what little demand there was to the bottom. Winchester's shareholders became reluctant to advance further funding to the company, already floundering beneath the weight of rising debts. In 1929 the Winchester Repeating Arms Company of Connecticut was "reorganized" and incorporated in Delaware to circumvent certain loans coming due. The Delaware scheme did not prevent its net value from plummeting, and on January 22, 1931, the company was put into receivership.

Here the Western Cartridge Company enters the story. That December it acquired Winchester with all "its properties, assets, business and good will" for $8,122,837.67. It was a seemingly strange and risky purchase, but in taking over the tarnished, bankrupt firm, Western had bought control of the country's largest owner of patents covering firearms and ammunition for pennies on the dollar. Western Cartridge traced its roots to Franklin Olin, an engineer who had been born in Vermont and founded a blasting-powder company in 1892 in East Alton, Illinois. Six years later Olin had expanded into making small-arms ammunition and formed the Western Cartridge Company. The Winchester fire sale brought an influx of investment but on a limited, cautious basis. Until the brand could be revived, the company could afford few extravagances . . . such as hiring too many green designers like Earle Harvey.[8]

Harold Brown, a friend of Pugsley's at Remington, offered Harvey an apprenticeship, and the young man, having realized that lecturing undergraduates on the delights of Chaucer and Dickens was never going to be in his future, quickly accepted it. His first day at work was on February 15, 1937, and he finished his apprenticeship eighty-two weeks later, soon after joining Savage Arms Company as an engineer. By this time, owing to Hitler's belligerence and the waning of the Depression, the arms business was emerging from its decades-long doldrums. In

January 1940 Harvey was detailed to the team making the tools, gauges, and fixtures required for the Thompson submachine gun. It was a living, but Harvey soon became bored with working with other people's designs and longed to join a research department that would allow him to innovate.

Finally on October 12, 1941, after myriad imprecations and back-channel maneuverings, Harvey secured a position at Springfield. Still a junior man, he was no Garand, not yet, and had certainly not been awarded his own workshop and staff. Instead, until March 1945 he punched his ticket sketching schematics for improving the M1's gas cylinder operation. In that month he received his reward, bestowed on him by an appreciative Studler: he was to be transferred to the latter's R&D office at the Pentagon. Harvey's timing was fortunate. Within the year Garand's T20 had been kiboshed, and Studler wanted a man who could take command of his secret new T25 rifle project.[9]

Studler intended to make the best gun in the world. It had to be, for the ambitious small-arms chief knew he was facing unexpected competition from the NATO allies, specifically Britain and Belgium. What he *didn't* know was that in 1947 in the Soviet Union a former army sergeant named Mikhail Timofeevich Kalashnikov was finishing work on the prototype of a new weapon called the AK-47.[10]

Kalashnikov had been born in November 1919, the son of Siberian peasants. Mechanically minded, he was a keen lock-picker, and coming into illegal possession of an American-made Browning pistol, he spent hours dismantling and refitting its intricate, solid parts. Drafted into the Red Army, he was assigned to a tank company and severely wounded in September 1941. While recuperating in hospital, Kalashnikov sketched his vision of an ideal instrument of revenge against the Nazi hordes.

It would be a rapid-fire submachine gun firing pistol-sized cartridges that was simple enough for an untrained, conscripted peasant to just pick up and use. It would also be cheaply produced out of machine-stamped steel and then riveted or welded together by the Soviet Union's beleaguered factories. Unlike the American Ordnance Department with its luxurious, hand-engineered tooling, gauges, and jigs, as well as its reputation for manufacturing weapons that were machine-milled, forged, and assembled to perfection, Kalashnikov believed he could massively increase production by designing a gun with loose tolerances; that is, its parts would not fit together anywhere near as finely as an American-made one.

Kalashnikov turned his sketch into a rough prototype and brought it to the Dzerzhinsky Ordnance Academy, where A. A. Blagonravov, a leading designer, had a look. He turned it down as too complex, but just as Harvey and Garand had been talent-spotted despite their initial failures, Blagonravov secured Kalashnikov a place at the Red Army's Small Arms Range directorate. There, having laid aside his submachine gun prototype, Kalashnikov worked on a fresh idea: an automatic carbine. Carbines are short-barreled, lightweight rifles that fire rifle ammunition and that are ideally used when portability and close-range lethality are essential. At the time paratroopers, commandos, and guerrillas alike swore by them. They also tended, at least in their automatic mode, to be a German specialty.

German tacticians had found that while submachine gun pistol ammunition was too underpowered for anything but short-range fighting, rifle ammunition was too powerful and heavy for really anything but long-range shooting. In urban combat, they discovered, the distance between opposing forces was usually anywhere between 100 and 330 yards and most often within 200 yards. Hitler's ballisticians began working on a compromise type of ammunition that would perform satisfactorily at these "intermediate" ranges. Their solution was called the PP Kurz (or "short"), otherwise known as a 7.92×33mm.

The figure "7.92" referred to the bullet's diameter, basically making it a .323-caliber, while "33" was the length of the casing. Until the Kurz's development, German rifle ammunition had measured 7.92×57mm— an altogether longer cartridge, in other words, and one with a higher recoil. By way of contrast, the submachine gun/pistol round was 9×19mm.

Thanks to the weight savings, the Kurz ammunition could be carried in great quantity and fired rapidly without overtaxing soldiers. The prototype gun that went with it was named the Maschinenkarabiner ("machine carbine") 1942 and was designed by Hugo Schmeisser, a master gun-maker with strong and enthusiastic connections to the Nazis. The following year the thirty-round MKb 42 was renamed the Maschinenpistole 43 (MP43) and then the MP44: Hitler's quirky dislike of carbines (a corporal in World War I, he would have been issued a regular Mauser rifle) had prompted his staff to obsequiously christen it a "machine pistol" to disguise its carbine characteristics. Hitler himself finally tried one out in the summer of 1944 and was so impressed that he dubbed it a *Sturmgewehr,* or "assault rifle," a name satisfying his demented dream of eternally attacking the world.

Hitler's Sturmgewehr 44, precursor of the Kalashnikov AK-47.

Nearly half a million Sturmgewehr 44s (StG44) were issued to the soldiers who were desperately trying, like King Canute, to rebuff the advancing Red tide on the Eastern Front between July 1944 and May 1945. During the war enormous numbers of weapons fell into the hands of the Russians—as would Schmeisser himself, their inventor, at the end of it. Schmeisser would go on to work in Kalashnikov's design-engineering department, returning to Germany in 1952.

The debt the AK-47 owes to Schmeisser's StG44 is an obvious one—it even looks like it: Kalashnikov adapted his automatic carbine to fit the Soviet version of the Kurz intermediate cartridge, the 7.62×39mm, approved directly by Stalin. Not quite an innovator, Kalashnikov was more a magpie inventor, borrowing bits and pieces from other weapons, simplifying them, and then combining them to forge something new. The AK-47's trigger mechanism and double-locking lugs, for instance, are actually based on those of Garand's M1.

In 1947, following years of modification and gradual improvements, Kalashnikov's masterpiece was approved for production. During this dawn of the Cold War, the Soviets went to extreme lengths to hide their invention from Western eyes. On maneuvers, soldiers were instructed to pick up their empty casings from the ground and to carry their weapons in pouches that obscured their contents' shape. Kalashnikov and his team were moved to "Izhevsk Motor Plant 524," a front for their gun factory, which by 1949 had made eighty thousand AKs in preparation for a possible massive land attack on Western Europe.[11]

For Moscow's postwar conscript army, the AK was perfectly suited. As its users were so expendable that they didn't even have to know how to clean it, the AK-47 didn't require an instruction manual; brutally utilitarian in its lines and cheaply welded together, the weapon perfectly exemplified the Stalinist worldview.

The Western Europeans too took their postwar cue from the StG44. In 1948 the British were the first, with the futuristic-looking EM-2, an experimental assault rifle built on a "bullpup" design (in which the chamber and magazine are behind the trigger and grip, thereby extending barrel length relative to overall weapon length). Intended to replace their obsolete Lee-Enfield rifles, whose basic pattern had been in service since 1902, the EM-2 used a .280-caliber, intermediate-range round.[12]

The British optimistically sent an army team to visit Colonel Studler, to sell him on the virtues of their .280 and, not uncoincidentally, their EM-2 rifle, which they hoped might be selected as a common NATO rifle. Not a chance. Studler, being an old Ordnance hand, could painfully recall the time in 1932 when General Douglas MacArthur, still alive and kicking (if busy reforming Japan), had come down hard on any suggestion of downshifting to a smaller caliber. Besides, he had his own pet .30-based T25 project in motion.

Brusquely, the Ordnance chief rejected both EM-2 and .280, saying that the latter was not a "full-power" round suited to the long-range shooting tradition of the U.S. Army, and sent the British on their way.[13] "There is something we British do like about you [Americans]," said a miffed Brigadier Aubrey Dixon, in charge of the visiting team. "When you state a conclusion, it is quite definite, and there can be no misunderstanding."[14] Less understatedly, one of his colleagues complained, "We've been Studlered again."[15]

The cold reception received by the British team raised hackles in

London, where Prime Minister Clement Attlee's Labour Party was divided between a Soviet-sympathizing faction and a working-class, patriotic wing. The former suspected (correctly, as it turned out) that the arms-standardization talks and the visit to the United States were a cover for organizing an anti-Moscow alliance; the latter were determined to buy British to restore national pride and keep jobs at home.[16]

As the NATO talks proceeded in the late 1940s, the kerfuffle over Studler's haughtiness disappeared—at least publicly. The British quietly developed their EM-2; the Americans, their T25. Sooner or later, both sides knew, there would be a showdown. Earle Harvey, unfortunately, was finding it difficult to proceed at anything even approaching a snail's pace. He was continually called off to perform other tasks, and he knew Springfield's production teams disliked the T25, for it could not be built on the existing M1 equipment. Worse, Studler had ordered him to reduce the prototype's weight to 6.8 pounds—nearly three pounds less than the M1's. It was a tall order, and a ridiculous one. When firing .30 ammunition on automatic, such a light gun would buck uncontrollably, and the recoil would leave soldiers' shoulders black and blue. The problem was insoluble. American ammunition had been developed for single-shot and semiautomatic use, not for firing long bursts. Something had to give. In the end it would be the T25 itself, once Studler realized he had made a colossal mistake.

In 1949–50, as rumors filtered back to the Pentagon that the British wanted to hold a trial between their EM-2 and Springfield's finest, Studler backed rapidly away from Harvey and the T25 project.[17] Funding was discreetly pared as Studler reinitiated work on Garand's canceled T20. Here at least was a rifle whose original version had been proved to work. Studler ordered that surviving prototypes be rebored to accommodate the light T65 round. His instruction was gleefully executed by Springfield's production branch. Since 100,000 T20s had been ordered in the waning days of World War II and the machinery already existed to mass-produce them, time was of the essence, owing not merely to Studler's desire to salve his amour propre in the threatened competition with the British but also to the rather more lethal threat rising in East Asia, where the Korean leader Kim Il-Sung was known to be building a gigantic army with Soviet aid. If war came (as it soon would), outnumbered American troops armed with M1s would be faced with a powerful enemy carrying automatics streaming over the 38th Parallel.

The much-vaunted British weapon, when it did arrive on these shores for trials on February 14, 1950, proved underwhelming. Unfortunately, the Garand T20s weren't ready in time, so Studler was forced to demonstrate Harvey's T25 instead—which proved more underwhelming still.[18] The one unexpected highlight was a Belgian contender that the British had brought to prove that their .280 ammunition was capable of being fired in a variety of guns. This was a new 8.5-pound, twenty-round weapon manufactured by Fabrique Nationale de Herstal (FN) and named the Fusil Automatique Léger (FAL, or "Light Automatic Rifle").

The FN-FAL performed as poorly as its British and American competitors, but Ordnance was impressed, primarily because it was hearing through back channels that the Belgians, not entirely in the spirit of European unity but certainly in the tradition of European perfidy, were willing to be "flexible" in the matter of caliber size.[19] To their minds, the Americans wielded the biggest stick in NATO, and if they refused to reduce their caliber to the British .280, then the odds of winning the subsequent squabble lay in Washington's favor. The billions of dollars flowing their way thanks to Marshall Plan largesse also helped decide the issue: Belgium would back the .30 as NATO's standard ammunition. It was never confirmed in writing, but the Belgians were given the distinct impression that the United States would adopt the FN-FAL as their service rifle in gratitude for Brussels's invaluable aid in this matter.

When they found out, the British were livid. Egged on by its nationalist backbenchers, the Labour government immediately declared that America and Europe could go hang: London was bulldoggedly sticking with the British-made EM-2 and the British-made .280. Nobody had been expecting such a full-throatedly patriotic reaction, though perhaps they should have: at the time Attlee's Labour Party was struggling for victory in the 1950 general election against Winston Churchill's Conservatives. On February 23 Labour emerged from the fray with a minuscule five-seat majority in the House of Commons. Attlee's hold on power was so tenuous that he was forced to call another election, scheduled for October 25, 1951.

Washington cheered when the results of that second election were announced: Churchill had won a workable majority. The new prime minister's credentials as a friend of America needed no explanation, and Churchill himself had declared that he believed Labour's posturing on the gun issue was hurting the country. It was more important, he felt, for the West to stick together, and that entailed working with the Americans to standardize NATO weapons.[20]

At base, the Anglo-American rifle controversy was not about a weapon, let alone about a .280 versus a .30 cartridge. It represented instead a tectonic shift in international relations, the passing of the torch of global supremacy from an empire to a republic. A bankrupt, exhausted Britain had emerged from the war with her possessions virtually intact but precariously so. She no longer had the will, nor the strength, nor the finances to govern a quarter of the world. The long process of decolonialization began. In 1947 India and Pakistan went their separate, independent ways; Burma and Ceylon followed a year later. By 1950 the mandate in Trans-Jordan had been terminated, Egypt evacuated, Palestine departed. Over the next two decades Britain would divest herself (or be divested by nationalist movements) almost completely of colonies in Africa, Asia, the Pacific, and the Caribbean. Churchill concluded that the world now belonged to the Americans, telling the House of Commons that "a decision to re-arm with a new rifle [is now] one of high policy, involving the world situation and the position of our Allies."[21]

To prepare the way for euthanizing the EM-2, British military officials began discreetly complimenting Garand's T20. During a demonstration on December 27, 1951, Colonel Kellet, of the British Joint Services Mission, commented that the rifle's performance was "extremely impressive compared to the M-1."[22] The big push was saved for Churchill's visit to President Truman in early January 1952. At the top of the agenda was Anglo-American unity in the new era, and topping that agenda was the question of caliber. A month later the result of their talks was revealed to all when, challenged by a Labour politician to clarify whether the Americans would be adopting the .280, Churchill tersely answered that he saw "no prospect of carrying out that process of conversion."[23] That

October NATO members announced that talks were proceeding on the use of the .30-caliber T65 cartridge as standard—to be rechristened the "7.62mm NATO" round.[24]

The final decision would be made at an international summit of NATO ministers in Paris scheduled for December 15, 1953.[25] In the meantime Studler had urgent business to finish: getting the T20 up to snuff so that he could pull off the double whammy of getting the Europeans to accept both the .30-caliber and an American-made rifle to fire it. The first thing he did? He rechristened it the T44, as a form of rebranding. The second thing? He resigned.

Over the past several years the colonel had found himself on the defensive regarding the .30 cartridge. Despite his best attempts, the military was coming reluctantly to the conclusion that maybe, just maybe, the Europeans had been right about downshifting to a lighter caliber. Was it possible that, in 1932, Pedersen had been right about the .276 and MacArthur wrong? It was a question that career officers felt they could safely raise now that President Truman had sacked the Great MacArthur in April 1951 for exceeding his military authority in Korea.

Following MacArthur's involuntary retirement, two internal reports analyzing Korean War performance inflicted further damage on the big-caliber, full-power advocates. The first was written by Donald Hall, a . civilian engineer with the Ballistics Research Laboratories (BRL) at the Aberdeen Proving Ground in Maryland. As the First World War had left behind a vast and miserable pool of human specimens on which to study the effects of bullets on the body, doctors had begun to revise their once-dismissive opinions on the lethality of small-caliber projectiles. Founded in 1938, the BRL had led the way in undermining the still-prevalent assumption that the extent of wounding depended on the mass and velocity of the projectile.[26]

Since 1945 the scientific examination of war wounds using high-speed film, spark shadowgrams, and microsecond roentgenograms seemed to confirm the importance of velocity, but it found that mass—mostly a function of bullet caliber—played a distinctly secondary role. This revelation rendered more intelligible the unexpected results of the 1928 Pig Board ballistics trials. What had surprised everybody at the time was the success of the Pedersen .276 versus the standard .30 in causing severe trauma. Many observers had not seriously believed that a high-velocity, small-caliber bullet could outperform the reigning champion.[27] Dismissed as a weird aberration, the Pig Board's conclusion that at short-to-intermediate ranges the smaller caliber was a killer was ignored for the next quarter-century, and the U.S. Army had stood firm with its .30.

During and after the Korean War, BRL experts reopened the case. In Hall's report, *An Effectiveness Study of the Infantry Rifle*, he determined that on the typical battlefield the range of fire infrequently rose beyond 500 yards, 120 yards being the optimum distance for a nice balance between the probability of a hit and the ability of the bullet to wound grievously. The upshot of Hall's work was that at the shorter ranges typical of the modern battlefield, a light, small-caliber, high-velocity bullet provided an equal or better rate of lethality than the hallowed .30—but with far less recoil.[28] By 1958 BRL would take this conclusion to an extreme by arguing that the best possible bullet would be a tiny .22-caliber 50-grainer zipping along at 3,500 feet per second.[29]

Hall's *Effectiveness Study* of March 1952 was followed three months later by a report collated by another civilian, Norman Hitchman, at the new Operations Research Office (ORO) at Johns Hopkins University. Entitled *Operations Requirements for an Infantry Hand Weapon*, Hitchman's report marked an early milestone in the growing scientification and quantification of war that mirrored what was happening at the Ford Motor Company.

In the nineteenth century army officers transformed businesses into their own image; in the twentieth, businessmen were instructing army officers on how to run their "corporation" along efficient principles. During the war the young Robert McNamara, eventually the secretary of defense but then teaching at the Harvard Business School, had joined the Army Air Forces' Office of Statistical Control, where he analyzed the efficacy of bombing. Afterward McNamara and his "Whiz Kid" colleagues joined the ailing Ford to install new management systems and implement control procedures along the most modern lines.

At this time, too—between 1945 and 1948—the air force created a "think tank" (the phrase had originated in Britain during the war) named Project RAND (Research and Development) to orchestrate the combined talents of its civilian mathematicians, engineers, aero-dynamicists, physicists, chemists, economists, and psychologists. The first great RAND report, ambitiously entitled *Preliminary Design of an Experimental World-Circling Spaceship,* was nothing if not an innovative solution to America's world-circling spaceship needs. (Sputnik, the first world-circling *satellite,* came along only eleven years later.)[30]

Hoping for a sheen of high-tech glamour, the army followed suit with the ORO in September 1948. Unlike RAND, which went fully independent of the air force in 1948, ORO was the result of a compromise between civilian demands for a high-level R&D agency separate from the army and the resistance of the heads of the army's old-established technical bureaus. (Ordnance was among ORO's loudest denouncers.) To soothe Ordnance's fears of a turf battle, the army directed ORO to focus only on studying tactical doctrine and new weapons while Ordnance kept its monopoly on *matériel* development. ORO, in other words, was pencil-and-paper Ideas; Ordnance was nuts-and-bolts Production.

Hence Studler regarded Hitchman's report as a threatening shot across his bow. Based on the army's own World War I and II files on some three million casualties, and supplemented by newer Korean material and interviews, the classified *Operational Requirements* report buttressed Donald Hall's by determining that three hundred yards was the rifle's effective limit and that the vast majority of kills took place under a hundred; and that small-caliber ammunition is more efficacious than larger. Other ORO researchers discovered that soldiers were aiming just one round out of their eight-shot M1 clips and believed, in true diehard fashion, that "the job of the rifleman is primarily to pour out as much lead as possible to keep the enemy's head down."

ORO's biostatistical analysis accordingly revealed that bullet wounds were not concentrated on the specific parts of the body where soldiers had been taught to aim (i.e., head, abdomen) but were instead randomly distributed. The dangerously revolutionary implication of this finding was that in an era of huge volume of fire, an enemy soldier was no more likely to be hit by a deliberately aimed bullet than by a random one. So what was the point of teaching marksmanship?

According to Hitchman's analysis, the army's famed standards of accuracy could be severely reduced—perhaps even to zero—without any

Annie Oakley was one of the finest shots in the world. Here she attempts a signature trick: Hitting an apple balanced atop her rather stoic hound's head.

The Russo-Turkish battle of Plevna in 1877 was the first time repeaters were pitted against single-shot rifles in a major clash, but its lessons were ambiguous. American companies, like Winchester, supplied the Turks. Here, Turkish officers inspect American rifles during a visit to the factories.

German-American leagues upheld
the marksmanship tradition in the late
nineteenth century and inspired the
creation of the National Rifle Association.

As the "cult of accuracy" spread
throughout the army after the
bloodletting of the Civil War,
the image of the marksman turned
more positive. Here, an unidentified
African-American soldier proudly
. sports his marksman badge and
sharpshooter medal.

Nowhere was marksmanship
more rigorously practiced than at the
Creedmoor range on Long Island,
New York. American teams defeated
the world and turned the sport into the
most popular one in the country. In a
variety of positions, the Americans are
fine-tuning their shots in preparation
for a match against the Irish.

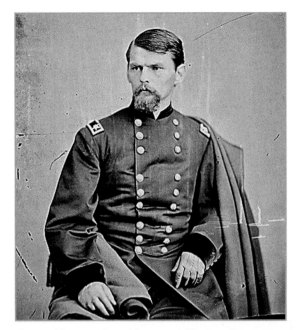

Emory Upton, whose ideas on military reform transformed the army from being a frontier police force into a fighting service capable of combating the finest European infantry.

General Nelson Miles (accompanied, at left, by Buffalo Bill) surveying a hostile Indian camp. Miles remained determined to preserve the army's traditional prerogatives. He would eventually be ousted as commanding general by the reform-minded President Theodore Roosevelt.

Theodore Roosevelt's fascination with firearms and the frontier influenced the course of American military history.

These two 1890 images are based on photographs snapped the moment the order "fire" was given. In the first case, French soldiers fired an 1874 rifle using regular gunpowder; in the second, they employed an 1886 gun loaded with the new, top secret smokeless powder. The regular gunpowder produced a murky cloud of smoke that rolled back into the men's faces, obscuring them from view (and obscuring theirs). The smokeless round resulted in a thin, hazy veil that almost instantly dissipated. At one hundred yards, even at its thickest, the puff was invisible. The "Smokeless Revolution" had arrived.

A Springfield Model 1903 outfitted with the revolutionary Pedersen device and magazine. The short-lived invention came just too late to influence the direction of World War I, but its rapid-fire capability threatened the army's "cult of accuracy."

A terrifying glimpse of firepower's future. At left, the soldier wears experimental armor pierced by pistol bullets; in the middle, a soldier exhibits hits by a regular rifle; and on the right, one can see the damage inflicted by a machine-gun. Nevertheless, the rifle could kill at greater range, economy, and accuracy.

General John Pershing presenting an award to a soldier for his performance in the 1919 Inter-Allied marksmanship competition. American shooting had reached its apogee, and U.S. troops (such as Sergeant Alvin York) were renowned for their lethal abilities.

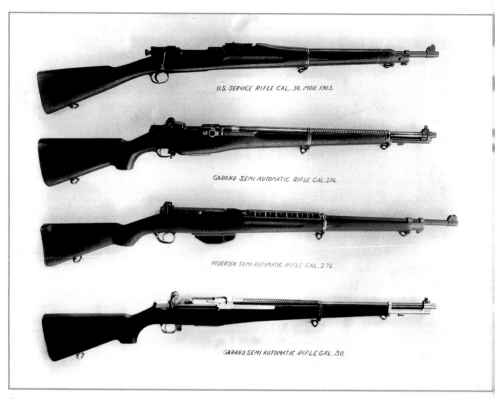

U.S. SERVICE RIFLE CAL. 30, MOD. 1903.

GARAND SEMI AUTOMATIC RIFLE CAL. 276.

PEDERSEN SEMI AUTOMATIC RIFLE CAL. 276

GARAND SEMI AUTOMATIC RIFLE CAL. 30.

During the 1920s and 1930s, competition was fierce in the race to replace the army's venerable Springfield Model 1903. The eventual winner, pictured at bottom in an early prototype, was John Garand's Semiautomatic Rifle Cal. 30—better known to millions of American servicemen as the M1.

John Garand working at one of his beloved machines at Springfield. As a government employee, he earned almost nothing from his creation, one of the most successful weapons of all time.

The impressive results of a 1930 test in which .276-caliber bullets were fired into a half-inch-thick steel plate. At the time, despite mounting evidence to the contrary, experts believed that small-caliber bullets were not sufficiently lethal for military use.

The T44 prototype, son of the M1 and father to the ill-fated M14. The debacle over the latter's introduction ended with the ignominious closure of Springfield Armory.

The M16, the deadly space-age weapon which initially suffered from production problems that led to jamming in battle.

The futuristic XM8 during testing. The kneeling soldier is using the version equipped with a grenade launcher, and the other, with the sharpshooter's model.

A soldier firing the M4, de facto successor to the M16 in Iraq.

The "light" version of the SCAR (SOF Combat Assault Rifle) now being deployed by U.S. Special Operations Command.

concordant diminution of hit-kill effectiveness. Most damagingly to Studler in the short run, however, was Hitchman's highly critical observation that Springfield's products were overpriced and overengineered. The T44 in particular, he said, was a wasteful extravagance.[31]

Adding to Studler's woes was a test in August 1953 at Fort Benning that the Pentagon had ordered as part of its unwritten deal with the Belgians to adopt their FN-FAL. Against the FN-FAL, the T44 flopped miserably, and the Infantry Board recommended that the project be terminated in favor of procuring the FN-FAL on an initially limited basis.[32] Having invested so heavily in the two successive failures of the T25 and T44, and assaulted from all sides by *civilian* analysts daring to question his military-bred expertise in all things Ordnance, Studler's position was untenable and he stepped down on August 31. (John Garand, disgusted by the T44 chaos, had retired four months before.)

On a broader level the 1950s reevaluation of the rifle, its uses, and its abilities marked a conceptual return to the early distinction between muskets and rifles that the advent of breech-loading weapons, metallic cartridges, and the cult of accuracy had obscured. Then the musket had been a rapid-firing, not overly accurate, short-range weapon issued to the general infantryman, and the rifle the long-range, single-shot-firing tool of the specialist. According to the new research, small-caliber automatic rifles ought to be employed as muskets, while higher-caliber rifles ought to be reserved for long-range sharpshooting by expert units. In a way, too, the controversies of the 1950s and later the 1960s were a rerun of the post–Civil War clash in the West between the progressive advocates of .45 single-shot rifles and those diehards who believed that rapid-firing weapons were sufficient for the close-in attacks endemic to the frontier.

The foremost advocate of the modern diehard approach was General S. L. A. Marshall (1900–77), son of a bricklayer and the author of the 1947 classic *Men Against Fire,* a book reprinting a remarkable series of articles he had written for *Infantry Journal.* Marshall, a short, stocky First World War veteran who discovered "that fire of any kind did not unnerve him," afterward worked as a reporter for the *Detroit News.* Working the beat, he honed his interview techniques and joined the Army Historical Branch as a major upon the outbreak of war. Seeking an explanation as to why and how men fight, Marshall trawled soldiers' memories in Europe and the South Pacific, interviewing them immediately following combat so that important details weren't forgotten and contradicting accounts detected. His *Infantry Journal* articles were enlightening and present a remarkable portrayal of the soldier at war, but one piece in particular, entitled "Ratio of Fire," especially stunned readers.

Marshall declared that, contrary to every assumption of the past and to the experience of the present, "not more than 15 percent of the men had actually fired at the enemy positions or personnel with rifles, carbines, grenades, bazookas, BARs, or machine guns during the course of an entire engagement." Even among "the most aggressive infantry companies," the "figure did not rise above 20 to 25 per cent of the total for any action."[33]

Marshall's solution was straightforward: teach men not to be afraid to fire. "Shoot fast, shoot often," might have been his motto, but only when subjected "to the thoroughness of control by the junior leaders." Officers should not regulate fire, he counseled, but instead should regulate the firers to ensure they opened up when ordered.[34] In almost every respect Marshall was the embodiment of the lately overshadowed diehard principles of intense, rapid-rate firepower combined with strict officer control to make sure the men didn't think too much for themselves. Marshall, however, thought very much of *himself,* and he was pleased to report that during the Korean War, thanks to the army's putting his training principles into action, the number of men firing their weapons had more than tripled, to 55 percent. By Vietnam, he later said, every man fired his weapon on frequent occasions.[35]

Some old soldiers dismissed Marshall's "15 percent" ratio-of-fire statistic as hogwash. Among them were General James Gavin, legendary commander of the 82nd Airborne Division during World War II; Harry Kinnard, who fought in every single one of the 101st Airborne Division's engagements and later commanded the First Cavalry Division in Vietnam; and General Bruce Clarke, who defended St. Vith during the Battle of the Bulge. Clarke denounced Marshall's numbers as "absolute nonsense."[36]

Indeed they were. It now appears that Marshall exaggerated them. His own assistant could not remember Marshall asking soldiers whether they had fired their weapons, and the general left behind no statistical record.[37] As for the apparent rise in the percentage of men firing at the enemy between 1945 and Korea, a more likely explanation than the alleged adoption of Marshall's vaguely expressed training methods is the army's organizational changes to the squad/platoon structure to ensure a higher ratio of machine-gunners to riflemen while teaching soldiers to more tightly bond and act together.[38]

Revelations of Marshall's misdemeanors would come later. Initially, however, as a result of Marshall's influence, the Infantry School at Fort Benning relaxed its marksmanship standards. In June 1951 Paul Cardinal published an exposé, in the NRA magazine *The American Rifleman,* of the trendy "aimless fire" doctrine and its dire effect on training. A year earlier, he revealed, the Infantry School had cut M1 shooting practice to just forty hours in its thirteen-week basic training course. (The Marines, holdouts as usual, had stuck to 150 hours.) The lack of training, said officers recently returned from Korea, was making American soldiers unconfident and hesitant in the face of "an enemy as determined and as numerous as the Chinese communists." They were too reliant on "automatic rifles, rocket guns, recoilless weapons and atom bombs" to do the killing for them.[39]

The Cardinal article caused a stir, especially among NRA readers. One of them, George Thomson of Minneapolis, sent eleven copies of the piece to congressmen from his state, and one of those contacted the Department of the Army for an explanation.[40] Within the year the Infantry School scurried away from its Marshall-induced methods and had upped rifle training to seventy-eight hours while placing renewed emphasis on accuracy. Fort Benning even reverted "to the Pershing World War I concept of an 'army of sharpshooters,'" according to Hanson Baldwin of the *New York Times*. The "World War II concept of spraying an entire area with a great volume of fire has been succeeded—in part, as a result of the lessons of Korea—by an emphasis upon marksmanship, on the basis that only the shots that hit count."[41] Irritated by the diversity of views and the sudden policy reverses, the army chief of staff General J. Lawton Collins vainly tried to steer a middle course by writing that "the primary job of the rifleman is not to gain fire superiority over the enemy but to kill with accurate, aimed rifle fire"—but only at short range, he added, confusingly.[42]

These internal debates, over aimed versus aimless, of fire volume versus fire moderation, of small caliber versus large caliber, may seem obtuse and obscure, but their importance cannot be exaggerated. It is from such controversies that military doctrine, economic might, foreign relations, and grand strategy are ultimately made. Culturally, too, they encapsulate the atmosphere of the early 1950s.

Americans had emerged from a hugely destructive and expensive world war only to find themselves involved in another, potentially world-ending one—against the forces of China and the Soviet Union. American leaders were alarmed at Communism's seemingly inexorable advance and just as worried that Americans were ill equipped to withstand it.

As millions of GIs handed in their M1s and headed home, they expected a change for the better in their living standards as part-payment for their sacrifices. They got it. Over the course of the 1950s the postwar boom increased the real weekly earnings of factory workers by 50 percent, the gross national product jumped by 51 percent, and a country with 6 percent of the world's population produced one-third of earth's goods and services. For the first time regular, normal Americans owned television sets (in 1946 there were 17,000 sets in the land; within three years Americans were buying 250,000 each *month)* and could afford to take their family vacations at Disneyland (founded in 1955), give their teenage kids enough of an allowance to buy an Elvis Presley LP, and buy the lady of the house dinner at a fashionable restaurant with a Diners Club card (first issued in 1950) as reward for all her diligent housework (helped by an array of vacuum cleaners, stainless-steel sinks, food mixers, coffeemakers, refrigerators, and washing machines).

Some members of the affluent society did not regard it with unalloyed admiration. Blacks were painfully aware of the underlying racial tensions of the time, while NRA members and pro-marksmanship soldiers became convinced that their fellow citizens were getting soft bellies from the good living. Teaching youths to shoot targets would increase their confidence, impart to them the meaning of manly character, and keep them on the straight and narrow.

In the 1950s the population drain from the countryside to the cities and suburbs—a third of Americans lived in the latter by 1960, up from 19.5 percent in 1940—was a particularly worrisome phenomenon for many: one can't hunt in Los Angeles, let alone in Levittown. If boys did not learn how to shoot at an early age, the legacy of the American Rifleman would die out. The rot had already seeped into society: those boys' teenage brothers were gyrating their hips to "Jailhouse Rock" and college freshmen had begun checking out those hep Beat poets.[43]

To the NRA, the decline of marksmanship within even the army said it all: affluence was forging wimps. "Let's admit," opined Bill Shadel, former *American Rifleman* editor, in the midst of the Korean War, "that we have become largely a nation of urbanites, dependent on machines and a proximity with our fellows. Even the farms have been caught in this dependency." In his experience "American soldiers, trained in formal tactics, are afraid of the dark, as infantile as that may sound! They are afraid of the woods, afraid of the terrain. They shun night attacks. They have shown themselves vulnerable to infiltration [and] encirclement." What trainees (and American males in general) needed was to learn the "art of the hunter," a tradition handed down by generations of frontiersmen who had needed no machines or middle-level office jobs to bring home the bacon and kill their foes. It was imperative, thought Shadel, to raise boys as junior riflemen and to teach them their "woodsmanship" so that they might be turned into "confident and self-reliant" warriors willing and able to defeat the Godless Red Menace.[44]

Another editorialist for *The American Rifleman* detected the origins of the decline of the frontier tradition in the rise of Marshall-style "aimless fire." The very idea led to loss of self-control and (quoting General Walsh of the National Guard Association) a "tendency to hoard ammunition; lack of motivation; fear of retaliation; indolence." Just as bad, the boom times had wrought unwholesome changes in the officer corps. "Not so many years ago the Army put great stress on training in rifle marksmanship," but these days, rued Walsh (and the editorialist), "the emphasis has been placed on careers [and] pay and promotion." The rat race and the greasy pole might be all right for the gray-flanneled

Company Man, but it was turning green-uniformed captains into money-hankering businessmen. In keeping with the religious tenor of the time—the Billy Graham Evangelistic Association and the Campus Crusade for Christ were founded in 1950 and 1951, and that decade saw the release of *The Robe, The Ten Commandments,* and *Ben-Hur*— Walsh spoke of soldiers having "faith" in their weapons and the "preaching of false doctrines regarding volume of fire and the elimination of marksmanship."[45] (Representative Donald Jackson of California, a Republican, made a still closer association between God and the gun in his NRA convention speech of 1951: While "the Savior of Mankind could probably never have competed at Camp Perry or any other international match . . . the moral rifle of His ideas changed history more than did any series of world conflicts ever concluded."[46] The cult of accuracy, it seems, had transubstantiated into a church.

The furor over aimless fire, the decline of sharpshooting, and civilian alarm over the future of American masculinity prompted the army to reexamine the prematurely terminated T44 project after the humiliating August 1953 Fort Benning tests (when it was bested by the Belgian FN-FAL). Dr. Fred Carten, Studler's replacement as head of Small Arms Research and Development, convinced the chief of staff, General Matthew Ridgway—himself a fan of the Springfield Model 1903 (he kept one in his jeep during the war)—that the entire basis for the Fort Benning finding had been flawed. Neither the T44 nor the FN-FAL had been tested in extreme arctic temperatures, and it was all too likely that a Soviet attack would occur, not in the prickly summer heat of Georgia, but during the winter.[47]

The T44 was revived and winterized—each part was lubricated, triggers were enlarged to fit mittened fingers, the wooden stock was reinforced with steel, a pressure-relief valve was added—by Springfield's mechanics and tested that October 1953 in Alaska. Unsurprisingly, the unwinterized FN-FAL fell behind and showed itself to be less dependable than the modified T44.[48]

Within Ordnance, however, it was an open secret that the T44 victory had been fixed. Even one of its firmest proponents in Carten's office, A. C. Bonkemeyer, confidentially told Colonel Rayle (the new head of Springfield's R&D division) not to bother making too many refinements to the T44 because it was "so close to being a dead duck, you would be better off to spend the funds and effort on future weapons."[49] He was referring to a rifle that was now being groomed as the next standard weapon of the U.S. Army.

Unattuned to the vagaries of arms procurement politics and unfamiliar with the vigor of the American sharpshooting tradition, the Belgians assumed the Alaska tests were nothing but a minor setback. They still naturally, if naïvely, expected the United States to come across and so took Washington's side at the NATO conference two months later. On December 15, 1953, NATO announced that the United States, Britain, Canada, France, and Belgium had settled on the T65 .30 cartridge as their standard round.[50]

Britain, led by an ailing Churchill, had sacrificed herself for the Cause. With the .30 decision finalized, the EM-2 rifle was a dead duck. Churchill, it was reported, even kept a .30-caliber FN-FAL (now called the FN-30) in his office at 10 Downing Street and had been driven to Kimble Range to test it for himself.[51] Churchill, like Lincoln and Theodore Roosevelt, was always very hands-on with weaponry. Back in the war, after the Normandy landings, he, Eisenhower, and General Omar Bradley had once held an impromptu M1-carbine shooting match. Churchill's target was set up 25 yards away, Ike's 50, and Bradley's 75. Sadly for posterity, said the last, "all the targets were tactfully removed before anyone could inspect them."[52] Back on form, Churchill learned to strip and reassemble the FN-30, swung its butt around the room like a club, and lunged forward with its bayonet attached. "The first time I did this sort of thing was as an army cadet in 1893," he told an aide.[53]

On January 19, 1954, Churchill announced to an angry House of Commons that Britain would adopt the FN-30 in the near future. The British "Tommy" would henceforth carry a Belgian rifle that fired American cartridges. Two weeks later the Labour Party submitted a resolution "that this House deplores the decision by Her Majesty's Government to adopt the Belgian FN rifle in place of the new British E.M.2 Rifle."[54] A bitter three-hour-long debate ensued. Accused of "weakness" for "not standing up to the Americans," and interrupted by catcalls from the backbenches, the aged prime minister retorted that the

Labourites were "always looking around in every controversy, even this one about rifles, to try to find fault with the Americans." Ultimately Churchill's embattled Conservatives and their allies managed to summon the strength to defeat the motion of censure by a vote of 266 to 232—a victory to be sure, but not a resounding one.[55]

The Belgians now expected Washington to follow through on its unwritten promise to issue the FN-30.[56] But it would not if the American backers of the T44 had their way.[57] Before any such decision was made, there had to be a final showdown between Springfield's king of all rifles and the Belgian pretender to the throne.[58]

In June 1954 Ridgway ordered that five hundred T44s and five hundred FN-30s be manufactured by the industrial division of Ordnance.[59] It then took three years—in addition to the decade the T44 had already been in development, and seven years for the FN-30—before one of them was finally chosen as the army's standard rifle. The T44 emerged as the early front-runner—the result of a massive push by armorers behind the scenes to tweak its mechanisms and improve its performance. The T44 also beat the FN-30 in the usual sand and mud trials and encountered half as many malfunctions as its rival.[60] Still, no firm decision was made, because while technical observers were impressed, the political calculus of the need to standardize NATO weapons and to reward Belgium and Britain for their loyalty was at the fore and only rose in importance the further up the chain of command one went. Army dissenters felt the T44 was too much of a marksman's weapon and simply out-of-date in an era where firepower mattered. Many knew, as well, that the T44's backers were disguising its flaws with cosmetic changes that would become horribly apparent only in combat. Nevertheless, at the very top of the chain—the White House—the exigencies of grand strategy and the global existential threat of Communism eventually trumped mere politics, and the T44 was awarded the laurel.

At a different time the T44 might have been subjected to more scrutiny, but alarmed at the titanic sums expended to fight an unpopular war in Korea and at the possible effects on American economic supremacy—the armed forces had ballooned from 1.5 million in 1950 to 3.6 million three years later—President Eisenhower had ordered a reassessment of U.S. Cold War strategy to replace the post-1945 focus on "containing" the Soviets at *all* points. The result was the "New Look" defense policy of October 1953 that stipulated the construction of an overwhelming nuclear force capable of "inflicting massive retaliatory damage by offensive striking power," to make Moscow think twice before embarking on any military adventures.[61]

Reflecting Eisenhower's wish to rely more heavily on this doctrine of Massive Retaliation (known to its detractors as "containment on the cheap"), funding for the army and navy was cut significantly while resources were transferred to the air force's Strategic Air Command (SAC), the new entity designated to deliver the nuclear payloads. By the end of 1953 SAC had completed eleven of the seventeen planned wings in its gigantic, long-range strike force.[62] On January 12, 1954, in a speech to the Council on Foreign Relations, Secretary of State John Foster Dulles publicly announced to the Soviets the new American strategy.

Within months, however, Dulles had begun fretting at the lack of flexibility inherent in the Massive Retaliation doctrine and its adverse effects on the United States' European allies, who understandably feared being vaporized alongside their Russian neighbors if a minor border incident somewhere in Asia spiraled into global thermonuclear war. All this hearty "talk of atomic attack," he advised, "tended to create 'peace at any price people' and might lead to an increase of appeasement sentiment in various countries."[63] That was precisely the opposite of what Washington desired of its allies.

Should nuclear war be the sole option available to punish the Soviets? he continued, grasping the inherent flaw of Massive Retaliation: though presented as a policy of strength, so long as the Soviets were willing to pull the American tail around the world on a limited basis, the doctrine actually weakened the United States. Without being able to draw on a variety of conventional, diplomatic, and nuclear options, the United States would be continually confronted by all-or-nothing decisions, and as the Soviets knew the Americans wouldn't dare push the button to punish a small infraction, Massive Retaliation diminished the credibility of the nuclear deterrent. Worse, the doctrine grew steadily less effective as the *Soviet* nuclear force expanded, thereby making the American homeland—and all those huge SAC bomber bases—vulnerable to a first-strike surprise attack. These facts, dutifully laid out, persuaded Eisenhower in late 1954 that Massive Retaliation had to be revised and a new, improved "New Look" developed that would rebalance the army–navy–air force relationship.

Matthew Ridgway's successor as chief of staff, General Maxwell D. Taylor, was "an aloof, handsome man with cool china blue eyes," wrote *Time* in a mash note masquerading as a cover story, "a knack for sketching a problem in broad perspective, and a talent for hammering out explicit courses of action." The son of a struggling lawyer in Keytesville, Missouri, Taylor was enthralled by the tales his grandfather had told of riding with Shelby's Confederate cavalry during the Civil War. He was determined to go to West Point, but when the time came, he kept his options open by applying to Annapolis as well. He failed the navy's entrance examination partly because he did not know where the Straits of Malacca were (he thought they were in Europe); but for that small geographical slip, Taylor might well have ended his days as an admiral. As it was, he graduated fourth in the West Point class of 1922 and joined the engineers, as many top-ranked West Pointers still did. There followed a brilliant military career (he was the first American general to invade Europe when he parachuted into Normandy on the night of June 6, 1944) and rapid promotion.[64] A former commander of the 101st Airborne and superintendent of West Point, he now took the battle directly to the enemy—defined as the *other* two fighting services but also including the president. His objective, he would write, was "to improve the combat readiness of the Army . . . and to improve its morale depressed as it was by the precedence given to the needs of the Navy and Air Force by the ex-Army man in the White House."[65]

Shrewdly predicting that the army would be called on to enforce America's interests abroad when nuclear annihilation seemed a measure somewhat too extreme, Taylor's first tactic was to turn himself into a supporter of what was being called the Flexible Response doctrine. In so doing (and by judicious leaking to the press), he managed to head off a dangerous proposal by Admiral Radford, chairman of the Joint Chiefs of Staff and an Eisenhower loyalist, to erase another 450,000 men from the army, leaving it with a rump of about 575,000.[66]

Taylor was greatly aided by Secretary of the Army Wilber Brucker, who gave speeches, galvanized the Association of the United States

Army into becoming a lobbying organization, and wrote articles extolling the virtues of the general infantryman whose rifle was "a decisive factor in keeping the Hammer and Sickle off our front lawn in the atomic age."[67] Together they kept the T44 front and center. American soldiers defending the American Way of Life around the world must have an American Rifle, they argued. Inexorably, official support for the FN-30 began to fall away, and with it any hope for the Belgians and the British to influence U.S. policy.

The renewed sense of urgency to adopt the T44 was also spurred by the very public unveiling of the Russian AK-47 during the Hungarian revolt in the fall of 1956 against the Communist government. When the Politburo decided to crush the rebels and send in the Red Army, the soldiers who arrived were seen to be carrying these strangely shaped rifles. American Ordnance officials took note but weren't quite sure what to make of them.[68] Probably through clandestine intelligence sources, they obtained a few samples for testing, but by then the momentum behind the T44 was too powerful to change direction or to start all over again with fresh designs.[69] On May 1, 1957, Brucker announced to the world that the twenty-round, newly dubbed "U.S. Rifle, 7.62mm, M14" had been selected as the new service weapon.[70]

Taylor retired in 1959, having emerged triumphant from his epic clash, of which the M14 rifle was its reigning symbol, but not without reigniting an unfortunate tradition of military politicking that had found its hero in General Nelson Miles (Theodore Roosevelt and Elihu Root's implacable enemy) and its praetorian apogee in Douglas MacArthur's impertinent questioning of the president's authority in Korea. Whereas Taylor's foe Admiral Radford had a rule not to send what he called "splits" upstairs to the secretary of defense, so as to preserve the chiefs' spirit of "consensus," Taylor's book *The Uncertain Trumpet,* published in 1960, publicly revealed his fights with the Joint Chiefs of Staff and the White House and turned the concept of rapid limited wars into a political issue to bludgeon Eisenhower.[71] Republicans and air force colonels, livid at Taylor's criticisms of Massive Retaliation, called it *The Unclean Strumpet.*[72] The witticism did them no good. In the 1960 presidential election, nearly every candidate condemned the New Look and pledged to reduce the role of the SAC.

The eventual victor, John F. Kennedy, in league with Secretary of Defense Robert McNamara, went furthest in calling for Flexible Response and an enhanced mission for the army. By first appointing Taylor "Military Representative to the President," and then recalling him to active duty and appointing him chairman of the Joint Chiefs of Staff, Kennedy explicitly supported not only an army buildup but an army capable of intervening in potential trouble spots. Khrushchev's declaration of January 6, 1961, that the USSR would back guerrilla-style "wars of national liberation" in those exact same trouble spots; then the Berlin Crisis of 1961–62, when the Soviets built their infamous wall; followed by the Cuban Missile Crisis of October 1962, demonstrated to Kennedy that Taylor had been right about Flexible Response and Eisenhower wrong to oppose it. As part of the Kennedy-era troop increases (during the Berlin Crisis the president requested an increase in army strength to one million men) and improvement in their combat readiness, Taylor augmented the government's counterinsurgency programs and expanded the army's Special Forces units. When Kennedy's assassination brought Lyndon Johnson to power in 1963, he thus found ready-made units prepared to "advise" in Vietnam. By 1964–65 Johnson had made the fateful decision to augment the U.S. presence there, all without escalating to a nuclear exchange.[73] The M14 rifle cast long shadows, it seems.

It also appeared to be accursed. Back in 1957, when the M14 was adopted, the Europeans had ended up with a cartridge they did not want but a rifle they did (the FN-FAL), whereas the Americans had a cartridge they did want but a rifle that few did. Because it was competing against the FN-FAL and the AK-47, the M14 acquired an unfortunate reputation for being a "bad" gun, though it wasn't. The M14 was far more accurate than either, and though it was condemned for being "uncontrollable" or for "kicking like a mule" when firing on automatic, with practice a soldier could accustom himself somewhat to the action. A correspondent for the *New York Times* who fired one at a demonstration in 1957 confirmed that "fully automatic fire with the new weapon is a fearsome business the first time. It fires at a rate of 750 rounds a minute, and the weapon leaps fearfully," but "after a second or third clip, however, the shooter, even a light one, can control the weapon's tendency to push steadily back and to the right."[74] On prolonged autofire, however, the

M14 was too wild to control so easily, so much so that it was issued with a "selector lock" that permitted only semiautomatic fire—a rather odd state of affairs.[75]

The tragedy of the M14 was not that it was a peasant enthroned as the king of rifles, but that it was a competent prince unexpectedly deposed by an abler heir exploiting his realm's turmoil. Because the M14 was destined to have the shortest lifetime of any army service weapon (even the Krag), historians have had an unfortunate tendency to portray its overthrow as inevitable. It is true that both the ORO and BRL's reports on smaller calibers had eroded the M14's rationale and subverted Ordnance's long-held assumption of expertise based on centuries-old experience. Hitherto, even after the humiliating experience of paying the Germans for the Springfield Model 1903 patents, Ordnance officers had cruised on their almost Masonic reputations as supremely competent technicians privy to the arcane secrets of ballistics and technical design. When a high priest of Ordnance emerged from his conclave and declared a particular rifle as the new service weapon, his Solomonic judgment could not be questioned.

Thanks to the ORO and BRL findings, however, everybody else was not assuming that any longer. The era had passed when Major Mordecai could survey Europe's gallimaufry of weapons and insist that the American way was superior, so much so that it should properly be the *only* way. No longer would patriarchal, airily superior attitudes like that of Civil War Ordnance chief James Ripley ("The United States musket, as now made, has no superior arm in the world") go entirely unchallenged by the public and the press simply because *he,* a lordly general, declared it so ("I say this with confidence, from my entire familiarity with the manufacture of these arms.")[76] In these modern times, by way of contrast, the BRL/ORO reports hinted that the development of the rifle did not necessarily follow a single track determined by the intelligent designers at Ordnance but could instead split off and evolve along diverse paths. Who was to say which was best, until the fittest survived? It was possible, nonetheless, that Ordnance's historical insistence on One Caliber, One Rifle, One Cartridge—a congenial worldview perfectly exemplified by the M14—would have, in the end, prevailed over its competitors. If BRL/ORO weakened Ordnance's foundations, what finally toppled the edifice and crushed the M14 was a factor that few had foreseen: Vietnam.

Quite aside from the accidental (Vietnam) and intellectual (ORO/BRL) issues that contributed to the M14's early demise was Ordnance's own mishandling of production. All might otherwise have been well, but Ordnance's flaws did much to persuade McNamara and his allies that the department was no longer capable of carrying out its duties. Once its credibility was shot, the end of Ordnance was surely nigh. As Ralph Waldo Emerson said, "Everything looks permanent until its secret is known."

Problems with the M14 production system arose almost immediately—rarely a good omen. Because Ordnance officials did not get even the preliminary paperwork ready for a month and a half after Brucker's approval in May 1957 and then languidly waited until November to finalize the rest, it was too late to include any estimates in the fiscal year (FY) 1958 budget, an omission that cost the M14 project critical momentum and allowed its rivals time to catch up. Already behind schedule, Ordnance officials rejected *five* requests by Springfield Armory engineers to draw up a detailed preproduction study—for a single weapon, the package might consist of thirty-five pounds of drawings and associated materials—of how to most economically mass-manufacture the rifle. By collecting all the available technical material at the outset and planning the manufacturing procedures, such studies caught potential bottlenecks, helped ensure quality control, and saved time later on during the pilot-production process. Ordnance officials in Washington, however, were more concerned with getting a move on *now* and gambled that the old M1 production lines were up to snuff. That the M14 could be made using already existing tools and equipment was what they had long assured the army, but as soon as work began, it was apparent that much of it dated from the late 1930s. Antiquated and worn out, nearly all the machine tools had to be purchased anew and refitted. Yet more time dripped away.

Not until March 1958, *ten months* after Brucker's announcement, did Ordnance admit its mistake and authorize the armory to carry out a preproduction survey. Now becoming distinctly alarmed at the delays, Ordnance stipulated that the engineers finish their report within six months rather than the typical twelve. To save time, they were ordered "to make only the most important changes to the drawings" and to leave out the small stuff. Ordnance should have sweated it, for as Harry Lynch of the armory's industrial division warned, there would be an "adverse effect on interchangeability and supply" if, as his superiors in Washington were demanding, such "minor" components as magazine improvements, rivets, pins, screws, and nuts were overlooked.[77] He was right. Even as the army blithely promised "plans . . . for a $35,000,000 program for quantity production," months passed by as armory engineers were forced to iron out unnecessary complications caused by Ordnance's corner-cutting.[78]

During hostile, closed-door interrogation by the House Defense Appropriations Subcommittee, Lieutenant General Arthur Trudeau, chief of army research and development, admitted that "money can buy many things, but it can't buy time—time lost through lengthy administrative procedures, deferred decisions, lack of vision, timidity, complacency, misdirected or fruitless effort, or through inadequate funding." Funnily enough, none of this self-criticism was directed at any of the technical departments, let alone the army. The culprit, instead, was the Eisenhower administration's budgetary process and its "attempt to keep defense spending always within fixed limits." The committee chairman, George Mahon, a Texas Democrat, cheerfully and opportunistically agreed and said he looked forward to President Kennedy's arrival in the White House. That was when, presumably, all these annoying budgetary restraints would vanish.[79]

It didn't happen. Before World War II much of Springfield's manufacturing capacity had been farmed out to private contractors in order to focus on engineering and research, so mass production of the M14 hinged on arranging terms and assuring quality control among the outside firms.[80] Ordnance, making the best of a bad deal, wanted just one company to make the M14, but the government stipulated two: the lowest bidder for the contract, and for pork-barrel reasons, a small firm situated in "a surplus labor area."

The winner of the low-bid contract was the Winchester-Western Division of the Olin Mathieson Chemical Corporation, which had claimed it could build the rifles for $68.75 each. Quite aside from Olin's very cozy relationship with Ordnance—the company already made the ball powder used for the weapons—the lowness of the bid should have raised suspicions that something did not quite add up. The average bid of the other leading eleven contenders was, after all, $108.73, nearly one-third more than Olin's figure.[81] As government regulations stated that the "surplus labor area" firm have the technical ability and financial wherewithal to produce the weapon *at the lowest bid,* Olin's dubious pricing must have had a dramatic effect on its smaller partner, which turned out to be Harrington & Richardson of Worcester, Massachusetts. Very quickly the price spiked from the projected $68.75 to a very-real-life $123.16, making a nonsense of the original budget. By that time, however, the delays were such that both Olin and Harrington received additional orders for, respectively, 81,500 and 70,082 extra rifles in the spring of 1960.[82]

Springfield soon began rejecting Harrington's rifles on the grounds that they were shoddily produced. Harrington had foolishly used non-specified steel to make its receivers, and as a result they disintegrated. Olin was also suffering major delays. In June 1960 it was noticed that Olin had not yet delivered a single rifle, and by mid-1961 only 12,894 M14s had been completed out of the *initial* order for 35,000 and no progress had been made on the follow-up order for 81,500.[83] Four years after the M14 had been adopted, just a single rifleman in ten was carrying one.[84]

This time when the Senate Appropriations Committee hauled up Defense Department officials in April 1961 to ask when these fabled M14s would be showing up, politicians were rather less sympathetic to the military's finger-pointing. General George Decker, the army chief of staff, blamed Olin's inability to set up a working automation line. Having recently received a $5 million contract to make 7.62mm NATO ammunition and under the impression that the army was looking out for their interests, Olin executives were livid at the betrayal. The company's vice president and general manager, W. Miller Hurley, lashed out at Decker by claiming that production lags were caused by *his* "delays in delivering of Government-owned equipment, plus difficulties in converting and rehabilitating this equipment, difficulties in obtaining certain materials specified by Army Ordnance and specification changes since the original contract." Senator Margaret Chase Smith, Republican of Maine, blamed both army and Olin equally for what she saw as collusion: "I don't want to see plants and concerns that don't produce and reasonably meet production schedules have their contracts perpetuated" so as to protect "a Democratic state that voted for a Democratic President."[85] The M14 was turning out to be a military-political fiasco.

Army secretary Elvis Stahr promised the committee that deliveries would be up to par by the end of the year even if the army would not be completely outfitted for another four years. In that case, one newspaper pointed out, if a war broke out anytime between now and 1965, the army would be sent to fight with a mixture of old and new rifles.[86] The Senate hearing could not have gone worse for the administration. In late July McNamara stepped into the ring and told the Senate Preparedness Committee that he thought "it was a disgrace the way the project was handled." No one could be left in any doubt that the secretary of defense was planning a root-and-branch purge of the Ordnance procurement and production system along Whiz Kid principles. "This is a relatively simple job, to build a rifle, compared to building a satellite or a missile system," he declared, "and yet this project languished for months—years, actually. I see no reason why we should expect it should be tolerated in the future."[87]

Soon afterward McNamara detailed Brigadier General Elmer Gibson to investigate the bottlenecks and inefficiences affecting mass production. He was ordered to knock some sense into the contractors. Gibson reported that he believed introducing a third competitor would stimulate Olin's and Harrington's juices, especially when coupled with a reform of the bidding process. There would be no more fixed-price bidding—a technique that had so often resulted in fabulously low initial figures, soon raised to fabulously high ones—and in its place would come "competitive negotiations" to arrive at a suitable price. To further encourage contractors to keep their bids reasonable from the outset, Gibson proposed ending the practice of price redeterminations: henceforth whatever sum a company originally quoted for its products and services could not be changed—even if, as a result of underbidding its competitors, the firm were to operate at a loss. Worse, if it fell behind on its deliveries, it would be hit with fines. Offering a carrot to accompany his sticks, Gibson introduced a bonus of $2.50 per rifle for each one made ahead of schedule.[88]

Just as McNamara seemed to be recovering from the Senate debacle, matters took a turn for the worse on August 13, 1961, the day the Soviets surprised the world by stringing miles of barbed wire between East and West Berlin. The wire was soon joined by a concrete wall and heavily armed guards at brand-new checkpoints and machine-gun towers. By happenstance a huge two-week war game (Exercise Swift Strike) had been scheduled in South Carolina three days hence. With 30,000 troops and four hundred aircraft participating, it was the greatest show since World War II. The Kennedy administration quickly turned Swift Strike into a demonstration of how, in the words of a military spokesman, American forces were "poised and ready for launching the required amount of striking power at any moment, anywhere"—like Berlin, for instance, if the Kremlin tried to move that wall a little westward. The Swift Strike exercise, while serving as a useful deterrent to Red Army adventurism, also publicly highlighted the embarrassing lack of M14s. A *Wall Street Journal* reporter present noticed that only members of the 101st Airborne were carrying these vaunted weapons; everyone else made do with "World War II vintage" M1s. Evidently trying to impress Khrushchev and his AK-47-armed border guards, Kennedy quickly ensured that the U.S. Berlin garrison was hurriedly issued with the scarce new rifles.[89]

The administration blamed Eisenhower's emphasis on nuclear-based Massive Retaliation for the conventional-forces shortfalls. Kennedy added $6 billion to the defense budget and proposed a 150 percent rise in the number of "anti-guerrilla forces" (i.e., Special Forces), while Congress quickly approved a 225,000-man increase in army strength and accelerated procurement of the necessary equipment (trucks, tactical air power, communications gear, and much more), including the M14.[90] At this point, with the Kremlin wagging Kennedy's tail, the Senate looking over McNamara's shoulder, and McNamara breathing down the army's neck, Ordnance had to come through on the M14 very, very rapidly.

That fall, for the first time, the army, McNamara, and Ordnance were bullish on their prospects. Most of the production kinks with Olin and

Harrington had by now been ironed out, and General Gibson's shake-up was shaping up. By October M14 production had risen from 9,000 per month to 44,000, and the rate was still increasing.[91]

Lagging M14 production ceased to be a danger that month when, following an eleven-company bidding war, the third M14 maker was announced: the newly merged Thompson-Ramo-Wooldridge (today called TRW) of Cleveland, Ohio. Learning from the armory shambles over the preproduction plans, TRW gathered a special team of engineers and manufacturing experts to draw up the schematics and construct the pilot production line. It took them six months and cost $200,000. The company's accountants precisely calculated the costs of the rifle ($85.54), and TRW rigidly stuck to that figure.

The contract stipulated that 100,000 M14s would be delivered, beginning in November 1962. Much to Ordnance's surprise, TRW began trucking first-rate, flawless rifles in October, a month ahead of schedule. Immediately afterward the company received an order for 219,691 more.[92] By the end of the year most army and Marine Corps formations had received large shipments of M14s.[93]

TRW's remarkable efforts brought the company no favors. On January 23, 1963, McNamara ordered a halt to further M14 purchases, killing the project just as it was hitting its stride.[94] The decision confirmed simmering rumors that the rifle was about to be chopped. As early as April 1962 Jack Lewis, the editor of *Gun World*, was writing that "high-placed Pentagon sources admit among themselves that adoption of the M-14 rifle for the armed forces has been a blunder based upon a comedy of errors." The magazine also alleged that "precisely how expensive this has been to the American taxpayer is one of those matters that goes ignored."[95] Not quite. The most widely cited estimate for the M14 was $5 million in development costs plus $130 million to produce it. And all for a rifle that was supposed to have been a simple, cheap replacement for its older brother, the M1.

The M16

Chapter 11

☆

GUNS OF THE
SPACE AGE

Soon after World War Two an aeronautical engineer, salesman, and self-described "gun nut" named George Sullivan had a genuinely brilliant idea.[1] When a Brussels-based arms dealer named Jacques Michault had told him about the Germans' wartime proficiency in assembling light rifles from stamped metal parts, Sullivan mentioned that the aviation industry was adopting a host of innovative materials that were also intended to reduce weight.

Michault later claimed that "together" the two men then "conceived the idea of an aluminum rifle using a stock of fiberglass."[2] At some point, a little later, Sullivan seems to have edged Michault out of the picture—the arms dealer returned to Europe and would later become a sales agent for the "aluminum rifle"—but Sullivan's contribution was always the greater of the two. It was he who realized that despite their technical improvements, from a design and materials perspective guns were stuck in the nineteenth century, what with their heavy wooden stocks, blocky steel receivers, and preindustrial aesthetics. By integrating mid-twentieth-century materials, Sullivan believed one could considerably lighten a standard rifle (aluminum, for instance, weighs less than one-third an equal volume of steel) and give it an extreme makeover (its anodized alloy parts and plastic furniture could be sold in any color combination, perfect for the burgeoning consumer market).

By the early 1950s and now in his late forties, Sullivan was chief patent counsel for the Lockheed Aircraft Corporation. In 1953, while attending a trade conference, he met Paul Cleaveland, the corporate secretary of the Fairchild Engine and Airplane Corporation, and by the by disclosed his idea about an aluminum rifle. Knowing that his boss, Fairchild president Richard Boutelle, was a gun enthusiast whose office did double duty as a trophy cabinet for his big-game kills, Cleaveland raised the concept with him. Branching out into small arms, they thought, might provide a profitable income stream for Fairchild should the airplane business falter.[3]

Boutelle asked Sullivan to come and see him. Together they decided to reconnaissance the arms industry by setting up a small unit—snappily called ArmaLite—in Hollywood, California. The firm was located in a building dubbed "George's Backyard Garage," and the original aim was to act not as a manufacturer but as a think tank—only with a profit incentive. Sullivan would use his aircraft-industry knowledge to create lightweight prototypes that would be licensed to makers. From the beginning ArmaLite's purpose was to focus on high-concept, radical design, and in keeping with that spirit Sullivan's first effort was dubbed the "Parasniper" (Sullivan seems to have had a genius for catchy names), an otherwise conventional-looking .308 bolt-action sporting rifle that, uniquely, used foam-filled fiberglass for its stock. Thanks also to its innovative aluminum barrel with a thin steel liner, the entire rifle (including scope) weighed just six pounds. Owing to ArmaLite's frugal setup, few of the "AR-1" rifles were made, prompting Sullivan to suggest to Boutelle in 1954 that he integrate the unit into Fairchild and turn it into a bona fide division of the company. Because Fairchild, thanks to its new missile and engine programs, was rolling in cash (Boutelle had pushed sales up from an anemic $30.5 million in 1948 to about $150 million), ArmaLite would then be assured of sufficient funding. Boutelle agreed, and on October 1, 1954, ArmaLite became a Fairchild subsidiary.[4]

Word that the air force was looking for a new survival rifle for its pilots attracted ArmaLite's attention.[5] The air force was keen to prove its independence from the two older fighting services and had decided to circumvent the cumbersome armory process. Ordnance's mooted M14 (or T44, as it was still called), it knew, would never fit the bill: it was too heavy, too unready, too *army*. What the air force wanted instead was an extremely lightweight rifle that would keep a downed pilot alive until he could be rescued. ArmaLite decided to throw its hat into the ring and submitted a .22 bolt-action with a four-shot magazine it called the AR-5. In keeping with ArmaLite's innovative ethos, the barrel and action could be detached and stored in the plastic stock. With the stock sealed, the rifle—which weighed an extraordinary 2.75 pounds—could *float*.

The air force was mightily impressed and quickly adopted it as the MA-1. Embarrassingly for Fairchild/ArmaLite, which publicly announced the sale and told reporters it had even produced civilian versions "in vivid colors—green or red, or a dazzling gold barrel with light blue stock," an actual purchase never followed, possibly owing to mechanical problems—it may not have floated as effortlessly as the company claimed—and only thirty were made.[6] From this episode, however, one thing was clear: ArmaLite needed to be less dreamy and more practical, and that meant finding skilled arms-makers to design the guns and veteran executives to sell them.

Sullivan happened to test ArmaLite prototypes at the Topanga Canyon Shooting Range in southern California. Near him, he noticed one day, there was a man firing what was obviously a homemade rifle. His name was Eugene Stoner (1922–97), a former Marine from Indiana who had fought in the Pacific during the war and was now living in Los Angeles. In 1945 he had worked in the machine shop of an aircraft-equipment maker before being promoted to design engineer. When he met Sullivan, he was making dental plates for a living. Stoner was also, evidently, a talented amateur armorer and had served in Aviation Ordnance during the war. Best of all, given ArmaLite's limited budget, he worked cheap. Stoner joined the firm as chief engineer.[7] He was soon joined by plastics specialist Charles Dorchester as day-to-day general manager of all development programs. In short order, ArmaLite had put in place the beginnings of a competent design-and-management team.

In 1955 ArmaLite geared up for war—against the T44/M14 and the FN-30, which was then being tested by the army through its cobweb of agencies. Daringly, ArmaLite believed it might enter a surprise contender for the crown that would knock out its rivals at the last minute. ArmaLite's entry, designed by Stoner and based on Sullivan's original concept, was called the AR-10. It was a gorgeous gun, a rifle of superlatives, a weapon bursting with design charisma. The AR-10 perfectly reflected its era and the society that had given it birth, just as the AK-47 did its. The AK's brutal Stalinist lines, sinister look, and cheap manufacturing mirrored its provenance in the Soviets' totalitarian state and in the shoddy manufacturing that nourished its empire.

A familiar form rendered startlingly modern, the high-style AR-10, on the other hand, resembled the jet-age, optimistic, newly affluent, Tupperwareified America of the 1950s, a place where, having broken free from the traditional stiff constraints of wood, stone, and steel, designers molded, bent, and formed plastics and alloys into increasingly abstract shapes. The Monsanto House of the Future—a plus-sign–shaped modernist structure on show at Disneyland between 1957 and 1967—was constructed almost entirely out of plastics, and its makers boasted that hardly any non-manmade materials were used.[8] Along the same lines, the AR-10's forestock and furniture, for instance, were made of fiberglass, and its two-part, hinged receiver of rustproof, lightweight aircraft-grade aluminum. Because aluminum was not as strong as steel, the rifle lacked the T44/M14's ruggedness, but it was sturdily built nonetheless, and it popularized the use of metal stamping in American rifle manufacturing. By isolating themselves from the historic Springfield-contractor nexus in Connecticut and the eastern seaboard, Stoner and his small team of engineers in California were able to pioneer innovative workarounds to preexisting obstacles, like the seeming inability to reduce weight drastically.

Externally, if the AK-47 reminded people of the dreary past, the

AR-10 looked futuristically cool, and today it remains, like any design classic, instantly recognizable—partly owing to its sleek lines and distinctive carrying handle that cleverly integrated the gun's rear sights (adjustable, in homage to America's marksman tradition, for windage), a detail clearly borrowed from the late British EM-2 rifle. And all this in a seven-pound automatic rifle firing the regulation .30-caliber NATO round with a twenty-shot magazine.

Its sole downside, so far as anyone could see, was that its light weight made muzzle climb inevitable when firing on automatic. Even so, Stoner succeeded in taming the rifle's potential uncontrollability by using a straight-line stock—a modification previously seen in Earle Harvey's T25—thus shifting the burden of recoil directly to the shooter's shoulder and allowing greater accuracy by reducing flinching.[9] Stoner was no aesthetician, but he achieved a lasting place in the pantheon of great gun men by combining the best bits and pieces of past rifles into a single machine.

At Springfield, the AR-10 met a hostile reception. Not only was the rifle a latecomer to the T44-FN trials, but *Time* and other news outlets, using information leaked by Fairchild, had been running articles critical of the armory process. ("The U.S. Army last week was still marching earnestly forward in search of a weapon it has been unable to perfect through ten years of research and testing: a new infantry rifle.")[10] By puffing this new "aluminum rifle" that had been developed "at no cost to the taxpayer" and that "gave promise of being superior" to the T44 and the FN, these helpful journalists unwittingly shot Fairchild in the foot.

The embarrassing articles infuriated the testers. When Sullivan brought two samples of his rifles to Springfield, an official told him they couldn't include them unless the government "owned" them. "I'll give them to you," Sullivan offered, naïvely. He was refused; the guns had to be purchased, and Sullivan had previously quoted a price of $500 for each. The army could not spare $1,000, he was told. Desperate to enter his rifles into the competition, Sullivan ate the loss and sold his two AR-10s for the princely sum of one dollar. (The uncashed check, framed, still hung on his office wall more than a decade later.)[11] Even with the AR-10s now in the running, another arsenal representative bluntly told Sullivan, "We'll send you home in one day with your parts in a basket." Sullivan also claimed that when one of the staff members reported of the AR-10 that "this is the best lightweight automatic rifle ever tested in the Springfield Armory," his boss erased it.[12]

The AR-10 tested well in every heat bar one, upon which it was sent home, though not in a basket: the six-thousand-round endurance test. The steel lining in the barrel was too thin, and the barrel became overheated and deformed. A week later Stoner had fixed the problem, but it was too late and the AR-10 was done.[13] Award for first place went to, as we've seen, the T44, adopted less than a year later as the M14.

Notwithstanding its barrel failure, the AR-10 found some interested parties abroad, but major customers eluded them.[14] ArmaLite had overhurried the AR-10 to get it ready for Springfield, and there remained a host of annoying bugs (mostly to do with flash suppression, extractor breakage, and ejection failure) that should have been caught earlier and dealt with. At the time, however, the Infantry Board happened to be run by Colonel Henry Nielsen, who had been struck by the civilian (the ORO and BRL) think tanks' emphasis on using small-caliber bullets to achieve volume of fire. Nielsen discussed his thoughts with General Willard Wyman, the commander of the First Division during the D-Day landings, then of the Ninth Corps in Korea, and later of the NATO Land Forces in southeastern Europe. In 1955 he had been appointed head of Continental Army Command (CONARC).[15] Privately, having seen an AR-10 demonstration for himself, Wyman had arrived at the same conclusion about small-caliber bullets. Neither man, of course, could go public with his misgivings: Nielsen was merely a colonel, and the Infantry Board was in any case officially committed to the M14 project, while a general in Wyman's position could not be seen as undermining settled policy.

Late in 1956 Wyman and Nielsen paid Stoner a quiet visit and outlined to him their idea of a perfect rifle. Could Stoner, they asked, adapt the AR-10 to fire a bullet smaller than the standard NATO 7.62mm/.30-caliber? The trio agreed that Stoner should begin—discreetly—a project that would allow the AR-10 to propel a 55-grain .22-caliber bullet at 3,250 feet per second.[16]

Thus was the genesis of the AR-15. As his colleagues Robert Fremont and L. James Sullivan struggled to downsize the AR-10 to chamber a smaller caliber, Stoner sought a suitable ammunition for his purposes. He settled on a common commercial round intended for varmints, the Remington .222. (Stoner's variant was actually a .223.) In the meantime Wyman talked privately to General Maxwell Taylor, the chief of staff, about postponing a decision on the T44 until the AR-15 could show its stuff.

Wyman's actions betray a man with nearly fifty years of conservative military experience behind him (he graduated from West Point in 1918) and one of utterly conventional taste. (Ethel, his wife, wrote cookbooks filled with local recipes that Wyman—a "tired little bear," she called him—dined on every single night.) Yet he introduced shockingly radical changes to the army, all while not unduly upsetting the upholders of the status quo. Perhaps he took after Ethel in this regard. At the zenith of mid-1950s American-cooking provincialism, she bravely managed to sneak a few exotic "foreign dishes"—"Teriyaki steak," helpfully described as "Japanese" by the *Washington Post,* and lasagna—into a cookbook entitled *Festival Foods of Virginia,* a collection of Jamestown-area culinary delights.[17]

Like Ethel and her delicious Teriyaki steak, in 1957 General Wyman smuggled an innovative program into the army's standard basic training for recruits through CONARC's Infantry Human Research Unit.[18] It was called Trainfire, and it implicitly accepted that modern warfare would be conducted at reduced ranges and would require more bullets. Older training programs had emphasized a soldier's levelheadedness to perfect the art and science of fine shooting under fire; the army filmed a training series in 1942–43 called *Rifle Marksmanship with the M-1 Rifle* in which the unflappable instructor advises his pupils not to blaze away in a firefight but to instead "stay cool and shoot straight . . . and you'll live to tell your girl about it." But in the Trainfire scheme teachers went to great lengths to demonstrate the animalistic fury and confusion of warfare.[19] They set targets at a maximum of three hundred yards—all the while keeping the true distance from the recruits—camouflaged them with brush, and manipulated them so they popped up and fell down at irregular intervals.[20] Wyman, contending that in combat there was never time to use a wind gauge and that targets never stood stock still, had his instructors stress that enemy soldiers were often detected by "smoke, flash, dust, noise or movement and usually are seen in a fleeting manner." The new program accordingly emphasized that soldiers use their senses and hunches to find their quarries. A major change was that recruits spent nearly one-third of their total basic training time of seventy-eight hours practicing their shooting skills at the abnormally close range of about twenty-five yards.

In that kind of close-quarters fighting, soldiers were taught not to be sparing of ammunition—bullets were cheaper than men—and to empty their clips into anywhere or at anything they suspected an enemy to be lurking (to "spray and pray"). Wyman, like the NRA, blamed the increasing number of rounds fired to produce a casualty on the "general decline in our male population's familiarity with the rifle": during the First World War an enemy casualty was produced for every 7,000 rounds expended, but in World War II that figure fell to one in 25,000, and during the Korean War to one in 50,000. But he, unlike the NRA, believed such statistics to be of minor interest. Of far greater influence was the introduction of "weapons with greater rates of fire and the doctrine of the volume of fire versus aimed fire." The horror stories about the decline of all-American marksmanship, thought the diehard-minded Wyman, were wrongheaded and irrelevant.[21]

(The Marines thought very differently and held the line for long-distance shooting practice. It was at this time, December 1956, that Marine recruit Lee Harvey Oswald, training on the range at five hundred yards, obtained a test score of 212—two points more than were needed to qualify him as "sharpshooter." When Oswald assassinated President Kennedy at distances of between 177 and 266 feet, his shots were easy ones.[22])

In the spring of 1957 Stoner informed Wyman that the gun was ready to be prototyped. In an instance of monumentally bad timing, Wyman ordered ten of them at the exact moment when Secretary of the Army Wilbur Brucker announced the adoption of the M14. Disappointed but undaunted, Wyman urged Stoner to continue developing the AR-15, and he would try to arrange a new set of tests—against the M14. In March 1958 the original ten rifles were ready.

Wyman by that time had succeeded in persuading chief of staff

Maxwell Taylor to give the rifle a chance. That summer Colonel Nielsen's Infantry Board put the AR-15 through its paces at Fort Benning. The Ordnance men who were in charge of the M14s were cheered, initially, by the M14's superior penetration, but the grins vanished when the AR-15 fired 3,578 rounds compared to the M14's 2,337 in the same amount of time. Embarrassingly, the "battle-ready," army-approved M14 malfunctioned at a rate of 16 rounds per 1,000, or *three* times that of the AR-15, a rifle in its mid-development stage. Moreover, the AR-15 had an almost supernatural lightness, upon which those who handled it inevitably commented. With 120 rounds in magazines, the AR-15's total weight was just 9.61 pounds, compared to 16.34 pounds for an M14 similarly equipped. Most devastatingly, the Infantry Board's subsequent report recommended the AR-15 as its "preferred replacement" for the brand-new M14.[23]

Ordnance had once before sunk a rival gun—the FN-FAL in 1953—by subjecting it to cold-weather testing. Now it was the AR-15's turn. For his part, Stoner had had no idea that any arctic tests were being conducted until someone at Fort Greely called him up and asked if he could send them a few spare parts. Stoner, who flew to Alaska as soon as he could, was horrified to discover that there were no instruction or maintenance manuals available. The staff had been cleaning and disassembling the weapons by guesswork and substituting homemade parts for precisely engineered ones—hence the awful report that the Testing Board subsequently submitted.[24]

The arctic imbroglio was the harbinger of worse things. Until then, despite the initial M14-announcement setback, the ArmaLite team had confidently felt they had both time and momentum on their side. How could any panel of objective observers fail to notice that an infantryman could carry up to 650 rounds of AR-15 ammunition, three times as many as the 220 NATO rounds borne by his M14-armed comrade?[25] Or that the AR-15 cost one-third less to make than the M14?[26]

But now, with the dire arctic report already distributed to the Pentagon brass, the Californians could not help but feel as if the M14 were running with the ball. Worse, their two staunchest allies—Wyman and Nielsen—had retired in the summer and fall of 1958, leaving them no one within the system who could propel the project forward.

General Maxwell Taylor was also getting really tired of the M14–AR-15 dilemma. In his opinion, this whole problem had been dealt with back in May 1957, when Brucker announced the adoption of the M14, and now here he was nearly two years later still dealing with it. For Taylor, too, the choice between sticking with the .30 or risking the .223 was more fraught with possible repercussions than it had been for General MacArthur in the early 1930s. In laying down his ruling that the .30 was here to stay, MacArthur had merely had American standards to consider; Taylor today had to think about the European reaction. Once, securing NATO agreement on the .30 cartridge had been cheered as a triumph for American ordnance expertise, but now it was locking generals, politicians, and arms-makers alike into an M14 cage that allowed them no escape. The cartridge and caliber could not yet again be changed. In February 1959, accordingly, he made the final decision. Unsurprisingly, he plumped for the M14. The army would not order a single AR-15.[27]

The news dealt a heavy body blow to ArmaLite. At a single stroke Fairchild was left with a $1.5 million hole in its books. That figure was what Boutelle had spent on development costs, and now it was a total write-off. In better years the huge loss could have been swallowed, but the last few had not been kind to Fairchild. Stretch-outs in military procurement had forced the company to lay off more than five hundred employees in early 1958, and on July 18 Boutelle had announced a $5 million half-year loss (causing the stock to plummet by 10 percent and prompting the New York Stock Exchange to suspend trading).[28] At the end of that benighted year, Fairchild declared a staggering net loss of $17,435,761 (against a $503,331 profit for 1957).[29] This red ink, coming on the heels of the canceled Goose missile program (and a few months before the shuttering of Fairchild's engine division), rendered Boutelle's position untenable, and in December 1958 he yielded his presidency and moved up to the post of vice chairman—essentially a short-time placeholding gig for him to save face before spending more time with his family.[30]

Taylor (and Boutelle, for that matter) had jumped the gun, so to speak. In May 1959 a delayed report from the respected Combat Developments Experimentation Center (CDEC) at California's Fort

Ord landed on Pentagon desks. CDEC had been tasked with applying new technologies to combat conditions and had, as part of its rubric, put the AR-15 through a series of tough simulated battlefield trials between November 1958 and February 1959. Its report was better than even the AR-15's staunchest advocates could have predicted or believed. A "five-to-seven-man squad equipped with [AR-15s] would have a greater target hit potential than an eleven-man squad armed with the M-14 rifle," it concluded before proposing the "early replacement of current rifles" with AR-15s. But this report came in three months after Taylor's decision. It was dead on arrival.[31]

By that time the embattled Fairchild had long since quit trying to sell the AR-15 to the army and just wanted to be rid of it. In what seems to have been Boutelle's final act as Fairchild's vice chairman, in January 1959 he oversaw the sale of the rifle's exclusive manufacturing and merchandising rights to Colt's Patent Firearms Manufacturing Company for the knockdown price of $75,000 and a 4.5 percent royalty on future sales.[32] It was an audacious move, especially for Colt, which was then itself perilously close to bankruptcy. The outbreak of peace in 1945 and the armistice following the Korean War were as bad for gun companies as the South's surrender in 1865. By 1954 Colt's annual profit was a miserable $246,670, and the work force had more than halved, to just 750.[33] The following year, exactly a century after Sam Colt had incorporated his business, the struggling arms-maker was taken over by Leopold Silberstein's Penn-Texas Corporation, later called Fairbanks Whitney after the financier was ousted when his own empire collapsed a few years later.[34] In a brave bid for solvency, the Colt board dispensed with its usual caution and threw the dice one last time.

For the ArmaLite fire sale, Boutelle appears to have been advised by Bobby MacDonald, a principal of Cooper-MacDonald of Baltimore. Cooper-MacDonald specialized in brokering sales of small arms, such as Colt pistols, Remington rifles, shotguns, and industrial-sized quantities of ammunition to a select and discerning international clientele, mostly in Southeast Asia, where such weaponry was always welcomed.

Colt gave MacDonald $5,000 to send him off on a sales tour of the Far East. Together with Stoner (who joined Colt as a consultant), MacDonald visited the Philippines, Malaya, Indonesia, Thailand, and

Burma. MacDonald had high hopes for his order book: he believed the "short stature," as he put it, of Asians would make the lightweight, low-recoil AR-15 a popular choice for their armies.

The arms merchant was half-right. While the AR-15s were wildly popular, not a single order came in. It turned out that these countries had signed military-assistance agreements with the United States, and the treaties stipulated that any models they purchased had to be in service with an American military or law enforcement entity. Because the Amazon of income generated by these deals—$9 billion between 1960 and 1964, $5 billion of which was in liquid cash—flowed back to the United States, these agreements aided the balance-of-payments deficit, propped up favored military contractors, and helped pay for the Pentagon's ever-rising international commitments. Indeed, by 1965 weapons exports were offsetting nearly half the cost of stationing U.S. forces around the world (excluding Southeast Asia).

What was good for General Motors, General Dynamics, and McDonnell Douglas was not, however, good for little ArmaLite, for even countries without such agreements were loath to buy weapons for which it might be difficult to obtain parts and ammunition. To their consternation, MacDonald and Stoner realized that without some kind of deal with a government agency, the AR-15 would never see a sale, no matter how much the Asians liked it.

On their return MacDonald made calls to the FBI, the navy, the Marines, and even the Secret Service (which actually bought two AR-15s and stashed them in the president's limousine, but removed them when someone pointed out that their spray-fire would kill too many bystanders). He reserved his greatest efforts, however, for the air force. Rumor had it that the service was seeking to replace its airbase security police's aged M1s and M2 carbines.[35]

The vice chief of staff of the air force at the time was General Curtis LeMay, sometimes known as "Bombs Away" LeMay and the unfortunate inspiration for George C. Scott's General Buck Turgidson character in *Dr. Strangelove*. LeMay had been the leading advocate of mass bombing offensives in the Second World War and afterward had turned the Strategic Air Command into the mirror of his views on Massive Retaliation. Blunt when he spoke, brooding when he didn't, bombastic all the time, but acknowledged even by his (many) enemies as the greatest sky captain of all time, LeMay was determined never to allow the air force to take its orders from the army. His insistence on air force independence and the necessity of annihilating the Soviets in a single, overwhelming offensive would naturally put him at odds with the Flexible Response doctrine pursued by the Kennedy administration. His particular bugbear would prove to be Secretary of Defense McNamara, though General Maxwell Taylor was up there on his hate list as well. Aside from being a keen aficionado of judo (he had acquired a taste for the sport while serving as MacArthur's assistant in Japan) and sports car racing, LeMay was an expert competitive shooter.[36] He was also friends with Boutelle—the two had been on safari to Africa together—and well acquainted with Bobby MacDonald.

Which is why it seemed the most natural thing in the world for Boutelle to invite the general to his July 4, 1960, barbecue at his farm outside Hagerstown, Maryland. The property was set up for some serious shooting. According to MacDonald, it had a "skeet field, trap field, archery, pistol ranges, you name it. It was beautifully equipped from a shooting angle."[37] Thoughtfully, the host provided three watermelons and a selection of AR-15s. Boutelle placed a watermelon at 50, 100, and 150 yards and asked LeMay to have a go. The general exploded the first and third of them. He walked over to the remains and, in MacDonald's enigmatic words, "put his hand down in there and picked this stuff up, and I won't say what he said, but it was quite impressive—he was impressed." When MacDonald asked whether he wanted to destroy the remaining watermelon, LeMay growled, "Hell no, let's eat it."[38]

From that moment on LeMay wanted AR-15s for the guards at his beloved Strategic Air Command bases. Nothing else would do, especially not M14s, which he'd already tried and disliked. Colt, in the meantime, began a public relations campaign designed to embarrass the M14 publicly and generate interest about its own AR-15. The crew-cut, gun-collecting George Strichman, in his late forties and a board member of the Jewish Theological Seminary of America, was the incoming president of Colt and a specialist in company turnarounds and modernization programs. (Some of Colt's machinery dated back to the Civil War.)[39] "We're up against the NIH factor," he announced. "Not

Invented Here. The [AR-15] rifle's basic problem was that it hadn't been invented by Army arsenal personnel." According to him, Ordnance "got the M14 adopted, then tried to cover their tracks. They resented the AR-15 being thrust upon them."[40] Colt publicists earned their pay. A highly influential article (even Kennedy read it) by the journalist A. J. Glass in the *New York Herald Tribune* caustically asserted that even some army officers considered the M14 to be "a major blunder . . . the result of an official Army ordnance policy . . . to get rid of short-range, light impact spray-fire weapons."[41] The long-standing idea that the M14 was an inherently poor weapon, it seems, had its genesis in a corporate rival spinning the complex story of its development into an easy-to-understand conspiracy theory about reactionary government officials and military experts crushing innovation wheresoever it could be found.

For the rest of 1960, as Colt and the indefatigable MacDonald pushed tame congressmen to ask questions, LeMay forged ahead with tests for the AR-15. At every turn, Ordnance was frustrated: the AR-15, now that the Colt engineers had tweaked whatever few bugs remained, was a terrific weapon in every way. Finally, in the summer of 1961, LeMay, newly elevated to the powerful position of air force chief of staff, believed he had secured enough proof of the AR-15's abilities to go ahead and request the purchase of eighty thousand of them. LeMay had miscalculated. He had been depending on the stream of complaints about M14 production delays to give him an advantage, but by the time he submitted his request, most of the problems at Winchester and at Harrington & Richardson had been mitigated.

With one rifle headache apparently dissipated, no one had any desire to invite a new one, and LeMay's order was turned down by the Pentagon, then by a House subcommittee on defense appropriations, and finally by President Kennedy himself.[42] Kennedy, who test-fired an AR-15 that fall, seems to have liked it but, being no gun expert, he was given the shakes by General Maxwell Taylor, who advised against having two calibers in service simultaneously. The AR-15, yet again, looked like a dead duck.

But not for long. On February 7, 1958, in the near-panic that followed the Soviet launch of Sputnik, Department of Defense directive 5105.15 had established the Advance Research Projects Agency (ARPA, though later better known as DARPA, the first letter standing for "Defense"). Proudly unbeholden to established military channels or traditions, ARPA's job was to develop, evaluate, and fund new technology for the Pentagon.

In the spring of 1961 ARPA embarked on Project AGILE, its task being to supply inventive fixes for use against Communist irregulars in Southeast Asia. (AGILE researchers would conceive a glider for cargo drops in the jungle, vehicles that could skim across rice paddies, shoes invulnerable to underwater bamboo spikes, and a weapon that would harness a cloud of charged particles and explode it using an electrical impulse.)[43]

Project AGILE was given top priority. The U.S. Military Assistance Advisory Group (MAAG), originally sent to Vietnam in the early 1950s to train the country's regular forces to withstand a North Vietnamese *conventional* attack, had underestimated the political and cultural impact of the new forms of guerrilla insurgency pursued by Hanoi after 1960. ("Any good soldier can handle guerrillas," army chief of staff George Decker had allegedly boasted to the president.) From that year onward, and especially under Kennedy, the American focus switched to counterinsurgency, paramilitary training, and special operations.

By October 1961, at the same time that Kennedy upped the number of military advisers in Vietnam, Colt's lobbying had attracted the attention of William Godel, a senior ARPA official. That month he sent ten AR-15s to Saigon to let Vietnamese allies and their American advisers try them out. The recipients were highly enthusiastic about these marvelous machines, and in the new year of 1962 a further shipment of a thousand AR-15s arrived, this time intended for actual field testing. In July the testers reported that it was the best "all around" firearm in existence.[44]

Heavily accounting for ARPA's cheerleading was the fact that none of these hard-bitten veterans in Vietnam had ever before witnessed the kinds of devastating wounds inflicted by the AR-15; none had thought such lethality possible in a rifle, particularly one firing a "varmint" round like the .223. As late as the mid-1980s, photographs of the victims remained classified. As an example of the horrific kills toted up by AR-15, consider the following files from the report:

☆ "One platoon from the 340 [South Vietnamese] Ranger Company was on an operation . . . and contacted 3 armed VC [Vietcong] in heavily forested jungle. . . . At a distance of approximately 15 meters, one Ranger fired an AR-15 full automatic hitting one VC with 3 rounds with the first burst. One round in the head took it completely off. Another in the right arm, took it completely off, too. One round hit him in the right side, causing a hole about 5 inches in diameter."

☆ "On 9 June a Ranger Platoon from the 40th Infantry Regt. was given the mission of ambushing an estimated VC Company. [Five VC were killed:]

1—Back wound, which caused the thoracic cavity to explode.
2—Stomach wound, which caused the abdominal cavity to explode.
3—Buttock wound, which destroyed all tissue of both buttocks.
4—Chest wound from right to left; destroyed the thoracic cavity.
5—Heel wound; the projectile entered the bottom of the right foot causing the leg to split from the foot to the hip.

These deaths were inflicted by the AR-15 and all were instantaneous except the buttock wound. He lived approximately five minutes."

☆ "On 13 April, a Special Forces team made a raid on a small village. In the raid, seven VC were killed. Two were killed by AR-15 fire. Range was 50 meters. One man was hit in the head; it looked like it exploded. A second man was hit in the chest, his back was one big hole."[45]

An historian who interviewed an officer who had been present during the field trials recalled that it was "impossible to take prisoners using the AR-15 because even minor wounds proved fatal."

The ARPA report's findings prompted its readers in Washington either to become convinced advocates of the AR-15 or to guffaw. Claims as to its lethality, the latter argued, were outlandishly absurd and clearly exaggerated. Their point was lent some credence by the inability of anybody to replicate the astounding results obtained in Vietnam. The Army Wound Ballistics Laboratory at Edgewood Arsenal used ballistic-gelatin blocks and anesthetized goats as stand-ins for Vietcong guerrillas but failed to reproduce the expected wounding characteristics. Had the ARPA reports been faked?

The anomaly was easily explained. The degree of "twist" in a barrel's grooved rifling governs how rapidly the bullet revolves as it races out of the muzzle, like a football spiraled by a quarterback. Twist is measured in terms of inches, so that a one in twelve-inch twist means that the bullet rotates around its axis once every foot; a one in ten-inch twist is thought to be "tighter" than a one in twelve, a one in fourteen, "looser." At its simplest, the tighter the barrel's twist, the faster a projectile spins and the stabler its flight. A stabilized bullet is more accurate than an unstable one, though when determining an appropriate twist for a particular bullet, its weight, velocity, and shape, as well as the range to target, weather, and barrel length, must be taken into account.

The Springfield Model 1903 and the M1 were both given, after much trial-and-error testing by Ordnance armorers, a twist of one in ten inches and the M14, one in twelve. In order to compensate for his .223 bullet's relative lack of striking energy by slightly destabilizing it, Stoner had suggested a looser twist of one in fourteen inches. Since he was expecting the AR-15 to be used almost exclusively at short ranges (25 to 150 yards), by wobbling its bullet a bit the energy differential wouldn't matter so much. This was because a relatively unstable bullet is more likely to fragment and tumble once it leaves the air and enters the denser medium of tissue. The .223 still would not hit as hard as the 7.62mm, but once inside it would cause greater damage.

The unreproducible, remarkable ARPA results were caused by Colt's antiquated machinery being unable to carve Stoner's specified rifling twist of one in fourteen inside the barrel. Instead, in these early models the barrelmen had plumped for one turn in sixteen or even eighteen inches. Stoner's original specification had ensured essentially stable flight with a touch of jiggle, but Colt's modification made the bullet travel at the ballistic equivalent of a bumblebee's erratic flight. The cumulative effect of the projectile's singular combination of instability, fragmentation, velocity, and hydrostatic shock when it collided with flesh, blood, and tissue was what produced the gushing, gaping wounds described in the ARPA report.[46]

The furor over the AR-15's performance—was it spectacular or not?—attracted Secretary of Defense McNamara's notice. In fact, McNamara had discreetly had his eye on the problem as early as December 27, 1961: it was he who had signed the order approving the ARPA shipment of one thousand AR-15s to Vietnam, bypassing Ordnance.[47] Owing to its M14 production delays, that corps had long since lost his confidence, and on May 8, 1962, McNamara merged it with six other technical bureaus—most of which dated back to the Revolutionary War and the early days of the Republic—into a single, sprawling entity called Army Matériel Command (AMC). At a stroke, the post of Chief of Ordnance had been abolished. (It would be resurrected in 1985.) The first head of AMC was General Frank Besson, originally commissioned in the Corps of Engineers (which was also vacuumed into the new command), his job being to improve production-and-supply efficiency.[48] Crucially, though, AMC would not be activated until August; until that time, everything would be in a state of confusion and ambiguity.

As of May 8, then, Curtis LeMay was confident that, with AMC existing but not operating, if he worked fast he could forge ahead with his plan to issue AR-15s to his Strategic Air Command guards before anyone could stop him. On May 15, exactly one week after AMC's creation, LeMay ordered 8,500 AR-15s.[49] By hook or by crook, the air force was going to use ARs. But would the army?

Not if the National Rifle Association had its way. In its May 1962 issue *American Rifleman* carried a piece on the AR-15 by Walter Howe and Colonel Edward Harrison, a retired Ordnance officer. They had tested the AR-15 for themselves and were confident that it was unsuitable for universal army use. The reviewers, adhering to the NRA's progressive marksmanship tradition, focused on the AR-15's bullet, which they found, correctly, "only weakly stable, much like a top which is spun barely fast enough to keep it upright." By suggesting that the bullet's twist be tightened to one in twelve, the authors were diminishing its lethality—perhaps by as much as 40 percent—in favor of imparting greater spin, improved stability, and of course, better accuracy over longer distances.[50] Since the aluminum gun was never designed for such ranges, however, there wasn't much call, thought the authors, for adopting the AR-15 in the first place. Stick with the M14 was the implicit message.

McNamara's computerlike mind, which operated on a binary system of one and zero, true or false, yes or no, heartily disliked these fuzzy, interminable debates between rival factions that he and his allies in the defense secretary's office suspected were hopelessly compromised by service turf battles and career interests. He wanted to know *which* rifle was definitively superior, not their pros and cons, the on-the-other-hands, and the pluses and minuses. Just give me a straight, honest, objective answer, he ordered Charles Hitch. The latter, being the Department of Defense's comptroller, a former RAND analyst, coauthor of 1960s *The Economics of Defense in the Nuclear Age,* and once-president of the Operations Research Society of America, was the perfect man for the job.[51] He, like McNamara, was predisposed to using logic to break down a problem into its constituent parts, producing a solution to each, and then adding the solutions together to arrive at a general answer.

Hitch immediately dragooned McNamara's favored systems analysts, operations researchers, and number crunchers into the effort and called up every file, every study in the Pentagon archives, that had anything to do with previous rifle controversies going back to the 1920s. His men scoured the old Pig Board's findings, broke down the BRL ballistics tests, parsed the ORO reports, dissected CDEC's 1959 observations. Then they compiled tables and accumulated figures covering every aspect of rifle development, from logistics to costs to capabilities. And at the end Hitch reported to McNamara on September 27, 1962, that "in combat the AR-15 is the superior weapon" to the M14.[52] Thank you, said McNamara, his own mind now made up.

Yet still no final decision was made, for the new secretary of the army, Cyrus Vance, asked his generals to come up with their own reasons to keep the M14 so that he could assert that Hitch had been biased.[53] For one, they suggested obligingly, what about our NATO partners? Switching to the .223 when we had forced them to adopt the .30 would cause untold damage to the alliance. Moreover, the M14 was decidedly superior in penetrative ability and was more lethal at ranges of four hundred yards and above. Lastly, 300,000 M14s were now being produced annually, and they estimated it would take Colt twenty-seven months to get AR-15 production ramped to acceptable levels.[54] (They did not, however, count on Colt's brilliant acquisition of the former machinist-turned-chief mechanical engineer of Thompson Ramo Wooldridge [TRW], Bill Goldbach, who had made gun history by delivering the company's initial M14 order *ahead* of schedule.)[55]

An exasperated McNamara, who had naïvely thought that at last he had an open-and-shut case against the M14—how he must have rued that flip comment back in 1961, that "this is a relatively simple job, to build a rifle, compared to building a satellite or a missile system"—sent Vance a memorandum on October 12. (Two days before, reconnaissance photos had been shown to Kennedy of Soviet nuclear missile installations on Cuba.) In the memo McNamara remarked that "I have seen certain evidence which appears to indicate that . . . we are equipping our forces with a weapon [M14] definitely inferior in firepower and combat effectiveness to the Soviet assault rifle."[56] There was only one thing to do: send the file upstairs to the White House for the president to decide. Two weeks later, just after the Cuban Missile Crisis, Kennedy read the Hitch Report and thoroughly quizzed McNamara on the issue. The only thing to do, they decided, was to pit the M14 directly, exhaustively, and definitively against the AR-15.

General Earl Wheeler, the new army chief of staff, was instructed to have a final report on McNamara's desk by the end of January 1963. As early as December, however, the tests had descended into an orgy of accusations of bias, rigging, and foul play—mostly orchestrated by Colt and its friends. Truth be told, there *was* bias, but it was generally inadvertent in nature, a product of the haste and poor planning that had gone into finishing the tests on time. To take one glaring example, in Georgia and Alaska the AR-15 flopped terribly. The reason was that the testers had, in the absence of any instructions from the Pentagon, used the standard 1954 performance yardsticks printed in their testing manuals, but these had been developed for the M1, not for small-caliber automatic weapons. One of them, for instance, required that rifles be tested for accuracy and penetration at 800 yards; the AR-15 had a maximum range of 500.

The fault lay not entirely on the army's side. Quality control at Colt and Remington (which made the AR-15 ammunition) was so poor that several rifles rattled themselves almost to pieces and loose bullets slipped out of shoddy cartridges. As a result, the malfunction rate of AR-15s, once enviably low, skyrocketed to eight times that of the M14. Bobby MacDonald, the excitable arms dealer who had a lot of money riding on these tests (over five to ten years, the army was forecasted to spend a billion dollars on two million rifles along with their ammunition, spare parts, and repair tools), angrily wrote to the two companies to accuse them of "deliberately sabotaging" their own products.[57]

So the supposedly "conclusive" tests had done nothing but create *more* confusion. They were about to become more so, for just after McNamara received Wheeler's now-useless report, the army's Small Arms Development Staff informed him that one of their secret programs was nearing completion. It was named SPIW, for Special Purpose Individual Weapon, and the small-arms people assured McNamara that, if approved, it would be ready for final testing by February 1964—by 1965, tops.[58] The defense secretary could not afford to ignore the SPIW. If it worked as spectacularly as Small Arms was telling him, it would outclass not only the M14 but the AR-15 and AK-47 as well. The SPIW would "leapfrog," according to Lieutenant General Dwight Beach, the chief of research and development, over any rifle in existence and solve the "Army small-arms muddle" (as "experts," quoted in the *New York Times*, put it). The SPIW certainly was radical: it would fire a cartridge crammed with inch-long .10-caliber flechettes, or nail-like darts that would disperse at immensely high speed and shred their target.

Such a revolutionary departure from a century's worth of hard-won experience with bullet-tipped metallic cartridges would naturally require significant technological innovations. To make the flechettes sufficiently lethal, they would have to be propelled faster than four thousand feet per second—a velocity at least one-third more than the AR-15's .223. So delicate were they, as well, that colliding with a drop of rain deformed them, and yet because they required extensive finishing for

accuracy, they cost a magnitude more than any bullet. "SPIW prototypes had the look of Rube Goldberg devices, and were usually just as
reliable," judged one expert.[59]

But they just *might* work. Could any secretary of defense leave himself
open to the charge that he had passed over what might have been the
greatest rifle of all time? The SPIW revelation left McNamara with three
options. *Safe:* he could ignore the AR-15 and continue M14 production
until the SPIW came online, if it ever did. *Risky:* terminate the M14 now
and issue AR-15s until the SPIW was ready, if it ever was. *Moderate:*
temporarily suspend M14 production and make a onetime purchase of
AR-15s to keep Colt in business and the Special Forces and LeMay off
his back until the SPIW came along. If it didn't, then reactivate the
M14.

McNamara settled on option three. In mid-1963 he approved a single
procurement of 85,000 AR-15s for the army and 19,000 for the air
force. The army's rifles were for "specialized" use, a euphemism for
Vietnam-theater Special Forces, airborne units, and CIA operatives
who reassured nervous State Department officials and American representatives at NATO headquarters that there was no danger of the AR-15
being distributed "universally" among troops—an act that would have
enraged the European allies, now lumbered with the .30/7.62mm. As for
the air force's consignment, it would serve to appease the combustive
LeMay until he retired in January 1965.

Accordingly, McNamara suspended production of the M14 come
July 1, 1964, and the military version of the AR-15 was dubbed the
M16.[60] The M14 was, nevertheless, not quite dead. More than a million
had either been manufactured or were on order, and Massachusetts
legislators (including both its senators, new boy Edward Kennedy and
old-timer Republican Leverett Saltonstall) were gearing up to defend
their constituents' jobs at Springfield Armory and at Harrington &
Richardson.[61] Even so, a *Wall Street Journal* headline nicely summarized
the story: "Order of $13,296,923 for New-Type Rifles Reflects Army's
Growing Dislike of M-14."[62]

The growing "like" for the M16 stemmed from two factors: the failure and cancellation of the SPIW and the mounting U.S. commitment
to Vietnam. When McNamara had scheduled M14 production to cease

in July 1964 and had put the M16 in stasis until the SPIW came along, the fighting in Vietnam still seemed more like a contained, controllable conflict than an escalating, expansive war. As late as the spring-summer of 1964, there was little reason to believe otherwise. Indeed, so confident was he that most of the 15,000 U.S. troops would be out of Vietnam within eighteen months, that on April 25 the secretary of defense told reporters he was "pleased" that Senator Wayne Morse (D-OR) was calling it "McNamara's War."[63] A week later McNamara declared that his staff was studying 8,000 defense installations and bases to see which ones could be closed.[64] Two weeks later a May 15 memorandum, in hindsight ironically entitled *Study of Rifle Readiness*, confirmed that there was to be "no more procurement of XM16E1 (AR15) rifles after the FY64 buy of 85,000."[65] There would be no need for them, apparently, in Vietnam or anywhere else.

Few predicted how rapidly the situation would change. On August 5, in response to two alleged attacks by North Vietnamese vessels on American warships in the Gulf of Tonkin, President Johnson put before Congress a resolution to allow him to take all necessary measures to prevent attacks on U.S. forces. Two days later it passed, in the House by 414 votes to nil, and in the Senate, 88 to 2. Henceforth American troops would be sent abroad in ever-rising numbers. Within the year there would be 60,000; by the end of 1965, 184,000; of 1966, 385,000; and of 1967, nearly half a million.[66]

All of these soldiers had to be armed with rifles. During the Tonkin Gulf crisis, however, the Pentagon had, to its horror, been caught short, partly because of McNamara's option three decision. Units were armed with no fewer than three "standard" rifles: some carried M1s authorized in 1936; others had been issued M14s, which some suspected were inferior to the AK-47s carried by the North Vietnamese enemy; and elite outfits were armed with the experimental, space-age M16. Since South Vietnamese units were carrying a variety of Browning Automatic Rifles, M2 carbines, cast-off submachine guns, and .30-caliber machine guns, American logisticians were tormented by the prospect of having to supply five different types of ammunition and parts across the Pacific and deep into the jungle.

It was time to reappraise the Pentagon's chaotic arms situation and put it back on track. Among McNamara's first decisions in this regard was to award Colt on November 3, 1964, a supplementary order of $4,305,750 for more M16s (33,500 for the air force, 240 for the navy, and 82 for the coast guard, plus $517,000 for spare parts).[67] The second, which came about three weeks later, was his announcement at a press conference that the Springfield Armory would be shuttered. Its death was hardly noticed by the country at large, for the armory was just one of ninety-five bases across thirty-three states and abroad that were being closed.[68]

McNamara's opponents were unwilling to allow Springfield to disappear. Instead they instigated a three-year fight to save the armory. Despite the pleas of Senator Kennedy, the Massachusetts House delegation, and Mayor Charles Ryan of Springfield, it did no good. Rock Island in Illinois took over some of the armory's research and development functions, but most (460 out of 480) of its highly skilled gunsmiths and civilian experts departed, took early retirement, or found jobs with military contractors, thus ignominiously bringing to an end 170 years' worth of hard-won tradition.[69] In the nineteenth century former Springfield employees had gradually diffused their skills to commercial firms around the country, but now this shortsighted closure of the armory instantly drained the pool of specialized small-arms talent and left behind few who could impart their knowledge to the next generation. Springfield Armory may have been slow and sometimes surly, but nobody had ever complained about the quality and workmanship of its Model 1903s, M1s, or M14s.

In some ways the end of Springfield was fated as soon as McNamara had joined the Pentagon. Its staff had been raised in the old Armory-Ordnance system of apprenticeship, inventive trial and error, and the vocational ethos of mechanics' school; that system was wholly at odds with the professional, rationalist, and primarily theoretical climate fostered by the defense secretary. Bill Davis, one of Ordnance's old-style civilian employees, believed that McNamara was uninterested in correcting the faults in the existing system but instead desired "to destroy the infrastructure itself, and rebuild within the hollow shell a system more in conformity with his own ideas." The secretary's "contempt for the Ordnance professional was undisguised at the less sophisticated lower levels outside Washington." His emissaries to Springfield, Rock Island, and Frankford "had no previous professional experience in the field of small arms [and] their qualifications consisted of, and apparently were limited to, advanced academic degrees, supreme confidence in their own intellectual superiority, virtually absolute authority as designated representatives of OSD [Office of the Secretary of Defense], and a degree of arrogance such as I have never seen before or since."[70] The times had certainly changed since the days when Andrew Jackson accused Ordnance men of being the intellectual snobs.

In the meantime General William Westmoreland, the new commander of U.S. forces in Vietnam, had been grappling with the M16 issue.[71] Having served General Paul Harkins as deputy commander since 1962, Westmoreland was familiar with the M16, but had, until late in the spring of 1965, assumed that it would always be only for specialist use. Thus "reports [of units, such as the 173rd Airborne Division, using the M16] are almost unanimously favorable," General Besson of AMC informed Vice Chief of Staff Creighton Abrams on April 5, "and there are no serious problem areas taken from [the] 82nd and 101st AB [Airborne Divisions], SF [Special Forces], etc." Neither man conceived that the M16 might be more widely issued, though Besson scribbled a private note for Abrams saying that "I honestly believe the M-16 is a better rifle [than the M14] for jungle and rice paddy warfare." For his part, Westmoreland was impressed by what he heard but wanted to see the rifle in more combat action before requesting additional numbers.

The Battle of Ia Drang that November provided him with the evidence he needed. Following a repulse at Plei Me, where North Vietnamese troops had assaulted a Vietnamese-American Special Forces camp, Colonel Hal Moore's First Battalion, Seventh Cavalry was ordered to pursue and eliminate the enemy. At Ia Drang, American forces entered into a new phase of the war by directly attacking massed formations of the North Vietnamese army rather than coping with Vietcong guerrillas.

As elite helicopter-borne air cavalry, the American battalion was armed with the scarce M16s.[72] Their rifles inflicted heavy casualties: at least fourteen hundred. When his platoon became pinned down by a machine gun in a bunker, for instance, Lieutenant Walter Marm, Jr., knew they would die if they stayed where they were. "The first thing I did was fire a grenade launcher at the bunker. Then I took two grenades and an M16 rifle and went straight up," he recalled. "I pulled the pin of a grenade and just lobbed it over. After it went off I went around to the left, saw some movements and fired. I fired six times, but didn't know then how many there were." The same lieutenant who had resisted his father's efforts to teach him how to box (he didn't like fighting, he explained) had killed, it turned out, eighteen men. He was awarded the Medal of Honor.[73]

Afterward Colonel Moore attended a meeting of senior commanders, wrote General Westmoreland in his memoirs, and "at the conclusion Moore held up an M-16 rifle, a newly developed, relatively light, fully automatic weapon. 'Brave soldiers and the M-16,' said Moore, 'brought this victory.'" Westmoreland added that when "Moore and many of his soldiers told me that the M-16 was the best individual infantry weapon ever made, clearly the American answer to the enemy's AK-47," he agreed that the M14 was too heavy for Vietnam and asked McNamara "as a matter of urgency to equip all American forces with the M-16 and then also to equip the ARVN [South Vietnamese army] with it."[74]

But Pentagon officials, Westmoreland believed, failed to see the urgency of his plea and did not approve his order for 170,000 M16s for U.S. forces and a request for 123,000 more for his Vietnamese allies. Part of the reason for the go-slow from Washington, particularly regarding rifles for ARVN units, was that McNamara was still uncertain whether American troops would be drawn down in Vietnam over the next couple of years. Once they were withdrawn, he was worried that the brand-new M16s supplied to the ARVN would find their way into the hands of the Communists. Publicly announcing a general M16 distribution would signal to Americans and Congress that President Lyndon Johnson was preparing for a long-term commitment to the beleaguered country. At the same time Colt was reaching what it called its "point of no return": without further orders of M16s to keep them in clover, its suppliers and the foundries would soon have to convert their machinery and production lines to other uses.[75] Worried that he might be left with a pile of M14s and no more M16s in that event, McNamara authorized 179,000 M16s but stipulated that just 9,000 of them were to be reserved for especially trustworthy ARVN allies.[76] Within three months Westmoreland was cabling home for more, 100,000 at a time.[77] Three months later, on June 16, 1966, Colt quietly announced that it had "received a definitive $45,035,407.50 contract" from the government to make 403,905 M16s.[78] The June 1966 contract marked the official end to the Pentagon's "onetime buy" policy for the M16.

Thus, try as McNamara might to keep a lid on ever-increasing demand for the M16, American troops arriving in Vietnam in ever-increasing numbers placed ever-increasing pressure on the Pentagon to make a final, incontrovertible, irreversible decision on the M16's status.[79] McNamara's placeholding option-three policy was slowly dissolving under the weight of changing realities. The June 1966 contract, for instance, would have to be amended 256 times during its three-year lifetime as the Pentagon struggled to keep pace with rising demand for M16s. By September 1967 *alone* the original 403,905 figure had more than doubled to 947,000 M16s, as the American military intervention in Vietnam deepened and there seemed no way to escape.[80]

As early as the winter of 1966 an embarrassed Pentagon was forced to admit that it had temporarily run short even of M14 rifles (it attributed the weapons deficit to "increased unit activations") and had been obliged to give trainees M1s taken from depot stocks.[81] Because M16s had still not been officially approved for general use in Vietnam, soldiers were being trained on M1s and M14s in the United States before picking up their M16s when they got to Vietnam. At the Marine Corps base at Camp Pendleton, California, it was reported, there were only between two hundred and four hundred M16s to go around, and each man who had been handed his orders for Vietnam received just a hundred rounds for practice.[82] Their unfamiliarity with the weapon, in combination with a ghastly error on the part of its manufacturers, led to calamitous incidents of jamming at critical moments.

One important aspect of the M16 of which recruits weren't aware was its propensity to fouling and susceptibility to dirt. Eugene Stoner had originally used Du Pont IMR4475 "stick" powder (its granules looked like tiny tubes) in his Remington-made ammunition, but in 1964–65 it was replaced by ball powder made by Ordnance's old friend Olin. At first glance ball powder was definitely a better bet: it burned longer and more slowly than IMR. On the downside, however, was that Stoner had originally designed the AR-15's gas-port reloading system near the muzzle to suit IMR and all its parts were conceived to function rhythmically at a cyclic rate of between 750 and 800 rounds per minute. Ball powder, because its slow, steady burn achieved constant pressure along the barrel, retained a relatively higher pressure at the muzzle than did IMR, whose fast initial combustion resulted in higher peak chamber pressure. As a result of the switch to ball powder, the gas-port was therefore forced to work harder and the cyclic rate was pushed up to a thousand rounds per minute or more, thereby increasing the likelihood of feed and ejection failures. Worse, even as the elevated cyclic rate strained the capacity of the rifle's mechanical components to keep synchronized, ball powder still burned when the gas-port was open, thereby searing and fouling the piece.[83]

With IMR, the M16 malfunctioned 3.2 times out of every thousand rounds; with ball powder, that figure sextupled to 18.5.[84] Though some have suspected a conspiracy by Ordnance to sabotage the hated M16 with bad powder, this view does not stand up to prolonged scrutiny: expert military and civilian representatives of all four fighting services and the defense secretary's office had approved the powder change. Their decision was the result more of confusion and hurry and carelessness than of anything else.[85]

The M16 jamming problem resulted in horrific, and all too often fatal, experiences. Specialist Galen Bungum remembered that at one point during a battle "I was crawling around looking for an M-16. I got my hands on one, and Specialist 5 Marlin T. Dorman said: 'That doesn't work; I'll get you another one.' Then he hollered: 'That doesn't work either.' I headed for a third rifle and PFC Donald Jeffrey hollered: 'It don't work!' Finally I did find an M-16 and some full magazines from our dead." Then there was Specialist Fourth Class Bob Towles, who said that "North Vietnamese troops shattered the foliage and headed straight for us, AK-47 rifles blazing, on the dead run. I selected the closest one and fired twice. I hit him but he refused to go down; he kept coming and shooting. I turned my M-16 on full automatic, fired, and he crumpled. I shifted to another target and squeezed the trigger. Nothing happened. The fear I felt turned to terror. I saw a cartridge jammed in the chamber. I removed it, reloaded, and began firing again." Towles suffered no more incidents during the firefight.[86]

Others were not so fortunate. During the vicious fighting in the hills surrounding Khe Sanh in early 1967 (a prelude to the more famous siege of a year later), the Marines bitterly joked that their newly issued M16s, owing to their plastic stocks, had been made by Mattel. Near battle's end, three Marines and a navy hospitalman were found dead, clustered together. "All three of their M16s had jammed," remembered Private Tom Huckaba. One of them had tried to free up the mechanism using the Bowie knife he had always carried. His friend "took the Bowie knife and stuck it in his belt. He was hit later on. We threw the knife away after that, figuring it was a jinx," said Robert Maras, another private.[87]

Initial reports of fatal M16 malfunctions sometimes made soldiers wistful for their M14s, but the issue should not be exaggerated. Hundreds and hundreds of millions of bullets would be fired using ball powder during the Vietnam War, and the introduction of a recoil buffer in December 1966 reduced the cyclic rate to a sustainable level. During tests in the Panama Canal Zone, new-model buffered M16s fitted with chrome-plated barrels (to reduce residue corrosion) and firing ball powder actually outperformed those firing a "stick" propellant successor to IMR.[88] In spite of the weapon's apparent problems, soldiers *wanted* M16s, and there were reports that GIs issued with M14s were spending $600 of their own pay to purchase black-market ArmaLites (list price: $100)—much as their Civil War ancestors had bought Spencers at their own expense.[89] Even the rifle's toughest critics had to admit that M16s could kill more men, more quickly, than an M14. Outside Khe Sanh, Corporal Thomas Wheeler of the Marines dropped to one knee, pulled the trigger of his M16, and killed four of the enemy in short order with a single magazine.[90] At Dak To in 1967 Specialist Fourth Class Bruce Benzene of the 173rd Airborne Brigade mowed down six North Vietnamese soldiers in one spray before being killed himself.[91]

When asked for his views, General S. L. A. Marshall, author of *Men Against Fire,* conceded that there had been operations where the failure rate had been high enough to warrant investigation, but he insisted that the M16 was the right gun for Vietnam fighting. Nevertheless, he correctly highlighted the principle that "it is not a perfect rifle. There is none such, and try as we will, we will not find one in the future."[92]

Because it had been rushed into production, and designed just as quickly, the M16 would require years' worth of finessing to work at 100 percent efficiency. This was unfortunate—and in the M16's case needless deaths were tragically suffered—but inevitable. The failure of advanced technology to deliver perfect performance from the outset had long dogged firearms development. When the Springfield Model 1873 rifle and its copper-cased .45-70s were introduced, noted arms historian Philip Shockley, some "failed to function when fired rapidly which was due to the softness of the . . . shell casing . . . Powder residue, gases and grease did foul the receivers . . . And jamming, if one can accept the contemporary comments, was constant."[93] And after the slaughter of Custer's Seventh at the Little Bighorn, newspapers charged that their Springfields' alleged cartridge-extraction defect left hundreds of troopers unable to fight when most desperately needed.[94]

M16 jamming there was, but the problem appears to have been exacerbated by soldiers not maintaining their weapons. This was not their fault. Those early arrivals who had been handed an M16 on their arrival in theater received virtually no advice on how and when to clean their weapon. One inspector reported that he "had never seen equipment with such poor maintenance . . . [On some rifles] you could not see daylight through the barrel. The barrels were rusty, and the chambers were rusty and pitted."[95] This oversight was entirely the army's responsibility: its own instruction manuals, which appeared to have been lifted verbatim from Colt promotional pamphlets, claimed that the M16 required hardly any upkeep, and while there were sufficient cleaning rods and patches in Vietnam, they were not properly distributed to soldiers.[96] At one point there was just one cleaning rod for every four soldiers; the "men in the rear" were donating them "to the grunts before we headed south so we'd have enough," recalled Navy Cross recipient Corporal Frederick Monahan.[97] Once the army got its act together in the late winter of 1966 and issued adequate instructions, the number of jams began rapidly declining.[98]

On December 6 of that year Westmoreland ordered a further 100,000

M16s—68,000 for the army, 32,000 for the Marines—and his request was granted the next day.[99] Eleven days later McNamara received the final word on the M16 for which he had been waiting. Dr. Jacob Stockfisch, an expert economist, had spent six months breaking down all available data and reported to the secretary of defense that the M14 ought to be immediately executed. In every test M16-armed teams were "superior to squads armed with 7.62mm weapons in target effects, sustainability of effects, and overall effectiveness."[100] At the end of the day, Stockfisch was merely confirming what everyone already knew: the rifle of today was the M16; that of the past, the M14. Crucially, Stockfisch's coup de grâce exemplified the dilution of the army's progressive-marksmanship tradition and its merging with the diehard way of war.

The end, now, was inevitable. McNamara directed that all M14s in Vietnam be replaced by M16s. Those M14s stockpiled in government armories, even brand-new ones, were destroyed by shearing them in half with a blowtorch, although a few were kept around for use as sniper rifles.[101] There remained, however, the question whether U.S. troops in Europe would also hand in their M14s. Dealing with NATO friends *and* Vietnamese foes simultaneously would be too painful a headache.[102] The chief of staff, General Harold Johnson, however, was asked to assure allies that soldiers in Europe would not carry M16s until at least 1972—long enough for Washington to arrange sufficient carrots and sticks to keep the Europeans docile.[103] On the first day of January 1967 Lieutenant General Victor Krulak confirmed to reporters that even the Marines, traditionally the holdouts in these matters, would be converting to M16s "in the spring."[104] On February 23, 1967, the U.S. government officially approved the M16 as its standard rifle.[105] The space-age gun remains in service to this day, but the Iraq War has resurrected, yet again, the question of the American rifle.

The HK 416

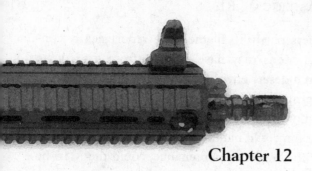

Chapter 12

THE RIFLE OF
THE FUTURE

At roughly seven in the morning on March 23, 2003, Iraqi soldiers and gunmen ambushed an American eighteen-vehicle convoy as it blundered, bewildered and lost after taking several wrong turns, through the outskirts of An Nasiriyah, an unremarkable city in the southeast. Of the thirty-three soldiers present, eleven were killed and seven were captured (including Private Jessica Lynch, later, most famously, rescued).

Four months later the army released its report on the destruction of the 507th Maintenance Company detachment. Buried in its pages lurks an implicit acknowledgment that malfunctioning M16s might well have contributed to the loss. Regarding six personnel who escaped under fire by maneuvering their vehicles past obstacles thrown up by the enemy, the report blandly notes that "most of the soldiers in this group report that they experienced weapons malfunctions." Elsewhere, Specialist James Grubb "returned fire with his M16 until wounded in both arms, despite reported jamming of his weapon." Sergeant James Riley "attempted to fire [Specialist Shoshana] Johnson's and [Specialist Edgar] Hernandez's M16s, but both jammed."

But what had caused the jamming? Were the weapons inherently

flawed, or were the soldiers partly to blame? The report gently concluded that these "malfunctions may have resulted from inadequate
individual maintenance in a desert environment."[1] In other words, the
M16s had not been kept properly cleaned and lubricated. Nevertheless,
it remained an open question whether these guns, originally developed
for jungle fighting in Vietnam, could handle the dust and sandstorms of
the Middle East. Even with excellent maintenance, could the M16 be
counted on to work? Surely, thanks to improved technology, there were
rifles available that did not require the rigorous, twice-a-day cleaning
demanded by the M16 for optimum performance. Was it time for the
United States to wave good-bye to the M16 after four decades of service?

The An Nasiriyah debacle reinvigorated a long-running debate over
the future of the M16. Since the end of the Vietnam War the M16 had
continued to suffer a reputation for underpoweredness (its 5.56mm
round was thought inferior in knockdown ability to the M14's and
AK-47's 7.62mm), and a vocal faction of soldiers, veterans, and gun experts had long demanded a bigger-caliber weapon to replace it. The
memory of some early models' disastrous failures in the middle of firefights was also not allowed to die. Nevertheless, there was never any
chance that the army would ditch the M16, especially after subsequent
modifications rectified many of the Vietnam version's flaws.

In any case, there was little call and less need for such a wholesale up-
grade. Between the mid-1970s and the beginning of Operation Iraqi
Freedom in the spring of 2003, M16s had not been used in heavy, sustained combat. The ground phase during the first Gulf War, for instance,
had lasted but one hundred hours, and the operations in Panama,
Grenada, Beirut, and Somalia had been small-scale. The Kosovo War in
1999, remarkably, had not even involved any ground troops. Overshadowed by more glamorous acquisitions like aircraft carriers, Bradley
Fighting Vehicles, and advanced fighter aircraft like the F-22 (budgeted
at $122 million each), the dull-as-dishwater M16 was considered per-
fectly satisfactory for the foreseeable future.

Instead, the army decided to postpone replacing the M16 until improved technology enabled a "great leap forward." In this scenario, instead of incrementally modifying the M16 in fits and starts as minor

issues arose, the service's next weapon would be a superadvanced, twenty-first-century rifle—the modern equivalent of the Ordnance Department's decision to cease patching up the old, sturdy Springfield .45 and adopt in its place the radical Krag rifle, which used the new .30 smokeless ammunition.

The prospect of just such a paradigm-smashing gun arose in the early 2000s with the advent of the Objective Individual Combat Weapon (OICW) project. As envisaged by its developers, Alliant Techsystems (ATK) and Heckler & Koch, what would be dubbed the XM29 was a dual 5.56mm rifle and 20mm airburst-munitions launcher that would allow the soldier to choose between firing a bullet directly at the enemy at close range and attacking him from up to a thousand yards away if he were in "defilade" (hidden behind a wall or other cover). Thanks to a programmable ballistics computer and range finder integrated into the titanium-composite weapon, the 20mm shell would explode at precisely the right distance and height to obliterate the foe. It was truly a Buck Rogers rifle that would shoot "above" corners, if not around them, though owing to its gigantic size (it was known as the "someone watched *Predator* too many times" gun), towering cost ($24,000), and inordinate weight (18 pounds), the XM29 would be a hard sell.[2]

In September 2002, despite several successful tests, these disadvantages were considered too onerous to overcome, and the program was split in two: an XM8 rifle component and a separate XM25 airburst component that would be developed independently. The XM8, it was assumed, would be America's next rifle for the coming generation.[3]

This daring scheme to sunder a once-unified weapons program and perfect its modules separately was intended to blast a shortcut through the jungles and mountains of red tape that constituted the Pentagon's traditional development and acquisitions process. If all worked out well, then at some point—say, when technology and materials science had matured sufficiently to allow major weight and cost reductions—the XM25 and the XM8 would be fused together again as the XM29.[4] Even if no such progress was made, however, the army would still end up with a superb rifle in record time—a prime consideration when an invasion of Iraq looked increasingly likely in early 2003.

This innovative technique was known as "spiral development," and it was diametrically different from the army's time-tested—but time-consuming—approach that called for releasing a full-fledged, working weapon and then fine-tuning it as bugs, kinks, and flaws were subsequently discovered. (The story of the M16 is a case in point.) Given time, the weapon would, theoretically at least, achieve the pitch of perfection. The ethos of spiral development, on the other hand, could be summarized as "build a little, test a little, build a little," and its primary advantages were speed and flexibility.[5] The spiral method tended to be preferred by those officials bestirred by the Revolution in Military Affairs (RMA) or "force transformation"—among whom numbered then–defense secretary Donald Rumsfeld.[6]

Following the end of the Cold War, Pentagon theorists conceived the RMA concept to justify a military metamorphosis that would be equal in impact to that executed by President Theodore Roosevelt and Secretary of War Elihu Root at the turn of the twentieth century. Under Roosevelt and Root, commanders had grappled with the conversion of the U.S. Army from its small, mobile structure and Indian-fighting duties into a large, European-style force committed to defending the homeland and its imperial possessions. Their successors wished to reverse the process: to transform the lumbering Cold War army, built to fight the Soviets in Europe, into a compact force that could be rapidly dispatched to world hotspots to stop trouble, protect American interests, and terminate the practitioners of "asymmetric warfare" (known as Indians in the days of Custer).

The Revolution in Military Affairs would be televised, quite literally—upon banks of networked monitors enabling "perfect situational awareness" of enemy positions and intentions in the designated "battlespace." Robots would be deployed into dangerous areas. "Smart" bombs would hit their targets precisely. Force would be applied exactly to the right spot, minimizing civilian casualties and military wastage. Many of the RMA's technical prognostications did come true—the Predator drones circling menacingly, invisibly overhead in Iraq and Afghanistan offer concrete proof of success—but the conceptual basis of "force transformation" would come undone in the Middle East.

While the RMA's advocates boasted that they looked to the future, they were in fact rooted deeply in the past. The RMA, in short, was little other than the return to power of the army's progressive school. Its exponents could even be considered the heirs of William Conant Church, the NRA founder and Creedmoor marksmanship enthusiast. In his case, the extravagant bloodiness of the Civil War and the technological innovation of the telescopic sight (which permitted one man to target a single officer) directed him to posit a future in which war was limited and "clean." When conducted by automonous specialists, not dragooned hordes of frightened youths pushed toward cannons' mouths, the once-immutable nature of warfare would alter for the better. War would be less hellish, more humanized. It would be quick, precise, and fought from a distance—up to a thousand yards with an expert sharpshooter behind the rifle. The trained technicians who today sit in air-conditioned comfort halfway around the globe guiding payloads to their targets by means of mouse and monitor incarnate Church's beguiling vision of tomorrow's army.

Nevertheless, as predicted by the rival diehard school of officers, and as the army would find in the trenches of France during the First World War, the eternal nature of battle did not change so much as the dreamers had imagined. The fog of war remained as murky as ever. Likewise, an element of millennial utopianism crept into much of the Beltway rhetoric involving "force transformation" and the liberating power of technology in the years before the attacks on the World Trade Center and the Pentagon. Modern diehards were less than impressed. "Bytes of information can be very valuable in war, but it's bullets that kill enemies," grumbled Marine Corps Lieutenant General Paul Van Riper.[7]

As Washington discovered in the aftermath of its superrapid, supertech toppling of the Taliban and its extraordinary military triumph in Iraq, it still needed boots on the ground—worn by 150,000 or so combat troops engaged in close-quarters urban gunfights against a gruesome array of insurgents and car bombers. It was a form of diehard, distinctly low-tech warfare that could not spare the time to perfect an experimental XM8. Indeed, the ever-shifting facts on the ground began overtaking the XM8's pace of progress. So while the original plan was to let the XM8 mature and eventually replace the M16, the M16 found itself losing out to competition from a most unexpected rival: its own cousin, the Colt-made M4 carbine, a virtually identical weapon to the M16 apart from its greatly shortened barrel.

The M4 had been introduced by Colt in 1991 and was adopted by the army three years later as a personal-defense weapon for support personnel (clerks, vehicle crews, staff officers). It was never intended to be anything more than a limited-distribution gun (rather as the M16 had once been envisioned as a Special Forces firearm). In 1996, for that reason, the army ordered a distinctly modest 9,861 M4s and 716 M4A1s (a version that allowed full autofire).[8]

In 2001, thinking that its compactness might serve admirably in certain types of mission, Special Operations Command (SOCOM) tested out the M4 but rejected it as unsuitable. It cited its "fundamentally flawed" and "obsolete" gas-tube system—based on that of the M16—as the main reason. The M16's gas system, which recycles the excess energy left by the bullet as it leaves the muzzle in order to prepare the next round for firing, has always been one of the weapon's weak points. Simple enough in concept, in practice the system blows dirty carbon, vaporized metals, and other impurities back into the receiver, thereby necessitating the constant cleaning for which the M16 has become notorious. The SOCOM report specifically linked a worrying "failure to extract" and "failure to eject" to the design. Though the army and Colt quickly took steps to reduce the problem, SOCOM remained adamant that the M4 was "never designed for the rigors of SOF [Special Operations Forces] use" and looked elsewhere.[9]

Nevertheless the M4 enjoyed a growing fan base. As early as April 2001 there were prescient warnings that the M16's length (39.5 inches, compared to the M4's 29.75 with its buttstock closed) was a hindrance when it came to clearing the enemy out of buildings. At such close ranges a carbine would kill just as efficiently as a full-size rifle.[10] Moreover, if urban combat—such as that experienced in Mogadishu—were to become more common, the M16 would prove irksome inside the cramped confines of a Humvee or Bradley, as soldiers sought a convenient, safe place to hold their weapons while the vehicles bounced over rocky roads or rounded tight corners. The M4 would be perfect for the job. In July 2002 another 26,064 were ordered.[11]

It is impossible to overestimate the importance of this lifeline to Colt. For decades the Hartford, Connecticut, firm had lurched from disaster to disaster, making for an unmissable capitalistic soap opera in real time. In the late 1980s its employees went on strike for four years, and it suffered bankruptcies, buyouts, restructurings, and lawsuits galore. Owing to its troubles, the company even lost the lucrative contract to build M16s for the military to its mortal enemy, Belgium-based FN Herstal.[12]

An accident in 1996 helped immeasurably in revivifying the firm's fortunes. After Colt received a modest contract to supply M4s, a navy office improperly distributed its secret blueprints to nearly two dozen competitors. Colt threatened to sue the government for up to $70 million, after which Washington agreed to make the firm the single-source supplier of the carbine to the military. (Rather enjoyably for Colt, FN Herstal challenged the arrangement but lost in federal court.)[13] No one then could have realized how lucrative this otherwise minor deal would become once Pentagon spending soared after September 11, 2001.

Having seen what was happening to its brethren—Winchester and Smith & Wesson—Colt would do *anything* to preserve this monopoly on M4 production. At the time, New Haven–based Winchester was on the ropes, a victim to falling consumer gun sales. It would eventually shut its doors in March 2006. Roughly 150 members of the International Association of Machinists, the descendants of those can-do gunsmiths who helped create the American industrial boom of the nineteenth century by diffusing their skills and knowhow countrywide, lost their jobs.[14]

As for Smith & Wesson, the Springfield stalwart was dismissed as stodgy by customers and a sellout by other gun-makers. (In 2000 the company agreed to certain gun-safety measures to settle federal and state lawsuits.) It had lost its contracts with police forces and the military. Tomkins, a London-based conglomerate, having bought the company in 1987 for $112.5 million and pumping in another $60 million to update the factory, sold it for a miserly $15 million to the Saf-T-Hammer Corporation in 2001.[15]

The army, likewise, was keen to shield Colt's products, and by extension its weapons policy, from adverse publicity. Intent on disproving post–An Nasiriyah criticisms of the M16, and the explosive charge that the M4's gas-tube system was fundamentally flawed, in mid-June 2003 the army dispatched a Small Arms Weapons Assessment team to Iraq to interview more than a thousand soldiers about their guns. The subsequent report found them highly enthusiastic about their M4s ("The M4 is by far the preferred individual weapon across the theatre of operations. Units that don't have it want it") and slightly less so about M16s, mostly owing to their awkwardness and some problems with their magazines. A couple of warnings were quietly inserted into the text, not least of which was the necessity of cleaning and lubricating weapons daily to avoid jamming—but crucially, this stricture applied to *all* types of guns (from the M9 pistol to the M249 machine gun), owing to the harsh desert environment that blew sand everywhere. In short, the team recommended that in the "near term" the M4 should replace every M16 in theater, but that was only, they implied, a stopgap solution for the relatively few troops the Pentagon was then forecasting would be needed to stabilize Iraq during the brief post-invasion occupation. In the "long term" a compact rifle specifically developed for urban combat ought to be developed.[16]

In the summer of 2003, as things stood, that rifle would be the XM8. That November the first thirty prototypes were delivered for preliminary testing at Aberdeen Proving Grounds in Maryland. Its prospects from the get-go were promising: in December, a spokesman claimed that "a retired soldier—who hadn't picked up a weapon in six years— picked up the XM8, during the live fire, and hit the target with his first shot. In fact, he hit the target with every shot. And that was from a standing position at 300 meters."[17]

Yet the XM8 was doomed for reasons beyond anyone's control or ken. Had the Iraq War ended at that moment, chances are that today American troops would be carrying "M8" rifles. But the war did not end—notwithstanding President George W. Bush's ill-starred decision to land on the deck of the aircraft carrier *USS Abraham Lincoln* in May 2003, with a "Mission Accomplished" banner fluttering behind him, or his equally ill-judged challenge to Sunni and Shi'ite guerrillas that July to "bring on" the fight. At the time it had seemed probable that U.S. soldiers would soon be coming home, where they would hand in their M4s and eventually be handed their new, high-tech rifles while waiting for their microprocessor-controlled airburst-munitions XM25 launcher to come online.

As it was, however, they urgently needed more M4s *now* to combat the terrorists who were planting IEDs by the roadside and to eliminate the gunmen infesting the alleys and backrooms of Baghdad. In August 2004, for that reason, another 125,804 M4s and M4A1s worth about $123 million were ordered from Colt.[18] The M4 was fast becoming the M16's de facto, if not de jure, replacement. To the chagrin of those who had for so long criticized the M16 as underpowered or prone to jamming, this creeping takeover by the M4 was the worst possible scenario.[19] Given that the M4 was merely an abbreviated M16, its apparently assured ascent to the throne was as terrible to contemplate as an ailing tyrant's son inheriting his crown.

But was the M4's sudden ascendancy as inexorable as it first appeared? As in some Wars of the Roses intrigue, powerful factions within the Pentagon were eager to play kingmaker for themselves. The most independent of these was SOCOM, which in November 2004 contracted with FN Herstal to manufacture a rifle niftily called the SCAR (Special Operations Combat Assault Rifle).[20] SOCOM was not answerable to the army and was able to demand and fine-tune its own specifications as it searched for a replacement for its M16s, M4s, and M14s.[21]

Beginning in September 2003, FN Herstal had worked hard to design a gun in record time: a folding sight requested by SOCOM, for instance, was added overnight and a push-button lock for it took just another few hours.[22] The SCAR would come in several versions, but the most important were the SCAR-L (for "light") and the SCAR-H (for "heavy"). The SCAR-L was a 5.56mm rifle whose standard barrel could be easily swapped out for one either longer (for sniper missions) or shorter (for close-quarters fighting). The SCAR-H, intended for longer-range work, was almost identical apart from its caliber—7.62mm—and the ability to adapt it to fire "battlefield pickup" AK-47 ammo in Iraq and Afghanistan. Special Operations troops would thus be able to live off the land for prolonged periods. The SCAR lacked the gorgeous lines of the XM8, but it worked magnificently.

Other elite units, such as Delta Force—which *was* answerable to the army though it received funding from SOCOM—went their own way during the Afghan fighting. Delta Force was satisfied with the M4 but felt its gas-tube system was unfixable. Like SOCOM, for a solution they approached an outside contractor—Heckler & Koch, a specialist at making broken guns work. (Its troubleshooting of the troublesome British SA80 rifle had been a notable success.) In 2004 the manufacturer perfected a modification to the upper receiver that replaced the gas-tube operation with a short-stroke gas piston like the one used in the SCAR.

The adaptation, which prevents carbon from being pushed back into the chamber, greatly reduces fouling (and therefore jamming) as well as wear and tear on parts. The modified gun was initially called the HKM4, but Colt launched a lawsuit in April 2004 charging the company with "trademark infringement, trade dress infringement, trademark dilution, false designation of origin, false advertising, patent infringement, unfair competition, and deceptive trade practices." So Heckler & Koch redubbed it the HK416—a cheeky play on the names of the rival M4 and M16, but one for which it could not be sued.

This kind of legal battle had been part of America's gun-making tradition ever since Dr. William Thornton, the head of the Patent Office, had defrauded the inventor John Hall back in about 1811. Colt president William Keys now played his expected role admirably by dismissing the Heckler & Koch product as a "knockoff" and reminding everyone that it was a German, not an American, firm.[23]

Leaving aside Heckler's spot of legal bother, Larry Vickers, a former Delta man who helped develop the gas-piston system, remembered that his colleagues were so overjoyed at the sight of the HK416 that they purchased the first five hundred right off the assembly line. Before letting the weapon see action in Afghanistan and Iraq, the arms-maker and Delta put "a quarter-of-a-million rounds through it," according to Vickers. "It had the right kind of testing—endurance firing to 15,000 rounds with no lubrication. It runs like a sewing machine."[24]

Given the real-world, proven quality of the HK416 and the SCAR, as well as the ubiquity of the M4, the prospects for the still-experimental XM8 were looking less rosy by the day. Ever since the XM8 had been split off from its airburst-munitions component three years before, some $33 million had been spent, attracting the attention of Pentagon auditors.[25] On May 27, 2005, the Department of Defense's inspector general issued a memo directing that the XM8 program be put on hold until the army offered more definitive proof that it needed a new rifle, particularly since it would cost more than $2 billion to purchase 800,000 of them when the time came to retire the M16 and M4.[26] Two months later the army complied, "temporarily suspending" further work on the XM8.[27] Just afterward, revealingly, Colt was awarded a contract for another 50,881 M4s (worth $52,509,192).[28]

In early October the inspector general submitted an exhaustive report on the project, devastatingly finding that his office could not be "assured that the OICW [XM8] satisfies warfighter needs, with measurable improvements to mission capability and operational support, in a timely manner." It also found manifold instances of financial mismanagement, faulty paperwork, and noncompliance with standard acquisition procedures.[29] By the end of the year the entire XM8 program had been shut down and ignominiously canceled.[30]

With this dangerous competitor unexpectedly taken off the board, 2006 turned out to be a fantastic year for Colt and its M4. That June the company received a rifle order worth $243 million, and in December an army-commissioned report by the Center for Naval Analyses (CNA) made for a wonderful Christmas present.[31] Despite what Colt's critics might say, and notwithstanding the HK416 and the SCAR lurking in the wings, the troops fighting in Iraq were cock-a-hoop over their M4s.

The CNA team interviewed 2,608 Iraq and Afghanistan veterans who had fought in at least one gun battle. Of all their weapons, they were "most satisfied" with the M4 (89 percent of soldiers agreeing). They also reported the highest levels of satisfaction overall with their weapon's accuracy, range, and rate of fire. Over half of them never suffered a stoppage of any kind (failure to fire, failure to feed, failure to eject or extract) with the M4s and M16s during their entire deployment in theater.

All welcome news to Colt, but the report also contained a few worrying remarks. About 20 percent of respondents *did* report incidents of stoppage with their M4s during a firefight. Now, while more than four-fifths of them were cleared almost immediately, one in five were not. The men carrying these M4s were either out of commission for a lengthy period or even had to withdraw.[32] In such life-or-death situations, surely

Colt's opponents were justified in demanding a 100 percent nonstoppage rate?

The tide began turning against Colt in the New Year of 2007. The most damaging attack came from the *Army Times* in a lengthy exposé uncompromisingly titled, "Better than M4, but you can't have one"—a reference to the HK416.[33] On March 23, confirming an earlier report in that newspaper observing that elite units were abandoning M4s in increasing numbers, a routine acquisition notice mentioned that a Special Forces battalion based in Okinawa had quietly bought eighty-four upper receivers to home-convert their M4s into HK416s.[34]

Sensing danger, Colt and the army quickly retaliated with a three-pronged attack. First, Colt's chief operating officer dispatched a missive on March 26 ravaging the *Army Times*'s contention that the M4 was fatally flawed. Then on March 29 the army insisted that with 225,000 of them already in the inventory and many more to be procured, the M4 was the "primary individual combat rifle for Infantry, Ranger, and Special Operations forces." Finally on April 6, just to make the point unmistakably clear, Colt received a $50,775,745 contract for M4s and M4A1s.[35]

Despite the bravado, the Colt letter implicitly acknowledged (but did not explicitly admit) that the M4's gas-tube system could be improved if necessary. In a possible attempt to forestall a patent-infringement suit by Heckler & Koch, Colt (accurately) said that there was nothing new about the company's gas-piston operation for the HK416; some of the experimental semiautomatic rifles of the 1920s had used them, and indeed Colt itself had "proposed" just such a system in the 1960s. "Today Colt Defense has the ability and expertise to manufacture in great numbers piston system carbines of exceptional quality should the U.S. military services initiate a combat requirement for this type of weapon."

The ball, then, was in the army's court. Given the word, Colt would junk the gas-tube version of the M4 and neutralize the HK416 threat by manufacturing its own piston-operated M4. By any estimation, this must have been unwelcome news at Heckler & Koch, now facing a second loss in the great carbine wars following the cancellation of its XM8.

The entry of Senator Tom Coburn (R-OK) into the debate evened the score. On April 12 the senator sent acting army secretary Pete Geren a letter questioning the service's plans to spend $375 million on nearly half a million M4s using Colt as the sole provider. "Considering the long standing reliability and lethality problems with the M16 design, on which the M4 is based, I am afraid that our troops in combat might not have the best weapon," Coburn wrote. "A number of manufacturers have researched, tested and fielded weapons which, by all accounts, appear to provide significantly improved reliability."[36]

Coburn's reference to the M16's alleged "lethality" problems and the vague intimation that the M4 had inherited them briefly reopened the controversy over the M16/M4 family's killing ability. The 2006 Center for Naval Analyses report had mentioned that 20 percent of M4 users had said they wanted more lethality in their rifle (some hopeful souls even requested hollowpoint bullets, which are illegal for military use) but had not gone into more detail.[37] That left four-fifths of all soldiers satisfied with the M4's lethality, a conclusion borne out by a finding three years earlier.

At that time, according to the 2003 Soldier Weapons report, "the majority of the soldiers interviewed that voiced or desired 'better knockdown power' . . . did not have actual close engagements." In contrast, when soldiers adhered to their training during close-quarters combat and landed what are known as "controlled pairs" (a chest and head shot, for instance) in vital areas, they had, in the bloodless words of the rapporteurs, "defeated the target without issue."[38] Subsequent laboratory testing concluded that though the M4, being a carbine, fired at a somewhat lower muzzle velocity than did the M16 (2,848 feet per second compared to 3,155), there was no significant difference in terminal bullet performance at the closer ranges—which is where most urban fighting takes place. Only at greater distances could one notice an increased degree of lethality in the M16's favor.[39] Even so, the compilers of the 2003 report specifically declared that they had heard no complaints about the M4's performance at ranges less than two hundred yards—which is about the outer perimeter of street combat.

The AK-47 gets grisly PR about having killed more people than any other gun—mostly a result of its widespread use by psychopathic regimes. But interestingly, in terms of deadliness the AK-47 suffers by way of comparison with the M4. Testing and unfortunate experience show that the AK's bullet, after entering human tissue, tends to take a straight path. It pushes in headfirst to a depth as great as ten inches, and for that reason many pass through the body in one piece, leaving behind less severe wounds. When hitting, say, the abdomen, an AK-47 projectile will cause the same "minimal" degree of disruption as a handgun bullet.

By way of contrast, an M4/M16 bullet, shot into the abdomen at less than two hundred yards, will penetrate headfirst for about 4.7 inches, then yaw to 90 degrees before breaking in half. The pointed half remains in one piece, but the base is torn into shards that perforate tissue in many places. This fragmentation and the yawing enhance lethality by creating more traumatic internal wounding.[40]

Bullet fragmentation combined with marksmanship produces a far more favorable kill ratio than the "spray-and-pray" tactics employed by untrained, undisciplined insurgents, who eventually realized in Iraq that directly confronting U.S. troops amounted to an involuntary suicide mission. Hence the shift toward Improvised Explosive Devices (IEDs) to inflict American casualties instead of risking close-quarters combat using their AKs.

Between September 2003 and October 2004, attacks on U.S. forces were roughly balanced between IEDs, direct fire, and indirect fire (mortars, generally). By 2005 insurgents were employing more IEDs. During that year, out of 674 combat deaths, 415 were caused by IEDs, or 61.6 percent. IEDs also inflicted 4,256 of the 5,941 wounded, or 71.6 percent.[41]

Killing and crippling were more certain with these terror bombs than with an AK-47. Since then the overall IED casualty rate has declined—as of April 2008, 1,682 U.S. soldiers have been killed by IEDs out of a total of 4,052 fatalities—to 41.5 percent (though there are monthly spikes), mostly as a result of increasingly effective suppression of enemy activity, improved IED detection, and the greater role played by Iraqi military and police forces.[42]

As American soldiers have come to realize in the centuries since the War of Independence, a successful army relies on warriors who are able to individually control their shooting while themselves serving in a disciplined unit observing the laws of war. The myriad attempts to forge *specifically American* soldiers en masse into *either* musket-wielding automatons *or* independently minded riflemen have all failed. Today, as a result, U.S. combat troops are the distant heirs of George Washington's beloved Virginia Regiment, which benefited as a fighting force from its colonel's dual emphasis on riflemen's skill and musketmen's drill. As the 2003 weapons report made clear, the M4 derives its lethality from the ability of its wielders to place controlled shots into the enemy's vital regions. Though there are times when maximum, unaimed suppressive fire using machine guns and artillery is warranted or necessary, the key to American success remains, as ever, a cadre of well-trained, self-motivated riflemen who keep their heads while their foes lose theirs amid the thousands of rounds wastefully shot into the air, brick, and dirt.

It could therefore be counted as an encouraging sign when, in February 2007, Brigadier General Terry Wolff, commander of the Military Assistance Training Team in Baghdad, announced that the United States would be issuing M16s and M4s to Iraqi army units to replace their AK-47s and would take them through a marksmanship course.[43]

They needed it. The Iraqi army suffered (and except among elite units, continues to suffer to an extent) from poor morale and discipline problems, mostly the by-product of decades of dreadful conscript practice, bad leadership, and worse training. These three elements are almost invariably integral to any military/paramilitary force armed with AK-47s, the genuine junk weapon of our time.[44] The intention now became to replace every single one of their AK-47s with an M16 or M4—some 165,000 of them.[45]

There were a few hiccups when recruits first received them: a U.S. trainer, according to the *Wall Street Journal,* "shook his head as several Iraqis gripped the M-16s as if they were AK-47s, causing their bullets to miss their targets by a long shot. 'This is not a Kalashnikov!' he shouted, using the nickname for an AK-47. 'You're using a precision weapon.'" Nevertheless, after they practiced some more, Master Sergeant Varon Martinez noticed that his once-raw apprentices began to act more like professional soldiers in firefights. "I saw them crouch on one knee and aim the weapon rather than just spraying," he told the *Journal.* "It was like, 'Wait. If I aim I can actually hit something. I don't need to just spray.' "[46]

The training does not always "take," perhaps because recruits tend to receive far less of it than do their American counterparts: the *New York Times* observed of recent streetfighting that "one big problem is that the Iraqi troops have responded to militia gunfire with such intense fusillades that the soldiers have endangered civilians, American soldiers and even their own forces." The lack of fire control prompted one American officer to radio in, "They are lighting up everything," before pleading, "Tell them to knock it off.")[47]

Ironically, while this was happening, Senator Tom Coburn's letter questioning whether the army's *own* procurement of M4s was having an effect. In July 2007 the army announced that it had "agreed to conduct testing of four carbine designs in an extreme dust environment."[48]

The competition was back on. Pitted against Colt's M4 would be the Heckler & Koch HK416, FN Herstal's SCAR, and—resurrected from the dead—the H&K also-ran XM8. In November, after twenty-five hours' exposure to heavy dust conditions designed to induce jamming and the firing of six thousand rounds through each rifle (there were ten of each model, making for a 60,000-round test) to simulate extreme combat and measure reliability, the results were in.

First place went to the XM8. Second place went to the SCAR. Third place went to the HK416. And in last place was . . . the M4.

It was, on the face of it, a terrible embarrassment for Colt and the army. The XM8 had suffered just 127 stoppages, the SCAR, 226, the HK416, 233, and the M4, a disastrous 882. Of the latter, 643 had been weapons-related (such as ejection and extraction failures) and 239 owing to problems with the magazines.[49] Yet all but nineteen stoppages— which would have required a skilled armorer to repair them if they had occurred in the field—were classed as being merely "minor" in character, which means they needed only about ten seconds to clear. By way of comparison, the XM8 suffered 11 major stoppages and 116 minor ones. Given that the SCAR catastrophically failed 16 times and the HK416 14 times, the M4's major-malfunction total of 19, while higher, was not way out of line.[50]

On the other hand, the M4 had jammed once in every 68 rounds compared to the XM8's once in 472. Since an M4 magazine holds 30 cartridges, the gunners were having to clear the rifle every third magazine or so. These tests were conducted under extreme conditions, however; active-duty soldiers were hardly likely to experience problems to anywhere near the same degree. But still, the apparent disparity between XM8 and M4 performance was troubling.

At base, nevertheless, the test proved nothing decisively one way or another. Even the M4's poor showing was not clear-cut, since earlier that summer an almost identical test comparing only M4s and M16s had resulted in just 307 stoppages for the carbine.[51] Eleven of them were classed as major ones, the same number later suffered by the first-place XM8. The sudden jump in total stoppages made it all the more likely that the winter round of tests had become inadvertently corrupted or that a vital factor had been overlooked. Indeed, the army confirmed that "the tests were undertaken at different times of the year; they were taken under different humidity conditions—it's not a humidity controlled chamber; the tests were undertaken by different crews."[52] There were also unverified rumors that the M4s and HK416s used in the tests had been off-the-shelf guns, whereas the XM8s and SCARs had been handcrafted to perfection, an advantage that would certainly have goosed the results.[53]

Even so, two concrete conclusions did suggest themselves. As the M4 had been the only rifle out of the four not to rely on the gas-piston design, and considering that Colt had already claimed it had such a system in the works, it would make sense for the army to authorize a modification in coming years. The other was that a significant proportion of the M4 stoppages could be eliminated by simply altering the magazine design. More than a quarter of them had been caused by weak springs and feeding problems. Accordingly, army officials soon announced that they were considering upgrading the M4's magazines.[54]

Those hoping that the test results would force the army to switch over from the M4 to an entirely new rifle—the HK416 or SCAR, perhaps— were bound to be disappointed. The army is irretrievably committed to the M4, not least owing to the practical difficulties of shifting tracks while a war is going on and M4s are streaming in ever greater numbers to deployed troops. In the past two years alone, 221,000 of them have been made (at a cost of $300 million), and the Pentagon has ordered another 136,000, worth $230 million.[55] Whether Colt will forever be the sole supplier is a different question: its exclusive production contract ends in June 2009, after which its rivals may compete for the business.

Another factor militating against the army adopting the SCAR or the HK416 is that both types of weapon were developed for use by Special Operations units accustomed to acquiring and customizing their own equipment. Accordingly, the quantities available are severely limited. "They can buy 50; we have to buy 50,000," said an army official. "We are wise to watch them and follow them and see what we can learn from them, but that doesn't mean that every time they get a new pair of boots that we need to get a new pair of boots." The number of SCARs contracted for by SOCOM might be as low as 20,000—a far cry and a huge production-straining jump from the 800,000-plus army-standard rifles that would be required.[56]

What is clear is that we are reaching the beginning of the end of the road in terms of current rifle development. It is a road upon which we have been traveling ever since eighteenth-century Pennsylvanian gunmakers broke free of the musket and perfected the flintlock rifle, and while breech-loaders, metallic cartridges, repeaters, and semiautomatics have speeded our way, the amber light is flashing up ahead.

At their broadest level, the summer and winter 2007 tests demonstrated that the qualitative, statistical, and operational differences among the four top-of-the-line rifles are but minute. One can tweak current firearm and projectile technology to enhance performance only so many ways before the marginal costs begin exceeding the marginal gains. The army is confronting the dilemma by relying on the M4 to tide things over until the arrival of a quantum technological breakthrough. "We think that somewhere around 2010, we should have enough insight into future technologies to take us in a direction we want to go for the next generation of small arms," said Colonel Robert Radcliffe, director of the Infantry Center's Directorate of Combat Developments at Fort Benning, Georgia.[57] What this breakthrough might consist of is an intriguing question, though almost certainly light, strong new materials (such as advanced polymers) and a great deal of computing power will be integrated into the weapon.

Before banking on 2010 as the date of the Great Leap Forward, we should cautiously remember the existence of the Pentagon's mass grave of failed futuristic projects: among others, the Special Project Individual Weapon (SPIW) program of the 1960s and the Advanced Combat Rifle scheme of the late 1980s both tried to conceive a flechette-firing rifle. And let us not forget the most recent enterprise, the Objective Individual Combat Weapon (OICW), which birthed the XM29.

Perhaps it will happen this time, perhaps it will not, but the likelihood is that for some years to come the rifle of the future will be the rifle of the past.

Note on Sources

As I wrote this book, the number of books and articles listed in the bibliography rose remorselessly. Between cataloguing primary sources, secondary volumes, scholarly articles, historical newspapers, old magazine pieces, government reports, and technical manuals I eventually hit the 40-page mark in Microsoft Word. Though subsequently winnowed down for publication, the bibliography remained resolutely long and we decided to excise it from the manuscript and make it freely available and downloadable as a PDF on my website:

www.alexrose.com

Endnotes, however, remain in place and the first mention of a given work in each chapter is cited in full–so if you're hankering to know the source of a quotation or fact you'll be able to find it without having to consult the bibliography.

Notes

Chapter 1

1. "[I am] in so grave . . . a mood [that] I fancy the skill of this gentleman's [Peale] pencil will be put to it in describing to the world what manner of man I am." Washington to Jonathan Boucher, May 21, 1772, quoted in D. S. Freeman, *George Washington: A Biography* (New York: Scribner's, 1948–57), p. 3:292. Unless otherwise noted, as in this case, references to Washington's correspondence pertain to letters kept in the Library of Congress.

2. This was the second day of a three-day exercise. On May 20 Washington had sat "to have my picture drawn," and the morning of May 22 he would be occupied having "my face" finished. See his entries in D. Jackson and D. Twohig, eds., *The Diaries of George Washington* (Charlottesville: University Press of Virginia, 1976–79), pp. 3:108–9.

3. On the artist, see J. J. Ellis's "Charles Willson Peale: Portrait of the American Artist as Virtuous Entrepreneur," in Ellis, *After the Revolution: Profiles of Early American Culture* (New York: W. W. Norton, 2002), pp. 41–71. Also C. C. Sellers, "Charles Willson Peale's Portraits of Washington," *Metropolitan Museum of Art Bulletin* 9, no. 6 (1951), pp. 147–55.

4. Freeman, *George Washington*, 3, p. 292. M. F. Perry, "Firearms of the First President," *American Rifleman* 104, no. 2 (1956), p. 34, says it was a musket but concedes that "identification is difficult." Given Washington's experience with rifles on the frontier and his exacting specifications—in the picture the weapon, with its trumpet-shaped ramrod and brass thimbles, certainly looks customized—it seems much more likely to me that it is a privately commissioned rifle and not a standard "military musket" (as Perry claims). Regarding the preferences of other military worthies of the time, compare a picture of General John Sullivan from about 1777. He's almost identically dressed, yet is wielding a spontoon, a type of halberd. He wears no firearms at all. See the picture in B. Dean, "On American Polearms, Especially Those in the Metropolitan Museum of Art," *Metropolitan Museum Studies* 1, no. 1 (1928), p. 35.

5. Jackson and Twohig, *Diaries of Washington,* p. 2:219, entry for March 5, 1770; Perry, "Firearms of the First President," p. 32; M. L. Brown, *Firearms in Colonial America* (Washington, D.C.: Smithsonian Institution Press, 1980), pp. 310, 324. Information on John Jost (Yost) is sparse. In 1785 a Caspar Jost—a relative, presumably—was working as a gunsmith in Lebanon, in Dauphin County, Pennsylvania. See H. J. Kauffman, *The Pennsylvania-Kentucky Rifle* (Harrisburg, Pa.: Stackpole, 1960), p. 272, but for a "John Yost," see p. 365.

6. The first officers to carry rifles into battle were apparently those of the British 95th Regiment during the Napoleonic Wars. See M. Urban, *Rifles: Six Years with Wellington's Legendary Sharpshooters* (London: Faber & Faber, 2003), p. 31.

7. John Adams to Abigail Adams, June 17, 1775, in C. F. Adams, ed., *Familiar Letters of John Adams and His Wife Abigail Adams During the Revolution, with a Memoir of Mrs. Adams* (1875; reprint, Freeport, N.Y.: Books for Libraries Press, 1970), pp. 65–66. Further, the

rifle "was little known in New England, and it may be said to have been confined to Pennsylvania and the colonies south, particularly to the western or border regions." See J.W.Wright, "The Rifle in the American Revolution," *American Historical Review* 29, no. 2 (1924), p. 294.

8. R. Held, *The Age of Firearms:An Illustrated History* (NewYork: Harper & Brothers, 1957), pp. 24–25.

9. Brown, *Firearms in Colonial America*, pp. 40–41.

10. G. Raudzens, "Outfighting or Outpopulating? Main Reasons for Early Colonial Conquests, 1493–1788," in Raudzens, ed., *Technology, Disease and Colonial Conquests, Sixteenth to Eighteenth Centuries: Essays Reappraising the Guns and Germs Theories* (Leiden [The Netherlands]: Brill, 2001), p. 41, curiously asserts that the Spaniards "seem to have had a rather higher proportion of advanced technology guns than was common in European armies in the 1490s." However, not only did the newcomers have relatively few firearms, but the ones they did have were primitive by European standards.

11. K. Hearn, "First Known Gunshot Victim in Americas Discovered," *National Geographic News,* June 19, 2007; J. N.Wilford, "Earliest GunshotVictim in NewWorld Is Reported," *NewYork Times,* June 20, 2007, p. A15.

12. See, for instance, D. Cahill, "The Long Conquest: Collaboration by Native Andean Elites in the Colonial System, 1532–1825," in Raudzens, *Technology, Disease and Colonial Conquests*, pp. 85–126.

13. H. P. Biggar, ed., *The Works of Samuel de Champlain* (Toronto: Champlain Society, 1922–36), pp. 2:97–100.

14. P. M. Malone, "Changing Military Technology Among the Indians of Southern New England, 1600–1677," *American Quarterly* 25, no. 1 (1973), p. 52; A. Starkey, "Conflict and Synthesis: Frontier Warfare in North America, 1513–1815," in G. Raudzens, *Technology, Disease and Colonial Conquests*, p. 64.

15. W. Bradford, *Of Plymouth Plantation, 1620–1647*, ed. S. E. Morison (NewYork: Alfred A. Knopf, 1963), p. 207.

16. W. Byrd, "History of the Dividing Line" (1728), in *TheWritings of ColonelWilliam Byrd of Westover inVirginia, Esq.*, ed. J. S. Bassett, (NewYork: Doubleday, Page & Co., 1901), pp. 97–98.

17. Bradford, *Of Plymouth Plantation*, p. 56.

18. Malone, "Changing MilitaryTechnology," pp. 53–57.

19. Quoted in C. P. Russell, *Firearms,Traps, and Tools of the Mountain Men* (NewYork: Alfred A. Knopf, 1967), p. 40, cited in L. A. Garavaglia and C. G. Worman, *Firearms of the American West (1803–1865, 1866–1894)* (1984; reprint, Niwot: University Press of Colorado, 1997–98), pp. 1:7–9.

20. R. F. Rosenberger and C. Kaufmann, *The Longrifles ofWestern Pennsylvania:Allegheny and Westmoreland Counties* (Pittsburgh: University of Pittsburgh Press, 1993), p. xx.

21. Quoted in Malone, "Changing MilitaryTechnology," p. 61.

22. S. L. Norman, *Guncotton to Smokeless Powder: The Development of Nitrocellulose as a Military Explosive, 1845–1929* (Unpub. Ph.D. diss., Brown University, 1988), pp. 23–25. See also esp. J. Leander Bishop, E. T. Freedley, and E.Young, *A History of Manufactures from 1608 to 1860* (Philadelphia: Edward Young & Co., 1864), p. 2:23n1; and A. P. Van Gelder and H. Schlatter, *History of the Explosives Industry in America* (New York: Columbia University Press, 1927), pp. 14–15, 29–30.

23. Van Gelder and Schlatter, *History of the Explosives Industry in America*, pp. 32–36.

24. See, for example, Washington's letter to Francis Fauquier, December 2, 1758, which urged "that a trade with the Indians should be upon such terms, and transacted by men of such principles, as would at the same time turn out to the reciprocal advantage of the colony and the Indians, and which would effectually remove those bad impressions that the Indians received from the conduct of a set of rascally fellows, divested of all faith and honor, and give us such an early opportunity of establishing an interest with them, as

would be productive of the most beneficial consequences, by getting a large share of the fur-trade." See also Kah-Ge-Ga-Gah-Bouh ("A Chief of the Ojibwa Nation"), "The American Indians," *American Whig Review* 9, no. 18 (1849), esp. p. 634.

25. Quoted in J. P. Reid, *A Better Kind of Hatchet* (University Park: Pennsylvania State University Press, 1976), pp. 194–96.

26. Quoted ibid., p. 195.

27. The best modern introduction to this subject is K. E. Holland Braund, *Deerskins and Duffels: The Creek Indian Trade with Anglo-America, 1685–1815* (Lincoln: University of Nebraska Press, 1993).

28. J. Underhill, "Newes from America; or, a New and Experimentall Discoverie . . ." (1638), in C. Orr, ed., *History of the Pequot War* . . . (Cleveland, Ohio: Helman-Taylor, 1897), p. 82.

29. R. Williams, "An Helpe to the Native Language of That Part of America Called New-England," in *The Complete Writings of Roger Williams*, ed. J. H. Trumbull (New York: Russell & Russell, 1963), p. 1:204. By way of comparison, between 1689 and 1713 about five percent of all able-bodied males in Massachusetts died fighting other Europeans; in a single year, 1690, around one thousand perished. Over the course of the 1740s one in five Massachusetts men between the ages of 18 and 40 died in battle. See J. Ferling, "The New England Soldier: A Study in Changing Attitudes," *American Quarterly* 33, no. 1 (1981), p. 34.

30. D. K. Richter, "War and Culture: The Iroquois Experience," in P. C. Mancall and J. H. Merrell, eds., *American Encounters,* 2d ed. (New York: Routledge, 2007), pp. 432–33.

31. "It is not for the sake of tribute . . . that they make war," remarked Cadwallader Colden, referring to the Five Nations (the Iroquois Confederacy, composed of the Seneca, Cayuga, Onondaga, Oneida, and Mohawk), "but from the notions of glory, which they have ever most strongly imprinted on their minds." Quoted in Richter, "War and Culture," p. 429. Roger Williams ascribed the outbreak of their wars to "mocking between their great ones" or "passion." See Williams, "Helpe to the Native Language," pp. 1:200–202.

32. J. Lawson, *The History of Carolina* . . . (London: T. Warner, 1718), p. 199.

33. Richter, "War and Culture," pp. 435–36. See also D. Gookin, *Historical Collections of the Indians in England* . . . (1674; reprint, New York: Arno Press, 1972), pp. 21–22.

34. Richter, "War and Culture," p. 434. See also J. Winthrop, *Winthrop's Journal: "History of New England,"* ed. J. K. Hosmer (New York: Charles Scribner's Sons, 1908), p. 2:80, on the trade in firearms.

35. Gookin, *Historical Collections of the Indians,* p. 27.

36. Richter, "War and Culture," pp. 436–37.

37. A good introduction to this broad subject is W. E. Lee, "Peace Chiefs and Blood Revenge: Patterns of Restraint in Native American Warfare, 1500–1800," *Journal of Military History* 71 (2007), no. 3, pp. 701–41.

38. A. T. Vaughan, *New England Frontier: Puritans and Indians, 1620–1675* (Boston: Little, Brown, 1965), p. 133.

39. A. J. Hirsch, "The Collision of Military Cultures in Seventeenth-Century New England," *Journal of American History* 74, no. 4 (1988), p. 1201.

40. See Vaughan, *New England Frontier,* p. 20.

41. On praying towns and English attempts at assimilation, see J. Axtell, "The English Colonial Impact on Indian Culture," and "The Indian Impact on English Colonial Culture," both in Axtell, *The European and the Indian: Essays in the Ethnohistory of Colonial North America* (New York: Oxford University Press, 1981).

42. C. Mather, *Souldiers Counselled and Comforted* . . . (Boston: Samuel Green, 1689), p. 28.

43. J. Ferling, "The New England Soldier: A Study in Changing Perceptions," *American Quarterly* 33, no. 1 (1981), p. 30.

44. H. St. J. de Crèvecoeur, "What Is an American?" in *Letters from an American Farmer and Sketches of Eighteenth-Century America,* ed. A. E. Stone (New York: Penguin, 1981), p. 72.

45. Axtell, "Indian Impact on English Colonial Culture," pp. 277–78.

46. Ibid.

47. Crèvecoeur, "What Is an American?" pp. 84–6.

48. R. W. Gilbert, *A Picture of the Pennsylvania Germans* (Gettysburg: Pennsylvania Historical Association, 1947), pp. 2–3.

49. A. D. Graeff, "The Pennsylvania Germans as Soldiers," in R. Wood, ed., *The Pennsylvania Germans* (Princeton, N.J.: Princeton University Press, 1942), p. 227.

50. Gilbert, *Picture of Pennsylvania Germans,* p. 4. On Franklin, see A. D. Graeff, "Pennsylvania, Colonial Melting Pot," in Wood, *Pennsylvania Germans,* p. 8.

51. Quoted in Graeff, "Pennsylvania, Colonial Melting Pot," p. 16.

52. Wright, "Rifle in American Revolution," p. 294; W. W. Greener, *The Gun and Its Development* (London: Cassell & Co., 9th ed., 1910, reprinted The Lyons Press, Guilford, Conn., 2002), pp. 620–26.; C. W. Sawyer, *Firearms in American History* (Boston: 3 vols. c. 1910–1939), pp. 2:32–38; Brown, *Firearms in Colonial America,* pp. 30, 262–63. J. G. W. Dillin, *The Kentucky Rifle: A Study of the Origins . . .* (Washington, D.C.: National Rifle Association of America, 1924), p. 15, claims that greased patches were introduced in America in the eighteenth century, but most authorities believe they were used in Germany for some time before that. See, for instance, B. W. Muir, "The Father of the Kentucky Rifle," *American Rifleman* 119 (January 1971), p. 76, who calls it a "myth."

53. A. Finkelstein, *The Grammar of Profit: The Price Revolution in Intellectual Context* (Boston: Brill, 2006).

54. Brown, *Firearms in Colonial America,* p. 28.

55. An introduction to the Jäger rifle's early years is Muir, "Father of the Kentucky Rifle," pp. 30, 75–79; also see Brown, *Firearms in Colonial America,* pp. 260–61.

56. There are a few isolated examples of rifle ownership in Virginia before the German emigration. When Ralph Wormeley died in 1702, he left behind twenty-one guns, including a "Rifile Gun," while Robert Spring (d. 1683) owned a "Screw Gun." Archaeologists have even discovered a rifle barrel abandoned sometime before 1640, making it probably the oldest in North America. H. B. Gill, *The Gunsmith in Colonial Virginia* (Williamsburg and Charlottesville: Colonial Williamsburg Foundation/University Press of Virginia, 1974), pp. 19–20.

57. Dillin, *Kentucky Rifle,* pp. 11–12, 17–18; Graeff, "Pennsylvania Germans as Soldiers," p. 230.

58. On the derivation of "Kentucky rifle," see (for the Daniel Boone thesis) Dillin, *Kentucky Rifle,* p. 1; for the "Hunters of Kentucky" thesis, see Kauffman's preface in *Pennsylvania-Kentucky Rifle,* and Rosenberger and Kaufmann, *Longrifles of Western Pennsylvania,* p. xiii. For the suggestion that "Kentucky rifle" was passed down orally, see Brown, *Firearms in Colonial America,* p. 264.

59. On the timing of the Jäger-Kentucky metamorphosis, see Kauffman, *Pennsylvania-Kentucky Rifle,* p. 8; Brown, *Firearms in Colonial America,* p. 264. Though Kauffman and Brown diverge on the exact date of certain developments, they agree that 1725 was the key year.

60. Rosenberger and Kaufmann, *Longrifles of Western Pennsylvania,* p. xvi.

61. The exact number of balls one could extract from a pound varied. I've used the most common figures, but authorities differ. For instance, Dillin, *Kentucky Rifle,* p. 36, says that a pound of lead sufficed for 16 balls for a .70 and 48 for a .45. Nevertheless, the difference in most cases between American and German rifles seems to have been a factor of three. See also Wright, "Rifle in American Revolution," p. 294; Sawyer, *Firearms in American History,* pp. 2:32–38.

62. G. Hanger, *Colonel George Hanger, to all sportsmen, and particularly to farmers and game-keepers . . .* (London: G. Hanger, 1814), pp. 125, 141–43.

63. Brown, *Firearms in Colonial America,* p. 268.

64. Dillin, *Kentucky Rifle,* pp. 59–60.

65. Brown, *Firearms in Colonial America,* p. 268.

66. C. W. Sawyer, *Our Rifles* (Boston: Williams, 1946), p. 13. Sawyer claims that it was Daniel Boone, but it was Crockett who was famous for naming his rifles Betsey. I have accordingly amended Sawyer but kept the anecdote. See, for instance, B. Ball, "The Most Famous Rifle of Texas! Recreating Colonel Crockett's rifle at the Battle of the Alamo," *Guns Magazine,* January 2004. (Ball spells it "Betsy," though Crockett, in his memoirs, says "Betsey." See *Life of Col. David Crockett, written by himself . . .* (Philadelphia: G. G. Evans, 1860).

67. J. Doddridge, *Notes on the Settlement and Indian Wars of the Western Parts of Virginia and Pennsylvania from 1763 to 1783, inclusive . . .* (1824; reprint Pittsburgh: J. S. Ritenour & W. T. Lindsey, 1912), pp. 123–24. Colonial Americans did not regard offhand shooting as "as any trial of the value of a gun; nor, indeed, as much of a test of the skill of a marksman." Modern attitudes are less strident. D. Anderson, "Offhand Shooting: A Rifleman's Primary Skill," *Guns Magazine* (July 2003), believes that "when you can shoot well offhand, you can almost certainly shoot very well from more stable positions."

68. Dillin, *Kentucky Rifle,* pp. 69–71. Successive experiments have confirmed the Kentucky's relative accuracy. In 1953 Cleves Howell Jr. found that a Jäger rifle circa 1730—one very similar to an early Kentucky—actually *outperformed* a modern .30-30 lever-action carbine at ranges of 50 and 100 yards. See Muir, "Father of Kentucky Rifle," p. 76.

69. B. P. Hughes, *Firepower: Weapons Effectiveness on the Battlefield, 1630–1850* (Staplehurst, U.K.: Spellmount, 1997), p. 59.

70. B. R. Lewis, *Small Arms and Ammunition in the United States Service* (Washington, D.C.: Smithsonian Institution, 1956), p. 90. For the British test, see J. W. Wright, "Some Notes on the Continental Army," *William and Mary Quarterly,* 2d ser., 11, no. 2 (1931), p. 88.

71. Some of the "Germans" in Lancaster were actually former French Huguenots, in particular the Ferree and LeFevre families, the survivors having escaped France after the revocation of the Edict of Nantes (1685). They moved to the Black Forest, near the Grand Duchy of Baden, and intermarried. The two families emigrated together and arrived in New York on December 31, 1708. They settled in Lancaster County in the fall of 1712. During their decades in Germany, Huguenots had learned their hosts' language and mingled easily with the other Germans in Lancaster. Dillin, *Kentucky Rifle,* pp. 19–22.

72. Kauffman, *Pennsylvania-Kentucky Rifle,* pp. 16–17.

73. Gill, *Gunsmith in Colonial Virginia,* pp. 18–19, 28–30.

74. Rosenberger and Kaufmann, *Longrifles of Western Pennsylvania,* p. xvii.

75. See Kauffman, *Pennsylvania-Kentucky Rifle,* p. 152.

76. Dillin, *Kentucky Rifle,* p. 23.

77. Gill, *Gunsmith in Colonial America,* pp. 19, 28–30.

78. Kauffman, *Pennsylvania-Kentucky Rifle,* p. 146.

79. Dillin, *Kentucky Rifle,* p. 25.

80. Cited in Brown, *Firearms in Colonial America,* p. 336.

81. M. Edgar, *Ten Years in Upper Canada in Peace and War, 1805–1815 . . .* (Toronto: William Briggs, 1890), p. 378.

82. Quoted in J. B. Whisker, *Arms Makers of Colonial America* (Selinsgrove, Pa.: Susquehanna University Press, 1992), p. 22.

83. On Chouteau, see Dillin, *Kentucky Rifle,* p. 89; on the Chickasaws, see Brown, *Firearms in Colonial America,* pp. 180, 286.

84. All cited in Whisker, *Arms Makers of Colonial America,* p. 22.

85. Rosenberger and Kaufmann, *Longrifles of Western Pennsylvania,* pp. xix–xx.

86. Brown, *Firearms in Colonial America,* p. 283; C. P. Russell, *Guns on the Early Frontiers . . .* (Lincoln/London: University of Nebraska Press, 1957), pp. 16–49.

87. Brown, *Firearms in Colonial America,* p. 284.

88. See, for instance, the photo and technical notes of a trade fusil, in Brown, *Firearms in Colonial America,* p. 282.

89. Ibid., p. 283.

90. "Colonel Bradstreet's thoughts on Indian affairs," December 4, 1764, in E. B. O'Callaghan et al., eds., *Documents Relative to the Colonial History of the State of New York, Procured in Holland, England, and France.* 15 vols. Albany, NY: Weed, Parsons, 1856–57. p. 7:692.

91. P. Haythornthwaite, *British Rifleman, 1797–1815* (Oxford [U.K.]: Osprey, 2002), p. 6.

92. "Victory and conquest did for a long time seem to stand neuter, and our condition and warfare not much unlike the conflict between Israel and Amelek in the Wilderness, nor can it be denied but that our enemies for a time had great success in their outrages, Providence as it were seeming to offer them opportunities of doing us much mischief, when we could find none of taking just revenge." W. Hubbard, *History of the Indian Wars in New England from the First Settlement to the Termination of the War with King Philip, in 1677,* ed. S. G. Drake (1677; reprint New York: Burt Franklin, 1971), pp. 2:259–60.

93. Cotton Mather, "Decennium Luctuosum: An History of Remarkable Occurrences . . . ," in C. H. Lincoln, ed., *Narratives of the Indian Wars, 1675–1699* (New York: Charles Scribner's Sons, 1913), p. 203.

94. Hubbard, *History of Indian Wars,* pp. 2:259–60.

95. P. M. Malone, *The Skulking Way of War: Technology and Tactics Among the New England Indians* (Lanham, Md.: Madison Books, 2000), pp. 21–22.

96. Forbes to Pitt, October 20, 1758, in A. P. James, ed., *Writings of General John Forbes Relating to His Service in North America* (Menasha, Wis.: Collegiate Press, 1938), p. 239.

97. Malone, *Skulking Way of War,* pp. 21–22.

98. L. V. Eid, " 'A kind of Running Fight': Indian Battlefield Tactics in the Late Eighteenth Century," *Western Pennsylvania Historical Magazine* 71, no. 2 (1988), pp. 155–56.

99. On the Indian reluctance to attack fortified positions, see J. K. Mahon, "Anglo-American Methods of Indian Warfare, 1676–1794," *Mississippi Valley Historical Review* 45, no. 2 (1958), p. 263.

100. D. J. Beattie, "The Adaptation of the British Army to Wilderness Warfare, 1755–1763," in M. Ultee, ed., *Adapting to Conditions: War and Society in the Eighteenth Century* (University: University of Alabama Press, 1986), p. 78.

101. Mahon, "Anglo-American Methods," p. 257, notes that Indians were never interested in acquiring bayonets—for "only disciplined bodies of soldiers could make effective use of them."

102. Doddridge, *Notes on Settlement,* pp. 122–23.

103. Ibid.

104. Gookin, D., *An Historical Account of the Doings and Sufferings of the Christian Indians in New England in the Years 1675, 1676, 1677 . . .* (1677). In *Archaeologia Americana: Transactions and Collections of the American Antiquarian Society* (1836), p. 442.

105. Axtell, "Indian Impact on English Colonial Culture," pp. 297–98.

106. Forbes to Pitt, October 20, 1758, in James, *Writings of General John Forbes,* p. 239.

107. Gookin, *Historical Account of Doings and Sufferings,* p. 442.

108. Hubbard, *History of Indian Wars in New England,* p. 1:87.

109. B. Church, *The History of the Eastern Expeditions of 1689, 1690, 1692, 1696, and 1704 Against the Indians and French,* (ed. H. M. Dexter), (Boston: J. K. Wiggin & Wm. Parsons Lunt, 1867), p. 132–33.

110. B. Church, *The History of King Philip's War,* ed. H. M. Dexter (1716; reprint Boston: John Kimball Wiggin, 1865), pp. 122–23.

111. Ibid., pp. 32–33, 121, 145, 176.

112. Regarding the makeup of Braddock's forces, see F. T. Nichols, "The Organization of Braddock's Army," *William and Mary Quarterly,* 3rd ser., 4, no. 2 (1947), pp. 125–47.

113. For a detailed description and analysis of the battle, see S. Pargellis, "Braddock's Defeat," *American Historical Review* 41, no. 2 (1936), pp. 253–69. On the number of the French and Indians, see Washington to Robert Dinwiddie, July 18, 1755.

114. Quoted in D. Higginbotham, *George Washington and the American Military Tradition* (Athens: University of Georgia Press, 1985), p. 8.

115. Anonymous letter dated July 25, 1755, in S. Pargellis, ed., *Military Affairs in North America, 1748–1765* (New York: D. Appleton-Century, 1936), p. 115.

116. All the while, the Indians had "pursued us butchering as they came as far as the other side of the river; during our crossing, they shot many in the water . . . and dyed the stream with their blood, scalping and cutting them in a most barbarous manner." See "The Journal of a British Officer," in C. Hamilton, ed., *Braddock's Defeat* (Norman: University of Oklahoma Press, 1959), p. 52.

117. Washington to John Augustine, July 18, 1755.

118. Washington to Dinwiddie, July 18, 1755.

119. "Journal of Captain Robert Cholmley's batman," in Hamilton, ed., *Braddock's Defeat,* quoted in Higginbotham, *Washington and the American Military Tradition,* p. 140n3.

120. Washington to Dinwiddie, July 18, 1755.

121. Ball to Washington, September 5, 1755.

122. Pargellis, "Braddock's Defeat," p. 267. Even as Washington's hopes of preferment were dashed, Captain Robert Orme (another Braddock aide) was quietly told that his career was at an end, and he resigned from the army within the year, as probably did another, Robert Dobson, whose name quickly disappeared from the officers' lists. The name and reputation of Lieutenant Colonel Ralph Burton, a Braddock favorite, was under a cloud for years, but he eventually became a major general in 1762. Conversely, those who commanded the vanguard enjoyed promotions (e.g., Colonel Thomas Gage—soon in charge of the British forces in North America—Major Russell Chapman, and Captain John Rutherfurd) within the next two years. Clearly London felt the fault lay with Braddock rather than with the vanguard, and his aides paid the price. On Washington's appointment as colonel, see Higginbotham, *Washington and the American Military Tradition,* 14; regarding fencing, see Freeman, *George Washington*: p. 2:204.

123. Diary entry, September 9, 1759, in J. C. Webster, ed., *The Journal of Jeffery Amherst in America from 1758 to 1763* (Chicago: University of Chicago Press, 1931), pp. 166–67.

124. Washington, General Orders, January 8, 1756.

125. Washington to Virginia Regiment officers, July 29, 1757.

126. Washington to Dinwiddie, August 3, 1757, and H. G. Unger, *The Unexpected George Washington: His Private Life* (Hoboken, N.J.: John Wiley & Sons, 2006), p. 32.

127. Mercer to Washington, August 17, 1757.

128. Washington to Dinwiddie, April 16, 1756.

129. Washington to John Robinson, April 7, 1756.

130. "I expect you will take great pains to make your soldiers good marks-men by teaching them to shoot at targets," he instructed. Washington to Virginia Regiment officers, July 29, 1757.

131. "Extract of a letter from an officer in Winchester, in Virginia, dated April 13, 1756," *New-York Mercury,* May 3, 1756, p. 3.

132. See Kauffman, *Pennsylvania-Kentucky Rifle,* p. 234. The rifles were probably made in Lancaster County, Pennsylvania.

133. Mackay to Washington, August 27, 1754, and also Washington to Sinclair, May 6, 1792.

134. Interestingly, this would not be the last time, and was perhaps not even the first, that Washington had to search for his property. Owning between 35 and 65 firearms over the course of his long life, he had a talent for misplacing or losing his weapons. In March 1776, while inspecting the American defenses overlooking Boston, he must have dropped a pistol somewhere. Despite multiple inquiries, the expensive pistol was not returned, but a little more than a year later he "mislaid or possibly lost" a much-treasured brass-barreled pistol that had been given to him by the late General Braddock. (After more

than a century it turned up in the collection of the U.S. Cartridge Company of Lowell, Massachusetts.) Perry, "Firearms of the First President," pp. 32–33; Brown, *Firearms of Colonial America,* p. 322.

135. On the purchase from Ashbrook of a rifle, see entry of that date in George Mercer's ledger of disbursements, March 20, 1757; on Baker in general and his estate, see Gill, *Gunsmith in Colonial Virginia,* pp. 19, 48, 70–71; and on Baker's relationship with the Virginia Regiment, see Baker's June 14, 1758, entry in the Virginia Colonial Militia Disbursement Book. On the skill needed to bore a barrel, see Dillin, *Kentucky Rifle,* pp. 45–48.

136. See Mahon, "Anglo-American Methods of Indian Warfare," p. 266. J. F. C. Fuller, *British Light Infantry,* (London: Hutchinson & Co., 1925) remains the standard, if flawed, work. See also P. E. Russell, "Redcoats in the Wilderness: British Officers and Irregular Warfare in Europe and America, 1740 to 1760," *William and Mary Quarterly,* 3d ser., 35, no. 4 (1978), pp. 628–52.

137. Forbes to Bouquet, June 27, 1758, in James, ed., *Writings of General Forbes,* p. 125.

138. Washington to Bouquet, July 3, 1758; Washington to Bouquet, July 13, 1758; and Bouquet to Washington, July 14, 1758. See also Washington to Adam Stephen, July 16, 1758, and Washington to Francis Halkett, same date.

139. See Washington to Adam Stephen, July 16, 1758, and to Francis Halkett, same date.

140. Washington to Bouquet, July 16, 1758.

141. Washington to Forbes, October 8, 1758.

142. In the words of General John Forbes, who always made an exception for Washington. Quoted in Higginbotham, *Washington and the American Military Tradition,* p. 28.

Chapter 2

1. *Pennsylvania Packet,* No. 201, August 28, 1775, quoted in J. G. W. Dillin, *The Kentucky Rifle . . .* (Washington, D.C.: National Rifle Association of America, 1924), pp. 81–82.

2. "Extract of a Letter to a Gentleman in Philadelphia, Dated August 1, 1775," in P. Force, ed., *American Archives: Consisting of a Collection of Authentick Records, State Papers . . .* (Washington, D.C., 1848–53), 4th ser., III, col. 2.

3. Ibid.

4. I was tempted to dismiss the plank-between-the-legs story as hyperbole until I found a rare copy of the memoirs of General Victor Collot's *A Journey in North America* in the New York Public Library. According to the general (died 1805), who met the residents of the Ohio and Mississippi Valleys after a buffalo hunt, "they had drunk plentifully of whisky, and though the greater number were intoxicated, they were amusing themselves in firing with carabines [i.e., rifles] against a piece of plank tied to a tree, which is called shooting at a mark. The board, probably ill fastened, fell at each shot; one of the party at length losing patience, took it up, and placing it between his legs, called out to his companions, 'Now fire away!' which they did immediately, and always with the same address; whilst he who held the board exclaimed at each shot, 'It is in!' This amusement, which lasted two hours without any accident taking place, may appear incredible to those who are not acquainted with the singular skill of these men; but it is sufficient to observe that they will aim at the head of a squirrel or a turkey and very rarely miss." See V. Collot, *A Journey in North America . . .* (1826; reprint and trans. O. Lange, Florence, Italy, 1924), pp. 1:172–73.

5. *Pennsylvania Packet,* no. 201, August 28, 1775, quoted in Dillin, *Kentucky Rifle,* p. 82.

6. Ibid.; see also "Extract of Letter to Gentleman," in Force, *American Archives,* III, col. 2.

7. See his entry in L. Edward Purcell, ed., *Who Was Who in the American Revolution* (New York: Facts on File, 1993). Thomas Jefferson alludes to an accusation against Cresap in his *Notes on the State of Virginia* (Richmond: J. W. Randolph, 1853), p. 68, but of this par-

ticular crime Cresap is today generally regarded as being (in Purcell's careful words) "relatively innocent." There is a lengthy appendix on the Cresap affair printed in the 1853 edition, "Relative to the Murder of Logan's family," no. 4, pp. 240–69.

8. W. C. Ford et al., eds., *Journal of the Continental Congress, 1774–1789* (Washington, D.C., 1904–37), p. 2:89.

9. "Extract of Letter to Gentleman," in Force, *American Archives,* III, col. 2. "All who go out to war under him do not only pay the most willing obedience to him as their commander, but in every instance of distress look up to him as their friend or father. A great part of his time was spent in listening to and relieving their wants, without any apparent sense of fatigue and trouble."

10. D. Higginbotham, *Daniel Morgan, Revolutionary Rifleman* (Chapel Hill: University of North Carolina Press, 1961), p. 23.

11. Leaving his family behind, Harrower shipped out to America on January 26, 1774, and died of an unknown disease in 1776. Harrower to James Craigie, August 28, 1775, printed in J. Harrower, "Diary of John Harrower, 1773–1776," *American Historical Review* 6, no. 1 (1900), p. 100.

12. H. L. Peterson, *Arms and Armor in Colonial America, 1526–1783* (Harrisburg, Pa.: Stackpole, 1956), p. 196. There is some dissension on the number of companies authorized. W. F. Dunaway, *The Scots-Irish of Colonial Pennsylvania* (Chapel Hill: University of North Carolina Press, 1944), pp. 160–61, says nine were raised in Pennsylvania. Thus in early 1776 the new Eighth Virginia Regiment was reserved for German-Americans from the outlying Shenandoah Valley, and it was, uniquely, permitted to raise as many rifle companies as it liked. R. K. Wright, *The Continental Army* (Washington, D.C.: Center of Military History, 1983), p. 70.

13. See note 57, attached to George Washington's letter to Continental Congress, September 21, 1775. Also the *Pennsylvania Gazette,* August 23, 1775, printed a report dated August 10 noting that "Col. Thompson of the Pennsylvania regiment of riflemen, and a number of young gentlemen, volunteers, from Philadelphia, are arrived. Also Captain Morgan's company in three 3 weeks from Virginia, being 600 miles."

14. General orders, August 13, 1776.

15. Higginbotham, *Daniel Morgan,* p. 93.

16. J. W. Wright, "Some Notes on the Continental Army," *William & Mary Quarterly,* 2nd ser., 11, no. 2 (1931), p. 97; Wright, *Continental Army,* p. 125.

17. Wright, "Some Notes on the Continental Army," p. 93.

18. Ibid., pp. 86–91.

19. Higginbotham, *Daniel Morgan,* p. 93.

20. A breechclout was a yard of cloth about eight or nine inches wide, ornamented with embroidery on the ends, and worn around the waist. From this makeshift Indian belt, strings hung that held up the leggins. It answered several other purposes, according to a contemporary. "In cold weather the mittens, and sometimes the bullet-bag, occupied the front part of it. To the right side was suspended the tomahawk and to the left the scalping knife in its leather sheath." Hunting shirts, made of canvas or linen, were "a kind of loose frock, reaching half way down the thighs, with large sleeves, open before, and so wide as to lap over a foot or more when belted. . . . The bosom of this dress served as a wallet to hold a chunk of bread, cakes, jerk, tow for wiping the barrel of the rifle, or any other necessary for the hunter or warrior." See J. Doddridge, *Notes on the Settlement and Indian Wars of the Western Parts of Virginia and Pennsylvania from 1763 to 1783, inclusive . . .* (1824; reprint (Pittsburgh: J. S. Ritenour and W. T. Lindsey, 1912), pp. 92–93. John Trumbull, who would later paint the famous picture *The Surrender of General John Burgoyne at Saratoga* (with Morgan featuring prominently at center right) described the "Virginia rifle-men" who arrived in Boston as wearing "an elegant loose dress reaching to the middle of the thigh, ornamented with fringes in various parts, and meeting the pantaloons of the same material and color, fringed and ornamented in a corresponding style. The officers wore the usual crimson sash over this, and around the waist, the straps, belts, &c., were black, forming, in my opinion, a very picturesque and elegant, as well as useful,

dress. It cost a trifle; the soldier could wash it at any brook he passed; and however worn and ragged and dirty his other clothing might be, when this was thrown over it, he was in elegant uniform." Quoted in D. Meschutt, "Portraits of Daniel Morgan, Revolutionary War General," *American Art Journal* 17, no. 3 (1985), p. 40.

21. J. Thacher, *Military Journal of the American Revolution* . . . (Boston: Cottons & Barnard, 1827), p. 33.

22. John Adams to Abigail Adams, June 17, 1775, in C. F. Adams, ed., *Familiar Letters of John Adams and His Wife Abigail Adams During the Revolution* . . . (1875; reprint Freeport, N.Y.: Books for Libraries Press, 1970), p. 66; Thacher, *Military Journal of American Revolution,* pp. 33–34.

23. In the August 17–19, 1775, issue, in M. W. Willard, ed., *Letters on the American Revolution, 1774–1776* (Cambridge, Mass.: Houghton Mifflin, 1925), pp. 165–67.

24. See H. Niles, ed., *Principles and Acts of the Revolution in America* . . . (1822; reprint Baltimore, Md.: W. O. Miles, 1876), pp. 264–68.

25. *Pennsylvania Gazette,* August 5, 1775, quoted in Dillin, *Kentucky Rifle,* p. 84.

26. *Pennsylvania Gazette,* August 16, 1775, quoted ibid.

27. *Pennsylvania Packet,* August 14, 1775, quoted ibid.

28. *Pennsylvania Gazette,* August 21, 1775, quoted ibid.

29. See J. Lukens to J. Shaw, September 13, 1775, and "Observations by Benjamin Thompson (afterward Count Rumford)," November 4, 1775, both in H. S. Commager and R. B. Morris, eds., *The Spirit of 'Seventy-Six: The Story of the American Revolution as Told by Participants,* 3d ed. (New York: DaCapo Press, 1995), p. 156.

30. Quoted in G. F. Scheer and H. F. Rankin, *Rebels and Redcoats* (Cleveland/New York: World, 1957), p. 86.

31. Washington, Orders to Rifle Detachment, August 16, 1775.

32. Scheer and Rankin, *Rebels and Redcoats,* p. 86. See also General Thomas Gage's letter to Lord Dartmouth, September 20, 1775, noting that "there are many Irish in the rebels' army, particularly amongst the riflemen, brought here from the frontiers of Virginia and Pennsylvania, who take every opportunity to desert to us, notwithstanding the danger and difficulty of doing it," quoted in D. Bailey, *British Military Flintlock Rifles, 1740–1840* (Lincoln, R.I.: Andrew Mowbray, 2002), p. 21.

33. George Washington, General Orders, September 16, 1775.

34. Lukens to Shaw, September 13, 1775, printed in Commager and Morris, *Spirit of 'Seventy-Six,* pp. 156–57; Washington, General Orders, September 13, 1775; September 11, 1775. Lukens and the official records give slightly different numbers for the mutineers: Lukens says there were 32, the general orders, 33. I have used the latter.

35. See the account in "Extract of a Letter from Cambridge, Dated July 31," in *Pennsylvania Gazette,* August 9, 1775, p. 2.

36. Washington to Congress, April 22, 1776.

37. In *Remembrancer, 1776,* quoted in Higginbotham, *Daniel Morgan,* p. 39n15.

38. M.J.P.Y.R.G. du M. Lafayette, *Memoirs, Correspondence, and Manuscripts of General Lafayette* . . . (London: Saunders and Otley, 1837), p. 1:252.

39. H. B. Gill, *The Gunsmith in Colonial Virginia* (Williamsburg and Charlottesville: Colonial Williamsburg Foundation/University Press of Virginia, 1974), p. 34.

40. "Letter from Richard Peters to Maryland Committee of Safety," October 26, 1776, in Force, *American Archives,* 5th ser., II, col. 1247.

41. On the gunpowder mills of the time, see J. L. Bishop, E. T. Freedley and E. Young, *A History of Manufactures from 1608 to 1860* . . . (Philadelphia: Edward Young & Co., 1861–64), pp. 23–25n1.

42. N. L. York, "Clandestine Aid and the American Revolutionary War Effort: A Reexamination," *Military Affairs* 43, no. 1 (1979), pp. 26–30; on the number of muskets produced each month, see Wright, "Some Notes on Continental Army," p. 87.

43. J. E. Hicks and F. P. Todd, "United States Shoulder Arms, 1795–1935," *Journal of the American Military History Foundation,* 1, no. 2, pt. 2 (1937), pp. 75–79. Over the course of the War, while French-made imports were overwhelmingly Charlevilles, there were some muskets made as long before as 1718 and a few as recently as 1777. See Wright, "Some notes on Continental Army," p. 87. See also J. E. Hicks, *Notes on United States Ordnance: Small Arms, 1776 to 1940* (Mount Vernon, N.Y.: James E. Hicks, 1940), plate 2.

44. York, "Clandestine Aid and American Revolutionary War Effort," pp. 26–30. Regarding the vital importance of these military supplies to the victory at Saratoga, see O. W. Stephenson, "The Supply of Gunpowder in 1776," *American Historical Review* 30, no. 2 (1925), p. 281.

45. Wright, *Continental Army,* p. 68.

46. Thus General Muhlenberg told Washington that his "whole regiment consists at present of riflemen; and the campaign we made to the southward last summer fully convinced me that on a march, where soldiers are without tents, and their arms continually exposed to the weather, rifles are of little use. I would therefore request your Excellency to convert my regiment into musketry." Muhlenberg to Washington, February 23, 1777, in H. A. Muhlenberg, *The Life of Major-General Peter Muhlenberg of the Revolutionary Army* (Philadelphia: Carey and Hart, 1849), pp. 72–74.

47. G. Johnston (Washington's aide-de-camp) to Muhlenberg, March 9, 1777, in Muhlenberg, *Life of Peter Muhlenberg,* p. 354.

48. Washington, General Orders, June 13, 1777. See also Wright, *Continental Army,* p. 108; Higginbotham, *Daniel Morgan,* pp. 55–57.

49. Washington to Morgan, June 13, 1777.

50. Washington to Morgan, August 16, 1777.

51. On Gates at Monongahela, see G. A. Billias, "Horatio Gates: Professional Soldier," in Billias, ed., *George Washington's Generals* (New York: William Morrow, 1964), pp. 81–82.

52. "Riflemen, as riflemen *only,* are a very feeble foe and not to be trusted alone any distance from camp; and at the out-posts they must ever be supported by regulars, or they will constantly be beaten in, and compelled to retire," judged one contemporary. On this subject, see G. Hanger, *Colonel George Hanger, to all sportsmen, and particularly to farmers and gamekeepers . . .* (London: G. Hanger, 1814), pp. 215, 199–200.

53. R. Lamb, *Memoir of His Own Life* (Dublin: J. Jones, 1811), p. 198. Robert Graves, author of *I, Claudius,* wrote an entertaining novelization of his story, *Sergeant Lamb's America* (New York: Random House, 1940).

54. Higginbotham, *Daniel Morgan,* pp. 69–70; "Journal of Lieutenant William Digby," September 19, 1777, in Commager and Morris, *Spirit of 'Seventy-Six,* p. 580.

55. Washington to Gates, September 24, 1777; Gates's reply, October 5, 1777.

56. J. R. Bright, "The Rifle in Washington's Army," *American Rifleman* 95 (August 1947), p. 10.

57. Quoted in Billias, "Horatio Gates," p. 95.

58. Quoted in D. Higginbotham, *War and Society in Revolutionary America: The Wider Dimensions of Conflict* (Columbia: University of South Carolina Press, 1988), p. 142.

59. Letter from Morgan, November 28, 1781, in anon., "A Recollection of the American Revolutionary War," *Virginia Historical Register and Literary Companion,* 6, no. 4 (1853), pp. 209–11. See also J. J. Graham, ed., *Memoir of General Graham with Notices of the Campaigns in Which He Was Engaged 1779–1801* (Edinburgh: R. & R. Clark, 1862), p. 70.

60. Higginbotham, *Daniel Morgan,* p. 73. On Murphy's singular scalping achievement, see Higginbotham, *War and Society,* p. 139.

61. "Recollections of Samuel Woodruff," in Commager and Morris, *Spirit of 'Seventy-Six,* p. 593.

62. Bright, "Rifle in Washington's Army," p. 9.

63. Quoted in C. Chenevix Trench, *A History of Marksmanship* (Chicago: Follett, 1972), p. 135n.

64. Hanger's interest in American affairs did not stop at its weapons. In his memoirs, published in 1801, he predicted that "one of these days the northern and southern powers of the States will fight as vigorously against each other as they have both united to do against the British." Quoted in Hanger's entry in the *Dictionary of National Biography* (1890 edition), which calls his memoirs "unsavoury."

65. Hanger, *To All Sportsmen,* pp. 122, 207–9, 210.

66. Thus, as he ironically put it, "the Americans . . . still continue to act in what we are pleased to call a cowardly manner, witness the efficacy of that matter on Bunker's Hill and the inaction of our troops have been obliged to preserve since that day." Quoted in A. Starkey, "Paoli to Stony Point: Military Ethics and Weaponry during the American Revolution," *Journal of Military History* 58, no. 1 (1994), p. 15. See also R. Lamb, *An Original and Authentic Journal of Occurrences During the Late American War from Its Commencement to the Year 1783* (1809; reprint New York: Arno Press/*New York Times,* 1968), pp. 27, 159.

67. Starkey, "Paoli to Stony Point," p. 13.

68. M. Van Creveld, *Technology and War from 2000 B.C. to the Present* (New York: Free Press, 1989), p. 17.

69. See illustrations printed in B. P. Hughes, *Firepower: Weapons Effectiveness on the Battlefield, 1630–1850* (Staplehurst, U.K.: Spellmount, 1997), pp. 86–91. There were another fourteen steps to perform after one had "given fire."

70. Hicks and Todd, "United States Military Shoulder Arms," p. 32n10 and 11; M. Urban, *Rifles: Six Years with Wellington's Legendary Sharpshooters* (London: Faber and Faber; 2003), p. 19. Dr. William Gordon, who described the battle in a missive from Roxbury (August 15, 1775) and printed it in his *The History of the Rise, Progress, and Establishment of the Independence of the United States of America . . .* (New York: Samuel Campbell, 1794), p. 1:352, noted that "the provincials have not a rifleman among them, not one being arrived from the southward; nor have they any rifle guns; they have only common muskets, nor are these in general furnished with bayonets; but then they are almost all marksmen, being accustomed to sporting of one kind or other from their youth."

71. Quoted in Dillin, *Kentucky Rifle,* p. 76.

72. J. Barker, *The British in Boston: Being the Diary of Lieutenant John Barker . . .* (Cambridge, Mass.: Harvard University Press, 1924), p. 43. It should be noted that no mention of such a diabolical plot has been found in any American source.

73. P. Haythornthwaite, *British Rifleman, 1797–1815* (Oxford, U.K.: Osprey, 2002), pp. 15–16.

74. Gage to Clephane, February 20, 1759, quoted in D. J. Beattie, "The Adaptation of the British Army to Wilderness Warfare, 1755–1763," in M. Ultee, ed., *Adapting to Conditions: War and Society in the Eighteenth Century* (University: University of Alabama Press, 1986), p. 74n51.

75. Quoted in Bright, "Rifle in Washington's Army," p. 10.

76. Quoted in F. Moore, *Diary of the American Revolution from Newspapers and Original Documents* (New York: Charles Scribner, 2, 1860), p. 1:350.

77. Diary entry, November 18, 1777, in G. D. Scull, ed., "The Montresor Journals," *Collections of the New-York Historical Society* 14 (1882), p. 477.

78. Interestingly, this view began as a politically progressive idea. In the seventeenth century, military theorists wanting to break away from the contemporary reliance on mercenaries (employed particularly brutally during the Thirty Years' War) and the medieval adulation of knights errant advocated professional armies subject to a chain of command and forbidden by strict discipline to loot and kill civilians. By the eighteenth century, such reforms were so deeply integrated into military practice that they had become regarded as conservative policies. On the original radicalism of professionalism, see G. E. Rothenberg, "Maurice of Nassau, Gustavus Adolphus, Raimondo Montecuccoli, and the

'Military Revolution' of the Seventeenth Century," in P. Paret, ed., *Makers of Modern Strategy* (Princeton, N.J.: Princeton University Press, 1986), p. 34.

79. In a letter to Washington, quoted in H. Rankin, "Anthony Wayne: Military Romanticist," in Billias, ed., *George Washington's Generals*, p. 263.

80. Starkey, "Paoli to Stony Point," pp. 7–9.

81. Quoted in Rankin, "Anthony Wayne," p. 273.

82. R. R. Palmer, "Frederick the Great, Guibert, Bülow: From Dynastic to National War," in Paret, ed., *Makers of Modern Strategy*, esp. pp. 91–105.

83. Hamilton to John Jay, March 14, 1779, in H. C. Syrett, ed., *The Papers of Alexander Hamilton* (New York: Columbia University Press, 1961–87), pp. 2:17–18.

84. Quoted in Paul David Nelson, "Citizen Soldiers or Regulars: The Views of American General Officers on the Military Establishment, 1775–1781," *Military Affairs* 43, no. 3 (1979), pp. 128, 129. On Wayne in particular, see Rankin, "Anthony Wayne," pp. 260–90.

85. A. D. Gaff, *Bayonets in the Wilderness: Anthony Wayne's Legion in the Old Northwest* (Norman: University of Oklahoma Press, 2004), pp. 26–27, 59–60. The *Reveries* were popular among several of Washington's generals, says Wright in, "Some Notes on the Continental Army," p. 84.

86. Jefferson to G. Fabbroni, June 8, 1778, in J. P. Boyd, ed., *The Papers of Thomas Jefferson* (Princeton, N.J.: Princeton University Press, 1950–), p. 2:198n1.

87. Gates's couplet is quoted in Billias, "Horatio Gates," p. 85.

88. Lee's broadside, "To the People of America," in E. Langworthy, ed., *The Life and Memoirs of the late Major General Lee . . .* (New York: Richard Scott, 1813), pp. 123, 128. In this view, Gates and Charles Lee were joined by the firebrand congressman Richard Henry Lee, who bragged that Virginia's six frontier counties alone could raise six thousand riflemen capable of hitting an orange at two hundred yards. Lee to Arthur Lee, February 24, 1775, in J. C. Ballagh, ed., *The Letters of Richard Henry Lee* (New York: Macmillan, 1911), pp. 1:130–31. Lee's brand of hearty patriotism would go on to enjoy a long life. In 1940 Senator Robert Reynolds of North Carolina declared that the mountain men of his fine state "learn to shoot from the time they put on knee pants" and "draw a bead on a squirrel a hundred yards away and aim at the right eye." That's why he wasn't afraid of "Hitler coming over here, because if he does, he will get the worst licking he ever had in his life, because our boys have been trained to shoot." Quoted in E. M. Coffman, "The Duality of the American Military Tradition: A Commentary," *Journal of Military History* 64, no. 4 (2000), p. 968.

89. Jefferson to Fabbroni, June 8, 1778, in Boyd, *Papers of Jefferson*, p. 2:195.

90. An excellent analysis of Lee's politics may be found in J. Shy, "Charles Lee," in Billias, *Washington's Generals*, esp. pp. 24–28, 46 (on his hatred of Hamilton).

91. Wayne to Mr. Peters (secretary of war), February 8, 1778, in C. J. Stillé, *Major-General Anthony Wayne and the Pennsylvania Line in the Continental Army* (Philadelphia: J. P. Lippincott, 1893), p. 118. "I never wish to see one—at least without a bayonet" was his blunt opinion of the rifle's place in modern warfare.

92. Greene to Colonel Cox, July 17, 1779, in Commager and Morris, *Spirit of 'Seventy-Six*, p. 723.

93. On Steuben, see the works by J. M. Palmer, *General von Steuben* (New Haven, Conn.: Yale University Press, 1937), and A. H. Bill, *Valley Forge: The Making of an Army* (New York: Harper & Brothers, 1952).

94. Wayne, for example, believed that "for want of [bayonets] the chief of the defeats we have met with ought in a great measure to be attributed." See letter to Peters of February 8, 1778, in Stillé, *Major-General Wayne*, p. 118.

95. Washington to John Banister, April 21, 1778.

96. General Orders, September 27, 1781, Washington Papers.

97. On Deckhard's (or Deckard's or Dickert's) provision of the rifles, see J. G. M. Ramsay, *The Annals of Tennessee to the End of the Eighteenth Century* (Charleston, S.C.: John Russell,

1853), p. 228. On the weather that day, see J. P. Collins, *Autobiography of a Revolutionary Soldier* (1859; reprint New York: Arno Press/*New York Times,* 1979), p. 51.

98. There is some confusion about whether Loyalists were also armed with rifles. The older interpretations—such as L. C. Draper, *King's Mountain and Its Heroes: History of the Battle of King's Mountain, October 7th, 1780, and the Events Which Led to It* (Cincinnati, Ohio: Peter G. Thomson, 1881), p. 237—claim that they were, but my view is that Draper was confused as to the difference between a rifle and a musket and carelessly used the more modern word to signify what he should have called a musket. The Tories under Ferguson's command were raised mostly in New York and New Jersey, in neither of which were rifles common. Perhaps a few of them did possess a looted or spare rifle, but they would have been used as muskets.

99. Quoted in Commager and Morris, *Spirit of 'Seventy-Six,* p. 1136. A slightly bowdlerized but subtly alternative version is in C. P. Russell, "The American Rifle at the Battle of King's Mountain" (1940), in the National Park Service, *Rifles and Riflemen at the Battle of King's Mountain,* online at www.cr.nps.gov/history/online_books/popular/12/ps12-2.htm.

100. Quoted in Draper, *King's Mountain,* p. 252.

101. B. R. Lewis, *Small Arms and Ammunition in the United States Service* (Washington, D.C.: Smithsonian Institution, 1956), p. 91.

102. Collins, *Autobiography of a Revolutionary Soldier,* p. 53.

103. "Account of Ensign Robert Campbell," in Draper, *King's Mountain,* p. 539.

104. Collins, *Autobiography of a Revolutionary Soldier,* p. 52.

105. "Account of Ensign Robert Campbell," in Draper, *King's Mountain,* p. 539.

106. Collins, *Autobiography of a Revolutionary Soldier,* p. 53. Ferguson had previously been badly wounded at the battle of Brandywine, leaving him with a permanent crook at the right elbow. That wound may explain Collins's observation that he saw the major's corpse with *two* broken arms; in fact, he may have broken the left falling from his horse, and Collins mistook the bent one for a new injury.

107. Russell, "American Rifle."

Chapter 3

1. Quoted in B. Hindle and S. Lubar, *Engines of Change: The American Industrial Revolution, 1790–1860* (Washington, D.C.: Smithsonian Institution Press, 1986), p. 254.

2. M. R. Smith, *Harpers Ferry Armory and the New Technology* (Ithaca, N.Y.: Cornell University Press, 1977), p. 19.

3. On Colt, see D. A. Hounshell, *From the American System to Mass Production, 1800–1932* (Baltimore, Md.: Johns Hopkins University Press, 1984), p.23.

4. As a result, the "American System" became so inextricably identified with specifically American business practice that when, in 1889, Mark Twain wanted to create his all-around Connecticut "Yankee of the Yankees" for his satirical novel of a nineteenth-century man who wakes up in King Arthur's Camelot and teaches his knights baseball, he invented none other than Hank Morgan (born and reared in Hartford, home of Colt's massive armory), who "went over to the great arms factory and learned my real trade; learned all there was to it; learned to make everything: guns, revolvers, cannon, boilers, engines, all sorts of labor-saving machinery." M. Twain, *A Connecticut Yankee in King Arthur's Court* (New York: Bantam Dell, 2005), p. 5.

5. H. Adams, *The Education of Henry Adams: An Autobiography* (Boston: Massachusetts Historical Society, 1918), p. 5. New universe or not, it did not save Robbins & Lawrence: the company went bankrupt a few years later after a series of financial miscalculations.

6. S. Wilentz, *Society, Politics, and the Market Revolution, 1815–1848* (Washington, D.C.: American Historical Association, n.d.); E. D. Genovese, *Roll, Jordan, Roll: The World the Slaves Made* (New York: Pantheon, 1974); W. B. Rothenberg, *From Marketplaces to a*

Market Economy: The Transformation of Rural Massachusetts, 1750–1850 (Chicago: University of Chicago Press, 1992); C. Sellers, *The Market Revolution: Jacksonian America, 1815–1846* (New York: Oxford University Press, 1991).

7. On the choice of Harpers Ferry, see Smith, *Harpers Ferry,* chap. 1. On Harpers Ferry, see also P. A. Chackel's *Culture Change and the New Technology: An Archeology of the Early American Industrial Era* (New York: Plenum, 1996).

8. C. W. Sawyer, *Our Rifles* (Boston: Williams, 1946), pp. 128–41; J. E. Hicks, *Notes on United States Ordnance: Small Arms, 1776 to 1940* (Mount Vernon: N.Y.: James E. Hicks, 1940), pp. 25–26; B. R. Lewis, *Small Arms and Ammunition in the United States Service* (Washington, D.C.: Smithsonian Institution, 1956), p. 8 (though Lewis calls it a Model 1804).

9. Smith, *Harpers Ferry,* pp. 70, 83.

10. The fullest analysis of Stubblefield's reign can be found in ibid., pp. 140–83.

11. Hall to Secretary of State James Monroe, March 21, 1817, quoted in R. T. Huntington, *Hall's Breechloaders* (York, Pa.: George Shumway, 1972), pp. 2–3.

12. The best summary of these post-Revolutionary debates is L. D. Cress's "Reassessing American Military Requirements, 1783–1807," in K. J. Hagan and W. R. Roberts, eds., *Against All Enemies: Interpretations of American Military History from Colonial Times to the Present Day* (Westport, Conn.: Greenwood Press, 1986), pp. 49–69.

13. See S. Forman, "Thomas Jefferson and Universal Military Training," *Military Affairs* 11, no. 3 (1947), pp. 177–78; and his "Why the United States Military Academy Was Established in 1802," *Military Affairs* 29, no. 1 (1965), pp. 16–28.

14. Amazingly, Hall had never heard of previous attempts. Indeed, he was being completely honest when, a little later, he wrote that "I invented the improvement in 1811, being at that time but little acquainted with rifles and being perfectly *ignorant of any method whatever* of loading guns at the breech, excepting that practiced with pocket pistols by unscrewing the barrel." Hall to Bomford, January 24, 1815, printed in Huntington, *Hall's Breechloaders,* pp. 269–70.

15. Ibid., p. 270.

16. Ibid., pp. 5, 8–9.

17. Smith, *Harpers Ferry,* p. 185; Huntington, *Hall's Breechloaders,* p. 9.

18. Hall to Captain John Morton, June 22, 1816, quoted in Huntington, *Hall's Breechloaders,* p. 11.

19. L. A. Garavaglia and C. G. Worman, *Firearms of the American West, (1803–1865, 1866–1894)* (Niwot, Colo.: University Press of Colorado, 1997–98), p. 1:6.

20. Hall to Morton, June 22, 1816, quoted in Huntington, *Hall's Breechloaders,* p. 11.

21. M. R. Smith, "Military Entrepreneurship," in O. Mayr and R. C. Post, eds., *Yankee Enterprise: The Rise of the American System of Manufacturers* (Washington, D.C.: Smithsonian Institution Press, 1981), p. 66.

22. See K. Alder's interesting "Innovation and Amnesia: Engineering Rationality and the Fate of Interchangeable Parts Manufacturing in France," *Technology and Culture* 38, no. 2 (1997), pp. 272–311.

23. See A. Halsey Jr. and J. M. Snyder, "Jefferson's Beloved Guns," *American Rifleman* 117 (November 1969), pp. 17–20.

24. Jefferson to Jay, August 30, 1785, in Thomas Jefferson Papers, Library of Congress, Washington, D.C.

25. Irvine to John Armstrong, June 12, 1813, in Hicks, *Notes on Ordnance,* p. 44.

26. Irvine to Whitney, October 26, 1813, ibid., p. 42.

27. Irvine to Whitney, November 17, 1813, ibid., p. 43.

28. Irvine to Armstrong, June 28, 1814, ibid., p. 43.

29. On Wadsworth, see C. W. Reed, "Decius Wadsworth, First Chief of Ordnance, U.S. Army, 1812–1821," pts. 1 and 2, *Army Ordnance* 24 (1943), pp. 527–30; and 25 (1943), pp. 113–16.

30. Smith, "Military Entrepreneurship," p. 68.

31. Smith, *Harpers Ferry,* pp. 107–8. On the pattern models for the Model 1816 musket, see the correspondence between Wadsworth and Roswell Lee, superintendent of Springfield throughout 1816 and 1818, in Hicks, *Notes on Ordnance,* pp. 49–51.

32. A recent narrative of the battle is R. V. Remini's *The Battle of New Orleans* (New York: Viking, 1999).

33. Quoted in J. W. Ward, *Andrew Jackson, Symbol for an Age* (New York: Oxford University Press, 1955), pp. 5–6.

34. See Sawyer, *Our Rifles,* p. 10.

35. C. Gayarré, *History of Louisiana* (New York: W. J. Widdleton, 1867), p. 4:452.

36. Quoted in H. W. Brand's excellent *Andrew Jackson: His Life and Times* (New York: Doubleday, 2005), pp. 275–76.

37. *National Intelligencer,* June 29, 1815, quoted in Ward, *Andrew Jackson,* p. 23.

38. Huntington, *Hall's Breechloaders,* p. 12. A. Hatch, *Remington Arms: An American Company* (New York/Toronto: Rinehart & Co., 1956), p. 60, unfairly castigates Talcott as a "man of resolute stupidity" owing to his report (expressed in a letter to William Wilkins, secretary of war between 1844 and 1845) that "a prejudice against all arms loading at the breech is prevalent among officers, and especially the dragoons," before going on to say that many of the patented types of arms then floating about "will ultimately all pass into oblivion." First, Talcott was merely reporting the true facts about many officers' distrust of breech-loaders, not discussing his personal views, which conformed with Ordnance policy. And second, it was a long-standing Ordnance complaint that inventors were claiming impossible feats for their patents, few of which bore out their assertions. As General Ripley would say during the Civil War, he wished they would all go away and leave it to the arsenals to get on with their work.

39. See P. G. Thompson, "Historical Importance of the Hall Breechloading Rifle in the Development of the American System of Manufacturing, Mass Production, Interchange-ability, and Industrial Education" (unpub. Ph.D. diss. Texas A&M University, 2002), p. 10.

40. Wadsworth to John C. Calhoun, November 16, 1818, in Huntington, *Hall's Breech-loaders,* p. 273.

41. "Extract of Report of Board of Officers," undated but pre–March 1819, in Huntington, *Hall's Breechloaders,* pp. 305–6.

42. Hall to Monroe, March 21, 1817, quoted in Smith, *Harpers Ferry,* p. 193.

43. Smith, *Harpers Ferry,* pp. 157–58.

44. Huntington, *Hall's Breechloaders,* p. 16; Wadsworth to Hall, March 18, 1819, ibid., p. 273. On competitive bidding, see Smith, *Harpers Ferry,* p. 163.

45. It wouldn't be until 1841, when Joseph Whitworth in Britain proposed universalizing the thread angle at 55 degrees and regulating the number of threads per inch for various diameters that the chaos subsided. Not for long, however, as in 1864 the American William Sellers introduced a new standard of a 60-degree thread with different pitches according to the length, while the Germans used 53 degrees and the Swiss 47.5 degrees.

46. Hall to Bomford, March 1, 1823, quoted in Huntington, *Hall's Breechloaders,* p. 32.

47. Hall to Bomford, December 17, 1824, ibid., pp. 275–76.

48. Hall to James Barbour, February 17, 1827, quoted ibid., p. 17. Unfortunately, because of a fire in 1836 that burned Hall's plans and the destruction of Harpers Ferry during the Civil War, hardly anything is known of what his machines actually looked like or did. See R. B. Gordon, "Simeon North, John Hall, and Mechanized Manufacturing," *Technology and Culture* 30, no. 1 (1989), p. 181.

49. "Notes of a Tour of Inspection," December 1822, quoted in Smith, *Harpers Ferry,* p. 198.

50. Hall to Bomford, December 17, 1824, in Huntington, *Hall's Breechloaders,* pp. 275–76. Thompson, "Historical Importance of the Hall Breechloading Rifle," pp. 108–9, agrees that 1824 was most probably the breakthrough year.

51. Hall to Bomford, January 16, 1827, in Huntington, *Hall's Breechloaders*, p. 276. He was slightly wrong about these figures. Between 1832 and 1839 the average cost would be $16.32, but still, it was close enough to the cost of a standard-issue musket to be more than acceptable, particularly considering the performance boost. See Smith, *Harpers Ferry*, p. 220.

52. Hall to Bomford, January 16, 1827, in Huntington, *Hall's Breechloaders*, p. 276. Between 1819 and 1835 Hall's final tally would amount to $432,899, or more than $9 million. Smith, *Harpers Ferry*, p. 221.

53. Huntington, *Hall's Breechloaders*, pp. 35–36.

54. Quoted in Smith, *Harpers Ferry*, p. 207.

55. All results extracted from "Report of the Staff of the Artillery School of Practice, Fortress Monroe, Virginia, on Comparative Firing Tests with Hall's Rifle, the Common Harpers Ferry Rifle, and the New Pattern Springfield Musket, Conducted July to November, 1826," dated December 11, 1826, in Huntington, *Hall's Breechloaders*, pp. 305–18.

56. Gordon, "Simeon North, John Hall," p. 183. I am grateful to Professor Gordon for his advice on this section. Thompson, "Historical Importance of Hall Breechloading Rifle," pp. 26ff., has a detailed section on the "flash gap."

57. Huntington, *Hall's Breechloaders*, p. 38.

58. Smith, *Harpers Ferry*, p. 209.

59. Huntington, *Hall's Breechloaders*, pp. 42–44.

60. Samuel Pepys mentions the compound in an entry dated November 11, 1663, in his famous diary. See H. B. Wheatley, ed., *The Diary of Samuel Pepys, M.A., F.R.S. . . .* (London: G. Bell and Sons, 1949), p. 1:319. Also F. Kurzer, "The Life and Work of Edward Charles Howard FRS," *Annals of Science* 56, no. 2 (1999), pp. 113–41.

61. W. W. Greener, *The Gun and Its Development*, 9th ed. (Guilford, Conn.: Lyons Press, 2002), pp. 112–13; D. Westwood, *Rifles: An Illustrated History of Their Impact* (Santa Barbara, Calif.: ABC-CLIO, 2005), pp. 65–66. Alternatively, Forsyth may have stayed in the gun-making business in London until 1852, but no one seems quite sure. See P. B. Sharpe, *The Rifle in America*, 3d ed. (New York: Funk & Wagnalls, 1953), p. 18.

62. "Joshua Shaw, Artist and Inventor: The Early History of the Copper Percussion Cap," *Scientific American*, August 7, 1869; also Sharpe, *Rifle in America*, pp. 19–20.

63. Westwood, *Rifles*, p. 68; Sharpe, *Rifle in America*, p. 19.

64. Greener, *Gun and Its Development*, p. 117.

65. Westwood, *Rifles*, p. 69.

66. Ibid., pp. 69–70.

67. See Bomford to Hall, September 3, 1836, in Huntington, *Hall's Breechloaders*, p. 283.

68. On Lucas's background and politics, see Smith, *Harpers Ferry*, pp. 258–62.

69. Quoted in Huntington, *Hall's Breechloaders*, p. 79.

70. Statira Hall to George Talcott, October 7, 1840; John Hall to Talcott, October 7, 1840; both in Huntington, *Hall's Breechloaders*, p. 291.

71. See Ward, *Andrew Jackson*, pp. 13–14. The Library of Congress has an 1815 copy of the broadside.

72. N. M. Ludlow, *Dramatic Life As I Found It . . .* (St. Louis: G. I. Jones & Co., 1880), pp. 237–38.

73. J. F. Cooper, *The Leatherstocking Tales*, ed. B. Nevius (New York: Library of America, 1985), pp. 2:870–81.

74. Cooper, *Leatherstocking Tales*, pp. 1:560, 567–68, 603.

75. F. Somkin, *Unquiet Eagle: Memory and Desire in the Idea of American Freedom, 1815–1860* (Ithaca, N.Y.: Cornell University Press, 1967), p. 4.

76. *London and Westminster Review*, 32, no. 1 (1832), p. 139.

77. Quoted in M. J. Heale, "The Role of the Frontier in Jacksonian Politics: David Crockett and the Myth of the Self-made Man," *Western Historical Quarterly* 4, no. 4 (1973), p. 405.

78. D. Crockett, *Life of Col. David Crockett written by himself* . . . (Philadelphia: A.A. Evans, 1860), pp. 224, 270; C. G. Loomis, "Davy Crockett Visits Boston," *New England Quarterly* 20, no. 3 (1947), pp. 396–400; B. Ball, "The Most Famous Rifle of Texas! Recreating Colonel Crockett's Rifle at the Battle of the Alamo," *Guns Magazine*, January 2004.

Chapter 4

1. "The Volcanic Repeating Rifle," *Frank Leslie's Illustrated Newspaper*, October 9, 1858, reprinted in J. E. Dizard, R. M. Muth, and S. P. Andrews Jr., eds., *Guns in America: A Reader* (New York: New York University Press, 1999), p. 48.

2. Author's count, using table "Classified List of Breech-Loading Fire-arms Patented in the United States," in E. H. Knight, *Knight's American Mechanical Dictionary*, 3 vols. (New York: Hurd & Houghton, 1877) pp. 1:855–60.

3. Quoted in M. R. Smith, "Army Ordnance and the 'American System' of Manufacturing, 1815–1861," in M. R. Smith, ed., *Military Enterprise and Technological Change: Perspectives on the American Experience* (Cambridge, Mass.: MIT Press, 1985), p. 40.

4. Hence the business world's motley collection of martial metaphors: all those corporate raiders, hostile takeovers, bidding wars, boardroom battles, target demographics, entrenched managements, scorched-earth defenses, bullet points, trade barriers, firing of employees, union battle lines, decisive leadership, the bleeding of red ink, marginal losses, industrial espionage, vulnerable or embattled companies, stock-price collapses, sneak attacks, morale-building exercises. Interestingly, the flow has in recent years run in the opposite direction: the army has begun to draw lessons from the business sector. According to a story in *Time* magazine, on the bookshelves "of nearly every Army office in the Pentagon, alongside military-history tomes, sits a stack of business books." Taking its cue from the success of Lean Six Sigma, a management concept conceived by Toyota and Motorola and employed most famously by Jack Welch at General Electric, the army has been raising productivity and efficiency at its arsenals, depots, and departments. "Lean and Mean," *Inside Business* supplement, *Time*, August 2006, pp. A1–A4.

5. H. Metcalfe, *The Cost of Manufactures and the Administration of Workshops, Public and Private* (New York: J. Wiley & Sons, 1885). See B. C. Hacker, "Engineering a New Order: Military Institutions, Technical Education, and the Rise of the Industrial State," *Technology and Culture* 34, no. 1 (1993), p. 15; W. H. Reid, "The Development of Henry Metcalfe's Card System of Shop Returns at Frankford Arsenal, 1880–1881," *Journal of Management* 12 (1986), pp. 415–23.

6. M. R. Smith, *Harpers Ferry Armory and the New Technology* (Ithaca, N.Y.: Cornell University Press, 1977), pp. 244–48. On Cincinnati's dominance, see N. Rosenberg, "Technological Change in the Machine Tool Industry, 1840–1910," *Journal of Economic History* 23, no. 4 (1963), p. 421.

7. J. W. Roe, *English and American Tool Builders* (New Haven, Conn.: Yale University Press, 1916), contains a number of interesting "genealogies" of mechanics and the geographical diffusion of their skills. See W. C. Scoville, "Minority Migration and the Diffusion of Technology," *Journal of Economic History* 11, no. 4 (1951), pp. 347–60, for a sixteenth-century example of this phenomenon.

8. N. Rosenberg, "Economic Development and the Transfer of Technology: Some Historical Perspectives," in T. S. Reynolds and S. H. Cutliffe, eds., *Technology and Culture: A Historical Anthology from "Technology and Culture"* (Chicago: University of Chicago Press, 1997), pp. 257–58.

9. The most important source for the influence of firearms on civilian development is Rosenberg, "Technological Change," pp. 427–31.

10. W. C. Leland and M. D. Millbrook, *Master of Precision: Henry M. Leland* (Detroit: Wayne State University Press, 1966); O. A. Hounshell, *From the American System to Mass Production, 1800–1832* (Baltimore, Md.: Johns Hopkins University Press, 1984), pp. 4–5.

11. D. R. Hoke, *Ingenious Yankees: The Rise of the American System of Manufactures in the Private Sector* (New York: Columbia University Press, 1990).

12. One has to be very careful not to assume a progressive, teleological direction to technological or manufacturing development. The road to Fordist mass production was by no means destined or designed, but by inherently writing as if it were, historians pass over alternative means of production, such as flexible specialization, in which small companies are able to keep up with changing market demand by rapidly updating and adapting existing machinery. On this point see C. Sabel and J. Zeitlin, "Historical Alternatives to Mass Production: Politics, Markets, and Technology in Nineteenth-Century Industrialization," *Past and Present* 108 (1986), pp. 133–76.

13. Regarding the role of the railroads at this time, see, for example, Alfred Chandler's work in *The Railroads: The Nation's First Big Business* (New York: Harcourt, Brace & World, 1965); and "The Railroads: Pioneers in Modern Corporate Business Administration," *Business History Review* 29, no. 1 (1965), pp. 16–40.

14. C. F. O'Connell Jr., "The Corps of Engineers and the Rise of Modern Management, 1827–1856," in Smith, ed., *Military Enterprise*, pp. 87–116.

15. C. Pursell, "Science and Industry," in G. H. Daniels, ed., *Nineteenth-Century American Science* (Evanston, Ill.: Northwestern University Press, 1972), p. 247. The most famous of these former West Pointers reaching for the glittering prizes available in the business world was George B. McClellan, subsequently general in chief of the Union Army during the Civil War. In 1857 he resigned his commission to become the vice president and chief engineer of the Illinois Central Railroad and later president of the Ohio and Mississippi Railroad. See S. W. Sears, *George B. McClellan: The Young Napoleon* (New York: Ticknor & Fields, 1988).

16. O'Connell, "Corps of Engineers," pp. 114–15.

17. Ibid., pp. 93–96.

18. R. A. Howard, "Interchangeable Parts Reexamined: The Private Sector of the American Arms Industry on the Eve of the Civil War," *Technology and Culture* 29, no. 4 (1978), pp. 637, 640. By midway through the Civil War, the output of these private makers was dwarfing that of the government armories. Whereas between 1851 and 1860, Harpers Ferry produced 93,271 guns and Springfield 125,222 for a total of 218,493, Colt alone made about 300,000 Ibid., pp. 634–5, n3.

19. B. Nosworthy, *The Bloody Crucible of Courage: Fighting Methods and Combat Experience of the Civil War* (New York: Carroll & Graf, 2003), pp. 27–28; C. Fuller, *The Rifled Musket* (Harrisburg, Pa.: Stackpole, 1958), pp. 3–4; and W. B. Edwards, *Civil War Guns: The Complete Story of Federal and Confederate Small Arms* (Harrisburg, Pa.: Stackpole, 1962), pp. 8–9.

20. The most important summary of these experiments is B. D. Steele, "Muskets and Pendulums: Benjamin Robins, Leonhard Euler, and the Ballistics Revolution," *Technology and Culture* 35, no. 2 (1994), pp. 348–82; and see also W. Johnson, "Benjamin Robins, F.R.S. (1707–1751): New Details of His Life," *Notes and Records of the Royal Society of London* 46, no. 2 (1992), pp. 235–52.

21. Chronologically speaking, it was W. Greener, an English gunsmith, who beat Minié to the punch. There were crucial differences between their bullets. In Greener's version, inside the bullet's front end there was a small wooden plug that, being thrust backward upon firing, pushed the rear of the bullet wider and filled the bore. During trials held by the 60th Rifles under Major Walcot, fifty Greener rounds were fired into sandbanks and recovered. They were found to have groove marks, demonstrating their expansive qualities. "The success of the trials," Walcot reported, "far surpassed the expectations of the military experts present. It was proved that the Greener bullet enabled rifles to be loaded as easily as smooth-bore muskets, whilst the range and accuracy of the rifle were retained." The authorities, however, disliked and rejected the bullet, believing it too complex for everyday use. Nevertheless, in yet another controversy over patents, Greener went on to sue Minié after the British government awarded the Frenchman £20,000; Greener claimed that Minié had copied his idea from reports in "the *Times,* or from my works, published in 1842 and 1846." Eventually, Greener was given £1,000 "for the first public suggestion of

the principle of expansion, commonly called the Minié principle, in 1836." The story is told in the famous book by his son, W. W. Greener, *The Gun and Its Development,* 9th ed. (reprinted Guilford, Conn.: Lyons Press, 2002), pp. 629–31.

22. J. K. Mahon, "Civil War Infantry Assault Tactics," *Military Affairs* 25, no. 2 (1961), p. 57.

23. Greener, *Gun and Its Development,* p. 633.

24. Rosenberg, "Economic Development and the Transfer of Technology," p. 255.

25. J. E. Hicks, *Notes on United States Ordnance: Small Arms, 1776 to 1940* (Mount Vernon, N.Y.: James E. Hicks, 1940), pp. 79–80. See also P. B. Sharpe, *The Rifle in America,* 3d. ed. (New York: Funk & Wagnalls, 1953), p. 21, for details on the conversion process. On the Model 1842, see Fuller, *Rifled Musket,* p. 3.

26. See Colonel H. K. Craig to Jefferson Davis, June 26, 1855, and Davis to Craig, July 5, 1855, in Fuller, *Rifled Musket,* p. 5.

27. Sharpe, *Rifle in America,* pp. 20–21.

28. See Craig to Davis, June 26, 1855, in Fuller, *Rifled Musket,* pp. 5–8. Craig, as an Ordnance man, was unwilling to support the immediate cessation of rifle production, believing that certain types should remain a specialized class of marksman's weapons. Also, C. W. Sawyer, *Our Rifles,* (Boston: Williams, 1946), pp. 148, 151.

29. On Sharps's employment with Hall, see G. S. Henig and E. Niderost, *Civil War Firsts: The Legacies of America's Bloodiest Conflict* (Mechanicsburg, Pa.: Stackpole, 2001), p. 72.

30. *Scientific American,* March 9, 1850.

31. Frederick Law Olmsted, the designer of Central Park in New York, traveled across Texas armed with a Sharps in 1853. He said that "at a single trial, without practice" he and his companions fired their weapons nine times. Quoted in L. A. Garavaglia and C. G. Worman, *Firearms of the American West (1803–1865, 1866–1894)* (1984–85; reprint Niwot: University Press of Colorado, 1997–98), p. 1:242.

32. W. R. Austerman, *Sharps Rifles and Spanish Mules: The San Antonio–El Paso Mail, 1851–1881* (College Station: Texas A&M University Press, 1985), p. 122. Some worried passengers might have gone a little overboard. Thus when in 1850 John Bartlett, the boundary commissioner charged with dealing with a Mexican-American border disagreement, left for the Southwest, his personal carriage was a wooden fortress on wheels ("what in New York is called a Rockaway"). From its ceiling hung a double-barreled shotgun, and to each door was strapped a large-caliber Colt six-shooter pistol. Bartlett and his companion (Dr. Webb) each carried a pair of Colt five-shooters, the driver was armed with two Deringer pistols, and close to Bartlett's hand at all times was a Sharps. "We were thus enabled," he wrote, "to discharge a round of thirty-seven shots without reloading; besides which, Sharp's [sic] rifle could be fired at least six times in a minute. J. R. Bartlett, *Personal Narrative of Explorations and Incidents in Texas . . .* (1854; reprint Chicago: Rio Grande Press, 1965), p. 1:48.

33. Austerman, *Sharps Rifles,* p. 38.

34. *New York Tribune,* February 8, 1856, quoted in W. H. Isely, "The Sharps Rifle Episode in Kansas History," *American Historical Review* 12, no. 3 (1907), p. 548. On the boxes of "Books," see pp. 552–53.

35. R. O. Boyer, *The Legend of John Brown: A Biography and History* (New York: Alfred A. Knopf, 1972), p. 111. Donors to the aid committees were sent a lithographed certificate quoting the Second Amendment, with two words in particular being highlighted: "A well regulated Militia being necessary to the Security of a FREE STATE the Right of the People to keep and bear Arms shall not be infringed." Isely, "Sharps Rifle Episode," pp. 548, 553.

36. Senate Report on John Brown's Harpers Ferry raid, June 15, 1860, 36th Congress, 1st Session, Report no. 278, reprinted as *Invasion at Harpers Ferry* (New York: Arno Press/New York Times, 1969), pp. 3, 7.

37. Mordecai is an obscure soldier, and finding information about him can be difficult. However, the biographical details in this section mostly come from Mordecai's useful memoir, written for his children's edification, which is printed in J. A. Padgett, ed., "The Life of Alfred Mordecai, as Related by Himself," *North Carolina Historical Review* 22,

no. 1 (1945), pp. 58–108. The Library of Congress has many of his papers, though in subsequent numbers of the *Historical Review,* Padgett prints Mordecai's private letters to his family dating from his time in Mexico. The sole detailed study of Mordecai's official affairs is S. L. Falk, "Soldier-Technologist: Major Alfred Mordecai and the Beginnings of Science in the United States Army," an unpublished Georgetown University Ph.D. dissertation (1959). A recent book narrates the interesting story of the Mordecai family (but deals cursorily with Alfred), and that is Emily Bingham's *Mordecai: An Early American Family* (New York: Hill & Wang, 2003).

38. A. Mordecai, *Military Commission to Europe in 1855 and 1856,* Senate Executive Document no. 60, 36th Congress, 1st Session (Washington, D.C.: G. W. Bowman, 1860). The report appended a lengthy translation by Mordecai's deputy, Captain Gorgas, of a work by a Saxon soldier, Captain Schön, on rifled small arms *(Das Gezogene Infanterie—Gewehr),* published in Dresden in 1855. Mordecai's conclusions were identical to Schon's. Gorgas would go on to become the head of ordnance for the Confederacy during the Civil War. For his background and experience, see F. E. Vandiver, "The Mexican War Experience of Josiah Gorgas," *Journal of Southern History* 13, no. 3 (1947), pp. 373–94.

39. For a typical argument along these lines, see *Hartford Daily Times,* September 9, 1874, in Dizard, Muth, and Andrews, *Guns in America,* p. 48.

40. Mordecai, *Military Commission to Europe,* p. 163.

41. A moderate Democrat, southern born, and an individual of robust "conservative opinions," Mordecai himself was nonetheless unsympathetic to slavery and would be torn over which side to support. Though he was offered senior posts by both Confederacy and Union, the anguished Mordecai resigned his commission and moved to Philadelphia. Regarding the outbreak of the Civil War, and Mordecai's thoughts on it, see S. L. Falk, "Divided Loyalties in 1861: The Decision of Major Alfred Mordecai," *Publication of the American Jewish Historical Society* 48, no. 3 (1959), pp. 147–69. Mordecai was by no means the only scientist with conflicted, complex views on slavery and secession; see, on this point, R. V. Bruce, *The Launching of Modern American Science, 1846–1876* (New York: Alfred A. Knopf, 1987), pp. 271–86.

42. On Jackson as self-made man, see J. W. Ward, *Andrew Jackson: Symbol for an Age* (New York: Oxford University Press, 1955), pp. 166–80; on Jackson and democracy, see R. V. Remini, *The Legacy of Andrew Jackson: Essays on Democracy, Indian Removal, and Slavery* (Baton Rouge and London: Louisiana State University Press, 1988), pp. 7–44.

43. Quoted in D. R. Beaver, "The U.S. War Department in the Gaslight Era: Stephen Vincent Benét at the Ordnance Department, 1870–91," *Journal of Military History,* 68, no. 1 (2004), p. 111.

44. *The Centennial of the United States Military Academy at West Point, New York* (1904; reprint New York: Greenwood Press, 1969), p. 1:496.

45. M. Cunliffe, *Soldiers and Civilians: The Martial Spirit in America, 1775–1865* (New York: Free Press, 1973), pp. 106–11. On Crockett's hostile view of West Point, see M. J. Heale, "The Role of the Frontier in Jacksonian Politics: David Crockett and the Myth of the Self-made Man," *Western Historical Quarterly* 4, no. 4 (1973), p. 417.

46. See "History of the Can" at www.cancentral.com/history.htm. D. Boorstin, *The Americans: The Democratic Experience* (New York: Random House, 1973), pp. 309–22, has an interesting section on "portable" food.

47. D. Westwood, *Rifles: An Illustrated History of Their Impact* (Santa Barbara, Calif.: ABC-CLIO, 2005), p. 29; Greener, *Gun and Its Development,* p. 114; J. G. Bilby, *A Revolution in Arms: A History of the First Repeating Rifles* (Yardley, Pa.: Westhome, 2006), pp. 49–50. Pauly's cartridges were laboriously made for a specific gun and thus were not uniform; this fact alone might have doomed them.

48. J. M. Fenster, "Seam Stresses," *Invention and Technology Magazine* 9, no. 3 (1994), has an interesting section on Hunt. Available online at www.americanheritage.com/articles/magazine/it/1994/3/1994_3_40.shtml.

49. "Loaded ball," Patent no. 5,701, August 10, 1848, which can be seen at the U.S. Patent and Trademark Office Web site, www.uspto.gov.

50. "Combined piston-breech and firing-cock repeating-gun," Patent no. 6,663, August 21, 1849; also Bilby, *Revolution in Arms*, p. 54; Edwards, *Civil War Guns*, p. 166.

51. "Improvement in breech-loading fire-arms," Patent no. 6,973, December 25, 1849; Bilby, *Revolution in Arms*, pp. 54–55; H. F. Williamson, *Winchester: The Gun That Won the West* (Washington, D.C.: Combat Forces Press, 1952), pp. 9–10. For an illustration of the Jennings, see either the patent application or the short article in *International Magazine*, January 1, 1852, online at www.researchpress.co.uk/firearms/usa/jennings/jennings.htm.

52. R. G. Jinks, *History of Smith & Wesson: No Thing of Importance Will Come Without Effort* (North Hollywood, Calif.: Beinfeld, 1977), pp. 1–3. Jinks notes (p. 8) that in June 1846, the Wesson company corresponded with Allen & Thurber of Norwich, Connecticut, where Smith was at the time employed. It's possible the two men first made contact there.

53. On Wesson's background, see Jinks, *Smith & Wesson*, pp. 5–13.

54. "Improvement in breech-loading fire-arms," Patent no. 8,317, August 26, 1851.

55. Bilby, *Revolution in Arms*, pp. 55–56; Westwood, *Rifles*, p. 30; Williamson, *Winchester*, p. 10. Edwards, *Civil War Guns*, p. 164, points out the dueling aspect.

56. "Improvement in fire-arms," Patent no. 10,535, February 14, 1854.

57. "Improvement in cartridges," Patent no. 11,496, August 8, 1854.

58. See "Stockholders of Volcanic Repeating Arms Company," in Williamson, *Winchester*, p. 462.

59. Williamson, *Winchester*, pp. 11–12.

60. Bilby, *Revolution in Arms*, pp. 57–58.

61. See "Making shirts," Patent no. 5,421, February 1, 1848.

62. Technically speaking, the first official Peacemaker was made in 1872 after Colt's death, but the colonel referred to his revolvers as "peacemakers" and endowed them with divine powers. In 1861, when his local minister's house was burgled, Colt sent him a letter (with a copy to the newspapers, of course): "I take the liberty of sending you a copy of my latest work on 'Moral Reform,' trusting that, in the event of further depredations being attempted, the perpetrators may experience a feeling effect of the moral influence of my work." In the accompanying package, there was a Peacemaker. (M. A. Bellesiles, *Arming America: The Origins of a National Gun Culture* [New York: Alfred A. Knopf, 2000], p. 430.) Colt, however, had not invented the term. In 1841 Cochran, a gun-maker, had described one of his products as "an American peacemaker," and three years later the twelve-inch iron cannon mounted on USS *Princeton* exploded, killing the secretaries of state and navy—its nickname was the Peacemaker. See Dizard, Muth, and Andrews, *Guns in America*, p. 52.

63. Bellesiles, *Arming America*, p. 354.

64. On Colt's background, see his entry in *American National Biography*; Sharpe, *Rifle in America*, pp. 184–85. The basic idea of having a movable or removable chamber was not entirely new. In the Middle Ages and Renaissance, heavy and light artillery pieces sometimes employed them, though it's doubtful Colt was aware of this. See K. DeVries and R. D. Smith, "Breech-loading guns with Removable Powder Chambers: A Long-lived Military Technology," in B. J. Buchanan, ed., *Gunpowder, Explosives and the State: A Technological History* (Aldershot [U.K.]/Burlington, Vt.: Ashgate, 2006).

65. "Improvement in fire-arms," Patent no. 9,430X, February 25, 1836.

66. On Colt's line about government patronage, see Dizard, Muth, and Andrews, *Guns in America*, p. 61.

67. Ibid., p. 62.

68. Garavaglia and Worman, *Firearms of the American West*, p. 1:141.

69. Dizard, Muth, and Andrews, *Guns in America*, pp. 64–65; Garavaglia and Worman, *Firearms of the American West*, p. 1:142.

70. Quoted in Sharpe, *Rifle in America*, p. 186.

71. Quoted in Garavaglia and Worman, *Firearms of the American West*, p. 1:145.

72. H. G. Houze, *Winchester Repeating Arms Company: Its History and Development from 1865 to 1981* (Iola, Wis.: Krause, 2004), p. 14; Williamson, *Winchester,* pp. 22–23. For a detailed look at Henry's background, see Edwards, *Civil War Guns,* p. 171.

73. "Improvement in magazine fire-arm," Patent no. 30,446, October 16, 1860.

74. Advertisement, reproduced in Edwards, *Civil War Guns,* p. 160.

75. On Spencer's background, see Bilby, *Revolution in Arms,* pp. 68–76 and W. A. Bartlett, "Lincoln's Seven Hits with a Rifle," *The Magazine of History with Notes and Queries,* vol. 19, no. 1 (1921), pp. 68–69.

76. Ripley's sparse biographical details can be found in R. V. Bruce, *Lincoln and the Tools of War* (Indianapolis/New York: Bobbs-Merrill, 1956), esp. chap. 2; his entry in *American National Biography;* and C. L. Davis, *Arming the Union: Small Arms in the Civil War* (Port Washington, N.Y.: National University Publications/Kennikat Press, 1973), p. 13. On his appointment as Ordnance chief, see Special Orders no. 115, April 23, 1861, *Official Records,* 3d ser., p. 1:102 (see note 86 below). His predecessor, Henry Knox Craig, had been forced out (or so he said) by means of a whirling and gnashing machination involving corrupt jobbers, political patronage, and war profiteering, much of it somehow orchestrated (according to the pro-Craig *New York Times*) by the newly arrived Ripley. (For the gory details, see *New York Times,* July 10, 1861.) Ripley's politics, however, are a bit of a mystery. Bruce, *Lincoln,* p. 29 and p. 305n., claims him as a Republican, saying that "Ripley was appointed to the superintendency at Springfield by a Whig administration, he promptly dismissed the Jacksonian paymaster, he feuded with the *Independent Democrat,* and he was removed under a Democratic administration and replaced by a Democratic politician." Fair enough, but an entertaining *New York Times* hit piece (there's no other word for it) of July 14, 1861, "inferred" that he had "no sympathy with Republicanism" and was "Pro-Slavery." (The anonymous author also managed to insinuate that he was a coward ("It is not known that [Ripley] was ever in a fight," and moreover, the Springfield Arsenal was "a place as far removed from the danger of assault by Mexican enemies as it is possible to conceive of.") Bruce's argument is the stronger of the two, and Ripley's unyielding support for the Union lends it additional credence. He also appears to have lacked any kind of Southern connections. It is unlikely, however, that Ripley was particularly partisan or ideological, and he seems to have been more of a technocrat than anything else.

77. *New York Times,* July 14, 1861: "Our bureaucratic hero had the address to secure a brevet for his skill in manipulating red tape."

78. On officer strength, see Davis, *Arming the Union,* p. 15; on clerks, ibid., p. 29.

79. Ibid., p. 30.

80. Ibid., pp. 133–34.

81. Bruce, *Lincoln,* pp. 131–43. On the "enemy-slaughtering" rifles, see W. O. Stoddard, *Inside the White House in War Times* (New York: Charles L. Webster & Co., 1890), p. 45.

82. *Scientific American,* September 19, 1863.

83. Davis, *Arming the Union,* pp. 46–47.

84. G. Perret, *Lincoln's War: The Untold Story of America's Greatest President as Commander in Chief* (New York: Random House, 2004), p. 147.

85. Quoted in Bruce, *Lincoln,* p. 36.

86. Ibid., pp. 33–34, 205.

87. James Ripley, "Notes on Subject of Contracting for Small-Arms," June 11, 1861, in *The War of the Rebellion: A Compilation of the Official Records of the Union and Confederate Armies* (Washington, D.C.: Government Printing Office, 1880–1901), 3d ser., pp. 1:264–65. Hereinafter known as *Official Records.* Later on, the commissioners looking into the matter of arms-contracting concurred: the Springfield rifle-musket was "the best infantry arm in the world." Report on Contracts by J. Holt and R. D. Owen, July 1, 1862, *Official Records,* 3d ser., p. 2:191. See also Ripley's comments in "The Small Arms of Our Armies," *San Francisco Bulletin,* May 30, 1862, p. 2: "The United States musket, as now made, has no superior arm in the world. I say this with confidence, from my entire familiarity with the manufacture of these arms."

88. H. L. Peterson, *Notes on Ordnance of the American Civil War, 1861–1865* (Washington, D.C.: American Ordnance Association, 1959), no page numbers. Mahon, "Civil War Infantry Assault Tactics," p. 58, says there were eighty-one different types of shoulder arm.

89. Ripley estimated the cost of a government-produced rifle-musket as $13.93 per arm, including bullet molds, wipers, screwdrivers, and other appendages; a privately produced cavalry carbine, on the other hand, cost $30, while a Colt revolver alone cost $25. See Ripley to Simon Cameron, June 8, 1861, *Official Records*, 3d ser., p. 1:260. By the fall of 1862, Ripley's estimate for a Springfield rifle-musket had risen, probably owing to inflation and the strictures of wartime demand, to $20. At that time early (if unreliable) Austrian, Prussian, and Belgian rifle-muskets cost as little as $10 to import (a good Enfield went for $19), while the price for a Sharps or Colt rifle was $42.50 and $45, respectively. War Department Report, "Supplement to Prices of Small-Arms," September 30, 1862, *Official Records*, 3d ser., p. 2:621.

90. Lieutenant Francis Shunk to Ripley, August 30, 1862, *Official Records*, 1st ser., pt. 3, pp. 12:767–68.

91. Ripley, "Notes," *Official Records*, 3d ser., p. 1:264.

92. One reason why the Henry failed to excite Ripley was Winchester's congenital inability to build more than 260 per month, even as late as 1865. Davis, *Arming the Union*, p. 90.

93. Ibid., pp. 73–74.

94. For a list and description, see Edwards, *Civil War Guns*, pp. 27–57.

95. Report by H. K. Craig for John Floyd, November 12, 1859, *Official Records*, 3d ser., p. 1:1.

96. Report by Ripley, "Principal Operations of the Ordnance Department," November 21, 1862, *Official Records*, 3d ser., pp. 2:849–59. For slightly different figures, see Letter, Simon Cameron to Edwin Morgan, September 27, 1861, *Official Records*, 3d ser., p. 1:544.

97. Howard, "Interchangeable Parts Reexamined," p. 635.

98. Davis, *Arming the Union*, p. 106.

99. In the 1830s Colonel Hawkins wrote that "the length, bend and casting of a [gun]stock must, of course, be fitted to the shooter, who should have his measure for them as carefully entered in a gunmaker's books, as that for a suit of clothes on those of his tailor." Quoted in Rosenberg, "Economic Development and the Transfer of Technology," p. 259.

100. On the North and South's differing conceptions of managerialism, see J. E. Clark, *Railroads in the Civil War: The Impact of Management on Victory and Defeat* (Baton Rouge: Lousiana State University Press, 2001).

101. On Gorgas, see F. E. Vandiver, *Ploughshares into Swords: Josiah Gorgas and Confederate Ordnance* (Austin: University of Texas Press, 1952); S. W. Wiggins, ed., *The Journals of Josiah Gorgas, 1857–1878* (Tuscaloosa/London: University of Alabama Press, 1995).

102. S. L. Falk, "Jefferson Davis and Josiah Gorgas, an Appointment of Necessity," *Journal of Southern History* 28 (1962), pp. 1:84–86.

103. He was officially appointed Ordnance chief on April 8. See Special Order no. 17, *Official Records*, 4th ser., p. 1:211.

104. Wiggins ed., *Journals of Josiah Gorgas*, p. 75.

105. F. E. Vandiver, "Makeshifts of Confederate Ordnance," *Journal of Southern History* 17, no. 2 (1951), p. 180. On the musicians' swords, see Bellesiles, *Arming America*, p. 418.

106. On the stripping of Harpers Ferry, see Smith, *Harpers Ferry*, pp. 319–20.

107. See Bellesiles, *Arming America*, p. 419.

108. Vandiver, "Makeshifts of Confederate Ordnance," p. 190.

109. Ibid., p. 185; W. Diamond, "Imports of the Confederate Government from Europe and Mexico," *Journal of Southern History* 6, no. 4 (1940), pp. 470–503. See also Fuller, *Rifled Musket*, pp. 2–3.

110. Vandiver, "Makeshifts of Confederate Ordnance," pp. 184–90.

111. Ibid., p. 193.

112. Bruce, *Lincoln,* p. 105.

113. Report by Lieutenant J. Green to Colonel J. Harris, commandant, Marine Corps, February 6, 1860, in Sharpe, *Rifle in America,* pp. 198–99.

114. Letter from Winchester, *Scientific American,* March 7, 1863.

115. Ibid.

116. *Scientific American,* September 19, 1863.

117. I. Tarbell, *The Life of Abraham Lincoln* (New York: Macmillan, 1924), p. 1:6.

118. Bruce, *Lincoln,* p. 39.

119. Ibid., p. 38. The *Annual* comprised 200 or 300 dense pages covering the year's technological developments around the world, as well as contributions from America's leading scientists. Lincoln was so fascinated with his copy—given to him by his law partner, William Herndon—that he immediately went out and purchased the entire set. "I have wanted such a book for years," Lincoln explained, "because I sometimes make experiments and have thoughts about the physical world that I do not know to be true or false. I may, by this book, correct my errors and save time and expense." Herndon to Weik, December 16, 1885, in E. Hertz, ed., *The Hidden Lincoln: From the Letters and Papers of William H. Herndon* (Garden City, N.Y.: Blue Ribbon Press, 1938), pp. 112–13.

120. G. B. McClellan, *McClellan's Own Story . . .* (London: Sampson Low, Marston, Searle & Rivington, 1887), p. 162.

121. *New York Times,* August 4, 1858; *Scientific American,* August 28, 1858.

122. H. C. Whitney, *Life on the Circuit with Lincoln* (1892; reprint Caldwell, Idaho: Caxton, 1940), p. 121. Whitney, interestingly, added that "he was equally inquisitive in regard to matters which obtruded on his attention in the moral world; he would bore to the center of any moral proposition, and carefully analyse and dissect every layer and every atom of which it was composed, nor would he give over the search till completely satisfied that there was nothing more to know, or be learned about it."

123. There is some debate as to what piece Lincoln carried. Traditionally, it is thought to have been an experimental Henry, though Bilby *(Revolution in Arms,* p. 67) points out that early, bronze-framed Henrys did not appear until April 1862. However, the Winchester historian Herbert Houze notes that iron-framed Henrys might have been available in May of 1861 as a result of Winchester contracting with Colt for a limited production run. The case can't be proven either way, and I think it perfectly possible that Lincoln had in his hands one of these rare Colt-made, primitive Henrys. Stoddard says Lincoln actually carried "a kind of Spencer"—which could easily be misidentified or misremembered as a Henry; Bilby, however, believes Stoddard might have confused this test with one conducted by Lincoln using a Spencer a year later. (Stoddard's anecdote can be found in his *Inside the White House,* p. 42.)

124. Stoddard, *Inside the White House,* p. 41.

125. Ibid., pp. 43–44. The anecdote regarding Mrs. Grady is in Bruce, *Lincoln,* p. 103n.

126. Ibid., p. 108.

127. Bilby, *Revolution in Arms,* p. 77; Bruce, *Lincoln,* p. 112. McClellan allusively explained later that at the time there weren't "a sufficient number of suitable officers to perform their duties at the various headquarters." The key word here was "suitable." Report by McClellan on the "Operations of the Army of the Potomac from July 27, 1861, to November 9, 1862," dated August 4, 1863, *Official Records,* 1st ser., p. 5:29.

128. Davis, *Arming the Union,* p. 124.

129. Quoted in Bruce, *Lincoln,* p. 167.

130. See the report in the *Pittsfield Sun,* January 30, 1862, p. 3; Davis, *Arming the Union,* p. 69.

131. Bruce, *Lincoln,* p. 168; E. A. Hitchcock, *Fifty Years in Camp and Field, the Diary of Major-General Ethan Allen Hitchcock, U.S.A.,* ed. W. A. Croffut (New York: G. P. Putnam's Sons, 1909), pp. 438–39. See also *New York Times,* January 30, 1862.

132. Hitchcock, *Fifty Years,* p. 441; Bruce, *Lincoln,* p. 169.

133. Bilby, *Revolution in Arms*, pp. 86–91; Edwards, *Civil War Guns*, p. 161.

134. It is sometimes alleged that Spencers were used at the beginning of the battle of Gettysburg, though without causing any casualties. William G. Adams Jr., in "Spencers at Gettsyburg: Fact or Fiction," *Military Affairs* 29, no. 1 (1965), pp. 41ff., casts doubt on the assertion.

135. Bilby, *Revolution in Arms*, p. 103. See also Edwards, *Civil War Guns*, p. 149.

136. For example, trooper Robert Trouax used "his Seven Shooting Spencer rifle, killing six rebels as they were crossing the [Rapidan] river." Quoted, with others, in Edwards, *Civil War Guns*, p. 150.

137. T. Dennett, ed., *Lincoln and the Civil War in the Diaries and Letters of John Hay* (New York: Dodd, Mead & Co., 1939), p. 82; Bruce, *Lincoln*, pp. 261–63; Bilby, *Revolution in Arms*, p. 119; "Lincoln and the Repeating Rifle," *Scientific American*, December 1921. Spencer's record of the day is reprinted in Edwards, *Civil War Guns*, p. 151, and see also Bartlett's transcript of an interview with Spencer, in "Lincoln's Seven Hits with a Rifle," *Magazine of History*, pp. 71–72. In 1883 the target board was donated by Spencer to the collection of Civil War and Lincoln relics in Springfield, Illinois, but was lost sometime between then and 1956, when an investigation of the inventory discovered it missing (Edwards, *Civil War Guns*, p. 152.)

138. *The New York Times* picked up early rumors on September 10, 1863.

139. *New York Times*, September 15, 1863.

140. *American National Biography* entry.

141. Davis, *Arming the Union*, pp. 140–41.

142. Report on the "Principal Operations of the Ordnance Department," October 22, 1864, *Official Records*, 3d ser., p. 4:802.

143. *Scientific American*, January 2, 1865.

144. The preceding section is heavily based on Nosworthy's brilliant chapter in *Bloody Crucible*, pp. 571–93; P. Griffith, *Battle Tactics of the Civil War* (New Haven, Conn./London: Yale University Press, 1987), pp. 145–50; and C. M. Wilcox, *Rifles and Rifle Practice* . . . (New York: D. Van Nostrand, 1859), pp. 236–37 (on hit rates). Wilcox rightly warns that these figures are not exact, but they nevertheless illustrate essential truths.

145. See Table 6.1, "Ranges of musketry fire," in Griffith, *Battle Tactics*, p. 147. Griffith points out (p. 148) that during the Second World and Korean Wars, the average combat range was about one hundred yards, while in Vietnam, that figure was even less. "There is therefore a fallacy in the notion," he says, "that longer-range weapons automatically produce longer-range fire."

146. Nosworthy, *Bloody Crucible*, pp. 571–93; Griffith, *Battle Tactics*, pp. 145–50.

147. Wilcox, *Rifles and Rifle Practice*. On the army copies, see G. D. Townsend (assistant adjutant general) to the publisher, June 28, 1859, reproduced in ibid., front matter.

148. W. L. Willard, *Comparative Value of Rifled and Smooth-bored Arms* (1863), quoted in Fuller, *Rifled Musket*, p. 9.

Chapter 5

1. P. D. Jamieson, *Crossing the Deadly Ground: United States Infantry Tactics, 1865–1899* (Tuscaloosa, Ala./London: University of Alabama Press, 1994), p. 25.

2. D. Rickey Jr., *Forty Miles a Day on Beans and Hay: The Enlisted Soldier Fighting the Indian Wars* (Norman: University of Oklahoma Press, 1963), pp. 234–35. On the Sioux and Crow, see J. S. Brisbin, ed., *Belden, the White Chief* . . . (Cincinnati and New York: C.F. Vent, 1874), pp. 440, 451; on the Pawnees, see R. I. Dodge, *The Plains of the Great West and Their Inhabitants* . . . (New York: G. P. Putnam's Sons, 1877), pp. 374–75; for Custer on Cheyennes, see Jamieson, *Crossing the Deadly Ground*, p. 30; on Crook's comment

about the Apaches, see J. H. Sears, *The Career of Leonard Wood* (New York: D. Appleton & Co., 1919), p. 28; and on the Comanches, E. A. Bode, *A Dose of Frontier Soldiering: The Memoirs of Corporal E. A. Bode, Frontier Regular Infantry, 1877–1882* ed. T. T. Smith (Lincoln: University of Nebraska Press, 1994), p. 144. Complicating matters still further was the sheer difficulty of distinguishing between friendly and hostile bands within even peaceful tribes; it was often impossible to know whether approaching horsemen would start shooting until they started shooting, let alone whether they would stay amicable if they sensed weakness. Captain Marcy, who wrote a helpful guidebook for "prairie travellers," advised that settlers never let Indians come too near, *even* if they seemed friendly or curious, for they were murderous at close quarters. Often, waving a rifle in the air or making hand-signals was enough to warn them off, he had found. R. B. Marcy, *The Prairie Traveller* . . . (New York: Harper & Brothers, 1859), p. 197. See also L. McMurtry, *Oh What a Slaughter: Massacres in the American West, 1846–1890* (New York: Simon & Schuster, 2005), p. 109.

3. Marcy, *Prairie Traveller,* p. 200.

4. In clashes between native Americans, "a single Indian of either tribe on his own ground counts himself the equal to at least three of the other," said Colonel Dodge, who knew his onions. Dodge, *Plains of Great West,* p. 375.

5. See L. M. Kane, trans., *Military Life in Dakota: The Journal of Philippe Régis de Trobriand* (St. Paul, Minn.: Alvord Memorial Commission, 1951), p. 64; J. G. Bourke, *On the Border with Crook* (London: Sampson, Low, Marston, Searle, & Rivington, 1892), p. 251; Jamieson, *Crossing the Deadly Ground,* pp. 37–38; F. W. Seymour, *Indian Agents of the Old Frontier* (New York: D. Appleton-Century, 1941), p. 235.

6. Marcy, *Prairie Traveller,* pp. 200–201.

7. Bode, *Dose of Frontier Soldiering,* p. 144.

8. W. T. Sherman, *Memoirs of General W. T. Sherman* (New York: D. Appleton & Co., 1875), p. 227.

9. R. M. Utley, *Cavalier in Buckskin: George Armstrong Custer and the Western Military Frontier,* rev. ed. (Lincoln: University of Oklahoma Press, 2001), p. 58.

10. Seymour, *Indian Agents,* pp. 241–42.

11. Quoted in ibid., pp. 58–59.

12. George Crook, "General Orders No. 8," October 24, 1876, quoted in C. King, *Campaigning with Crook* (1890; reprint Norman: University of Oklahoma Press, 1964), p. 158.

13. Quoted in J. W. Vaughn, *Indian Fights: New Facts on Seven Encounters* (Norman: University of Oklahoma Press, 1966), p. 231. Vaughn's account (pp. 14–90) is the most comprehensive one available. See S. S. Calitri, " 'Give Me Eighty Men': Shattering the Myth of the Fetterman Massacre," *Montana: The Magazine of Western History,* Autumn 2004, for a revisionist angle.

14. Bourke, *On the Border with Crook,* p. 107. Fort Bowie was "filled with such inscriptions as 'Killed by the Apaches,' 'Met his death at the hands of the Apaches,' 'Died of wounds inflicted by Apache Indians,' and at times 'Tortured and killed by Apaches. One visit to that cemetery was warranted to furnish the most callous with nightmares for a month."

15. Vaughn, *Indian Fights,* p. 70.

16. Calitri, " 'Give Me Eighty Men,' " and J. H. Cook, *Fifty Years on the Old Frontier as Cowboy, Hunter, Guide, Scout, and Ranchman* (Norman, Okla.: University of Oklahoma Press, 1992 ed.), p. 198; E. D. Belish, "American Horse (Wasechun-Tashunka): The Man Who Killed Fetterman," *Annals of Wyoming* 58 (Spring 1991), pp. 54–67.

17. Quoted in R. M. Utley, *Frontier Regulars: The United States Army and the Indian, 1866–1891* (New York: Macmillan, 1973), p. 109 n30.

18. Vaughn, *Indian Fights,* p. 69.

19. Brisbin, *Belden,* pp. 377–78.

20. S. Gibson, "The Wagon Box Fight" in G. R. Hebard and E. A. Brininstool, *The Bozeman Trail* . . . (1922; reprint New York: AMS Press, 1978), pp. 2:39–71.

21. M. Littman, "The Wagon Box Fight as I Saw It," in Hebard and Brininstool, *Bozeman Trail*, pp. 2:72–82.

22. King, *Campaigning with Crook*, pp. 135–36.

23. Quoted in L. A. Garavaglia and C. G. Worman, *Firearms of the American West (1803–1865, 1866–1894)*, 2 vols. (1984–85; reprint Niwot: University Press of Colorado, 1997–98), pp. 2:355.

24. Seymour, *Indian Agents*, pp. 39–40, 48; Garavaglia and Worman, *Firearms of American West*, p. 2:361.

25. J. H. Taylor, *Sketches of Frontier and Indian Life on the Upper Missouri and Great Plains*, 3d ed. (Bismarck, N.D.: J. H. Taylor, 1897), pp. 62–63.

26. Brisbin, *Belden*, p. 393.

27. A. Garcia, *Tough Trip Through Paradise, 1878–1879*, ed. B. H. Stein (1967; reprint Moscow: University of Idaho Press, 2001), pp. 150–53.

28. J. C. Cremony, *Life Among the Apaches* (San Francisco: A. Roman & Company, 1868), p. 194.

29. J. E. Parsons and J. S. du Mont, *Firearms in the Custer Battle* (Harrisburg, Pa.: Stackpole, 1953), p. 31. See also, for further examples, D. G. McCrady, *Living with Strangers: The Nineteenth-Century Sioux and the Canadian-American Borderlands* (Lincoln: University of Nebraska Press, 2006).

30. Garavaglia and Worman, *Firearms of American West*, p. 2:362, 356.

31. F. B. Linderman, *Plenty-Coups: Chief of the Crow* (1930; reprint Lincoln: University of Nebraska Press, 1962), pp. 106–7. It took time for warriors accustomed to molding their own ammunition from lead and pouring powder down the muzzle to familiarize themselves with the new metallic cartridges. Henry Stanley, soon to set off for Africa to find the vanished explorer Dr. Livingstone, was in Nebraska at the time and was told that several Spencer-armed Indians, "not being posted in the breech-loading business," had injured their hands after trying to pound the explosive metallic cartridges down the barrel. H. M. Stanley, *My Early Travels and Adventures in America and Asia* (1895; reprint London: Gerald Duckworth & Co., 2001), pp. 135–36.

32. "Official Report of the Engagements with Indians on the 4th and 11th Ultimo," August 15, 1873, by Custer, printed in E. B. Custer, *"Boots and Saddles," or, Life in Dakota with General Custer* (1885; reprint Norman: University of Oklahoma Press, 1961), p. 247. Three years later Richard Hughes was touring the Black Hills and recorded that "the adult [Ogalallas] were splendidly armed—indeed much better than the average man of our party—their guns being mostly Sharps' or Winchester rifles of late pattern." R. B. Hughes, *Pioneer Years in the Black Hills*, ed. A. W. Spring (Glendale, Calif.: Arthur H. Clark Co., 1957), pp. 41–42.

33. C. Windolph, *I Fought with Custer . . .* (New York: Charles Scribner's Sons, 1947), p. 92. Windolph had emigrated from Germany and joined the Seventh Cavalry in 1870. He won the Medal of Honor during the fight on Reno's Hill while exposing himself to heavy hostile fire as he covered a water-fetching party. On Indian armament at the battle, see Parsons and Du Mont, *Firearms in the Custer Battle*, pp. 26–27. Their account corresponds with Windolph's. During the subsequent Court of Inquiry, Major Reno testified that "the Indians had Winchester rifles and the column made a large target for them and they were pumping bullets into it."

34. D. D. Scott, R. A. Fox Jr., M. A. Connor, and D. Harmon, *Archaeological Perspectives on the Battle of the Little Bighorn* (Norman: University of Oklahoma Press, 1989), p. 119.

35. Crook quoted in Jamieson, *Crossing the Deadly Ground*, p. 44.

36. Quoted in Garavaglia and Worman, *Firearms of American West*, p. 2:366.

37. J. B. Gillett, *Six Years with the Texas Rangers, 1875–1881* (Austin, Tex.: Von Boeckmann-Jones Co., 1921), pp. 68–69; R. I. Dodge, *Our Wild Indians: Thirty-three Years' Personal Experience Among the Red Men of the Great West* (Hartford, Conn.: A. D. Worthington & Co., 1882), p. 423. Alternatively, the Indians soaked the heads off matches and arranged

the phosphorus in a circle at the base of the cartridge; it was hoped that when the rim was struck, the lit phosphorus would ignite the powder. W. R. Austerman, "Guns of Many Voices," *Wild West Magazine,* October 1990, p. 7.

38. Quoted in Garavaglia and Worman, *Firearms in American West,* p. 2:378.

39. Ibid., pp. 2:370–71, 375, 377.

40. Rickey, *Forty Miles a Day,* pp. 299–300.

41. G. Custer "Official Report of the Engagements with Indians on the 4th and 11th Ultimo," August 15, 1873, in Custer, *"Boots and Saddles,"* pp. 237–48.

42. Even muzzle-loaders could still be found, not least because they could fire virtually any caliber or unorthodox type of ammunition that came to hand. Private James Lockwood laughed to recall that in the "Hayfield Fight" of August 1867—when thirty soldiers and civilians held out, in grand Rorke's Drift style, against a force of hundreds of Cheyenne— one of his comrades saw an Indian sneak into a wagon to gulp down molasses. Short of ammo, he threw a handful of .32-caliber pistol cartridges ("copper shells and all") down the barrel of his trusty old Springfield .58 muzzle-loader and blasted the intruder (Vaughn, *Indian Fights,* p. 102). As late as 1883 the Pittsburgh firm of James Bown & Sons ran an advertisement claiming that "in some parts it is very difficult to get cartridges for breech loaders. But you can always get powder, lead and caps in the most remote part of the world, and this is why we claim the muzzle-loader is better." Quoted in A. Halsey's review of Henry Kauffman's *The Pennsylvania-Kentucky Rifle* in *Technology and Culture* 6, no. 1 (1965), p. 127.

43. Quoted in Garavaglia and Worman, *Firearms of American West,* pp. 2:136, 133. See also D. D. Smits, "The Frontier Army and the Destruction of the Buffalo: 1865–1883," *Western Historical Quarterly* 25, no. 3 (1994), pp. 315, 320, for Cody's hunting.

44. Gillett, *Six Years with the Texas Rangers,* pp. 203–4.

45. The previous section on ballistics and cartridges based on Garavaglia and Worman, *Firearms of American West,* pp. 2:141–52; and Chuck Hawks's article, "Buffalo Cartridges of the American Frontier," at www.chuckhawks.com/buffalo_cartridges.htm.

46. Dodge, *Plains of Great West,* p. 137.

47. A. Hatch, *Remington Arms: An American Company* (New York/Toronto: Rinehart & Co., 1956), pp. 38–39. P. B. Sharpe, *The Rifle in America,* 3d ed. (New York: Funk & Wagnalls, 1953), p. 284, disagrees and says Eliphalet possessed a "dry sense of humor."

48. Hatch, *Remington Arms,* pp. 48–61; Sharpe, *Rifle in America,* pp. 284–87, 304.

49. W. B. Edwards, *Civil War Guns: The Complete Story of Federal and Confederate Small Arms* (Harrisburg, Pa.: Stackpole Co., 1962), pp. 190–96; Hatch, *Remington Arms,* pp. 77–82; Sharpe, *Rifle in America,* pp. 288–89, 305.

50. Sharpe, *Rifle in America,* p. 291. On Hartley's background and business career, see Edwards, *Civil War Guns,* p. 71.

51. Hatch, *Remington Arms,* p. 131.

52. "Mrs. Frances Hartley dead," *New York Times,* April 23, 1909, p. 9. The couple had four children.

53. Sharpe, *Rifle in America,* p. 292; H. F. Williamson, *Winchester: The Gun That Won the West* (Washington D.C.: Combat Forces Press, 1952), p. 66; Hatch, *Remington Arms,* pp. 109–11. On Frankford's experiments, see Sharpe, *Rifle in America,* pp. 32–33. Regarding the dictatorial Berdan, he was loathed by many of his men in the two Sharpshooter regiments. In July 1862, five company-level officers requested his removal from command. P. Katcher, *Sharpshooters of the American Civil War, 1861–65* (Oxford, U.K.: Osprey, 2002), p. 29.

54. Hatch, *Remington Arms,* pp. 135–36.

55. J. Dunn, "Egypt's Nineteenth-Century Armaments Industry," *Journal of Military History* 56, no. 2 (1997), pp. 231–54; Hatch, *Remington Arms,* pp. 142–45. The Mahdi's remark is quoted in F. Nicoll, *The Sword of the Prophet: The Mahdi of Sudan and the Death of General Gordon* (Sutton, U.K.: Stroud, 2004), pp. 88–89.

56. Hatch, *Remington Arms,* pp. 142–45. Dunn, "Egypt's Nineteenth-Century Armaments Industry," p. 244, disagrees with Hatch on the subject of the Paris Exposition, saying that the Remington was awarded the silver medal.

57. For these figures, see Sharpe, *Rifle in America,* pp. 305–6. On the French figure, see R. I. Wolf, *Arms and Innovation: The United States Army and the Repeating Rifle, 1865–1900* (Unpub. Ph.D diss.; Boston University, 1981), p. 63.

58. Sharpe, *Rifle in America,* p. 293. Remington sales have, I think, been greatly exaggerated; some authorities put the number as high as one million.

59. Dunn, "Egypt's Nineteenth-Century Armaments Industry," p. 253.

60. When Sergeant John Ryan of Company M was overseeing the burial detail for the Seventh Cavalry three days later, he found that "under the General's body were four or five brass cartridge shells which I picked up, they were what he used in his Remington rifle." Quoted in Parsons and Du Mont, *Firearms in the Custer Battle,* p. 19. Ryan was himself a crack shot: he carried a custom-made .45-caliber Sharps telescopic rifle. Noted in G. Michno, "Battle of Little Bighorn: Were the Weapons the Deciding Factor?" *Wild West,* online at www.historynet.com/magazines/wild_west/3035316.html?page=1&c=y. Ironically, though Custer liked to "brag on" his skills as a hunter (in the words of a colleague accompanying his 1874 Black Hills hunting expedition), he "did no shooting that was notable." See Garavaglia and Worman, *Firearms of American West,* p. 2:161.

61. Dodge, *Plains of Great West,* pp. 133, 137.

62. J. Cloud, "Why the Buffalo Roam," *Time,* March 15, 2007.

63. In 1882 James McNaney and his brother decided to become buff runners; their shopping list is printed in Garavaglia and Worman, *Firearms of American West,* pp. 2:200–201; and see also Hatch, *Remington Arms,* p. 156.

64. A. Barra, *Inventing Wyatt Earp: His Life and Many Legends* (New York: Carroll & Graf, 1998), p. 31. Dodge's *Plains of the Great West* has an informative section on buffalo running, pp. 134–39.

65. Garcia, *Tough Trip Through Paradise,* p. 184.

66. F. Collinson, *Life in the Saddle,* ed. M. W. Clarke (Norman: University of Oklahoma Press, 1963), p. 55.

67. Hatch, *Remington Arms,* pp. 156–57; on Malcolm sights, see Sharpe, *Rifle in America,* pp. 168–69.

68. Collinson, *Life in the Saddle,* p. 55.

69. Smits, "Frontier Army," p. 320.

70. Sharpe, *Rifle in America,* p. 217.

71. Hatch, *Remington Arms,* pp. 180–83. On Remington's losses, see Sharpe, *Rifle in America,* p. 294.

72. For prices, see Edwards, *Civil War Guns,* p. 400, and also pp. 403–4.

73. Collinson, *Life in the Saddle,* p. 12.

74. G. Riley, *The Life and Legacy of Annie Oakley* (Norman: University of Oklahoma Press, 1994), p. 68; S. Kaspar, *Annie Oakley* (Norman: University of Oklahoma Press, 1992), pp. 184–85.

75. See C. Tefertiller, *Wyatt Earp: The Life Behind the Legend* (New York: John Wiley & Sons, 1997), pp. 116–17.

76. Austerman, "Guns of Many Voices," p. 4.

77. See, for example, Sergeant W. J. L. Sullivan, *Twelve Years in the Saddle for Law and Order on the Frontiers of Texas,* quoted in G. Shirley, *West of Hell's Fringe: Crime, Criminals, and the Federal Peace Office in Oklahoma Territory, 1889–1907* (Norman: University of Oklahoma Press, 1978), pp. 345, 347, where Sullivan notes that he and his comrades were using Winchesters when hunting down a band of desperadoes.

78. N. C. Wilson, *Treasure Express: Epic Days of the Wells Fargo* (New York: Macmillan, 1936), pp. 112–13.

79. Quoted in Garavaglia and Worman, *Firearms of American West,* p. 2:122.

80. Stanley, *My Early Travels and Adventures in America and Asia,* pp. 144–45.

81. There is some debate on the exact numbers. Some commentators have declared the number of Spencers as high as 230,000. I have used those given in C. Fuller, *The Rifled Musket* (Harrisburg, Pa.: Stackpole Co., 1958), p. 1, and confirmed by Edwards, *Civil War Guns,* p. 144, but see also A. M. Beck's detailed "Spencer's Repeaters in the Civil War" (1998), online at www.rarewinchesters.com/articles/art_spencercivilwar.shtml.

82. Williamson, *Winchester,* p. 58; Houze, *Winchester,* p. 69. Uncharacteristically for the arms business, the ending of Spencer's story was a happy one. During the war Spencer had continued to dabble with his beloved machines and in 1862, finding Ripley immovable, had turned his attention to developing a horseless carriage consisting of a steam engine, boiler, and steering wheel grafted onto a buggy. Spencer claimed he could keep pace with racehorses at the track—though the puffing contraption terrified them—but bad roads severely impeded the vehicle's speed and he returned to firearms. In the 1870s he invented an automatic screw machine, which he patented in September 1873 and licensed to Pratt & Whitney for a great deal of money. Bored again, he and Sylvester Roper developed a pump-action shotgun in 1882 and established the new Spencer Arms Company. Though lauded in Europe, sales were slack and the company went bust, taking much of Spencer's wealth with it. He then (again) invented an improved screw machine in 1891 and remade his fortune. He continued to work until the week of his death in January 1922, aged eighty-nine and with forty-two patents to his name. Two years before he met the great celestial mechanic, Spencer took up aviation, and made more than twenty flights. See Spencer's entry in *American National Biography;* his obituary in *New York Times,* January 15, 1922; and Patent no. 143,306, September 30, 1863, available at the U.S. Patent and Trademark Office Web site, www.uspto.gov.

83. Williamson, *Winchester,* p. 474. Winchester was ruthless toward competitors. According to Houze, *Winchester,* p. 63, in 1865 "he learned that Isaac Hartshorn, the India Rubber magnate, was filing a patent suit against the Burnside Rifle Company, a manufacturer of the Spencer Repeating Rifle, the Henry Rifle's chief rival, Winchester secretly purchased Hartshorn's patent while the suit was still in progress. With pure Machiavellian foresight, Winchester knew that if the matter was decided in Hartshorn's favor, Winchester could then, by proxy, dictate the terms of settlement. After Hartshorn's claim was determined to be valid in 1866, Winchester requested payment of damages to be made in machinery, thus forcing the Burnside Company out of the firearms business."

84. Ibid., pp. 22–25, 14; J. G. Bilby, *A Revolution in Arms: A History of the First Repeating Rifles* (Yardley, Pa.: Westholme, 2006), p. 224.

85. Garavaglia and Worman, *Firearms of American West,* pp. 2:123–29; Houze, *Winchester,* p. 46; Williamson, *Winchester,* pp. 47–50.

86. An enduring mystery was exactly how they had acquired all these weapons, since, upon inquiry, no one claimed responsibility for any arms transfers. The *Army and Navy Journal,* remarking upon this strange and universal silence in the aftermath of a massacre, published an ironic editorial advising the Winchester company to "prosecute the Indians for infringement of their patent." After all, since "the agency people and the traders solemnly affirm that they don't furnish them," it could only be inferred that the Indians were making them in their own secret factories. If Oliver Winchester "could get out a preliminary injunction, restraining the Indians from the use of his rifle, it might be of signal service to our troops in the next engagement" (*Army and Navy Journal,* July 22, 1876). Lurking furtively behind the *Journal*'s jokes was the implication that the respected Mr. Winchester was no stranger to slightly dubious arms dealing, if on a relatively minor level and mostly because American arms-makers were desperate to find new markets once the Civil War ended. Thus, back in 1865, using a French agent named François de Suzanne as an intermediary, he had sold one thousand prototype, King-adapted Henrys to Emperor Maximilian of Mexico, the Paris-backed monarch then causing conniptions in Washington over untoward French influence on the U.S. border. The guns were run from New York to Cuba and then shipped to Mexico, neatly avoiding American officials' scrutiny. Following the invocation of the Monroe Doctrine, Winchester, alarmed that revelations about the dodgy deal might return to haunt him (and hurt domestic sales), sold the same number of Model 1866s to Benito Juárez, the U.S.-backed republican rebel

who toppled Maximilian. Houze, *Winchester*, pp. 41, 59. Ultimately, Winchester shipped just seven hundred rifles to Mexico before the fall of the emperor; the French government requested that the remainder be sent to Le Havre. Ibid., pp. 61–62.

87. Garavaglia and Worman, *Firearms of American West*, p. 2:40.

88. Quoted in ibid., p. 2:186.

89. Quoted in ibid., p. 2:202. Hopalong Cassidy, the great cowboy himself (albeit a fictional one created by Clarence Mulford in 1904), was at one with Hiram. In the 1906 adventure, *Bar-20* (New York: A. L. Burt, 1906), p. 243, Mulford captured the single-shot/repeater debate that had evidently been the ruin of many a friendship: "Winchesters were Mr. Cassidy's pet aversion and Mr. Connors' most prized possession, this difference of opinion having upon many occasions caused hasty words between them. Mr. Connors, being better with his Winchester than Mr. Cassidy was with his Sharps, had frequently proved that his choice was the wiser but Mr. Cassidy was loyal to the Sharps and refused to be convinced."

90. L. Wallace, "A Buffalo Hunt in Northern Mexico," *Scribners Monthly*, March 1879, pp. 713–24. On Wallace's background, see R. M. Utley, *Four Fighters of Lincoln County* (Albuquerque: University of New Mexico Press, 1986), pp. 61–77.

91. G. O. Shields, "Antelope Hunting in Montana," *Harper's New Monthly Magazine* 69, no. 411 (August 1884), pp. 364–69.

92. See Sharpe, *Rifle in America*, p. 295.

93. "Improvement in breech-loading fire-arms," Patent no. 35,947, July 22, 1862, available at the U.S. Patent Office Web site. On the history of the company, see Edwards, *Civil War Guns*, p. 36.

94. Sharpe, *Rifle in America*, p. 78.

95. H. Bodinson, "The Martini-Henry: But Whatever Happened to Mr. Peabody?" *Guns Magazine*, December 2005.

96. Ibid.; Williamson, *Winchester*, pp. 64–65. Estimates differ on the number of Peabody-Martinis in Turkish hands during the war. I have used the figure given in J. Grant's authoritative "The Sword of the Sultan: Ottoman Arms Imports, 1854–1914," *Journal of Military History* 66, no. 1 (2002), p. 15.

97. Williamson, *Winchester*, pp. 55–57; 63–65.

98. This description of Plevna is based on R. T. Trenk Sr., "The Plevna Delay: Winchesters and Peabody-Martinis in the Russo-Turkish War," *Man at Arms* 19, no. 4 (1997), available online at www.militaryrifles.com/Turkey/Plevna/ThePlevnaDelay.html. I have adjusted downward Trenk's estimation that the first Russian casualties on July 30 occurred at three thousand yards. On this point, see W. C. Church, "American Arms and Ammunition," *Scribners Monthly* 19, no. 3 (January 1880), p. 436, who quotes contemporary sources regarding the ranges.

99. Church, "American Arms and Ammunition," p. 436.

100. Williamson, *Winchester*, p. 74, and see associated table of prices.

101. W. H. Becker, "American Manufacturers and Foreign Markets, 1870–1900: Business Historians and the 'New Economic Determinists,'" *Business History Review* 47, no. 4 (1973), pp. 466–81, provides a good overview of the issues concerned.

Chapter 6

1. "Col. Berdan's Sharp-shooters," *New York Times*, August 7, 1861, p. 8.

2. On Confederate rifle training, see P. Katcher, *Sharpshooters of the American Civil War, 1861–65* (Oxford, U.K.: Osprey, 2002), pp. 46–48.

3. H. D. Langley, ed., *To Utah with the Dragoons and Glimpses of Life in Arizona and California, 1858–1859* (Salt Lake City: University of Utah Press, 1974), p. 73.

4. D. C. McChristian, *An Army of Marksmen: The Development of United States Army Marksmanship in the Nineteenth Century* (Fort Collins, Colo.: Old Army Press, 1981), pp. 10–11.

5. J. H. Moore, ed., "Letters from a Santa Fe Army Clerk, 1855–1856," *New Mexico Historical Review* 40, no. 2 (1965), p. 143.

6. McChristian, *Army of Marksmen*, pp. 11–17; H. P. Walker, "The Enlisted Soldier on the Frontier," in J. P. Tate, ed., *The American Military on the Frontier: The Proceedings of the 7th Military History Symposium*: (Washington, D.C.: Office of Air Force History, 1978), pp. 124–25.

7. Quoted in McChristian, *Army of Marksmen*, p. 39. McChristian says that Gibbon was "obviously twenty-five years behind the times in his attitude towards tactics," which I think too dismissive. See a different view in H. M. Stanley, *My Early Travels and Adventures in America and Asia* (1895; reprint London: Gerald Duckworth & Co., 2001), p. 137. There the journalist-traveler Stanley says that Gibbon was "one of the most brilliant officers in the army."

8. Quoted in C. M. Robinson, *General Crook and the Western Frontier* (Norman: University of Oklahoma Press, 2001), p. 183.

9. Cited in J. W. Vaughn, *With Crook at the Rosebud* (Harrisburg, Pa.: Stackpole, 1956), p. 191. J. W. Vaughan, *Indian Fights: New Facts on Seven Encounters* (Norman: University of Oklahoma Press, 1966), pp. 117–44, has an analysis of the campaign.

10. J. Finerty, *War-path and Bivouac, or the Conquest of the Sioux: A Narrative . . .* (1890; reprint Norman: University of Oklahoma Press, 1994), pp. 92–93.

11. Walker, "Enlisted Soldier," p. 119.

12. McChristian, *Army of Marksmen*, pp. 22–24.

13. Quoted in C. King (who was there), *Campaigning with Crook* (1890; reprint Norman: University of Oklahoma Press, 1964), p. 120.

14. Quoted in L. A. Garavaglia and C. G. Worman, *Firearms of the American West (1803–1865, 1866–1894)*, 2 vols. (1984–85; reprint Niwot: University of Colorado, 1997–98), p. 2:44.

15. G. W. Wingate, *Manual for Target Practice, Including . . .* (New York: W. C. & F. P. Church, 1872). On Wingate's background, see J. G. Wilson and J. Fiske, eds., *Appleton's Encyclopaedia of American Biography* (New York: D. Appleton & Co., 1889), p. 574.

16. J. Parker, *The Old Army Memories, 1872–1918* (Philadelphia: Dorrance & Co., 1929), p. 18. On the international flavor of the army at the time, see King, *Campaigning*, p. 7.

17. R. M. Utley, *Frontier Regulars: The United States Army and the Indian, 1866–1891* (New York: Macmillan, 1973), p. 74.

18. H. Blumenthal, "George Bancroft in Berlin: 1867–1874," *New England Quarterly* 37, no. 2 (1964), pp. 224–41; D. F. Bowers, "Hegel, Darwin, and the American Tradition," in Bowers, ed., *Foreign Influences in American Life: Essays and Critical Bibliographies* (Princeton, N.J.: Princeton University Press, 1944), pp. 146–71.

19. Sherman to S. A. Hurlbut, May 26, 1874, quoted in Utley, *Frontier Regulars*, p. 66. During the Civil War American tactics manuals (such as Hardee's *Rifle and Light Infantry Tactics*) continued to be based on French military regulations and procedures, but with decreasing emphasis on, or at least acknowledgment of, their provenance. See J. Luvaas, "A Prussian Observer with Lee," *Military Affairs* 21 no. 3 (1957), p. 107. General Grant, who believed that Hardee's volume on tactics was "a mere translation from the French with Hardee's name attached," confessed unguiltily that he never got past the first lesson. U.S. Grant, *Personal Memoirs* (New York: Modern Library, 1999), pp. 128–29.

20. There were two major newspapers that stood up for France, the *Boston Post* and the *New York World*. The *Post* thought that Napoleon III had "kept France in the path of progress," and warned that Prussia was not as liberal as its defenders believed; in fact, it was nothing other than a despotism. By way of contrast, the *New York Times* opined that Germany was a republic and France, an imperialist state. The *World* trod a middle line between the two, saying that France was indeed an imperialist power while cautioning that Prussia was run by a warmongering "North German Caesar," and it told off the *Times* for "converting Count Bismarck and King William into apostles of progress and freedom." See

C. E. Scheiber, *The Transformation of American Sentiment Toward Germany, 1870–1914* (Boston, Mass.: Cornhill, 1923), pp. 14–24. By 1870, in any case, the French lacked much of a cheerleading constituency in this country—at least in the North; the "aristo-cratic" South was more sympathetic. At this time there were 151,203 foreign-born, emi-grant Germans living in New York (plus 50,746 in Philadelphia and 49,446 in Boston), compared to just 8,240 French in New York, 2,471 in Philadelphia, and 615 in Boston. Owing to their overwhelming preponderance, Germans naturally enjoyed greater sway in politics, diplomacy, and public opinion than did their French cousins. E. N. Curtis, "American Opinion of the French Nineteenth-Century Revolutions," *American Historical Review* 29, no. 2 (1924), p. 264n56.

21. Quoted in C. Brinton, *The Americans and the French* (Cambridge, Mass.: Harvard University Press, 1968), p. 68.

22. The "makeup" story extended right back to the creation of the United States—and even then it probably enjoyed something of a pedigree. In 1780, when Dr. Ezra Stiles, the pres-ident of Yale College, and his friend William Channing visited Newport, Rhode Island, to watch the French troops disembarking, they were surprised to discover that "neither offi-cers nor men are the effeminate beings we were heretofore taught to believe them." (Quoted in A. R. Rosenthal, "The Gender-Coded Stereotype: An American Perception of France and the French," *French Review* 72, no. 5 (1999), p. 905). In this regard, I once heard a story that in the pre-1914 Austro-Hungarian army a regulation, sternly adminis-tered, stated that no officer under field rank was permitted to wear rouge or to powder his face. I have no idea how true this is. However, in his recent *World War I: A Short History,* Norman Stone observes that the Romanian army was so unaccustomed to war that ju-nior officers were ordered not to wear eye shadow into battle. See P. Brendon, "Trench Warfare," *Guardian,* July 7, 2007.

23. On this subject see Rosenthal, "Gender-Coded Stereotype," pp. 897–908. French food enjoyed, or suffered, the sole honor of being cuttingly designated as "cuisine" to distin-guish it from down-home Yankee fare. During the 1840 election Whig backers of William Henry Harrison would claim their man subsisted, like any good American frontiersman, on "raw beef without salt" while his dandified competitor Martin Van Buren gorged him-self, like some modern-day Caligula, on such foreign fripperies as celery, cauliflower, and strawberries. D. Boorstin, *The Americans: The Democratic Experience* (New York: Random House, 1973), p. 323.

24. For a detailed examination of the politics and *Kultur* of German emigrants, see T. Jaehn, *Germans in the Southwest, 1850–1920* (Albuquerque: University of New Mexico Press, 2005), esp. chap. 3.

25. On the date of the NRA's formation, see the extremely helpful "condensation of General Wingate's memoirs of the National Rifle Association," which had been published around the turn of the century in its journal. G. W. Wingate, "Early Days of the NRA: Recollections of the National Rifle Association," pt. 1, *American Rifleman* 99, no. 5 (May 1951), p. 32.

26. M. Derthick, *The National Guard in Politics* (Cambridge, Mass.: Harvard University Press, 1965), pp. 18–20.

27. Wingate, "Early Days of the NRA," pp. 32–33.

28. See Wingate's pamphlet, "Programme for Opening of Range of the National Rifle Association, at Creedmoor, Queens Co., L.I." (National Rifle Association, 1873), and "Early Days of the NRA," p. 33.

29. There is some dispute over numbers. Most sources give the figure in the text; Wingate, "Early Days of the NRA," p. 34, states there were eight men and two reserves.

30. For a technical discussion of the Remington and Sharps rifles, see D. F. Butler, "Match Rifles: Then and Now," *American Rifleman* 119, no. 1 (January 1971), pp. 70–72.

31. There is some dispute on this point. Wingate says it was ginger ale.

32. Wingate, "Early Days of the NRA," p. 35, states that the Americans won by a single point. Other sources say it was by three.

33. Except where otherwise noted, this lengthy section on the formation of the NRA, Wingate and Church, the *Schützenbünde*, and Creedmoor is based on a variety of sources, including R. S. Gilmore, " 'Another Branch of Manly Sport': American Rifle Games, 1840–1900," in K. Glover, ed., *Hard at Play: Leisure in America, 1840–1940* (Amherst: University of Massachusetts Press, and Rochester, N.Y.: Strong Museum, 1992), pp. 93–111; A. Hatch, *Remington Arms in American History* (New York: Rinehart & Co., 1956), pp. 159–66; and D. Minshall's series, "Creedmoor and the International Matches," available online at www.researchpress.co.uk/targets/creedmoor/01creedmoor_nra.htm.

34. On closer inspection, the American victory in 1874, while impressive, was not decisive. After all, if Milner hadn't flubbed his shot, the Irish would have won. Any doubts were roughly shoved aside in the return match the following year, this time held near Dublin. Using the same weapons, and shooting under the same conditions, the Americans whipped their rivals 967 to 929 before fifty thousand spectators. In 1876's Grand Centennial Match the NRA invited the "riflemen of the world" to test themselves against American mettle. This time Canada, Scotland, Ireland, and Australia took up the challenge, but they too went home defeated. (The scores: United States, 3,126; Ireland, 3,104; Scotland, 3,062; Australia, 3,062; and Canada 2,923.) The high point for the Irish was the unbelievable performance of Milner, who was still embarrassed about his gaffe two years before and determined to avenge it. At the Centennial he hit the bull's-eye fifteen times out of fifteen for maximum points. But just in case anyone still doubted that Americans were the best shots and the deadliest riflemen in the world, the United States brought home another trophy the following week, again defeating the Irish. That still left the old enemy, the British, who had arrogantly stayed aloof from competing against their former colony since 1860, when Queen Victoria used a Whitworth muzzle-loader to fire the opening shot (at four hundred yards) of the first all-Britain competition. In May 1877, using muzzle-loaders, the Americans took them out 3,334 to 3,242. Following the 1877 match general interest in target shooting on the East Coast slowly declined as bicycling and automobiling took off. In 1878 and 1879 no matches were held, and while an Ireland-American competition in June 1880 resulted in an American victory, one against the British a month later at Wimbledon was a catastrophe for the transatlantic visitors: to the Britons' 1,646 points, the Americans scored an anemic 1,568. In 1882 and 1883 the Americans, commanded by Colonel Bodine, traveled to Britain and were ignominiously defeated twice. Butler, "Match Rifles," p. 70; Wingate, "Early Days of the NRA," pt. 2, *American Rifleman* 99, no. 6 (June 1951), pp. 40–41; and various pages in Minshall, "Creedmoor and the International Matches."

35. D. Rickey, Jr., *Forty Miles a Day on Beans and Hay: The Enlisted Soldier Fighting the Indian Wars* (Norman: University of Oklahoma Press, 1963), p. 104n21; McChristian, *Army of Marksmen*, pp. 34, 37; Walker, "Enlisted Soldier," p. 126.

36. The sources most useful for this section have been R. C. Brown, "General Emory Upton—The Army's Mahan," *Military Affairs* 17, no. 3 (1953), pp. 125–31; S. E. Ambrose, "Emory Upton and the Armies of Asia and Europe," *Military Affairs* 28, no. 1 (1964), pp. 27–32; D. J. Fitzpatrick, "Emory Upton and the Citizen Soldier," *Journal of Military History* 65, no. 2 (2001), pp. 355–89; Upton's entry in *American National Biography*. See also S. E. Ambrose, *Upton and the Army* (Baton Rouge: Louisiana State University Press, 1964). And for the view that Upton was too German-minded for American consumption and that his doctrines were poisonous to civilian-military relations, see R. F. Weigley, "The Soldier, the Statesman, and the Military Historians," *Journal of Military History* 58, no. 4 (1999), esp. pp. 812–14. Fitzpatrick (above) is much more sympathetic. M. A. Weitz, "Drill, Training, and the Combat Performance of the Civil War Soldier: Dispelling the Myth of the Poor Soldier, Great Fighter," *Journal of Military History* 62, no. 2 (1998), pp. 263–89, backs the Uptonian point of view.

37. Quoted in P. D. Jamieson, *Crossing the Deadly Ground: United States Infantry Tactics, 1865–1899* (Tuscaloosa, Ala./London: University of Alabama Press, 1994), p. 64.

38. T. L. McNaugher, *The M16 Controversies: Military Organizations and Weapons Acquisition* (New York: Praeger, 1984), p. 18.

39. Read the thrilling details in T. T. S. Laidley, *Reply to the Charge of Infringement of Colonel Wingate's Copyright* (Boston: Mills, Knight & Co., 1879).

40. McChristian, *Army of Marksmen*, pp. 41–43, 46.

41. Ibid., p. 43.

42. Quoted in McNaugher, *M16 Controversies*, p. 18.

43. P. A. Clarke, "Skirmish Line Target Practice in the Regular Army," *Harper's Weekly* 33, no. 1714 (October 26, 1889), p. 862; McChristian, *Army of Marksmen*, p. 52; Jamieson, *Crossing Deadly Ground*, pp. 56–59.

44. McChristian, *Army of Marksmen*, p. 82.

45. D. D. Smits, "The Frontier Army and the Destruction of the Buffalo: 1865–1883," *Western Historical Quarterly* 25, no. 3 (1994), p. 318.

46. R. Gilmore, " 'The New Courage': Rifles and Soldier Individualism, 1876–1918," *Military Affairs* 40, no. 3 (1976), p. 99.

47. McChristian, *Army of Marksmen*, pp. 47–58. On the creation of the "expert" class, see Gilmore, "The New Courage," p. 99.

48. Garavaglia and Worman, *Firearms of the American West*, p. 2:31; McChristian, *Army of Marksmen*, pp. 53–54.

49. Upton having suffered from excruciating headaches (perhaps psychosomatic) for many years, his doctor believed he might have a brain tumor, though others cited depression and still others his "chronic catarrh."

50. Utley, *Frontier Regulars*, p. 15.

51. On this subject, see S. P. Huntington, *The Soldier and the State: The Theory and Politics of Civil-Military Relations* (Cambridge, Mass.: Harvard University Press, 1957), pp. 222–30.

52. Quoted in Wingate, "Early Days of the NRA," pt. 2, p. 39.

53. *Congressional Record* 18:295 (December 20, 1886), quoted in Derthick, *National Guard*, pp. 20–21.

54. Quoted in R. M. Utley, "The Contribution of the Frontier to the American Military Tradition," in J. P. Tate, ed., *The American Military on the Frontier: The Proceedings of the 7th Military History Symposium* (Washington, D.C.: Office of Air Force History, 1978), p. 3.

55. Utley, *Frontier Regulars*, pp. 19–22; E. M. Coffman, "Army Life on the Frontier, 1865–1898," *Military Affairs* 20, no. 4 (1956), p. 200n42. "Unless there should be a war," mourned one young lieutenant, "I could not possibly be promoted to a Captaincy under 15 to 20 years from now." Quoted in P. Karsten, "Armed Progressives: The Military Reorganizes for the American Century," in Karsten, ed., *The Military in America: From the Colonial Era to the Present* (New York: Free Press, 1986), p. 259.

56. Rickey, *Forty Miles a Day*, pp. 51, 61.

57. Ibid., pp. 67–68.

58. E. A. Bode, *A Dose of Frontier Soldiering: The Memoirs of Corporal E. A. Bode, Frontier Regular Infantry, 1877–1882*, ed. T. T. Smith (Lincoln: University of Nebraska Press, 1994), pp. 19, 197n4, 123–24.

59. Utley, *Frontier Regulars*, pp. 23, 16; Rickey, *Forty Miles a Day*, pp. 143–47.

60. King, *Campaigning with Crook*, pp. 154–55. Custer, as always, had an innovative solution to curbing the problem. Imprisonment with hard labor and tattooing a large D on the left hip was the regulation punishment for captured deserters, but when thirty-five of his men deserted on a single day in 1867, he sent troopers after them with orders to bring back as many corpses—not prisoners—as possible. The bullet-holed dead were strung up prominently in the center of the camp. Waverers subsequently decided to stick with Custer rather than take their chances against him. M. Merington, ed., *The Custer Story: The Life and Intimate Letters of General George A. Custer and His Wife* (New York, 1950), p. 205, quoted in Coffman, "Army Life," p. 199. On punishment, see Rickey, *Forty Miles a Day*, pp. 153–55.

61. Coffman, "Army Life," pp. 198–99.

62. Rickey, *Forty Miles a Day*, pp. 156–65. For more on army life by a contemporary, see J. S. Brisbin, ed., *Belden, the White Chief; or, Twelve Years . . .* (Cincinnati and New York: C. F. Vent, 1874), pp. 408–20.

63. Bode, *A Dose of Frontier Soldiering*, pp. 40–41.

64. For these quotes, see J. Pettegrew, "'The Soldier's Faith': Turn-of-the-Century Memory of the Civil War and the Emergence of Modern American Nationalism," *Journal of Contemporary History* 31, no. 1 (1996), pp. 49–73.

65. See "The Soldier's Faith," in Karsten, *Military in America*, pp. 203–7. Stephen Crane's *The Red Badge of Courage* appeared the same year. Please don't be so silly, thought Walt Whitman, who remarked that the Civil War was "about nine hundred and ninety-nine parts diarrhea to one part glory." Quoted in V. J. Cirillo, *Bullets and Bacilli: The Spanish-American War and Military Medicine* (New Brunswick, N.J.: Rutgers University Press, 2004), p. 33.

66. King, *Campaigning with Crook*, p. 39. "Yellow Hair" is often mistranslated as "Yellow Hand." See L. McMurtry, "Inventing the West," in *Sacagawea's Nickname: Essays on the American West* (New York: New York Review Books, 2001), p. 24.

67. W. B. Skelton, "Army Officers' Attitudes Toward Indians, 1830–1860," *Pacific Northwest Quarterly* 67, no. 3 (1976), pp. 113–24; T. C. Leonard, "Red, White and the Army Blue: Empathy and Anger in the American West," *American Quarterly* 26, no. 2 (1974), pp. 178ff.

68. King, *Campaigning with Crook*, p. 30.

69. Quoted in Rickey, *Forty Miles a Day*, p. 317.

70. Quoted in Leonard, "Red, White and the Army Blue," p. 186.

71. N. A. Miles, *Personal Recollections and Observations of General Nelson A. Miles* (1896; reprint New York: Da Capo Press, 1969), p. 346. On Miles's politics, see W. B. Skelton's review of R. Wooster, *Nelson A. Miles and the Twilight of the Frontier Army* (Lincoln: University of Nebraska Press, 1993), in *American Historical Review* 99, no. 4 (1994), pp. 1393–94.

72. Miles, *Personal Recollections*, pp. 317–18. According to a hostile obituary of Geronimo in the *New York Times* in 1909 ("crafty, bloodthirsty, incredibly cruel and ferocious, he was all his life the worst type of aboriginal American savage"), it was only when Miles "showed him the white man's uses of the steam engine and telegraph" that he "acknowledged the uselessness of contending further against the military authorities of the United States." "Geronimo," *New York Times*, February 18, 1909.

73. See W. S. Nye, *Carbine and Lance: The Story of Old Fort Sill*, 3d ed. (Norman: University of Oklahoma Press, 1969), p. 250.

74. W. C. Church, "American Arms and Ammunition," *Scribners Monthly* 19, no. 3 (1880), p. 436.

75. Quoted in Jamieson, *Crossing Deadly Ground*, p. 64.

76. Quoted in Garavaglia and Worman, *Firearms of American West*, p. 2:44.

77. H. W. S. Cleveland, "Rifle-clubs," *Atlantic Monthly* 10, no. 59 (September 1862), p. 306.

78. Quoted in A. Trachtenberg, *The Incorporation of America: Culture and Society in the Gilded Age* (New York: Hill & Wang, 1982), p. 70.

79. On the army-navy game, see S. W. Pope, "An Army of Athletes: Playing Fields, Battlefields, and the American Military Sporting Experience, 1890–1920," *Journal of Military History* 59, no. 3 (1995), p. 439, and pp. 440–41 for Wingate's activities; W. C. Church, "Foot-ball in Our Colleges," *Century* 47, no. 2 (1893), pp. 315–16.

80. G. S. Patton, *War As I Knew It* (1947; reprint Boston/New York: Houghton Mifflin, 1995), p. 336.

81. For a summary of these incidents, see Trachtenberg, *Incorporation*, pp. 39–40.

82. J. K. Mahon, "Civil War Infantry Assault Tactics," *Military Affairs* 25, no. 2 (1961), p. 62, citing F. N. Maude, "Evolution of Modern Infantry Tactics," *Lectures*, Aldershot Military Society, no. 78 (London, 1908), p. 14.

83. "Col. Berdan's Sharp-shooters," *New York Times,* August 7, 1861; Katcher, *Sharpshooters of Civil War,* pp. 14–15.

84. Quoted in Gilmore, "New Courage," p. 99.

85. Ibid. As late as 1917 Ely, by then a colonel, was still trying to interest the army in his admittedly intriguing invention. He did succeed in attracting to his standard *Scientific American,* which ran a long but undetailed article about what Ely was calling his "battle control" device. He claimed that when it had been tested at the School of Musketry, the evidently progressive director had decided not to adopt it because, said Ely, the mechanism was "not an instrument of precision." Precision, added the magazine, is "a hobby of this school." Anon., "The Battle Control for the Rifle," *Scientific American* 97, no. 25 (December 22, 1917), p. 474.

86. Gilmore, "New Courage," p. 99; Jamieson, *Crossing Deadly Ground,* pp. 75–76.

87. On the evolution of the Springfield after the Civil War, the Allin system, ballistics developments, and internal Ordnance politics—all of which combined to produce the 1873 Springfield—see R. I. Wolf, *Arms and Innovation: The United States Army and the Repeating Rifle, 1865–1900* (Unpub. Ph.D. diss., Boston University, 1981), pp. 32–41, 48, 5–65, 70–73; Garavaglia and Worman, *Firearms of American West,* pp. 2:11, 16–17; "Improvement in Breech-Loading Fire-arms," Patent no. 49,959, September 19, 1865 (available at the U.S. Patent and Trademark Office website); T. T. S. Laidley to A. Dyer, January 22, 1866, in J. E. Hicks, *Notes on United States Ordnance: Small Arms, 1776 to 1940* (Mount Vernon, N.Y.: James E. Hicks, 1940), pp. 90–91; C. W. Sawyer, *Our Rifles* (Boston: Williams, 1946), p. 168; R. Pinckney, "The Tragedy of the Trapdoor Springfield," *Invention and Technology* 10, no. 4 (1995), available online at www.americanheritage.com/articles/magazine/it/1995/4/1995_4_28_print.shtml; W. H. Hallahan, *Misfire: The History of How America's Small Arms Have Failed Our Military* (New York: Charles Scribner's Sons, 1994), pp. 200–1; Proceedings of a Board of Officers, January 1869, Brig. Gen. P. V. Hagner presiding, extracts in Hicks, *Notes on Ordnance,* pp. 91–92.

88. Wolf, *Arms and Innovation,* pp. 93, 87.

89. Thus, in the words of one, magazine fire should be used "only at close quarters and for very short periods." Quoted in Gilmore, "New Courage," p. 101n23.

90. On the introduction of Bessemer steel and metallurgy, see Wolf, *Arms and Innovation,* pp. 104–5.

91. H. F. Williamson, *Winchester: The Gun That Won the West* (Washington, D.C.: Combat Forces Press, 1952), pp. 51, 62.

92. Quoted in Wolf, *Arms and Innovation,* p. 114.

93. In fact, for its Model 1876 "Centennial" rifle, Winchester did hit its target of .45, and even used the same cartridge case as the army's, but only by using a lighter bullet (350 grains instead of 405) and compensating for its loss of hitting power by increasing the powder charge to 75 grains. Ultimately, though, the '76's weak toggle-link breech mechanism could not happily accommodate the cartridge, and sales were relatively poor—at least compared to its legendary predecessor, the Model 1873. Only with the advent of the Model 1886 lever-action would Winchester finally be able to handle the government-mandated ammunition. See P. B. Sharpe, *The Rifle in America,* 3d ed. (New York: Funk & Wagnalls, 1953), pp. 232–35. The Model 1873 continued to be produced until the remarkably late date of 1924. (The Model 1876 was dropped in 1897.) Domestic sales of the M1873 were 720,610, compared with 123,211, but foreign sales would have greatly increased the former figure. See also B. N. Canfield, "Nineteenth-Century Military Winchesters," *American Rifleman* (March 2001), p. 38. The Model 1886 was the first Winchester repeater that John M. Browning was called upon to design, and his solution to the toggle-link's fragility was to replace it with a far more solid mechanism. So marvelous was his rethinking of a problem that had dogged Winchesters for decades that his weapon could fire cartridges even larger than the government stipulated: up to .45-90 initially and rising to a monstrous .50-110-450 by 1895.

94. Biographical material based on D. R. Beaver, "The U.S. War Department in the Gaslight Era: Stephen Vincent Benét at the Ordnance Department, 1870–91," *Journal of Military*

History 68, no. 1 (2004), pp. 107–8. On *The Dust Which Is God,* see C. E. Purinton's review, *Journal of Bible and Religion* 14, no. 2 (1946), p. 126.

95. Quoted in Wolf, *Arms and Innovation,* p. 118.

96. H. Metcalfe, *The Ordnance Department, U. S. Army, at the International Exhibition, 1876* (Washington, D.C.: Government Printing Office, 1884), pp. v, vii, 844–46, 860, quoted in Wolf, *Arms and Innovation,* p. 125. On the exhibition as a whole, see R. W. Rydell, *All the World's a Fair: Visions of Empire at American International Expositions, 1876–1916* (Chicago: University of Chicago Press, 1984), pp. 10–37.

97. S. Brinckerhoff and P. Chamberlin, "The Army's Search for a Repeating Rifle, 1873–1903," *Military Affairs* 32, no. 1 (1968), p. 21; H. G. Houze, *Winchester Repeating Arms Company: Its History and Development from 1854 to 1981* (Iola, Wis.: Krause, 2004), pp. 97, 104; Williamson, *Winchester,* p. 70; Sharpe, *Rifle in America,* p. 235.

98. C. Windolph, *I Fought with Custer: The Story of Sergeant Windolph . . .* (1947; reprint Lincoln: University of Nebraska Press, 1987), p. 92; J. E. Parsons and J. S. du Mont, *Firearms in the Custer Battle* (Harrisburg, Pa.: Stackpole, 1953), p. 16; Wolf, *Arms and Innovation,* p. 137.

99. See General Godfrey's conclusion that "when cartridges were dirty and corroded, the ejectors did not always extract the empty shells from the chambers, and the men were compelled to use knives to get them out. When the shells were clean no great difficulty was experienced," in his authoritative memoir, "Custer's Last Battle," originally published in *Century* (January 1892) and reprinted in W. A. Graham, *The Custer Myth: A Source Book of Custeriana* (New York: Bonanza Books, 1953), pp. 146–47.

100. D. D. Scott, R. A. Fox Jr., M. A. Connor, and D. Harmon, *Archaeological Perspectives on the Battle of the Little Bighorn* (Norman: University of Oklahoma Press, 1989), p. 114, contains the results of these recent investigations. It's worth pointing out that the *Indians* must also have suffered from jamming—and probably more often, owing to the troopers' more stringent cleaning and oiling discipline when back at barracks. In the aftermath of the annihilation, General Nelson Miles wrote, as they traveled to avenge Custer's death, his men "occupied themselves in polishing their cartridges . . . or in cleaning their rifles." Miles, *Personal Recollections,* p. 215.

101. See R. M. Utley, *Custer and the Great Controversy: The Origin and Development of a Legend* (1962; reprint Lincoln: University of Nebraska Press, 1988), pp. 39–40.

102. Sharpe, *Rifle in America,* p. 236; Wolf, *Arms and Innovation,* pp. 146–51, 154; Canfield, "Military Winchesters," p. 39.

103. Brinckerhoff and Chamberlin, "Army's Search," p. 22; Wolf, *Arms and Innovation,* pp. 162–70; Canfield, "Military Winchesters," p. 39. Interestingly, the Hotchkiss did find a zealous admirer in Geronimo; during his surrender negotiations in 1886 army assistant surgeon Leonard Wood—future commander of the Rough Riders, of San Juan Hill fame—briefly lent him one. Having never seen a Hotchkiss, Geronimo was curious and asked to shoot some rounds. Wood, a little nervous as to the chieftain's intentions, recalled that he showed him how it worked and Geronimo "fired at a mark, just missing one of his own men, which he regarded as a great joke, rolling on the ground, laughing heartily and saying 'good gun.'" J. H. Sears, *The Career of Leonard Wood* (New York: D. Appleton & Co., 1919), pp. 44–45. The original anecdote seems to have first been printed in Miles, *Personal Recollections,* pp. 513–14.

104. Quoted in Hallahan, *Misfire,* p. 225.

105. Sharpe, *Rifle in America,* p. 69.

106. Quoted in Wolf, *Arms and Innovation,* p. 120.

107. Ibid., pp. 158–62.

108. On Lee's mechanism, see D. Westwood, *Rifles: An Illustrated History of Their Impact* (Santa Barbara, Calif.: ABC-CLIO, 2005), p. 94.

109. "Improvement in magazine fire-arms," Patent no. 221,328, November 4, 1879, available at the U.S. Patent and Trademark Office Web site.

110. Wolf, *Arms and Innovation,* pp. 187–207; Brinckerhoff and Chamberlin, "Army's Search," pp. 24–26.

111. Westwood, *Rifles*, pp. 95–103. On Mauser being present at Plevna, see Hallahan, *Misfire*, p. 224.

112. "For an Army Rifle," *New York Times*, December 23, 1890, p. 3.

Chapter 7

1. See R. E. Rice, "Smokeless Powder: Scientific and Institutional Contexts at the End of the Nineteenth Century," in B. J. Buchanan, ed., *Gunpowder, Explosives and the State: A Technological History* (Aldershot [U.K.]/Burlington, Vt: Ashgate, 2006), p. 355.

2. "Sconbein's [*sic*] Explosive Cotton," *Scientific American* 2, no. 8 (November 14, 1846), pp. 58, 64.

3. "Gun Cotton," *Scientific American* 3, no. 3 (October 8, 1847), p. 22, quoted in S. L. Norman, *Guncotton to Smokeless Powder: The Development of Nitrocellulose as a Military Explosive, 1845–1929* (Unpub. Ph.D. diss., Providence, R.I.: Brown University, 1988), p. 42. Norman's doctoral thesis is the essential reference text on this subject.

4. "Flying Cotton," *Scientific American* 2, no. 16 (January 9, 1847), p. 125. In the same issue the editors mentioned that E. W. Kent, a chemist of 116 John Street, New York, had provided them with a sample of this "wonderful article." The guncotton was "as white and delicate in appearance, as the raw material, and would not be suspected of having been subjected to chemical process."

5. "Sconbein's [*sic*] Explosive Cotton," p. 64.

6. "Cotton Powder," p. 79. On his use at home, see J. A. Padgett, ed., "The Life of Alfred Mordecai, as Related by Himself," *North Carolina Historical Review* 22, no. 1 (1945), pp. 58–108. Interestingly, some superstitious backwoodsmen were convinced that black powder was actually more powerful than guncotton. For an example, see T. Aber and S. King, *Tales from an Adirondack County* (Prospect, N.Y.: Prospect Books, 1961), p. 189.

7. "The explosive cotton," *Scientific American* 2, no. 13 (December 19, 1846), p. 101; Norman, *Guncotton to Smokeless Powder*, p. 115.

8. Norman, *Guncotton to Smokeless Powder*, pp. 63–64, 80, 120.

9. "Foreign Correspondence No. Two," *Scientific American* 2, no. 10 (November 28, 1846), p. 77.

10. Norman, *Guncotton to Smokeless Powder*, pp. 70–71.

11. Quoted in ibid., p. 115.

12. P. A. Clarke, "Skirmish Line Target Practice in the Regular Army," *Harper's Weekly* 33, no. 1714 (October 26, 1889), p. 862.

13. Referring to French exercises, *Scientific American* observed that "it will now be necessary to substitute subdued colors for their red pantaloons and other bright accouterments, as the absence of smoke renders the gay figures of the men very conspicuous when in action." *Scientific American* 62, no. 15 (April 12, 1890), p. 226, quoted in Norman, *Guncotton to Smokeless Powder*, p. 198.

14. G. Hartcup, *Camouflage: A History of Concealment and Deception in War* (New York: Charles Scribner's Sons, 1980), p. 12.

15. Norman, *Guncotton to Smokeless Powder*, p. 53.

16. Ibid., pp. 55–56, 60, 67–71.

17. Ibid., pp. 74, 116–23.

18. R. Amiable, "Scientific Reasoning and the Empirical Approach at the Time of the European Invention of Smokeless Powder," in B. J. Buchanan, ed., *Gunpowder, Explosives and the State: A Technological History* (Aldershot [U.K.]/Burlington, Vt.: Ashgate, 2006), esp. pp. 346–52.

19. *Scientific American* 63, no. 6 (August 9, 1890), p. 89.

20. On these powders and developments, see P. G. Sanford, *Nitro-explosives: A Practical Treatise Concerning the Properties, Manufacture, and Analysis of Nitrated Substances . . .* , 2d ed. (London: Crosby Lockwood & Son, 1906), pp. 179–80, 191, 193.

21. *Scientific American* 61, no. 25 (December 7, 1889), p. 353. On military attachés, see R. I. Wolf, *Arms and Innovation: The United States Army and the Repeating Rifle, 1865–1900* (Unpub. Ph.D. diss., Boston University, 1981), p. 227.

22. On the rivalry between Ordnance and private enterprise, see D. R. Beaver, "The U.S. War Department in the Gaslight Era: Stephen Vincent Benét at the Ordnance Department, 1870–91," *Journal of Military History* 68, no. 1 (2004), pp. 118–20. On the Whitney and Remington buyouts, H. G. Houze, *Winchester Repeating Arms Company: Its History and Development from 1854 to 1981* (Iola, Wis.: Krause, 2004), pp. 133, 139, 143.

23. Norman, *Guncotton to Smokeless Powder*, pp. 124–25, 132.

24. Unfortunately his optimism was almost perfectly mistimed. When the Spanish-American War erupted in 1898, the army assuredly enjoyed powder enough for its 28,000 regulars—Frankford by now could turn out seven million cartridges annually—but not for the hundreds of thousands of men who enlisted during the war's first six months. The subsequent investigation in the Senate was a nasty one, with populist politicians and army technocrats tangling over who was to blame for the fiasco. In a rerun of the Jacksonian years, Ordnance officers found themselves accused of discriminating against small entrepreneurs and agglomerating power to the department; they in turn charged Congress with starving the department of funds for decades and thus could not have been expected to produce the quantities needed.

   The most extraordinary aspect of the affair is the relatively tiny amounts of powder that contemporaries were fighting over in that innocent era before the industrial age of slaughter. In 1893, for instance, Ordnance had contracted the Leonard Smokeless Powder Company of New York and the California Powder Works (of which Du Pont was a minority stockholder and later owner) to provide lump amounts of 5,000 pounds and 15,000 pounds, respectively, of propellant. In 1906 at Picatinny Arsenal, the army's brand-new powder plant in New Jersey, it was imagined that 1,000 pounds a day was a major achievement. Two years later Picatinny had upped that figure to an impressive 3,000 pounds daily. Now, skip forward a mere decade, to the Great War. By the time the Armistice with Germany was signed on November 11, 1918, American factories and arsenals were producing 525,000 pounds of smokeless powder *per day*. Had the war lasted into 1919, the great arsenal near Nashville, Tennessee (built on the site of Andrew Jackson's house), would alone have been making one million pounds daily. Norman, *Guncotton to Smokeless Powder*, pp. 129–55; Wolf, *Arms and Innovation*, p. 265; S. Brown, *The Story of Ordnance in the World War* (Washington, D.C.: James William Bryan Press, 1920), pp. 97–98.

25. An extended analysis of the physics of air resistance is given in J. S. Hatcher, *Hatcher's Notebook: A Standard Reference Book for Shooters, Gunsmiths, Ballisticians, Historians, Hunters and Collectors*, 2d ed. (Harrisburg, Pa.: Stackpole, 1957), pp. 551–58.

26. "For an Army Rifle," *New York Times*, December 23, 1890, p. 3.

27. J. Carmichel, "Happy 100th Birthday, .30-06," *Outdoor Life*, April 2006, p. 53.

28. Quoted in Wolf, *Arms and Innovation*, p. 232.

29. "Magazine Small Arms," *New York Times*, September 5, 1892.

30. Quoted in S. Brinckerhoff and P. Chamberlin, "The Army's Search for a Repeating Rifle, 1873–1903," *Military Affairs* 32, no. 1 (1968), p. 29.

31. Wolf, *Arms and Innovation*, pp. 238–41.

32. "New Army Rifle," *New York Times*, September 4, 1892.

33. Brinckerhoff and Chamberlin, "Army's Search," p. 28.

34. P. M. Shockley, *The Krag-Jørgensen Rifle in the Service* (Aledo, Ill.: World-Wide Gun Report, 1960), pp. 6–7; P. B. Sharpe, *The Rifle in America*, 3d ed. (New York: Funk & Wagnalls, 1953), p. 105; Wolf, *Arms and Innovation*, pp. 264, 278; J. Poyer, *The Krag Rifle and Carbine* (Tustin, Calif.: North Cape Publications; 2002), p. 155.

35. The *New York Times* was very annoyed at these tactics by arms-makers. See "Delaying the New Rifle: Inventors Who Have Succeeded in Postponing the Change," February 12, 1893, and editorial of February 25, 1893. Brinckerhoff and Chamberlin, "Army's Search" p. 29n55; Wolf, *Arms and Innovation*, pp. 254–60.

36. Wolf, *Arms and Innovation*, pp. 247–48.

37. Ibid., p. 262.

38. On these figures and the accompanying illustration, see V. L. Mason, "New Weapons of the United States Army," *Century* 49, no. 4 (February 1895), pp. 571–72.

39. The conflict between the army and the National Guard on the eve of the war is exhaustively covered in G. A. Cosmas, "From Order to Chaos: The War Department, the National Guard, and Military Policy, 1898," *Military Affairs* 29, no. 3 (1965), pp. 105–22.

40. See Wolf, *Arms and Innovation*, pp. 270–71. On the Krag's rate of fire, Shockley, *Krag-Jørgensen Rifle*, pp. 19, 31; V. S. Mason, "New Weapons of the United States Army," *Century* 49, no. 4 (February 1895), p. 572.

41. T. Roosevelt, *The Rough Riders: An Autobiography*, ed. L. Auchincloss (New York: Library of America, 2004), p. 15.

42. H. Irving Hancock, *What One Man Saw; Being the Personal Impressions of a War Correspondent in Cuba* (New York: Street & Smith, 1898), quoted in Shockley, *Krag-Jørgensen Rifle*, p. 18.

43. P. D. Jamieson, *Crossing the Deadly Ground: United States Infantry Tactics, 1865–1899* (Tuscaloosa, Ala./London: University of Alabama Press, 1994), pp. 138–39.

44. R. H. Davis, *The Cuban and Porto Rican Campaigns* (New York: Charles Scribner's Sons, 1898), p. 208.

45. On Wood, see Shockley, *Krag-Jørgensen Rifle*, p. 17; see also Jamieson, *Crossing Deadly Ground*, p. 147.

46. Davis, *Cuban and Porto Rican Campaigns*, p. 149.

47. General George S. Patton would later call the technique "marching fire" and believed that "the proper way to advance, particularly for troops armed with that magnificent weapon, the M-1 rifle, is to utilize marching fire and keep moving. This fire can be delivered from the shoulder, but it is just as effective if delivered with the butt of the rifle halfway between the belt and the armpit. One round should be fired every two or three paces. The whistle of the bullets, the scream of the ricochet, and the dust, twigs, and branches which are knocked from the ground and the trees have such an effect on the enemy that his small-arms fire becomes negligible." G. S. Patton, *War As I Knew It* (1947; reprint Boston/New York: Houghton Mifflin, 1995), p. 339.

48. F. Funston, *Memories of Two Wars: Cuban and Philippine Experiences* (New York: Charles Scribner's Sons, 1911), pp. 199–200.

49. In a manner similar to the enemy's being shot in the face, after Las Guasimas, Roosevelt wrote in his *Rough Riders*, "when we arrived at the buildings, panting and out of breath, they contained nothing but heaps of empty cartridge-shells and two dead Spaniards, shot through the head." Roosevelt, *Rough Riders*, p. 82 and pp. 108, 112; Shockley, *Krag-Jørgensen Rifle*, pp. 17–27. On the operations of the Rough Riders, see D. S. Pierson, "What the Rough Riders Lacked in Military Discipline, They Made Up for with Patriotic Fervor and Courage," *Military History* 15, no. 2 (1998).

50. Funston, quoted in Jamieson, *Crossing Deadly Ground*, pp. 132–33; Roosevelt, *Rough Riders*, pp. 100–101, 86. General Merritt, commanding the Volunteers in the Philippines, also felt that the black-powder .45 Springfield was a better weapon for killing than the Krag. See Wolf, *Arms and Innovation*, p. 276.

51. Anon., "Wounds and Disease at the Front," *Journal of the American Medical Association* 31, no. 5 (July 30, 1898), p. 250.

52. Davis, *Cuban and Porto Rican Campaigns*, pp. 207–8.

53. These figures are taken from V. J. Cirillo, *Bullets and Bacilli: The Spanish-American War and Military Medicine* (New Brunswick, N.J.: Rutgers University Press, 2004), pp. 34–37, except for the Civil War abdomen-wound rate, which can be found in D. C. Smith,

"Military Medicine," in J. E. Jessup and L. B. Ketz, eds., *Encyclopedia of the American Military* (New York: Charles Scribner's Sons, 1994), p. 3:1597.

54. N. Senn, "The Modern Treatment of Gunshot Wounds in Military Practice," *Journal of the American Medical Association* 31, no. 2 (July 9, 1898), pp. 46–55.

55. The material on wounds and projectile behavior is mostly based on several works by Martin Fackler, M.D., and on E. N. Harvey et al., "Mechanism of Wounding," in J. C. Beyer, ed., *Wound Ballistics* (Washington, D.C.: Office of the Surgeon General, Department of the Army, 1962). See especially M. L. Fackler and P. J. Dougherty, "Theodor Kocher and the Scientific Foundation of Wound Ballistics," *Gynecology and Obstetrics* 172 (February 1991), pp. 153–60; M. L. Fackler, "What's Wrong with the Wound Ballistics Literature, and Why," Letterman Army Institute of Research Report no. 239 (July 1987); M. L. Fackler, "Ballistic Injury," *Annals of Emergency Medicine* 15 (December 1986), pp. 1451–55; and M. L. Fackler, J. S. Surinchak, and J. A. Malinowski, "Bullet Fragmentation: A Major Cause of Tissue Disruption," *Journal of Trauma* 24 (1984), pp. 35–39. D. Lindsey, "The Idolatry of Velocity, or Lies, Damn Lies, and Ballistics," *Journal of Trauma* 20 (1980), pp. 1068–69, is also key. For the Longmore quote and the statistic on Civil War perforating-chest wounds, see Smith, "Military Medicine," pp. 1597–98; and for the anecdote about the attaché in Manchuria, see Shockley, *Krag-Jørgenson Rifle*.

56. Mason, "New Weapons," p. 572.

57. Shockley, *Krag-Jørgensen Rifle*, pp. 50–54.

Chapter 8

1. W. R. Roberts, "Reform and Revitalization, 1890–1903," in K. J. Hagan and W. R. Roberts, eds., *Against All Enemies: Interpretations of American Military History from Colonial Times to the Present* (Westport, Conn.: Greenwood Press, 1986), pp. 198–201. Good summaries of the tussle between commanding generals and the secretary of war can be found in E. Ranson, "Nelson A. Miles as Commanding General, 1895–1903," *Military Affairs* 24, no. 4 (1965–66), pp. 181–82; P. L. Semsch, "Elihu Root and the General Staff," *Military Affairs* 27, no. 1 (1963), pp. 16–18. See also R. F. Weigley, *History of the United States Army* (Bloomington: Indiana University Press, 1984), pp. 138, 285–90.

2. G. A. Cosmas, "Military Reform After the Spanish-American War: The Army Reorganization Fight of 1898–1899," *Military Affairs* 35, no. 1 (1971), pp. 12–18; and Cosmas, "From Order to Chaos: The War Department, the National Guard, and Military Policy, 1898," *Military Affairs* 29, no. 3 (1965), pp. 105–22. On Miles's background in Boston, see R. M. Utley's introduction to N. A. Miles, *Personal Recollections and Observations of General Nelson A. Miles* (1896; reprint New York: Da Capo Press, 1969), p. vi.

3. "Army Reorganization," *New York Times*, December 9, 1898, p. 6; Ranson, "Nelson A. Miles," pp. 188–89; Weigley, *History of the Army*, pp. 311–12.

4. "Roosevelt was a youngster. He didn't know much about business or business affairs. He got caught in a little inconsistency of an affidavit about his tax," wrote Root later, not completely believably. See P. C. Jessup, *Elihu Root* (New York: Dodd, Mead & Co., 1938), pp. 1:198–99.

5. Ibid., pp. 1:215–17.

6. E. Morris, *The Rise of Theodore Roosevelt* (New York: Coward, McCann & Geohagen, 1979), pp. 481–514.

7. Jessup, *Elihu Root*, p. 1:254.

8. Work on the subject of Taylorism is voluminous. For the basics, see R. Kanigel's excellent biography, *The One Best Way: Frederick W. Taylor and the Enigma of Efficiency* (New York: Viking, 1997); D. Nelson, *Frederick W. Taylor and the Rise of Scientific Management*

(Madison, Wis.: University of Wisconsin Press, 1980); H. L. Schachter, *Frederick Taylor and the Public Administration Community: A Reevaluation* (Albany, N.Y.: State University of New York Press, 1989); and of course, Taylor's *The Principles of Scientific Management* (1911), available online at www.eldritchpress.org/fwt/taylor.html.

9. Quoted in R. W. Stewart, ed., *American Military History: The United States Army and the Forging of a Nation, 1775–1917* (Washington, D.C.: Center of Military History, United States Army, 2005), p. 369.

10. Jessup, *Elihu Root*, p. 1:223.

11. Ibid., p. 1:242. See also L. Cantor, "Elihu Root and the National Guard: Friend or Foe?" *Military Affairs* 33, no. 3 (1969), p. 363.

12. Semsch, "Root and General Staff," pp. 19–20; Jessup, *Elihu Root*, pp. 1:241–43. Roosevelt was "delighted with Upton's book, and I think you rendered a great service in publishing it." However, he felt that Upton emphasized too much "length of service" by "regulars": these terms "amount to nothing whatever" without good, competent leadership. See Roosevelt to Root, February 16, 1904, in L. Auchincloss, ed., *Theodore Roosevelt: Letters and Speeches* (New York: Library of America, 2004), pp. 313–15.

13. Jessup, *Elihu Root*, pp. 1:252–53.

14. Quoted in Semsch, "Root and General Staff," p. 22. On Root's initial attempt to work with Miles, see Jessup, *Elihu Root*, p. 1:244. *Harper's Weekly* ("This Busy World," April 12, 1902, p. 478) believed that Miles should retire sooner rather than later so that he could "go out amid an immense clamor of tomtoms."

15. Semsch, "Root and General Staff," pp. 23–24; R. Morris, *Theodore Rex* (New York: Random House, 2001), p. 99.

16. The bitterness between Roosevelt and Miles was boundless. Thus Harvard's award of an honorary degree to Miles may have been "preposterous," and his complaints that American troops had abused Filipinos strikingly hypocritical considering (as Roosevelt told him to his face) that "when he was in command against the Sioux at the time of the Pine Ridge outbreak . . . the troops under his command had at Wounded Knee committed a massacre," but ultimately Miles could only genuinely be a "very bad man . . . if the opportunity came and his abilities were sufficient." Perhaps no criticism is more damning in life or politics than dismissal as being too inept to be dangerous. Miles, for his part, cruelly hinted in a speech in June 1901 that Roosevelt had not, in fact, been at San Juan Hill. Roosevelt to Owen Wister, July 20, 1901, pp. 234–36; to Root, February 18, 1902, pp. 246–47; and to John Hay, July 22, 1902, pp. 253–54, in Auchincloss, ed., *Roosevelt Letters and Speeches*; for Miles's insinuation, see Jessup, *Elihu Root*, p. 1:245. Roosevelt's view, put most succinctly, was that Miles was a "scoundrel." See Roosevelt to Hay, August 9, 1903, p. 277. On the succeeding developments surrounding the bill, see Semsch, "Root and General Staff," pp. 25–27.

17. Exercised by Roosevelt's remark, *Harper's Weekly* admitted that the old general had "been consistently bombastic and condescending and generally a nuisance" but declared that his long service record made him an undeserving recipient of the president's "snub of the snubbiest sort." Editorial, "President Roosevelt and General Miles," *Harper's Weekly*, August 22, 1903, p. 1359. Even after his own supporters complained at the slight, Roosevelt suggested to Root that he submit an official memorandum noting that Miles had "played the part of traitor to the army and therefore to the nation. His intriguing disloyalty should be made manifest so that there can be no mistake about it in the future." Ultimately, according to Root's biographer, the war secretary's "order transferring [Miles] from the active to the retired list was purely formal and contained no word of praise for past services." Jessup, *Elihu Root*, pp. 1:249–50.

18. Roosevelt to Root, October 19, 1899, in E. E. Morison, ed. *The Letters of Theodore Roosevelt* (Cambridge, Mass.: Harvard University Press, 1951), p. 2:1085.

19. Roosevelt to Wood, June 4, 1904, in Morison, *Letters of Roosevelt*, p. 4:820. For his background, see Crozier's entry in *American National Biography*.

20. "Capt. Crozier Is Ineligible," *New York Times*, September 25, 1901, p. 3.

21. Quoted in Jessup, *Elihu Root,* p. 1:185.

22. "Capt. Crozier to Be Promoted," *New York Times,* October 3, 1901, p. 5.

23. "Capt. William Crozier Now Chief of Ordnance," *New York Times,* November 23, 1901, p. 5.

24. "The Chief of Ordnance," *New York Times,* May 4, 1902, p. 6.

25. "Agree on Gen. Crozier," *New York Times,* June 20, 1902; "Crozier for Another Term," *New York Times,* November 19, 1905, p. 3.

26. W. H. Hallahan, *Misfire: The History of How America's Small Arms Have Failed Our Military* (New York: Charles Scribner's Sons, 1994), p. 269.

27. Roosevelt to Lodge, March 27, 1901, in Morison, *Letters of Roosevelt,* pp. 2:31–32.

28. Hallahan, *Misfire,* p. 266.

29. Ibid., p. 267; W. S. Brophy, *The Springfield 1903 Rifles: The Illustrated, Documented Story . . .* (Harrisburg, Pa.: Stackpole, 1985), p. 2.

30. Report by Major John Greer, October 2, 1900, in J. E. Hicks, *Notes on United States Ordnance: Small Arms, 1776 to 1940* (Mount Vernon, N.Y.: James E. Hicks, 1940), pp. 110–11.

31. See Brophy, *Springfield 1903,* pp. 16–17.

32. "Favors Rifle Practice Among Schoolboys," *New York Times,* January 28, 1906, p. 8.

33. Roosevelt to William Howard Taft, January 4, 1905, in Morison, *Letters of Roosevelt,* pp. 4:1090–91.

34. Brophy, *Springfield 1903,* p. 20.

35. J. S. Hatcher, *Hatcher's Notebook: A Standard Reference Book for Shooters, Gunsmiths, Ballisticians, Historians, Hunters and Collectors,* 2d ed. (Harrisburg, Pa.: Stackpole, 1957), p. 2.

36. Brophy, *Springfield 1903,* pp. 20, 30; Hatcher, *Hatcher's Notebook,* p. 2.

37. Hatcher, *Hatcher's Notebook,* p. 2.

38. "New Bullet for the Army," *New York Times,* August 10, 1906, p. 5.

39. "A New and Deadly Bullet for the Army," *Harper's Weekly,* October 20, 1906, p. 1509.

40. Brophy, *Springfield 1903,* pp. 34, 37; Hatcher, *Hatcher's Notebook,* p. 3.

41. "Cartridge feed pack for magazine guns," Patent no. 402,605, May 7, 1889.

42. "Cartridge-holder for magazine-guns," Patent no. 482,376, September 13, 1892; "Cartridge-pack for magazine-guns," Patent no. 547,932, October 15, 1895.

43. Hallahan, *Misfire,* p. 274.

44. Ibid., pp. 274–75; J. A. Stockfisch, *Plowshares in Swords: Managing the American Defense Establishment* (New York: Mason & Lipscomb, 1973), p. 53; R. I. Wolf, *Arms and Innovation: The United States Army and the Repeating Rifle, 1865–1900* (Unpub. Ph.D. diss., Boston University, 1981), p. 281. See also E. C. Ezell, *The Search for a Lightweight Rifle: The M14 and M16 Rifles* (Unpub. Ph.D. diss., Cleveland, Ohio: Case Western Reserve University, 1969), pp. 38–39n37 for additional details.

45. "Projectile for hand-firearms," Patent no. 841,861, January 22, 1907; Hallahan, *Misfire,* p. 276.

46. On this point see H. G. J. Aitken, *Scientific Management in Action: Taylorism at Watertown Arsenal, 1908–1915* (Princeton, N.J.: Princeton University Press, 1985), pp. 57–60.

47. Ibid., pp. 56, 61, 66, 70.

48. Ibid., pp. 68–108.

49. Ibid., pp. 135–85.

50. Ibid., pp. 229–34.

51. Hallahan, *Misfire,* p. 277.

52. S. Brown, *The Story of Ordnance in the World War* (Washington, D.C.: James William Bryan Press, 1920), pp. 14, 17, 35.

53. Aitken, *Scientific Management*, p. 238.

54. On the Enfield, see Hatcher, *Hatcher's Notebook*, pp. 13–14, 16; E. C. Crossman, "Uncle Sam's New Infantry Rifle: How the British Arm of 1914, Chambered for Our Cartridge, Compares with Our Old Springfield," *Scientific American* 117, no. 22 (December 1, 1917), p. 408.

55. Brophy, *Springfield 1903*, pp. 232–37.

56. Hallahan, *Misfire*, pp. 277–78.

Chapter 9

1. In his 1902 report, quoted in J. S. Hatcher, *The Book of the Garand* (1948; reprint Highland Park, N.J.: Gun Room Press, 2000), p. 13. As early as 1663–64 an English "lawyer and virtuoso" named Dudley Palmer had (probably) originated this economical concept when he proposed a theoretical firearm that could "shoot as fast as it could be and yet be stopped at pleasure, and wherein the motion of the fire and bullet was made to charge the piece with powder and bullet, to prime it, and to pull back the cock." Palmer had outlined his idea in the *Philosophical Transactions of the Royal Society, 1663–1664*, quoted in M. L. Brown, *Firearms in Colonial America: The Impact on History and Technology, 1492–1792* (Washington, D.C.: Smithsonian Institution Press, 1980), p. 144. On Palmer, see M. Hunter, "The Social Basis and Changing Fortunes of an Early Scientific Institution: An Analysis of the Membership of the Royal Society, 1660–1685," *Notes and Records of the Royal Society of London* 31, no. 1 (1976), p. 84.

2. Hatcher, *Book of Garand*, p. 13.

3. Ibid., pp. 14–15.

4. Ibid., pp. 2–5, 15.

5. H. E. Eames, *The Rifle in War* (Fort Leavenworth, Kans.: U.S. Cavalry Association, 1909), pp. 42–43.

6. Ibid., pp. 108–9.

7. R. Gilmore, "'The New Courage': Rifles and Soldier Individualism, 1876–1918," *Military Affairs* 40, no. 3 (1976), pp. 99–100.

8. See especially D. Minshall, "Creedmoor and the International Matches," available online at www.researchpress.co.uk/targets/creedmoor/01creedmoor_nra.htm. Also, G. W. Wingate, "Early Days of the NRA: Recollections of the National Rifle Association," pt. 2, *American Rifleman* 99, no. 6 (June 1951), pp. 39, 46.

9. S. W. Brookhart, *Rifle Training for War* (Washington, D.C.: National Rifle Association/U.S. Government Printing Office, 1919), pp. 5–11. This pamphlet was published after the war but it exemplified pre-1914 thinking.

10. On this now-forgotten achievement, see G. M. Chinn's Bureau of Ordnance–sponsored *The Machine Gun: History, Evolution, and Development of Manual, Automatic, and Airborne Repeating Weapons* (Washington, D.C.: U.S. Government Printing Office, 1951), p. 1:268.

11. Editorial, "Maneuvers and Marksmanship," *American Rifleman* 87, no. 12 (December 1939), p. 4.

12. J. J. Pershing, *My Experiences in the World War* (New York: Frederick A. Stokes, 1931), p. 1:153.

13. Pershing to Baker, October 4, 1917, ibid., p. 1:189; see esp. pp. 1:151–53. See also war diary, December 19, 1917, in *United States Army in the World War, 1917–1919* (Washington, D.C.: U.S. Government Printing Office, 1948), p. 2:117; extract from a meeting of the War Cabinet, December 21, 1917, pp. 2:123–24ff.; Pershing to chief of staff, January 1, 1918, p. 2:132; and Pershing letter, February 6, 1918, p. 2:196: "We should begin to make plans to carry out necessary construction leading up to what is to become the American sector."

14. Quoted in "Good Advice from General Pershing: Importance of the Rifle," *Army and Navy Journal* 55, no. 7 (October 13, 1917), p. 232.

15. In a cable to National Guard instructors, October 3, 1917, quoted in ibid.

16. *Notes on Training for Rifle Fire in Trench Warfare* (Washington, D.C.: U.S. Government Printing Office, 1917), pp. 6–7.

17. E. C. Crossman, "German Military Rifle Practice," *Scientific American* 116, no. 5 (February 3, 1917), pp. 126, 137.

18. See, for instance, Brookhart, *Rifle Training for War*, p. 7: "The best defense or offense against the machine gun is in the training of more and better snipers."

19. This section was heavily based on D. D. Lee's excellent *Sergeant York: An American Hero* (Lexington: University Press of Kentucky, 1985). But see also J. Perry's useful *Sgt. York: His Life, Legend and Legacy: The Remarkable Untold Story of Sergeant Alvin C. York* (Nashville, Tenn.: Broadman & Holman, 1997); and S. K. Cowan, *Sergeant York and His People* (New York: Funk & Wagnalls, 1922).

20. Perry, *Sgt. York*, p. 72.

21. Biographies of York, especially the earlier ones, invariably follow this line. Sam Cowan's *Sergeant York and His People* (published in 1922) devotes much space to revealing York's Tennessee background, connecting him to Andrew Jackson (including a photograph of York visiting the president's tomb), and describing the idyllic lives of the inhabitants of the townspeople and farmers of the valley. As David Lee points out (*Sergeant York*, p. 98), however, his biographers tended to play down York's particularly fiery brand of fundamentalist Christianity in favor of a generic notion of Christian faith.

22. As Newton Baker, the secretary of war, put it, battle had become "an industrial art conducted like a great modern integrated industry." Quoted in Lee, *Sergeant York*, p. 50.

23. On this point, see of course Cowan, *Sergeant York and His People*, as well as T. Skeyhill's *Sergeant York: His Own Life Story and War Diary* (Garden City, N.Y.: Doubleday, Doran, & Co., 1928) and *Sergeant York: Last of the Long Hunters* (Philadelphia: John C. Winston, 1930).

24. V. Hicken, *The American Fighting Man* (New York: Macmillan, 1969), p. 106.

25. Cowan, *Sergeant York and His People*, pp. 154–55.

26. D. Crockett, *Life of Col. David Crockett, Written by Himself . . .* (Philadelphia: G. G. Evans, 1860), pp. 237–38 (for a detailed description of shooting for beef), p. 194.

27. As a result, Bradley wrote, "I had the staff set up a short-range firing course in the woods with partially concealed cans for targets. The men had to traverse this wooded course, spot the cans and shoot quickly. It was a radical departure from the standard static long-distance firing range." Another time, when Churchill and Eisenhower visited, they held an impromptu shooting match using the new M1 carbines. Churchill's target was set up 25 yards away, Ike's 50, and Bradley's 75. Sadly for posterity, 'all the targets were tactfully removed before anyone could inspect them.' " O. N. Bradley and C. Blair, *A General's Life* (New York: Simon & Schuster, 1983), p. 107. On the shooting match, see photo no. 30 in the insert.

28. Cowan, *Sergeant York and His People*, pp. 23, 152.

29. Quoted in G. Sheffield, *Forgotten Victory: The First World War—Myths and Realities* (London: Review, 2002), pp. 253–54.

30. On Pershing's tactics, see ibid., pp. 252–56. By mid-April 1918 Pershing was looking forward to "the possibility of open warfare being substituted for trench warfare." See cable of April 12, in *United States Army in the World War*, p. 2:320.

31. So arresting were the bloody news reports from the front that even Crossman, *Scientific American*'s accuracy fanatic, had to accept that "superiority of fire" could no longer refer exclusively to superiority of marksmanship but instead referred to the practice of sending sufficient bullets toward the enemy to make him keep his head down so that bayonet-armed troops could advance rapidly. Pershing, *My Experiences*, pp. 1:11–12; T. L. McNaugher, *The M16 Controversies: Military Organizations and Weapons Acquisition* (New York: Praeger, 1984), p. 27n35.

32. "General Principles Governing the Training of Units of the American Expeditionary Forces," in *United States Army in the World War*, p. 2:296.

33. The preceding section is based on J. S. Hatcher's article, "Our War Secret: The Pedersen Device; the Springfield Was to Be a Miniature Machine Gun in 1919," in the May–June 1932 issue of *Army Ordnance*, which is reprinted almost in full in W. S. Brophy, *The Springfield 1903 Rifles: The Illustrated, Documented Story . . .* (Harrisburg, Pa.: Stackpole, 1985), pp. 156–64; and also Hatcher's similar article, "The Pedersen Device," *American Rifleman* 80, no. 5 (May 1932), pp. 7–9, 36. There were two types of Pedersen device, which I have conflated here for the sake of simplicity: the Mark I, which was designed for use with Springfield rifles, and the Mark II, for use with Enfields. The army ordered 133,450 Mark I devices and 500,000 Mark IIs. On the number of demobilized soldiers in the U.S. Army, see R. F. Weigley, *History of the United States Army* (Bloomington: Indiana University Press, 1984), p. 396; and on the postwar boards, Hatcher, *Book of Garand*, p. 34. Details of Pedersen's life are difficult to discover, but his Wikipedia entry, based primarily on material in L. L. Ruth, *War Baby!: The U.S. Caliber .30 Carbine* (Cobourg, Ont.: Collector Grade, 1992), is useful.

34. Hatcher, *Book of Garand*, p. 42.

35. "Information for inventors desiring to submit semiautomatic shoulder rifles for test to the Ordnance Department," February 11, 1921, in Hatcher, *Book of Garand*, p. 46.

36. J. S. Hatcher, "The Military Semiautomatic rifle," *American Rifleman* 80, no. 3 (1932), pp. 11–17; Hatcher, *Book of Garand*, pp. 17–25.

37. Hatcher, *Book of Garand*, pp. 57–60. Pedersen also did his bit for postwar belt-tightening: the smaller cartridge cut down on lead, brass, and powder to the tune of 3,500 pounds of lead, 6,400 of brass, and 2,750 of powder for every million produced. That doesn't sound like much until one considers that in the Second World War 47 billion rounds of ammunition would be manufactured, thereby potentially saving 82,250 tons of lead, 150,400 tons of brass, and 64,625 tons of gunpowder.

38. "Summary of Progress to 1925: History and Present Status of Postwar Development of Small Arms," Ordnance memorandum, March 31, 1925, in Hatcher, *Book of Garand*, pp. 63–64. See also "Springfield to Turn Out Semi-Automatic Rifles," *Washington Post*, January 16, 1927, p. R11.

39. On Pedersen's work methods, see Hatcher, *Book of Garand*, p. 66, and on the Browning anecdote, p. 67.

40. Ibid., pp. 68–71.

41. "Novel Rapid-Firing Shoulder Rifle Is Success in Tests," *Washington Post*, May 16, 1926, p. S14. On the start of the tests, see Hatcher, *Book of Garand*, p. 72. Pedersen would file a patent for an updated version about a year later. See "Magazine rifle" (and associated drawings), Patent no. 1,737,974, June 9, 1927 (granted December 3, 1929). He submitted another soon afterward: "Rifle," Patent no. 1,866,722, November 29, 1930 (granted July 12, 1932). Both are available at the United States Patent and Trademark Office Web site.

42. The biography of Garand is collated from the obituary in the *New York Times*, February 17, 1974, p. 67; "Inventor of Garand Rifle Dies at 86," *Washington Post*, February 17, 1974, p. D13; his entry in the *American National Biography*; and Hatcher, *Book of Garand*, pp. 25–31. J. McCarten's hitherto overlooked profile of Garand, "The Man Behind the Gun," *New Yorker*, February 6, 1943, pp. 22–28, is immensely useful and contains many anecdotes (such as the list of journals to which he subscribed) not seen elsewhere. On Garand's accent, see "Garand's Gun: Modest Inventor Is Bewildered by Fame His Rifle Has Drawn," *Newsweek*, December 4, 1939, p. 18.

43. McCarten, "Man Behind the Gun," pp. 22, 28.

44. See Hatcher, *Book of Garand*, pp. 41, 53–54, for additional technical details. A summary of the mechanism is provided on pp. 62–63.

45. "Two New Types of Rifles Given Trials by Army," *Washington Post*, November 1, 1925, p. AF8. The second type of gun was a Thompson Autofire, but it became apparent that, while it was functional, it wasn't what the army was looking for. On the delivery of arms

to Fort Riley, see "Shoulder Rifle Sent to Army for Tests," *Washington Post,* June 13, 1926, p. S12.

46. "Summary of Progress to 1925," in Hatcher, *Book of Garand,* pp. 62–64.

47. "New Rifle May Make Every Doughboy Machine Gunner," *Washington Post,* June 25, 1923, p. 1.

48. Report of the Pig Board, in Hatcher, *Book of Garand,* p. 81. "New Garand Type Rifle Is Expected After Army Tests," *Washington Post,* December 11, 1927, p. R9, notes that Frankford Arsenal was mildly interested in .256s. See also "Army Develops Two New Rifles with .276 Caliber," *Washington Post,* July 15, 1928, p. R7.

49. Though Ordnance officers tended to prefer the .30, line officers were more open-minded about the .276. Major General Herbert Crosby, the chief of cavalry, was reportedly "inclined to favor the smaller caliber for his arm of the service," and his infantry counterpart Major General Robert Allen was "understood to be of the opinion" that he had not yet seen decisive proof of the superiority of the .30 over the .276. "Springfield to Turn Out Semi-Automatic Rifle," *Washington Post,* January 16, 1927, p. R11.

50. Hatcher, *Book of Garand,* pp. 74–75.

51. Report of the Semiautomatic Rifle Board, 1st Series, September 21, 1928, in Hatcher, *Book of Garand,* p. 85. There were also representatives of the Engineers, Medical Corps, General Staff Field Artillery, Coast Artillery, and Ordnance, of course. "Army Develops Two New Rifles with .276 Caliber," *Washington Post,* July 15, 1928, p. R7.

52. Hatcher, *Book of Garand,* p. 91.

53. Accordingly, Pedersen had repatented his invention before he left for Europe. "Rifle," Patent no. 1,866,722, November 29, 1930 (granted July 12, 1932).

54. "Infantry Report on the T3E2 (Garand)," in Hatcher, *Book of Garand,* pp. 99–100.

55. See "Characteristics of Pedersen and Garand Caliber .276 Semiautomatic Rifles," part of the report by the Semiautomatic Rifle Board, 3d series, December 9, 1931, in Hatcher, *Book of Garand,* pp. 101–6.

56. Hatcher, *Book of Garand,* p. 110.

57. Shulman to president of the board, February 25, 1932, in ibid., pp. 110–11.

58. G. Perret, *Old Soldiers Never Die: The Life of Douglas MacArthur* (New York: Random House, 1996), pp. 150, 172–76; R. K. Griffith, Jr., "Quality Not Quantity: The Volunteer Army During the Depression," *Military Affairs* 43, no. 4 (1979), pp. 171–77. At this time the congressionally mandated size of the regular army was 118,750 officers and men. Weigley, *History of United States Army,* p. 401.

59. W. Manchester, *American Caesar: Douglas MacArthur, 1880–1964* (Boston: Little, Brown & Co., 1978), p. 153; Weigley, *History of United States Army,* p. 414.

60. Quoted in Weigley, *History of United States Army,* p. 403.

61. In 1924, when both departmental budgets reached their nadir, Ordnance received $5,812,180 out of the War Department's $256,669,118 (or 2.26 percent of the total); in 1940 the latter's budget had "merely" tripled to $813,816,590, but Ordnance's had rocketed to $176,546,788, or thirtyfold. See Table I, "Total Appropriations for the Ordnance Department Compared with Total Appropriations for the Military Activities of the War Department," in E. C. Ezell, *The Search for a Lightweight Rifle: The M14 and M16 Rifles* (unpub. Ph.D. diss., Cleveland, Ohio: Case Western Reserve University, 1969), p. 64.

62. V. Cunningham, *British Writers of the Thirties* (Oxford: Oxford University Press, 1988), pp. 200–201. See also Martin Ceadel's important essay, "Popular Fiction and the Next War, 1918–1939," in F. Gloversmith, ed., *Class, Culture and Social Change: A New View of the 1930s* (Brighton, [U.K.]: Harvester Press, 1980), pp. 161–84.

63. G. Godwin, *Empty Victory* (London: John Long, 1932), and "Miles" (Stephen Southwold), *The Gas War of 1940* (London: Eric Partridge, 1931). See also B. Stableford, "Man-made Catastrophes," in E. S. Rabkin, M. H. Greenberg, and J. D. Olander, eds., *The End of the World* (Carbondale: Southern Illinois University Press, 1983), p. 122; I. F. Clarke, *Voices Prophesying War, 1763–3749* (Oxford: Oxford University Press, 1992); "N. Bell" (Stephen Southwold), *My Writing Life* (London: A. Redman, 1955), p. 148.

64. J. F. C. Fuller, *War and Western Civilization, 1832–1932* (London: Duckworth, 1932), p. 250; M. Ter Borg, "Reducing Offensive Capabilities—The Attempt of 1932," *Journal of Peace Studies* 29, no. 2 (1992), pp. 145–60; D. Richardson, "The Geneva Disarmament Conference, 1932–1934," in Richardson and G. Stone, eds., *Decisions and Diplomacy: Essays in Twentieth-Century International History in Memory of George Grün and Esmonde Robertson* (London: Routledge, 1995), pp. 60–82. Hoffman Nickerson reported that "the delegate of the microscopic Dominican Republic, strutting his little hour on the world stage, solemnly said that since 'the League of Nations desires to spread among the childhood and youth of the world ideals of peace, fraternity and international co-operation—the Dominican Republic . . . has the honour to propose . . . to all the countries here represented that they should agree to prohibit the manufacture of warlike toys.'" Nickerson, *Can We Limit War?* (London: Arrowsmith, 1933), p. 181.

65. Many governments had attended in the first place only in order to placate their pacifist constituencies and to show off their "good citizen" badges to an admiring world, but compared to the cynicism of the American and European governments, the honest attitude of the Afghans was refreshing. On the first day of the conference, desperate to distract himself from an interminable speech by its president about "the number of committees that had been formed," Sir Samuel Hoare (a senior British politician) asked the Afghans sitting near him why they were attending. They told him "that they were short of arms, and that they thought at a Disarmament Conference there would be a chance of picking up second-hand munitions cheap." Hoare to R. MacDonald, February 4, 1932, quoted in S. Hoare [Viscount Templewood], *Nine Troubled Years* (London: Collins, 1954), pp. 123–25. For more details on the subjects of future war and the Disarmament Conference, see A. Rose, *Radar Strategy: The Air Dilemma and British Politics, 1932–1937* (Unpub. Ph.D. diss., Cambridge [U.K.] Cambridge University, 1996), esp. chaps. 1 and 2.

66. See the section on budgets in Hatcher, *Book of Garand*, pp. 106–8.

67. Perret, *Old Soldiers*, p. 170. The famous gold-braided cap was actually acquired a little later, when MacArthur was appointed a field marshal by the Filipino government. See Manchester, *American Caesar*, p. 172.

68. Quoted in Perret, *Old Soldiers*, p. 173.

69. Ibid., pp. 163–65; Manchester, *American Caesar*, p. 157.

70. On this process, see Hatcher, *Book of Garand*, pp. 111–14.

71. Quoted in Weigley, *History of United States Army*, p. 417.

72. Roosevelt's views on guns had shifted considerably. In 1932, as governor of New York, he had vetoed bills to repeal two measures enacted in October 1931 to require the photographing and fingerprinting of all applicants for permits to carry pistols. The thinking at the time was that such laws would curb gang activity and racketeering, though as it turned out, relatively few felons consented to being photographed and fingerprinted by the police and so continued to acquire guns illegally. During his presidency the National Firearms Act of 1934 and the Federal Firearms Act of 1938 became law. Both acts were primarily concerned with collecting excise taxes and regulating interstate commerce of certain types of weapons. Editorial, "How FDR Really Felt About Guns," *American Rifleman* 114, no. 11 (November 1966), p. 36; see also General Omar Bradley's endorsement in "A Message to the Members of the National Rifle Association," *American Rifleman* 99, no. 6 (June 1951).

73. The preceding section based on Colonel James Hatcher's lecture to the Army Industrial College on February 20, 1939, printed in his brother's *Book of Garand*, pp. 115–18. On the process of making a cartridge, see V. C. Royster, "How Long Will Defense Take?" *Wall Street Journal*, July 18, 1940, p. 11.

74. D. Wilhelm, "What 'on Order' Means," *Reader's Digest*, October 1940, p. 34. This article, condensed from *Forbes*, differs from Hatcher's figures in a few minor respects. I have tended to use Hatcher's.

75. Based on figures taken from Hatcher, *Book of Garand*, pp. 119, 153; Wilhelm, "What 'on Order' Means," p. 35; Royster, "How Long Will Defense Take?" p. 11; "Rifle and Submachine Gun Output Now at 1,500 Daily," *Wall Street Journal*, July 18, 1941, p. 6.

On Winchester, see "Report on the Garand," *Time,* March 24, 1941. For references to outsourcing to Winchester, Remington, and Savage, see "U.S. Reported Placing Orders with Private Firms for New Rifle," *Wall Street Journal,* April 6, 1939, p. 4.

76. J. A. McWethy, "Machine Tool Makers Work Night and Day to Meet Defense Demand but Unfilled Orders Continue to Pile Up," *Wall Street Journal,* May 16, 1941, p. 8.

77. Hatcher, *Book of Garand,* covers this episode on pp. 128–29.

78. "Battle Efficiency of Garand Rifle Provokes Controversy," *Evening Star,* February 22, 1940, in Hatcher, *Book of Garand,* pp. 132–33.

79. "Wanted: A Rifle," *Time,* May 6, 1940, has a summary of Ness's findings. See also F. C. Ness, "M1 (Garand Semi-Automatic) Rifle," *American Rifleman* 88, no. 5 (May 1940), pp. 43–45.

80. See, for instance, F. C. Ness's in-depth "The New Johnson Rifle," *American Rifleman* 86, no. 11 (November 1938), pp. 3–7, 37. Ness was so positive about the Johnson that he thought that even if the army had selected the Garand, American civilians should purchase a Johnson and familiarize themselves with it so they would be ready "in case of a national emergency." See also Ness's column *Dope Bag* (on the Rotary-Johnson semiautomatic) in *American Rifleman* 87, no. 12 (December 1939), pp. 42–43.

81. On Johnson's background, see www.johnsonautomatics.com/Biography.htm, and the obituaries (from *Boston Globe* and *American Rifleman*).

82. For these numbers, see table I in Hatcher, *Book of Garand,* p. 143.

83. The cross words were Hatcher's, ibid., p. 137. Until two years before publishing this book, Hatcher had been a director of the NRA (and he remained its magazine's technical editor), so he was obliged to be quite discreet about his views on the Garand-Johnson affair.

84. Based on reports in the Washington *Times-Herald,* May 10, 1940, in Hatcher, *Book of Garand,* p. 138, and "Questions for Defense," *Time,* May 20, 1940.

85. "Semi-Automatic Demonstration," *American Rifleman* 88, no. 6 (June 1940), p. 32. Johnson would go on to invent a moderately successful light machine gun. (It was issued in small numbers to specialized Marines and army units.) He frequently visited the Ordnance Department, to which he transferred as a reservist in 1949; that same year he joined Winchester as an adviser when the company agreed to buy his struggling Johnson Automatics firm. In 1951 he acted as a weapons consultant to the Pentagon, and later to ArmaLite, before dying of a heart attack during a business trip to New York in 1965, aged fifty-five. See his obituaries at www.johnsonautomatics.com/Biography.htm.

86. For an example of unvarnished pro-Garandism, see "The Garand Rifle," *American Rifleman* 90, no. 12 (December 1942), pp. 37–38.

87. The most detailed breakdown of the Marine Corps results may be found in Hatcher, *Book of Garand,* pp. 141–53; "Report on the Garand," *Time,* March 24, 1941; and "Marine Corps Rifle Tests," *American Rifleman* 89, no. 5 (May 1941), pp. 5–10. *Time* magazine was consistently hostile to the Garand, calling its relative lack of ruggedness a "grave indictment" and menacingly warning that weapons that performed satisfactorily in tests all too often failed in the field. "Report on the Garand," *Time,* March 24, 1941.

88. "Bataan Proves Garand Worth," *Washington Post,* February 23, 1942, p. 2; "Garand Rifle Praised by Gen. MacArthur," *New York Times,* February 23, 1942, p. 1. In its editorial, "The Garand in Action," February 26, 1942, p. 18, the *Times* observed that the Garand's performance bore out MacArthur's 1932 decision to scrap the .276 and keep the .30. It meant that "the Philippine army did not have to be provided with ammunition of several different sizes for its small arms." See also the *Washington Post*'s editorial, "Garand's Test," of the same date, p. 10.

89. Personal memoir, in Hatcher, *Book of Garand,* p. 248.

90. M. M. Johnson, Jr., "The M1 Rifle," reprinted in *Marine Corps Gazette* 85, no. 4 (April 2001), p. 51. The Springfield Model 1903 to this day (and justifiably so) retains a fervent fan base. In 1951, for instance, the *Washington Post* ran an editorial about "arms standardization" that offhandedly remarked that the Springfield "did not stand up to trench conditions" in the First World War, only to be assaulted by a fusillade of angry letters

claiming its superiority in all things. The editorial board issued an apology the very next day for casting an "aspersion" on this fine rifle. See "Arms Standardization," August 15, 1951, p. 10, and "Springfield, 1903," August 16, 1951, p. 6. The latter article noted that General Matthew Ridgway preferred to keep a Springfield in his personal jeep rather than a Garand, but this choice was regarded as rather an eccentric one.

91. On Rupertus, White, and the genesis of the Creed, see the USMC History Division briefings, "My Rifle—The Creed of a United States Marine," online at www.tecom.usmc.mil/HD/Frequently_Requested/Marines%27_Rifle_Creed.htm, and "History of Marine Corps Recruit Training," online at www.tecom.usmc.mil/HD/Frequently_Requested/Recruit_Training.htm.

92. J. N. George, *Shots Fired in Anger*, quoted in Hatcher, *Book of Garand*, pp. 141–42.

93. Personal correspondence, ibid., p. 242.

94. Personal correspondence, ibid., p. 244.

95. George, *Shots in Anger*, pp. 247–62.

96. In a letter to the chief of Ordnance, quoted in Ezell, *Lightweight Rifle*, p. 26.

97. McCarten, "Man Behind the Gun," p. 22.

Chapter 10

1. "U.S., Canada and Britain in Standard Arms Pact," *Los Angeles Times*, May 20, 1951, p. 21.

2. E. C. Ezell, *The Search for a Lightweight Rifle: The M14 and M16 Rifles* (Unpub. Ph.D. diss., Cleveland, Ohio: Case Western Reserve University, 1969), p. 94.

3. Ibid., pp. 91–92, 95.

4. Ibid., p. 68n105; B. N. Canfield, "The M14: John Garand's Final Legacy," *American Rifleman* 150, no. 6 (August 2002), p. 50.

5. On Studler's background, see Ezell, *Lightweight Rifle*, pp. 85–88. See also the obituary of Mildred Studler in the *Washington Post*, June 14, 1957, p. B2.

6. On Studler's participation in sports, see "Army to Promote Golf and Tennis at Posts," *Washington Post*, April 7, 1925; and www.wbtahorseshows.org/about.htm. The description is from T. McCullough, "Colonel's Real 'Man Behind' All Those Guns," *Washington Post*, April 15, 1945, p. B2.

7. On ball powder, see "9 billion cartridges produced by Western," *New York Times*, December 23, 1943, p. 27; Ezell, *Lightweight Rifle*, pp. 98–100. The Olin companies went through a confusing succession of names. For the sake of clarity, I have generally referred to it as Olin Industries, its name between 1944 and 1954 (when it became Olin Mathieson Chemical Corporation). Canfield, "M14," p. 52.

8. On Winchester at this time, see H. F. Williamson, *Winchester: The Gun That Won the West* (Washington, D.C.: Combat Forces Press, 1952), pp. 345–90. Pugsley contributed the book's epilogue. After the dry 1930s Pugsley went on to become a director of Western Cartridge and Olin.

9. Ezell, *Lightweight Rifle*, pp. 101–11. Ezell interviewed Harvey several times. On Pugsley's background, see Williamson, *Winchester*, p. 283.

10. Much of the following biographical material and weaponry background is based on L. Kahaner's illuminating *AK-47: The Weapon That Changed the Face of War* (Hoboken, N.J.: John Wiley & Sons, 2007), pp. 9–30.

11. It would be only in 1956 that Moscow was forced to reveal its infantry superweapon to the world when Kalashnikov-armed Red Army soldiers crushed the Hungarian rebellion, leaving some fifty thousand dead. Much to Nikita Khrushchev's delight, and to Kalashnikov's no doubt, the AK-47 performed magnificently in the narrow alleys and compact streets of Budapest. With nothing more to hide, the USSR began exporting its propaganda triumph in a metal case to whichever "fraternal countries" asked for it.

China, Poland, Yugoslavia, Bulgaria, and East Germany were among the first beneficiaries, but the weapon, partly because untrained irregulars—even children—could lay down heavy, if unbelievably inaccurate, fire at ranges up to 330 yards, took off among Moscow-backed guerrilla, outlaw, and terrorist outfits in Africa, the Middle East, and South America.

12. C. Aubrey Dixon, "The NATO Rifle: A British Statement on the Development of a Shoulder Weapon for the North Atlantic Treaty Organization," *American Rifleman* 100, no. 1 (January 1952), p. 17.

13. As bitterly related by Aubrey Dixon (who was present), ibid., pp. 17, 40.

14. Ibid., p. 40.

15. Quoted in W. H. Hallahan, *Misfire: The History of How America's Small Arms Have Failed Our Military* (New York: Charles Scribner's Sons, 1994), p. 421.

16. E. C. Ezell, "Cracks in the Post-war Anglo-American Alliance: The Great Rifle Controversy, 1947–1957," *Military Affairs* 38, no. 4 (1974), pp. 138–41, is the best summary of the dispute.

17. Ezell, *Lightweight Rifle*, pp. 199–202.

18. Ibid., pp. 189–92.

19. Belgium held a demonstration of its FAL near Antwerp before about one hundred NATO officers in the late summer of 1951. The Belgian hosts, said the *New York Times,* "contend their new weapon is less complicated than its British counterpart," was 25 percent cheaper, could fire single shots or automatically, could pierce a steel helmet at 1,100 yards, and was almost as accurate as an M1—all music to Ordnance's ears. "New Belgian Rifle Enters Gun Controversy; Less Complex than Britain's Makers Say," *New York Times,* September 7, 1951, p. 5.

20. Ezell, "Cracks in Post-war Alliance," p. 139.

21. Quoted in ibid., p. 140.

22. "New Light Rifle Meets Tests but Production Is Not Near," *New York Times,* December 28, 1951, p. 1.

23. Quoted in Ezell, "Cracks in Post-war Alliance," p. 140.

24. "Many NATO Arms Are Standardized," *New York Times,* October 12, 1952, p. 9; Canfield, "M14," p. 52.

25. "NATO Choice of Standard Rifle Snagged," *Los Angeles Times,* November 23, 1952, p. A6.

26. E. N. Harvey et al., "Mechanism of Wounding," in J. C. Beyer, ed., *Wound Ballistics* (Washington, D.C.: Office of the Surgeon General, Department of the Army, 1962), pp. 144–46. The second edition of L. A. La Garde's *Gunshot Injuries* appeared in 1916; L. B. Wilson's contribution to the government-printed *The Medical Department of the U.S. Army in the World War,* titled *Firearms and Projectiles: Their Bearing on Wound Production,* came out in 1927; and the English translation (from German) of the first volume of C. Cranz and K. Becker's exhaustive *Handbook of Ballistics* was printed in London in 1921. See footnotes 8–10 in Harvey et al., "Mechanism of Wounding," p. 145.

27. Report printed in J. S. Hatcher, *The Book of the Garand* (1948; reprint Highland Park, N.J.: Gun Room Press, 2000), p. 81.

28. On BRL, see T. L. McNaugher, *The M16 Controversies: Military Organizations and Weapons Acquisition* (New York: Praeger, 1984), p. 55; R. B. Stevens and E. C. Ezell, *The Black Rifle: M16 Retrospective* (Toronto: Collector Grade Publications, 1987) pp. 7–8; Hallahan, *Misfire,* pp. 428–29.

29. McNaugher, *M16 Controversies,* p. 57.

30. See http://rand.org/about/history/ and V. Campbell, "How RAND Invented the Postwar World," *Invention & Technology,* Summer 2004, pp. 50–59.

31. For a summary of Hitchman's report, see Stevens and Ezell, *Black Rifle,* pp. 9–10; Hallahan, *Misfire,* p. 432; for ORO in general, plus the quoted results of "other ORO researchers," McNaugher, *M16 Controversies,* pp. 53–54; and especially Ezell, *Lightweight Rifle,* pp. 284–93. Also W. L. Whitson, "The Growth of the Operations Research Office in

the U.S. Army," *Operations Research* 8, no. 6 (1960), pp. 809–24. An excellent summary of the origins and development of the field is A. V. Grant, "Operations Research and Systems Analysis," in J. E. Jessup and L. B. Ketz, eds., *Encyclopedia of the American Military* (New York: Charles Scribner's Sons, 1994), esp. 3:1961.

32. "No further consideration [should] be given US Rifles, Caliber .30, T-44 and T-44E1," according to "Report of Board #3, Project #2495: Lightweight Rifle and Ammunition," August 3, 1953, quoted in McNaugher, *M16 Controversies,* p. 69n1.

33. S. L. A. Marshall, *Men Against Fire: The Problem of Battle Command* (1947; reprint Norman: University of Oklahoma Press, 2000), pp. 50–63.

34. Ibid., p. 82.

35. Ibid., p. 2.

36. Ibid., pp. 2–3.

37. On this subject see F. Smoler, "The Secret of the Soldiers Who Didn't Shoot," *American Heritage* 40, no. 2 (1989).

38. K. C. Jordan, "Right for the Wrong Reasons: S.L.A. Marshall and the Ratio of Fire in Korea," *Journal of Military History* 66, no. 1 (2002), pp. 135–62.

39. P. Cardinal, "Marksmanship and the U.S. Army," *American Rifleman* 99 (June 1951), pp. 14–17, 19.

40. Editorial, "Army Marksmanship," *American Rifleman* 99, no. 12 (December 1951).

41. H. W. Baldwin, "Infantry Adjusts Role," *New York Times,* November 23, 1953, p. 17.

42. See D. Liwanag, "Improving Army Marksmanship: Regaining the Initiative in the Infantry's Half Kilometer," *Infantry Magazine,* July/August 2006; McNaugher, *M16 Controversies,* p. 61 and n35.

43. There are more recent manifestations of this opinion. One newspaper has reported that "hunting is on the decline across the nation as participation has fallen over the last three decades" (down from 19.1 million in 1975 to 12.5 million in 2006). There are different explanations for the phenomenon: "Wildlife officials and environmental researchers" cite "rural depopulation, higher gas prices, and the increased leasing of land by small exclusive clubs or the posting of 'No Hunting' signs by private land owners"; others, however, note the "prevalence of single-parent homes, where the father is not present to pass down the tradition, and the growing popularity of indoor activities that offer immediate gratification, like the Internet, video games and movies." See I. Urbina, "To Revive Hunting, States Turn to the Classroom," *New York Times,* March 8, 2008, p. A1.

44. B. Shadel, "What Price Riflemen?" *American Rifleman* 99, no. 3 (March 1951), pp. 31–32.

45. Editorial, "Aimless Fire," *American Rifleman* 99, no. 9 (September 1951).

46. D. L. Jackson, "The Man with a Rifle," *American Rifleman* 99 (December 1951), pp. 13–15.

47. On Carten's background, see Ezell, *Lightweight Rifle,* p. 210n45. Ridgway's keeping of a Model 1903 in his car is noted in the editorial "Springfield, 1903," *Washington Post,* August 16, 1951, p. 6.

48. Hallahan, *Misfire,* pp. 434–37.

49. Quoted in Ezell, *Lightweight Rifle,* p. 210.

50. ".30-caliber Bullet Adopted for NATO," *New York Times,* December 16, 1953, p. 5.

51. Baldwin, "The Belgian Rifle Case," *New York Times,* February 4, 1954, p. 8; "Churchill Out on Range to Test Disputed Rifle," *New York Times,* January 26, 1954, p. 6.

52. O. N. Bradley and C. Blair, *A General's Life* (New York: Simon & Schuster, 1983), p. 107.

53. B. Welles, "Churchill Faces Commons Fight on Decision to Use Belgian Rifle," *New York Times,* January 29, 1954, p. 4.

54. Ezell, "Cracks in Post-war Alliance," p. 141.

55. "Churchill Chides Laborites for Seeking 'Faults' of U.S.," *New York Times,* February 2, 1954, p. 1.

56. "Britain Will Adopt Belgian Rifle Favored by U.S. for Use by NATO," *New York Times,* January 20, 1954, p. 1. Rather presciently, one of Churchill's leading Labour opponents

on the issue, Woodrow Wyatt (later, ironically, to become one of Margaret Thatcher's most unabashed conservative admirers), had predicted during the recent rifle debate that there was "no evidence that the United States would agree within the next ten years to adopt the new Belgian rifle." Quoted in "Churchill Chides Laborites," p. 1.

57. See H. W. Baldwin's reports, "Standard Rifle Far Off," *New York Times,* May 6, 1954, p. 17; and "The Belgian Rifle Case," *New York Times,* February 4, 1954, p. 8. Baldwin, as the newspaper's military editor-correspondent, had good connections inside the Pentagon and discreetly served as a conduit for the Joint Chiefs of Staff's views. See Ezell, *Lightweight Rifle,* p. 181n74.

58. Baldwin, "Standard Rifle Far Off," p. 17.

59. Ezell, *Lightweight Rifle,* p. 222.

60. Ibid., pp. 216–37.

61. National Security Council, "Basic National Security Policy," NSC 162/2, October 30, 1953.

62. H. S. Wolk, "The 'New Look,' " *Air Force Magazine* 86, no. 8 (August 2003), pp. 80–83. In a classic case of *just* missing the boat, by 1955 Massive Retaliation was so widely known that Hollywood made a not-bad movie, *Strategic Air Command,* starring Jimmy Stewart as the heroic pilot of a B-36 nuclear bomber who gets to fly a brand-new B-47 Stratojet. The movie appeared more than a year after Massive Retaliation's zenith of popularity.

63. J. L. Gaddis, "The Unexpected John Foster Dulles: Nuclear Weapons, Communism, and the Russians," in R. H. Immerman, ed., *John Foster Dulles and the Diplomacy of the Cold War* (Princeton, N.J.: Princeton University Press, 1990), pp. 47–78. See also his cautious article, "Policy for Security and Peace," *Foreign Affairs* 32 (April 1954), pp. 353–64.

64. "Chief of Staff," *Time,* July 28, 1961.

65. M. D. Taylor, *Swords and Plowshares* (New York: W. W. Norton & Co., 1972), p. 166.

66. See R. H. Cole et al., *The Chairmanship of the Joint Chiefs of Staff* (Washington, D.C.: Joint History Office, Office of the Chairman of the Joint Chiefs of Staff, 1995), pp. 52–53.

67. D. Van Ee, "From the New Look to Flexible Response, 1953–1964," in K. J. Hagan and W. R. Roberts, eds., *Against All Enemies: Interpretations of American Military History from Colonial Times to the Present* (Westport, Conn.: Greenwood Press, 1986), p. 331.

68. Kahaner, *AK-47,* pp. 27–28.

69. Hallahan, *Misfire,* p. 462.

70. "Rifle to Replace Four Army Weapons," *New York Times,* May 2, 1957, p. 15; Canfield, "M14," p. 53.

71. Cole et al., *Joint Chiefs of Staff,* pp. 12, 18.

72. "Chief of Staff," *Time.*

73. Van Ee, "From the New Look to Flexible Response," pp. 334–37. On the creation of Special Group Counterinsurgency, see Taylor, *Swords and Plowshares,* pp. 200–201.

74. M. James, "New Small Arms Shown by Army," *New York Times,* August 15, 1957, p. 2.

75. Canfield, "M14," p. 54.

76. Ripley's remark is quoted (uncritically) in "The Small Arms of Our Armies," *San Francisco Bulletin,* May 30, 1862, p. 2.

77. Ezell, *Lightweight Rifle,* pp. 246–54. On the weight of a typical production package, see W. J. Howe and E. H. Harrison, "The Modern Springfield Armory," *American Rifleman* 107, no. 9 (September 1959), p. 22. The timing of this highly favorable article is illuminating: it was printed in the NRA's house journal at the height of the M14 production imbroglio. Colonel Harrison, the coauthor, was a retired Ordnance man.

78. "Mass Output Is Set on New Army Rifle," *New York Times,* September 6, 1958, p. 8.

79. J. G. Norris, "Probers Hear Red Tape Slows Arms Progress," *Washington Post,* April 18, 1960, p. 1.

80. On Springfield's "farming out," see J. S. Hatcher, *The Book of the Garand* (1948; reprint Highland Park, N.J.: Gun Room Press, 2000), p. 118.

81. See Table 8, "Bids Submitted by Prospective Producers of the M14 Rifle, 1958," in Ezell, *Lightweight Rifle*, p. 255.

82. Table 9, "Procurement Orders for the M14 Rifle," and Table 10, "Production Prices for the M14 Rifle by Producer," in Ezell, *Lightweight Rifle*, p. 269. J. G. Norris, "Rifle Production Rising but Army Funds Shrink," *Washington Post*, December 28, 1961, p. A7, has a slightly different figure for the increased sum, $114.

83. J. Raymond, "M-14 Rifle Output Now Satisfies U.S.; Delays Overcome," *New York Times*, October 16, 1961, p. 1.

84. "Only 1 of 10 in Army Has Its M-14 Rifle," *Washington Post*, June 25, 1961, p. A14.

85. "Army, Olin Mathieson Unit Agree Output of M-14 Rifle Lags; Each Blames Other," *Wall Street Journal*, April 20, 1961, p. 4.

86. "Only 1 of 10 in Army Has Its M-14 Rifle," p. A14.

87. Raymond, "M-14 Rifle Output," p. 1.

88. Ezell, *Lightweight Rifle*, pp. 267–68.

89. L. Kraar, "Army Maneuvers Show Gaps in Preparedness for Any Shooting War," *Wall Street Journal*, August 17, 1961, p. 1. Ezell, *Lightweight Rifle*, p. 344, notes that the 5,000 troops in besieged Berlin carried M1s, as did the 1,500 reinforcements sent to aid them.

90. On the defense preparations, see T. Wicker, "President Defends Arms Stand; Asks His Critics to Be Specific," *New York Times*, October 12, 1961, p. 20; Kraar, "Army Maneuvers," p. 1.

91. Raymond, "M-14 Rifle Output," p. 1.

92. Ezell, *Lightweight Rifle*, pp. 272–76.

93. Canfield, "M14," p. 95.

94. Ezell, *Lightweight Rifle*, p. 282.

95. "Experts Study Infantry Weapon to Replace M-14," *Washington Post*, January 30, 1963, p. A7.

Chapter 11

1. There is little material available on Sullivan. The article "Plastic Rifle Designed by Angeleno Passes Test," *Los Angeles Times*, February 11, 1957, p. 31, contains a few nuggets as well as a photo, and J. Hartt, "Deadly AR-15 Rifles Born with $999 Loss," *Los Angeles Times*, January 3, 1966, adds a bit more.

2. Michault's role at this early stage is shrouded in obscurity. See R. B. Stevens and E. C. Ezell, *The Black Rifle: M16 Retrospective* (Toronto: Collector Grade, 1987), pp. 19–20.

3. Indeed, at the time Fairchild was taking an enormous gamble that its new forty-seat turboprop F-27, which it had licensed from Fokker in the Netherlands, would replace the fabled Douglas DC-3 as the nation's number-one civilian airliner. Though built in significant numbers, the F-27 ultimately could not compete against the DC-3's ingrained customer base, let alone its versatility, thriftiness, and hardiness. See "Flight of the Friendship," *Time*, April 21, 1958. This article also mentions Boutelle's "trophy-filled office."

4. These very early days in the history of ArmaLite are covered in D. T. McElrath, "Golden Days at ArmaLite," *American Rifleman* 152, no. 12 (December 2004) and the official history of the company, "A Historical Review of ArmaLite," available online at www .armalite.com. On Fairchild's sales figures, see "Flight of the Friendship," *Time*.

5. As a former Air Corps major, Boutelle might have heard about this some time before his army-connected competitors did. Another probable information conduit was through Boutelle's senior management team, which enjoyed strong connections with the Air Force: the consumer-relations director had actually outranked the corporate president back in the day. See "Flight of the Friendship," *Time*; on his senior managers, see R. P.

Cooke, "Fairchild: A Small Firm Made Big by Making Bigger Planes; It May Be the First to Top Wartime Production," *Wall Street Journal,* November 6, 1950, p. 6.

6. On the number manufactured, see "The Aluminum Rifle," *Time,* December 3, 1956. On the colorful civilian models, "New and Lighter Rifles Signal Fairchild's Entry in Arms Field," *Washington Post,* November 27, 1956, p. A14.

7. McElrath, "Golden Days"; and "Historical Review of ArmaLite." Wikipedia has a useful entry giving Stoner's sparse biographical details. See also D. Shea, "Father of the AR-15," *American Rifleman* 145, no. 12 (November/December 1997), pp. 39, 54–55, 62, for a technical appreciation.

8. On the Monsanto House of the Future, see R. Chittum, "Castles in the Air," *Wall Street Journal,* May 14, 2007, p. R10.

9. On the M16, see "Aluminum Rifle," *Time*; T. L. McNaugher, *The M16 Controversies: Military Organizations and Weapons Acquisition* (New York: Praeger, 1984), p. 51; E. C. Ezell, *The Search for a Lightweight Rifle: The M14 and M16 Rifles* (Unpub. Ph.D. diss., Cleveland, Ohio: Case Western Reserve University, 1969), pp. 299–302, 424–28; "Historical Review of ArmaLite"; McElrath, "Golden Days." The Web site www.world .guns.ru/assault/as16-e.htm has much useful information. Melvin Johnson, perhaps questionably given his business connections with the firm (he was the East Coast consult-ant for ArmaLite), wrote a positive article on the AR-10 for *Ordnance* magazine in 1955 (though it was not printed until May–June 1957). On Johnson's article, see Stevens and Ezell, *Black Rifle,* p. 28.

10. "Aluminum Rifle," *Time.*

11. Hartt, "Deadly AR-15 Rifle."

12. Quoted in W. H. Hallahan, *Misfire: The History of How America's Small Arms Have Failed Our Military* (New York: Charles Scribner's Sons, 1994), pp. 446–47.

13. McNaugher, *M16 Controversies,* p. 51; Stevens and Ezell, *Black Rifle,* pp. 36–40.

14. Stevens and Ezell, *Black Rifle,* pp. 40, 49–51.

15. "Gen. Willard Wyman Dies at 71; Led Normandy Invasion Force," *New York Times,* March 30, 1969, p. 85.

16. McNaugher, *M16 Controversies,* pp. 58–59.

17. C. B. Hughes, "Virginia's Festival Foods," *Washington Post,* September 27, 1957, p. C1.

18. "Chicagoan with Trainfire Unit," *Daily Defender,* June 13, 1957, p. 5.

19. These lengthy training films are available for viewing online at www.archive.org/details/ Rifle_Marksmanship_with_M1_Rifle_Part_1.

20. See the description in H. W. Baldwin, "The New Fort Dix," *New York Times,* November 12, 1959, p. 14.

21. D. Liwanag, "Improving Army Marksmanship: Regaining the Initiative in the Infantry's Half Kilometer," *Infantry Magazine,* July/August 2006; W. G. Wyman, "Army Marksmanship Today," *Infantry* 48, no. 3 (July–September 1958), pp. 6–14. For discus-sion of the impact of Trainfire and the place of competitive marksmanship, see the inter-esting pro and con discussion between Lieutenant Colonel T. J. Sharpe, "Competitive Marksmanship: It Pays Off!" pp. 24–26, 66 and Captain J. R. Semmens, "Competitive Marksmanship: The Price of the Prizes!" pp. 25–27, 67 in *Infantry* 49, no. 3 (July–September 1959).

22. Summarized Sergeant Zahm of the Marine Corps School's Markmanship Training Unit, "I would say in the Marine Corps he [Oswald] is a good shot, slightly above average, and as compared to the average [civilian] male of his age . . . that he is an excellent shot." *Report of the President's Commission on the Assassination of President Kennedy* (Washington, D.C.: U.S. Government Printing Office, 1964), esp. pp. 189–92, 581–82, 586.

23. McNaugher, *M16 Controversies,* p. 63; Stevens and Ezell, *Black Rifle,* p. 66; Hallahan, *Misfire,* pp. 450–51. On the relative weights, see Table 13, "Comparative Description of the AR-15 and M14 Rifles," in Ezell, *Lightweight Rifles,* p. 306.

24. Stevens and Ezell, *Black Rifle,* p. 75; Hallahan, *Misfire,* pp. 458–59.

25. On the amount of ammunition a soldier could carry, see Hallahan, *Misfire,* p. 457.

26. See figure given in "Order of $13,296,923 for New-Type Rifles Reflects Army's Growing Dislike of M-14," *Wall Street Journal*, November 6, 1953, p. 7.

27. McNaugher, *M16 Controversies*, pp. 66–67; Ezell, *Lightweight Rifle*, p. 311.

28. "Fairchild Engine Reports Layoff of 500; Says Job Rolls Still Top '57," *Wall Street Journal*, February 11, 1958, p. 17; "Fairchild Stock Drops as Loss Is Predicted," *Washington Post*, July 19, 1958, p. D6.

29. "Fairchild Engine Had First Quarter Loss, Cites Cost of Closing Plant," *Wall Street Journal*, April 23, 1959, p. 3; "Fairchild Engine," *New York Times*, February 13, 1960, p. 24.

30. "Boutelle Quits Posts," *New York Times*, January 22, 1959, p. 48. See also A. R. Hammer, "New Chief Expected Next Week for Fairchild Engine & Airplane," *New York Times*, February 2, 1961, p. 37.

31. McNaugher, *M16 Controversies*, p. 67.

32. On the sale details, Stevens and Ezell, *Black Rifle*, p. 81; "Historical Review of ArmaLite"; McElrath, "Golden Days."

33. E. Grant, *The Colt Legacy: The Colt Armory in Hartford, 1855–1980* (Providence, R.I.: Mowbray, 1982), p. 172.

34. "Colt's New Rifle," *Time*, November 22, 1963. For more details on the "boardroom battles," see "Change at Fairbanks Whitney," *Time*, October 26, 1962, and Grant, *Colt Legacy*, pp. 174–79.

35. McNaugher, *M16 Controversies*, pp. 76–77, 106n6; Stevens and Ezell, *Black Rifle*, p. 82 (MacDonald's "small-statured" comment, in his testimony, is on p. 83); Hallahan, *Misfire*, pp. 464–66; L. Kahaner, *AK-47: The Weapon That Changed the Face of War* (Hoboken, N.J.: John Wiley & Sons, 2007), p. 46. See W. C. Westmoreland, *A Soldier Reports* (Garden City, N.Y.: Doubleday & Co., 1976), p. 158, for his remark about the M1. On arms exports offsetting the cost of overseas forces, see J. A. Huston, "The Military-Industrial Complex," in J. E. Jessup and L. B. Ketz, eds., *Encyclopedia of the American Military* (New York: Charles Scribner's Sons, 1994), pp. 3:1695–96.

36. On LeMay, see T. M. Coffey, *Iron Eagle: The Turbulent Life of General Curtis LeMay* (New York: Crown Publishers, 1986); W. J. Boyne, "LeMay," *Air Force Magazine* 81, no. 3 (March 1998).

37. Quoted in Hallahan, *Misfire*, p. 466.

38. On this celebration of the nation's birthday, see Kahaner, *AK-47*, p. 44; Stevens and Ezell, *Black Rifle*, p. 87; Hallahan, *Misfire*, p. 467; McNaugher, *M16 Controversies*, p. 78 (on Boutelle and LeMay's relationship, see p. 106n10).

39. On Strichman, see "Change at Fairbanks Whitney," *Time*, and the obituary (he died, aged seventy-two, of cancer) in *New York Times*, April 26, 1989.

40. Quoted in Ezell, *Lightweight Rifle*, p. 313.

41. A. J. Glass, "The M14: Best Army Rifle—or a 'Major Ordnance Blunder,'" *New York Herald Tribune*, June 26, 1961.

42. McNaugher, *M16 Controversies*, pp. 79–80; Hallahan, *Misfire*, p. 470.

43. McNaugher, *M16 Controversies*, p. 83. Useful summaries of AGILE can be found in W. Beecher, "Unconventional Wars Spur U.S. to Develop Some Unusual Devices," March 24, 1964, p. 1; and "Weapons Sought for Remote Wars," *New York Times*, January 27, 1964, p. 2.

44. The report is printed in full in Stevens and Ezell, *Black Rifle*, pp. 101–6.

45. Quoted ibid., p. 107.

46. This section is based on Table 14, "Comparative Performance Date for the 7.62mm NATO (.30) and 5.56mm (.223) Cartridges," in Ezell, *Lightweight Rifle*, pp. 315–18; McNaugher, *M16 Controversies*, pp. 84, esp. 108–9n34. Lastly, though I don't entirely agree with his conclusions, the article by Major Anthony Milavic, "The Last 'Big Lie' of Vietnam Kills U.S. Soldiers in Iraq," at www.americanthinker.com/2004/08/the_last_big _lie_of_vietnam_ki.html, August 24, 2004, contains important extracts from the ARPA report and is a valuable resource in its own right. J. Fallows, "M-16: A Bureaucratic

Horror Story," *Atlantic,* June 1981, p. 60, quotes Stoner on the instability issue: "There is the advantage that a small or light bullet has over a heavy one when it comes to wound ballistics . . . What it amounts to is the fact that bullets are stabilized to fly through the air, and not through water, or a body, which is approximately the same density as the water. And they are stable as long as they are in the air. When they hit something, they imediately go unstable . . . If you are talking about .30-caliber [like the bullet used in the M-14], this might remain stable through a human body . . . While a little bullet, being it has a low mass, it senses an instability situation faster and reacts much faster . . . this is what makes a little bullet pay off so much in wound ballistics."

47. Hallahan, *Misfire,* p. 472.

48. On Besson, see his obituary in *Washington Post,* July 18, 1985, p. C6.

49. Regarding the order, see McNaugher, *M16 Controversies,* p. 85.

50. W. J. Howe and E. H. Harrison, "The ArmaLite AR-15 Rifle," *American Rifleman,* May 1962, pp. 17–23. For the 40 percent figure, see Ezell, *Lightweight Rifle,* p. 335, and J. Fallows, "M-16: A Bureaucratic Horror Story," *Atlantic,* June 1981, p. 61. According to McNaugher, *M16 Controversies,* p. 109n44, "because Col. Harrison was a retired ordnance officer, most of the AR15's advocates saw this article as little more than Army propaganda." Interestingly, LeMay was not unaverse to changing the barrel twist to one in 12. This was because, in cold weather, increased air density amplified the bullet's tumbling and many of LeMay's SAC bases were in northern Europe and the far north. (Ezell makes this point on p. 335.)

51. On Hitch's background, see Grant, "Operations Research and Systems Analysis," in Jessup and Ketz, eds., *Encyclopedia of the American Military,* pp. 3:1966–70.

52. McNaugher, *M16 Controversies,* pp. 85–86; Stevens and Ezell, *Black Rifle,* p. 109.

53. See McNaugher, *M16 Controversies,* p. 109n38.

54. Ibid., p. 87.

55. Grant, *Colt Legacy,* p. 185.

56. J. Raymond, "M-14 Rifle Output Now Satisfies U.S.; Delays Overcome," *New York Times,* October 16, 1961, p. 1; McNaugher, *M16 Controversies,* p. 88.

57. McNaugher, *M16 Controversies,* pp. 91–96. On MacDonald's furious reaction, Stevens and Ezell, *Black Rifle,* p. 115. Based mostly on a minute of a meeting held at AMC headquarters on October 22, 1962, which noted that "the U.S. Army Infantry Board will conduct only those tests that will reflect adversely on the AR-15," Hallahan, *Misfire,* argues (pp. 482–84) that the tests were deliberately skewed by the army to favor the M14. McNaugher, however, claims the bias was inadvertent. The AMC remark, incidentally, was firmly denied, and, moreover, it seems an odd thing to record if one is intent on conspiracy. According to Ezell, *Lightweight Rifle,* p. 323, regarding the statement, "there was no further evidence to support this seeming bias." For the one-billion-dollar estimate, see W. Beecher, "Billion Dollar Bang: The Pentagon Prepares to Choose Her Rifle from Among Four Models," *Wall Street Journal,* July 24, 1964, p. 1.

58. The SPIW was announced in "New Developments: New Infantry Method," *Ordnance,* May–June 1963, p. 714, cited in McNaugher, *M16 Controversies,* p. 97. For the change in date, see McNaugher, p. 117.

59. Ibid., p. 117; H. W. Baldwin, "Army Tests Dart-Throwing, Hand-held Weapon," *New York Times,* March 15, 1964, p. 25.

60. Ezell, *Lightweight Rifle,* p. 326. An extremely early army training film of the XM16E1 (the trial version of the weapon) can be viewed at www.archive.org/details/Rifle556mmXM16E1OperationandCycleof FunctioningTF93663.

61. W. Beecher, "Choice of Basic Rifle Stirs Pentagon Debate in an Age of Missiles," *Wall Street Journal,* July 2, 1963, p. 1.

62. The story was printed on November 6, 1963, p. 7. See also an editorial, "A Shot in the Dark," *Wall Street Journal,* November 19, 1963, p. 18.

63. " 'McNamara's War' Tag OKd by Defense Chief," *Los Angeles Times,* April 25, 1964, p. 15.

64. "All U.S. Bases Studied for Possible Cuts," *Los Angeles Times*, May 2, 1964, p. 9.

65. Quoted in McNaugher, *M16 Controversies*, p. 116.

66. On these figures, see *American Military History* (Washington, D.C.: Center of Military History, U.S. Army, 1989), p. 642.

67. "Colt's, Inc., Is Awarded $4,305,750 Army Order; GE Receives Contracts," *Wall Street Journal*, November 3, 1964, p. 5. The breakdown for the order is noted in Stevens and Ezell, *Black Rifle*, p. 157.

68. "Brooklyn Navy Yard Will Close," *New York Times*, November 20, 1964, p. 1. See also "Navy Yards at Brooklyn, Portsmouth, N.H., to Close, 2 on West Coast to Merge in Big Pentagon Cutbacks," *Wall Street Journal*, November 20, 1964, p. 3. The *Journal* mentioned Springfield just once, in a comprehensive, small-type catalog of all the closures.

69. On the number of employees who did not go to Rock Island, see Ezell, *Lightweight Rifle*, p. 385.

70. Quoted in Stevens and Ezell, *Black Rifle*, p. 99.

71. On Westmoreland's career and background, see "Combat-Ready General," *New York Times*, April 27, 1964, p. 6.

72. See, for instance, H. G. Moore and J. L. Galloway, *We Were Soldiers Once . . . and Young: Ia Drang: The Battle That Changed the War in Vietnam* (New York: Random House, 1992), passim.

73. For a profile of Hal Moore, see "Pursuer of Vietcong," *New York Times*, January 31, 1968, p. 9; and for details on Lieutenant Marm's exploits, "Charges Vet Foe to Show Way to Mates," *Chicago Tribune*, November 25, 1965, p. B6; "Didn't Like Fighting, Gets Valor Award," *Los Angeles Times*, November 18, 1966, p. 17; "Lieutenant, Iadrang Hero, Wins the Medal of Honor," *New York Times*, December 20, 1966, p. 6. There's a small discrepancy in the number of casualties ascribed to Marm. Moore and Galloway, *We Were Soldiers Once*, p. 124, states that there was an NVA officer and eleven soldiers.

74. W. C. Westmoreland, *A Soldier Reports* (Garden City, N.Y.: Doubleday & Co., 1976), p. 158. See also Moore and Galloway, *We Were Soldiers Once*, pp. 197–98.

75. Stevens and Ezell, *Black Rifle*, pp. 196–97.

76. McNaugher, *M16 Controversies*, p. 124.

77. See photo caption adjacent to "Foe Opens Truce-zone Arms Trail," *Washington Post*, March 19, 1966, p. A15.

78. "Colt Wins 45 Million M-6 [*sic*] Rifle Contract," *Chicago Tribune*, June 19, 1966. Details of the contract are printed in Stevens and Ezell, *Black Rifle*, p. 205. Working out how many weapons were ordered, paid for, and received is a complex business. The clearest summary of all previous orders can be found in the table printed in E. H. Harrison, "M14 and M16 Rifles," *American Rifleman* 114, no. 4 (April 1966), p. 57. At the time of writing total orders amounted to 328,299 M16s and XM16E1s. Until its decommissioning, says Harrison, 1,380,346 M14s were made. (Exact estimates differ slightly.)

79. A perceptive summary of the situation is W. Beecher, "Army Seeks a Rifle to Replace the M-14, Found Erratic in Vietnam Fighting," *New York Times*, June 26, 1966, p. 38.

80. See June 1966 contract details printed in Stevens and Ezell, *Black Rifle*, p. 205. There is a great deal of ambiguity regarding exact numbers, partly owing to secrecy and the continual changes to the Colt contract. I have used the 947,000 figure quoted in the article, "Unit of Colt Industries Gets $25,871,701 Award for Army's M16 Rifle," *Wall Street Journal*, September 5, 1967, p. 11. Whereas Stevens and Ezell, p. 205, state that Colt's total income from the amended contract was $91,682,159.88, I have used the *Journal*'s figure of $106,198,738.

81. "Pentagon Reports Shortage of Rifles for Last Two Months," *New York Times*, November 24, 1966, p. 6.

82. "Rep. Ichord Says M-16 Dispute Threatens Morale in Vietnam," *New York Times*, June 1, 1967, p. 3.

83. The mechanics of IMR, ball powder, and the cyclic rate is discussed in McNaugher, *M16 Controversies*, pp. 146–47.

84. Fallows, "M-16: A Bureaucratic Horror Story," p. 63.

85. For this view, see ibid. and, though I disagree with some of its conclusions ("American troops in Vietnam were equipped with a rifle their superiors knew would fail when put to the test."), the highly illuminating *National Defense*, p. 77. Most subsequent work on the M16 has tended to follow this line; e.g., Hallahan, *Misfire*, p. 516, goes so far as to write that the "points of condemnation sound like a historical bill of particulars against all the other eras of Ordnance Department history—including the regimes of Ripley and Benét, and Flagler and Buffington and Crozier—right through the regimes of Studler and Carten." The "confusion" argument forwarded by McNaugher, *M16 Controversies*, pp. 135–70, esp. p. 137, decisively routs the opposition.

86. Though the authors do not remark on these jammings (and a few more), Bungum and Towles's stories can be found in Moore and Galloway, *We Were Soldiers Once*, pp. 89, 242, respectively.

87. E. F. Murphy, *The Hill Fights: The First Battle of Khe Sanh* (New York: Ballantine Books, 2003), pp. 47, 206.

88. On these tests, see McNaugher, *M16 Controversies*, p. 160.

89. Kahaner, *AK-47*, p. 50.

90. Murphy, *Hill Fights*, p. 129.

91. E. F. Murphy, *Dak To: the 173rd Airborne Brigade in South Vietnam's Central Highlands, June–November 1967* (Navato, Calif.: Presidio Press, 1993), p. 248.

92. Quoted in Stevens and Ezell, *Black Rifle*, pp. 274–75.

93. Originally in P. Shockley, *The Trap-door Springfield in the Service*, quoted in Stevens and Ezell, *Black Rifle*, p. 209.

94. See, for instance, General Godfrey's comment that "when cartridges were dirty and corroded, the ejectors did not always extract the empty shells from the chambers, and the men were compelled to use knives to get them out. When the shells were clean no great difficulty was experienced." His authoritative recollection of the battle is reprinted in W. A. Graham, *The Custer Myth: A Source Book of Custeriana* (New York: Bonanza Books, 1953), esp. pp. 146–47, and also D. D. Scott et al., *Archaeological Perspectives on the Battle of the Little Bighorn* (Norman: University of Oklahoma Press, 1989), p. 113.

95. Quoted in McNaugher, *M16 Controversies*, p. 140.

96. Ezell, *Lightweight Rifle*, pp. 370–71. Alternatively, "official Army inquiries placed the blame for this situation on Colt's, which, they asserted, shipped the rifle to Vietnam with promotional literature stating that the M16 could not 'malfunction under any condition, including rain, snow, and mud.' Colt's personnel denied this, although literature making precisely these claims was indeed printed for the AR15. Whether such literature was shipped with the weapon to Vietnam, whether it found its way to Vietnam in some other fashion, or whether the Army simply was trying to blame Colt's for its own omissions is impossible to determine." McNaugher, *M16 Controversies*, pp. 169–70n65.

97. Murphy, *Hill Fights*, pp. 48, 107.

98. On bullet "sweating," see Ezell, *Lightweight Rifle*, p. 371.

99. Hallahan, *Misfire*, p. 511; Ezell, *Lightweight Rifle*, p. 350.

100. Quoted in McNaugher, *M16 Controversies*, p. 121.

101. B. N. Canfield, "The M14: John Garand's Final Legacy," *American Rifleman* (August 2002), p. 95.

102. Ezell, *Lightweight Rifle*, pp. 328–30.

103. McNaugher, *M16 Controversies*, p. 127.

104. "Marines in Viet Will Get Lighter Rifles," *Chicago Tribune*, January 2, 1967, p. A2.

105. There is some confusion over the date of the adoption. Many Web sites state that it was February 28. I have used the date given in Stevens and Ezell, *Black Rifle*, p. 224.

Chapter 12

1. Special Report, *Attack on the 507th Maintenance Company, 23 March 2003, An Nasiriyah, Iraq,* July 2003, pp. 12–14, available online at www.army.mil/features/507thMaintCmpy/.

2. Quoted in "The USA's M4 Carbine Controversy," December 20, 2007, online at www.defenseindustrydaily.com/the-usas-m4-carbine-controversy-03289/. See also C. R. Schoenberger, "You've Got Bang!" *Forbes,* June 11, 2001, pp. 138–39.

3. See Office of the Inspector General, Department of Defense, *Acquisition of the Objective Individual Combat Weapon,* Report D-2006-004, October 7, 2005, p. 2; also Appendix F, "Project Manager Soldier Weapons Memorandum for XM8 Carbine," pp. 48–49.

4. M. Cox, "Too Late, XM8: Doomed Carbine the Victim of Army Infighting," *Army Times,* June 1, 2007.

5. J. Jackson, "Pentagon Backs Spiral Development," *Washington Technology,* June 9, 2003.

6. See W. M. Arkin, "Spiraling Ahead," *Armed Forces Journal,* February 2006.

7. Quoted in ibid.

8. "M4 Carbine Contracts Announced to Date," appendix A of "USA's M4 Carbine Controversy"; P. Leicht, "M4A1 Rifle Delivers Flexibility," *Leatherneck,* October 2004, pp. 34–35.

9. In a classified report entitled "M4A1 5.56mm Carbine and Related Systems Deficiencies and Solutions: Operational and Technical Study with Analysis of the Alternatives." Portions are cited in M. Cox, "Better than M4, But You Can't Have One," *Army Times,* posted online March 1, 2007. (There are earlier postings of this article dating from late February.) A letter submitted by Colt's chief operating officer in response to the piece, dated March 26, notes that the army disagreed with the SOCOM findings, adding that the company's subsequent improvements "eliminate[d] those few problems." The letter can be found at www.colt.com/mil/news.asp or at the *Army Times* Web site.

10. See C. R. Wonson, "Replacing the M16A2: A New Rifle for the 21st Century," *Marine Corps Gazette,* April 2001, pp. 20–23.

11. "M4 Carbine Contracts Announced to Date," appendix A of "USA's M4 Carbine Controversy."

12. M. Remez, "Colt on the March," *Hartford Courant,* December 5, 2004, pp. D1–2.

13. On the case, see R. Lardner, "Reliability, Cost of U.S. Forces' Standard Rifle under Scrutiny," *Washington Post,* April 27, 2008, p. A11.

14. J. M. Moran and R. Kalra, "Winchester Aims to Close a Factory, End an Era," *Hartford Courant,* January 18, 2006, pp. A1, A5; D. Haar, "Farewell Bids at Winchester," *Hartford Courant,* September 28, 2006, pp. A1, A7.

15. Worse was to come. Three years later Smith & Wesson's chairman, James Minder, resigned after it was revealed that in the 1950s and 1960s he had participated in an armed-robbery spree and had spent fifteen years in jail. Convicted felons, even ones running gun companies, are banned from owning or possessing firearms. Fate, however, would be kinder to S&W than to Winchester. Soon afterward Michael Golden, the new president, reoriented the company toward military and police sales, hired new marketing and sales executives, beefed up its lobbying, and aggressively pursued exports, thereby greatly driving up revenue and profits. L. Wayne, "Armed and Competitive: Military Sales Help Smith & Wesson Fight Its Way Back," *New York Times,* April 11, 2006, pp. B1, B4; R. Thurman, "Smith & Wesson Launches Aggressive Strategy," *Shooting Industry,* August 2005.

16. Project Manager Soldier Weapons, *Soldier Weapons Assessment Team Report 6-03,* July 31, 2003, pp. 1–64. Similar views on the M4 were expressed in a report by Lieutenant Colonel Jim Smith, *Operation Iraqi Freedom: PEO Soldier Lessons Learned,* May 15, 2003; available online at www.globalsecurity.org/military/library/report/2003/index.html.

17. Quoted in H. Kennedy, "Army Tests New Rifle That Could Replace M16, M4," *National Defense,* February 2004, p. 42.

18. "M4 Carbine Contracts Announced to Date," appendix A of "USA's M4 Carbine Controversy." For the contract sum, see I. Kemp, "Assault Rifles in a 5.56mm Evolution," *Armada International*, 2, April–May 2007, pp. 36–38, 40.

19. For a typical example of anti-M4 writing, see S. Koehl's article, "Army Get Your Gun: Why Our Troops Use an Inferior Rifle," *Weekly Standard Online*, April 25, 2008.

20. News release dated November 30, 2004, online at www.fnherstal.com/html/NEWS.htm.

21. See F. Colucci, "Custom-Designed Rifle Aims to Fit Commandos' Special Needs," *National Defense*, July 2005.

22. Ibid.

23. See news release "Colt Challenges Rivals' Illegal Marketing Practices," April 21, 2004, online at www.colt.com/mil/news.asp; "Colt Sues to Block 'Copycat' M4 Rifles," *Hartford Courant*, April 22, 2004. In late 2006 Bushmaster, another company sued by Colt, won its case. The judge also ruled that "M4" was not a federal trademark. R. Huntingdon, "Bushmaster Beats Colt," *American Handgunner*, November–December 2006.

24. Quoted in Cox, "Better than M4." Vickers's own account, dating from June 2006, of the development of the HK416 may be found online at www.hkpro.com/hk416.htm. For more, see K. Hackathorn, "HK416 5.56mm," *Special Weapons for Military and Police* (2006), pp. 36–41.

25. Cox, "Better than M4."

26. The memorandum is printed as appendix C in Inspector General, *Acquisition of Objective Combat Weapon*, pp. 36–38; Cox, "Too Late, XM8."

27. See www.defenseindustrydaily.com/oicw-individual-weapon-rfp-temporarily-suspended-0898/, dated July 22, 2005, though the suspension went into effect on July 19.

28. IPR Strategic Business Information Database, August 8, 2005.

29. Inspector General, *Acquisition of Objective Combat Weapon*.

30. Inspector General, Department of Defense, *Program Management of the Objective Individual Combat Weapon Increment* I, Report D-2006-123, September 29, 2006, pp. 7, 52.

31. Kemp, "Assault Rifles in a 5.56mm Evolution." Another end-of-year bonus was the declaration, at a major military conference by the commanding general of the U.S. Army Infantry Center and School at Fort Benning, that the M4 was "one of the highlighted success stories in combat operations in Iraq and Afghanistan." Cited in letter by retired Marine Corps major general James Battaglini, chief operating officer of Colt, March 26, 2007, online at www.colt.com/mil/news.asp.

32. Center for Naval Analyses, *Soldier Perspectives on Small Arms in Combat*, Report CRM D0015259.A2, December 2006, pp. 14, 1–2, 17–18.

33. Cox, "Better than M4."

34. M. Cox, "Newer Carbines Outperform M4 in Dust Test," *Army Times*, posted online on December 19, 2007. Regarding the Okinawa acquisition, see C. Lowe, "Army Won't Field Rifle Deemed Superior to M4," Military.com, posted April 6, 2007.

35. James Battaglini, Colt Defense chief operating officer, letter to the editor, March 26, 2007, online at www.colt.com/mil/news.asp; "Army Position: M4 Carbine Is Soldier's Battlefield Weapon of Choice," news release, March 29, 2007, online at www.army.mil/-newsreleases/2007/03/29/2471-army-position—m4-carbine-is-soldiers-battlefield-weapon-of-choice/; IPR Strategic Business Information Database, April 22, 2007.

36. Quoted in C. Lowe, "Senator Tells Army to Reconsider M4," Military.com, April 30, 2007.

37. CNA, *Soldier Perspectives on Small Arms*, pp. 29–30.

38. Project manager, *Soldier Weapons Assessment Team Report 6-03*, p. 7.

39. P. J. Doughterty and B. K. Matthews, "Comparison of M-16A2 and M-4 Wounding Potential," *Military Medicine* 172, no. 8 (2007), pp. 871–74.

40. M. L. Fackler, "Ballistic Injury," *Annals of Emergency Medicine* 15 (December 1986), pp. 1451–55; and Fackler, "Wounding Patterns of Military Rifle Bullets," *International Defense Review* 1 (1989), pp. 59–64.

41. A. H. Cordesman, *Iraq's Evolving Insurgency: The Nature of Attacks and Patterns and Cycles in the Conflict* (Washington, D.C.: Center for Strategic and International Studies, February 3, 2006), pp. ii–iii, 3.

42. These statistics are available online at www.icasualties.org.

43. Press conference February 21, 2007, transcript available online at www.mnf-iraq.com/index.php?option=com_content&task=view&id=10403&Itemid=128. The Iraqi government made the original $750 million request for small arms (50,250 M16s and the same number of M4s), ammunition, equipment, armored vehicles, and helicopters in September 2006 ("Up to $750M in Weapons and Support for Iraq," *Defense Industry Daily*, September 21, online at www.defenseindustrydaily.com/up-to-750m-in-weapons-support-for-iraq-02643/.

44. On Iraqi army problems, see for instance M. Gordon, "Iraqi Unit Deserts Post, Despite American's Plea," *New York Times*, April 16, 2008, p. 1; and M. Kramer, "Desertion or Break? An Iraqi Gives His Side," *New York Times*, April 17, 2008.

45. C. Lowe, "Iraqi Army to Ditch AK-47s for M-16s," Military.com, February 27, 2008.

46. Y. J. Dreazen and G. Jaffe, "Plan to Sell Iraqis M-16s Triggers New Controversy," *Wall Street Journal*, October 8, 2007.

47. Gordon, "Iraqi Unit Deserts Post"; on training time, see Dreazen and Jaffe, "Plan to Sell Iraqis M-16s."

48. C. Lowe, "Army Agrees to M4 Sand Test Shoot-off," Military.com, July 27, 2007.

49. M. Cox, "Newer Carbines Outperform M4 in Dust Test," *Army Times*, posted online December 19, 2007.

50. From a chart, "Slide 6," reproduced in the most exhaustive dissection of the test at http://elementsofpower.blogspot.com/2008/01/extreme-dust-test-m4-and-others.html, entry for January 1, 2008. The blog is maintained by an experienced Air Force tester and lead engineer. For the definition of major and minor stoppages, see J. D. Leipold, "Soldiers Confident in M4 Despite Test," *Infantry Magazine*, January–February 2008.

51. Lowe, "M4 Carbine Fares Poorly."

52. Quoted in Leipold, "Soldiers Confident in M4 Despite Test."

53. This "inside skinny" was published by David Crane, "Colt M4 Carbine Finishes Last in Latest U.S. Army Small Arms Reliability Test," online at www.defensereview.com/modules.php?name=News&file=article&sid=1077, December 18, 2007.

54. M. Cox, "M4 May Get Tougher Barrel, Better Mags," *Army Times*, posted online on December 17, 2007.

55. Lardner, "Reliability, Cost of U.S. Forces' Standard Rifle."

56. Quoted in Cox, "Better than M4."

57. Quoted in Cox, "Better than M4." In another article (Lowe, "M4 Carbine Fares Poorly") Radcliffe is quoted as saying, "We know there are some pretty exciting things on the horizon with technology . . . so maybe what we do is stick with the M4 for now and let technologies mature enough that we can spin them into a new carbine." He added, "It's just not ready yet. But it can be ready relatively rapidly."

Photo Credits and Permissions

TEXT

INSERT

Insert page 1 Matchlock. *Library of Congress, Prints and Photographs Division*
Kentucky rifle. *National Museum of American History, Smithsonian Institution*

Insert page 2 Hall breech-loader. *National Museum of American History, Smithsonian Institution*
Toolbox. *National Museum of American History, Smithsonian Institution*
Mordecai. *Library of Congress, Prints and Photographs Division*

Insert page 3 Industrialization wrought (I): *National Archives (156-RDI-4)*
Industrialization wrought (II): *National Archives (156-RDI-4)*

Insert page 4 John Brown Sharps rifle. *National Museum of American History, Smithsonian Institution*
Lincoln's Henry rifle. *National Museum of American History, Smithsonian Institution*
California Joe. *Library of Congress, Prints and Photographs Division*

Insert page 5 Ripley. *National Park Service, Springfield Armory NHS, Photograph 5583-SA.2*
Dyer. *National Park Service, Springfield Armory NHS, Photograph 5586-SA.1*
1867 breechloading tests. *Library of Congress, Prints and Photographs Division*

Insert page 6 Spencer repeater. *National Museum of American History, Smithsonian Institution*
Winchester Model 1866: *National Park Service, Springfield Armory NHS, SPAR 1454*
Jesse James rifle. *Library of Congress, Prints and Photographs Division*

Insert page 7 Indian cartoon. *Library of Congress, Prints and Photographs Division*
Indian-decorated rifle. *National Park Service, Springfield Armory NHS, SPAR 756*

Insert page 8 Buff-running. *Library of Congress, Prints and Photographs Division*
Aftermath of buff-running craze. *National Archives (79-M-1B-4)*

Insert page 9 Annie Oakley. *Buffalo Bill Historical Center, Cody, Wyoming; P94.1P.94.1*
Turks at gunmaking factory. *Picture Collection, The Branch Libraries, The New York Public Library, Astor, Lenox and Tilden Foundations*

Insert page 10 German-American league march. *Library of Congress, Prints and Photographs Division*
African-American soldier. *Library of Congress, Prints and Photographs Division*
Creedmoor range. *Library of Congress, Prints and Photographs Division*

Insert page 11 Emory Upton. *National Archives (111-B-5877)*
Nelson Miles and Buffalo Bill. *National Archives (111-SC-85680)*

Insert page 12 Teddy Roosevelt. *Library of Congress, Prints and Photographs Division*
Two shots of soldiers firing regular and smokeless powder. "Smokeless Powder," *The Manufacturer and Builder, September 1890*

Insert page 13 Pedersen device. *National Park Service, Springfield Armory NHS, SPAR 1324 (Rifle), 1325 (Pedersen Device), and 1326 (Magazine)*
Three men wearing armor. *National Archives (111-SC-19271)*
Pershing handing out medal. *National Archives (120-RPM-08)*

Insert page 14 Four prototype rifles. *National Archives (156-RD-285)*
John Garand. *National Archives (156-RDI-5)*

Insert page 15 Steel plate with bullet holes. *National Archives (156-RD-41)*
T44 prototype rifle. *National Park Service, Springfield Armory NHS, SPAR 3937*
M16 rifle. *National Museum of American History, Smithsonian Institution*

Insert page 16 Two men firing XM8s. *Released by Program Executive Office Soldier/U.S. Army*
Man firing M4 with casing flying out. *Released by the U.S. Department of Defense/U.S. Air Force*
Light version of the SCAR. *Courtesy of FNH USA*

Acknowledgments

In writing this book, I have incurred many debts, and here I can but partially repay them. I promise, a check for the full amount is in the mail, but my primary creditors are: David Smith, who runs the New York Public Library's marvelous Allen Room; Mark Lee, Mark Lamster, and Susan Jacoby, denizens of said room and my fellow scriveners; Professor Robert Gordon of Yale University and John O'Rear for their expert advice; David Miller, associate curator, Division of Military History and Diplomacy, at the Smithsonian Institution's National Museum of American History, for allowing me the privilege of entering the hallowed Gun Room and for helping me obtain some wonderful new images of some wonderful old rifles; Daniel Wilson for helping to sell a book about some wonderful old rifles; and, finally, Alex MacKenzie, park ranger at the National Park Service–supervised Springfield Armory National Historic Site, who went out of his way (during a move, no less) to take photos of Springfield's vast inventory of weaponry.

I also greatly owe the staff of the New York Public Library's Milstein Division of United States History, Local History, and Genealogy for ferrying up piles of books on all manner of musketry, as well as the librarians at the Rare Books Room, the Pforzheimer Collection, and the Science, Industry, and Business Library.

For the look, feel, and "sound" of *American Rifle*, I'm hopelessly indebted to three people: John Flicker, my editor, who aided in structuring the manuscript; the designer Virginia Norey, who performed magic on my messy collection of photos; and Janet Biehl, the copy editor, who performed surgery on my predilection for passive-voice sentences.

Also invaluable to the Team Rose effort was Emma Parry, my agent at Fletcher & Parry, who shepherded *American Rifle* from a vaguely expressed idea ("Hey, a book about guns might be interesting") to a definitely expressed one ("Hey, a book about rifles *is* interesting") and then prevailed upon the publisher to take a chance.

Without family, books can't be written. Mine has always been a source of inspiration and a rock of support. My parents, Olivia, Zoë, and Ari, as well as Erna, David, Carolyn, Liz, Chad, Kyla, Iliana, Ben, and Jaime—all have aided immeasurably and I cannot thank them enough.

The person who aided most immeasurably of all, in all things bright and beautiful, in all things wise and wonderful, is, of course, my beloved Rebecca—to whom this book is dedicated. Without her encouragement, I would have quit halfway through.

Index

Born in the United States, Alexander Rose was raised in Australia and Britain. A military historian and former journalist, he is the author of *Washington's Spies: The Story of America's First Spy Ring,* and his writing has appeared in *The New York Observer, The Washington Post, Studies in Intelligence,* and many other publications. His website is www.alexrose.com.

Photo: © S. Nancy Upham